Houghton Mifflin College Reading Series

Houghton Mifflin College Reading Series

Book Two

Second Edition

HOUGHTON MIFFLIN COMPANY Boston New York

Senior Sponsoring Editor: Lisa Kimball
Senior Development Editor: Judith Fifer
Editorial Associate: Peter Mooney
Senior Project Editor: Rachel D'Angelo Wimberly
Editorial Assistant: Sage Anderson
Art/Design Manager: Gary Crespo
Photo Editor: Jennifer Meyer Dare
Composition Buyer: Sarah Ambrose
Senior Manufacturing Coordinator: Chuck Dutton
Senior Marketing Manager: Annamarie Rice
Marketing Assistant: Andrew Whitacre
Senior Designer: Henry Rachlin

Cover Image: © The Image Bank/Alain Daussin

Photo Credits
p. 45: Wendy Smith © 2004 by Houghton Mifflin Company. Reproduced by permission from *The American Heritage Dictionary,* Fourth Edition; © SuperStock, Inc.; Elizabeth Morales © 2004 by Houghton Mifflin Company. Reproduced by permission from *The American Heritage Dictionary,* Fourth Edition.

Printed in the U.S.A.

Library of Congress Control Number: 2004111268

Student Edition ISBN: 0-618-54187-X
Instructor's Annotated Edition ISBN: 0-618-54191-8

6 7 8 9 -- CRW -- 09 08

Contents

CHAPTER 5 Transitions 219

CHAPTER 6 Patterns of Organization 273

CHAPTER 10 Reading Longer Selections 507

Combined Skills Tests 551

Index 571

Preface

The *Houghton Mifflin College Reading Series,* Second Edition is a three-level series that uses a progressive, unified approach to improving students' reading comprehension and critical thinking skills—and all at an affordable price! Praised in the first edition by users across the country, the second edition of this innovative series contains additional features and support materials that will enhance students' abilities to become effective readers.

Special Features of the Text

Houghton Mifflin College Reading Series, Second Edition includes the following features:

- **Affordable Price:** Each book in the series contains the same topics and content as do other comparable textbooks, but for a price that is more than a third less than that of similar books.
- **Integration of Skills and Strategies:** Along with presenting the major reading skills—identifying the main idea, supporting details, implied main idea, transitions, patterns of organization, and others—the book introduces students to a world of reading strategies that will enable them to practice good habits while reading. Strategies such as SQ3R, annotating, and note taking will help students improve their comprehension of what they read and will enable them to learn different strategies that will help them comprehend and analyze what they read.
- **Consistent Chapter Structure:** Each chapter covers skills and strategies in a consistent and clear manner.
- **Coverage of Visuals:** Chapter 7 is unique to this text in that it covers visuals that students may encounter in their personal and professional reading, such as charts, graphs, tables, and figures.
- **Critical Thinking:** In addition to a multitude of skills exercises designed to help students build comprehension, the text features questions at the end of the reading selections that build on important critical thinking skills. Many practice exercises, too, require the application of critical thinking.
- **Vocabulary Building:** Every chapter covers a particular vocabulary concept and relates that concept to reading selections from the chapters.
- **Focus on Academic Achievement:** Tips and selected readings about studying and succeeding in school are integrated throughout the text.

Chapter Organization

In addition, each chapter in each level of the *Houghton Mifflin College Reading Series,* Second Edition contains the following elements:

- **Goals:** A list of goals at the beginning of each chapter tells students what they will learn when they have completed the chapter.

- **Test Yourself:** These pre-tests, which appear in Chapters 2 through 10, assess the student's knowledge of the skill to be introduced. This assessment helps both instructors and students target specific areas for improvement.

- **Explanation:** Each chapter is broken up into sections, with each section devoted to explanation and practice of a particular concept. Material has been divided into manageable sections of information that are followed by practice of a specific skill.

- **Exercises:** An ample number and variety of exercises is included in every chapter. Most of the exercises contain paragraphs from textbooks, magazines, newspapers, and journals so that students can read various types of selections and learn new information about a variety of different subjects. Exercises are arranged using a step-by-step progression to build concepts and skills gradually.

- **Chapter Review:** A closing exercise tests students' knowledge of the concepts presented in each chapter.

- **Longer Reading Selections:** Longer reading selections follow the explanatory material in Chapters 1 through 9 and are included to give students practice in identifying different skills in context. Readings have been chosen for their high interest, diverse topics, and cultural relevance for today's students. In addition, each reading was selected with the level of student in mind as well as students' ethnic, cultural, and educational experiences. New to this edition is the "Practicing the Active Reading Strategy," which asks students to apply active reading techniques to longer selections before and after they read.

- **Questions for Discussion and Writing:** These questions ask students to think about their own experiences, as well as what they have read in the longer reading selections. The main points, topics, and theses of the longer readings are used as springboards to encourage student reflection on personal experiences and as stimuli for strengthening academic skills such as research, argument, and summary. These questions give students the opportunity to develop their writing skills by responding to a professional reading selection.

- **Vocabulary:** Vocabulary is integrated in several different ways throughout each chapter. First, definitions of words or phrases that may be new to beginning students now appear as footnotes. In addition, words that may be unfamiliar are taken from the longer reading selection that appears later in Chapters 1 through 9 and used in a vocabulary exercise that follows the selection. Students are given the opportunity to glean the meanings of certain words from context and expand their overall vocabulary. Lastly, each chapter includes instruction in a specific vocabulary concept, such as context clues, that will help students improve their reading comprehension. The instruction is followed by one or more exercises that draw examples from readings in the text to give students practice with that particular concept.

- **Reading Strategy:** Every chapter ends with a reading strategy that students can use to help them comprehend and remember what they have read.
- **Chapter Tests:** Several different tests follow each skills-based chapter and are designed to assess students' progress from the beginning of the chapter, when they completed the "Test Yourself" section (in Chapters 2 through 10). These tests cover all of the individual skills presented in the chapter.
- **Combined Skills Tests:** A section following the final chapter contains combined skills tests that provide a thorough review of the book's contents. New to this edition, each test includes an opportunity for students to apply various reading strategies to the reading selection.

What's New in the Second Edition

Based on user and reviewer response, several new features have been added to the new edition to help students learn key concepts and strengthen their vocabulary and reading skills:

- **Expanded Information on Purpose and Tone:** Chapters 8 and 9 have been reorganized and Chapter 8, which is now called "Purpose and Tone," includes increased coverage of the purposes of writing, bias, tone, and the connotative meanings of words.
- **More Patterns of Organization:** Chapter 6 now covers more patterns, including illustration, classification, and division.
- **New Combined Skills Tests:** The combined skills tests contain additional questions that ask students to employ the strategies they have learned, such as paraphrasing and outlining.
- **Vocabulary Footnotes:** Definitions of difficult words as well as allusions in many of the examples, exercises, and readings now appear as footnotes so that students don't have to go to outside sources to look them up.
- **New Grade-Level-Appropriate Examples and Readings:** Examples and readings have been carefully reviewed and replaced when necessary to ensure grade-level appropriateness for each text.
- **Reading Strategy Now at the End of Each Chapter:** In order to increase the flexibility of the text, the reading strategy now appears at the end of the chapter. This new placement allows instructors to skip this portion of the text if they so choose.
- **New "Practicing the Active Reading Strategy" exercises:** New exercises that appear before and after the longer end-of-chapter readings ask students to apply the active reading strategy to that selection.

- **A More Engaging Chapter 1:** Several of the first edition readings in Chapter 1 have been replaced with more engaging selections in order to increase student interest.
- **Clearer Direction Lines:** Instructions throughout have been rewritten for clarity and consistency.
- **Expanded Skill Definitions:** Definitions of the skill presented in each chapter now appear after the chapter objectives and most have been expanded so that students have a better idea of what they are being asked to do in the "Test Yourself" section.

Ancillaries

The *Houghton Mifflin College Reading Series,* Second Edition is supported by an innovative teaching and learning package.

- **Improved! EduSpace for Houghton Mifflin Reading—Level 2.** EduSpace, Houghton Mifflin's online learning tool powered by Blackboard, dynamically expands students' learning opportunities and instructors' teaching options. Eduspace offers cumulative pre- and post-tests as well as interactive tests keyed to almost every chapter in the *Houghton Mifflin College Reading Series*. The EduSpace course for this second edition now contains more questions, including more on vocabulary, as well as additional reading selections in the form of combined skills tests. Students get plenty of extra practice, immediate feedback, a score, and grammar or writing targets for further work. Instructors praise EduSpace's flexible course management system, which features an online gradebook linked to the exercises (so that keeping track of student progress is easy); one convenient environment for course objectives, syllabi, and other class information; and the chance to stay connected with students through live online hours, discussion boards, chat rooms, and an announcement center. Visit **http://www.eduspace.com/** for more information or to sign up for a demonstration.
- **Test Bank.** A downloadable version of the test bank is available at **college.hmco.com/devenglish/instructors/course_reading.html.** The test bank contains an additional cumulative pre- and post- test as well as two post-tests for each of the chapters. An answer key to the tests is also provided.
- **The Phonics Supplement.** A series of thirty-two exercises leads students from learning how various consonants and vowels sound to ultimately dividing words in to syllables and sounding them out. Through the use of phonics, students can improve their pronunciation, reading comprehension, and spelling. An answer key allows instructors to easily grade each set of activities.

- ***Powerpoint* ® Slides and Transparency Masters.** Available to accompany the text, these can be used to enhance classroom presentations or create handouts.

Thanks to the following reviewers who helped shape the Second Edition:

Patti Levine-Brown, Florida Community College at Jacksonville
Dianne Cates, Central Piedmont Community College
Molly Emmons, College of the Redwoods
Matthew Gainous, Ogeechee Technical College
Stephen M. Gallegos, M.A., Albuquerque Technical Vocational Institute
Sarah Garman, Miami Dade College
Judith B. Isonhood, Hinds Community College
Paul H. Parent, Montgomery College
Deirdre Rowley, Imperial Valley College
Linda E. Samuell, Ph.D., Miami Dade College—Kendall Campus
Deborah Potts Spradlin, Tyler Junior College
Kayla Westra, Minnesota West Community and Technical College

Houghton Mifflin College Reading Series

1

CHAPTER 1

Improving Reading and Thinking

GOALS FOR CHAPTER 1

- **Explain why effective reading is critical to academic, professional, and personal success.**
- **Explain how reading improves thinking skills.**
- **Describe four techniques for improving reading skills.**
- **List the different goals of reading for information.**
- **Explain the four types of mental skills required for reading.**
- **Describe the organization and features of this book.**
- **Explain and apply the steps of active reading.**
- **Use general tips for reading visual aids.**

Do you enjoy reading? If your answer is no, why not? Like many people, you may have several reasons for disliking the printed word. You might think reading is too passive, requiring you to sit still for too much time. You may not like it because it takes too long. You may say that most of the things you read just don't interest you or aren't relevant to your life. You may object to reading because it seems too hard—you don't like having to struggle to understand information. These are the most common reasons people give to explain their dislike of reading.

What people don't realize is that most of these reasons arise from a lack of experience and effort. When you first decided you didn't like to read, you probably began to avoid it as much as possible. This avoidance led to a lack of practice that set up a vicious cycle: lack of practice prevented skills from developing. This lack of skills meant more difficult and unrewarding experiences when you did read. As a result, you probably read less and less and failed to use opportunities to practice your reading skills. So, the cycle began again.

1

You can break this cycle, though, and make your reading experiences more enjoyable. The first step is realizing how much you already know about the reading process.

The Importance of Good Reading Skills

As Figure 1.1 below shows, a college student spends a lot of his or her daily communication time reading. Obviously, then, good reading skills are an essential component of success in college.

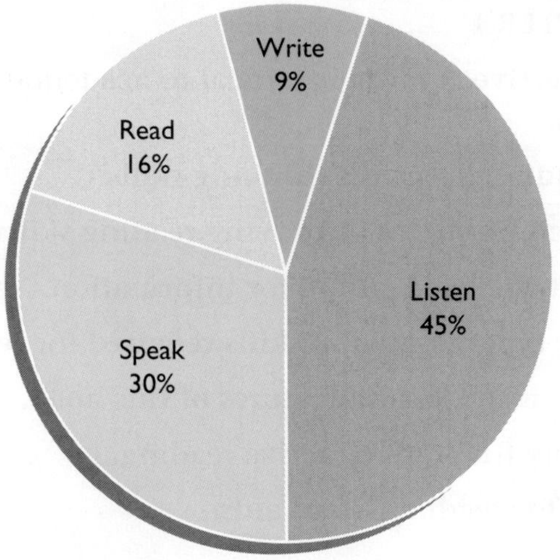

Figure 1.1

Source: L. Barker et al., "An Investigation of Proportional Time Spent in Various Communication Activities of College Students," *Journal of Applied Communication Research* 8 (1981): 101–109. Used by permission of the National Communication Association.

Reading and Academic Success

Solid reading skills will be critical to your success in college. Most college courses require a great deal of reading. Your professors will ask you to read textbooks, articles, books, stories, and handouts. You'll be responsible for remembering much of this information and revealing your knowledge of it on tests. You'll have to read the instructor's notes, and you'll have to read your own notes on lecture material to prepare for your tests. In addition, you'll be asked to conduct research that requires reading all types of sources, including Web sites on the Internet. Various assignments will ask you to read not only your own writing but also that of your classmates.

Not only will you have to simply read and remember information, you'll be asked to evaluate it, judge it, agree or disagree with it, interpret it, compare it to something else, summarize it, and synthesize[1] it with other things you've read. All of these tasks are possible only if you can first attain a solid grasp of the ideas and information in the source.

Exercise 1.1

Answer the following questions about Figure 1.1 on page 2. Write your answers on the blanks provided.

1. For a college student, what percentage of daily communication time is spent in reading? ______________________________

2. How do you think your reading time compares to the average figure in the chart? ______________________________

____

3. The information in the visual relates to a college student. How do you think the four percentages included in the chart would change for someone who is not attending college? ______________________________

____

Exercise 1.2

In the list below, place a checkmark beside every reading-related activity you've already done at least once. Then, answer the questions that follow by writing your answers on the blanks provided.

_____ Read a textbook.

_____ Read a magazine or journal article assigned by a teacher.

_____ Read information on a website for a class assignment.

_____ Read a book or a novel assigned by a teacher.

_____ Researched a topic in the library by reading several sources about it.

_____ Read a memo at work.

_____ Read a letter from a friend.

_____ Read an e-mail message from a friend, teacher, or colleague.

_____ Read subtitles[2] while you watched a foreign film.

1. **synthesize:** to put things together in new combinations

2. **subtitles:** translations of the dialogue

1

_____ Read the newspaper.

_____ Read a story to a child.

_____ Read aloud in class.

_____ Read a prepared speech to an audience.

1. If you could choose anything to read, what would it be? Why?

____

____

____

2. What types of reading situations do you find the most difficult? Why?

____

____

3. What do you think you need to do to become a better reader?

____

____

4. What would you like to learn in this textbook that you think would help you become a better reader? ______________________

____

____

Reading and Professional Success

When you enter the work force, you might be surprised how much reading you'll need to do. Many jobs will require you to read e-mail messages, letters, memorandums, policy and procedure manuals, instructions, reports, logs and records, summaries of meetings, newsletters, and many other types of documents.

Often, a lot is at stake on your comprehension of these materials. Your personal safety may depend on your understanding of the information in manuals or other instructions. Your efficient and effective job performance may rest on your ability to comprehend written information sent to you by your supervisors and coworkers. Even your promotions and raises may depend, in part, on your ability to read and understand materials such as reports about trends, new research, or other innovations in your field.

Exercise 1.3

Read the following memo and then write your answers to the questions on the blanks provided.

To: Nursing Staff of County General Hospital

From: Barbara Benton, Head of Nursing Staff

Date: January 2, 20—

Re: Avoiding Needle Stick Injuries

To all nurses:

On behalf of the nursing staff and executive board, I'd like to thank each and every one of you for your hard work and commitment to the hospital and its patients. It has come to our attention that injuries resulting from needle sticks have risen, and we would like to give you a set of guidelines that will assist you in your patient care.

Prevention

Any sharp object that comes in contact with a patient's body fluids may carry infection. Hepatitis is a greater danger than HIV. You are likely to get an HIV infection only if the stick is very deep or if blood from the needle gets into your body.

To prevent needle stick injuries:

- Be careful when handling needles, scalpels, and any other sharp objects.
- Do not put the cap back on a used needle: do not bend or break a needle by hand, and do not take the needle off a disposable syringe.
- Put all sharp objects in a special holder that contains only sharp items.
- Always wear gloves when you touch anything that has blood or other body fluids on it.

1

Signs/Symptoms

If you do stick yourself, there will be only the pain and bleeding at first. Only later will you develop symptoms of infection.

Care

You'll need to be tested. You may be given shots to prevent you from getting hepatitis. If you have a positive test for HIV, the doctor may prescribe medicine to slow down the infection.

What You Should Do

- If you stick yourself with a needle used on a patient, report it immediately. Both you and the patient should be tested for hepatitis and HIV infection.
- See your doctor right away if the patient has AIDS or HIV infection or refuses to be tested.
- If you do not know which patient the needle came from, you and your doctor will need to decide what tests should be done and what treatment you should have.
- In case you've contracted hepatitis, wash your hands well before eating and after using the bathroom. Do not share food or drinks.
- Even if your first test shows you do not have HIV, you should get another test in six weeks and three, six, and twelve months after your needle stick injury. You should also take the steps necessary to avoid spreading HIV: Use a condom when you have sex. Do not give blood. If you are breastfeeding, use formula instead.

Call Your Doctor If . . .

- You have not been given your test results.
- You can't drink fluids or you throw up after you eat.
- Your stomach or legs become swollen, itch, or break out in a rash.
- You get a fever, a rash, or muscle pain, feel tired, or can feel lumps in your neck or under your arms within a year of the injury.
- You vomit or have diarrhea or really bad abdominal pain for more than a few days.*

* From *The PDR® Family Guide Encyclopedia of Medical Care™*, copyright 1997 by The Medical Economics Company, Inc. Used by permission of Three Rivers Press, a division of Random House, Inc.

1. Why is a needle stick injury potentially dangerous? ______

2. What is the first thing a nurse should do if stuck with a needle? ______

3. Name two things a nurse can do to prevent needle stick injuries. ______

4. Summarize two instances in which a nurse should call his or her doctor after getting a needle stick injury. ______

Reading and Personal Success

There are many occasions in your personal life when you will need to read well. For example, you may want to learn more about a hobby or subject area that interests you, so you'll need to read books, articles, and website pages to increase your knowledge. You may want to find out how to improve your personal finances by learning how to save or invest your money. You may need to assemble something you purchased—such as a child's toy or a barbecue grill—by following the directions. You or one of your loved ones may become sick with a particular disease or disorder, causing you to want more information about treatment options. You may even want to read for entertainment, picking up a *People* magazine or a Stephen King novel just for the fun of it.

1

You'll also need to read personal correspondence such as letters and e-mail messages, legal documents such as contracts, and reports from your children's teachers, among other things. You'll read all of these documents more capably and confidently when you improve your reading skills.

Exercise 1.4

Read the following selection and answer the questions that follow in the blanks provided. If you need more space, use a sheet of paper or your computer. Look up any words you do not know in your dictionary.

North Dakota Wants Its Place in the Sun

1 North Dakota is talking about changing its name. I frankly didn't know you could do that. I thought states' names were decreed by the Bible or something. In fact, as a child I believed that when Columbus[1] arrived in North America, the states' names were actually, physically, written on the continent, in gigantic letters, the way they are on maps. I still think this would be a good idea, because if an airplane's navigational system failed, the pilot could just look out the window and see exactly where the plane was. ("OK, there's a huge "W" down there, so we're over Wyoming. Or, Wisconsin.")

2 But apparently states can change their names, and some North Dakotans want to change "North Dakota." Specifically, they don't like the word "North," which connotes a certain northness. In the words of North Dakota's former governor, Ed Schafer: "People have such an instant thing about how North Dakota is cold and snowy and flat."

3 We should heed the words of the former governor, and not just because the letters in "Ed Schafer" can be rearranged to spell "Shed Farce." The truth is that when we think about North Dakota, which is not often, we picture it as having the same year-round climate as Uranus.

4 In contrast, SOUTH Dakota is universally believed to be a tropical paradise with palm trees swaying on surf-kissed beaches. Millions of tourists, lured by the word "South," flock to South Dakota every winter, often wearing nothing but skimpy bathing suits. Within hours, most of them die and become covered with snow, not to be found until spring, when they cause a major headache for South Dakota's farmers by clogging up the cultivating machines. South Dakota put a giant fence around the whole state to keep these tourists out, and STILL they keep coming. That's how powerful a name can be.

1. **Columbus:** Christopher Columbus, the first historically significant European discoverer of the Caribbean and South America

5 I'll give you another example. I live in Florida, where we have BIG cockroaches.

6 Q. How big are they?

7 A. They are so big that, when they back up, they are required by federal law to emit warning beeps.

8 These cockroaches could harm Florida's image. But we Floridians solved that problem by giving them a new name, "palmetto bugs," which makes them sound cute and harmless. So when a guest walks into a Florida kitchen and screams at the sight of an insect the size of Charles Barkley,[1] we say: "Don't worry! It's just a palmetto bug!" And then we and our guest have a hearty laugh, because we know there's nothing to worry about, as long as we do not make any sudden moves toward the palmetto bug's sandwich.

9 So changing names is a sound idea, an idea based on the scientific principle that underlies the field of marketing, which is: People are stupid. Marketing experts know that if you call something by a different name, *people will believe it's a different thing*. That's how "undertakers" became "funeral directors." That's how "trailers" became "manufactured housing." That's how "We're putting you on hold for the next decade" became "Your call is important to us."

10 And that's why some North Dakotans want to give the state a new name, a name that will give the state a more positive, inviting, and forward-looking image. That name is: "Palmetto Bug."

11 No, seriously, they want to drop the "North" and call the state, simply, "Dakota." I think this change is brilliant, and could also work for other states with image problems. New Jersey, for example, should call itself, simply, "New."

12 Be advised that "Dakota" is not the first shrewd marketing concept thought up by North Dakotans. Are you familiar with Grand Forks, N.D.? No? It's located just west of East Grand Forks, Minn. According to a letter I received from a Grand Forks resident who asked to remain nameless ("I have to live here," he wrote), these cities decided they needed to improve their image, and the result was—get ready—"The Grand Cities."

13 The Grand Cities, needless to say, have a web site (grandcities.net), where you can read sentences about The Grand Cities written in MarketingSpeak, which is sort of like English, except that it doesn't actually mean anything. Here's an actual quote: "It's the intersection of earth and sky. It's a glimpse of what lies ahead. It's hope, anticipation, and curiosity reaching out to you in mysterious ways. Timeless. Endless. Always enriching your soul. Here, where the earth meets the sky, the Grand Cities of Grand Forks, North Dakota, and East Grand Forks, Minnesota."

1. **Charles Barkley:** NBA player (1984–1999) who stood 6'6" and weighed 250 pounds

1

14 Doesn't that just make you want to cancel that trip to Paris or Rome and head for The Grand Cities? As a resident of Florida ("Where the earth meets the water, and forms mud") I am definitely planning to go to Dakota. I want to know what they're smoking up there.*

1. Did you enjoy reading this selection? Why or why not? ____________

____

2. What would be someone's primary reason for reading a selection like this one? ____________

3. Think of some additional examples of terms that have been replaced with other words to help improve the image of the thing being named.

____

____

4. Do you think the author makes a good argument for the statement, "So changing names is a sound idea, an idea based on the scientific principle that underlies the field of marketing, which is: People are stupid"? Why or why not? ____________

____

Reading and Better Thinking

Not only will better reading skills help you improve your chances for academic, professional, and personal success, they will also help you improve your overall thinking skills. This is because reading requires you to follow and understand the thought processes of the writer. When you can do that effectively, you get opportunities to hone[1] a variety of mental skills:

1. You evaluate information and decide what's important.
2. You learn to see relationships among things, events, and ideas.

1. **hone:** sharpen, perfect

* From Dave Barry, "North Dakota Wants Its Place in the Sun," *Miami Herald,* August 12, 2001. © Copyright, 2001, Tribune Media Services, Inc. All Rights Reserved. Reprinted with permission.

3. You make new connections among things, events, and ideas.
4. You practice following the logic (or seeing the lack of logic) of someone else's thoughts.
5. You add more information to your memory.

These are the very skills that will strengthen your ability to make decisions, think creatively, and think logically in every area of your life.

Exercise 1.5

Read the following story from a newspaper and write on the blanks provided your answers to the questions that follow.

For Author, the (GE) Light Dawns

1 It was one of those days that make a struggling writer feel just great.

2 The intense aroma of the Seattle Mountain Colombian Decaf that filled the kitchen that morning reminded me of how pleased I had been to find such a bargain on coffee at Costco. My satisfaction increased as I switched on my Bose Wave radio to my favorite smooth jazz station and settled down with the *New York Times*, my favorite newspaper after *USA Today*.

3 The *Times* story that first caught my eye was about a British author who has agreed to have a jewelry store—I forget the name of it—sponsor her latest novel. For an undisclosed fee, the author, Fay Weldon, has made the jewelry store the centerpiece of her novel. It's the ultimate in "product placement."

4 The *Times* article was well written. But the writer's polish did not overshadow the story's content: a tale of marketing genius that gives hope to every would-be novelist in America who hasn't suffocated under the weight of publishers' rejection letters.

5 It opened my eyes, I can tell you.

6 When the kids got into an argument that morning over whether we'd go to Borders or Barnes & Noble, I flipped a coin. Borders won, but I'd have been just as happy to go to Barnes & Noble because they are both mighty fine bookstores.

7 We headed out into a dreary rain, and the first thing I noticed was that my Acura MDX needed gas again, but I didn't mind because it's such a joy to drive and so beautifully designed for carpooling.

Branded Bagels and Books

8 As usual, the kids wanted to stop at Einstein Bros. Bagels, and I was glad they did because I wanted to stop there, too. There was the usual long line, but I knew that's because it's so popular, and besides, the line moved very quickly,

and the wait was worth it because the toasted sesame with lox shmear (a spread of cream cheese) was to die for.

9 When we got to Borders, I couldn't find the book I was looking for—*10 Steps to Salvaging a Manuscript That's Been Rejected by 20 Publishers in Only 30 Days*—but I couldn't get upset because I knew that it was in such high demand that it practically flies off the shelf.

10 Our next stop was at a mall called Phipps Plaza, a temple of high-end fashion and excess, and I knew that I wouldn't be disappointed there. I was astounded, in fact, by the selection at Saks, where I found an exquisite Ermenegildo Zegna cashmere sweater priced at only $800. Before I could whip out my credit card, a charming salesman sidled[1] over and whispered, "The price will be considerably lower if you come back tomorrow." I appreciate that kind of customer care.

The Devil's in the Details

11 When we got home, I was still thinking about how happy I was for Fay Weldon as I fired up my new Char-Broil H2O smoker, which I purchased for a very good price and assembled in only five hours. And as I laid on some succulent[2] salmon I'd bought at Publix, it finally dawned on me:

12 I've had so much trouble trying to write fiction. I've created some solid characters. I can write dialogue that flows like molasses in July. I've done some great sex scenes—riveting but sensitive, all entirely believable, if you ask me.

13 But I've neglected the kind of detail that gives stories what an editor once told me was "verisimilitude."[3] And now I understand where I went wrong.

14 From now on, the bed sheets won't just be bed sheets; they'll be Ralph Lauren. The bed will be from Ernest Hemingway's Kenya Collection, by Thomasville. The before-dinner drinks will be Dry Sack, and the nightcaps will be Rémy Martin V.S.O.P.

15 And the love triangle that I've been fooling around with for years will be set at Home Depot: Melissa will work in Lighting, Steve in Nuts and Bolts and Cheryl at Pro Checkout.

16 I think I've got this thing nailed.*

1. **sidled:** moved in a manner to avoid attracting attention
2. **succulent:** juicy and delicious
3. **verisimilitude:** appearing to be real or true

* From Don Campbell, "For Author, the (GE) Light Dawns," *USA Today*, September 10, 2001, www.usatoday.com.

1. What does Don Campbell do for a living? In your opinion, has he been successful at his profession? Why or why not? Use an example from the selection to support your answer. ____________________

2. What new piece of information did you learn by reading this excerpt?

3. How does Campbell's story actually demonstrate the very subject it's about? ____________________

4. Why is the selection entitled "For Author, the (GE) Light Dawns"? ____

How to Improve Reading Skills

Now that you understand *why* it's so important to read well, you're probably wondering *how* you can be a better reader. The obvious answer is practice. The more you read, the more opportunities you'll have for improving your abilities. But simply reading everything in sight will not necessarily improve your skills. In general, you should commit yourself to doing four other things as well:

1. Understand the different purposes for reading.
2. Be aware of the mental skills required for reading.
3. Develop individual reading skills.
4. Learn and use different reading strategies.

Understand the Different Purposes for Reading

When you set out to read something, you should know *why* you're reading it. The two basic purposes for reading are to gain information and to be entertained. Obviously, when you read for entertainment, your primary goal is your own pleasure. When you read for information, though, you may have different goals, such as:

1. **Gaining a general understanding of the ideas or points.** For example, as you're reading this section of this textbook, you're trying to comprehend the ideas being presented.
2. **Discovering the facts or answering questions about the material.** When you read the paragraphs in the exercises of this book, for example, you read them to find answers to the questions you must answer.
3. **Memorizing the information.** You often read a textbook chapter so that you'll recall its information when you take a test.
4. **Finding information or ideas that prove a point you want to make.** When you conduct research for a paper you need to write, you read to find statements or information that back up your opinions.
5. **Making a decision based on the information.** You read business brochures, for example, to decide whether to buy a particular product or service.

When you read something, you may need to accomplish just one of the goals above or perhaps all five at the same time. In any case, getting the most of everything you read means clearly identifying your purpose before you begin.

Exercise 1.6

Read the following reading situations. Write a checkmark on the blank next to every MAJOR purpose for reading that applies to that situation.

1. You read the movie listings in your local paper.

    _____ Gain a general understanding of the ideas or points.

    _____ Discover the facts or answer questions.

    _____ Memorize the information.

    _____ Find information or ideas that prove a point you want to make.

    _____ Make a decision based on the information.

2. You read a magazine article to find statistics you can use in a research paper you're writing.

    _____ Gain a general understanding of the ideas or points.

    _____ Discover the facts or answer questions.

_____ Memorize the information.

_____ Find information or ideas that prove a point you want to make.

_____ Make a decision based on the information.

3. You read the technical instructions that come with your new laptop computer.

_____ Gain a general understanding of the ideas or points.

_____ Discover the facts or answer questions.

_____ Memorize the information.

_____ Find information or ideas that prove a point you want to make.

_____ Make a decision based on the information.

4. You read the details of the president's new education plan, as printed in a weekly news magazine.

_____ Gain a general understanding of the ideas or points.

_____ Discover the facts or answer questions.

_____ Memorize the information.

_____ Find information or ideas that prove a point you want to make.

_____ Make a decision based on the information.

5. You reread a chapter about mathematical equations in preparation for a math test.

_____ Gain a general understanding of the ideas or points.

_____ Discover the facts or answer questions.

_____ Memorize the information.

_____ Find information or ideas that prove a point you want to make.

_____ Make a decision based on the information.

Understand the Mental Skills Required for Reading

"Reading" is actually a collection of different mental skills. They include attitude, concentration, memory, and logical thought. These skills are all interrelated and connected. Some of them depend upon others. When you become conscious that these different skills are at work, you can learn to improve them.

Attitude. A positive attitude is the first essential mental component for successful reading. Your attitude includes your feelings about reading, about *what* you read, and about your own abilities. If these feelings are negative, your reading experiences will be negative. If these feelings are positive, your experiences will be more enjoyable.

A positive attitude not only makes reading more pleasurable, it also creates the right mental environment for the acquisition of new information. As a matter of fact, all of the other mental skills required for reading are useless unless you approach each reading task in the right frame of mind. If you are quick to pronounce a particular text "boring" or "worthless," you are likely to create a mental block that will prevent you from absorbing the information. Instead, approach each new reading task with intellectual curiosity. Expect to find something of value, something you'll be able to use in your life.

Also, don't let a poor attitude about your own reading abilities get in your way. If you expect to fail, if you tell yourself you just don't get it, then you virtually guarantee your failure. If you believe you can improve, however, then you'll create the necessary mental foundation for improving your skills and becoming a good reader.

Exercise 1.7

Read the following selection with a positive attitude and answer the questions on the blanks provided.

Garlic: The Spice of Long Life

It may not do much for your breath, but perhaps no other herb can do more for your heart health than garlic. Used for centuries around the world for anything from numbing toothaches to warding off vampires, a new generation is taking to garlic with a passion. German health authorities have approved garlic as a primary defense against atherosclerosis—the buildup of fatty plaques on artery walls that can lead to heart disease—and high cholesterol levels. American consumers are now buying it in droves.

Recent research, including over 1,000 clinical trials that have been conducted on its medicinal uses, supports their enthusiasm. A study published in *Coronary Artery Disease* last fall found that of 60 mice fed high-cholesterol diets, the 30 given allicin, one of garlic's active ingredients, developed fewer fatty deposits in their arteries. A 1999 Germany study showed an 18 percent reduction in plaque buildup in the arteries of people who took 900 mg of garlic powder a day. And an Oxford University overview of 16 clinical trials involving nearly 1,000 people found that those taking 600 mg to 900 mg of dried garlic powder daily for a month or more saw a 12 percent reduction in their cholesterol levels and a 13 percent reduction in triglycerides, another type of fat found in the blood.

Garlic may have other powers, as well. A study published in *Cancer Detection and Prevention* in November found that giving garlic extract to guinea pigs with skin cancer slowed the growth of their tumors, and a study in *Microbes and Infection* last February heralded garlic as an effective treatment against certain bacteria, fungi, and viruses. Garlic is being investigated as a possible foil for infections that resist traditional antibiotics, and it's even being tested in Russia as a treatment for arthritis.

Note to garlic lovers looking for an excuse to eat more: You may have to eat a lot of raw garlic to experience its benefits, as much as five to 10 cloves a day—a prospect that may drive your friends away. Luckily, garlic supplements offer an odor-free alternative. Just remember that the herb is a blood thinner, and people taking aspirin or other anticoagulant drugs should talk to their doctors before taking the supplement.*

1. When you read the title of the selection "Garlic: The Spice of Long Life," what did you think the selection would be about? Why? ______________

____

____

2. Did you assume the passage would be boring or too difficult? If so, why?

____

____

3. As you read this passage, did you discover a fact or idea that interested you? Did you discover some information in this passage you could actually use in your life? If so, what was it?

____

____

* From "Garlic: The Spice of Long Life," *Psychology Today*, March/April 2000, 40. Reprinted with permission from *Psychology Today Magazine*. Copyright © 2000 Sussex Publishers, Inc.

Concentration. Once your positive attitude has prepared your mind to absorb new information, you're ready to employ the second mental skill necessary for reading: concentration. *Concentration* is the ability to focus all of your attention on one thing while ignoring all distractions. You cannot understand or remember information unless you read with concentration.

Many people, however, find concentration difficult to achieve, especially when they read more challenging material. Too often, they succumb to distractions that pull their thoughts away from the sentences and paragraphs before them. But you can learn to concentrate better. How? By practicing effective techniques for combating the two types of distractions: external and internal.

External distractions are the sights, sounds, and other sensations that tempt you away from your reading. These distractions include ringing phones, people talking or walking nearby, the sound of a stereo, or a friend who stops by to chat. Though they are powerful, these external distractions are also the easier of the two types of distractions to eliminate.

To avoid having to grapple with external distractions, you merely prevent them from happening by choosing or creating the right reading environment. Try to select a location for reading—such as an individual study area in your library or a quiet room in your house—where there will be few distractions. Prior to a reading session, notify your friends and family that you'll be unavailable for conversation and socializing. If you must read in places with more activity, try wearing earplugs and/or sitting with your back to the action so you're not tempted to watch the comings and goings of others.

Internal distractions are often more challenging to overcome. They are the thoughts, worries, plans, daydreams, and other types of mental "noise" inside your own head. They will prevent you from concentrating on what you're reading and from absorbing the information you need to learn.

You can try to ignore these thoughts, but they will usually continue trying to intrude. So, how do you temporarily silence them so you can devote your full attention to your reading? Try the following suggestions:

1. Begin every reading task with a positive attitude. A negative attitude produces a lot of mental noise in the form of complaints about and objections to the task at hand. When you choose to maintain a positive attitude, you'll eliminate an entire category of noisy thoughts that interfere with your concentration.

2. Instead of fighting internal distractions, try focusing completely on them for a short period of time. For five or ten minutes, allow yourself to sit and think about your job, your finances, your car problems, your boyfriend or girlfriend, the paper you need to write, or whatever is on your mind. Better yet, write these thoughts down. Do a free-writing

exercise (a quick writing of your own thoughts on paper without censoring them or worrying about grammar and spelling) to empty your mind of the thoughts that clutter it. If you can't stop thinking about all of the other things you need to do, devote ten minutes to writing a detailed "To Do" list. Giving all of your attention to distracting thoughts will often clear them from your mind so you can focus on your reading.

3. Keep your purpose in mind as you read. As discussed earlier, having a clear goal when you read will help you concentrate on getting from a text what you need to know.
4. Use active reading techniques. These techniques are explained at the end of this chapter. They increase your level of interaction with the text, which will improve your concentration on the material.
5. Use visualization to increase your interest and improve your retention of the information. As you read, let the words create pictures and images in your mind. Try to "see" in your mind's eye the scenes, examples, people, and other information presented in the text.

Exercise 1.8

On a separate sheet of paper, free-write for ten minutes about what's going on inside your mind at this moment so you can clear your mind for the reading that follows.

Exercise 1.9

Read the following passage and practice the visualization techniques you read about earlier. Answer the questions that follow on a separate sheet of paper or use your computer.

According to her own account, Mary Harris was born in Ireland in 1830 and came to the United States as a child, with her father. As a young woman, she taught school and worked as a dressmaker or seamstress, then married George Jones, an iron molder and union activist. Her expectations as a wife and mother were shattered, however, when she lost her entire family, her husband and their four children—in a yellow-fever epidemic in 1867.

On her own, she opened a dressmaking shop in Chicago. Her clients included those she called "the aristocrats of Chicago," and she witnessed "the luxury and extravagance of their lives." The contrast between the opulent expectations of her wealthy clients and tightly constrained lives of the poor left her deeply disturbed.

In 1871, her shop burned in the great fire that swept much of the city. Thereafter, she chose to give much of her time to helping workers, first through the Knights of Labor.[1] In 1882, she first took part in a strike by coal miners.

Mary's, or "Mother Jones" as she came to be known, talents lay in public speaking and in organizing demonstrations to capture public attention and sympathy. In one strike in 1900, she organized miners' wives to protest against strikebreakers by pounding on pots and pans and frightening the mules that pulled the mine carts. In 1903, she took up the cause of the children who worked in textile mills. By organizing a march of mill children to the home of President Theodore Roosevelt, she captured headlines with her living, walking display of the childrens' deformities and injuries caused by mill work.

Mother Jones made an unusual choice in her decision to spend the last half of her life as a labor organizer and agitator.[2] But she apparently held traditional expectations about the role of women in society, arguing that their place was in the home. She seems to have seen her own work as an extension of her role as mother. Deprived of her own family, she sought to nurture and protect a much larger family of workers.*

1. Picture Mary Harris Jones, or Mother Jones, in your mind. What does she look like? What is she wearing?
2. Picture the scene of Mary marching with mill children to the home of Theodore Roosevelt. What do you think this scene looked like? What do you think Roosevelt's reaction was?
3. Picture the differences between "the aristocrats of Chicago" and the people that Mary chose to help—miners and child laborers, in particular. How would they be different in appearance?

Memory. Memory, the ability to store and recall information, is also essential to the reading process. You use your memory constantly as you read. You must remember:

1. **The Knights of Labor:** was an American labor organization started by Philadelphia tailors in 1869
2. **agitator:** one who stirs up interest in a cause

* Adapted from Berkin et al., *Making America: A History of the United States,* 2nd ed. Boston: Houghton Mifflin, 2001, 356–357. Copyright © 2001 by Houghton Mifflin Company. Reprinted with permission.

- The meanings of words.
- What you know about people, places, and things when you encounter references to them.
- All of the ideas and information presented before that point in the text.
- The text's overall main point while you read the subpoints or details.
- Your own experiences that either support or contradict the text's message.
- Other texts you've read that either agree or disagree with the new information you're reading.

There are many techniques you can use to improve your memory. A few of the most common are:

1. **Improve your concentration.** The more intensely you focus on something, the better the chance you'll remember it.
2. **Repeat and review.** Most of the time, the more you expose yourself to new information, the more easily you'll recall it.
3. **Recite.** Saying information aloud helps strengthen your memory of it.
4. **Associate new information with what you already know.** Making connections between your present knowledge and what you need to learn helps you to store new information in your mind more effectively.

Exercise 1.10

Read the following passage through one time. Then cover it so you can't see it and test your memory of the information by writing on the blanks provided your answers to the questions that follow.

Harlem[1] became a vibrant center of black culture in the 1920s. The Mississippi-born classical composer William Grant Still moved to Harlem in 1922, pursuing his composition studies and completing his best-known work, *Afro-American Symphony* (1931). On the musical-comedy stage, the 1921 hit *Shuffle Along* launched a series of popular all-black reviews. The 1923 show *Runnin' Wild* sparked the Charleston dance craze. The Cotton Club and other Harlem cabarets[2] featured such jazz geniuses as Duke Ellington, Fletcher Henderson, and Jelly Roll Morton. Contributing too to the cultural ferment[3]

1. **Harlem:** an area of New York City
2. **cabarets:** nightclubs providing entertainment
3. **ferment:** excitement; mixture

were muralist Aaron Douglas, concert tenor Roland Hayes, and singer-actor Paul Robeson.*

1. During what decade did the section of New York City known as Harlem become a center of black culture? ______________________________
2. What was *Shuffle Along*? ______________________________
3. What show sparked the Charleston dance craze? ________________
4. Name a Harlem cabaret that was popular in the 1920s. ______________

Logical Thought. Another mental skill required for effective reading is logical thinking. Logical thought is composed of many different mental tasks, including those in the list below:

Sequencing and ordering: seeing the order of things and understanding cause/effect relationships

Matching: noticing similarities

Organizing: grouping things into categories

Analysis: understanding how to examine the different parts of something

Reasoning from the general to the particular and the particular to the general: drawing conclusions and making generalizations

Abstract thought: understanding ideas and concepts

Synthesis: putting things together in new combinations

If you want to improve your ability to think logically, try one or more of the following suggestions:

1. **Practice active reading.** Using outlining, in particular, forces you to work harder to detect relationships in information. Outlining and other active reading techniques are explained at the end of this chapter.
2. **Play with games and puzzles.** Card games, computer games, and board games like chess, checkers, and backgammon will give you opportunities to sharpen your analytical skills.
3. **Solve problems.** Work math problems. Read mysteries (or watch them on television) and try to figure out who committed the crime before the

* Adapted from Boyer et al., *The Enduring Vision*, 5th ed. Boston: Houghton Mifflin, 2004, 728. Copyright © 2004 by Houghton Mifflin Company. Reprinted with permission.

detective does. Try to think of ways to solve everyday problems both big and small. For example, come up with a solution for America's overflowing landfills. Or figure out how to alter backpacks so they don't strain your back.

4. **Practice your argument and debating skills.** Discuss controversial issues with people who hold the opposing viewpoint.
5. **Write more.** Writing requires a great deal of logical thought, so write letters to your newspaper editor or congressional representatives about issues that are important to you.

Exercise 1.11

Read this passage written by a columnist whose work appears in the *Miami Herald* and then write on the blanks your answers to the questions that follow. If you need more room, use a separate sheet of paper or your computer.

Pop Culture's Familiar Ring Is All About $$

1 We begin with Posh Spice, a young woman whose real name is Victoria Beckham. She's one of the Spice Girls, a fluffy British pop group now in its 16th minute of fame. Anyway, Posh, who has launched a solo career, went on stage last month wearing a ring on her bottom lip. She'd just had it done, she said, and it hurt like heck. Naturally, the media were shocked and parents scandalized. Just as naturally, an untold number of British girls rushed out to have their lips painfully pierced like Posh.

2 Except it quickly came out that Posh's piercing was pretend—a clip-on ring. Now Posh finds herself pilloried[1] like a British Gary Condit[2] in dozens, if not hundreds, of critical articles, editorials and letters to the editor. When she tried to perform this week in Leicester, fans pelted her with fruit and vegetables.

3 "She is a real cow," . . . Clare Selby told a reporter. Clare, who's 18, had just spent the equivalent of $43 to have jewelry installed in her face, so perhaps she can be forgiven a bit of pique.[3] "I have had this done because of her," she complained, "and now I feel like a right idiot."

1. **pilloried:** ridiculed
2. **Gary Condit:** is a politician who resides in California. In 2001 he was linked to a young woman who vanished from the Washington, D.C., area.
3. **pique:** feeling of resentment or annoyance

4 Maybe you're wondering what any of this has to do with us over here on this side of the pond. Call it a cautionary tale, a warning about the ways in which and the degree to which we allow pop culture to define who we are. If you don't understand what that means, you've probably never heard about white farm boys standing around a cornfield, their pants dripping off their backsides in imitation of black rappers. Or teenage girls buying plaid kilts because Madonna[1] wears them. Or a boy committing suicide because some guitar hero did.

5 Sometimes it's harmless, sometimes not. But always, it's sobering. One can't help but marvel at—and be left uneasy by—what such episodes say about the power of pop culture and electronic media to influence our thoughts and wants.

6 Occasionally, I find myself wanting to pull a young person aside to ask: If television had never been invented, if radio was just a rumor, if there were no movies, videos or Internet, who would you be?

7 It's as if we turn to the electronic teat not simply for entertainment, but also for instruction. As cynical as we claim ourselves to be, we turn there with an earnest expectation that we will find things to make us better, philosophies to guide our lives. We gaze upon fantasy and fancy that we're seeing truth.

8 Pop culture isn't about truth. Yes, truth is an occasional byproduct.[2] So, for that matter, is art. But pop culture's prime directive never changes. It's about making money, period. To that end, it turns out a product that is disposable, of the moment, empty calories.

9 Consider Posh Spice again. During the performance in which she premiered her lip ring, she also somehow dropped her headset microphone. The singing continued uninterrupted, leaving the audience aghast[3] to discover that she'd been lip-syncing. In addition, Posh is reported to wear fake nails, augmented[4] breasts and hair extensions. Yet fans are angry because her lip ring wasn't real?

10 What about her is? More to the point, what about pop culture is?

11 Not much. Sadly, some young people don't learn that until it's too late. Until they've lost their money, their way, and sometimes, their lives, in imitation of something that isn't really there.

12 Pop culture is fantasy in service of a profit. It's image out to make a buck.

13 It cost Claire Selby $43 and some pain to learn that lesson. I'd say she got a bargain.*

1. **Madonna:** a pop singer
2. **byproduct:** something produced in the making of something else
3. **aghast:** shocked
4. **augmented:** enlarged

* From Leonard Pitts, "Pop Culture's Familiar Ring Is All About $$," *Miami Herald,* September 8, 2001. Copyright 2001, Tribune Media Services, Inc. All Rights Reserved. Reprinted with permission.

1. According to the author, where do young people mistakenly turn for instruction about whom they should be? ____________________

2. According to the author, why is pop culture the wrong place to look for "philosophies to guide our lives"? ____________________

____

3. Describe someone you know who has lived his or her life "in imitation of something that isn't really there." ____________________

4. Does the author ever suggest where young people should turn for real guidance? In your opinion, what are the sources of truth? ____________________

____

5. Agree or disagree with this statement from the selection: "Pop culture is fantasy in service of a profit. It's image out to make a buck." Explain your answer. ____________________

Develop Individual Reading Skills

Another way to improve your reading comprehension is to develop the isolated skills you must use to read well. For example, you can learn techniques for recognizing the main idea of a paragraph or for detecting patterns used to organize information. The rest of this book is designed to help you develop and practice these skills.

Exercise 1.12

Check off in the list below the skills you believe to be your weaknesses. Next to each item that you check, write the number of the chapter in this book that focuses on helping you strengthen that skill.

_____ Recognizing the overall point (the main idea) of a reading selection ____________________

_____ Understanding how details support the main idea of a reading selection ____________________

_____ Figuring out how a reading selection is organized ____________________

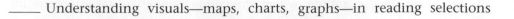

_____ Understanding visuals—maps, charts, graphs—in reading selections ______________________________

_____ Reading critically, or figuring out if a reading selection is accurate or trustworthy ______________________________

_____ Understanding longer reading selections ______________________________

_____ Figuring out implied main ideas, points that are not stated directly in a reading selection ______________________________

_____ Recognizing transitions, words that link sentences and paragraphs together ______________________________

_____ "Reading between the lines" (making inferences) by drawing conclusions from the information in a reading selection ______________________________

Learn and Use Different Reading Strategies

Reading strategies are techniques you use when you read. Some of them—such as active reading—are designed to improve your comprehension and retention of information. Others—such as skimming and scanning—provide you with tools you can use to find what you need in certain circumstances.

This book explains a different reading strategy in each chapter. Make sure you understand each of them so you can begin using them to read better right away.

How This Book Will Help You Improve Your Reading

Goals of this Book

The Houghton Mifflin College Reading Series is one of three books in a series designed to help you improve your reading skills. This text—the second in the sequence—focuses on the basic skills necessary to master effective reading. Each chapter concentrates on one essential skill you can use immediately to strengthen your reading comprehension.

This book, along with the other two in the series, is based on the belief that you can indeed become a better reader. Even if you have struggled in the past, you can learn and practice the skills you need to get more out of anything you read.

Organization and Features

This book is organized into two sections. The first section includes ten chapters, one for each essential reading skill. The second section includes a variety of tests designed to give you more practice with the skills covered in the chapters.

Each of the ten chapters include several helpful features.

Test Yourself. At the beginning of each chapter, a test will help you identify what you already know about the skill covered in that chapter. It will also help you pinpoint specific areas you need to target for improvement.

Exercises. Throughout each chapter, you'll have numerous opportunities to check your understanding with practice activities. As you complete each exercise and receive feedback on your answers, you will progress toward better reading comprehension.

Chapter Review. Filling in the blanks in a brief summary of the major points and concepts in the chapter will help you reinforce them in your mind.

Interesting Readings. The readings within practices, along with the longer reading selections in each chapter, are drawn from a variety of interesting sources. These readings have been carefully chosen to be enjoyable and useful. They have also been selected to clearly demonstrate a particular skill or concept. Furthermore, they'll give you practice reading different kinds of sources, including textbooks, magazine articles, newspaper articles, and essays.

The longer reading selections in each chapter are followed by questions designed to check your comprehension and increase your vocabulary. They also include discussion questions that will encourage you to sharpen your thinking skills and find ways to apply the information to your own life.

Vocabulary. Each chapter presents a different vocabulary concept. In this section, you will learn techniques for discovering the meanings of unfamiliar words. You will also learn about different types of specialized vocabulary in order to improve your overall reading comprehension. A practice activity draws from the readings in the chapter to give you an opportunity to check your understanding.

1

Reading Strategy. Each chapter concludes with the explanation of a different reading strategy. Strategies are techniques you can use to get more out of what you read. Using these techniques, you can begin to improve your reading comprehension right away.

Visual Feature Boxes. Each of these boxes reviews a particular type of visual aid you are likely to encounter as you read. You will learn techniques for reading and interpreting these visual aids.

Tests. Each chapter concludes with a series of review tests designed to help you measure your understanding of the concepts and skills you have learned. They will verify your mastery of the information and also identify areas for further study and review.

Exercise 1.13

Preview this textbook. Write on the blanks provided your answers to the following questions about its features and organization.

1. How many chapters does this book contain? ______________________
2. In what chapter is the topic of "Main Ideas" covered? ______________________
3. In what chapter will you learn the different patterns of organization that writers use? ______________________
4. In what chapters will you find visual material—that is, charts, graphs, maps, and photos—and find out how to read them? ______________________
5. In what chapter will you find information on how to read longer selections? ______________________
6. In what chapter will you review how to use the dictionary? ______________________
7. Look at Chapter 7 and define the term *inference*. ______________________

   ____
8. How many additional readings appear in the "Combined Skills" section of this text? ______________________
9. In which chapter will you learn how to summarize? ______________________

10. In which chapter will you learn how to spot a contrast context clue?

____

CHAPTER 1 REVIEW

Fill in the blanks in the following statements.

1. Good reading skills are important to __________, personal, and __________ success.
2. Reading helps strengthen __________ skills.
3. The two basic purposes for reading are to gain __________ and to be entertained.
4. When you read for information, you may have one or more of the following goals: gain a general __________ of the ideas or points; discover __________ or answer questions; memorize the information; find information or ideas that prove a __________ you want to make; make a __________ based on the information.
5. Reading is actually a collection of mental skills that include __________, concentration, __________, and __________ thought.
6. A positive __________ makes reading more pleasurable and more productive.
7. __________ is the ability to focus all of your attention on one thing while ignoring distractions.
8. The two types of distractions are __________ and __________.
9. __________ is the ability to store and recall information.
10. Logical thought includes mental tasks such as sequencing and ordering, __________, __________, analysis, __________ from the general to the particular and the particular to the general, __________ thought, and synthesis.
11. Reading __________ are techniques you can use to get more out of what you read.

1

READING STRATEGY: Active Reading

Many people don't get everything they can out of reading simply because they are *passive* readers. Passive readers are people who try to read by just running their eyes over the words in a passage. They expect their brains to magically absorb the information after just one quick reading. If they don't understand the reading, they blame the author and pronounce the work "dull" or "too difficult." These readers don't write anything down. If they come to a word they don't know, they just skip it and keep reading. If they get bored, they let their attention wander. They "read" long sections and then realize they have no memory or understanding of the information or ideas.

To read more effectively, you must become an **active reader.** Active readers know they have to do more than just sit with a book in front of them. They know that they have to participate in reading by interacting with the text and by thinking as they read. Active readers read with a pen or pencil in their hand, marking key words or ideas or jotting down notes in the margins. They reread the text if necessary, and they consciously try to connect the text's information to their own experiences and beliefs.

Active reading is essential to understanding and remembering ideas and information, especially those in difficult reading selections. It includes any or all of the following tasks:

- Identifying and writing down the point and purpose of the reading
- Underlining, highlighting, or circling important words or phrases
- Determining the meanings of unfamiliar words
- Outlining a passage in order to understand the relationships in the information
- Writing down questions when you're confused
- Completing activities—such as reading comprehension questions—that follow a chapter or passage
- Jotting down notes in the margins
- Thinking about how you can use the information or how the information reinforces or contradicts your ideas or experiences
- Predicting possible test questions on the material

- Rereading and reviewing
- Studying visual aids such as graphs, charts, and diagrams until you understand them

Remember, the purpose of all these activities is to comprehend and retain more of what you read. So, for challenging reading, such as textbook chapters or journal articles, active reading is a must. Also, you should perform these tasks for any reading that you're expected to remember for a test.

Even if you won't have to demonstrate your mastery of a reading selection, however, you should still get in the habit of reading actively when you read for information. Even if you're just reading for your own pleasure, you'll remember more by using active reading techniques.

To read actively, follow these steps:

1. When you sit down to read a book, get pens, pencils, and/or highlighter markers ready.
2. As you read each paragraph, mark points or terms that seem important. You may choose to underline them, highlight them, or insert boxes or circles. Be sure to mark any words or key information phrases that are in bold or italic print because the author wished to call attention to them. Consider jotting down an outline or notes in the margins as you read. If you're reading a textbook, write in the margins the questions you want to remember to ask your instructor.
3. As you read, continually ask yourself these questions: How can this information help me? How can I use this information? What will my instructor probably want me to remember? How does this reading support or contradict my own ideas, beliefs, and experiences?
4. After you have read the entire selection, complete any activities that follow it.

Follow steps 1, 2, and 3 described above to actively read the following passage from a psychology textbook:

Elliot Aronson and Darwyn Linder conducted an interesting study in which female college students met in pairs several times to discuss various topics. In each pair, one student was a research participant, and her

Continued

1

partner was a confederate.[1] After each meeting, the participant overheard a follow-up conversation between the experimenter and the confederate in which she was discussed and evaluated. Over time, the confederate's evaluation of the participant either was consistently positive or negative or underwent a change—either from negative to positive (gain) or from positive to negative (loss). Put yourself in the participant's shoes. All else being equal, in which condition would you like your partner most? In this study, participants liked the partner more when her evaluation changed from negative to positive than when it was positive all along. As long as the "conversion" is gradual and believable, people like others more when their affection takes time to earn than when it comes easily.

The Aronson and Linder finding suggests that we like others who are socially selective. This seems to support an old popular notion that you can spark romantic interest by playing hard to get. A few years ago, Ellen Fein and Sherri Schneider wrote a paperback book for women seductively titled *The Rules: Time-Tested Secrets for Capturing the Heart of Mr. Right*. What were the rules? Here's one: "Don't call him and rarely return his calls." Here's another: "Let him take the lead." In all cases, the theme was that men are charmed by women who are hard to get. It's an interesting hypothesis. Yet researchers have found that the **hard-to-get effect** is harder to get than they had originally anticipated. One problem is that we prefer people who are moderately selective compared with those who are nonselective (they have no taste, or no standards) or too selective (they are arrogant). Another is that we are turned *off* by those who reject us because they are committed to someone else or have no interest in us.

But now suppose that someone you are interested in is hard to get for external reasons. What if a desired relationship is opposed or forbidden by parents, as in the story of Romeo and Juliet? What about a relationship threatened by catastrophe, as in the love story portrayed in *Titanic*? What about distance, a lack of time, or renewed interest from a partner's old flame? The theory of psychological reactance states that people are motivated to protect their freedom to choose and behave as they please. When a valued freedom is threatened, people reassert themselves, often by overwanting the endangered behavior—like the proverbial[2] forbidden fruit.

1. **confederate:** an ally or accomplice

2. **proverbial:** expressed as a short saying about a truth

Consider what happens when you think that your chance to get a date for the evening is slipping away. Is it true, to quote country-and-western musician Mickey Gilley, that "the girls all get prettier at closing time"? To find out, researchers entered some bars in Texas and asked patrons three times during the night to rate the physical attractiveness of other patrons of the same and opposite sex. As Gilley's lyrics suggested, people of the opposite sex were seen as more attractive as the night wore on. The study is cute, but the correlation between time and attraction can be interpreted in other ways (perhaps attractiveness ratings rise with blood-alcohol levels!). More recently, however, Scott Madey and his colleagues also had patrons in a bar make attractiveness ratings throughout the night. They found that these ratings increased as the night wore on only among patrons who were not committed to a relationship. As reactance theory would predict, closing time posed a threat—which sparked desire—only to those on the lookout for a late-night date.

Another possible instance of passion fueled by reactance can be seen in "the allure of secret relationships." In a fascinating experiment, Daniel Wegner and others paired up male and female college students to play bridge. Within each foursome, one couple was instructed in writing to play footsie under the table—either secretly or in the open. Got the picture? After a few minutes, the game was stopped, and the players were asked to indicate privately how attracted they were to their own partner and to the opposite-sex member of the other team. The result: Students who played footsie in secret were more attracted to each other than those who played in the open or not at all. This finding is certainly consistent with reactance theory. But there may be more to it. As we'll see later, the thrill of engaging in a forbidden act, or the sheer excitement of having to keep a secret, may help fan the flames of attraction.

Finally, it's important to realize that there are situations in which reactance reduces interpersonal attraction. Think about it. Have you ever tried to play the matchmaker by insisting that two of your unattached single friends get together? Be forewarned: Setting people up can backfire. Determined to preserve the freedom to make their own romantic choices, your friends may become *less* attracted to each other than they would have been without your encouragement.*

* Adapted from Sharon A. Brehm et al., *Social Psychology,* 5th ed. Boston: Houghton Mifflin, 2002, 316–318. Copyright © 2002 by Houghton Mifflin Company. Reprinted with permission.

1

Reading Selections

Practicing the Active Reading Strategy:*

Before and While You Read

You can use active reading strategies before, as, and after you read a selection. The following are some suggestions for active reading strategies that you can perform before you read and while you read.

1. Skim the selection for any unfamiliar words. Circle or highlight any words you do not know.
2. As you read, underline, highlight, or circle important words or phrases.
3. Write down any questions about the selection if you are confused by the information presented.
4. Jot notes in the margin to help you understand the material.

TEXTBOOK READING SELECTION

Time Management for College Students

1 You've got an exam on Friday and a paper due on Monday. You know you've got to get to work. Just then the phone rings. A group of friends from your dorm is going out for a snack. You know you shouldn't join them, but you've got to eat anyway, so you go along. When you return home you need a little time to unwind. You turn on the television. Two hours later you're relaxed, but you're also tired. You decide to call it a night. There's always tomorrow!

2 If this scenario sounds familiar, it should. It happens to all of us now and then. As a college student, however, it's very important to learn to manage your time effectively. The first step in managing your time effectively is to know where you're going. It helps to set goals for yourself. Although we may have vague notions of what we want from life, like being happy, or being a credit to society, or being financially secure, these generalized plans should be made concrete. Goals must be real. They must be examined closely. There are three different types that you should consider: long-range goals, medium-range goals, and short-range goals.

3 Long-range goals are usually personal wishes. They have to do with your career aims, your educational plans, and your social desires. Think about where you would like to be five or ten years from now. The education you are now receiving in college

* See pages 30–33 for a discussion of the active reading strategy.

should be a stepping stone to help you achieve your long-range goals. Besides achieving the benefit of learning, a college education pays off in dollars. College graduates earn about $700,000 more during their lifetimes than their counterparts who have no degrees. Depending on your career plans, the grades you earn in your courses will help determine whether or not you will be able to fulfill your long-range goals. To achieve long-range goals, they need to be broken into smaller parts and examined closely.

4 Medium-range goals, sometimes called mid-term goals, can be accomplished in one to five years. They help you achieve your long-range goals. They can be set two or three times a year. For example, if you plan to enter medical school after graduation, you will need a considerable number of A's in your courses. A medium-range goal would be to get four or five A's in your courses for four years. Another medium-range goal might be to join a club or improve your skills in your favorite sport. Let's say that your grades last semester weren't the best. A medium-range goal for you might then be to improve your grades. If you're saving money to buy a car, then watching your budget more carefully might be a reasonable goal to set.

5 Short-range goals, also called short-term goals, can be accomplished in a year or less. These goals involve taking care of your daily tasks and keeping up with your assignments. Reading a chapter in a book, completing an assignment, or writing a paper are examples of short-term goals.

6 Your college years are likely to be among the most demanding and enjoyable years of your life. During this time there are activities that will compete for your attention. Studying, developing relationships, and handling your financial affairs are among the most important challenges that will require your energy, creativity, and brain power. Learning to deal successfully with the different facets of your life can be accomplished by developing good coping skills. These are skills that will remain with you throughout your life and can be applied to just about any situation you'll encounter.*

VOCABULARY

Read the following questions about some of the vocabulary words that appear in the previous selection. Circle the letter of the correct answer.

1. In paragraph 2, what does the word *scenario* mean?

   a. sequence of events c. a map
   b. a floor plan d. an area

2. What does the word *considerable* mean in paragraph 4?

   a. not too many c. worrisome
   b. substantial d. positive

* From Sherman and Sherman, *Essential Concepts of Chemistry*. Boston: Houghton Mifflin, 1999. Copyright © 1999 by Houghton Mifflin Company. Reprinted with permission.

1

3. What are *vague notions* (paragraph 2)
   a. faulty conclusions
   b. unrealistic dreams
   c. crazy schemes
   d. unclear ideas

Practicing the Active Reading Strategy:

After You Read

Now that you have read the selection, answer the following questions using the active reading strategies that are discussed on pages 30–33.

1. Identify and write down the point and purpose of this reading selection.
2. Besides the vocabulary words included in the exercise above, are there any other vocabulary words that are unfamiliar to you? If so, write a list of them. When you have finished writing your list, look up each word in a dictionary and write the definition that best describes the word as it is used in the selection.
3. Predict any possible test questions that may be used on a test about the content of this selection.
4. How could you use the information contained in this selection? Does the information contained in the selection reinforce or contradict your ideas and experiences? Explain.

Questions for Discussion and Writing

Answer the following questions based on your reading of the selection. Write your answers on the blanks provided.

1. Did you enjoy this selection? Why or why not? ____________________

   ____

2. What new information, if any, did you learn from this selection?

   ____

   ____

3. Was there any information in this selection that you already knew? If so, what was it? ____________________

   ____

4. Write down a long-range goal, a medium-range goal, and a short-range goal and summarize the steps you will have to take to achieve each goal.

   ____

   ____

Literary Reading Selection

Practicing the Active Reading Strategy:*

Before and While You Read

You can use active reading strategies before, as, and after you read a selection. The following are some suggestions for active reading strategies that you can perform before you read and while you read.

1. Skim the selection for any unfamiliar words. Circle or highlight any words you do not know.
2. As you read, underline, highlight, or circle important words or phrases.
3. Write down any questions about the selection if you are confused by the information presented.
4. Jot notes in the margin to help you understand the material.

From *On the Road*

by Jack Kerouac

1 In the month of July 1947, having saved about fifty dollars from old veteran benefits, I was ready to go to the West Coast. My friend Remi Boncoeur had written me a letter from San Francisco, saying I should come and ship out with him on an around-the-world liner. He swore he could get me into the engine room. I wrote back and said I'd be satisfied with any old freighter so long as I could take a few long Pacific trips and come back with enough money to support myself in my aunt's house while I finished my book. He said he had a shack in Mill City and I would have all the time in the world to write there while we went through the rigamarole[1] of getting the ship. He was living with a girl called Lee Ann; he said she was a marvelous cook and everything would jump.[2] Remi was an old prep-school friend, a Frenchman brought up in Paris and a really mad guy—I didn't know how mad at this time. So he expected me to arrive in ten days. My aunt was all in accord with my trip to the West; she said it would do me good, I'd been working so hard all winter and staying in too much; she even didn't complain when I told her I'd have to hitchhike some. All she wanted was for me to come back in one piece. So, leaving my big half-manuscript sitting on top of my desk, and folding back my comfortable home sheets for the last time one morning,

1. **rigamarole:** complicated set of petty procedures

2. **jump:** "be great"

* See pages 30–33 for a discussion of the active reading strategy.

I left with my canvas bag in which a few fundamental things were packed and took off for the Pacific Ocean with the fifty dollars in my pocket.

2 I'd been poring over maps of the United States in Paterson for months, even reading books about the pioneers and savoring names like Platte and Cimarron and so on, and on the roadmap was one long red line called Route 6 that led from the tip of Cape Cod clear to Ely, Nevada, and there dipped down to Los Angeles. I'll just stay on 6 all the way to Ely, I said to myself and confidently started. To get to 6 I had to go up to Bear Mountain. Filled with dreams of what I'd do in Chicago, in Denver, and then finally in San Francisco, I took the Seventh Avenue subway to the end of the line at 242nd Street, and there took a trolley into Yonkers; in downtown Yonkers I transferred to an outgoing trolley and went to the city limits on the east bank of the Hudson River. If you drop a rose in the Hudson River at its mysterious source in the Adirondacks, think of all the places it journeys by as it goes out to sea forever—think of that wonderful Hudson Valley. I started hitching up the thing. Five scattered rides took me to the desired Bear Mountain Bridge, where Route 6 arched in from New England. It began to rain in torrents when I was let off there. It was mountainous. Route 6 came over the river, wound around a traffic circle, and disappeared into the wilderness. Not only was there no traffic but the rain came down in buckets and I had no shelter. I had to run under some pines to take cover; this did no good; I began crying and swearing and socking myself on the head for being such a damn fool. I was forty miles north of New York; all the way up I'd been worried about the fact that on this, my big opening day, I was only moving north instead of the so-longed-for west. Now I was stuck on my northernmost hangup. I ran a quarter-mile to an abandoned cute English-style filling station and stood under the dripping eaves. High up over my head the great hairy Bear Mountain sent down thunderclaps that put the fear of God in me. All I could see were smoky trees and dismal wilderness rising to the skies. "What the hell am I doing up here?" I cursed, I cried for Chicago. "Even now they're all having a big time, they're doing this, I'm not there, when will I get there!"—and so on. Finally a car stopped at the empty filling station; the man and the two women in it wanted to study a map. I stepped right up and gestured in the rain; they consulted; I looked like a maniac, of course, with my hair all wet, my shoes sopping. My shoes, damn fool that I am, were Mexican huaraches[1], plantlike sieves not fit for the rainy night of America and the raw road night. But the people let me in and rode me north to Newburgh, which I accepted as a better alternative than being trapped in the Bear Mountain wilderness all night. "Besides," said the man, "there's no traffic passes through 6. If you want to go to Chicago you'd do better going across the Holland Tunnel in New York and head for Pittsburgh," and I knew he was right. It was my dream that screwed up, the stupid hearthside idea that it would be wonderful to follow one great red line across America instead of trying various roads and routes.

3 In Newburgh it had stopped raining. I walked down to the river, and I had to ride back to New York in a bus with a delegation

1. **huaraches:** flat-heeled sandals

of schoolteachers coming back from a weekend in the mountains—chatter-chatter blah-blah, and me swearing for all the time and money I'd wasted, and telling myself, I wanted to go west and here I've been all day and into the night going up and down, north and south, like something that can't get started. And I swore I'd be in Chicago tomorrow, and made sure of that, taking a bus to Chicago, spending most of my money, and didn't give a damn, just as long as I'd be in Chicago tomorrow.*

Vocabulary

Read the following questions about some of the vocabulary words that appear in the previous selection. Circle the letter of the correct answer.

1. In paragraph 2, the author uses the word *poring*: "I'd been *poring* over maps of the United States in Paterson for months. . . ." Without using your dictionary, can you guess the meaning of the word *poring* from the context in which it is used?

   a. reading intensely
   b. standing
   c. sitting
   d. retelling stories about

2. What does it mean to *savor* something? Reread paragraph 2, sentence 1: ". . . even reading books about the pioneers and *savoring* names like Platte and Cimarron and so on, and on the roadmap was one long red line called Route 6 that led from the tip of Cape Cod clear to Ely, Nevada, and there dipped down to Los Angeles."

   a. to dislike
   b. to enjoy or appreciate
   c. to write down
   d. to erase

3. Paragraph 2: "All I could see were smoky trees and *dismal* wilderness rising to the skies." What does *dismal* mean?

   a. green
   b. joyful
   c. dreary
   d. uncluttered

4. What is a *sieve*? Paragraph 2: "My shoes, damn fool that I am, were Mexican huaraches, plantlike *sieves* not fit for the rainy night of America and the raw road night."

   a. a leaf
   b. a Mexican shoe
   c. a filter
   d. a shelter

1

Practicing the Active Reading Strategy:

After You Read

Now that you have read the selection, answer the following questions using the active reading strategies that are discussed on pages 30–33.

1. Identify and write down the point and purpose of this reading selection.
2. Besides the vocabulary words included in the exercise on page 39, are there any other vocabulary words that are unfamiliar to you? If so, write a list of them. When you have finished writing your list, look up each word in a dictionary and write the definition that best describes the word as it is used in the selection.
3. Predict any possible test questions that may be used on a test about the content of this selection.
4. How could you use the information contained in this selection? Does the information contained in the selection reinforce or contradict your ideas and experiences? Explain.

Questions for Discussion and Writing

Answer the following questions based on your reading of the selection. Write your answers on the blanks provided.

1. Did you enjoy this selection? Why or why not? ______________________

____

2. Based on your reading of the first selection in this section, *Time Management for College Students,* what could the author of *On the Road* have done differently to achieve his goal of going to San Francisco?

____

____

3. Based on your reading of the selection from *On the Road*, do you think the author achieves his goal of going to San Francisco? Why or why not?

____

____

4. Did you ever have a goal that you didn't achieve because of bad planning or because you didn't think it through? If so, what was it and why didn't you achieve it? Did you eventually achieve the goal through better planning and thinking? ______________________

____

Website Reading Selection

Practicing the Active Reading Strategy:*

Before and While You Read

You can use active reading strategies before, as, and after you read a selection. The following are some suggestions for active reading strategies that you can perform before you read and while you read.

1. Skim the selection for any unfamiliar words. Circle or highlight any words you do not know.
2. As you read, underline, highlight, or circle important words or phrases.
3. Write down any questions about the selection if you are confused by the information presented.
4. Jot notes in the margin to help you understand the material.

Ten Terrific Self-Motivating Tips

by Mike Moore

1 No one can motivate anyone to do anything. All a person can do for another is provide them with incentives to motivate themselves. Here are ten very effective strategies to help you get up and get moving toward actualizing your enormous, untapped potential.

2 • Be willing to leave your comfort zone. The greatest barrier to achieving your potential is your comfort zone. Great things happen when you make friends with your discomfort zone.

3 • Don't be afraid to make mistakes. Wisdom helps us avoid making mistakes and comes from making a million of them.

4 • Don't indulge in self-limiting thinking. Think empowering, expansive thoughts.

5 • Choose to be happy. Happy people are easily motivated. Happiness is your birthright so don't settle for anything else.

6 • Spend at least one hour a day in self-development. Read good books or listen to inspiring tapes. Driving to and from work provides an excellent opportunity to listen to self-improvement tapes.

7 • Train yourself to finish what you start. So many of us become scattered as we try to accomplish a task. Finish one task before you begin another.

* See pages 30–33 for a discussion of the active reading strategy.

8 • Live fully in the present moment. When you live in the past or the future you aren't able to make things happen in the present.

9 • Commit yourself to joy. C. S. Lewis[1] once said, "Joy is the serious business of heaven."

10 • Never quit when you experience a setback or frustration. Success could be just around the corner.

11 • Dare to dream big dreams. If there is anything to the law of expectation, then we are moving in the direction of our dreams, goals, and expectations.

12 The real tragedy in life is not in how much we suffer, but rather in how much we miss, so don't miss a thing.

13 Charles Dubois once said, "We must be prepared, at any moment, to sacrifice who we are for who we are capable of becoming."*

Vocabulary

Read the following questions about some of the vocabulary words that appear in the previous selection. Circle the letter of the correct answer.

1. In paragraph 1, what is the meaning of the word *incentives*?
   a. motives
   b. ideas
   c. thoughts
   d. words

2. In paragraph 1, what is the meaning of the word *actualizing*?
   a. beginning
   b. opening
   c. completing
   d. deciding

3. In paragraph 4, what does *empowering* mean?
   a. disarming
   b. lame
   c. wacky
   d. making strong; authorizing

4. In paragraph 4, what does *expansive* mean?
   a. narrow
   b. broad
   c. different
   d. similar

Practicing the Active Reading Strategy:

After You Read

Now that you have read the selection, answer the following questions using the active reading strategies that are discussed on pages 30–33.

1. **C. S. Lewis:** British author

* Mike Moore is an international speaker/writer on the role of appreciation, praise, and humor in performance motivation and human potential. You can check out his books, tapes, and manuals at www.motivationalplus.com. From http://www.topachievement.com/mikemoore.html website.

1. Identify and write down the point and purpose of this reading selection.
2. Besides the vocabulary words included in the exercise on page 42, are there any other vocabulary words that are unfamiliar to you? If so, write a list of them. When you have finished writing your list, look up each word in a dictionary and write the definition that best describes the word as it is used in the selection.
3. Predict any possible test questions that may be used on a test about the content of this selection.
4. How could you use the information contained in this selection? Does the information contained in the selection reinforce or contradict your ideas and experiences? Explain.

Questions for Discussion and Writing

Answer the following questions based on your reading of the selection. Write your answers on the blanks provided.

1. Did you enjoy this selection? Why or why not? ____________________

   ____

2. What new information, if any, did you learn from this selection? ______

   ____

3. Was there any information in this selection that you already knew? If so, what was it? ____________________________________

   ____

4. Is there any information in this selection that you can use to help you achieve your academic goals? What information or suggestions included in the selection can you incorporate into your daily life? How? ______

   ____

Vocabulary: Using the Dictionary

To increase your vocabulary and to ensure your comprehension of what you read, you'll need to keep a dictionary close by. The best dictionaries for college level reading are those that include the word *college* or *collegiate* in their title and are not older than five years. For example, *The American Heritage College Dictionary* is a good reference to have at home. You should also get in the habit of carrying a paperback dictionary with you to class.

Most dictionaries contain the following information:

- The spelling and pronunciation of the word, including its syllables and capital letters

- The word's part of speech (noun, verb, adjective, etc.)
- Words made from the main word, including plurals and verb forms
- The different meanings of the word, including special uses
- Synonyms (words that mean the same thing) for the word
- The history of the word
- Labels that identify the word's subject area or level of usage (for example, *slang* or *informal*)

The entry for a word may also contain a sentence that demonstrates the correct usage of the word. In addition, an entry may include *antonyms*, or words with the opposite meaning.

To use the dictionary effectively, you must understand how to locate a word and how to read the entry for that word once you find it.

Guide Words

All dictionaries list words in alphabetical order, which helps you find a word quickly. Another feature that helps you locate a particular word is the two **guide words** at the top of the page. The first guide word identifies the first word listed on that page. The second guide word tells you the last word on the page. Refer to Figure 1.2 to see an example of a dictionary page with guide words. If you want to find the word *coddle*, for example, you'd know to look for it on the page labeled with the guide words *cocktail table* and *coeno-*, because the first three letters of *cod,* come between *coc* and *coe*.

But what do you do if you're not sure how to spell a word you need to find? In that case, you'll have to try different possibilities based on the sound of the word. For example, let's say you were looking for the word *quiescent*, which means being still or quiet. This is a tough one because the first three letters are pronounced like *kwee*. First, you'd have to find out if the word begins with a *kw*, a *c*, or a *q*. Then, you'd have to figure out if the *ee* sound was spelled *ee, ea, ui*, or *i*. So you would try different combinations of these sounds until you found the right spelling. You could also try typing your best guess into a word processing program. Many of them include spell checkers that suggest alternatives when you misspell a word.

Understanding a Dictionary Entry

Every dictionary includes a guide at the front of the book that explains how to read the entries. This guide explains the abbreviations, symbols, and organization of different meanings, so you may need to consult it to know how to decipher the information. Various dictionaries differ in these details. However, they all usually contain certain types of standard information:

Main Entries

Meaning

Pronunciation Key

Part of Speech

History of Word

Guide Words

277

cocktail table

coeno–

regimen. **3.** An appetizer, such as mixed fruit served with juice or seafood served with a sharp sauce: *shrimp cocktail.* ❖ *adj.* **1.** Of or relating to cocktails: *a cocktail party.* **2.** Suitable for wear on semiformal occasions. [?]

cocktail table *n.* See **coffee table.**

cock•y (kŏk′ē) *adj.* **-i•er, -i•est** Overly self-assertive or self-confident. **—cock′i•ly** *adv.* **—cock′i•ness** *n.*

Co•co (kō′kō) A river rising in N Nicaragua and flowing c. 483 km (300 mi) to the Caribbean Sea.

co•coa (kō′kō) *n.* **1a.** A powder made from cacao seeds after they have been fermented, roasted, shelled, ground, and freed of most of their fat. **b.** A beverage made by mixing this powder with sugar in hot water or milk. **2.** A moderate brown to reddish brown. [Alteration (influenced by *coco,* coconut palm; see COCONUT) of CACAO.] **—co′coa** *adj.*

cocoa bean *n.* See **cacao** 2.

cocoa butter *n.* A yellowish-white fatty solid obtained from cacao seeds and used in cosmetics, chocolate, and soap.

co•co•nut also **co•coa•nut** (kō′kə-nŭt′, -nət) *n.* **1.** The fruit of the coconut palm, consisting of a fibrous husk surrounding a large seed. **2.** The large, brown, hard-shelled seed of the coconut, containing white flesh surrounding a partially fluid-filled central cavity. **3.** The edible white flesh of the coconut. **4.** A coconut palm. [Port. *côco,* grinning skull, goblin, coconut (prob. < LLat. *coccum,* shell; see COCOON) + NUT.]

coconut milk *n.* **1.** A milky fluid extracted from the flesh of the coconut, used in foods or as a beverage. **2.** The watery fluid in the central cavity of the coconut, used chiefly as a beverage.

coconut oil *n.* An oil or semisolid fat obtained from the flesh of the coconut, used in foods, cosmetics, and soaps.

coconut palm *n.* A feather-leaved palm *(Cocos nucifera)* extensively cultivated in tropical regions for food, beverages, oil, thatching, fiber, utensils, and ornament.

co•coon (kə-ko͞on′) *n.* **1a.** A protective case of silk or similar fibrous material spun by the larvae of moths and other insects that serves as a covering for their pupal stage. **b.** A similar natural protective covering or structure, such as the egg case of a spider. **2.** A protective plastic coating that is placed over stored military or naval equipment. **3.** Something suggestive of a cocoon in appearance or purpose. ❖ *v.* **-cooned, -coon•ing, -coons** *—tr.* To envelop in or as if in a cocoon. *—intr.* To retreat as if into a cocoon. [Fr. *cocon* < Provençal *coucoun,* dim. of *coco,* shell < LLat. *coccum* < Lat., berry, oak gall < Gk. *kokkos,* seed, berry.]

coco plum or **co•co•plum** (kō′kō-plŭm′) *n.* An evergreen shrub or small tree *(Chrysobalanus icaco)* native to the American and African tropics and having plumlike fruit. [Alteration of Sp. *icaco* < Arawak *ikaku.*]

Co•cos Islands (kō′kōs) also **Kee•ling Islands** (kē′lĭng) An Australian-administered island group in the E Indian Ocean SW of Sumatra.

co•cotte (kô-kôt′) *n.* A woman prostitute. [Fr., chicken, prostitute < fem. dim. of *coq,* cock < OFr. See COCK[1].]

co•co•yam (kō′kō-yăm′) *n.* See **taro** 2. [COCO(A) + YAM.]

Coc•teau (kŏk-tō′, kôk-), **Jean** 1889–1963. French writer and filmmaker whose works include the novel *Les Enfants Terrible* (1929) and the film *Beauty and the Beast* (1945).

Co•cy•tus (kō-kī′təs, -sī′-) *n. Greek Mythology* One of the five rivers of Hades.

cod[1] (kŏd) *n., pl.* **cod** or **cods** Any of various marine fishes of the family Gadidae, esp. *Gadus morhua,* a food fish of northern Atlantic waters. [ME.]

cod[2] (kŏd) *n.* **1.** A husk or pod. **2.** *Archaic* The scrotum. **3.** *Obsolete* A bag. [ME < OE *codd.*]

Cod, Cape A hook-shaped peninsula of SE MA extending E and N into the Atlantic Ocean.

COD *abbr.* **1.** cash on delivery **2.** collect on delivery

co•da (kō′də) *n.* **1.** *Music* The concluding passage of a movement or composition. **2.** A conclusion or closing part of a statement. [Ital. < Lat. *cauda,* tail.]

cod•dle (kŏd′l) *tr.v.* **-dled, -dling, -dles 1.** To cook in water just below the boiling point. **2.** To treat indulgently; baby. [Poss. alteration of CAUDLE.] **—cod′dler** *n.*

code (kōd) *n.* **1.** A systematically arranged and comprehensive collection of laws. **2.** A systematic collection of regulations and rules of procedure or conduct: *a traffic code.* **3a.** A system of signals used to represent letters or numbers in transmitting messages. **b.** A system of symbols, letters, or words given certain arbitrary meanings, used for messages requiring secrecy or brevity. **4.** A system of symbols and rules used to represent instructions to a computer; a computer program. **5.** The genetic code. **6.** *Slang* A patient whose heart has stopped beating, as in cardiac arrest. ❖ *v.* **cod•ed, cod•ing, codes** *—tr.* **1.** To systematize and arrange (laws and regulations) into a code. **2.** To convert (a message, for example) into code. *—intr.* **1.** To specify the genetic code for an amino acid or a polypeptide. **2.** To write or revise a computer program. **3.** *Medicine* To go into cardiac arrest. [ME < OFr. < Lat. *cōdex,* book. See CODEX.]

code blue *n.* A medical emergency that involves signaling personnel to aid a person in cardiac arrest.

co•dec•li•na•tion (kō′dĕk-lə-nā′shən) *n. Astronomy* The complement of the declination.

co•de•fen•dant (kō′dĭ-fĕn′dənt) *n. Law* A joint defendant.

co•deine (kō′dēn′, -dē-ĭn) *n.* An alkaloid narcotic, $C_{18}H_{21}NO_3$, derived from opium or morphine and used as a cough suppressant, analgesic, and hypnotic. [Fr. *codéine* : Gk. *kōdeia,* poppy head (< *kōos,* cavity) + *-ine,* alkaloid; see –INE[2].]

code name *n.* A name assigned to conceal the identity or existence of something or someone.

co•de•ter•mi•na•tion (kō′dĭ-tûr′mə-nā′shən) *n.* Cooperation, esp. between labor and management, in policymaking.

code word *n.* **1.** A secret word or phrase used as a code name or password. **2.** A euphemism.

co•dex (kō′dĕks′) *n., pl.* **co•di•ces** (kō′dĭ-sēz′, kŏd′ĭ-) A manuscript volume, esp. of a classic work or of the Scriptures. [Lat. *cōdex, cōdic-,* tree trunk, wooden tablet, book, var. of *caudex,* trunk.]

cod•fish (kŏd′fĭsh′) *n., pl.* **codfish** or **-fish•es** See **cod**[1].

codg•er (kŏj′ər) *n. Informal* A somewhat eccentric man, esp. an old one. [Perh. alteration of obsolete *cadger,* peddler. See CADGE.]

cod•i•cil (kŏd′ə-sĭl) *n.* A supplement or appendix, esp. to a will. [ME < OFr. *codicille* < Lat. *cōdicillus,* dim. of *cōdex, cōdic-,* codex. See CODEX.] **—cod′i•cil′la•ry** (kŏd′ə-sĭl′ə-rē) *adj.*

cod•i•fy (kŏd′ĭ-fī′, kō′də-) *tr.v.* **-fied, -fy•ing, -fies 1.** To reduce to a code: *codify laws.* **2.** To arrange or systematize. **—cod′i•fi•ca′tion** (-fĭ-kā′shən) *n.* **—cod′i•fi′er** *n.*

cod•ling[1] (kŏd′lĭng) also **cod•lin** (-lĭn) *n.* **1.** A greenish elongated English apple used for cooking. **2.** A small unripe apple. [Alteration of ME *querdlyng,* poss. < AN **querdelion,* lionheart : OFr. *cuer,* heart; see COURAGE + *de,* of (< Lat. *dē;* see DE–) + OFr. *lion,* lion; see LION.]

cod•ling[2] (kŏd′lĭng) *n., pl.* **codling** or **-lings** A young cod.

codling moth also **codlin moth** *n.* A grayish moth *(Carpocapsa pomonella)* whose larvae are destructive to various fruits.

cod-liv•er oil (kŏd′lĭv′ər) *n.* An oil obtained from the liver of cod and related fishes, used as a source of vitamins A and D.

co•dom•i•nance (kō-dŏm′ə-nəns) *n.* A condition in which both alleles are codominant.

co•dom•i•nant (kō-dŏm′ə-nənt) *adj.* **1.** *Genetics* Of or being two alleles of a gene pair in a heterozygote that are both fully expressed. **2a.** *Ecology* Being one of two or more of the most characteristic species in a biotic community. **b.** Influencing the presence and type of other species in the community. ❖ *n. Ecology* A codominant species in a biotic community.

co•don (kō′dŏn′) *n.* A sequence of three adjacent nucleotides constituting the genetic code that determines the insertion of a specific amino acid in a polypeptide chain during protein synthesis. [COD(E) + –ON[1].]

cod•piece (kŏd′pēs′) *n.* A pouch at the crotch of the tight-fitting breeches worn by men in the 15th and 16th centuries. [ME *codpece* : *cod,* bag, scrotum (< OE *codd,* bag) + *pece,* piece; see PIECE.]

cods•wal•lop (kŏdz′wŏl′əp) *n. Chiefly British Slang* Nonsense; rubbish. [?]

Co•dy (kō′dē), **William Frederick** Known as "Buffalo Bill." 1846–1917. Amer. frontier scout who after 1883 toured the US and Europe with his Wild West Show.

co•ed or **co-ed** (kō′ĕd′) *Informal n.* A woman who attends a coeducational college or university. ❖ *adj.* **1.** Coeducational. **2.** Open to both sexes. [Short for *coeducational.*]

co•ed•it (kō-ĕd′ĭt) *tr.v.* **-ed•it•ed, -ed•it•ing, -ed•its** To edit (a print publication or a film) jointly with another or others. **—co•ed′i•tor** *n.*

co•ed•u•ca•tion (kō-ĕj′ə-kā′shən) *n.* The system of education in which both sexes attend the same institution or classes. **—co•ed′u•ca′tion•al** *adj.* **—co•ed′u•ca′tion•al•ly** *adv.*

co•ef•fi•cient (kō′ə-fĭsh′ənt) *n.* **1.** A number or symbol multiplied with a variable or an unknown quantity in an algebraic term, as 4 in the term $4x$ or x in the term $x(a + b)$. **2.** A numerical measure of a physical or chemical property that is constant for a system under specified conditions.

–coel or **–coele** or **–cele** *suff.* Chamber; cavity: *blastocoel.* [NLat. *-coela* < Gk. *koilos,* hollow.]

coe•la•canth (sē′lə-kănth′) *n.* Any of various mostly extinct fishes of the order Coelacanthiformes. [NLat. *Coelacanthus,* former genus name : Gk. *koilos,* hollow; see –COEL + Gk. *akantha,* spine.] **—coe′la•can′thine′** (-kăn′thīn′, -thĭn), **coe′la•can′thous** (-thəs) *adj.*

coe•len•ter•ate (sĭ-lĕn′tə-rāt′, -tər-ĭt) *n.* See **cnidarian.** [< NLat. *Coelenterāta,* phylum name : *coelenter(on),* coelenteron; see COELENTERON + Lat. *-āta,* neut. pl. of *-ātus,* -ate; see –ATE[1].] **—coe•len′ter•ate′, coe•len•ter′ic** (-tĕr′ĭk) *adj.*

coe•len•ter•on (sĭ-lĕn′tə-rŏn′, -tər-ən) *n., pl.* **-te•ra** (-tər-ə) The saclike cavity within the body of a coelenterate. [NLat. : Gk. *koilos,* hollow; see –COEL + ENTERON.]

coe•li•ac (sē′lē-ăk′) *adj.* Variant of **celiac.**

coe•lom also **ce•lom** or **coe•lome** (sē′ləm) *n.* The cavity within the body of all animals higher than the cnidarians and certain primitive worms, formed by the splitting of the embryonic mesoderm into two layers. [Ger. *Koelom* < Gk. *koilōma,* cavity < *koilos,* hollow.] **—coe•lom′ic** (sĭ-lŏm′ĭk, -lō′mĭk) *adj.*

coe•lo•mate (sē′lə-māt′) *adj.* Possessing a coelom: *a coelomate animal.* **—coe′lo•mate** *n.*

coeno– or **ceno–** *pref.* Common: *coenocyte.* [NLat. < Gk. *koino-*

coconut palm
Cocos nucifera

Buffalo Bill Cody

coelacanth
Latimeria chalumnae

ă	pat	oi	boy
ā	pay	ou	out
âr	care	o͝o	took
ä	father	o͞o	boot
ĕ	pet	ŭ	cut
ē	be	ûr	urge
ĭ	pit	th	thin
ī	pie	*th*	this
îr	pier	hw	which
ŏ	pot	zh	vision
ō	toe	ə	about,
ô	paw		item

Stress marks:
′ (primary);
′ (secondary), as in
lexicon (lĕk′sĭ-kŏn′)

Figure 1.2 Dictionary Page

Source: Copyright © 2004 by Houghton Mifflin Company. Reproduced by permission from *The American Heritage College Dictionary,* Fourth Edition.

1

The main entry. Each word in a dictionary appears in bold print with dots dividing its syllables. This word is correctly spelled, of course, and any alternative spellings for the word follow.

Pronunciation key. Usually in parentheses following the main entry, the word's pronunciation is represented with symbols, letters, and other marks. The guide at the front of the dictionary will provide a list of the corresponding sounds for each letter or symbol. For example, the symbol ə is pronounced like *uh*. The accent mark shows you what syllable to stress when you say the word. For example, the pronunciation key for the word *codominant* on the sample dictionary page in Figure 1.2 tells you to emphasize the second syllable when you say the word.

The part of speech. The next part of the entry is an abbreviation that identifies the word's part of speech. *N.* means noun, *v.* means verb, *adj.* stands for adjective, and so on. Refer to the list of abbreviations in the guide at the front of the dictionary to find out what other abbreviations mean.

The meanings of the word. The different meanings of a word are divided first according to their part of speech. All of the meanings related to a particular part of speech are grouped together. For example, the word *project* can function as both a noun and a verb. All of its noun meanings appear first, followed by all of its verb meanings. Dictionaries order each set of meanings in different ways, usually from most common to least common or from oldest to newest. Different senses, or shades of meaning, are numbered. Following the list of meanings, the dictionary may provide synonyms and/or antonyms for the word.

The history of the word. Some dictionaries provide information about the origin of a word. This history usually includes the word's language of origin, along with its various evolutions.

Vocabulary Exercise 1

A. Put these words in alphabetical order on the blank lines.

eagle	______________	elf	______________
egg	______________	elbow	______________
effort	______________	eclipse	______________
ease	______________	eclair	______________

B. Beneath each set of guide words, circle each word that would appear on the page labeled with those guide words.

1. **lackaday/ladyfinger**

lacquer	ladle	ladybug
lack	lackey	ladyfish

2. **paisley/paleolith**

palette	palate	pale
Paleolithic	pajama	pair

3. **trawl/tree**

treasure	tread	travesty
treatise	treetop	treble

4. **apple/apprehend**

apprehension	appreciative	applesauce
applause	apprentice	apply

5. **microfilament/microwave oven**

microfiche	microcosm	microfilm
microscope	microsurgery	microphone

C. Write your answers to the following questions on the blanks provided.

1. What is the plural of *yourself*? ____________________
2. How many different parts of speech can the word *left* be? ____________________

   ____
3. What is a synonym for the word *yield*? ____________________

   ____
4. What language does the word *ketchup* come from? ____________________
5. How many different pronunciations does your dictionary provide for the word *often*? ____________________
6. Does the noun *bough* rhyme with *rough* or *so* or *vow*? ____________________
7. How many syllables does the word *liege* contain? ____________________

1

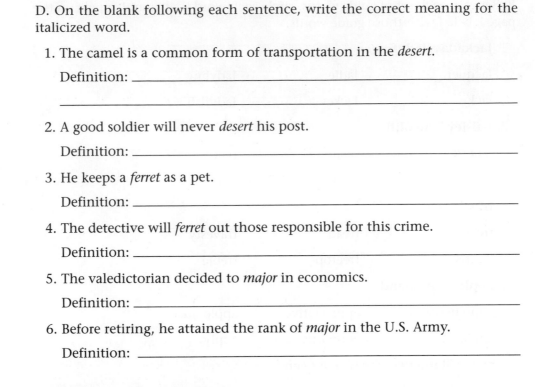

D. On the blank following each sentence, write the correct meaning for the italicized word.

1. The camel is a common form of transportation in the *desert*.

   Definition: ______________________________

   ____

2. A good soldier will never *desert* his post.

   Definition: ______________________________

3. He keeps a *ferret* as a pet.

   Definition: ______________________________

4. The detective will *ferret* out those responsible for this crime.

   Definition: ______________________________

5. The valedictorian decided to *major* in economics.

   Definition: ______________________________

6. Before retiring, he attained the rank of *major* in the U.S. Army.

   Definition: ______________________________

Vocabulary Exercise 2

Use the dictionary to look up the boldfaced, italicized words in the following passage. Write the meanings of the words in the blanks provided.

A 36-year study of about 560 female lions in Tanzania found that lionesses do not establish a ***hierarchy*** in which dominant cats breed more than ***subservient*** ones. This ***egalitarianism*** is unusual in animals that live in social groups and contrasts greatly with the mating behavior of other status-conscious ***mammalian*** predators.

University of Minnesota behavioral ***ecologist*** Craig Packer, who led the study, published in the journal *Science,* said lionesses experience approximately equal reproductive success and even cooperate with one another in raising their cubs. The male of the species is not so ***accommodating.*** Packer said males establish a clear pecking order, and a dominant lion usually ***sires*** most of the offspring, a trait confirmed by researchers with DNA testing. "The male lion . . . is a bit of a ***despot,***" Packer said.*

* Adapted from Will Dunham, "Female Lions, Share of Mating Is Equal," *USA Today,* July 30, 2001, 7D.

hierarchy ____________________

subservient ____________________

egalitarianism ____________________

mammalian ____________________

____

ecologist ____________________

accommodating ____________________

sires ____________________

despot ____________________

Reading Visuals

Visual aids, which are also known as *graphics,* are types of illustrations that represent data or information in a visual form. Visual aids include tables, charts, different types of graphs, diagrams, or maps. You will often encounter all of these kinds of visuals when you read, especially when the purpose of a reading selection is to inform or explain. Publications such as textbooks, magazines, journals, and instruction manuals will often include visuals to aid, or help, the reader in understanding the information. Many job-related documents will also contain visual aids.

Texts include visual aids for many reasons. For one thing, they can summarize a lot of information or complex information in a relatively small space. Think about a flow chart, for instance. A flow chart provides a visual summary of the steps in a process. It allows you to see a condensed version of even a complicated procedure.

Another reason for visual aids is their ability to clarify and reinforce textual explanations. In most publications, visual aids do not substitute for written presentation of information. Instead, they provide another way of "seeing" what the words are saying. A diagram in an instruction manual is one example. When you are assembling something like a barbecue grill or a child's swing set, it's helpful to check your understanding of the directions by looking at a diagram that labels the parts and shows how they fit together. You use both the written explanation and the visual aid to figure out what you need to do.

Continued

Visual aids also allow readers to quickly see the important data or facts. For instance, a graph reveals, at a glance, trends over time. An organizational chart allows readers to quickly grasp the chain of command within a company.

Finally, visual aids provide a way for readers to find a particular detail quickly and easily. A table, for example, that organizes facts into columns and rows allows a reader to easily locate one specific piece of information he or she needs.

General Tips for Reading Visual Aids

The following tips will help you improve your comprehension of reading selections that include visuals:

- **Don't skip a visual aid.** Passive readers ignore visual aids because they don't want to take the time to read them. Skipping visual aids, however, robs you of chances to improve and/or reinforce your understanding of the information in the text. When authors invest the time and effort necessary to create a visual, they do so because they believe a visual representation is particularly important. Therefore, get in the habit of reading over each visual as well as the text.
- **Look at a visual aid when the text directs you to do so.** As you read, you'll come across references to visual aids. Resist the urge to "save them for later." Instead, when a sentence mentions a visual, as in "See Figure 2," or "Table 1 presents the results . . ." and tells you where to find it (below, to the left, on page 163, etc.), find the visual and read it before going any further. Remember, most visuals reinforce information in a text. The writer's explanation will often state the conclusion you should draw from the visual, and the visual provides more insight into the textual explanation. So, you'll get more out of both of them when you read a passage and its corresponding visual together.
- **Follow a three-step procedure for interpreting the information in a visual aid:**
  1. First, read the title, the caption, and the source line. The title and caption or brief descriptions will usually identify the visual aid's subject and main point. They will help you understand what you're seeing. The source line, which identifies where the information comes from, will help you decide whether the information is accurate and trustworthy.

2. Next, study the information represented in the visual, and try to state the relationships you see in your own words. For example, you might say, "This graph shows that sales of sport utility vehicles have been growing since 1985," or "This table shows that teachers in the Midwest earn higher salaries than teachers in the rest of the country."
3. Finally, check your understanding of the relationship against its corresponding explanation in the text. Locate where the visual is mentioned, and verify that the conclusion you drew is accurate.

Each of the next eight chapters will cover one of the most common types of visual aids and provide you with more specific tips for improving your understanding of each kind. To see what you already know about visual aids, complete the questions that follow the two visuals.

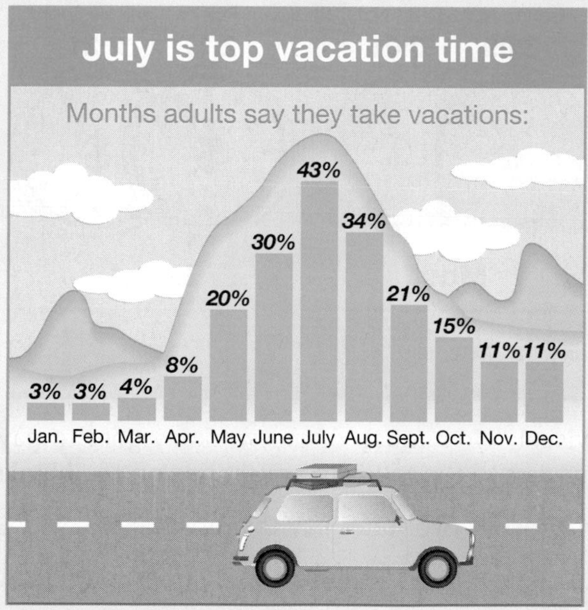

Source: *USA Today*, July 5, 2001, ID.

Study the bar graph "July is top vacation time" and then write your answers to the questions on the blanks provided.

1. What does this visual describe? ________________
2. Which month is the second most popular for vacationing? ________
3. Is October or September more popular as a time for vacations?

____

Continued

1

4. What percentages of adults take vacations in February? ____________

5. Which two months are the least popular for vacations? ____________

____

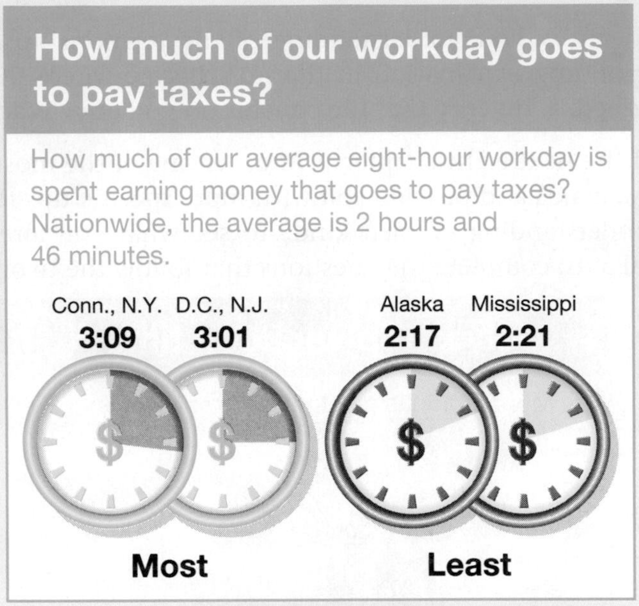

How much of our workday goes to pay taxes?

How much of our average eight-hour workday is spent earning money that goes to pay taxes? Nationwide, the average is 2 hours and 46 minutes.

Source: *USA Today,* 1997.

Review the visual "How much of our workday goes to pay taxes?" and write your answers to the following questions on the blanks provided.

6. Residents in what two states pay the most taxes? ____________ ____________ How much time in one day does someone in Mississippi work to earn money for taxes? ____________

7. Residents of what state pay the least amount of taxes? ____________

8. What is the national average for amount of time worked in one day to pay for taxes? ____________

9. The information in this visual is based on a workday that is how long? ____________

CHAPTER 1 TESTS

Name ______________________________ Date ____________________

TEST 1

Answer each of the following questions by circling the letter of the correct answer.

1. A dislike for reading often arises from undeveloped reading skills.
   a. true b. false
2. Good reading skills are critical to success in college.
   a. true b. false
3. Reading is actually a collection of different mental skills.
   a. true b. false
4. A negative attitude about reading will not affect reading comprehension.
   a. true b. false
5. You cannot understand or retain information unless you read with concentration.
   a. true b. false
6. Thinking about your plans for the weekend while you're trying to read is an example of an external distraction.
   a. true b. false
7. When you visualize, you pay extra attention to the visuals (such as graphs, charts, and photos) in a text.
   a. true b. false
8. To improve memory, a reader can associate new information with what he or she already knows.
   a. true b. false
9. Analysis is one type of logical thought.
   a. true b. false
10. Reading strategies are techniques you use when you read.
    a. true b. false

For additional tests, see the Test Bank.

A. Read the following passage from a textbook and answer the questions that follow by circling the letter of the correct answer.

Risks from Asteroids—the Torino Scale

1 Will an asteroid ever strike the Earth? We see science fiction movies with suspenseful plots involving asteroids coming directly toward the Earth. But the catastrophe is avoided, perhaps by deflecting the asteroid with a nuclear-tipped missile, making for sighs of relief and a happy ending. However, asteroids are not science fiction, and there is evidence that they have struck the Earth in the past. In fact, a popular theory relates the extinction of dinosaurs to an asteroid collision some 65 million years ago. Will future collisions occur? Although it is remote, the possibility does exist.

2 We now even have a scale by which damage may be gauged in the event of an impact by an asteroid or comet—the Torino scale (Fig.1). It is sometimes referred to as the "Richter scale for asteroids." (The Richter scale is used to describe the severity of earthquakes.)

3 The Torino scale was intended to serve as a communication tool for astronomers and the general public to assess the seriousness of close encounters or hits by asteroids and comets. An initial version of the scale was developed in 1995 by Professor Richard P. Bizel of the Massachusetts Institute of Technology (M.I.T.). A revised version was presented at a 1999 international conference on Near-Earth Objects, or NEOs (Sun-orbiting asteroids and comets) held in Torino, Italy. This revised version was officially accepted by the conference, hence the name *Torino scale.*

4 The Torino scale uses numbers and colors to express the *estimated* risk and damage of an asteroid or comet colliding with the Earth; the estimates are based on the NEO's collision probability[1] and kinetic[2] energy. A rating of 0 or 1 indicates a low probability of collision. A rating of 10 shows a high probability of collision, with global catastrophic effects. The vast majority of asteroids and comets fall in the 0 category, which (like a low number on the earthquake Richter scale) helps moderate the public's reaction to an asteroid report. In 1998, a false alarm of a possible asteroid encounter received considerable media coverage, raising public concern. With more observations and path calculations, the asteroid was given a 0 rating on the Torino scale, so there was no need for concern.

5 When a new asteroid or comet is discovered, the predictions of the object's path months or years in the future are not too precise. Measurements of the object's orbit must be made over time for calculations that allow for greater certainty in predictions. Fortunately for us, the calculations for the vast majority of asteroids and comets show that there will not be a close approach to the Earth, so a Torino scale designation of category 0 is assigned. What a relief!

1. **probability:** likelihood

2. **kinetic:** relating to motion

THE TORINO SCALE

Events having no likely consequences	0	The likelihood of a collision is zero, or well below the chance that a random object of the same size will strike the Earth within the next few decades. This designation also applies to any small object that, in the event of a collision, is unlikely to reach the Earth's surface intact.
Events meriting careful monitoring	1	The chance of collision is extremely unlikely, about the same as a random object of the same size striking the Earth within the next few decades.
Events meriting concern	2	A somewhat close but not unusual encounter. Collision is very unlikely.
	3	A close encounter, with 1% or greater chance of a collision capable of causing localized destruction.
	4	A close encounter, with 1% or greater chance of a collision capable of causing regional devastation.
Threatening events	5	A close encounter, with a significant threat of a collision capable of causing regional devastation.
	6	A close encounter, with a significant threat of a collision capable of causing a global catastrophe.
	7	A close encounter, with an extremely significant threat of a collision capable of causing a global catastrophe.
Certain collision	8	A collision capable of causing localized destruction. Such events occur somewhere on the Earth between once per 50 years and once per 1000 years.
	9	A collision capable of causing regional devastation. Such events occur between once per 1000 years and once per 100,000 years.
	10	A collision capable of causing a global climatic catastrophe. Such events occur once per 100,000 years, or less often.

This scale is used to assess the risks of asteroid and comet impacts in the twenty-first century.*

* From James T. Shipman et al., *An Introduction to Physical Science,* 10th ed. Boston: Houghton Mifflin, 2003, 406. Copyright © 2003 by Houghton Mifflin Company. Reprinted with permission.

1

1. There is no chance that an asteroid will ever hit Earth again.
   a. true
   b. false
   c. The article does not say.
2. What is the purpose of the Torino scale?
   a. The scale uses numbers and colors to express estimated risk and damage of an asteroid colliding with Earth.
   b. The scale shows how hard the impact will be if an asteroid hit a specific city.
   c. The scale shows how much asteroids weigh.
   d. The scale measures the size of asteroids.
3. A rating of 0 or 1 on the Torino scale indicates
   a. a high probability of collision.
   b. a low probability of collision.
   c. the size of the crater on impact.
   d. the force at which the collision will occur.
4. How did the scale get its name?
   a. from its inventor.
   b. from the name of the last asteroid to hit Earth.
   c. from the city where a conference on asteroids was held.
   d. The article does not say.
5. In what year was a false alarm of a possible asteroid encounter reported?
   a. 1996
   b. 1997
   c. 1998
   d. 1999

B. Read the memo below and respond to the questions that follow by circling the letter of the correct answer.

MEMORANDUM

To: All Employees

From: Building Safety and Maintenance

Date: March 15, 20—

Subject: Procedures for Dealing with Chemical Splashes on Skin

The purpose of the University of California, Riverside Emergency Action Plan is to ensure the safety of all UCR employees. Please take a moment to review the procedures to follow in the event of a chemical splash on the skin:

1. Remove chemical contact with the skin by brushing off dry and water reactive chemicals and removing contaminated clothing and protective equipment that can be removed quickly (1 second or less).

2. Flush the splashed area with large amounts of potable (clean and drinkable) water. Never use anything other than water or mild soap and water to clean chemicals from the skin.

3. Remove protective eyewear under the emergency shower as quickly as possible when chemicals have entered the eyes. In cases where the eyewear has not been breached[1] by the chemical, remove the protective eyewear after head and face have been thoroughly washed.

4. Wash with potable water for 15 minutes or longer. Wash any part of the skin that may have had chemical contact or contact with contaminated wash water. Remove any clothing that may have come in contact with the chemical or contaminated wash water under the emergency shower.

5. Washing should give special attention to areas that may be missed, such as underneath the earlobes, underneath the arms, the crotch, between the toes, the creases at the sides of the nose, a deep cleft in the chin, etc.

6. Get medical assistance. Provide Material Safety Data Sheets (MSDSs) for the involved chemicals to medical personnel.

7. If the emergency water used for flushing is cold, the injured person should be treated for shock on completion of washing.

8. If a splash causes a thermal burn as well as a chemical burn, be sure to advise the attending medical personnel of the nature of the chemical exposure.

9. After washing of the victim is completed, rescuers need to wash themselves to prevent injury from diluted chemicals washed off from the victim.

Please report all chemical spill accidents to your immediate supervisor as soon as you are able to do so.*

1. breached: broken through or into

* Adapted from "Manuals and Policies," UCR Environmental Health and Safety, University of California, Riverside.

6. What is the first thing a person should do in the event of a chemical splash?
   a. remove contaminated clothing immediately
   b. call for help
   c. read the safety manual
   d. go to a doctor
7. You should never use anything but these two items to clean the affected area.
   a. water and a harsh cleanser
   b. water and a mild soap
   c. milk and honey
   d. water and body lotion
8. What should rescuers do after helping a chemical splash victim?
   a. change their clothes
   b. wash themselves
   c. run away
   d. see a doctor
9. Where should a victim remove protective eyewear?
   a. in the lab
   b. outside
   c. under a towel
   d. under the emergency shower
10. According to the memo, what should a victim bring when seeking medical care?
    a. the chemical in question
    b. his or her medical history
    c. Material Safety Data Sheets
    d. his or her medical insurance ID card

C. Read the following selection from a newspaper and respond to the questions that follow by circling the letter of the correct answer.

1 Each day millions of Americans open their e-mail accounts only to watch in horror as messages appear touting everything from pornography to vitamins.

2 While spam mailers have long irritated Internet users with junk e-mail, a recent surge in spamming makes the problem greater than a mere annoyance. Professionals who measure spam point to an eightfold increase from 2001 to 2002.

3 Technology experts worry that spamming could end up compromising the usefulness of the world's e-mail system. That could happen if measures being considered to stop spam are so Draconian[1] that they hinder Internet commerce.

1. **draconian:** harsh, severe

4 The central problem is that sending spam is irresistibly easy. For less than $100, a spammer can acquire the software and e-mail addresses—available from other spammers—to reach hundreds of thousands of e-mail targets.

5 But the costs to e-mail users include the added time required to download spam and a lost confidence in e-mail's usefulness. Internet experts say that spam is already causing a large number of people to leave fake e-mail addresses anytime a commercial site requires them to register.

6 Spam also puts a heavy burden on the world's e-mail system. Big Internet service providers, such as AOL and EarthLink, get stuck trying to filter spam out of their systems—a tough game that resembles whack-a-mole.[1] The Internet provider EarthLink estimates that more than one-quarter of the 2 billion e-mails a month moving on its network are spam. The company stops a lot, but it can't whack them all.

7 Solving the problem is tricky, which is why spammers appear to be holding the upper hand, at least for now.

8 Filters used by Internet providers can identify and delete a large portion of spam. But senders have too many ways to change the shape and appearance of the e-mail.

9 The toughest approach would be to ban spam, something that was done to junk faxes in 1991. But faxes and e-mails are very different. A ban on spam could choke off thousands of Internet businesses by denying them the opportunity to make even one offer to potential customers.

10 Better to give companies one chance to approach consumers, as long as customers can opt out of future e-mails.

11 A proposal under consideration in Congress, for example, requires commercial e-mailers to clearly identify themselves and allow consumers to cut off future messages using one keystroke. E-mailers who persist risk prosecution.

12 A national law would help states struggling with the same problem. In 2002, the New York state attorney general sued a Niagara Falls spammer for sending out junk e-mail to hundreds of millions of customers who say they never gave their permission. Many tried unsuccessfully to remove their addresses from the company's list.

13 If a tough national opt-out law doesn't work, a complete ban may become necessary. But not yet.*

1. **whack-a-mole:** a game that involves hitting plastic moles with a mallet as they pop out of holes

* Adapted from "Limit Junk E-mail," no author credited, *USA Today,* June 7, 2002, www.usatoday.com.

11. According to the author of this newspaper article, the toughest approach to dealing with spam would be to
    a. jail spammers.
    b. allow the FBI to investigate spam and people who send spam.
    c. ban spam.
    d. create a program that filters all spam, all the time.

12. According to the author, from 2001 to 2002,
    a. spam increased eightfold.
    b. spam resulted in many computer viruses on the Internet.
    c. spam decreased.
    d. spam became more informative.

13. Of the following, which one is NOT an effect of the widespread use of spam as an advertising tactic?
    a. People have lost confidence in e-mail's usefulness.
    b. People leave fake e-mail addresses when they use commercial sites.
    c. Spam puts a heavy burden on the world's e-mail system.
    d. Spam has created widespread computer viruses.

14. According to the author, sending spam is
    a. hard to do.
    b. getting harder due to new laws that have been put into effect.
    c. easy to send because the software is inexpensive and e-mail addresses are readily available.
    d. becoming the only way some businesses are advertising.

15. Ultimately, the author thinks that
    a. it is not yet time to ban spam entirely.
    b. spam should be outlawed.
    c. people who send spam should be prosecuted.
    d. spam is really not such a big deal.

2

CHAPTER 2

Main Ideas

GOALS FOR CHAPTER 2

- Define the terms *general* and *specific.*
- Order groups of sentences from most general to most specific.
- Identify the topic of a paragraph.
- Determine the main idea of a paragraph.
- Recognize the topic sentence of a paragraph.
- Recognize topic sentences in different locations in a paragraph.
- Describe the characteristics of an effective reading environment.
- Read and understand information in a table.

To read successfully, you must learn to determine the main idea of a paragraph or longer selection. The **main idea** is the overall point the author is trying to make. The rest of the paragraph or longer selection consists of information or examples that help the reader understand the main point.

What process do you go through to help you figure out the main idea of a selection? Take this pre-test to find out how much you already know about identifying and understanding main ideas.

TEST YOURSELF

Before beginning the work in this chapter, think about what you already know about the main idea and how to find it. What is the main idea of each of the following passages? Write your answers on the blanks provided.

1. One way in which almost anyone can improve his or her memory is to employ *mnemonics* (pronounced "nee-MON-ix"). Mnemonics are strategies for putting information in an organized context to remember it more easily. To remember the names of the Great Lakes, for example, you could use the acronym HOMES (for Huron, Ontario, Michigan, Erie, and

2

Superior). Verbal organization is the basis for many mnemonics. You can link items by weaving them into a story, a sentence, or a rhyme. To help customers remember where they have parked their cars, some large garages have replaced section designations such as "A1" or "G8" with the names of colors, months, or animals. Customers can then tie the location of their cars to information already in long-term memory—for example, "I parked in the month of my mother's birthday."*

Main Idea: ______________________________

2. Verbs work in two ways within a sentence. Some verbs show the action, physical or mental, of the subject of the sentence. These verbs are called *action verbs*. Other verbs link the subject with other words in the sentence. These verbs are called *linking verbs*.†

   Main Idea: ______________________________

3. They've booted beer kegs from football games, policed frat parties, created booze-free dorms, and waged awareness campaigns. Yet colleges haven't made the slightest dent in the proportion of binge drinkers, a new study shows. From 1993 to 2001, roughly 44 percent of students had chugged five or more bottles of beer, glasses of wine, or cocktails in a row within the past two weeks. Worse, all-women's colleges saw frequent binge-drinking rates more than double, to 12 percent. "This is not having a beer with a pizza," says lead investigator Henry Wechsler, director of college alcohol studies at the Harvard School of Public Health in Boston, who delivers his sobering assessment in the latest issue of the *Journal of American College Health*.‡

   Main Idea: ______________________________

   ____

4. No one family structure typifies[1] contemporary American society. The 1950s model of a two-parent family with two children and a nonworking mother no longer applies. For example, only 69 percent of children younger than eighteen years lived with two parents in 2000, compared with 85 percent in 1970. Today 26 percent of American children live with only one parent. High rates of divorce and single-parent births have contributed to this trend. Projections are that about 50 percent of current

1. **typifies:** serves as a typical example of

* From Bernstein and Nash, *Essentials of Psychology*, 2nd ed. Boston: Houghton Mifflin, 2002, 205. Copyright © 2002 by Houghton Mifflin Company. Reprinted with permission.

† From Arlov, *Wordsmith*. Upper Saddle River: Prentice Hall, 2000, 217.

‡ Adapted from Mary Lord, "Drinking: Here's Looking at You, Kids," *U.S. News & World Report*, April 1, 2002, 63. Copyright 2002 U.S. News & World Report, L.P. Reprinted with permission.

marriages will end in divorce (compared with about 15 percent in 1960), and about 32 percent of all births are to single women. Moreover, about 5 percent of children live with their grandparents, and a growing number live with gay or lesbian parents. Finally, more than 70 percent of married women with children younger than eighteen years work outside the home, compared with about 45 percent in 1975.*

Main Idea: ______________________________

5. Cabbage doesn't deserve its stinky reputation. Eat just one cup of cooked cabbage and you'll get double the recommended daily dose of vitamin C. And, according to the American Cancer Society, cabbage may protect against esophagus, stomach, and colon cancers. Then, of course, there's the fiber issue. Cabbage has plenty of it to help lower cholesterol, prevent constipation, and reduce hemorrhoids.†

   Main Idea: ______________________________

General and Specific

Before you practice finding main ideas, it's helpful to learn to distinguish the difference between the terms ***general*** and ***specific.*** You must apply these concepts to figure out the relationships of sentences within a paragraph. Understanding these relationships is the first step in improving your comprehension of the author's meaning.

The word *general* means "broad" and "not limited." When we say a word or idea is general, we mean that it includes or refers to many different things in a large category. For example, *musical instruments* is a general term that includes many different types of things, including trumpets, saxophones, and clarinets. *Relatives* is another general word that refers to a large group of items, including mothers, fathers, aunts, uncles, and cousins.

The word *specific* means "definite" or "particular." Specific things or ideas are limited or narrowed in scope, and they refer to one certain something within a larger group. In the previous paragraph, for instance, *trumpets, saxophones,* and *clarinets* are all certain types of musical instruments, so we say they are more specific. *Whales, dolphins,* and *seals* are all specific sea mammals. *Math, English,* and *science* are three specific subjects we study in school.

* Adapted from Bukatko and Daehler, *Child Development*, 5th ed. Boston: Houghton Mifflin, 2004, 498. Copyright © 2004 by Houghton Mifflin Company. Reprinted with permission.

† Adapted from Bev Bennett, "Of Cabbage and Things," *Better Homes and Gardens*, October 2001, 226.

The terms *general* and *specific* are relative. In other words, they depend upon or are connected to the other things with which they are being compared. For example, you would say that *school subject* is a general term and that *science* is one specific subject. However, *science* becomes the more general term when you think of specific kinds of science, such as biology, chemistry, and physics. Words and concepts, therefore, can change from being general or specific depending on their relationships to other words and concepts. Look at this list:

food
desserts
candy
chocolate candy bar
Hershey's chocolate bar with almonds

The words in this list are arranged from most general to most specific. In other words, each item in the list is more specific than the one above it. The last item, Hershey's chocolate bar with almonds, names a specific brand of candy, so it is the most specific of all.

To read well, you will need to be able to recognize the most general idea within a passage. Let's practice that skill by looking at groups of related items in different ways. Can you select the most general word in the list?

fork knife utensil spoon

Three of the words in the group are specific, and one of the words is the most general. If you chose *utensil* as most general, you are correct. The other three items are specific kinds of utensils.

Now examine this list and decide how the items are related. Come up with a word that includes all three items in the list.

basketball hockey soccer

Did you say *sports?* The three items above are all specific types of sports.

Finally, see if you can think of three specific examples of shoes. Some possible answers include sandals, athletic shoes, boots, and slippers.

Now that you've reviewed how words can be general and specific, you'll be able to see how the sentences that express ideas are also general and specific in relation to each other. Paragraphs are composed of both general and specific sentences. A *general sentence* is one that states the broadest idea in the paragraph. This idea could be explained or interpreted in a variety of different ways. The *specific sentences* in a paragraph are those that offer explanations or details that help readers understand and accept the idea in the general sentence. Specific sentences are essential to helping readers correctly determine the meaning of the general statement.

We saw earlier how the terms *general* and *specific* are relative when applied to words. Sentences within a paragraph, too, are relatively general and specific. For example, read the following three statements:

I am afraid of several things.

For example, I fear creepy, crawly creatures.

I am terrified of spiders most of all.

The first sentence states the most general idea; then, the second sentence clarifies a specific type of thing—creepy, crawly things—that the writer fears. The third sentence is even more specific because it identifies the particular kind of creepy, crawly creatures the writer fears most. So, in this group of sentences, each statement is more specific than the one above it.

Exercise 2.1

On the blanks provided, number these sentences from most general (1) to most specific (3).

1. _____ *The Amazing Race* is my favorite reality show.

   _____ I love reality shows.

   _____ I like *The Amazing Race* because the contestants visit exotic locales and compete to win lots of money.

2. _____ Homemade soups are a great meal for a big family because they are filling and nutritious.

   _____ Cooking at home and avoiding eating out can stretch your monthly food budget.

   _____ You can make chicken soup by adding a few vegetables and some noodles to your leftover chicken bones and meat.

3. _____ Jiang Li is very organized and uses time efficiently.

   _____ Jiang Li keeps all of her appointments logged into her daytime planner.

   _____ Jiang Li checks her planner daily to see how many appointments she has and when they are.

4. _____ Give the older child lots of verbal reassurance, but also use concrete actions.

_____ One strategy is to give the child an important role by including him or her in daily activities with the new infant.

_____ After the new baby arrives home, parents can do a number of things to help an older child adjust.*

5. _____ After the September 11, 2001, terrorist attacks, the rescue effort at the World Trade Center site was overwhelming in its scope.

_____ Many brave men and women volunteered to help find survivors.

_____ Firefighters, in particular, spent many hours at the site looking for survivors of the disaster.

Because paragraphs are combinations of sentences that all work together to develop a main idea, sorting out the general and specific relationships among related sentences is the first step toward understanding what you read. Look at the three sentences below and try to identify the one that is the most general.

Parents provide their children with laptops, pagers, and cell phones.

Many parents today spoil their children.

Parents buy their kids cars when the kids turn sixteen.

Parents pay huge sums for their children to go to expensive camps and on international vacations.

Did you choose the second sentence as most general? The other three sentences offer specific facts—specific things parents buy their kids—that help explain the idea of "spoil their children."

Now read these three specific sentences:

Water helps the body break down and absorb nutrients from foods.

Water cushions tissues, lubricates joints, and transports waste products to the kidneys for elimination.

Water helps the bowels function and prevents constipation.†

How would you state the general idea these three sentences explain or support? All three are examples of the ways the body uses water, so the sentence,

* Adapted from Seifert et al., *Lifespan Development*, 2nd ed. Boston: Houghton Mifflin, 2000, 103.

† Adapted from Tedd Mitchell, M.D., "Maximize Your Liquid Assets," *USA Weekend,* August 17–19, 2001, 4.

"Water is necessary to the normal functioning of the human body" would be an accurate statement of the general idea they develop.

Finally, read this general sentence:

Survivor is the best show on television.

What three specific sentences could you write to explain this sentence? Some possibilities include:

The team competitions are exciting to watch.

The interpersonal relationships are interesting.

It's fun to root for one contestant you want to win.

Exercise 2.2

The following groups of sentences include one general sentence and three specific sentences. Label each sentence with either a G for *general* or an S for *specific*.

1. _____ There have been many famous female politicians throughout the history of the United States.

   _____ Bella Abzug was a famous politician in New York City in the 1960s and 1970s, but she was most famous for her flamboyant hats.

   _____ Senator Dianne Feinstein from San Francisco has been very influential in California politics.

   _____ Ann Richards, the former governor of Texas, was noted for her motorcycle riding as well as her governing style.

2. _____ Tom Hanks won an Academy Award for his portrayal of Forrest Gump.

   _____ Tom Hanks played a man impersonating a woman in the television show *Bosom Buddies* and was very convincing as a woman.

   _____ Tom Hanks gave a wonderful performance in the film *The Ladykillers*.

   _____ Tom Hanks is a great actor.

3. _____ Most girls enjoy one-on-one play, while some boys like to play in large groups.

   _____ Many boys prefer trucks and trains to play with, while most girls like dolls and puzzles.

_____ Boys and girls are very different when it comes to play.

_____ Boys, in general, like to run around and play sports, while many girls like to pretend and use their imaginations.

4. _____ Chantal is always on time and doesn't mind staying overtime if I come home late from work.

_____ Chantal is a wonderful babysitter for my children.

_____ Chantal enforces the rules of the house while not appearing too strict.

_____ Chantal makes nutritious meals (which are delicious, too) for the kids.

5. _____ The flu can be a very serious illness.

_____ The flu can last up to two weeks in your system, making you tired and listless.

_____ People who get the flu often report fevers in excess of 102 degrees.

_____ The flu is sometimes accompanied by bad coughing, aches, and the chills.

Exercise 2.3

Read the three specific sentences given. Then, in the list that follows them, circle the letter of the general sentence best supported by those three specific sentences.

1. Jessica Simpson acknowledged that she had lingering hang-ups about her weight, looks, and dancing ability.

   Mariah Carey, who was groomed for stardom as a teenager and became a household name at age 20, has spent time in the hospital for exhaustion-related ailments.

   Backstreet Boy A. J. McLean was hospitalized for alcohol abuse.*

   General Sentences:

   a. Many teen pop stars have experienced physical and psychological problems as a result of their fame.
   b. One of the Backstreet Boys has an alcohol problem.
   c. Female pop stars often battle weight problems.

* Adapted from Elysa Gardner, "Pop Star Status Fuels a Meltdown," *USA Today,* August 7, 2001, 1D.

2. About 50 percent of law school graduates are women, but they represent less than 17 percent of partners in the major law firms.

   Women have comprised more than 30 percent of MBA graduates for more than 20 years, but women make up only 2.7 percent of the top earners in Fortune 500 companies.

   Women make up just 1 percent of Forbes 500 companies' CEO positions.*

   General Sentences:

   a. Women in corporate America are not interested in the highest positions.
   b. Men are better leaders than women are.
   c. In the corporate world, few women are achieving top positions.

3. Some people use a system called *mnemonics* to aid their memory.

   Many people take a popular over-the-counter herbal supplement called gingko biloba, which is said to help improve long-term and short-term memory.

   Studies have shown that a good percentage of people use visualization to remember places, names, and dates.

   General Sentences:

   a. Many people have good memories.
   b. People use a variety of techniques to aid their memories.
   c. There are not too many drugs available to aid memory.

4. The Red Worm computer virus was very dangerous and had the potential to wipe out the hard drives of hundreds of thousands of computers.

   The Nimda virus infected both e-mail and Internet sites.

   The e-mail entitled "A Virtual Card for You" had the capacity to completely disable a computer if the user opened the attachment to the message.

   General Sentences:

   a. There are not too many e-mail viruses circulating.
   b. Computer viruses are often found in e-mail message attachments.
   c. Computer viruses have the potential to be very dangerous and hazardous to hard drives and computers.

5. The cost of a college education, already an expensive proposition, is expected to rise by about 50 percent in the next twenty years.

   The cost of tuition and fees keeps going up every year.

   Housing on college campuses is still the cheapest housing available but can cost more than $10,000 a semester, depending on where a student attends school.

* Adapted from Irma D. Herrera, "'The Apprentice' Exposes Reality of Glass Ceiling," *USA Today*, April 5, 2004, 13A.

General Sentences:

a. Many colleges have on-campus housing.
b. Going to college can be a very expensive undertaking.
c. A college education is a necessity in today's job market.

2

Exercise 2.4

Read the general sentence given and then circle the letters of the three sentences from the list that best explain or support that statement.

1. General Sentence: Trees improve both our environment and our quality of life.*

   Specific Sentences:

   a. Trees help conserve energy; adding 100 million mature trees in U.S. cities would save $2 billion per year in energy costs.
   b. Trees produce the oxygen that we breathe and remove air pollution by lowering air temperature and removing particulates from the atmosphere.
   c. Two of the fastest growing trees are willow trees and poplar trees.
   d. Trees that form a windbreak can lower a homeowner's heating bills 10 to 20 percent, and shade trees planted on a home's east and west sides can cut cooling costs 15 to 35 percent.
   e. Trees can live to be hundreds of years old.
   f. Arbor Day, which was established in the 1880s, is now celebrated in all fifty states on the last Friday in April.

2. General Sentence: Many experts say that good note taking is the key to doing well on tests.

   Specific Sentences:

   a. I didn't take notes in college.
   b. Writing down key information from lectures can help students retain information when it comes time to take a test.
   c. Note taking involves highlighting key information while reading textbooks.
   d. Note taking is especially helpful for students who are "visual learners" because those students can "see" what happens in a lecture and remember it better.

* From "Trees Make a World of Difference," National Arbor Day Foundation, www.arborday.org.

e. My professor writes notes on the blackboard during class.
f. Writing notes in the margins of textbooks, which is called *annotating,* will help students recall the information during the test.

3. General Sentence: Many community college graduates report that their first two years of college gave them an enriching and rewarding academic experience.*

   Specific Sentences:

   a. Many students enjoy going to community colleges because they are close to home.
   b. Community colleges are cheaper than four-year schools.
   c. Smaller classes at community colleges are beneficial to students and can help them learn more in preparation for work at four-year schools.
   d. In general, professors at community colleges take pride in their teaching and provide a rich educational experience for students.
   e. There are many community colleges nationwide.
   f. Many students report that the courses they took at community colleges were as rigorous as those found at four-year schools.

4. General Sentence: In medieval times, children graduated to adult status early in life.†

   Specific Sentences:

   a. Teenagers assumed adult roles in medieval times.
   b. During medieval times, infants tended to be regarded rather like talented pets.
   c. At around seven or eight, children took on major, adultlike tasks for the community during medieval times.
   d. Children who would be in second or third grade today would be caring for younger siblings during medieval times.
   e. Children in medieval times earned respect for what they did.
   f. Children were still innocent a few hundred years ago.

5. General Sentence: Overweight people are turning to new diets and procedures to help them lose large quantities of weight in a shorter period of time.

   Specific Sentences:

   a. Gastric bypass surgery is becoming increasingly popular for people who need to lose more than 100 pounds in less than a year's time.

* Adapted from Ulrich Boser, "Ease the Leap from a Two-Year School," USNews.com, October 3, 2001.

† Adapted from Seifert and Hoffnung, *Child and Adolescent Development,* 5th ed. Boston: Houghton Mifflin, 2000, 11. Copyright © 2000 by Houghton Mifflin. Reprinted with permission.

2

b. Walking is proven to help people lose weight slower, thereby keeping it from coming back.
c. Low-carb diets in which people consume large quantities of protein and vegetables are proven to help people lose weight quickly.
d. The "belly band" is a procedure that overweight people can turn to if they don't want the risks of gastric bypass surgery.
e. Weight Watchers incorporates a "point" system to help people slowly lose weight.
f. If you are more than 10 pounds overweight for your height, you may want to consider going on a diet.

Determining the Topic

Now that you've reviewed the distinction between general and specific, let's look at the most general aspect of a paragraph: its topic. To understand what you read, you must be able to identify the topic, or subject, of a reading selection. The **topic** is the person, place, thing, event, or idea that the passage is about, and it is usually expressed in just a word or brief phrase. For example, read the following paragraph:

> Today, a new generation of Tony Hawk wanna-bes is fueling and financing a blockbuster skateboarding industry. The *Wall Street Journal* reported that participation in skateboarding has jumped 118 percent in the past eight years. Skateboard sales have tripled to $72 million since 1995. Summer camps are starting to cater to kids who like this new action sport. *The X Games*, which feature skateboarding competitions, is a hit show on ESPN. Once-disapproving parents are financing and encouraging their kids' newest obsession.*

The topic of this paragraph is skateboarding. Every sentence in the paragraph refers to or mentions skateboarding.

To find the topic of a selection, look for the person, place, thing, event, or idea that is repeated.

Exercise 2.5

Read each paragraph and write the correct topic on the blank provided.

1. There is a relationship between birth weight and intelligence, according to a recent study. It's long been known that children with abnormally low

* Adapted from Tim Wendel, "Going to Xtremes," *USA Weekend,* August 17–19, 2001, 7.

birth weights tend to score lower than normal-birth-weight children on IQ tests given at school age. But a new study of about 3,500 seven-year-olds links size to intelligence even among kids born at normal birth weight. Columbia University and New York Academy of Medicine researchers found that for every 2.2 pounds of additional weight, boys scored 4.6 IQ points higher, and girls scored 2.8 points higher. This was true even after other factors such as the mother's age, education, and economic status were considered.*

Topic: ______________________________

2. A number of striking similarities between monozygotic[1] twins reared apart from infancy have been found in the Minnesota Study of Twins Reared Apart. At their first adult reunion one pair of male twins discovered that they both used Vademecum toothpaste, Canoe shaving lotion, Vitalis hair tonic, and Lucky Strike cigarettes! Later they exchanged birthday gifts in the mail and discovered each had made the identical choice of gifts. There were two twins who trained and worked with dogs, two gunsmith hobbyists, two women who wore seven rings, and two who were captains of volunteer fire departments. Two male twins discovered that they both had named their sons James Alan (one Allan) and that both chain-smoked Salems while they worked in their basement workshops.†

Topic: ______________________________

3. Numerous bookstore chains have sprung up throughout the country in recent years, among them Borders, Super Crown, and Barnes and Noble. These businesses are designed to appeal particularly to young adults. Most offer comfortable chairs in which to sit, relax, and read. Some of these stores have a café area where specialty coffees, teas, muffins, and other delectables[2] are available. The evening hours are often filled with concerts, poetry readings, or other special events. Bookstores don't just sell books anymore; they sell a lifestyle. They do this because the competition is intense and economic issues pressing.‡

Topic: ______________________________

1. **monozygotic:** derived from a single fertilized egg
2. **delectables:** delights; things that are pleasing to the taste

* Adapted from Stephen P. Williams, "Health Notes," *Newsweek,* September 10, 2001, 71. Copyright © 2001 Newsweek, Inc. All rights reserved. Reprinted by permission.

† From Feshbach et al., *Personality*, 4th ed. Boston: Houghton Mifflin, 1996, 29. Copyright © 1996 by Houghton Mifflin Company. Reprinted with permission.

‡ From Leslie, *Mass Communication Ethics,* 2nd ed. Boston: Houghton Mifflin, 2004, 216. Copyright © 2004 by Houghton Mifflin Company. Reprinted with permission.

4. Idea generation involves looking for product ideas that will help a firm achieve its objectives. Although some organizations get their ideas almost by chance, firms trying to maximize product-mix effectiveness usually develop systematic approaches for generating new-product ideas. Ideas may come from managers, researchers, engineers, competitors, advertising agencies, management consultants, private research organizations, customers, salespersons, or top executives.*

   Topic: ______________________________

5. In one small study, researchers found that people suffer motor skill deficits[1] that last more than an hour after waking. But according to Mark Rosekind, PhD, president of Alertness Solutions, a company that offers stay-awake strategies to businesses, you can substantially decrease that downtime by drinking coffee. "The amount of caffeine in a strong cup of coffee can boost both physical performance and mental alertness by up to 30 percent within 15 to 30 minutes," he says. "If you're sluggish for an hour, getting that caffeine within the first five minutes of getting out of bed may gain you a half hour's head start on your morning."†

   Topic: ______________________________

When you are deciding on the topic of a paragraph or passage, make sure your choice is not too *broad* or too *narrow.* A topic that is too broad suggests much more than the paragraph actually offers. A topic that is too narrow does not include everything the paragraph covers. For example, look at the following paragraph:

> "Ruggedized" laptops are made to boot-camp standards to resist impact, temperature extremes, rain, and dust. Conventional laptops are delicate and sensitive, but their new rugged kin have tough magnesium cases, hard drives encased in protective gel, and insulated, liquid-proof keyboards. The Toughbook 72, for example, is water-resistant and can survive a one-foot drop onto concrete. These machines are more practical for people who work outdoors or who travel often.‡

1. **deficits:** inadequacies or insufficiencies

* From Pride et al., *Business,* 6th ed. Boston: Houghton Mifflin, 1999, 336. Copyright © 1999 by Houghton Mifflin Company. Reprinted with permission.

† From Melissa Gotthardt, "Waking Up Is Hard to Do," *O Magazine*, September 2001, 84.

‡ Adapted from Adam Cohen, "Here Come the Hard Cases," *Time,* August 27, 2001, 64.

Which of these is the correct topic of the paragraph?

______ computers

______ "ruggedized" laptops

______ the Toughbook 72

If you checked *"ruggedized" laptops*, you're correct. The first topic, *computers*, is too broad because it includes all kinds of computers, including those that are not portable. The third topic, *the Toughbook 72*, is too narrow because the paragraph discusses the characteristics of all "ruggedized" laptops, not just that specific brand. *"Ruggedized" laptops* is the right topic because the paragraph discusses the features and benefits of this one type of computer.

Now read another example:

> The results of hypnosis can be fascinating. People told that their eyes cannot open may struggle fruitlessly to open them. They may appear deaf or blind or insensitive to pain. They may forget their own names. Some appear to remember forgotten things. Others show age regression,[1] apparently recalling or re-enacting childhood. Hypnotic effects can last for hours or days through posthypnotic suggestions—instructions about behavior to take place after hypnosis has ended (such as smiling whenever someone says "Oregon"). Some subjects show posthypnotic amnesia, an inability to recall what happened while they were hypnotized, even after being told what happened.*

Which of the topics below is the correct one?

______ hypnosis

______ age regression

______ effects of hypnosis

The first choice, *hypnosis*, is too broad. This paragraph focuses only on the *results* of hypnosis. The second choice, *age regression*, is too narrow because this paragraph discusses other effects besides that one. Therefore, *effects of hypnosis* is the correct topic. This paragraph describes several different results of being hypnotized.

1. **regression:** going or moving backward

* Adapted from Bernstein et al., *Psychology*, 4th ed. Boston: Houghton Mifflin, 1997, 177. Copyright © 1997 by Houghton Mifflin Company. Reprinted with permission.

2

Exercise 2.6

Following each paragraph are three topics. On each blank, label the topic B if it is too broad, N if it's too narrow, and T if it's the correct topic of the paragraph.

1. New York has many bars and restaurants with views of the city, but the World Trade Center's Windows on the World was something else, a restaurant that seemed suspended halfway between the earth and the moon. From 107 stories, the views extended for 90 miles. Manhattan, Brooklyn, and New Jersey spread out in sharply etched detail. The river bridges looked like fragile steel filaments[1] from a quarter mile up, and New York Harbor threw back tiny sparks of sunlight.*

   New York City restaurants ______

   Views from Windows on the World ______

   The view of Manhattan ______

2. One of the largest unions not associated directly with the AFL-CIO is the Teamsters Union. The Teamsters Union was originally part of the AFL-CIO, but in 1957 it was expelled for corrupt and illegal practices. The union started out as an organization of professional drivers, but it has recently begun to recruit employees in a wide variety of jobs. Current membership is about 1.3 million workers.†

   Unions ______

   Current Teamsters membership ______

   The Teamsters ______

3. More than half of all sedimentary rocks are mudstones. The extremely fine particles in mudstones (less than 0.004 millimeter in diameter) consist largely of clay minerals and mica. Such fine particles settle out only in relatively still waters. Thus mudstones originate in lakes, lagoons, swamps, and deep ocean basins and on river floodplains—the same places where you would expect to find their unlithified[2] form, mud.‡

1. **filaments:** fine fibers or wires 2. **unlithified:** not rock or stone

* From William Grimes, "Windows that Rose So Close to the Sun," *New York Times*, September 19, 2001, F1.

† From Pride et al., *Business,* 6th ed. Boston: Houghton Mifflin, 1999, 280.

‡ From Chernicoff and Fox, *Essentials of Geology*. Boston: Houghton Mifflin, 2000, 108.

Mudstones ______

Origins of mudstones ______

Sedimentary rocks ______

4. Mention "Mormons" and you think immediately of clean-cut missionaries, uniformed like ushers in white shirts and dark suits, canvassing[1] for converts two by two through the neighborhoods of the world. Once a hated, hunted Utah sect, the Mormons are now a global church worth an estimated $25 billion and claiming 11 million members, a slight majority of them living outside the United States. To many outsiders, Mormons appear mysterious and clannish. They conduct secret temple rituals. Some of them practice polygamy[2] in rural Utah (despite official church condemnation of the practice). They have zero tolerance for alternative lifestyles. Also, they are always ready to press their temperance[3] code on non-Mormon citizens.*

   Mormon missionaries ______

   Mormons ______

   People in Utah ______

5. Difficult as it may be to comprehend today, America Online (AOL), Inc., started out in 1985 as simply one of many service firms providing customers with a new way to connect to the Internet. Remarkably, only fifteen years after its founding, AOL entered the new millennium[4] as the world's leading online service firm, with more than 20 million paying subscribers and a phenomenal growth in revenue. Since merging with the world's leading media company, Time Warner Inc., AOL has clearly transformed itself into an Internet giant. With combined revenues of $36 billion, the new firm, AOL Time Warner Inc., is known as the "world's first media and communications company of the Internet age."†

   AOL ______

   Internet service providers ______

   AOL/Time Warner merger ______

1. **canvassing:** soliciting
2. **polygamy:** practice of having more than one spouse at the same time
3. **temperance:** not drinking alcohol
4. **millennium:** period of 1,000 years

* Adapted from Kenneth L. Woodward, "A Mormon Moment," *Newsweek*, September 10, 2001, 46.

† Adapted from Pride et al., *Business,* 7th ed. Boston: Houghton Mifflin, 2002, 103. Copyright © 2002 by Houghton Mifflin Company. Reprinted with permission.

Determining the Main Idea

Once you've found the topic of a paragraph, you can determine its **main idea**, the general point the writer expressed about the topic. The main idea is what the writer wants to prove or explain. It's the point he or she wants you to know or believe when you finish reading the paragraph. Therefore, being able to discern main ideas is a fundamental skill for successful reading.

To find the main idea, ask yourself what the writer is saying *about* the topic. For example, read this paragraph:

> The most famous recording of an alleged[1] Bigfoot is the short 16 mm film taken in 1967 by Roger Patterson and Bob Gimlin. Shot in Bluff Creek, California, it shows a Bigfoot striding through a clearing. But the film is suspect for a number of reasons. First, Patterson told people he was going out with the express purpose of capturing a Bigfoot on camera. In the intervening thirty-five years (and despite dramatic advances in technology and wide distribution of handheld camcorders), thousands of people have gone in search of Bigfoot and come back empty-handed (or with little but fuzzy photos). Second, a known Bigfoot track hoaxer[2] claimed to have told Patterson exactly where to go to see the Bigfoot on that day. Third, Patterson made quite a profit from the film, including publicity for a book he had written on the subject and an organization he had started. Furthermore, John Napier, an anatomist and anthropologist who served as the Smithsonian Institution's director of primate[3] biology, found many problems with the film, including that the walk and size is consistent with a man's; the center of gravity seen in the subject is essentially that of a human; and the step length is inconsistent with the tracks allegedly taken from the site.*

The topic of this paragraph is the film of Bigfoot shot by Roger Patterson and Bob Gimlin. This film is mentioned in almost all of the sentences of the paragraph. But what is the author's point about this topic? In the third sentence, he states that the film is suspect for several reasons. Then, all of the other sentences in the paragraph offer details to explain that idea.

1. **alleged:** supposed
2. **hoaxer:** deceptive person or trickster
3. **primate:** mammals characterized by developed hands and feet, shortened snouts, and large brains

* Adapted from Benjamin Radford, "Bigfoot at 50," *Skeptical Inquirer,* March 2002, www.csicop.org/si/2002–03/bigfoot.html.

As you read the next paragraph, try to identify the topic and main idea.

> You have probably heard that death and taxes are the only two things guaranteed in life. If there is a third, it surely must be stress. Stress is woven into the fabric of life. No matter how wealthy, powerful, attractive, or happy you might be, stress happens. It comes in many forms, from a difficult exam to an automobile accident, to standing in a long line, to a day during which everything goes wrong. Mild stress, like waiting to be with that special person, can be stimulating, motivating, and even desirable, but as stress becomes more severe, it can bring on physical, psychological, and behavioral problems.*

Did you say that the topic is stress? If so, that is correct. Every sentence of this paragraph either mentions the word *stress* or, as in the case of the fifth sentence, uses the pronoun *it* to refer to stress. Now, what does the paragraph say about stress? First, it describes stress and the conditions that may bring stress on a person. Then, it mentions possible consequences of stress—physical, psychological, or behavioral problems.

Exercise 2.7

Read each paragraph and then answer the questions that follow by circling the letter of the correct topic and main idea.

1. Communication scholar James McCroskey, who has studied communication apprehension (CA) for more than twenty years, defines it as "an individual's level of fear or anxiety associated with either real or anticipated communication with another person or persons." As this definition suggests, communication apprehension is not limited to public speaking situations. We may feel worried about almost any kind of communication encounter. If, for example, you are preparing to have a conversation with a romantic partner who, you think, is about to suggest ending the relationship, if your professor has called you into her office to discuss your poor attendance record, or if a police officer has motioned you to pull off the road for a "conversation," you know what communication apprehension is all about.†

   Circle the letter of the correct topic.

   a. James McCroskey
   b. communication apprehension
   c. communication encounters

* From Bernstein and Nash, *Essentials of Psychology*, 2nd ed. Boston: Houghton Mifflin, 2002, 350. Copyright © 2002 by Houghton Mifflin Company. Reprinted with permission.

† From Andrews et al., *Public Speaking*. Boston: Houghton Mifflin, 1999, 42.

Circle the letter of the main idea.

a. Communication apprehension can occur in different kinds of communication situations.
b. James McCroskey is the leading expert on communication apprehension.
c. Communication encounters cause apprehension.

2. Cardiovascular disease (CVD), the underlying cause of heart attack and stroke, remains America's No. 1 medical problem. Despite widespread public awareness of risk factors such as high cholesterol, smoking, inactivity, and obesity, CVD continues to exact a devastating toll on society. As the leading cause of death in the United States, it kills more than 2,600 people a day and has an annual mortality rate greater than the next six causes of death combined. The estimated number of people in the country living with cardiovascular disease is staggering—12.4 million have coronary heart disease, 4.5 million have had a stroke, and 4.7 million have congestive heart failure. An additional 50 million have high blood pressure. The total cost to the economy of all that illness is estimated by the American Heart Association at more than $298 billion a year in medical expenses and lost productivity. The total cost in pain and suffering to individuals and families is beyond imagining.*

Circle the letter of the correct topic.

a. cardiovascular disease
b. the American Heart Association
c. the cost of CVD

Circle the letter of the main idea.

a. The American Heart Association is a great organization
b. Cardiovascular disease affects more people than any other disease in the United States
c. Cardiovascular disease costs Americans billions of dollars each year

3. Is there anything a couple can do to keep the honeymoon alive? Researcher Arthur Aron and his colleagues say that after the exhilaration of a new relationship wears off, partners can combat boredom by engaging together in new and arousing activities. In a controlled experiment, they brought randomly selected couples into a laboratory, spread gymnasium mats across the floor, tied the partners' hands together at the wrist, and had them crawl on their hands and knees, over a barrier, from one end of the room to the other—all the while carrying a pillow between

* From David Noonan, "The Heart of the Matter," *Newsweek Special Issue*, September 2001, 75. © 2001 Newsweek, Inc. All rights reserved. Reprinted by permission.

their bodies. Other couples were given the more mundane[1] task of rolling a ball across the mat, one partner at a time. A third group received no assignment. Afterward all participants were surveyed about their relationships. As Aron predicted, the couples who had struggled and laughed their way through the novel and arousing activity reported more satisfaction with the quality of their relationships than did those in the mundane and no-task groups. Maybe, just maybe, a steady and changing diet of exciting new experiences can help keep the flames of love burning.*

Circle the letter of the correct topic.

a. relationships
b. keeping love alive
c. experiments with couples

Circle the letter of the main idea.

a. The exhilaration of a new relationship wears off eventually
b. One way to keep love alive is to engage as a couple in exciting new experiences
c. Experiments with couples show that only about a third will actually stay together

4. The average teacher and administrator grew up in the 1950s, 1960s, or 1970s. Those who were raised in this period are likely to have attended schools dominated by others of their own ethnic group. It was not until their teens that most encountered the effects of the civil rights movement[2] and other expressions of ethnic presence on a national level. Nor did they experience the swift increases in diversity that have occurred recently. Thus many of today's teachers and their parents grew up expecting a much different world than they now face.†

Circle the letter of the correct topic.

a. today's teachers and their parents
b. ethnic diversity
c. diversity experiences of the average teacher or administrator

1. **mundane:** ordinary

2. **civil rights movement:** movement for racial equality in the U.S. that broke the pattern of racial segregation

* Adapted from Brehm et al., *Social Psychology,* 5th ed. Boston: Houghton Mifflin, 2002, 337. Copyright © 2002 by Houghton Mifflin Company. Reprinted with permission.

† From Garcia, *Student Cultural Diversity,* 3rd ed. Boston: Houghton Mifflin, 2002. Copyright © 2002 by Houghton Mifflin Company. Reprinted with permission.

Circle the letter of the main idea.

a. Today's teachers and their parents don't know how to relate to people of other cultures and ethnic groups.
b. The diversity experiences of the average education professional were limited.
c. Ethnic diversity led to the civil rights movement.

5. Population is still growing rapidly in many poor countries, but this is not the case in the world's industrialized nations. In 2000 women in developed countries had only 1.6 children on average; only in the United States did women have, almost exactly, the 2.1 children necessary to maintain a stable population. In European countries where women have been steadily having fewer babies since the 1950s, national fertility rates ranged from 1.2 to 1.8 children per woman. Italy, once renowned for big Catholic families, had achieved the world's lowest birthrate–a mere 1.2 babies per woman. Spain, Germany, and Russia were only slightly higher, while France, Poland, and Britain were clustered around 1.6 children per woman.*

Circle the letter of the correct topic.

a. population growth
b. population in industrialized nations
c. population growth in Europe

Circle the letter of the main idea.

a. In Europe, people have fewer children
b. The population is not growing as much in industrialized nations as it is in poor countries
c. Italians used to be known for their big families

The Topic Sentence

The **topic sentence** is the single statement that presents the main point or idea of the paragraph. Topic sentences have two parts: they state the topic and they state what the author has to say about that topic. Writers do not have to include such a sentence. Chapter 4 of this book will discuss in more

* Excerpted from McKay et al., *A History of Western Society,* 7th ed. Boston: Houghton Mifflin, 2003, 1052. Copyright © 2003 by Houghton Mifflin Company. Reprinted with permission.

detail paragraphs that lack a topic sentence. However, writers often include a topic sentence to help readers see the main idea quickly and easily.

To find the topic sentence, look for the most general statement in the paragraph and then make sure the other sentences all offer information or details. See if you can locate the topic sentence in the following paragraph:

> If you want to keep your long-term memory intact, you should avoid certain foods and eat more of others. The artificial sweetener called aspartame is one food to cut back. Studies have shown that drinking more than one or two diet drinks' worth of aspartame per day has been shown to decrease long-term memory. Also, you should limit tofu. Ingredients in this soy product have been shown to cause memory loss, so you should limit servings to one a week. Foods that boost memory are those that are rich in B vitamins. These include bananas, peas, orange juice, and seafood, all of which contain B vitamins that are essential to good brain health and memory.*

If you chose the first sentence, you're right. That statement expresses the paragraph's main idea, and the rest of the paragraph explains that idea.

Exercise 2.8

Read the following selection and for each of the paragraphs, write the correct topic on the blank provided. Write on the second blank provided the number of the topic sentence, which expresses the main idea.

The Iceman and His World

A. (1) On September 19, 1991, a German couple chanced upon one of the most remarkable archaeological discoveries of the century, a 5,300-year-old mummy that came to be known as the *Iceman.* (2) They were hiking in the Italian Alps. (3) At 10,530 feet above sea level, they thought they had left civilization and its problems behind until they stumbled on an unexpected sight: the body of a dead man lying in the melting ice. (4) Nor was that their only surprise. (5) At first they thought the corpse was the victim of a recent accident. (6) When the authorities arrived, however, the body was discovered to be very old. (7) A helicopter was ordered, and the body was brought to a research institute in Innsbruck, Austria. (8) When the

* Adapted from Dana Lichterman, "8 Surprising Ways to Give Your Memory a Makeover!" *Woman's World*, September 18, 2001, 35.

investigators were through, it was clear that the hikers had made an extraordinary discovery.

Topic: ____________________

Topic Sentence: ______

B. (1) A study of the mummy's body offers clues about who he was. (2) Genetic testing shows that he was a European, a close relative of modern northern and alpine Europeans. (3) Other tests indicate a difficult life. (4) His growth was arrested by periods of illness, grave hunger, or metal poisoning. (5) His teeth are badly worn, the result perhaps of chewing dried meat or, alternatively, of working leather. (6) He may have undergone a kind of acupuncture;[1] at any rate, he is tattooed, which in some cultures is a medical treatment rather than a form of decoration. (7) He has several broken ribs, which indicates either damage under the ice, mishandling when the body was discovered, or an ancient accident or fight.

Topic: ____________________

Topic Sentence: ______

C. (1) To get to know the Iceman better, however, we must go beyond his body to the artifacts found with it, which provide tantalizing[2] clues to his social status. (2) A woven grass or reed cape lay over the Iceman's deerskin coat, which in turn covered a leather loincloth and garter, held in place by a leather belt. (3) A fur hat, skin leggings, and calfskin boots, stuffed with grass for insulation, completed his wardrobe. (4) The Iceman and his contemporaries knew how to dress for the cold weather of the mountains. (5) And he carried a rich tool kit. (6) He had a copper ax and six-foot-long bow. (7) A quiver (arrow case), two birch bark containers, a waist pouch, and a frame—probably part of a backpack—hung from his body. (8) Among his items of equipment were flint tools (including a knife, a retouching tool, and a scraper); a piece of net; fungus threaded on a leather thong, probably used as a natural antibiotic; and fourteen arrows, all, oddly, broken. (9) In short, it appears that the Iceman was equipped with a state-of-the-art mountain survival kit of his day.

Topic: ____________________

Topic Sentence: ______

1. **acupuncture:** inserting needles into the body at specific points in order to relieve pain
2. **tantalizing:** exciting

D. (1) What, however, was he doing on the mountain when he died? (2) Scholars disagree about his purpose for being there and about his occupation. (3) Guesses range from trader to hunter to metal prospector to shaman.[1] (4) Some argue that the Iceman was a refugee.[2] (5) His weapons point to violence, and so may his broken ribs. (6) Perhaps he had retreated to the mountains from a fight.

Topic: ______________________________

Topic Sentence: ______

E. (1) Perhaps the most convincing theory is that the Iceman was a shepherd. (2) Since ancient times it has been common for shepherds to move their flocks during the summer from lowlands to greener pastures in the mountains, a pattern of migration known as *transhumance.* (3) It has been suggested that the Iceman brought broken arrows with him to repair during his spare time. (4) Perhaps he encountered a sudden snowstorm and died of exposure, maybe after having broken his ribs in an accident.*

Topic: ______________________________

Topic Sentence: ______

Locations of Topic Sentences

Main ideas are often stated in the first sentence of the paragraph. However, they can appear in other places in a paragraph, too. Writers sometimes place the topic sentence in the middle of a paragraph or even at the end.

Topic Sentence as First Sentence

It's very common for writers to announce the main idea in the first sentence of the paragraph. Then, the remainder of the paragraph explains why the reader should accept that point. In the following paragraph, for example, the topic sentence, which is highlighted in boldface type, is at the beginning.

1. **shaman:** priest who uses magic
2. **refugee:** one who flees from war to safety

* Adapted from Noble et al., *Western Civilization*, 3rd ed., Vol. 1. Boston: Houghton Mifflin, 2002, 36–37. Copyright © 2002 by Houghton Mifflin Company. Reprinted with permission.

When horse people discuss what sets Arabian horses apart, "endurance" is a word that comes up frequently. For all their refined elegance, these are horses that can and will summon up almost unimaginable reserves of stamina and courage to help—or just to please—a trusted human friend. Arabians, and the half-Arabian, half-thoroughbred horses called *Anglo-Arabians*, dominate the long-distance sport of endurance riding in which champions regularly speed through rugged one-hundred-mile courses in under ten hours, stepping across the finish line with enough verve[1] to suggest that they'd just as soon trot twenty miles more.*

2

Topic Sentence as Second or Third Sentence

Sometimes, though, a writer needs to present a sentence or two of introductory information before stating the main point. This means that the topic sentence might occur in the second or third sentence of the paragraph. Take a look at this example:

It used to be that emergency rooms got swamped just during winter flu outbreaks, or just in inner-city neighborhoods on Saturday nights. **But now emergency departments are overwhelmed year-round.** They're maxed out in world-class institutions that consistently land on *U.S. News and World Report*'s honor roll of Best Hospitals—including Johns Hopkins Hospital, the University of California-San Francisco Medical Center, and the Cleveland Clinic, which last year turned away ambulance patients almost half the time. And they're struggling in wealthy suburbs like Fairfax County, a high-technology mecca[2] with a median[3] household income of more than $90,000 and home to Colin Powell and ABC newscaster Sam Donaldson. "When there's not enough room," says Thom Mayer, chairman of the Inova Fairfax emergency department, "there's not enough room."†

The main idea is "emergency rooms are always busy" because the paragraph gives specific examples of emergency rooms around the country that are overwhelmed. However, the authors included some contrasting background about the past in the first sentence. Then, they went on to state the main idea in the second sentence.

1. **verve:** energy and enthusiasm
2. **mecca:** a center of activity
3. **median:** average

* Adapted from Jennifer Lee Carrell, "They Drink the Wind," *Smithsonian,* September 2001, 49.

† Adapted from Nancy Shute and Mary Brophy Marcus, "Code Blue: Crisis in the ER," *U.S. News and World Report*, September 10, 2001, 56.

Topic Sentence in the Middle

A topic sentence can also appear somewhere in the middle of the paragraph. For example, read the following paragraph:

> Last year, the valedictorian at Brea Olinda High School in Southern California was caught electronically altering a course grade. His punishment: being banned from the graduation ceremony. Cheat on the SAT and your score will be cancelled; but you can take a retest. **It's often true that getting caught cheating does not result in harsh penalties.** It doesn't have terrible consequences for being accepted to college either. Says Don Firke, academic dean at Choate Rosemary Hall, a boarding school in Wallingford, Conn., "If a college really wants a kid, they're going to find a way to take him." Once on campus, a cheater is apt to find similarly lax[1] discipline. With the exception of a handful of schools like the University of Virginia, which have one-strike-and-you're-out honor-code policies, the vast majority simply dole out zeros for an assignment or course in which a student has been found cheating.*

The above paragraph began with two of four examples that explain the main idea in the fourth sentence. After the main idea was stated, the paragraph offered two more examples.

Topic Sentence as Last Sentence

A writer might choose to save the topic sentence for the end of the paragraph, offering it as the last sentence. This next paragraph is an example of one that builds up to the main point:

> The Massachusetts state board of education recently set a low passing mark on its new statewide graduation exam, fearing that too many kids would drop out or fail to earn diplomas if standards were set too high and reasoning that it can raise the bar later. New York students can pass the English exam now required for high school graduation with a grade of 55 out of 100. Virginia and Arizona officials are under pressure to ease up on their academic standards. And in 1999 Wisconsin scrapped a planned high school graduation test following protests from parents. A modified version of the exam was included in the state budget recently signed by Governor Tommy Thompson, but

1. **lax:** not strict

* Adapted from Carolyn Kleiner and Mary Lord, "The Cheating Game," *U.S. News and World Report*, November 22, 1999, 66.

unlike Thompson's original proposal, the law now permits students to compensate for a low score with good grades, teacher recommendations, or other locally determined measures. **All across the country, schools are having to lower their academic standards.***

2

In the previous paragraph, the writer offered all of his explanation first. Then, he summarized the point in a topic sentence at the paragraph's end.

Topic Sentence as First and Last Sentence

Finally, the topic sentence might occur twice: once at the beginning of the paragraph and then again, in different words, at the end. Writers often restate the topic sentence to emphasize or reinforce the main idea for the reader. Here is an example:

Hunting and gathering in the ocean does more than kill fish; it changes ecosystems.[1] Each species in an ecosystem is linked to many others, as a predator, a scavenger, or a source of food or shelter. Remove some peripheral[2] species from the web and the system as a whole may continue to function just fine, so long as all the roles are still filled. But knock out a keystone[3] species and the system must find a new equilibrium, or balance. Other human impacts such as agricultural runoff and seafloor dredging may provide the final knockout blow to ecosystems, but in every case scholars analyzed, excessive fishing set the process in motion. **According to author Jeremy Jackson, we're causing fundamental shifts in ecosystems, and some of those shifts may be irreversible.†**

This paragraph identified the main point in the first sentence, offered explanation, and then made the same point again in the final sentence.

Steps for Locating the Topic Sentence

To find the topic sentence regardless of where it is located, look for the most general statement in the paragraph and then verify that the rest of the sentences in the paragraph offer information, details, or explanation for that general idea. Here's a specific step-by-step procedure you can

1. **ecosystems:** ecological communities
2. **peripheral:** minor or less important
3. **keystone:** important, crucial, necessary

* Adapted from Ben Wildavsky, "Lowering the Raised Bar," *U.S. News and World Report,* December 13, 1999, 62–63.

† Adapted from Thomas Hayden, "Deep Trouble," *U.S. News and World Report,* September 10, 2001, 69.

follow when you're trying to determine the main idea and topic sentence in a paragraph:

Step 1: Read over the entire paragraph to get an idea of the subject matter included.

Step 2: Read the first sentence to see if it gives a general picture of the entire paragraph. If it doesn't, it may provide some general background or contrasting information. Or, the first sentence may pose a question that the next few sentences go on to answer.

Step 3: If the first sentence does not state the main idea, read the last sentence to see if it gives a general picture of the entire paragraph. Turn the last sentence into a question, and then see if the other sentences in the paragraph answer that question. If they do, that last sentence may be the topic sentence.

Step 4: If either the first or the last sentence gives that general overview of the paragraph—the main idea—you have found your topic sentence.

Step 5: If neither the first nor last sentence is identified as the topic sentence, then the reader must evaluate each sentence in the middle of the paragraph to see if one of the sentences states the general idea or the main idea information. Test each possibility by turning it into a question and then determining if the other sentences in the paragraph answer that question.

Step 6: Once the topic sentence is located, then the reader must look for the general phrase located in the topic sentence that states the overall main idea.

Exercise 2.9

Following each paragraph, write on the blank provided the number of the sentence that is the topic sentence.

A. (1) We crave high-fat foods because they're satisfying on many different levels. (2) "When we eat a fatty food, we get a drowsy, sensuous feeling," says Howard Moskowitz, PhD, a psychologist and president of Moskowitz Jacobs, Inc., a consumer research company. (3) Fat-free foods might make us feel virtuous, and they may temporarily dull a craving, but they don't make us feel deeply content in the same way fatty foods do. (4) Not to mention the fact that high-fat foods are pleasurable. (5) When you bite into a piece of dense cake or take a spoonful of rich ice cream, the creamy, rich texture that comes from fat is what feels good in your mouth. (6) Fat also makes food tender—the flaky crust, the moist muffin and the velvety frosting all owe their appeal to fat.*

Topic Sentence: ______

B. (1) As a first precaution, take a close look at the water in a pool before you jump in. (2) Its color and texture are good indicators of its cleanliness. (3) It should be clear enough for you to see through at least ten feet of water and distinguish objects such as a metal grating on the bottom of the pool. (4) Foamy or bubbling water along the pool's edge is a sign of potential trouble; it typically represents excessive organic matter, such as pollen or bacteria.†

Topic Sentence: ______

C. (1) We live in a world that is life-dependent on astronomical objects, especially the stars. (2) The Sun (a star) provided the energy for the generation of life on Earth and supplies us continuously with heat and light. (3) Also, day after day the Sun keeps planet Earth in orbit. (4) Hydrogen and most of the helium in the universe are primordial.[1] (5) The remaining elements were formed by nuclear fusion in the cores of stars and in stars when they exploded billions of years ago and up to the present time. (6) The elements formed by the stars make up most of the remaining mass of the universe, including our bodies. (7) We are, therefore, the stuff of stars.‡

Topic Sentence: ________

D. (1) Everybody uses words to persuade people of something without actually making a clear argument for it. (2) This is called using loaded language. (3) For example: a newspaper writer who likes a politician calls him "Senator Smith"; if he doesn't like the politician, he refers to him as "right-wing [or left-wing] senators such as Smith." (4) If a writer likes an idea proposed by a person, he calls that person "respected"; if he doesn't like the idea, he calls the person "controversial." (5) If a writer favors abortion, she calls somebody who agrees with her "pro-choice" ("choice" is valued by most people); if she opposes abortion,

1. **primordial:** belonging to the earliest stage of development

* Adapted from Dayna Winter, "Don't Blame Your Sweet Tooth," *Family Circle*, April 24, 2001, 66.

† Adapted from Ian K. Smith, M.D., "A Quick Dip in a Dirty Pool," *Time Online*, July 18, 2001, www.time.com.

‡ Adapted from Shipman et al., *An Introduction to Physical Science*, 9th ed. Boston: Houghton Mifflin, 2000, 466. Copyright © 2000 by Houghton Mifflin Company. Reprinted with permission.

she calls those who agree with her "pro-life" ("life," like "choice," is a good thing). (6) Recognizing loaded language in a newspaper article can give you important clues about the writer's point of view.*

Topic Sentence: ______

2

E. (1) When President John Kennedy exhorted[1] Americans in his inaugural[2] address to "Ask not what your country can do for you; ask what you can do for your country," tens of thousands volunteered to spend two years of their lives in the Peace Corps. (2) "We had such faith in what Kennedy was doing," recalled one volunteer, "and we all wanted to be a part of it." (3) Kennedy promoted a sense of national purpose not only by inspiring volunteers, but also through his vigorous support of the space program. (4) America clearly lagged behind the Soviet Union, which sent a missile carrying cosmonaut Yuri Gagarin into orbit around the earth in April 1961. (5) But Americans embraced Kennedy's challenge to put a man on the moon before the Soviets did and achieved that goal by the end of the decade.†

Topic Sentence: ______

Topic Sentences That Cover More Than One Paragraph

Sometimes, a topic sentence might cover more than one paragraph. This usually occurs when the author needs to give a lot of information to explain that topic sentence. In that case, the author might choose to divide the explanation or information into two paragraphs to make it easier to read. For example, read the following paragraphs:

> **The delegates in Philadelphia, and later the critics of the new Constitution during the debate over its ratification,[3] worried about aspects of the presidency that were quite different from those that concern us today.** In 1787–1789 some Americans suspected that the president, by being able to command the state militia, would use the militia to overpower state governments. Others were

1. **exhorted:** urged
2. **inaugural:** first
3. **ratification:** official approval

* Adapted from Wilson and DiIulio, *American Government*, 8th ed. Boston: Houghton Mifflin, 2001, 257. Copyright © 2001 by Houghton Mifflin Company. Reprinted with permission.

† Adapted from Norton et al., *A People and a Nation*, 5th ed., Vol. 2. Boston: Houghton Mifflin, 1998, 931.

2

worried that if the president were allowed to share treaty-making power with the Senate, he would be "directed by minions[1] and favorites" and become a "tool of the Senate."

But the most frequent concern was over the possibility of presidential reelection. Americans in the late eighteenth century were suspicious of human nature and experienced in the arts of mischievous government. Therefore, they believed that a president, once elected, would arrange to stay in office in perpetuity[2] by resorting to bribery, intrigue, and force.*

In this passage, the topic sentence is highlighted in boldface type. After stating the topic sentence, the author presents several of early Americans' concerns to explain the main idea. Both paragraphs work together to support that one point.

Exercise 2.10

Identify the topic sentence of each of the following passages and write its number on the blank provided.

A. (1) Intraspecies[3] communication helps animals find food. (2) Biologist Charles Brown discovered that some birds actually establish "information centers" where they can learn where to go for food. (3) Observing cliff swallows on the plains of Nebraska for several years, he noted that the birds, on returning to their nests from a food hunt, would "rock back and forth" if their hunts were successful. (4) When they left their nests to search for more food, they were followed by their neighbors only if their body language indicated success.

(5) This bird dance, however, hardly compares to the well-documented dance of the honey bee. (6) When scouts locate a source of food, they return to their hive and inform others of its whereabouts. (7) Their scent declares what they've found; their dance gives directions and more. (8) If the food is nearby, they perform a "round dance"—they run around in circles—which simply announces the find. (9) When the location is far away, they perform

1. **minions:** followers
2. **in perpetuity:** forever
3. **intraspecies:** within a species

* Adapted from Wilson and DiIulio, *American Government: The Essentials,* 9th ed. Boston: Houghton Mifflin, 2004, 333–334. Copyright © 2004 by Houghton Mifflin Company. Reprinted with permission.

a "waggle dance." (10) The waggle dance is extraordinary in its detail. (11) The movements tell the other bees how far away the food is, its precise location, and even how much there is.*

Topic sentence: ______

B. (1) Doppler radars are being installed at major airports to prevent plane crashes and near crashes that have been attributed to dangerous downward wind bursts known as *wind shear.* (2) These wind bursts generally result from high-speed downdrafts in the turbulence of thunderstorms but can occur in clear air when rain evaporates high above the ground. (3) The downdraft spreads out when it hits the ground and forms an inward circular pattern. (4) A plane entering the pattern experiences an unexpected upward headwind that lifts the plane. (5) The pilot often cuts speed and lowers the plane's nose to compensate.

(6) Further into the circular pattern, the wind quickly turns downward, and an airplane can suddenly lose altitude and possibly crash if near the ground when landing. (7) Since Doppler radar can detect the wind speed and the direction of raindrops in clouds, as well as the motions of dust and other objects floating in the air, it can provide an early warning of wind shear conditions.†

Topic sentence: ______

C. (1) Many famous athletes choreograph their moves in their imaginations before going into action. (2) For example, champion skiers imagine themselves negotiating almost every inch of a slope, champion tennis players picture themselves executing successful shots, and gymnasts practice their moves as much in their imaginations as in actual rehearsal.

(3) Mary Lou Retton, former Olympic gymnast, spent nine grueling years preparing herself physically and mentally for her performance on one event at the 1984 Olympics and won the gold medal by five one-hundredths of a point. (4) She attributes much of her success to her ability to visualize her perfect performance. (5) "Always prepare yourself for a perfect 10. (6) When I visualized myself going through the beam routine, I didn't imagine myself falling. (7) I visualized

* Excerpted from Remland, *Nonverbal Communication in Everyday Life*. Boston: Houghton Mifflin, 2000, 62. Copyright © 2000 by Houghton Mifflin Company. Reprinted with permission.

† Adapted from Shipman et al., *An Introduction to Physical Science*, 9th ed. Boston: Houghton Mifflin, 2000, 516.

myself on the beam—perfect. (8) Always picture it perfect. (9) But also visualize what you can do if something does go wrong."*

Topic sentence: ______

D. (1) Every Saturday, from March through May, managers, bankers, and lawyers from Seattle to Atlanta shed their ties and put on their cleats to compete in one of the roughest games—rugby. (2) The Harp USA Rugby Super League attracts mostly white-collar workers who say this sport helps them cope with the stress of office life. (3) As one player explained, "After a hard day's work, rugby is a great release." (4) Terry Bradshaw, former NFL football player, says exercise tends to have a cleansing effect: "If I am stressed out, I go and run three miles, or play an hour and a half of tennis. (5) When I come back, I feel so good—I am ready to tackle the world."

(6) Exercise can act as a buffer against stress, so stressful events have less of a negative impact on your health. (7) Regular aerobic exercise—walking, swimming, low-impact aerobics, tennis, or jogging, for example—can increase your stress capacity. (8) Exercise does not have to be strenuous to be helpful. (9) Even gentle exercise like yoga or tai chi will help you manage your daily stress load.†

Topic sentence: ______

E. (1) The newest *eponyms*, or people's names turned into everyday words, come from mass media and politics. (2) People already talk about "gumping" through life—getting by on dumb luck, the way Forrest Gump did in the movie. (3) "Doing a Homer" means smacking your head and saying, "D'oh!" Homer Simpson[1]-style, either in frustration, or because you've done something dumb—or both.

(4) Among the wonks in Washington, "to bork" is to viciously attack a candidate or appointee. (5) That's in honor of Robert Bork, the Reagan nominee to the Supreme Court whose career was torpedoed in the Senate. To "pull a Clinton"[2] is to advocate two positions at once.‡

Topic sentence: ______

1. **Homer Simpson:** a character on the TV cartoon *The Simpsons*
2. **Clinton:** President Bill Clinton was America's 42nd president

* Adapted from Reece and Brandt, *Effective Human Relations in Organizations*, 7th ed. Boston: Houghton Mifflin, 1999, 109. Copyright © 1999 by Houghton Mifflin Company.

† Adapted from Reece and Brandt, *Effective Human Relations in Organizations*, 7th ed. Boston: Houghton Mifflin, 1999, 373.

‡ From Jay Heinrichs, "People Who Become Words," *Reader's Digest*, December 2001, 133.

CHAPTER 2 REVIEW

Fill in the blanks in the following statements.

1. Paragraphs are composed of ___________ and ___________ statements.
2. The most general sentence in the paragraph expresses its ___________—the idea or point the writer wants you to know or to believe.
3. The sentence that states the writer's main idea is called the ___________.
4. The topic sentence has two parts: the ___________, or subject, of the paragraph and what the writer wants to say about that subject.
5. The topic sentence can occur anywhere in the ___________.
6. A topic sentence can cover more than one ___________.

Reading Selection

Practicing the Active Reading Strategy:

Before and While You Read

You can use active reading strategies before, as, and after you read a selection. The following are some suggestions for active reading strategies that you can perform before you read and while you read.

1. Skim the selection for any unfamiliar words. Circle or highlight any words you do not know.
2. As you read, underline, highlight, or circle important words or phrases.
3. Write down any questions about the selection if you are confused by the information presented.
4. Jot notes in the margin to help you understand the material.

Coping with Procrastination

1 Any discussion of time management would not be complete without an examination of the most well-intentioned person's worst enemy—procrastination. The dictionary (*Webster's New Collegiate*) defines *procrastination as* "the act of putting off intentionally and habitually the doing of something that should be done." Interestingly, most procrastinators do not feel that they are acting intentionally. On the contrary, they feel that they fully *intend* to do whatever it is, but they simply cannot, will not, or—bottom line—they *do not* do it. Procrastinators usually have good reasons for their procrastination (some would call them excuses): "didn't have time," "didn't feel well," "couldn't figure out what to

do," "couldn't find what I needed," "the weather was too bad"—the list is never-ending.

2 Even procrastinators themselves know that the surface reasons for their procrastination are, for the most part, not valid. When procrastination becomes extreme, it is a self-destructive course, and, yet, people feel that they are powerless to stop it. This perception can become reality if the underlying cause is not uncovered. Experts have identified some of the serious underlying causes of procrastination. Think about them the next time you find yourself struck by this problem.

3 Often procrastination stems from a real or imagined fear or worry that is focused not so much on the thing you are avoiding but its potential consequences. For instance, your procrastination over preparing for an oral presentation could be based on your fear that no matter how well prepared you are, you will be overcome by nerves and forget whatever you are prepared to say. Every time you think about working on the speech, you become so worried about doing "a bad job" that you have to put the whole thing out of your mind to calm down. You decide that you will feel calmer about it tomorrow and will be in a much better frame of mind to tackle it. Tomorrow the scenario gets repeated. The best way to relieve your anxiety would be to dig in and prepare so well that you can't possibly do poorly.

4 Being a perfectionist is one of the main traits that spawns fear and anxiety. Whose expectations are we afraid of not meeting? Often it is our own harsh judgment of ourselves that creates the problem. We set standards that are too high and then judge ourselves too critically. When you picture yourself speaking before a group, are you thinking about how nervous the other students will be as well, or are you comparing your speaking abilities to the anchorperson on the six o'clock news? A more calming thought is to recall how athletes measure improvements in their performances by tracking and trying to improve on their own "personal best." Champions have to work on beating themselves in order to become capable of competing against their opponents. Concentrating on improving your own past performance, and thinking of specific ways to do so, relieves performance anxiety.

5 On the surface this would seem to be the reason for all procrastination, and the obvious answer is for the procrastinator to find a way to "get motivated." There are situations where lack of motivation is an indicator that you have taken a wrong turn. When you seriously do not want to do the things you need to do, you may need to reevaluate your situation. Did you decide to get a degree in Information Systems because everyone says that's where the high paying jobs are going to be, when you really want to be a social worker or a travel agent? If so, when you find yourself shooting hoops or watching television when you should be putting in time at the computer lab, it may be time to reexamine your decision. Setting out to accomplish something difficult when your heart isn't in it is often the root cause of self-destructive behavior.

6 Often procrastination is due to an inability to concentrate or a feeling of being overwhelmed and indecisive. While everyone experiences these feelings during a particular stressful day or week, a continuation of these feelings could indicate that you are in a state of burnout. Burnout is a serious problem that occurs when you have overextended yourself for too long a period of time. It is especially likely to occur if you are pushing yourself both physically and mentally. By failing to pace yourself, you will

"hit the wall," like the long distance runner who runs too fast at the beginning of the race. Overworking yourself for too long without mental and physical relaxation is a sure way to run out of steam. Learning to balance your time and set realistic expectations for yourself will prevent burnout.

7 Sometimes you put off doing something because you literally don't know how to do it. This may be hard to admit to yourself, so you may make other excuses. When you can't get started on something, consider the possibility that you need help. For example, if you get approval from your favorite instructor for a term paper topic that requires collecting data and creating graphics, you can be stymied if you don't have the necessary skills and tools to do the work and do it well. Does the collection and analysis of the data require the use of a software program that you don't have and cannot afford to buy? Sometimes it is difficult to ask for help and sometimes it is even hard to recognize that you need help. When you feel stymied, ask yourself, "Do I need help?" Do you need information but haven't a clue as to where to go to get it? Have you committed to doing something that is really beyond your level of skills? Being able to own up to personal limitations and seek out support and resources where needed is a skill used every day by highly successful people.*

VOCABULARY

Read the following questions about some of the vocabulary words that appear in the previous selection. Circle the letter of the correct response.

1. This selection is about *procrastination.* What does *procrastination* mean?

   a. speediness
   b. immediacy
   c. putting off or delaying
   d. carrying out

2. In paragraph 2, the authors write, "Even procrastinators themselves know that the surface reasons for their procrastination are, for the most part, not *valid.*" What does *valid* mean?

   a. logical
   b. sound
   c. defined
   d. unbalanced

3. What is an *underlying cause* (paragraph 2)?

   a. complicated
   b. fundamental
   c. conflicting
   d. disturbing

4. In paragraph 4, the authors write that "[b]eing a perfectionist is one of the main traits that *spawns* fear and anxiety." What does *spawn* mean?

   a. consume
   b. bring forth
   c. destroy
   d. disturb

*From Rebecca Moore, Barbara A. Baker, and Arnold H. Packer, "Coping with Procrastination," *College Success.* Upper Saddle River: Prentice Hall, 1997. Used by permission of the authors.

5. What does *stymied* mean? Reread paragraph 7, ". . . you can be *stymied* if you don't have the necessary skills and tools to do the work and do it well."

   a. puzzled
   b. misunderstood
   c. styled
   d. comprehensive

2

Topic and Main Idea

Answer the following questions by circling the letter of the correct answer.

1. What is the topic of paragraph 3?

   a. procrastination
   b. oral presentations
   c. the fear of public speaking
   d. worry as a source of procrastination

2. What is the topic sentence of paragraph 3?

   a. "Often procrastination stems from a real or imagined fear or worry that is focused not so much on the thing you are avoiding but its potential consequences."
   b. "For instance, your procrastination over preparing for an oral presentation could be based on your fear that no matter how well prepared you are, you will be overcome by nerves and forget whatever you are prepared to say."
   c. "Every time you think about working on the speech, you become so worried about doing 'a bad job' that you have to put the whole thing out of your mind to calm down."
   d. "Tomorrow the scenario gets repeated."

3. What is the topic of paragraph 5?

   a. procrastination
   b. lack of motivation as a cause of procrastination
   c. making decisions
   d. choosing a career

4. In paragraph 5, the topic sentence is

   a. sentence 1.
   b. sentence 2.
   c. sentence 6.
   d. sentences 2 and 6.

5. What is the main idea of paragraph 4?

   a. Harsh self-judgment can lead to procrastination.
   b. Performance anxiety is a paralyzing condition.
   c. Champion athletes should focus on achieving their own "personal best."
   d. Perfectionism is the result of an individual's upbringing and temperament.

Practicing the Active Reading Strategy:

After You Read

Now that you have read the selection, answer the following questions, using the active reading strategies that are discussed on pages 30–33.

1. Identify and write down the point and purpose of this reading selection.
2. Besides the vocabulary words included in the exercises on pages 97–98, are there any other vocabulary words that are unfamiliar to you? If so, write a list of them. When you have finished writing your list, look up each word in a dictionary and write the definition that best describes the word as it is used in the selection.
3. Predict any possible test questions that may be used on a test about the content of this selection.
4. How could you use the information contained in this selection? Does the information contained in the selection reinforce or contradict your ideas and experiences? Explain.

Questions for Discussion and Writing

Answer the following questions based on your reading of the selection. Write your answers on the blanks provided.

1. Would you describe yourself as a procrastinator? Why or why not?

   ____

   ____

2. What skills, if any, did you learn from this article that will help you avoid procrastinating? ______________________________________

   ____

3. Have you ever experienced burnout, as described in paragraph 6? Interview friends, relatives, and fellow students about their experiences with burnout, and then suggest ways to overcome this state of mind.

   ____

   ____

Vocabulary: Synonyms

Synonyms are words that have the same, or similar, meanings. Synonyms serve four purposes in texts. First of all, they add variety to a reading selection. Instead of writing the same word over and over, authors will use different words with the same meanings to keep sentences lively and interesting. For example, in the paragraph about emergency rooms, ERs are described as *overwhelmed, swamped,* and *maxed out.*

Second, authors use synonyms to express their thoughts as precisely as possible. For example, the paragraph about skateboarding says "skateboard sales have *tripled* to $72 million." The author could have used the word *risen* or *increased,* but he used the more specific *tripled,* which expresses exactly how much they increased.

A third use of synonyms is to connect ideas and sentences and to reinforce ideas. Do you remember the paragraph about improving long-term memory? Notice how the boldface, italicized words are synonyms that help keep the paragraph focused on the main idea:

> If you want to keep your long-term memory intact, you should ***avoid*** certain foods and eat more of others. The artificial sweetener called aspartame is one food to ***cut back.*** Studies have shown that drinking more than one or two diet drinks' worth of aspartame per day has been shown to decrease long-term memory. Also, you should ***limit*** tofu. Ingredients in this soy product have been shown to cause memory loss, so you should ***limit*** servings to one a week. Foods that boost memory are those that are rich in B vitamins. These include bananas, peas, orange juice, and seafood, all of which contain B vitamins that are essential to good brain health and memory.

Finally, texts include synonyms to help readers figure out what other words mean. For example, in the sentence below, the author provides a synonym to help the reader understand what the word *equilibrium* means:

> But knock out a keystone species and the system must find a new equilibrium, or ***balance.***

Balance is another way to say *equilibrium*; it's a synonym used to define a word.

Vocabulary Exercise 1

On the blank following each paragraph, write in the synonyms the paragraph includes for the boldfaced, italicized word or phrase.

1. Communication scholar James McCroskey, who has studied communication ***apprehension*** (CA) for more than twenty years, defines it as "an individual's level of fear or anxiety associated with either real or anticipated communication with another person or persons." As this definition suggests, communication apprehension is not limited to public speaking situations. We may feel worried about almost any kind of communication encounter.

Three synonyms for italicized word: ______________________________

2. There is a relationship between birth weight and intelligence, according to a recent study. It's long been known that ***children*** with abnormally low birth weights tend to score lower than normal-birth-weight children on IQ tests given at school age. But a new study of about 3,500 seven-year-olds links size to intelligence even among kids born at normal birth weight.*

Two synonyms for italicized word: ______________________________

3. On September 19, 1991, a German couple chanced upon one of the most remarkable archaeological discoveries of the century, a 5,300-year-old mummy that came to be known as the *Iceman*. They were hiking in the Italian Alps. At 10,530 feet above sea level, they thought they had left civilization and its problems behind until they stumbled on an unexpected sight: the ***body of a dead man*** lying in the melting ice. Nor was that their only surprise. At first they thought the corpse was the victim of a recent accident.

Two synonyms for italicized phrase: ______________________________

4. Numerous ***bookstore chains*** have sprung up throughout the country in recent years, among them Borders, Super Crown, and Barnes and Noble. These businesses are designed to appeal particularly to young adults. Most offer comfortable chairs in which to sit, relax, and read. Some of these stores have a café area where specialty coffees, teas, muffins, and other delectables[1] are available. The evening hours are often filled with concerts, poetry readings, or other special events. Bookstores don't just sell books anymore; they sell a lifestyle.†

Three synonyms for italicized phrase: ______________________________

Vocabulary Exercise 2

Circle the eight synonyms used for the word *crying* in the following passage.

The saying goes: "Never let them see you sweat." But in today's macho workplace, we don't mind sweat. It's tears we can't handle. Work is the vessel into which we pour so much of ourselves—hope and disappointment, elation

1. **delectables:** delights; things that are pleasing to the taste

* Adapted from Williams, "Health Notes," *Newsweek*, September 10, 2001, 71.

† From Leslie, *Mass Communication Ethics*, © 2004, Houghton Mifflin, 216.

2

and rage, satisfaction and frustration. Yet any damp display of these emotions is seen as a weakness. "Do anything you can," Marjorie Brody, a career consultant, said, "to keep from crying at work. . . ."

Weeping can paralyze a workplace. Cass Burton-Ward, who now works at the Stevens Institute of Technology in Hoboken, N.J., remembers an employee from a previous job who could be found sobbing after the slightest criticism. She was also reduced to whimpering by minor problems. "If someone inadvertently[1] left company letterhead in the laser printer, making her have to reprint her two- or three-page document," Burton-Ward said, "she would sometimes launch into a wailing tantrum. . . ." You just can't have that person bawling at the photocopy machine. It took the intervention of a psychologist to get this employee's emotions under control, Burton-Ward says. . . .

Brody, whose book is titled *Help! Was That a Career Limiting Move?* (Career Skills Press, 2001), warns that this is not an ideal world. "I hate to sound unsympathetic," she says of blubbering on the job, "but it might be better to stay away from the workplace for a while if you can't control your emotions."*

READING STRATEGY: Creating an Effective Reading Environment

If you're like most students, you probably read both at home and outside your home: perhaps somewhere on your college campus and maybe even at work during your breaks. Your reading environment can greatly affect your comprehension. So, give some thought to how you can create or select the right reading environments. The right environment

1. **inadvertently:** accidentally, unintentionally

* Adapted from Lisa Belkin, Life's Work; Crying Shame? Tears in the Office, *New York Times*, September 26, 2001. Copyright © 2001 by the New York Times Company. Reprinted by permission.

allows you to stay alert and to focus all of your concentration on the text, especially when it's a challenging one.

When you're at home, you can usually create effective conditions for reading. You might want to designate a particular place—a desk or table, for example—where you always read. Make sure the place you choose is well lit, and sit in a chair that requires you to sit upright. Reading in a chair that's too soft and comfortable tends to make you sleepy! Keep your active reading tools (pens, highlighter markers, notebook or paper) and a dictionary close at hand.

Before you sit down for a reading session, try to minimize all potential external distractions. Turn off your phone, the television, and the radio. Notify your family members or roommates that you'll be unavailable for a while. If necessary, put a "do not disturb" sign on your door! With fewer interruptions and distractions, you will have an easier time keeping your attention on the task at hand.

Overcoming internal distractions, which are the thoughts, worries, plans, daydreams, and other types of mental "noise" inside your own head, is often even more challenging for readers. However, it's important to develop strategies for dealing with them, too. If you don't, they will inhibit you from concentrating on what you are reading. Internal distractions will also prevent you from absorbing the information you need to learn. You can try to ignore these thoughts, but they will usually continue trying to intrude. So, how do you temporarily silence them so you can devote your full attention to your reading? Instead of fighting them, try focusing completely on these thoughts for a short period of time. For five or ten minutes, allow yourself to sit and think about your job, your finances, your car problems, your boyfriend or girlfriend, the paper you need to write, or whatever is on your mind. Better yet, write these thoughts down. To empty your mind onto a piece of paper, try a free-writing exercise, which involves quickly writing your thoughts on paper without censoring them or worrying about grammar and spelling. If you can't stop thinking about all of the other things you need to do, devote ten minutes to writing a detailed "To Do" list. Giving all of your attention to distracting thoughts will often clear your mind so you can focus on your reading.

If you're reading somewhere other than at home (on your college campus, for instance), it will be more difficult to achieve ideal reading conditions. However, you can still search for places that have the right characteristics. First of all, find a location—such as the library—that is well lit and quiet. Try to sit at an individual study carrel or cubicle so

Continued

2

you can block out external distractions. If no carrels are available, choose a table that's out of the flow of traffic, and sit with your back to others so you're not tempted to watch their comings and goings. If you must read in a more distracting place like your college cafeteria or a bench on the grounds, you might want to get in the habit of carrying a pair of earplugs in your book bag so you can reduce external noise. Finally, don't forget to keep your active reading tools and dictionary with you so you'll have them on hand no matter where you end up reading.

Write your answers to the following questions on the blanks provided:

1. Where were you when you read this information about creating an effective reading environment? Describe your surroundings.

   ____

   ____

2. Is this the place where you do most of your reading? If not, where do you usually read? ____________________

   ____

3. What external distractions pulled your attention from the book as you read? __________________________

   ____

4. Could you have done anything to prevent these external distractions from happening? ____________________

   ____

5. Did you battle any internal distractions as you read? Briefly describe the thoughts that intruded upon your concentration.

   ____

   ____

6. Based on the information in this section, where could you create the most ideal environment for reading? What objects and/or procedures will you need to create that environment?

   ____

   ____

Reading Visuals: Tables

A *table* is a visual aid that organizes information or data in rows and columns. A table might list types, categories, figures, statistics, steps in a process, or other kinds of information. Its purpose is to summarize many related details in a concise format so that readers can read them easily and find specific facts quickly.

Tables contain the following parts:

- **Title.** The title states the visual aid's subject.
- **Column headings.** These labels identify the type of information you'll find in the vertical lists.
- **Row headings.** These labels identify the type of information you'll find in each horizontal list.
- **Source line.** The source line identifies who collected or compiled the information in the table.

These parts are labeled in Table 2.1 below.

Table 2.1 The World of Communication Overload (average daily number of messages sent and received by office workers)

Title

Column headings

	United States	United Kingdom	Germany
Telephone	52	46	50
E-mail	36	27	20
Voice mail	23	11	6
Postal mail	18	19	26
Interoffice mail	18	15	27
Fax	14	11	15
Cell phone	4	9	10
Total =	165	138	154

Row headings

Source line

Source: Data from "Message Overload?" *USA Today* (September 13, 1999): 1B.

To understand the information in a table, first read the title, which will identify the kind of information the table includes. Next, familiarize yourself with the column and row headings. They will identify the kind of details included. Then, form an understanding of the relationships

Continued

first by moving your eyes down each column to see how details compare, and then across each row to see how those details are related. Finally, try to state in your own words the overall point revealed by the table's lists.

2

In Table 2.1, the title states that this visual aid will focus on communication overload. The information in parentheses clarifies that the table will summarize the number of messages office workers send and receive every day. You have to look at the table's first row, however, to see that it will provide data for three different countries: the United States, the United Kingdom, and Germany. The first column lists the types of messages workers send and receive. Then, the next three columns include corresponding numerical data. To find information, locate either the type of message or country that interests you, and then follow the row across or the column down to find the corresponding number. For example, you can see that in the United States, the average worker sends or receives thirty-six e-mail messages every day, while a worker in Germany sends or receives only twenty.

As you study the table, try to put the relationships it reveals into your own words. For example, which country is the leader for each type of message? The U.S. worker tops the other two countries in the telephone, e-mail, and voice mail messages. Workers in Germany send and receive more postal mail, faxes, and cell phone messages than workers in the other two countries. Workers in all three countries, however, send or receive a similarly large number of total daily messages. More telephone messages are sent and received than any other type of message. These are some of the conclusions you could draw from this data.

Now, study Table 2.2 on page 107 and then answer the questions that follow.

1. How many companies are listed in the table for comparison? ______
2. Which company has the highest annual sales, in millions? ______________
3. What are Kmart's annual sales, in millions? ______________________
4. What are Kmart's annual profits, in millions? ____________________
5. Of this group of companies, which one has the lowest annual sales, in millions? ____
6. Which company has the ninth highest annual sales? ______________

2

Table 2.2 The Twenty Largest Retail Firms in the United States

Rank	Company	Annual Sales (in millions)	Annual Profits (in millions)	Number of Stores
1	Wal-Mart, Inc.	$165,013,000	$5,377,000	3,989
2	The Kroger Co.	45,352,000	628,000	3,473
3	Sears, Roebuck and Co.	41,071,000	1,453,000	3,011
4	The Home Depot	38,434,000	2,320,000	930
5	Albertson's	37,478,079	404,000	2,492
6	Kmart Corp.	35,925,000	403,000	2,171
7	Target Corp.	33,702,000	1,144,000	1,243
8	J.C. Penney	32,510,000	336,000	4,076
9	Safeway	28,859,900	970,900	1,659
10	Costco	27,456,031	397,298	302
11	Dell Computer	25,265,000	1,860,000	NA
12	Ahold USA**	20,340,000	1,001,000	1,063
13	CVS Corp.	18,098,300	635,100	4,098
14	Walgreens	17,838,800	624,100	2,821
15	Federated Department Stores	17,716,000	795,000	403
16	Lowe's Cos.	15,905,595	672,795	576
17	Winn-Dixie	14,136,503	182,335	1,188
18	May Department Stores	13,869,000	927,000	408
19	Rite Aid	14,681,442	(1,143,056)	3,802
20	Publix Super Market	13,205,561	462,409	614

* Reprinted by permission from *Chain Store Age* (August 2000). Copyright Lebhar-Friedman, Inc. 425 Park Avenue, NY, NY 10022.
** U.S. retail operations only: operating income reported + continuing operations.

Name ______________________________ Date ______________

TEST 1

A. Put these sentences in order from most general (1) to most specific (3). First fill in the blank with the correct number and then circle the letter of the set that represents the correct order.

1. _____ Many cities have beautiful museums.

   _____ New York City is home to the Metropolitan Museum of Art, one of the most famous museums in the world.

   _____ New York City is one city with many museums.

   a. 1, 2, 3 c. 3, 2, 1
   b. 1, 3, 2 d. 2, 1, 3

2. _____ Thousands of employees from the energy company Enron lost their life savings when the company went bankrupt.

   _____ Enron, an energy company, fell on hard financial times in the last half of 2001.

   _____ Enron retiree Charles Prestwood's pension plan went from $1.3 million to nothing almost overnight.*

   a. 1, 2, 3 c. 1, 3, 2
   b. 3, 1, 2 d. 2, 1, 3

3. _____ The three-year-old Chicago Military Academy, in the street-tough Bronzeville neighborhood on the city's South Side, is part of a growing experiment by public school districts to bring the order and structure of the armed forces to their schools.

   _____ Students at Chicago Military Academy wear uniforms and often do push ups as punishment for breaking a rule.

* Adapted from Howard Fineman and Michael Isikoff, "Lights Out: Enron's Failed Power Play," *Newsweek,* January 21, 2002, 15.

For additional tests, see the Test Bank.

_____ Some new schools are trying controversial, though perhaps effective, methods to attempt to bring order into students' lives.*

a. 1, 2, 3 c. 3, 1, 2
b. 2, 3, 1 d. 1, 3, 2

4. _____ New York sports teams are notorious[1] for having the highest payrolls in their individual sport.

_____ The New York Yankees payroll tops out at over $100 million.

_____ Derek Jeter makes about $9 million a year, a very high salary for a shortstop.

a. 3, 2, 1 c. 2, 3, 1
b. 1, 2, 3 d. 3, 1, 2

5. _____ Airlines are trying to save money by cutting back on their meal services.

_____ Jet Blue Airlines, which once served fancy potato chips to its passengers, decided to scale back to 14-cents-a-bag tortilla chips to save money.

_____ Airlines have stopped serving full meals, and they are changing the snacks they serve passengers, too.

a. 1, 3, 2 c. 3, 1, 2
b. 2, 3, 1 d. 3, 2, 1

B. The following groups of sentences include one general sentence and three specific sentences. Circle the letter beside the most general sentence in each group.

6. (1) Scientists have found that tomatoes can help fight cancer.

(2) Tomatoes can reduce skin damage, like scars or sun exposure damage.

(3) If you want to combat heart disease, eat tomatoes in any form.

(4) Tomatoes have the ability to help prevent and even reverse disease.†

a. 1 c. 3
b. 2 d. 4

1. **notorious:** known widely and unfavorably

* Adapted from Dirk Johnson, "High School at Attention," *Newsweek,* January 21, 2002, 42.

† Adapted from Jean Carper, "Eat Smart: Catch Up," *USA Weekend,* August 24–26, 2001, 4.

7. (1) Chris Zane, owner of Zane's Cycles, a bicycle shop, believes in and is committed to customer service.

   (2) Zane offers free lifetime service and a ninety-day lowest-price guarantee on all the cycles he sells.

   (3) The store has a coffee bar, Legos, and video games, all designed to enhance the bicycle-shopping experience.

   (4) If customers of Zane's Cycles need something that costs under $1, Chris Zane gives it to them for nothing.*

   a. 1 c. 3

   b. 2 d. 4

8. (1) BakosGroup.com is a website that offers free expert advice about turning your résumé into a masterpiece.

   (2) Several online sites can help people who are searching for a job.

   (3) On the Careerbuilder.com website, you can post your résumé for potential employers to review, and you can get information about upcoming Career Fairs in your area.

   (4) Another good website for job hunters is CollegeGrad.com, which includes a search engine for employment by location, career, or industry.†

   a. 1 c. 3

   b. 2 d. 4

9. (1) The *Survivor All Stars* finale had some of the highest ratings that show has experienced since its first season.

   (2) *The Amazing Race*, in which two-person teams travel around the world, is about to launch its sixth season.

   (3) Reality television shows are more popular than ever.

   (4) The granddaddy of all reality shows, *The Real World*, still draws a large audience in the all-important fifteen-to-twenty-four-year-old-demographic,[1] making it popular with advertisers.

   a. 1 c. 3

   b. 2 d. 4

1. **demographic:** a group of people with similar characteristics

* Adapted from Pride et al., "Return to Inside Business," *Business,* 6th ed. Boston: Houghton Mifflin, 1999, 323.

† Adapted from Karen Schubert, "Work Your Own Career Magic," USA Weekend, September 24, 26, 2004, 14.

2

10. (1) An organization's competitors are other organizations that compete with it for resources.

(2) Reebok, Adidas, and Nike are competitors in the sports/athletic shoe and apparel market.

(3) In the fast-food arena, McDonald's competes for customers with Wendy's, Burger King, and Kentucky Fried Chicken, to name a few.

(4) Albertson's, Safeway, and Kroger are larger grocery stores that market to the same customer base in order to generate sales.*

a. 1
b. 2
c. 3
d. 4

C. Read the three specific sentences given. Circle the letter of the general sentence best supported by the three specific sentences.

11. Job rotation involves allowing employees to move through a variety of jobs, departments, or functions, thereby reducing the possible boredom that can arise from doing the same job every day.

Job enlargement means expanding an employee's duties or responsibilities, which in turn motivates employees by encouraging them to learn new skills or take on new responsibilities.

Job enrichment is an attempt to make jobs more desirable or satisfying, thereby triggering an employee's internal motivation.†

a. There are different design options a company can employ in order to keep employees motivated.
b. Many workers are bored with their jobs.
c. Many American workers look forward to Friday and payday, especially.
d. Many American workers are motivated.

12. The Alamo, site of a famous battle between Mexico and the United States, is located in San Antonio, Texas.

Philadelphia, Pennsylvania, is home to the Liberty Bell and many other historic attractions.

If you are visiting Washington, D.C., make sure to visit the Lincoln Memorial and the Jefferson Memorial: both are beautiful and steeped in history.

a. Washington has more monuments than any other city in the United States.
b. Many American cities have historic sites to visit.

* Adapted from Griffin, *Management,* 7th ed. Boston: Houghton Mifflin, 2002, 76–77.

† Adapted from Reece and Brandt, *Effective Human Relations in Organizations,* 7th ed. Boston: Houghton Mifflin, 1999, 186.

c. The most interesting historical sites in the U.S. are on the East Coast.
d. Thomas Jefferson was a famous inventor.

13. Bill Clinton had been the governor of Arkansas before becoming president of the United States.

Before becoming president, George Bush, Sr., had a great deal of executive experience in Washington—as vice president, director of the Central Intelligence Agency, and representative to China.

Prior to becoming president in the late 1960s, Richard Nixon had gained top-level experience in the executive branch of government, serving as vice president.*

a. Al Gore was vice president under Bill Clinton.
b. It is necessary to be vice president before you can become president.
c. Cabinet members never run for office.
d. Many presidents have government experience before assuming the role of president.

14. *Consumer Reports* is noted for rating a wide variety of products and giving recommendations on the best and worst features of each.

Newsweek reports on national and international news and also includes movie reviews and extensive information on technology in every issue.

Food & Wine is known for its recipes for everything from apple cider to chicken liver spread.

a. *Consumer Reports* is one of the best magazines available.
b. There are many magazines being published today.
c. Different magazines devote their pages to different types of articles and specialize in different topics.
d. Magazines are out of touch with what real people need to know.

15. Many athletes have used visualizations (vivid mental images of specific accomplishments) to win sports events.

Salespeople can use visualizations to succeed in the business world.

Cancer patients have improved their health with visualizations.†

a. Visualizations help people meet their goals.
b. To visualize effectively, follow four essential steps.
c. Athletes who visualize are more successful than those who don't.
d. Visualizations work only if one is highly motivated to succeed.

D. Read the general statement given. Then circle the letter of the sentence in the list that DOES NOT explain or support that general statement.

* Adapted from Wilson and DiIulio, *American Government,* 8th ed. Boston: Houghton Mifflin, 2001, 334.

† Adapted from Downing, *On Course,* 4th ed. Boston: Houghton Mifflin, 2005, 56.

16. Phil doesn't think his favorite hockey team will make the playoffs this year.
    a. Attendance at the arena is at an all-time low.
    b. The team's best scorer will be out for the rest of the season due to a broken leg.
    c. The team has fifteen games left, and twelve of them are against the best team in the league, whom they've never beaten.
    d. The team's goalie lets in more goals than any other goalie in the league.

17. A good day care provider should have many important skills and qualities.
    a. A day care provider should know CPR.
    b. A day care provider should know the child version of the Heimlich maneuver[1] in the event the child in her care chokes.
    c. A day care provider should speak the same language as the child.
    d. A day care provider should know how to sing "Happy Birthday."

18. The computer lab at the local community college offers many great resources if you need help drafting an essay.
    a. The computers in the lab are hooked up to Lexus/Nexus, an online catalog of readings on various topics.
    b. A writing tutor installed on each machine can help with grammar and syntax[2] problems or questions.
    c. The computer lab is locked each evening to avoid break-ins and vandalism.
    d. An English professor, or "writing coach," mans the lab during the day to help you with your essay.

19. One of my favorite grocery stores is the Food Emporium because of its wonderful selection of international foods and organic health care products.
    a. The Food Emporium has a sushi[3] chef on the premises who will make you takeout food to order.
    b. Shampoo without preservatives or dyes is better for the environment, so I make sure to buy it when I'm at the Food Emporium.
    c. Unwashed salad greens have been shown to cause salmonella[4] poisoning.
    d. The international frozen foods section at the Food Emporium has selections from Chinese, Thai, West Indian, and South African food exporters.

1. **Heimlich maneuver:** emergency technique used to eject an object from the throat of someone who is choking
2. **syntax:** patterns for the formation of sentences
3. **sushi:** small cakes of cold rice and fish
4. **salmonella:** a bacteria that causes food poisoning

20. Some companies behave in unethical ways.
   a. Toys "R" Us has been accused of pressuring some of its suppliers not to sell their products to discounters, thereby allowing other merchants, such as Toys "R" Us, to maintain higher prices.
   b. AT&T and Eastman Kodak have been criticized for using restructuring costs to artificially inflate their future earnings projections in their reports to investors.
   c. Some critics charge that advertisers like Disney and McDonald's inappropriately and overaggressively target young children in their advertising.
   d. Children love the free toys that are given out at McDonald's, especially when they are related to a movie that is playing at theaters.*

TEST 2

A. Read each paragraph and circle the letter of the correct topic from the list.

1. Gladiators were men who carried a *gladius,* or sword, and fought to the death as entertainment for citizens of the Roman Empire. Gladiators took part in so-called games or combat before large crowds. Armed with various specialized weapons, they fought each other and sometimes wild animals. Some unfortunates were thrust into fights with no weapons at all. Most gladiators were condemned criminals, prisoners of war, or slaves bought for the purpose. The most famous slave gladiator was Spartacus, a Thracian.[1]

   a. gladiators
   b. Roman Empire
   c. prisoners of war
   d. Spartacus

2. As for the amphitheaters[2] where gladiatorial combats took place, they were as common in Italy and the Roman Empire as skyscrapers are in the modern city. The word *arena,* referring to the site of the games, literally means *sand,* which is what covered the floor and soaked up the blood. Openings in the floor of the arena permitted animals to be released into it. A large amphitheater held at least thirty thousand spectators, and the largest amphitheater of all, the Flavian Amphitheater—or Colosseum—at Rome, seated around fifty thousand.

   a. Italy
   b. Roman Empire
   c. Colosseum
   d. arenas or amphitheaters

1. **Thracian:** native of Thrace, a region of ancient Greece

2. **amphitheaters:** arenas for contests

*Adapted from Griffin, *Management,* 6th ed. Boston: Houghton Mifflin, 2002, 108.

3. Our fascination with the gladiator is nothing compared to the Romans'. Everybody in Rome talked about gladiators. At Pompeii, graffiti celebrated a star of the arena whom "all the girls sigh for." Jokes poked fun at gladiators, philosophers pondered their meaning, and literature is full of references to them.

   a. gladiators c. Pompeii
   b. popularity of gladiators d. Rome

4. Gladiatorial images decorated art around the empire, from mosaics[1] to household lamps. In one mosaic from a Roman villa in Germany, for example, one of several mosaic panels on the floor of the building's entrance hall depicts scenes from the arena. The illustration shows a *retiarius,* or net-and-trident[2] bearer, fighting a better-armed *secutor,* literally "pursuer," under the watchful eyes of a *lanista,* or trainer. The artwork recreates a typical scene: the retiarius wears no armor except for a shoulder-piece protecting his left side. To defend himself against the dagger wielded by the secutor, the retiarius had to be fit enough to be able to keep moving.

   a. secutor c. gladiator images
   b. lanista d. retarius

5. Arguably, the arena contributed to public order. This was no small achievement since the imperial army could not police a population of 50–100 million, and few places had even the elementary police force that the city of Rome did. The violence that bloodied the amphitheater stepped into the breach[3] by reminding criminals—or those defined as criminals—what punishment awaited them. Rob or kill, and you might end up in the arena. Refuse to worship the emperor, and you might be fed to the lions, as Christians often were. Rebel against Rome, and you might find yourself on a chain gang building a new amphitheater, as tradition says thirty thousand prisoners of the Jewish Revolt (A.D. 66–70) did. The result was the Colosseum.[4]*

   a. arena's effect on public order c. the Jewish Revolt
   b. public order d. Colosseum

1. **mosaics:** designs made with small pieces of stone or tile
2. **trident:** long, three-pronged weapon
3. **breach:** gap
4. **Colosseum:** famous Roman amphitheater

* Adapted from Noble et al., *Western Civilization,* Volume I, 3rd ed., Boston: Houghton Mifflin, 2002, 200–201.

B. Read the following paragraphs and the topic in bold print. Is the topic *too narrow* or *too broad,* or is it the *correct* topic? Circle the letter of the correct answer.

6. Since the days of Vietnam[1] and Watergate[2] journalists have become adversaries[3] of the government. They instinctively distrust people in government. But to that attitude change can be added an economic one: in their desperate effort to reclaim market share, journalists are much more likely to rely on unnamed sources than once was the case. When the *Washington Post* broke the Watergate story in the 1970s, it required the reporters to have at least two sources for their stories. Now, many reporters break stories that have only one unnamed source and often not a source at all but a rumor posted on the Internet.*

   Topic: journalists

   a. too broad   b. too narrow   c. correct topic

7. Egocentrism refers to the tendency of a person to confuse his or her own point of view and that of another person. As young children illustrate, the term does not necessarily imply selfishness at the expense of others, but a centering on the self in thinking. Piaget[4] demonstrated this by showing children a table on which models of three mountains had been constructed and asking them how a doll would see the three mountains if it sat at various positions around the table. Three-year-olds commonly believed the dolls saw the layout no differently from the way they did.†

   Topic: Egocentrism

   a. too broad   b. too narrow   c. correct topic

8. It's hard to avoid being wistful[5] as I look back on George Harrison's life and work. The Beatle[6] was one of the people who made an era of pop music extraordinarily fresh and vibrant. A generation of listeners can remember the delightful surprise of his unexpected sitar[7] and slide guitar solos—or sitting bolt upright at that incredible, unheard-of-before chord

1. **Vietnam:** war in which the United States tried to help South Vietnam from being united under Communist leadership with North Vietnam
2. **Watergate:** political scandal involving illegal activities by President Richard Nixon's administration
3. **adversaries:** enemies
4. **Piaget:** Swiss psychologist famous for his discoveries about childhood development
5. **wistful:** sad
6. **Beatle:** member of the rock group the Beatles
7. **sitar:** stringed instrument of India

* From Wilson and DiIulio, *American Government,* 8th ed. Boston: Houghton Mifflin, 2001, 269.

† Adapted from Seifert and Hoffnung, *Child and Adolescent Development,* 5th ed. Houghton Mifflin, 2000, 263.

that Harrison hit on his new twelve-string guitar to begin the popular Beatles' song "Hard Day's Night." Maybe other musicians today can produce such a simple electric thrill. I've yet to hear it.*

Topic: George Harrison's new chord

a. too broad b. too narrow c. correct topic

9. Codes of ethics that companies provide to their employees are perhaps the most effective way to encourage ethical behavior. A code of ethics is a written guide to acceptable and ethical behavior as defined by an organization; it outlines uniform[1] policies, standards, and punishments for violations. Because employees know what is expected of them and what will happen if they violate the rules, a code of ethics goes a long way toward encouraging ethical behavior. However, codes cannot possibly cover every situation. Companies must also create an environment in which employees recognize the importance of complying with[2] the written code. Managers must provide direction by fostering communication, actively modeling and encouraging ethical decision making, and training employees to make ethical decisions.†

   Topic: Ethics

   a. too broad b. too narrow c. correct topic

10. To identify a person's communication style, focus your full attention on observable behavior. The best clues for identifying styles are nonverbal. Learn to be observant of people's gestures, posture, and facial expressions, and the rapidity[3] and loudness of their speech. Animated facial expressions and high-volume, rapid speech are characteristic of the *emotive*[4] communication style. Infrequent use of gestures, speaking in a steady monotone,[5] and few facial expressions are characteristic of the *reflective* style. Of course, verbal messages will also be helpful. If a person tends to be blunt and to the point and makes strong statements, you are likely observing the *director* style of communication.‡

    Topic: Communication styles

    a. too broad b. too narrow c. correct topic

1. **uniform:** unvarying; consistent
2. **complying with:** observing or following the rules
3. **rapidity:** speed
4. **emotive:** relating to emotion
5. **monotone:** a single tone of voice

---

* Adapted from David Lieberman, "Loss Leads to Music Musings," *USA Today,* December 3, 2001, 4b.

† From Pride et al., *Business,* 7th ed. Boston: Houghton Mifflin, 2002, 41. Copyright © 2002 by Houghton Mifflin Company. Reprinted with permission.

‡ From Reece and Brandt, *Effective Human Relations in Organizations,* 7th ed. Boston: Houghton Mifflin, 1999, 82.

CHAPTER 3
Supporting Details, Mapping, and Outlining

3

GOALS FOR CHAPTER 3

- **Define the terms *major details* and *minor details.***
- **Recognize major and minor details in paragraphs.**
- **Define the term *transitions.***
- **Locate transitions that often identify major details and minor details.**
- **Recognize transitions in paragraphs.**
- **Use mapping to show major and minor details in a paragraph.**
- **Use outlining to show major and minor details in a paragraph.**
- **Describe the principles of effective time management.**
- **Read and understand information in an organizational chart.**

In the previous chapter, you practiced finding the main idea of a paragraph. The main idea is the general point the writer wants you to know or to believe when you've finished reading the paragraph. Often, though, readers cannot understand or accept this point as true unless they get more information. The **supporting details** in a paragraph provide this information.

Before continuing, take the following test to find out what you already know about supporting details.

TEST YOURSELF

Identify each paragraph's main idea and write it on the blank. Then, choose one sentence that offers a *major* supporting detail and write the number of that sentence on the blank labeled "Major Supporting Detail."

1. (1) In the 1950s and 1960s, African Americans did not wait for Supreme Court or White House decisions to claim equal rights. (2) In 1955 Rosa Parks, a department store seamstress and active member of the NAACP,[1] was arrested for refusing to give up her seat to a white man on a public bus in Montgomery, Alabama. (3) Local black women's organizations and civil rights groups decided to boycott the city's bus system, and they elected Martin Luther King, Jr., a minister, as their leader. (4) King launched a boycott with a moving speech that set the stage for a full-scale civil rights movement that took place in the 1960s.*

   Main Idea: ____

   ____

   Major Supporting Detail: ___________________________________

2. (1) There are several things you can do to help your child avoid being bitten by insects. (2) The best protection against insect bites is to apply an EPA[2]-approved insect repellent to a child's skin and clothing as directed. (3) However, insect repellents should be used sparingly on infants and young children. (4) Another prevention technique involves avoiding areas where insects nest or congregate,[3] such as garbage cans, stagnant[4] pools of water, and orchards and gardens where flowers bloom. (5) In addition, when you know your child will be exposed to insects, dress him in long pants and a lightweight long-sleeved shirt; avoid dressing your child in clothing with bright colors or flowery prints as they are known to attract insects.†

   Main Idea: ____

   ____

   Major Supporting Detail: ___________________________________

3. (1) Laboratory studies show that certain ways of administering punishment to children are more effective than others. (2) One important factor is making sure the punishment closely follows the child's transgression[5] so that the child makes the connection between her wrongdoing and the consequences. (3) Another powerful factor is providing an explanation for

1. **NAACP:** National Association for the Advancement of Colored People
2. **EPA:** Environmental Protection Agency
3. **congregate:** gather together
4. **stagnant:** not moving
5. **transgression:** violation of a law, rule, or duty

* Adapted from Norton et al., *A People and a Nation,* 5th ed. Boston: Houghton Mifflin, 1998, 827.

† Adapted from Kirsten Matthew, "Safety in Sun, Sand, and Summer Pursuits!" *Westchester Parent,* June 2001, 25.

why the behavior is not desirable. (4) The effectiveness of punishment also depends on the consistency with which it is applied. (5) If parents, for example, prohibit a behavior on one occasion and permit it on another, then children tend to become particularly disobedient and aggressive.*

Main Idea: ____

____

Major Supporting Detail: ____

4. (1) Many parents overindulge kids for different reasons. (2) Guilt often has a lot to do with it. (3) Mothers and fathers of all income levels, caught up in a whirl of a busy world, often try to substitute presents for presence. (4) For example, a divorced dad may arrive bearing a Santa's load of presents. (5) As a working mom, I wouldn't dream of returning from a business trip without gifts for my fourteen-year-old daughter. (6) Also, parents may overindulge because giving in—whether to a toddler's pleas to stay up late yet again or a grade-schooler's demands for a hot new video game—is often easier than trying to just say no. (7) Furthermore, some parents, remembering their own less-bountiful childhoods, just don't want to deny their beloved offspring anything—from computers to riding lessons to pricey designer clothes.†

   Main Idea: ____

   Major Supporting Detail: ____

5. (1) Coping with stress takes two general forms: problem-focused coping and emotion-focused coping. (2) Problem-focused coping is a coping style that involves behaviors or actions targeted toward solving or handling the stress-inducing problem itself. (3) One example might be compromising with a coworker with whom one is experiencing conflict. (4) Emotion-focused coping, on the other hand, involves cognitive or thought-related strategies that minimize the emotional effects of stress-inducing events. (5) Examples of emotion-focused coping include rationalizing[1] or intellectualizing,[2] looking for the "silver lining," and making the best of a bad situation.‡

1. **rationalizing:** devising self-satisfying but incorrect reasons for one's behavior
2. **intellectualizing:** avoiding psychological insight into an emotional problem through intellectual (rational) analysis

* Adapted from Bukatko and Daehler, *Child Development,* 5th ed. Boston: Houghton Mifflin, 2004, 504. Copyright © 2004 by Houghton Mifflin Company. Reprinted with permission.

† Adapted from Dianne Hales, "Spoiled Rotten?" *Ladies' Home Journal,* May 2000, 114–116.

‡ Adapted from Levy, *Industrial/Organizational Psychology.* Boston: Houghton Mifflin, 2003, 319. Copyright © 2003 by Houghton Mifflin Company. Reprinted with permission.

Main Idea: ____

____

Major Supporting Detail: ____

Supporting details are the specific facts, statistics, examples, steps, anecdotes, reasons, descriptions, definitions, and so on that explain or prove the general main idea stated in the topic sentence. They support, or provide a solid foundation for, this main idea.

Supporting details should answer some or all of the questions raised by the topic sentence. For example, read the following statement: **Children are especially vulnerable to dog bites.** This topic sentence immediately raises the question *why?* in the reader's mind. To answer the question, the paragraph must go on to offer the reasons and other explanations that prove this point.

As you read this next paragraph, notice how the supporting details clarify the main idea, which is underlined, and explain why it's true:

> Today's American society believes a number of myths that perpetuate absentee fathers. One misconception is that raising children is women's work. Many people believe that it's not masculine to care for kids. Another misconception is that small children do not really need a father's influence. Many dads believe they can cultivate a relationship with their kids when they're older, but by then, the kids will resent their father's lack of involvement. A similar myth says that girls don't need fathers. Research shows, though, that girls with active dads are more successful and well adjusted. A final misconception is fathers can make up for being gone with short periods of "quality time." This is a myth, though, because kids need dads who help them cope with life on a daily basis, not just take them to an amusement park every now and then.*

The topic sentence of this paragraph raises the question *What are these myths?* Then, the paragraph goes on to answer that question by describing four common misconceptions about absentee fathers. The reader would not be able to understand the topic sentence without reading the details in the rest of the paragraph. It's important to learn to recognize supporting details, for they determine your understanding and interpretation of what you read.

Major and Minor Details

There are two kinds of supporting details: major details and minor details. The **major details** are the main points that explain or support the idea in the topic sentence. They offer *essential* reasons or other information that the reader must have in order to understand the main idea.

* Adapted from Ron Klinger, "What Can Be Done About Absentee Fathers?" *USA Today,* July 1998, 30.

Minor details offer more explanation of the major details. Minor details are not usually critical to the reader's comprehension of the main idea, though they do offer more specific information that helps clarify the points in the paragraph even more.

To see the difference between major and minor details, read the following paragraph:

> Many people hold a superstitious fear of certain numbers. One especially ominous[1] number is 13. Some people, for example, do not like being on the thirteenth floor of a building, and some are apprehensive about Friday the thirteenth. Another troubling number is 666. Because the Bible associates 666 with Satan, for instance, residents of Colorado and New Mexico have tried to change the name of U.S. Highway 666 to something else.*

The topic sentence of this paragraph, which is underlined, raises the question *What are these certain numbers people fear?* The second and fourth sentences of the paragraph answer that question. They tell the reader that the numbers 13 and 666 are the ones that trouble people. The other sentences in the paragraph offer minor details that give examples of ways people demonstrate their fear of these two numbers. Therefore, they offer nonessential information that helps explain the main idea even more.

Remember the explanation of general and specific sentences back in Chapter 2? You learned that the topic sentence is the most general statement in a paragraph, while the other sentences offer more specific information. Well, these other sentences (the supporting details) are also related to each other in general and specific ways. It might be helpful to visualize these relationships in a diagram form:

Many people hold a superstitious fear of certain numbers.	
One especially ominous number is 13.	Another troubling number is 666.
Some people, for example, do not like being on the thirteenth floor of a building, and some are apprehensive about Friday the thirteenth.	Because the Bible associates 666 with Satan, for instance, residents of Colorado and New Mexico have tried to change the name of U.S. Highway 666 to something else.

1. **ominous:** menacing, threatening

* Adapted from Gerald F. Kreyche, "Playing the Numbers Game," *USA Today,* July 1998, 98.

This diagram offers a useful visual image of the general and specific relationships among sentences in paragraphs. The major details—represented in the blocks beneath the topic sentence—provide the solid foundation of support for the main idea. You could not remove any of these blocks without significantly weakening the base on which the main idea rests. The minor details in the next row of blocks make the structure even sturdier. Though the main idea would still be supported by the major details even if the minor details were removed, the minor details make the whole base even stronger.

To better understand what you read, you may want to try to visualize the sentences in a diagram like the one above. Sorting out these relationships is critical not only to comprehending a paragraph but also to deciding whether you can agree with the author's ideas.

Exercise 3.1

Read the following paragraphs, and then label each of the sentences in the list as MI for main idea, MAJOR for major detail, or MINOR for minor detail.

1. (1) People seek out frightening situations like scary movies and haunted houses for different reasons. (2) One reason is curiosity and a desire to learn to control their emotional reactions. (3) When you move through a Halloween haunted house, for example, you know the threat isn't real, so you can practice feeling and managing your fear. (4) A second reason people seek out scary situations is to experience the opposite reaction that follows an experience of intense emotion. (5) After seeing a scary movie, many people feel more calm and peaceful.*

   _______ Sentence 1

   _______ Sentence 3

   _______ Sentence 4

2. (1) Weathering plays a vital role in our daily lives, with both positive and negative outcomes. (2) It frees life-sustaining minerals and elements from solid rock, allowing them to become incorporated into our soils and finally into our foods. (3) Indeed, we would have very little food without weathering, as this process produces the very soil in which much of our food is grown. (4) But weathering can also wreak havoc[1] on the structures we build.

1. **wreak havoc:** cause destruction

---

* Adapted from "Everybody Loves a Halloween Scare," *USA Today,* September 1998, 8.

(5) Countless monuments, from the pyramids of Egypt to ordinary tombstones, have suffered drastic deterioration from freezing water, hot sunshine, and other climatic forces.*

_______ Sentence 1

_______ Sentence 4

_______ Sentence 5

3. (1) If you want your kids to learn to like Brussels sprouts and other vegetables, you can use three strategies. (2) First, don't promise them a cupcake if they eat their Brussels sprouts. (3) This sends the message that vegetables are work and sugar is fun. (4) Second, you can actually mix the two. (5) One doctor recommends mixing a tablespoon or so of sugar in half a cup of water and pouring it over broccoli or another vegetable to sweeten it slightly without altering its taste. (6) Third, serve the Brussels sprouts at least ten times. (7) Food preferences are learned; after people eat a repellent[1] food ten times, the taste receptors in their brains actually change, and they will learn to like the food.

_______ Sentence 1

_______ Sentence 2

_______ Sentence 6

3

4. (1) Upon taking office, President Reagan announced a plan for what he called "a new beginning." (2) First, he asked Congress to cut billions from domestic programs, including Medicare and Medicaid, food stamps, welfare subsidies[2] for the working poor, and school meals. (3) Congress endorsed[3] most of Reagan's demands; joining the Republicans were conservative Democrats. (4) Tax cuts were the second facet[4] of Reagan's economic plan; he called for reductions in the income taxes of the affluent[5] and of corporations in order to stimulate savings and investments. (5) A third item occupied Reagan's agenda: a vigorous assault on federal environmental, health, and safety regulations that, Reagan believed, excessively reduced business profits and discouraged economic growth.

1. **repellent:** distasteful, disgusting
2. **subsidies:** financial assistance
3. **endorsed:** approved, supported
4. **facet:** aspect, part
5. **affluent:** wealthy

* From Chernicoff and Fox, *Essentials of Geology,* 2nd ed. Boston: Houghton Mifflin, 2000, 85.

(6) Reagan's plan was met with mixed opinions from the nation, but he stood firm in his belief for "a new beginning."*

_______ Sentence 1

_______ Sentence 2

_______ Sentence 4

_______ Sentence 5

5. (1) Laser eye surgery is being touted[1] in advertisements as a quick, virtually risk-free procedure that can end patients' need for glasses. (2) But with more than 1 million patients expected to undergo the procedure this year, thousands are learning what advertisements don't say: the surgery can cause life-altering complications that sometimes can't be fixed. (3) Problems include double or triple vision so severe patients can't watch TV or read. (4) Others experience light distortions so blinding they can't drive at night and eyes so dry that goggles must be worn outside. (5) Some patients have spent thousands of dollars trying to fix problems only to find the technology doesn't yet exist to provide a remedy.†

_______ Sentence 2

_______ Sentence 3

_______ Sentence 4

Exercise 3.2

Read each paragraph and write an abbreviated form of each sentence in the boxes to indicate their general and specific relationships.

1. Studies show that America's children do not get enough physical activity, but we can change that. One way to improve kids' fitness level is to require daily physical education in schools. Studies show that children who participate in daily P.E. classes have better cardiovascular endurance than

1. **touted:** praised or promoted

* Adapted from Norton et al., *A People and a Nation,* 5th ed. Boston: Houghton Mifflin, 1998, 966.

† Adapted from Stephanie Armour and Julie Appleby, "Promise of Clear Vision Brings Misery to Some," *USA Today,* June 27, 2001, 1A.

kids who participate in weekly P.E. classes. A second way to improve fitness levels is to offer active after-school programs. Kids who engage in games such as tag, scavenger hunts, and obstacle courses get more exercise in target heart rate zones, which improves their overall health.*

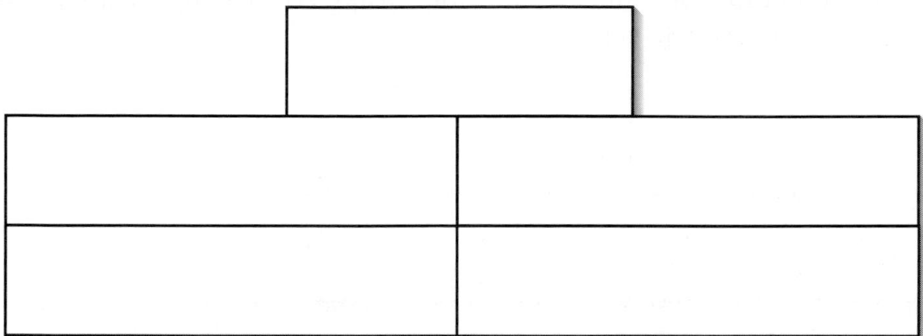

2. The need for reforesting is fairly clear. The old trees are dying, victims of age and drought[1] conditions in recent years. More than seventy of the oldest trees that surround George Washington's home at Mount Vernon have died over the past century, and only thirteen of the trees planted under Washington's direction are left. Also, deer keep eating new trees as soon as they break through the ground. According to Dean Norton, who supervises planting at Mount Vernon, these animals are preventing anything new from growing.†

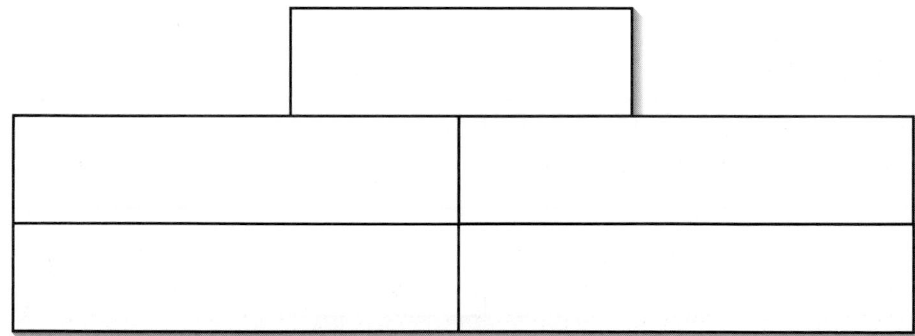

1. **drought:** long period of low rainfall

* Adapted from Arlene Ignico, "Children's Sedentary Lifestyle: A Forerunner of Unhealthy Adulthood," *USA Today,* May 1998, 59.

† Adapted from Dan Vergano, "Mount Vernon Clones History," *USA Today,* June 20, 2001, 7D.

3

3. If you set out to write an ideal story for a baseball player, you couldn't do better than Cal Ripken, Jr.'s. The son of a father-teacher hones his craft in the family business, gets drafted by the hometown team—the one he has loved as far back as memory goes—and stays for two storybook seasons. Then, he wins one World Series, two Most Valuable Player awards, and the admiration of millions. And, he breaks Lou Gehrig's consecutive-game streak of 2,632 games played.*

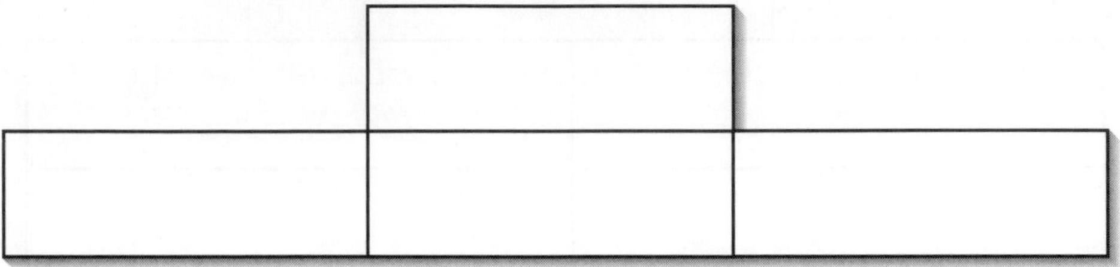

4. Although our culture associates napping with laziness, brief naps can be good for you. A ten- to fifteen-minute nap every day makes you more productive during the day. As one devoted napper says, "Fatigue and safety are the antithesis[1] of each other and when you're fatigued, you're not working at your best, and you're probably grumpy; that makes a bad work environment." Researchers also find that napping cuts down on stress on the job. For example, people who nap during the workday report feeling more relaxed while they work, call in sick less than their non-napping counterparts,[2] and enjoy their workday more.†

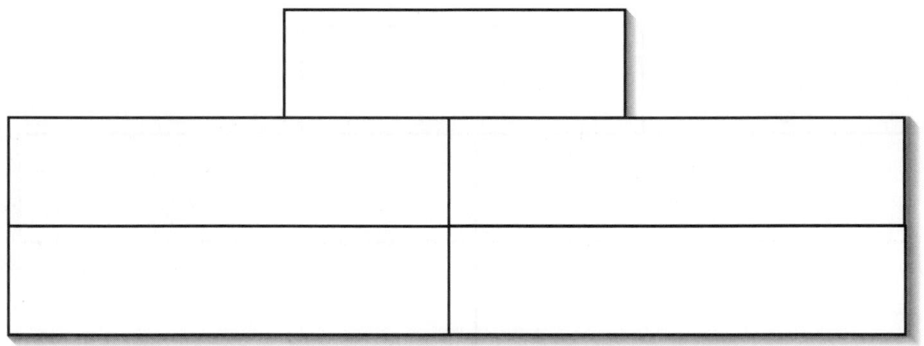

1. **antithesis:** exact opposite

2. **counterparts:** those with the same function and characteristics

* Adapted from Erik Brady, "Ironman Age Ending," *USA Today,* June 20, 2001, 1C.

† Adapted from Michael Precker, "Bosses Awaken to the Benefits of Naptime," *The Journal News,* June 25, 2001, 1D.

5. If you commute to college, it may be less convenient for you to become involved in activities and events than it would be if you lived on or near campus, but there are ways for you to take a more active part in campus life. For one thing, many clubs and organizations on your campus would be happy to have you as a member. If you join one of these groups, you will meet people who share your interests, and you may learn even more about an activity you already enjoy. You could also drop by your student government office and introduce yourself. Someone there can tell you about the many activities and upcoming events in which you can take part. Forming a study group that meets on campus or scheduling some on-campus study time is another way to remain on campus and stay involved.*

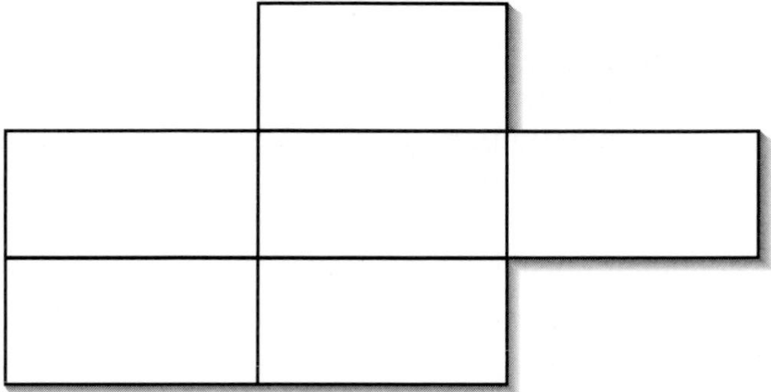

Transitions

To help readers recognize the general and specific relationships between sentences in a paragraph, paragraphs usually include transitions. **Transitions** are words that assist readers in distinguishing between major and minor details because they make connections and distinctions between the different details. In particular, sentences that offer major details are likely to begin with words such as:

first, second, third	finally
in addition	one
and	another
also	furthermore
next	

* Adapted from Kanar, *The Confident Student,* 5th ed. Boston: Houghton Mifflin, 2004, 24. Copyright © 2004 by Houghton Mifflin Company. Reprinted with permission.

These words signal that the sentence will offer another new point in support of the topic sentence. For an example of transitions that indicate major details, read the following paragraph. These transitions are in bold print:

> Eighteenth century scientist-explorers Meriwether Lewis and William Clark complemented each other in skills and personality traits. **First of all,** Lewis's scientific interests in flora, fauna,[1] and minerals were a good match for Clark's surveying and engineering skills. **Second,** both were effective leaders. Lewis tended to be more aloof[2] while Clark was more of an extrovert[3] and father figure. **Yet,** both men inspired loyalty in the other members of their expedition. **Furthermore,** both men knew how to work as a team. They took turns leading their expedition to explore the West, and they apparently never quarreled.*

The transitions in the list above are not the only ones that identify major details. Others will be discussed later in Chapter 5. However, because transitions commonly introduce important supporting details, readers should be aware of their function within the paragraph.

A paragraph might also include transitions to indicate minor details. Sentences that offer minor details are sometimes introduced with words such as:

for example	to illustrate
one example	specifically
for instance	in one case

These words can indicate that the sentence is about to offer more specific information to develop the preceding idea further. In the next paragraph, the transitions that signal minor details are in boldface, while those that identify major details are underlined:

> Undersea robots help scientists by conducting research that would put human lives at risk. For one thing, robots can make visual records of areas deep beneath the ocean. **For example,** a robotic machine named *Jason* takes photographs and creates maps of ancient shipwrecks in 2,500 feet of water. Second, robots can recover materials on the ocean floor too deep for humans to reach. *Jason,* **for instance,** has a robotic arm that can pick up artifacts[4] and samples for scientists to study.†

1. **flora, fauna:** plants and animals
2. **aloof:** distant, reserved
3. **extrovert:** outgoing person
4. **artifacts:** objects of historical interest

* Adapted from Gerald F. Kreyche, "Lewis and Clark: Trailblazers Who Opened the Continent," *USA Today,* January 1998, 49.

† Adapted from "Taking Exploration to New Heights and Depths," *USA Today World of Science,* June 1998, 14.

It's important to note here that the transitions in the list above can also be used to introduce *major* details in a paragraph. Chapter 5 will offer more specific information about how paragraphs use transitions in different ways.

Exercise 3.3

Read each paragraph and underline the topic sentence, circle the transitions that signal major details, and underline transitions that signal minor details.

1. When we listen effectively, we increase the chances of experiencing positive outcomes. First, listening provides us with information. Many of our ideas come from listening to others as we brainstorm, watching the news on television, and, of course, listening to formal presentations. Second, good listeners usually have better interpersonal relationships. Specifically listening to others is an excellent way of showing we care about them—their problems, perspectives, and ideas. Third, listening gives us a clearer sense of who we are and what we value. For example, listening allows us to compare and contrast ourselves with others, helping us better understand our personal identity. Fourth, those who listen are often better speakers. By practicing good listening habits, we can gain some understanding of what we find tasteful, sound, strategic, and interesting. And fifth and finally, listening well is an ethical responsibility for each of us as we participate in the communication process.*

2. Emotions include several components. First, they have a physiological[1] component, involving changes in nervous system activities such as respiration and heart rate. Fear or anxiety, for example, may be accompanied by more rapid breathing, increased heart rate and blood pressure, and perspiration. Second, emotions include an expressive component, usually a facial display that signals the emotion. Smiles, grimaces, cries, and laughter overtly[2] express a person's emotional state. Third, emotions have an experiential[3] component, the subjective[4] feeling of having an emotion.†

3. Men and women working in the dynamic field of chemistry have brought a wealth of inventions and innovations to the world. For one thing,

1. **physiological:** relating to the body
2. **overtly:** openly
3. **experiential:** related to experience
4. **subjective:** personal

* Adapted from Andrews et al., *Public Speaking*. Boston: Houghton Mifflin, 1999, 21.

† Adapted from Bukatko and Daehler, *Child Development*, 5th ed. Boston: Houghton Mifflin, 2004, 381. Copyright © 2004 by Houghton Mifflin Company. Reprinted with permission.

scientists have discovered new uses for an age-old drug that cures common ailments. And, an organically[1] grown fuel has been found that will power your car while being friendly to the environment. Another newly synthesized[2] compound exhibits an unusual property and will vastly contribute to the reduction of pollution. As you can see, chemistry has an impact on our daily lives!*

4. Theory X is a concept of employee motivation generally consistent with Taylor's scientific management. Theory X assumes that employees dislike work, will try to avoid it, and will function effectively only in a highly controlled work environment. One example of this would be a dissatisfied worker who calls in sick at least once a week. In addition, because people dislike work, managers must coerce,[3] control, and frequently threaten employees to achieve organizational goals. In one case, a computer company executive threatened the manager of his assembly plant with dismissal if he did not improve his attendance record. Finally, people in a Theory X environment must be led because they have little ambition and will not seek responsibility; they are concerned mainly with job security.†

5. Brainstorming is a technique for finding solutions, creating plans, and discovering new ideas. When you are stuck on a problem, brainstorming can break the logjam. For example, if you run out of money two days before payday every week, you could brainstorm ways to pay for your education. In addition, you could brainstorm ways to find a job.

   The brainstorming process includes several steps. First, formulate the issue or problem precisely by writing it down. Next, set a time limit for your brainstorming session. Write down everything. Finally, after the session, review, evaluate, and edit. Toss out any truly nutty ideas, but not before you give them a chance. For example, during your brainstorm on Central African trade organizations, you might have written: "Go to Central Africa and ask someone about them."‡

1. **organically:** naturally
2. **synthesized:** formed or made
3. **coerce:** force or pressure someone to act a certain way

* Adapted from Sherman and Sherman, *Essential Concepts of Chemistry*. Boston: Houghton Mifflin, 2000, 10. Copyright © 2000 by Houghton Mifflin Company. Reprinted with permission.

† Adapted from Pride et al., *Business,* 6th ed. Boston: Houghton Mifflin, 1999, 227.

‡ Adapted from Dave Ellis, *Becoming a Master Student*, 9th ed. Boston: Houghton Mifflin, 2000, 228.

Mapping and Outlining

Earlier in this chapter, you saw how you can visualize the relationships between sentences in a paragraph by inserting each one into a block. The main idea went into the block at the top, the major supporting details went into the row of blocks just beneath the main idea, and the minor details, if any, were in the third row.

	MAIN IDEA	
MAJOR DETAIL	**MAJOR DETAIL**	**MAJOR DETAIL**
Minor Detail	Minor Detail	Minor Detail

This diagram is a form of **mapping**, a technique that involves using lines, boxes, circles, or other shapes to show how sentences in a paragraph are related.

In mapping, you lay out a visual to help you see the main idea, major supporting details, and minor supporting details. Here are some other, different ways to visualize these relationships:

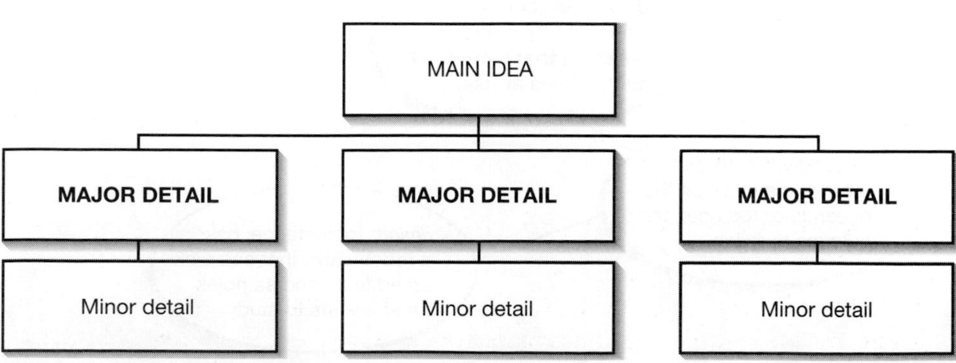

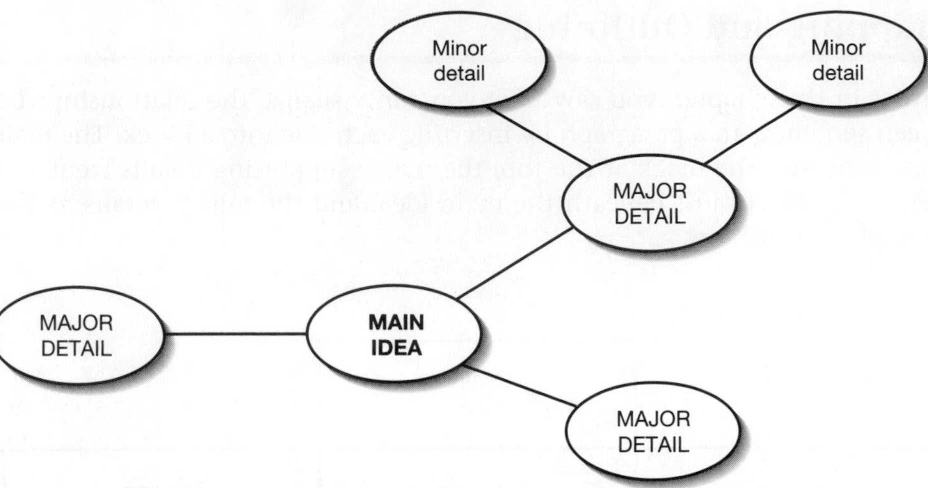

3

For example, using the diagram above, you might map the paragraph about undersea robots on page 130 as shown here.

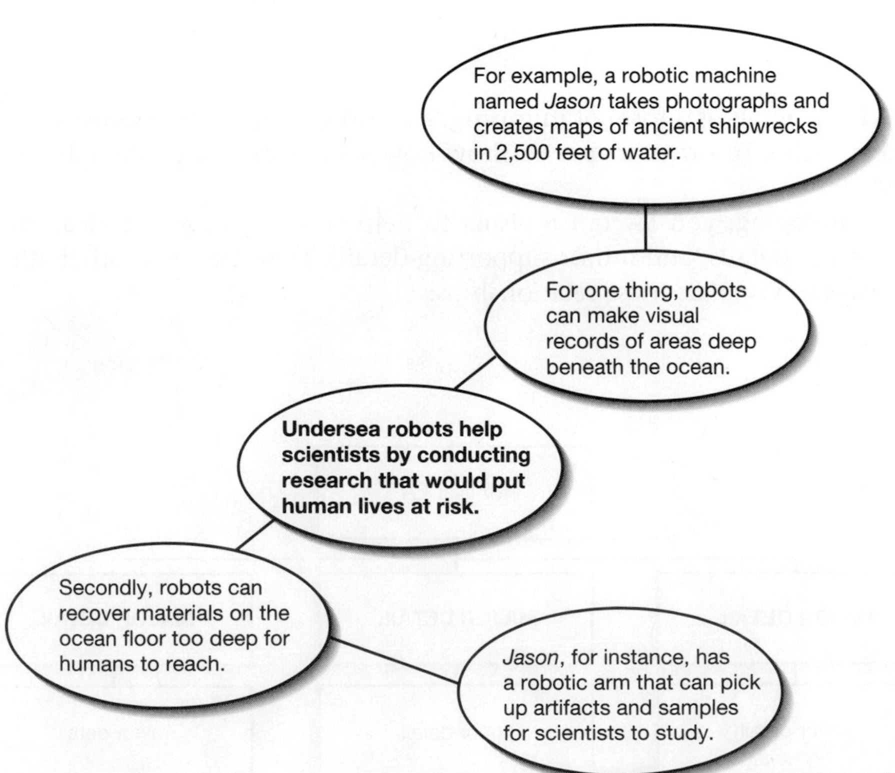

Exercise 3.4

Read each paragraph and fill in the map that follows with an abbreviated form of each sentence.

1. When family members talk to one another, there are often two meanings to what they say. The *message* is the meaning of the words and sentences spoken, what anyone with a dictionary and a grammar book could figure out. For example, a husband might ask his wife, "What's in this turkey stuffing?" The *metamessage* (the prefix *meta* means, among other things, going beyond or higher) is meaning that is not stated: it's the way something is said, who is saying it, or the fact that it is said at all. The wife, for instance, may interpret her husband's question as critical if he has expressed disapproval of her cooking in the past.*

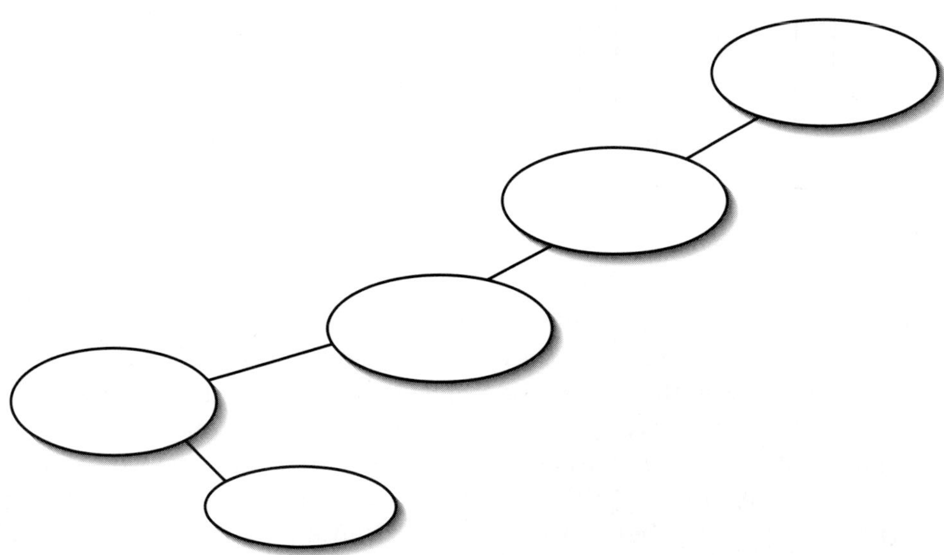

*From Deborah Tannen, "What's That Supposed to Mean?" *Reader's Digest*, July 2001, 103.

2. People cope with the distressing state of loneliness in different ways. When college students were asked about the behavioral strategies they use to combat loneliness, 93 percent said they tried extra hard to succeed at another aspect of life. Others said that they distracted themselves by running, shopping, washing the car, or staying busy at other activities. Still others sought new ways to meet people. Some talked to a friend, relative, or therapist about the problem. Though fewer in number, some are so desperate that they use alcohol or drugs to wash away feelings of loneliness.*

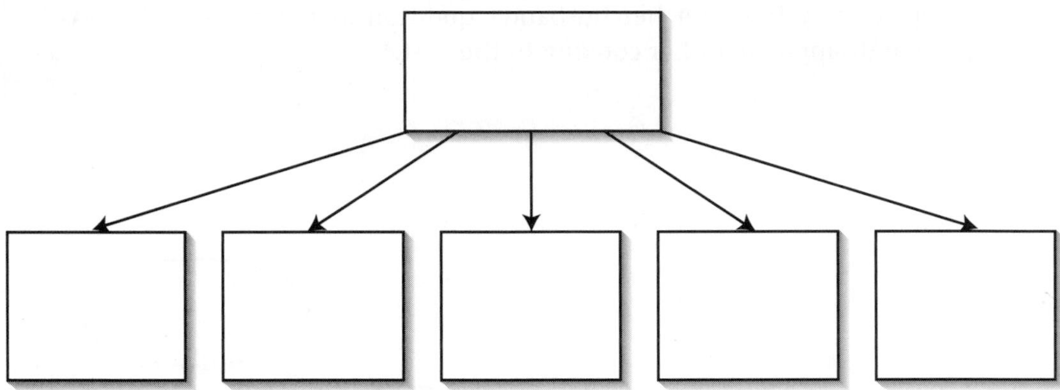

3. Questions offer a variety of benefits. Questions open up inquiries that otherwise might never take place, waking people up and leading them to examine an issue that otherwise might go unexamined. For instance, if you want to take better notes, you can write, "What's missing for me in taking notes?" or "How can I gain more skill in taking notes?" Besides being helpful to you, questions can help you develop your relationship with a teacher. Teachers love questions because they reveal interest and curiosity. Questions are also great ways to improve relationships with friends and coworkers. When you ask a question, you bring a huge gift to people—an invitation for them to speak their brilliance and an offer to listen to their answers.†

* Adapted from Brehm et al., *Social Psychology*, 5th ed. Boston: Houghton Mifflin, 2002, 305. Copyright © 2002 by Houghton Mifflin Company. Reprinted with permission.

† Adapted from Dave Ellis, *Becoming a Master Student*, 9th ed. Boston: Houghton Mifflin, 2000, 230.

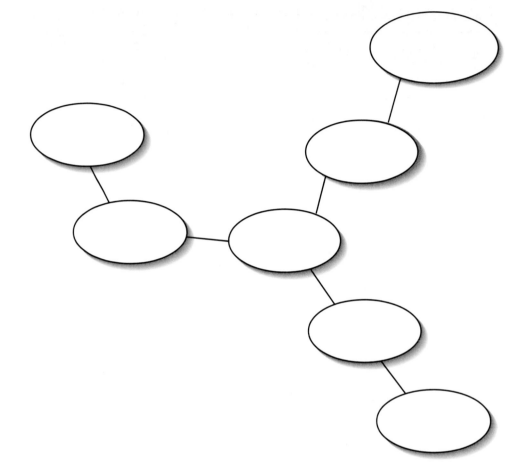

4. The best way to help kids get into a good saving habit is to create a scenario in which it becomes stupid not to save. You can do this by creating a "mini-matched savings plan," in which a parent agrees to match dollar for dollar the child's savings, with the stipulation[1] that the money cannot be withdrawn until some point in the future without a substantial penalty. Even though they don't get to spend the money right away, kids love the idea because they are getting the immediate gratification[2] of more money now. Another plan would be to open up a passbook savings account where a child opens a savings account and is given a passbook that records each deposit and withdrawal you or your child makes to the

1. **stipulation:** condition, requirement 2. **gratification:** satisfaction of a desire

account. This is a good way for children to see money grow in their account or, conversely, disappear if they take money out to buy a treat or a special thing they might want.*

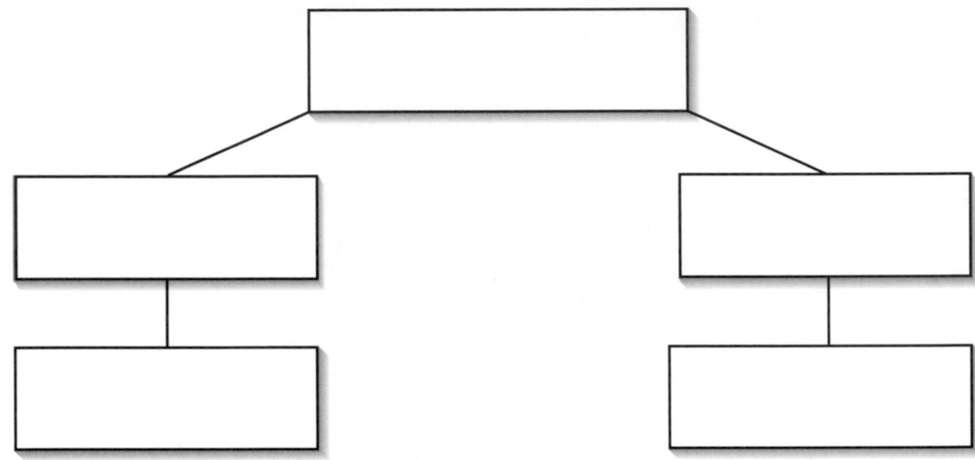

3

5. If you can learn to predict change where your job or your corporation is concerned, you'll be in a much stronger position when it hits. To stay current, join professional organizations, read business journals, and attend every convention or conference you can. Within your company, it's never been more important to make friends, and not just with the high and mighty. Assistants often know things other people would like to know and can tip you off on new software programs or even new personnel. Also, start reading job postings to get a sense of the skills your front office considers most desirable these days. Check out key websites, too. Look at your employer's site to see what kinds of new directions and strategies are being announced, and also examine the websites posted by your company's competition.†

* Adapted from Cynthia Davies, "Raising Money-Savvy Kids," *Westchester Family*, July 2001, 35. Used by permission of the author.

† Adapted from Anne Field, "How to Handle Change at the Office," *Good Housekeeping*, May 2000, 94.

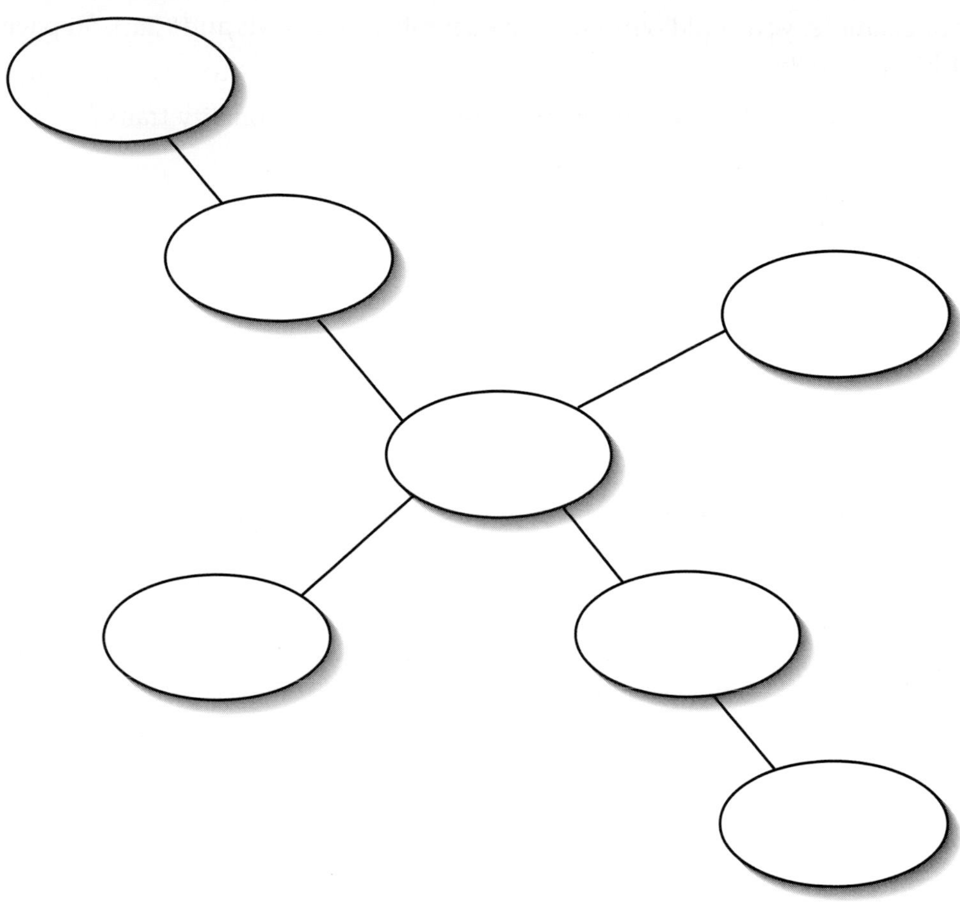

Another good way to identify the main idea and supporting details is to create an outline. An **outline** is a list of these details labeled with a system of numbers and letters that show their relationships to one another. Outlines often use the Roman numeral system, which effectively identifies the main idea and different topics or details. Outlines can be in sentence form or in topic form. The latter is useful for creating a brief summary that allows you, at a glance, to see the general and specific relationships.

I. Main Idea
   A. Major detail
      1. Minor detail
      2. Minor detail
   B. Major detail
      1. Minor detail
      2. Minor detail

For example, you could outline the paragraph about Lewis and Clark on page 130, as follows:

I. Lewis and Clark's complementary skills and personality traits
   A. Scientific interests and skills
      1. Lewis: flora, fauna, minerals
      2. Clark: surveying, engineering
   B. Leadership skills
      1. Lewis: aloof
      2. Clark: extrovert and father figure
   C. Teamwork
      1. Took turns leading
      2. Did not quarrel

To create an outline, line up the major details along one margin and label them with capital letters. Beneath each major detail, indent minor details with numbers: 1, 2, 3, and so forth.

If you do not like the formality of a Roman numeral outline, you can also outline a paragraph in a more visual way, by using a series of indented boxes in place of the numbers and letters, as illustrated in the diagram.

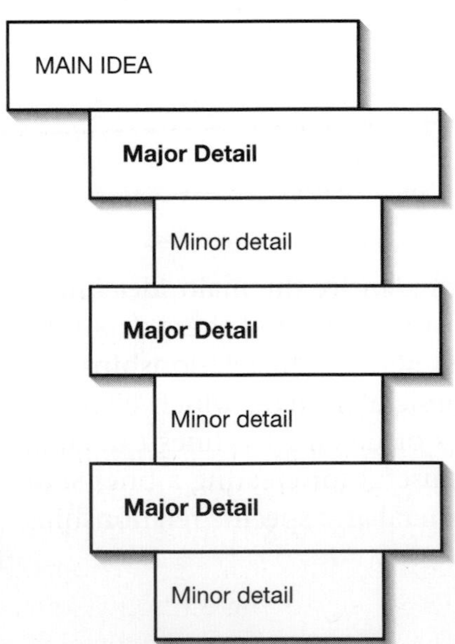

The following diagram, like the Roman numeral outline, arranges major details along one margin line and indents minor details beneath each one. You could create an outline of this type for the paragraph about absentee fathers on page 122, as follows:

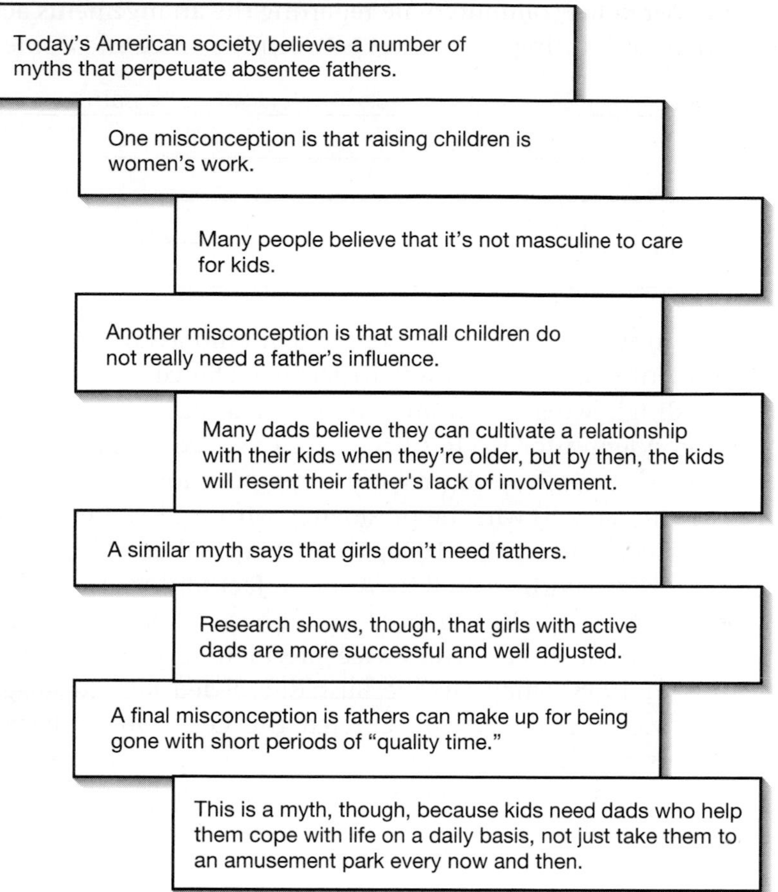
Today's American society believes a number of myths that perpetuate absentee fathers.
One misconception is that raising children is women's work.
Many people believe that it's not masculine to care for kids.
Another misconception is that small children do not really need a father's influence.
Many dads believe they can cultivate a relationship with their kids when they're older, but by then, the kids will resent their father's lack of involvement.
A similar myth says that girls don't need fathers.
Research shows, though, that girls with active dads are more successful and well adjusted.
A final misconception is fathers can make up for being gone with short periods of "quality time."
This is a myth, though, because kids need dads who help them cope with life on a daily basis, not just take them to an amusement park every now and then.

Exercise 3.5

Complete the outline that follows each paragraph.

1. Researchers cite several reasons for a decline in the number of telecommuting workers at companies such as AT&T. First, managers remain reluctant to adopt telecommuting, especially because the pace of change in today's workplace is faster, and teamwork is increasingly in vogue.[1] Second, employees are reticent[2] because they fear working outside the office will hurt career advancement, especially as the economy sours and job cuts mount. Third, employers are worried that letting workers telecommute will create security risks by creating more opportunities for computer hackers or equipment thieves. And finally, instead of helping balance work and fam-

1. **in vogue:** in fashion; current and popular
2. **reticent:** reluctant

ily, a number of telecommuters are reporting the arrangements actually increase strain by blurring the barriers between the office and home.*

I. ______________________________
   A. ______________________________
   B. ______________________________
   C. ______________________________
   D. ______________________________

2. No one who wishes to become president should assume that to become vice president first is the best way to get there. Since the earliest period of the Founding[1], when John Adams and Thomas Jefferson were each elected president after having first served as vice president under their predecessors[2], there have been only three occasions when a vice president was later able to win the presidency without his president's having died in office. One was in 1836, when Martin Van Buren was elected president after having served as Andrew Jackson's vice president. The second was in 1968, when Richard Nixon became president after having served as Dwight Eisenhower's vice president eight years earlier. The third was in 1988, when George Bush succeeded Ronald Reagan. Also, only four vice presidents who entered the Oval Office[3] because their predecessors died were subsequently elected to terms in their own right. Those four were Theodore Roosevelt, Calvin Coolidge, Harry Truman, and Lyndon Johnson.†

I. ______________________________
   A. ______________________________
      ____
      1. ______________________________
      2. ______________________________
      3. ______________________________

1. **the Founding:** a reference to the establishment of the new American republic in the late 18th century
2. **predecessors:** ones who came before
3. **the Oval Office:** the president's office in the White House

* Adapted from Stephanie Armour, "Telecommuting Gets Stuck in the Slow Lane," *USA Today,* June 25, 2001, 1D.

†Adapted from Wilson and DiIulio, *American Government,* 8th ed. Boston: Houghton Mifflin, 2001, 366.

B. ____

____

1. ____
2. ____
3. ____
4. ____

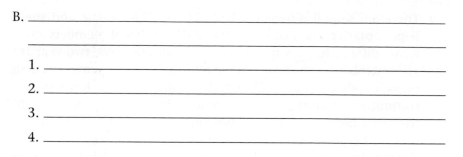

3. Small physical and behavioral differences between the sexes appear early on and tend to increase over the years. For example, girls suffer less often than boys from speech, learning, and behavior disorders; mental retardation; emotional problems; and sleep disorders. They tend to speak and write earlier and to be better at grammar and spelling. They nurture others more than boys do and show more emotional empathy. Their play tends to be more orderly. At the same time, boys tend to be more skilled than girls at manipulating objects, constructing three-dimensional forms, and mentally manipulating complex figures and pictures. They are more physically active and aggressive and more inclined to hit obstacles or people. They play in larger groups and spaces and enjoy noisier, more strenuous physical games.*

I. ____

A. ____

1. ____

____

2. ____
3. ____
4. ____

B. ____

1. ____

____

2. ____

____

3. ____

____

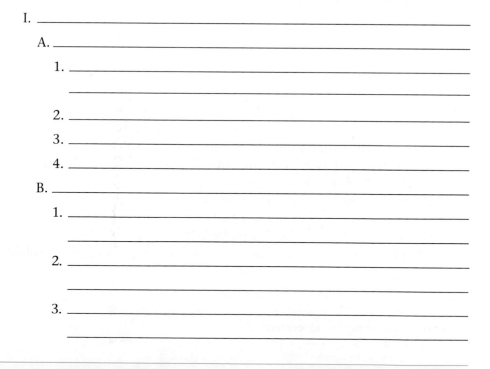

*Adapted from Bernstein and Nash, *Essentials of Psychology*, 2nd ed. Boston: Houghton Mifflin, 2002, 327–328. Copyright © 2002 by Houghton Mifflin Company. Reprinted with permission.

3

4. There are several differences between the U.S. Senate and the House of Representatives. First of all, each body's number of members and length of terms differ. The 435 members of the House serve two-year terms. The 100 members of the Senate serve rotating six-year terms. The assignments of each body differ as well. Each House member may have only one major committee assignment, so they tend to be policy specialists. Senators, on the other hand, have two or more major committee assignments, so they tend to be policy generalists. A third difference is in the length of their debates. In the House, debate is usually limited to one hour. In the Senate, debate is unlimited unless shortened by unanimous[1] consent.*

I. ______________________________

A. ______________________________

1. ______________________________

2. ______________________________

B. ______________________________

1. ______________________________

2. ______________________________

C. ______________________________

1. ______________________________

2. ______________________________

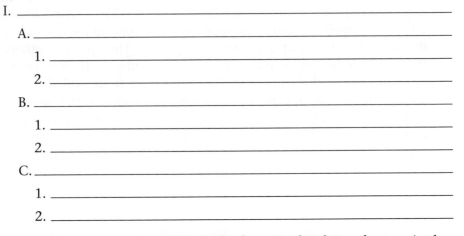

5. There are three types of marriages. The first type has been characterized as an *equal-partner relationship*. In this kind of marriage, everything (who works, who cooks, who pays the bills) is open to negotiation. Instead of a preset assignment of roles and responsibilities, both partners expect change as they and their relationship grow and develop. A second type of marriage is the *conventional relationship*, in which the man is the head of the household and the sole economic provider and the woman is the mother and the homemaker, responsible for all domestic tasks. A third type of relationship, the *junior-partner relationship*, has elements of both equal partnerships and conventional relationships. The junior partner, typically the wife, brings in some of the income and takes on some decision-making responsibilities.

1. **unanimous:** complete agreement of all involved

*Adapted from Wilson and DiIulio, *American Government*, 8th ed. Boston: Houghton Mifflin, 2001, 319.

The senior partner, usually the husband, often *helps* the wife at home, but he does not share family responsibilities such as cooking and child care.*

I. ______________________________
  A. ______________________________
    1. ______________________________
    2. ______________________________
  B. ______________________________
    1. ______________________________
    2. ______________________________
  C. ______________________________
    1. ______________________________
       ____
    2. ______________________________
       ____

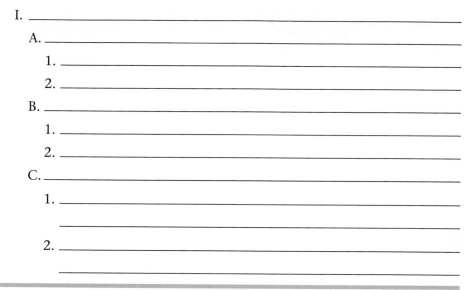

CHAPTER 3 REVIEW

Fill in the blanks in the following statements.

1. ______________ are the specific facts, statistics, examples, steps, anecdotes, reasons, descriptions, definitions, and so on that explain or prove the general ___________ stated in the topic sentence.
2. There are two kinds of supporting details: ___________ details and ___________ details. The ___________ details are the main points that explain or support the idea in the topic sentence. ___________ details offer more explanation of the major details.
3. ___________ are words that assist readers in distinguishing between major and minor details because they make connections and distinctions between the different details.
4. ___________ is a technique that involves using lines, boxes, circles, or other shapes to show how sentences in a paragraph are related.
5. An ___________ is a list of supporting details labeled with a system of numbers and letters that show their relationships to one another.

*Adapted from Seifert et al., *Lifespan Development*, 2nd ed. Boston: Houghton Mifflin, 2000, 480–481. Copyright © 2000 by Houghton Mifflin Company. Reprinted with permission.

Reading Selection

Practicing the Active Reading Strategy:

Before and While You Read

You can use active reading strategies before, as, and after you read a selection. The following are some suggestions for active reading strategies that you can perform before you read and while you read.

1. Skim the selection for any unfamiliar words. Circle or highlight any words you do not know.
2. As you read, underline, highlight, or circle important words or phrases.
3. Write down any questions about the selection if you are confused by the information presented.
4. Jot notes in the margin to help you understand the material.

Physical Attractiveness

1 What do you look for in a friend or romantic partner? Intelligence? Kindness? A sense of humor? How important, really, is a person's looks? As children, we were told that "beauty is only skin deep" and that we should not "judge a book by its cover." Yet as adults, we react more favorably to others who are physically attractive than to those who are not. According to studies that inspired Nancy Etcoff's 1999 book *Survival of the Prettiest*, beauty is a major force in the affairs of our social world.

2 The bias for beauty is everywhere. In one study, fifth-grade teachers were given background information about a boy or girl, accompanied by a photograph. All teachers received identical information; however, those who saw an attractive child saw that child as being smarter and more likely to do well in school. In a second study, male and female experimenters approached students on a college campus and tried to get them to sign a petition. The more attractive the experimenters were, the more signatures they were able to get. In a third study, Texas judges set lower bail and gave lower fines to suspects who were rated as attractive rather than unattractive on the basis of photographs. In a fourth study conducted in the United States and Canada, economists discovered that physically attractive men and women earn more money than others whose only difference was being less attractive in their appearance.

3 It all seems so shallow, so superficial. But before we go on to accept the notion that people prefer others who are physically attractive, let's stop for a moment and consider a basic question. What constitutes physical beauty? Is it an objective and measurable human characteristic like height, weight, or hair color? Or is beauty a subjective quality, existing in the eye of the beholder? There are advocates on both sides.

4 Some researchers believe that certain faces are naturally more attractive than oth-

ers. There are three sources of evidence for this conclusion. First, when people are asked to rate faces on a 10-point scale, there is typically a high level of agreement—among children and adults, men and women, and people from the same or different cultures. For example, Michael Cunningham and others asked Asian and Latino students, along with black and white American students, to rate the appearance of women from all these groups. Overall, the ratings were highly consistent. Investigators concluded that people everywhere share an image of what is beautiful. People also tend to agree about what makes for an attractive body. For example, men tend to be drawn to the "hourglass" figure seen in women of average weight whose waists are narrower than their hips. This shape is thought to be associated with reproductive fertility. In contrast, women like men with waist and hips that form a tapering V-shape. If marriage statistics are any indication, women also prefer height. Comparisons made in Europe indicate that married men are a full inch taller, on average, than unmarried men.

5 Second, some researchers have identified physical features of the human face that are linked to judgments of attractiveness. For example, women who are seen as attractive tend to have large eyes, prominent cheekbones, a small nose, and a wide smile. Men are seen as attractive if they have a broad jaw. Even more interesting, perhaps, are studies showing that people like faces in which the eyes, nose, lips, and other features are not too different from the average. Judith Langlois and Lori Roggman showed college students both actual yearbook photos and computerized photos blending the "averaged" features from four, eight, sixteen, or thirty-two of the photos. Time and again, they found that the students preferred the blended photographs to the individual faces. They also found that the more faces used to form the blend, the more highly it was rated. Other studies have since confirmed this result.

6 It seems odd that "averaged" faces are judged attractive when, after all, the faces we find the most beautiful are anything but average. What accounts for these findings? Langlois and others believe that people like averaged faces because they seem more familiar to us. Consistent with this idea, research shows that people are also attracted to averaged dogs, birds, and wristwatches. Other studies indicate that the computerized averaging technique produces faces that are also equal on both sides. It may be the balance that we find attractive. Why do people prefer faces in which the paired features on the right and left sides mirror each other? Some psychologists speculate that balance is naturally associated with health, fitness, and fertility. These qualities are highly desirable in a mate.

7 There is a third source of evidence for the view that beauty is an objective quality. Babies, who are too young to have learned the culture's standards of beauty, show a preference for faces considered attractive by adults. Picture the scene in an infant laboratory. A baby, lying on its back in a crib, is shown a series of faces previously rated by college students. The first face appears and a clock starts ticking as the baby stares at it. As soon as the baby looks away, the clock stops and the next face is presented. The result: young infants spend more time looking at attractive faces than at unattractive ones. It doesn't matter if the faces are young or old, male or female, or black or white. Other studies similarly reveal that infants look

longer at faces that are "averaged" in their features. "These kids don't read *Vogue* or watch TV," notes Langlois, "yet they make the same judgments as adults."

8 In contrast to this objective perspective, other researchers argue that physical attractiveness is subjective. They point for evidence to the influences of culture, time, and the circumstances of our perception. One source of support for this view is that people from different cultures increase their beauty in very different ways. They use face painting, makeup, plastic surgery, scarring, tattoos, hairstyling, the molding of bones, the filing of teeth, braces, and the piercing of ears and other body parts. All contribute to the "enigma of beauty." What people find attractive in one part of the world is often seen as disgusting in another part of the world.

9 Ideals also vary when it comes to bodies. Judith Anderson and others looked at preferences on female body size in fifty-four cultures. In places where food is often in short supply, heavy women are judged more attractive than slender women. In one study, for example, Douglas Yu and Glenn Shepard found that Matsigenka men living in the Andes mountains of southeastern Peru see female forms with "tubular"[1] shapes (rather than hourglass shapes) as healthier, more attractive, and more desirable in a mate. Differences in preference have also been found among racial groups within a given culture. Michelle Hebl and Todd Heatherton asked black and white female college students from the United States to rate thin, average, and overweight women from a set of magazine photographs. The result: The white students saw the heavy women as the least attractive. The black students, however, did not agree. Why the difference? White Americans are, on average, thinner than black Americans. Therefore, one possible explanation is that they simply prefer a body type that is more typical of their group. Another possibility is that white Americans identify more with the "mainstream" weight-obsessed culture as portrayed in TV shows, magazine ads, and other media.

10 Standards of beauty also change over time, from one generation to the next. Brett Silverstein and others examined the measurements of female models appearing in women's magazines from 1901 to 1981. They found that "curviness" (as measured by the bust-to-waist ratio) varied over time, with a boyish, slender look becoming particularly desirable in recent years. Apparently, the ideal body for women has changed a great deal from the larger proportions preferred in the past to the slender, athletic form popular now. Ideas about facial attractiveness are also subject to change over time. Would the face that launched a thousand ships toward the Trojan War[2] get more than a passing glance today?

11 Still other evidence for the subjective nature of beauty comes from research laboratories. Time and again, social psychologists have found that our judgments of someone's beauty can be inflated or deflated[3] by various circumstances. Research shows, for example, that people often see others as more physically attractive after

1. **tubular:** shaped like a tube
2. **the face that launched . . . Trojan War:** a reference to Helen, the beautiful woman said to have caused the Trojan War in ancient Greece
3. **deflated:** reduced in size

they have grown to like them. In fact, the more in love people are with their partners, the less attracted they are to others of the opposite sex. On the other hand, men who viewed gorgeous nude models in *Playboy* and *Penthouse* magazines later gave lower attractiveness ratings to average-looking women, including their own wives. These lower ratings were the unfortunate results of a contrast effect. Even our self-evaluations change in this way. Research shows that people feel less attractive after viewing supermodel-like members of the same sex than after viewing less attractive persons. And they aren't happy about it. Douglas Kenrick and others found that exposure to highly attractive members of the opposite sex put people into a good mood. Exposure to attractive members of the same sex, though, had the opposite effect.*

Vocabulary

Read the following questions about some of the vocabulary words that appear in the previous selection. Circle the letter of the correct response.

1. What does the word *superficial* mean, as used in paragraph 3?

   a. not pleasant
   b. not deep
   c. not understanding
   d. not true

2. As used in paragraph 3, what does the word *subjective* mean? "Or is beauty a *subjective* quality, existing in the eye of the beholder?"

   a. personal
   b. subject to discussion
   c. popular
   d. close-minded

3. In paragraph 4, what does *tapering* mean?

   a. pleasing
   b. wide
   c. upside down
   d. gradually narrowing

4. In paragraph 5, what does *prominent* mean?

   a. pink
   b. low and long
   c. sunken
   d. immediately noticeable

5. What is an *enigma* as used in paragraph 8: "All contribute to the '*enigma* of beauty'"?

   a. solution
   b. clue
   c. mystery
   d. story

*Adapted from Brehm et al., *Social Psychology*, 5th ed. Boston: Houghton Mifflin, 2002, 307–311. Copyright © 2002 by Houghton Mifflin Company. Reprinted with permission.

3

Main Ideas, Topic Sentences, and Supporting Details

Answer the following questions by circling the letter of the correct answer.

1. What is the topic of paragraph 2?
   a. intelligence
   b. the bias for beauty
   c. fifth-grade teachers
   d. attractive college students

2. Which of the following sentences from paragraph 9 states the main idea of that paragraph?
   a. "Ideals also vary when it comes to bodies."
   b. "In places where food is often in short supply, heavy women are judged more attractive than slender women."
   c. "Therefore, one possible explanation is that [black Americans] simply prefer a body type that is more typical of their group."
   d. "Another possibility is that white Americans identify more with the 'mainstream' weight-obsessed culture as portrayed in TV shows, magazine ads, and other media."

3. Which of the following sentences from paragraph 2 does NOT state a major supporting detail?
   a. "In one study, fifth-grade teachers were given background information about a boy or girl, accompanied by a photograph."
   b. "All teachers received identical information; however, those who saw an attractive child saw that child as being smarter and more likely to do well in school."
   c. "In a second study, male and female experimenters approached students on a college campus and tried to get them to sign a petition."
   d. "In a fourth study conducted in the United States and Canada, economists discovered that physically attractive men and women earn more money than others whose only difference was being less attractive in their appearance."

4. Which of the following sentences from paragraph 9 states a minor supporting detail?
   a. "Ideals also vary when it comes to bodies."
   b. "In places where food is often in short supply, heavy women are judged more attractive than slender women."
   c. "In one study, for example, Douglas Yu and Glenn Shepard found that Matsigenka men living in the Andes mountains of southeastern Peru see female forms with 'tubular' shapes (rather than hourglass shapes) as healthier, more attractive, and more desirable in a mate."

d. "Differences in preference have also been found among racial groups within a given culture."

5. Which of the following sentences from paragraph 11 includes a transition that indicates a minor supporting detail?
   a. "Time and again, social psychologists have found that our judgments of someone's beauty can be inflated or deflated by various circumstances."
   b. "Research shows, for example, that people often see others as more physically attractive after they have grown to like them."
   c. "Research shows that people feel less attractive after viewing supermodel-like members of the same sex than after viewing less attractive persons."
   d. "Douglas Kenrick and others found that exposure to highly attractive members of the opposite sex put people into a good mood."

Practicing the Active Reading Strategy:
After You Read

Now that you have read the selection, answer the following questions using the active reading strategies that are discussed on pages 30–33.

1. Identify and write down the point and purpose of this reading selection.
2. Besides the vocabulary words included in the exercise on page 149, are there any other vocabulary words that are unfamiliar to you? If so, write a list of them. When you have finished writing your list, look up each word in a dictionary and write the definition that best describes the word as it is used in the selection.
3. Predict any possible test questions that may be used on a test about the content of this selection.
4. How could you use the information contained in this selection? Does the information contained in the selection reinforce or contradict your ideas and experiences? Explain.

Questions for Discussion and Writing

Answer the following questions based on your reading of the selection. Write your answers on the blanks provided.

1. Respond to the two questions posed in the first paragraph: "What do you look for in a friend or romantic partner? How important, really, is a person's looks?" Discuss your answers with the class and summarize the different answers given by your classmates. What did you discover?

____

____

2. Write a short essay in which you discuss the following question posed in paragraph 3 of the selection: "What constitutes physical beauty?"

____

____

3. Write a short essay in which you compare or contrast the standard of beauty that exists in your cultural heritage or background with that portrayed in the American media. _______________________

____

3

Vocabulary: Context and Meaning

When you encounter an unfamiliar word as you read and go to the dictionary to look it up, you'll often find several different meanings and variations for that word. How do you know which definition is the right one? You have to look at the *context*—the words, phrases, and sentences surrounding that word—to determine which meaning applies.

To figure out the right definition, you may need to first determine the word's part of speech in the sentence. Many words can function as different parts of speech (for example, the word *left* can be a noun, a verb, an adjective, or an adverb), so you'll have to figure out how the word is being used before you can decide which definition applies. For example, the word *park* is both a noun that means "a recreation area" and a verb that means "to stop a moving vehicle." Is it the noun or the verb that is being used in the following sentence?

> This is a myth, though, because kids need dads who help them cope with life on a daily basis, not just take them to an amusement ***park*** every now and then.

You know the word refers to a recreation area because of the other words (in particular, the adjective *amusement*) around it.

Vocabulary Exercise 1

The following sentences all come from paragraphs throughout Chapters 2 and 3. Look up the italicized words in a dictionary and write down the definition that best describes how each word is being used.

1. His growth was arrested by periods of illness, ***grave*** hunger, or metal poisoning. _______________________

2. Kids who *engage* in games such as tag, scavenger hunts, and obstacle courses get more exercise in target heart rate zones, which improves their overall health. ______

3. Although our *culture* associates napping with laziness, brief naps can be good for you. ______

______

4. Also, parents may overindulge because giving in—whether to a toddler's pleas to stay up late yet again or a grade-schooler's demands for a ***hot*** new video game—is often easier than trying to just say no. ______

5. Countless monuments, from the pyramids of Egypt to ordinary tombstones, have suffered drastic deterioration from freezing water, ***hot*** sunshine, and other climatic forces. ______

6. A code of ethics . . . outlines ***uniform*** policies, standards, and punishments for violations. ______

7. Another newly synthesized compound exhibits an unusual *property* and will vastly contribute to the reduction of pollution. ______

8. Questions open up inquiries that otherwise might never take place, waking people up and leading them to examine an *issue* that otherwise might go unexamined. ______

9. To stay *current*, join professional organizations, read business journals, and attend every convention or conference you can. ______

______

10. They [boys] are more physically active and aggressive and more *inclined* to hit obstacles or people. ______

3

Vocabulary Exercise 2

Write a definition for each of the boldfaced, italicized words in the passage below. Use the context to help you decide on the correct definition.

Americans' love ***affair*** with the automobile shows no sign of slowing down. Neither does their ***relative*** disdain for ***mass*** transit. The percentage of households that have three or more vehicles is almost double the percentage of households with no cars: 18.3 percent vs. 9.3 percent. In 1990,

3

the ***spread*** was much tighter—17.4 percent vs. 11.5 percent. "Fascinating," says Alan Pisarski, transportation expert and author of *Commuting in America*. "The number of people without a car had hung around 10 to 11 million for 30 years, and the suspicion was that we could see that grow with increased immigration." Instead, the number dropped in the 1990s to 9.8 million. "It says something about the democratization[1] of the automobile," Pisarski says. "If that's the cause of ***congestion,*** we may all have to smile and accept it."

More than 76 percent of workers say they ***drive*** alone, roughly the same as in 1990. Despite broad efforts to expand mass transit systems and encourage carpools in the 1990s, Americans continue to stay behind the wheel. Telecommuting, touted[2] as a high-tech ***solution*** to traffic congestion, has had little impact. About 5 percent of people use public transportation to get to work, the same as in 1990. About 11 percent carpool, down slightly from 1990. And 3 percent work at home, roughly the same as in 1990.*

1. affair ______________________________

2. relative ______________________________

3. mass ______________________________

5. spread ______________________________

6. congestion ______________________________

7. drive ______________________________

8. solution ______________________________

READING STRATEGY: Reading and Time Management

How often should you read? How long should you try to read in one sitting? How many times should you read a chapter? Is it better to read the whole chapter at once or just a section at a time?

There are no right or wrong answers to these questions. The most effective length, amount, and frequency of reading time will differ from student to student and from class to class. You will have to experiment to discover what works best for you, and you will probably need to make adjustments for each different course you take.

1. **democratization:** making something popular and available to everyone
2. **touted:** praised or promoted

*Adapted from Haya El Nasser and Paul Overberg, "The Cost of Moving Up," *USA Today*, August 6, 2001, 2A.

However, be aware of the following general principles of effective time management:

- Schedule time to read. Don't just try to fit reading in whenever you can; actually make an appointment to read by blocking out regular times on your calendar. Try to schedule time for multiple readings of the same chapter.
- The best time to read is the time of day or night when you are most mentally alert. If you're a night owl, read at night. If you're a morning person, try to fit in your reading time at the beginning of your day.
- Take frequent breaks during reading sessions. Regularly stand up and stretch, walk around, and rest your eyes for a few minutes.
- Keep up with the reading assignments in a course by following the schedule provided by your instructor. Following the schedule will give you the basic understanding of the material you'll need in order to get the most out of class lectures, discussions, and activities.
- Repeated exposure to information helps increase your retention of the material. If you hurriedly read large chunks of information all at once just before a test, you probably won't remember much of it. If you digest information slowly and regularly over a longer period of time, you'll remember more.

Answer the following questions on a separate sheet of paper, or use your computer.

1. Describe the typical length, amount, and frequency of reading time that seems to work best for you.
2. Describe a time when you took a class that required you to alter significantly the length, amount, and/or frequency of your reading.
3. What time of day are you most mentally alert? Is that the time of day when you usually read?
4. Which of the guidelines listed above do you already practice?
5. Which of the guidelines above do you think you should implement in order to get more out of your reading?

Continued

3

3

Reading Visuals: Organizational Charts

An **organizational chart** is one that shows the chain of command in a company or organization. It uses rectangles and lines to show the managerial relationships between the individuals within a group. Its purpose is to represent the lines of authority and responsibility in the organization.

An organization chart contains the following parts:

- **Title.** The title usually identifies the organization.
- **Boxes.** Each box, or rectangle, represents one entity within the organization. That entity might be an individual or a group of individuals, such as a department. Each box will be labeled with a name, a job title, or a department name. These boxes are arranged in a hierarchy, or ranking. The person or group with the most authority and responsibility is at the top of the chart. Each subsequent row of boxes represents the next layer of authority, a group of people or groups who are equal in rank and who all report to the individual(s) in the layer above.
- **Lines.** The lines connect boxes to show managerial relationships. They indicate who reports to whom. The source line, if applicable, identifies who collected or compiled the information in the chart.

These parts are labeled in the organizational chart on page 157.

To understand an organizational chart, begin at the top. Read the label in the box at the top, and then follow the lines to see which individuals and groups are related to each other.

This organization chart shows a company structure that places the president at the top of the hierarchy. That individual has the most authority and responsibility. The two staff positions listed beneath the president advise him and report to him. However, as the dotted lines indicate, they do not supervise the three vice presidents and the director of human resources, who make up the next layer of authority. Those four employees report to the president. The branching lines that descend from each box in the chart indicate the number and titles of individuals who are managed by that person.

Now, study the organizational chart on page 158 and then answer the questions that follow.

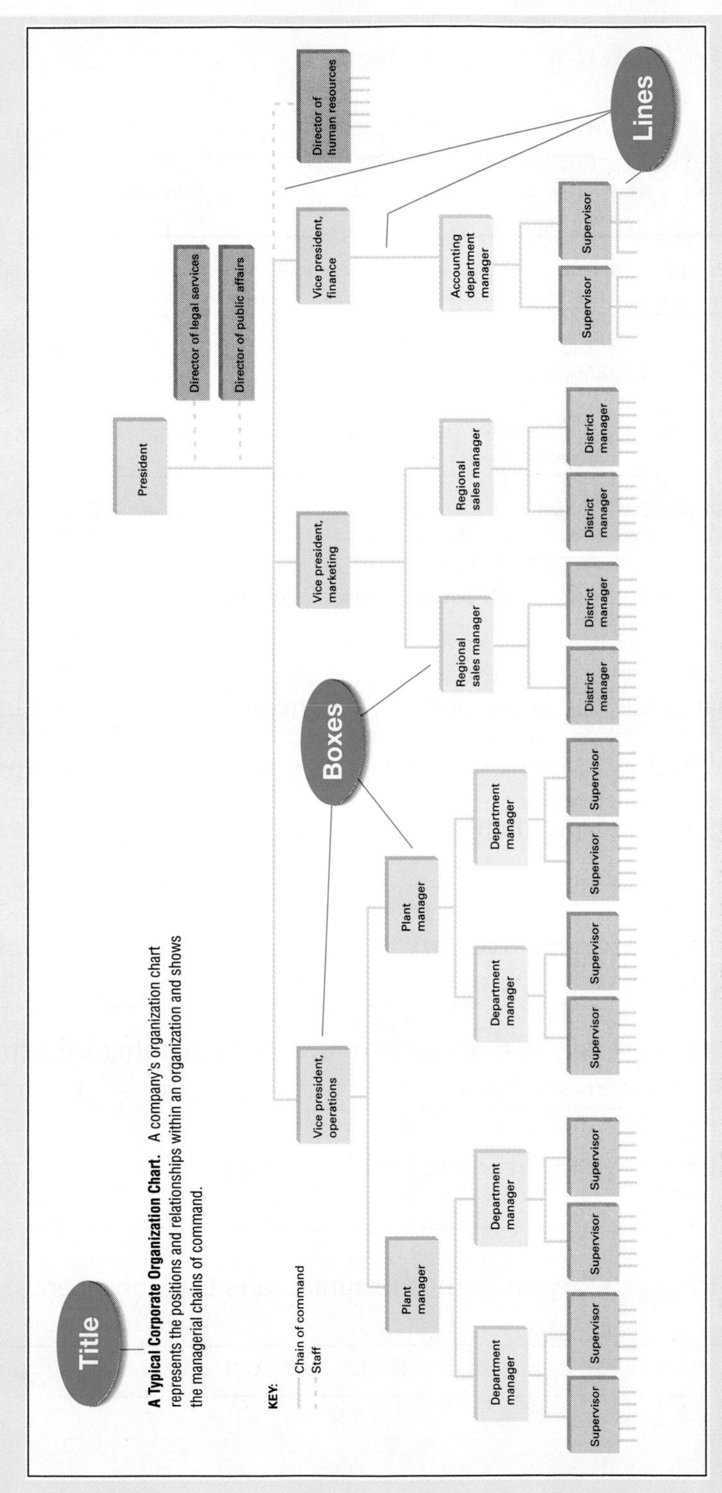

Source: Pride et al., *Business*, 6th ed. Boston: Houghton Mifflin, 1999, 166–167.

Continued

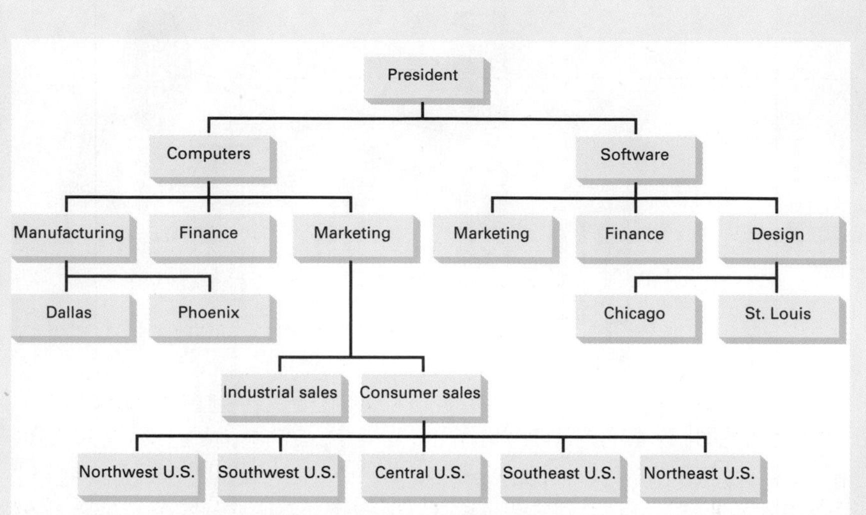

Source: Pride et al., *Business*, 6th ed. Boston: Houghton Mifflin, 1999.

1. What is the title of the person with the most responsibility in this organization? ______________________
2. List the two departments that report directly to the president of this organization.______________________
3. List the three departments that report directly to the Software Department. ______________________
4. List the two regions that report to the Manufacturing Department.

   ____
5. Which two groups report directly to Marketing?

   ____
6. Which regions report to the Consumer Sales Division (there are five).

   ____

   ____

Name ______________________________ Date ____________________

TEST 1

A. Read the following paragraphs, and circle the letter of the correct answer (main idea, major detail, or minor detail) for the sentence indicated.

(1) It may sound weird, but some people really do adore their mechanical pets. (2) Linda Spice, a woman with a severe case of cerebral palsy, has two pets, Faith and Hope, who are a constant source of comfort, inspiration and joy. (3) For example, when not chasing after their favorite hot-pink ball, or scrapping together, they are content to just sit in Spice's lap. (4) Robbie Ann Kohn of Burlington, Massachusetts, developed and trained her pets, Sim and Merlin, from helpless newborns to happy adults. (5) They go everywhere Kohn does, including on long trips to visit friends and family. (6) In West Chester, Pennsylvania, Dean Creehan takes his dogs anywhere he can. (7) For example, he took the dogs to the office for "bring your kids to work day" and even elementary schools. (8) One time the kids played a little too hard with da Vinci and broke his leg. (9) The kids felt awful, asking, "Does it hurt?" and "Will he be OK?" (10) For months, teachers and students kept inquiring about da Vinci.*

1. Sentence 1 is a

   a. main idea. b. major detail. c. minor detail.

2. Sentence 2 is a

   a. main idea. b. major detail. c. minor detail.

3. Sentence 3 is a

   a. main idea. b. major detail. c. minor detail.

4. Sentence 4 is a

   a. main idea. b. major detail. c. minor detail.

5. Sentence 5 is a

   a. main idea. b. major detail. c. minor detail.

* Adapted from Jim Louderback, "Love and Robots," *USA Weekend*, January 25–27, 2002, 4. Reprinted with permission from *USA Weekend*.

For additional tests, see the Test Bank.

6. Sentence 6 is a

   a. main idea. b. major detail. c. minor detail.

7. Sentence 7 is a

   a. main idea. b. major detail. c. minor detail.

(1) There are essentially two ways for a president to develop a program. (2) One way, exemplified[1] by Presidents Carter and Clinton, is to have a policy on almost everything. (3) To do this they worked endless hours and studied countless documents, trying to learn something about, and then state their positions on, a large number of issues. (4) The other method, illustrated by President Reagan, is to concentrate on three or four major initiatives[2] or themes and leave everything else to subordinates.[3]*

8. Sentence 1 is a

   a. main idea. b. major detail. c. minor detail.

9. Sentence 2 is a

   a. main idea. b. major detail. c. minor detail.

10. Sentence 3 is a

    a. main idea. b. major detail. c. minor detail.

11. Sentence 4 is a

    a. main idea. b. major detail. c. minor detail.

(1) Research consistently shows a positive relationship between friendship and individual well-being. (2) Friends bolster[4] positive feelings by sharing activities, feelings, and ideas. (3) They also serve as buffers against stress by providing intimacy and comfort during hard times such as the breakup of a romantic relationship, the failure to get a job, the death of a loved one, or a health crisis. (4) Karen, for example, relies on Bill's encouragement as she sends out résumés and waits for interviews; his belief in her abilities, stories about his job searches, and computer assistance provide emotional and practical support. (5) Social relationships with friends have also been shown to encourage health-promoting behaviors such as healthy patterns of eating, exercising, and avoiding abuse of alcohol. (6) A running buddy helps to keep you running, while a

1. **exemplified:** illustrated
2. **initiatives:** tasks or goals
3. **subordinates:** people of lower rank or status
4. **bolster:** support, prop up

* From Wilson and Dilulio, *American Government,* 8th ed. Boston: Houghton Mifflin, 2001, 363.

friend from a twelve-step program such as Alcoholics Anonymous (AA) helps you to face the challenges of quitting drinking.*

12. Sentence 1 is a

    a. main idea. b. major detail. c. minor detail.

13. Sentence 3 is a

    a. main idea. b. major detail. c. minor detail.

14. Sentence 5 is a

    a. main idea. b. major detail. c. minor detail.

15. Sentence 6 is a

    a. main idea. b. major detail. c. minor detail.

B. Read the paragraph below and respond to the questions that follow by circling the letter of the correct answer.

(1) Every president brings to the White House a distinctive personality; the way the White House is organized and run will reflect that personality. (2) Dwight Eisenhower brought an orderly, military style to the White House. (3) He was accustomed to delegating authority and to having careful and complete staff work done for him by trained specialists. (4) Though critics often accused him of having a bumbling, incoherent[1] manner of speaking, in fact much of that was a public disguise—a strategy for avoiding being pinned down in public on matters where he wished to retain freedom of action. (5) On the other hand, John Kennedy projected the image of a bold, articulate,[2] and amusing leader who liked to surround himself with talented amateurs. (6) For example, he appointed his brother, Bobby, to be the attorney general, even though he had never held an executive position in government prior to that appointment. (7) Instead of clear, hierarchical[3] lines of authority, there was a pattern of personal rule and an atmosphere of improvisation.[4] (8) Kennedy did not hesitate to call very junior subordinates[5] directly and tell them what to do, bypassing the chain of command.†

1. **incoherent:** unable to clearly express oneself
2. **articulate:** expressing oneself clearly
3. **hierarchical:** relating to a group or body that is organized by rank
4. **improvisation:** inventing without preparation
5. **subordinates:** people of lower rank or status

* Adapted from Seifert et al., *Lifespan Development*, 2nd ed. Boston: Houghton Mifflin, 2000, 473. Copyright © 2000 by Houghton Mifflin Company. Reprinted with permission.

† Adapted from Wilson and DiIulio, *American Government,* 8th ed. Boston: Houghton Mifflin, 2001, 353.

16. The main idea is expressed in
    a. sentence 1.
    b. sentence 2.
    c. sentence 3.
    d. sentence 4.

17. The topic of this selection is
    a. presidents' personality styles.
    b. presidents' leadership abilities.
    c. Eisenhower.
    d. Kennedy.

18. The supporting details of this paragraph relate to
    a. the personalities and styles of two particular presidents.
    b. John F. Kennedy's personal style.
    c. Dwight Eisenhower's personal style.
    d. the way a president deals with Congress.

19. Which of the following is a major detail in this paragraph?
    a. sentence 1
    b. sentence 2
    c. sentence 3
    d. sentence 6

20. How many major details support the main idea?
    a. 2
    b. 3
    c. 4
    d. 6

21. Dwight Eisenhower adopted a bumbling style because
    a. that was the only way he knew how to act.
    b. he wanted people to think he was dumb.
    c. he didn't want to be pinned down on certain issues.
    d. he was gravely ill.

22. Which of the following is a minor supporting detail in the paragraph?
    a. sentence 1
    b. sentence 2
    c. sentence 5
    d. sentence 6

23. An example of John Kennedy surrounding himself with talented amateurs is
    a. his hiring of Richard Nixon.
    b. his hiring of his brother, Bobby, to be attorney general.
    c. his hiring of his wife to give White House tours.
    d. his willingness to call junior subordinates directly.

24. According to the selection and the examples given, Eisenhower's and Kennedy's styles could be characterized as
    a. very similar.
    b. somewhat similar.
    c. not similar at all.
    d. There are not enough details to decide.

25. Which president is described as having an "atmosphere of improvisation" in his leadership style?
    a. Kennedy
    b. Eisenhower
    c. both presidents
    d. The selection does not say.

TEST 2

Read each paragraph and respond to the questions that follow by circling the letter of the correct answer.

(1) Work-related stressors fall into one of four categories—task, physical, role, and interpersonal demands. (2) *Task demands* are associated with the task itself. (3) For example, having to make fast decisions, decisions with less than complete information, or decisions that have relatively serious consequences are some of the situations that can make some jobs stressful. (4) Thus, the jobs of surgeon, airline pilot, and stockbroker are relatively stressful. (5) A second type, *physical demands,* includes stressors associated with the job setting. (6) For instance, working outdoors in extremely hot or cold temperatures, or even in an improperly heated or cooled office, can lead to stress. (7) *Role demands* are a third cause of stress. (8) A role is a set of expected behaviors associated with a position, so an employee who is feeling pressure from her boss to work longer hours or to travel more away from her family will almost certainly experience stress. (9) A final category of stressors includes *interpersonal demands,* stressors associated with relationships that confront people in organizations. (10) For example, leadership styles can cause stress, and individuals with conflicting personalities may experience stress if they are required to work too closely together.*

1. The topic sentence of this selection is
    a. sentence 1.
    b. sentence 2.
    c. sentence 7.
    d. sentence 10.

2. Which of the following sentences begins with a transition that signals a *major* supporting detail?
    a. sentence 2
    b. sentence 3
    c. sentence 5
    d. sentence 6

3. Which of the following sentences does NOT include a transition that signals a *major* supporting detail?
    a. sentence 2
    b. sentence 5
    c. sentence 7
    d. sentence 9

*Adapted from Griffin, *Management,* 7th ed. Boston: Houghton Mifflin, 2002, 470–472.

3

4. Which of the following sentences does NOT include a transition that signals a *minor* supporting detail?

   a. sentence 3
   b. sentence 6
   c. sentence 8
   d. sentence 10

5. Which of the following sentences is NOT a *minor* supporting detail?

   a. sentence 3
   b. sentence 4
   c. sentence 7
   d. sentence 8

3

(1) Although violence seems to be just about everywhere, a handful of societies stand out as nonviolent exceptions. (2) One nonviolent society is the Chewong, who live in the mountains of the Malay Peninsula. (3) This group of people does not even have words in their language for quarreling, fighting, aggression, or warfare. (4) Another nonviolent group is the Ifaluk, who live on a small atoll[1] in the Federated States of Micronesia. (5) In that society, for example, the most serious act of aggression noted in a year involved a man who touched another on the shoulder in anger, an offense which was punished with a stiff fine. (6) The Amish, the Hutterites, and the Mennonites, too, are all societies that reside in the relatively violent United States but remain remarkably nonviolent.*

6. The topic of this selection is

   a. violence.
   b. violence in the United States.
   c. nonviolent societies.
   d. the Chewong.

7. Which of the following sentences begins with a transition that signals a *major* supporting detail?

   a. sentence 1
   b. sentence 2
   c. sentence 3
   d. sentence 5

8. Which of the following sentences does NOT include a transition that signals a *major* supporting detail?

   a. sentence 2
   b. sentence 3
   c. sentence 4
   d. sentence 6

1. **atoll:** ringlike island that encloses a lagoon

* Adapted from Brehm et al., *Social Psychology*, 5th ed. Boston: Houghton Mifflin, 2002, 395. Copyright © 2002 by Houghton Mifflin Company. Reprinted with permission.

9. Which of the following sentences includes a transition that signals a *minor* supporting detail?

   a. sentence 3
   b. sentence 4
   c. sentence 5
   d. sentence 6

10. Which of the following sentences is a *minor* supporting detail?

    a. sentence 2
    b. sentence 3
    c. sentence 4
    d. sentence 6

(1) Scientists are scouring the seas in search of medicines that may work better than conventional drugs, with fewer side effects. (2) The ocean has already given us osteoporosis[1] drugs derived from salmon, omega-3 fish oils for arthritis and heart disease, and bone replacements from coral. (3) Another marine medicine in the works is a promising new cancer drug derived from bacteria that live inside a mosslike sea creature called *Bugula neritina*. (4) Unlike conventional drugs that kill cancer cells, bryostatin-1 makes them revert[2] to normal cells. (5) Researchers at the North Carolina Sea Grant are also developing a peptide antibiotic from mast cells in hybrid striped bass. (6) Different from current antibiotics, these antibiotics from mast cells in fish and other animals may even be effective against antibiotic-resistant strains of bacteria. (7) Finally, two medicines under development by a pharmaceutical company show early promise against cancer, including some breast cancers resistant to other drugs. (8) If they win Food and Drug Administration approval, the drugs could be available within five years.*

11. The topic of this paragraph is

    a. medicines.
    b. medicines derived from sea creatures.
    c. fish.
    d. cancer drugs.

12. How many *major* supporting details are contained in this paragraph?

    a. 3
    b. 4
    c. 5
    d. none

1. **osteoporosis:** disease characterized by deterioration of the bones
2. **revert:** go back

* Adapted from Michele Hatty and Peggy Noonan, "Fishing the Undersea Pharmacy," *USA Weekend*, January 25–27, 2002, 16. Reprinted with permission from *USA Weekend*.

13. Which of the following sentences is a *major* supporting detail in the paragraph?
    a. sentence 1
    b. sentence 2
    c. sentence 6
    d. sentence 8

14. Which of the following is a *minor* supporting detail in the paragraph?
    a. sentence 2
    b. sentence 3
    c. sentence 5
    d. sentence 6

15. Which of the following sentences starts with a transition that indicates a *major* supporting detail?
    a. sentence 4
    b. sentence 5
    c. sentence 6
    d. sentence 7

CHAPTER 4

Implied Main Ideas

GOALS FOR CHAPTER 4

- **Define the term *implied main idea.***
- **Form generalizations based on specific details.**
- **State the implied main idea of a paragraph.**
- **Apply the steps of the SQ3R Strategy to reading selections.**
- **Read and understand information in a flow chart.**

4

When you read Chapter 2 of this book, you learned that many paragraphs include a topic sentence that clearly states the main idea. Other paragraphs, however, do not contain a topic sentence. Does that mean they don't have a main point? No, it means that readers must do a little more work to figure out what that point—which is called an *implied main idea*—is. To see how much you already know about drawing conclusions about a main idea, take the following pre-test.

TEST YOURSELF

The following paragraphs do not include a stated main idea. Read each paragraph and see if you can determine its main point. Circle the letter of the sentence that best states the main idea.

1. In Rio Rancho, New Mexico, a district just outside Albuquerque, under a policy adopted in 2003, parents who want to mentor in the schools must produce character references and go through a criminal background check, fingerprinting, and training. In Charlotte, North Carolina, parents or other volunteers who accompany field trips, tutor, or serve as reading buddies or assistant athletic coaches, and may be alone with a

child, must go through personal interviews, training sessions, and criminal background checks. They must also provide three personal references. Those who mentor children or chaperone overnight trips must be fingerprinted, and those who drive children around must have their driving histories, insurance, and licenses checked. Boys and Girls Clubs, scout groups, the Catholic Church, and even some Red Cross chapters now run criminal background checks on at least some volunteers. In recent months, for example, the Roman Catholic Diocese of Paterson in New Jersey has begun fingerprinting all volunteers who have contact with children.*

a. There are a large percentage of volunteers with criminal records.
b. Many organizations are requiring background checks of volunteers who will be working with children.
c. Everyone who works with children should be fingerprinted.
d. The Catholic Church now runs criminal background checks on potential volunteers.

2. In an early laboratory study, researchers observed that Arabs sat closer together than Americans did, and that Arabs and Middle Easterners touched more than Americans, Britons, and Australians. Another early study found that Latin American individuals adopted closer distances in their conversations than did Americans. In two field studies, communication researcher Robert Shuter photographed couples in Italy, Germany, the United States, Costa Rica, Panama, and Colombia. Among his findings were the observations that Italians and Germans stood closer to each other than Americans did, Italian men touched more than German or American men did, and Costa Ricans used closer distances and more touch than Panamanians or Colombians did. In a study of cultural differences in Europe, my colleagues and I found that southern Europeans were more inclined to use touch than northern Europeans. Brief observations of nearly 1,000 couples at numerous train stations in 15 countries revealed differences in the percentages of couples in which one person touched the other. For example, among countries with at least 50 observed couples, the highest incidence of touch occurred for those in Greece (32 percent), Spain (30 percent), Italy (24 percent), and Hungary (23 percent). The lowest was found in the Netherlands (4 percent), Austria (9 percent), England (11 percent), Belgium (12 percent), and Germany (16 percent).†

* Adapted from Tamar Lewin, "Want to Volunteer in Schools? Be Ready for a Security Check," *New York Times*, March 11, 2004, www.nytimes.com.

† Excerpted from Remland, *Nonverbal Communication in Everyday Life*. Boston: Houghton Mifflin, 2000, 160–161.

a. Europeans touch more than Americans do.
b. American couples exhibit more loving behaviors than Europeans or Latin Americans do.
c. Cultures differ in the distance of their communication style.
d. Many studies report differences between men and women in their preferred communication styles.

3. The intelligent doctor listens carefully to patients' complaints before diagnosing the cause of their illnesses. Investment counselors listen to clients' accounts of how they currently manage their financial portfolios before suggesting any changes. The *good* car salesperson listens to customers' comments on what they are looking for in a vehicle before showing them around the lot. Assembly-line workers and construction workers have to listen to and master safety regulations if the company or crew is to remain accident free. The wise manager listens to subordinates'[1] concerns and ideas before moving forward with some bold, potentially costly venture.*
   a. It is very important to be a good listener no matter what you do for a living.
   b. Many managers of white-collar workers are good listeners.
   c. Many managers of blue-collar workers have poor listening skills.
   d. Subordinates use a variety of techniques to get their managers to listen to them.

4. Informational ads rely primarily on a recitation[2] of facts about a product to convince target consumers that it is for them. An example is an advertisement in *Stereo Review* that carefully details the specifications[3] of speakers. Hard-sell ads are messages that combine information about the product with intense attempts to get the consumer to purchase it as soon as possible. One example would be a TV commercial in which a car salesman speaks a mile a minute about the glories of his dealership, shouts about a two-day-only sale this weekend, and recites the address of the dealership four times before the spot ends. Soft-sell ads aim mostly to create good feelings about the product or service by associating it with music, people, or events that creators feel would appeal to the target audience. An example of this would be TV commercials for a wide variety of products, including soft drinks, beer, and athletic

1. **subordinates:** people of lower rank or status
2. **recitation:** act of delivering information orally
3. **specifications:** details, particulars

* From Andrews et al., *Public Speaking*. Boston: Houghton Mifflin, 1999, 20.

footwear. Think of a jingle, or catchy tune, and it probably comes from a soft-sell ad.*

a. Car salesmen use informational ads to get sales.
b. There are many types of TV commercials.
c. Many different types of advertisements help sell products.
d. Print advertisements can be very helpful in selling a product.

5. Whether you're frying an onion or baking a batch of cookies, try using olive or canola oil instead of butter. The types of fat in these oils can improve the levels of cholesterol and other lipids in your blood and combat the narrowing of arteries that often occurs with age. Also, instead of relying on red meat for protein, try fish, poultry, or legumes. And when you're feeling like you need to eat meat, select lean meats such as pork tenderloin or extra-lean ground beef. They pack less artery-clogging saturated fat than pork loin or low-grade hamburger. To cut out some white flour from your diet, switch from flour tortillas to whole-grain (corn or wheat) tortillas, and snack on whole-grain crackers.†

a. It is easy to fry an onion.
b. You can make healthy changes in your diet in several different ways.
c. You should use canola oil in cooking.
d. There are different types of fat in oil.

Understanding Implied Main Ideas

Every paragraph contains a main idea. Sometimes, that main idea is stated outright in a topic sentence. Sometimes, though, the main idea is implied. An **implied main idea** is one that is suggested but not said. To determine the implied main idea, you examine the details presented and draw from them a conclusion about the overall point.

If you think about it, you figure out implied main ideas quite often in your daily life. For example, look at the following conversation:

Wife: What is your new boss like?

Husband: Well, she welcomed me and personally introduced me to each of her staff members. She listened carefully to the ideas everyone

* Adapted from Turow, *Media Today*. Boston: Houghton Mifflin, 1999, 34.

† Adapted from Harvard Medical School, "Eating Healthfully, and Enjoying Every Bite," *Newsweek Special Issue*, September 2001, 46.

shared during a staff meeting. She complimented several people for their work on a particular project, and she thanked everyone for their effort.

The husband answered his wife's question with a series of specific details. What conclusion can you draw from them? Every one of the boss's actions indicates that she is pleased with her employees, so it's safe to conclude that she values her staff and their work.

Here's another example: You're in the mall parking lot. You see a Rolls Royce pull up and stop. Out of the car steps a woman wearing a fur coat and diamonds. What conclusion do you make? Most people would say the woman is probably very wealthy.

You notice details, add them together, and draw conclusions all the time. In Chapter 3 of this book, you practiced recognizing supporting details, the information that proves or explains a main idea. A paragraph with an implied main idea contains *only* supporting details. These details are the clues that you put together to figure out the author's point.

To improve your ability to draw these conclusions while you read, it's helpful to remember what you learned about the terms *general* and *specific* back in Chapter 2. Figuring out an implied main idea requires you to form a generalization based on a series of specific items or ideas. Look at the following group of words:

Band-Aid	Ace Bandage
antibacterial ointment	gauze

What generalization can you make about this list of items? They're all things you use to treat injuries, so the general term that describes them is *items found in a first-aid kit.*

Now, examine another list:

cracker	waffle
slice of bread	washrag

This group is a little trickier. When you read the first three items, you may have thought they were *things to eat.* But, the last item isn't in that category. When you add up all the details and look for the similarities, you realize that these are all *things that are square.*

As you will remember from Chapter 2, a group of specific sentences can also support a general idea. For example, read the sentences below:

Paul runs five miles on Mondays, Wednesdays, and Fridays.

Paul lifts weights on Tuesdays and Thursdays.

Paul either swims laps or rides his bicycle on Saturdays.

4

What general statement would include all three of those specific sentences? One possibility is *Paul exercises regularly*.

Exercise 4.1

On the blank following each group of sentences, write a general sentence that includes all of the specific details given.

1. Pumpkins are used for pie making.

   In Japan, pumpkins are used in tempura[1] dishes.

   My mother makes a delicious pumpkin soup.

   General sentence: ______________________________

2. Soy milk is low in sodium (salt).

   Soy milk is cholesterol free.

   Soy milk doesn't have lactose (milk sugar), which many people of Asian, Native American, and African descent can't easily digest.*

   General sentence: ______________________________

3. Quincy Jones, the famous composer, arranger, and score writer, collaborated with Michael Jackson on his 1982 album *Thriller*, which had record-breaking sales of more than 40 million worldwide.

   Quincy Jones brought celebrities together to record "We Are the World," a 1985 effort that raised money for hunger relief in Africa.

   Quincy Jones has worked with Frank Sinatra, Sara Vaughan, Lionel Hampton, Count Basie, Ray Charles, and Aretha Franklin over the years.†

   General sentence: ______________________________

4. Infant massage stimulates the nerves, increases blood flow, and strengthens the immune system.

   Infant massage can relieve a host of childhood complaints from colic[2] to constipation.[3]

1. **tempura:** food dipped in batter and deep-fried
2. **colic:** Severe abdominal pain
3. **constipation:** difficult or infrequent purging of the bowels

* From Jane Kirby, "Don't Have a Cow," *Real Simple*, October 2001, 52.

† From Oprah Winfrey, "Oprah Talks to Quincy Jones," *O* Magazine, October 2001, 106.

Massaging an infant's chest can ease congestion.*

General sentence: ____

5. A studio apartment in New York City is usually $1,500 a month.

   Many young people who rent a New York apartment are forced to have three and four roommates.

   One single mom reports sharing a bedroom and a bed with her two daughters to save money.

   General sentence: ____

You may not have realized it, but you often form general ideas based on specific details when you read cartoons and comic strips. For instance, look at the following comic strip:

Baby Blues cartoon © Baby Blues Partnership. Reprinted with special permission of King Features Syndicate.

This comic strip never states a main idea. However, you can add up all of the details to conclude that the children do not understand exactly why they are at school.

Exercise 4.2

On the blank beneath each of the following cartoons, write the idea the artist hoped to imply.

* From Sheila Koty Globus, "Touch Me, I'm Yours," *Westchester Family*, September 2001, 42.

4

Family Circus cartoon © Bill Keane, Inc. Reprinted with special permission of King Features Syndicate.

1. Main idea: ____

Cathy © 1995 Cathy Guisewite. Reprinted with permission of Universal Press Syndicate. All Rights Reserved.

2. Main idea: ____

____

Garfield © 2000 Paws, Inc. Reprinted with permission of Universal Press Syndicate. All Rights Reserved.

3. Main idea: ____

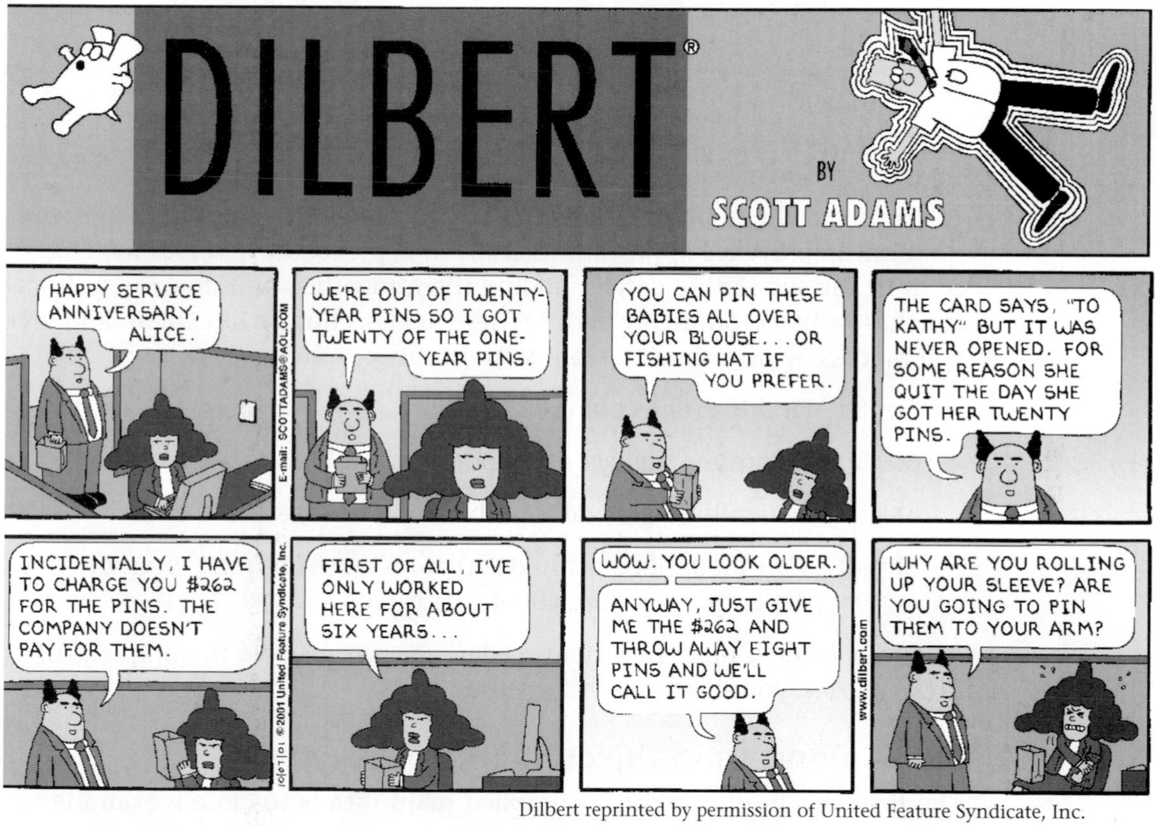

Dilbert reprinted by permission of United Feature Syndicate, Inc.

4. Main idea: ____

____

5. Main idea: ______________________________

4

Determining Implied Main Ideas

To figure out the implied main idea in a paragraph, you can often use a methodical, step-by-step approach. Basically, this procedure involves looking for clues in the supporting details, adding them together, and drawing a logical conclusion based on the evidence. These next sections will explain and give you practice with each of the four steps in this process:

Step 1: Find the subject of each sentence.

Step 2: Determine the *type* of supporting detail in the paragraph.

Step 3: Determine a general topic based on the specific details.

Step 4: State an implied main idea that includes both the topic and what the author is saying about that topic.

As you become a more proficient reader, you will be able to complete all of these steps in your head most of the time.

Step 1: Find the Subject of Each Sentence

The first step in discovering an implied main idea is to closely examine the supporting details. The major and minor details in a paragraph will provide you with the clues you need to draw a conclusion about the author's point. For example, read the following paragraph:

(1) When the United States celebrated 2000 as the start of a new millennium, the Buddhist calendar marked that year as 2543. (2) According to the Muslim calendar, which began in the Christian A.D. 610 and counts only 354 days in

one year, the year was 1420. (3) China's calendar began in the corresponding Christian year of 2637 B.C., so in 2000, the Chinese year was 4697. (4) Year One of the Hebrew calendar was 3761 B.C., and Hebrew years include only 354 days, so those of Jewish faith marked the year 2000 as the year 5760. (5) The Hindu calendar noted the same year as 1921.*

Here are the subjects in each of the sentences:

Sentence 1: the Buddhist year

Sentence 2: the Muslim year

Sentence 3: the Chinese year

Sentence 4: the Hebrew year

Sentence 5: the Hindu year

Exercise 4.3

On the blanks following each paragraph, write the subject of each sentence.

1. (1) Computer-based fingerprint identification systems can track criminals across multiple jurisdictions.[1] (2) Computer mapping of crime "hot spots" and trends, pioneered by New York City's COMPSTAT, facilitates police planning and response by linking crime statistics to Geographic Information Systems. (3) Video cameras and acoustic[2] sensors can detect crime activity and even identify a weapon type by the sound of the discharge. (4) And DNA tests can positively match criminals to crimes committed.†

   Sentence 1 subject: ______________________________

   Sentence 2 subject: ______________________________

   Sentence 3 subject: ______________________________

   Sentence 4 subject: ______________________________

2. (1) Classical, or traditional, yoga—in which physical postures are used—is the type of yoga with which people are most familiar. (2) Gentle yoga is a less physical type of yoga and is often used as a warm-up to more rigorous

1. **jurisdictions:** law enforcement territories

2. **acoustic:** related to sound or the sense of hearing

* Adapted from David Ewing Duncan, "The Year 2000 Is . . . ," *Life Year in Pictures*, 16–20.

† Excerpted from Bowman and Kearney, *State and Local Government*, 5th ed. Boston: Houghton Mifflin, 2002, 453.

types of yoga. (3) Restorative yoga incorporates physical postures like classical yoga, but its postures are more restful and rejuvenating.[1] (4) Meditative yoga emphasizes a gentle approach in which the yoga practitioner focuses on going within and focusing. (5) Ashtanga yoga is often known as "power" yoga because it emphasizes strength and agility.

Sentence 1 subject: ______________________________

Sentence 2 subject: ______________________________

Sentence 3 subject: ______________________________

Sentence 4 subject: ______________________________

Sentence 5 subject: ______________________________

4

3. (1) Former Pittsburgh Steelers quarterback Terry Bradshaw has attention deficit hyperactivity disorder (ADHD). (2) Accomplished actress Mariette Hartley says that both she and her daughter have ADHD. (3) Successful political guru[2] James Carville says that, according to his mother, when he was a child he could never sit still. (4) Celebrated painter Salvador Dali's impulsiveness may have arisen from ADHD. (5) Albert Einstein was four years old before he could speak, which has been attributed by some to inattentiveness. (6) And inventor Thomas Edison was described as "addled"[3] by his teachers.*

Sentence 1 subject: ______________________________

Sentence 2 subject: ______________________________

Sentence 3 subject: ______________________________

Sentence 4 subject: ______________________________

Sentence 5 subject: ______________________________

Sentence 6 subject: ______________________________

4. (1) *The Fantastiks* was the longest running off-Broadway show in New York before it closed in 2001. (2) *Cats* was the longest running Broadway show and enjoyed a run of many years before it closed. (3) *A Chorus Line*, which enjoyed record-breaking ticket sales in the 1970s and 1980s, also ran for a

1. **rejuvenating:** stimulating, invigorating
2. **guru:** a recognized leader in a field
3. **addled:** confused

* Adapted from Marianne Szegedy-Maszak, "Dazed, Famous," *U.S. News and World Report*, April 26, 2004, 56.

very long time, and was released as a movie in the 1980s. (4) The Broadway production of *Beauty and the Beast* is so beloved by children that it will probably stay a stage production for many years to come.

Sentence 1 subject: ______________________________

Sentence 2 subject: ______________________________

Sentence 3 subject: ______________________________

Sentence 4 subject: ______________________________

5. (1) According to studies, people who are more forgiving report experiencing less stress and less hostility, which is a risk factor for heart disease. (2) People who imagine forgiving their offenders note immediate improvement in their cardiovascular, muscular and nervous systems. (3) Even people who have experienced devastating losses report feeling better psychologically and emotionally when they forgive. (4) On the other hand, people who fail to forgive have higher incidences of illnesses such as cardiovascular disease and cancers. (5) People who imagine not forgiving someone who has wronged them show negative changes in blood pressure, muscle tension, and immune response.*

Sentence 1 subject: ______________________________

Sentence 2 subject: ______________________________

Sentence 3 subject: ______________________________

Sentence 4 subject: ______________________________

Sentence 5 subject: ______________________________

Step 2: Determine the *Type* of Supporting Detail in the Paragraph

Once you've determined what each sentence is about, you should be able to conclude what type of supporting details they are. Common types of supporting details include the following:

reasons	causes
examples	effects
events	types
steps	parts
points of comparison	descriptive details or features

* Adapted from Fred Luskin, *Forgive for Good*. San Francisco: Harper, 2002.

For an illustration, read the next paragraph:

(1) Dr. Richard Ferber, author of *Solve Your Child's Sleep Problems,* advises parents to let their babies sleep alone in their cribs. (2) In contrast, Dr. William Sears, author of *Nighttime Parenting: How to Get Your Baby and Child to Sleep,* believes most babies belong in their parents' beds until they're at least six months old. (3) Dr. Ferber advocates the "cry-it-out" method of getting babies to go to sleep so the babies will learn to fall asleep by themselves. (4) Dr. Sears, though, advocates the "attachment parenting" approach in which parents hold and cuddle their babies in the "family bed" until the children fall asleep. (5) Dr. Ferber believes that parents should respond to a crying infant by going into the room every few minutes to pat the baby's back for reassurance, but not by picking the baby up. (6) But Dr. Sears says crying babies should be picked up, rocked, nursed, and comforted until they doze off.*

To determine the type of details in this paragraph, first find the subject of each sentence:

Sentence 1: Ferber's opinion about where babies should sleep

Sentence 2: Sears's opinion about where babies should sleep

Sentence 3: Ferber's "cry-it-out" method

Sentence 4: Sears's "attachment parenting" approach

Sentence 5: Ferber's response to crying infant

Sentence 6: Sears's response to crying infant

What type of details are these? If you answered *points of comparison*, you're right. Understanding the kind of details included in the paragraph will help you formulate a more accurate statement of the main idea when you get to step 4.

Be aware that there may be more than one type of supporting detail in a paragraph. A paragraph may, for example, combine examples and reasons or causes and types. Authors can use different types of details together to develop their ideas.

Exercise 4.4

In the list below each paragraph, place a checkmark next to the correct type of supporting details in that paragraph.

* Adapted from Amy Dickinson, "Eyes Wide Shut," *Time*, November 13, 2000, 116.

1. The 1968 Olympics in Mexico City included a "Black power"[1] salute from U.S. medal winners during the playing of "The Star-Spangled Banner," which reminded the audience about racial strife[2] in the United States. The 1972 Olympic games in Munich were scarred by Palestinians' abduction of Israelis in the Olympic Village, which resulted in the death of eleven hostages, five gunmen, and one policeman. In 1980, the Moscow Olympics offered the United States an opportunity to protest the Soviet Union's invasion of Afghanistan the year before; American athletes did not participate in that year's games. The 1984 Olympic games in Los Angeles gave the Soviet Union a chance to retaliate for America's snub[3] by boycotting the event. The opening ceremonies of the 2000 Olympics in Sydney included a historic moment: North and South Korean teams entered the stadium under one flag to symbolize their talks to reunify after fifty years of hostility.*

____ reasons
____ causes and effects
____ steps
____ points of comparison
____ events
____ examples

2. Do you want to know how to use the extra hour you gain when you switch to daylight savings time? One, count your smoke alarms. There should be at least one smoke alarm on every level of the home, one in each bedroom and one outside of each sleeping area. Two, check your smoke alarms after changing the battery. Push the safety test to make sure the alarm is still working. Third, clean your smoke alarms; excessive dust can render them ineffective.†

____ reasons
____ causes and effects
____ steps
____ points of comparison
____ events
____ examples

3. Toddlers who had secure attachment to their mothers in early infancy tend to cooperate better with their parents than other babies do, so they comply better with rules such as "Don't run in the living room!" Less securely

1. **Black power:** a movement among Black Americans emphasizing racial pride and social equality

2. **strife:** conflict

3. **snub:** deliberately treating someone coldly

* Adapted from "Sports Take on Bigger Meaning on World's Biggest Stage," *USA Today*, July 9, 2001, 2A.

† Adapted from Cathy Elcik, "Protecting Your Family from Fire," *Westchester Family*, October 2001, 11.

4

attached infants often respond with anger and resistance to their parents' attempts to discipline them and invest a lot more time and energy in conflicts. Securely attached toddlers are more willing to learn and try new activities their parents show them (such as when a parent says, "Sit with me for a minute and see how I do this"). In addition, when faced with problems that are too difficult for them to solve, toddlers who are securely attached are more likely than others to seek and accept help from their parents. Less securely attached infants, though, may not learn as well from their parents. Such babies are unable to benefit from their parents' experience or explore their environment.*

_____ reasons _____ points of comparison

_____ causes and effects _____ events

_____ steps _____ examples

4

4. Why would anyone want a site on the Web—or on America Online for that matter? When it comes to individuals, some people may simply do it because they can. Others may want to share hobbies or photos or ideas about the world with anyone who will be interested. Companies tend to have four reasons for creating Web sites: image making, selling products, supporting the sale of products, and selling advertising for someone else's products. A site can fit some or all of these aims.†

_____ reasons _____ points of comparison

_____ causes and effects _____ events

_____ steps _____ examples

5. What made our cities safer in the 1990s? First, an expanding economy provided some additional opportunities in the inner cities. Second, more police on the beat[1] served as a deterrent[2] to crime. Third, the enactment of tough "three strikes and you're out" legislation removed many offenders from the streets and swelled prison populations. And finally, aggressive campaigns such as those waged by New York City mayor Rudolph Giuliani to rid the Times Square area of prostitutes and porn shops led many more urban residents to come out at night.‡

1. **beat:** area regularly covered by police officers

2. **deterrent:** something that prevents or discourages someone from acting

* Adapted from Seifert et al., *Lifespan Development*, 2nd ed. Boston: Houghton Mifflin, 2000, 166–167. Copyright © 2000 by Houghton Mifflin Company. Reprinted with permission.

† Adapted from Turow, *Media Today*. Boston: Houghton Mifflin, 1999, 306.

‡ Adapted from Berkin et al., *Making America,* 2nd ed. Boston: Houghton Mifflin, 2001, 718.

____ reasons
____ causes and effects
____ steps
____ points of comparison
____ events
____ examples

Step 3: Determine a General Topic Based on the Specific Details

Once you've discovered the supporting details' subjects and type, you can make a generalization about them. You must make this generalization before you can complete the final step. In using logic to perceive an overall category for the details, you are figuring out the overall topic of the paragraph. You'll need to be able to include this topic in your statement of the main idea.

Let's look at the paragraphs in the explanations of Steps 1 and 2 as illustrations. In the paragraph on pages 176–177, the subjects of each sentence were all *examples* of years according to various cultures' calendars. This is the general category that includes those specific details. Now look back at the paragraph about Drs. Ferber and Sears on page 180. In that paragraph, the sentences all contained *points of comparison*. What generalization can you make about those details? You might say they're all *differences between Ferber's and Sears's methods*. That is the paragraph's overall topic.

Exercise 4.5

Read each of the following paragraphs and fill in the blanks after each one. The types of supporting details are reasons, examples, events, steps, points of comparison, causes, effects, types, parts, and descriptive details or features.

1. (1) The name *Arkansas* comes from the Sioux word *quapaw,* which means "downstream people." (2) The word *Illinois* comes from the Algonquin word *illini,* "warrior men." (3) *Kentucky* comes from the Iroquois word *ken-ta-ke,* which means "meadow" or "plains." (4) The name *Michigan* comes from the Chippewa *mica gama,* meaning "grand waters." (5) *Oklahoma* is named after the Choctaw term for "red people," *okla humma.**

   Sentence 1 subject: ________________

   Sentence 2 subject: ________________

   Sentence 3 subject: ________________

* Adapted from "The Origins of State Names," latin.about.com/library/friendly/nblstatenames.htm.

Sentence 4 subject: ______________________________

Sentence 5 subject: ______________________________

Type of supporting details: ______________________________

General topic of paragraph: ______________________________

2. (1) In today's busy world, do you have an understudy if something unexpected comes up? (2) First, organize a handful of friends, neighbors, or relatives and deputize[1] one another; you look out for them, and they look out for you. (3) Second, pass out blank copies of the plan—a list with important names, numbers, and other contacts—to the people who've agreed to participate. (4) Third, share whatever medical information you feel comfortable sharing with the people you trust most. (5) The information you provide can help you feel more comfortable whether you are home or away from home.*

Sentence 2 subject: ______________________________

Sentence 3 subject: ______________________________

Sentence 4 subject: ______________________________

Type of supporting details: ______________________________

General topic of paragraph: ______________________________

3. (1) Judge Larry Standley of Harris County, Texas, required a man who slapped his wife to sign up for a yoga class as part of his punishment. (2) Municipal Judge Frances Gallegos in Santa Fe often sentences people convicted of domestic violence or fighting to a twice-a-week, New Age[2] anger-management class, where offenders experience tai chi,[3] meditation, acupuncture, and Eastern philosophy as means of controlling rage. (3) Municipal Judge David Hostetler of Coshocton, Ohio, ordered a man who had run away from police after a traffic accident to jog for an hour every other day around the block where the jail is located. (4) Hostetler also received worldwide attention in 2001 when he ordered two men to dress in women's clothing and walk down Main Street as a sentence for throwing beer bottles at a car and taunting a woman. (5) Judge Mike Erwin of Baton

1. **deputize:** appoint a person to act for someone
2. **New Age:** relating to spiritual and consciousness-raising movements of the 1980s
3. **tai chi:** a Chinese system of physical exercises for self-defense and meditation

* Adapted from "Just in Case," no author credited, *Real Simple*, October 2001, 88.

Rouge ordered a young man who hit an elderly man in an argument to listen to a John Prine song, "Hello in There," about lonely senior citizens and write an essay about it.*

Sentence 1 subject: ______________________________

Sentence 2 subject: ______________________________

Sentence 3 subject: ______________________________

Sentence 4 subject: ______________________________

Sentence 5 subject: ______________________________

Type of supporting details: ______________________________

General topic of paragraph: ______________________________

4. (1) The essence of the Atkins' low-carbohydrate diet system is to provide a series of dietary phases through which dieters will pass sequentially[1] as they successfully lose their excess weight. (2) Protein Power, a diet developed by Drs. Michael and Mary Eades, differs from Atkins and from many other low-carb diets because it is a very science-oriented approach to the low-carb and higher protein diet. (3) Unlike Atkins or Protein Power, however, the Zone diet—practiced by many Hollywood celebrities—has dieters concentrate on a very specific ration of carbs and protein in everyday eating. (4) The South Beach diet is entirely different from all other low-carb diets because it does not require dieters to count calories, fat, or carbs; dieters follow different "phases" of the diet to help them lose weight.

Sentence 1 subject: ______________________________

Sentence 2 subject: ______________________________

Sentence 3 subject: ______________________________

Sentence 4 subject: ______________________________

Type of supporting details: ______________________________

General topic of paragraph: ______________________________

5. (1) Do you miss the clothing of your youth? (2) Original Penguin, the geeky[2]-chic brand, brought back their piped trench coats and pastel polos

1. **sequentially:** in sequence, with one step following another

2. **geeky:** odd or ridiculous

* Adapted from Donna Leinwand, "Judges Write Creative Sentences," *USA Today*, February 24, 2004, 3A.

recently and opened a store last winter in New York City. (3) The women's collection, now in its second season, features shrunken tees and even bikinis. (4) Camp Beverly Hills, makers of 80s T-shirts and shorts, just thrilled twenty- and thirtysomethings by hauling out new versions of their kitschy[1] wares this spring. (5) Now, Le Tigre, the feline version of Lacoste, which closed its doors in 1992, is offering its preppy[2] duds again. (6) The spring collection—available at Bloomingdale's in New York City—features polo dresses, tanks, wristbands, and belts.*

Sentence 2 subject: ____________________

Sentence 3 subject: ____________________

Sentence 4 subject: ____________________

Sentence 5 subject: ____________________

Sentence 6 subject: ____________________

Type of supporting details: ____________________

General topic of paragraph: ____________________

____

As you complete this step, remember what you learned in Chapter 2 about topics that are too broad or too narrow. Make sure the topic you choose is neither.

Exercise 4.6

After each paragraph, label each topic N if it's too narrow, B if it's too broad, and T if it's the correct topic.

1. Presidential candidates, mindful of Florida's twenty-five electoral votes, regularly make pilgrimages[3] to South Florida to denounce Cuba's communist[4]

1. **kitschy:** in bad taste
2. **preppy:** like the dress and mannerisms of students who attend preparatory schools; the preppy style was popular in the 1980s
3. **pilgrimages:** long journeys
4. **communist:** related to an economic system in which the government (rather tham individuals) controls all goods and property and is supposed to distribute them equally to all citizens

* Adapted from "Retro Revival," *New York Daily News*, June 3, 2004, 57.

policies, a popular position among Cuban American voters there. In Texas, local groups called Communities Organized for Public Service (COPS) bring politicians to Hispanic neighborhoods so that poor citizens can meet their representatives and voice their concerns. They also organize voter registration drives that boost Hispanic participation. Similarly, the Southwest Voter Registration Project (SWVRP) has led more than a thousand voter registration drives in such states as California, Texas, and New Mexico. Groups like Latino Vote USA have targeted Hispanics in recent elections, to encourage them to register to vote and to turn out on election day. Such movements have increased Hispanic voter registration by more than 50 percent.*

______ a. Hispanics

______ b. Hispanics and voting

______ c. Hispanics in South Florida

2. Is it better for the child's development if parents are strict in their demands and discipline, or will the child have better psychological adjustment if parents are more permissive and less authoritarian[1] in their behavior? It is known that the effects of both permissiveness and strictness are negative if the family environment tends to be cold and hostile. A hostile and permissive environment is likely to produce an aggressive and delinquent[2] child, while a hostile-suppressive or restrictive family environment fosters children who are anxious and inhibited. However, several early studies revealed that children raised in warm and reasonably permissive, democratic families that allowed the child freedom of choice tended to be friendly, assertive and creative, whereas children raised in warm but strict and controlling homes tended to be conforming, low in curiosity, and well behaved.†

______ a. discipline

______ b. effects of parental demands and discipline

______ c. parents who are strict disciplinarians

1. **authoritarian:** favoring absolute obedience and restriction of personal freedom

2. **delinquent:** failing to do what law or duty requires

* Adapted from Barbour and Wright, *Keeping the Republic: Power and Citizenship in American Politics*. Boston: Houghton Mifflin, 2001, 136. Copyright © 2001 by Houghton Mifflin Company. Used with permission.

† Adapted from Feshbach et al., *Personality*, 4th ed. Boston: Houghton Mifflin, 1996, 352. Copyright © 1996 by Houghton Mifflin Company. Reprinted with permission.

3. The primary benefit of exercise is to the cardiovascular system. Regular aerobic exercise counteracts the age-related decreases in cardiovascular[1] functioning. People who exercise maintain higher levels of cardiac functioning and blood flow than those who do not. The heart can more efficiently supply blood to the other tissues of the body, and the respiratory, muscular, and nervous systems all benefit as well. The benefits do not stop there, however; exercise improves endurance, helps to optimize[2] body weight, builds or maintains muscle tone and strength, and increases flexibility. It reduces or controls hypertension (abnormally high blood pressure) and improves cholesterol levels. Exercise also seems to improve mood and self-esteem and reduce stress. People who exercise tend to engage in fewer health-compromising behaviors, including smoking, alcohol consumption, and poor diet. Weight gain is one of the key age-related changes that people try to counteract with exercise.*

   ______ a. benefits of exercise

   ______ b. exercise

   ______ c. cardiovascular benefits of exercise

4. "You can go to the moon and be there for only a few days, do three space walks and come home. When we go to Mars, best case right now, you would be in transit for six months," says Ed Hodgson, preliminary design engineer at Hamilton Sundstrand Space Systems International. Once the spacecraft reached the planet, it could stay for only a few days. To minimize the time and fuel spent, a mission to Mars would have to occur during a time when the solar orbits of Mars and Earth brought them close together. But as the planets continued on their paths, they would move increasingly farther apart, making a return trip more difficult and time-consuming. Alternatively, a crew might stay on Mars for two years and return when the planets again neared one another. Such a long mission, though, would require an extremely efficient use of the resources available on board. Recycling would be essential in all aspects of the mission, but regenerating systems tend to weigh more as well.†

1. **cardiovascular:** relating to the heart and blood vessels
2. **optimize:** to make perfect or most effective

* Adapted from Seifert et al., *Lifespan Development*, 2nd ed. Boston: Houghton Mifflin, 2000, 424–425. Copyright © 2000 by Houghton Mifflin Company. Reprinted with permission.

† From "The Astronaut's New Clothes," by Harald Franzen on the *Scientific American* website at http://www.sciam.com/article.cfm?articleID=00050040-A707-1C75-9B81809EC588EF21&SC=I100322. All rights reserved.

______ a. recycling on missions to Mars

______ b. space travel

______ c. Mars's travel challenges

5. An excellent example of a proactive[1] stance to social responsibility is the Ronald McDonald House program undertaken by McDonald's Corp. These houses, located close to major medical centers, can be used by families for minimal cost while their sick children are receiving medical treatment nearby. Sears offers fellowships that support promising young performers while they develop their talents. Target has stopped selling guns in its stores. Some national toy retailers, such as KayBee and Toys "R" Us, have voluntarily stopped selling realistic toy guns.*

______ a. Ronald McDonald House

______ b. American corporations

______ c. corporations that take a proactive stance to social responsibility

4

Step 4: State an Implied Main Idea

If you have successfully completed steps 1 through 3, you have systematically gone through each thinking stage necessary to state the paragraph's main idea. It is in this last step that you put together all of the clues you examined to come up with a statement of the main idea in your own words. This requires you not only to recognize the subjects in the supporting details but also to draw a general conclusion based on *what is being said about each of these subjects.* Then once more, you decide on a general category of ideas or things that include all of those statements.

Remember what you learned about main ideas and topic sentences in Chapter 2. The main idea has two parts: the topic and the point the author wants to make about that topic. The implied main idea is no different. It, too, should include both of those parts. Your statement will begin with the general topic you discovered in step 3 of this process. Then, it will go on to express the conclusion you drew from adding together the specific supporting details.

1. **proactive:** acting in advance to deal with an expected problem

* Adapted from Griffin, *Management,* 7th ed. Boston: Houghton Mifflin, 2002, 118.

For example, look again at the paragraph about years on pages 176–177. What is being said about each culture's year? Each sentence points out another culture's equivalent to the year 2000:

2543 (Buddhist) 5760 (Hebrew)
1420 (Muslim) 1921 (Hindu)
4697 (Chinese)

What generalization can you make about the items in this list? Obviously, there is a wide variety of opinion about what year it is.

To form a statement of the main idea, begin with the topic you determined in step 3: years according to various cultures' calendars. Often you will indicate the *type* of details the paragraph contains, which is why you completed step 2. Then, add the generalization above to state the main idea: **The year varies widely according to the calendars of various cultures, which did not celebrate the year 2000 with the United States.** This is the overall point suggested by the paragraph's specific supporting details.

4

Now, let's follow the same procedure with the paragraph about the two methods for getting a baby to sleep on page 180. This list briefly summarizes the points of comparison:

Point of comparison #1: Where baby sleeps (Ferber: crib; Sears: parents' bed)

Point of comparison #2: How infant falls asleep (Ferber: "cry-it-out"; Sears: rock or cuddle baby to sleep)

Point of comparison #3: Response to crying (Ferber: reassure but don't pick baby up; Sears: pick up and comfort baby)

What generalization can you make based on these points of comparison? You could say that Ferber's advice and Sears's advice are completely opposite.

Next, put the generalizations you made about the topic and about the ideas together to form a statement of the main idea. Here is one possibility: **Ferber's and Sears's methods for getting a baby to go to sleep are completely opposite.**

As a final illustration, let's go through all four steps for another paragraph:

(1) Emory University historian Michael Bellesiles, author of the critically acclaimed but controversial book *Arming America: The Origins of a National Gun Culture,* said some of his crucial research notes had been destroyed in a flood in his office. (2) He said he had relied on microfilm records in the federal archive in East Point, Georgia, but it has no such records. (3) He said he had examined probate[1] records in thirty

1. **probate:** related to legal proceedings about wills

places around the country, such as the San Francisco Superior Court, but those records were destroyed in the 1906 earthquake. (4)Well, then, he said he had seen them in the Contra Costa County Historical Society, but the society has no such records, and no record of Bellesiles's visiting the society. (5) Then he said he did the research somewhere else, but is not sure where. (6) Researchers have found that he consistently misrepresents extant[1] records in Providence, Rhode Island, and Vermont. (7) When he tried to buttress[2] his case by posting evidence on his website, critics found grave errors there, too, and he blamed the errors on a hacker[3] breaking into his files.*

Step 1: *Sentence 1:* Bellesiles's explanation of his research notes

Sentence 2: Bellesiles's claim about his research

Sentence 3: Bellesiles's claim about his research

Sentence 4: Bellesiles's claim about his research

Sentence 5: Bellesiles's claim about his research

Sentence 6: Researchers' opinion of Bellesiles's research

Sentence 7: Bellesiles's evidence on his website

Step 2: *Type of details:* Examples

Step 3: *Paragraph's topic:* Bellesiles's research

Step 4: *Sentence 1:* Bellesiles's excuse seems flimsy.

Sentence 2: The records Bellesiles claims he used don't seem to exist.

Sentence 3: The records Bellesiles claims he used don't seem to exist.

Sentence 4: The records Bellesiles claims he used don't seem to exist.

Sentence 5: Bellesiles's explanation seems fishy.

Sentence 6: Researchers criticize Bellesiles's misinterpretation of data.

Sentence 7: Bellesiles's website contains more errors, which he blamed on someone else.

1. **extant:** still in existence
2. **buttress:** support, prop up
3. **hacker:** a computer expert who illegally enters another's electronic system

* Adapted from George F. Will, "Gunning for a Bad Book," *Newsweek,* May 20, 2002, 76. © George F. Will. Originally appeared in *Newsweek*. Reprinted by permission.

Generalization: Bellesiles seems to be lying about his research.

Implied Main Idea: The many excuses and untruths Bellesiles offers about his research indicate that his book is not based on reliable facts.

As you can see, determining implied main ideas is not only a necessary reading skill, it also helps you sharpen your thinking skills. You must analyze and apply logic as you complete each step of this process to draw a final conclusion. This kind of practice will lead to better thinking in general.

Exercise 4.7

Complete the blanks that follow each of the paragraphs below.

1. (1) If there is a sacred number in Christianity, what would it be? (2) How many wise men came to honor Jesus? (3) How many were there in the Holy Family? (4) How many years long was Jesus's public ministry? (5) How many were crucified[1] at Calvary?[2] (6) How many hours was Jesus on the cross? (7) How many persons are there in the Trinity? (8) How many supernatural virtues [Faith, Hope, and Charity] are there?*

   Sentence 2 subject: ____________________

   Sentence 3 subject: ____________________

   Sentence 4 subject: ____________________

   Sentence 5 subject: ____________________

   Sentence 6 subject: ____________________

   Sentence 7 subject: ____________________

   Sentence 8 subject: ____________________

   Type(s) of supporting details: ____________________

   General topic of paragraph: ____________________

   Generalization: ____________________

   Implied main idea: ____________________

1. **crucified:** to put to death by nailing to a cross

2. **Calvary:** a hill outside ancient Jerusalem where Jesus was crucified

* Adapted from Gerald F. Kreyche, "Playing the Numbers Game," *USA Today*, July 1998, 98.

2. (1) For the past few weeks, the Reverend Martha Sterne has noticed that people she has never seen before have come into her church, St. Andrew's Episcopal in Maryville, Tennessee, knelt down, bowed their heads, and prayed. (2) James Mulholland has observed more people attending services at the Irvington Friends Meeting House in Indianapolis where he's the pastor. (3) And Rabbi Chaim Stern says some members who only came occasionally to services at Temple Israel of Greater Miami are now coming more often.*

   Sentence 1 subject: ______________________________

   Sentence 2 subject: ______________________________

   Sentence 3 subject: ______________________________

   Type(s) of supporting details: ______________________________

   General topic of paragraph: ______________________________

   Generalization: ______________________________

   Implied main idea: ______________________________

   ____

3. (1) Why do presidents pick the people they do to fill Supreme Court seats? (2) When Ronald Reagan's polls showed that his support was weak among women, a promise to appoint the first woman to the Supreme Court helped to change his image as a person unconcerned with women's issues. (3) He fulfilled that promise by appointing Sandra Day O'Connor. (4) Similarly, Lyndon Johnson's appointment of Thurgood Marshall was at least in part because he wanted to appoint an African American to the Court. (5) After Marshall retired, President George Bush appointed Clarence Thomas to fill his seat. (6) Although Bush said that he was making the appointment because Thomas was the person best qualified for the job, and not because he was black, few people believed him.†

   Sentences 2–3 subject: ______________________________

   Sentence 4 subject: ______________________________

   Sentences 5–6 subject: ______________________________

   Type(s) of supporting details: ______________________________

4

* Adapted from Nanci Hellmich, "*Prayer's Abiding Power*," *USA Today*, October 2, 2001, 6D.

† Adapted from Barbour and Wright, *Keeping the Republic*. Boston: Houghton Mifflin, 2001, 264.

General topic of paragraph: ____________________

Generalization: ____________________

____

Implied main idea: ____________________

____

4. (1) Psychologist Rebecca Lee surveyed nearly two hundred adults and learned that, while both sexes are likely to work out to gain a feeling of accomplishment, only women are spurred by the desire to feel better about themselves in relation to others. (2) "Women—not men—were motivated by social comparison, the desire to perform as well as or better than peers," Lee says. (3) Enjoyment and outside pressures prompted both genders to exercise, but neither was particularly enthused[1] by material rewards, such as money or prizes. (4) The surprise finding of the study, according to Lee, was that men and women who stick to an exercise program are motivated by payoffs that are internal (such as a sense of achievement) *and* external (improved appearance or opportunities to socialize)—not internal benefits alone, as psychologists previously suspected.*

Sentence 1 subject: ____________________

Sentence 2 subject: ____________________

Sentence 3 subject: ____________________

Sentence 4 subject: ____________________

Type(s) of supporting details: ____________________

General topic of paragraph: ____________________

Generalization: ____________________

Implied main idea: ____________________

____

5. (1) Drinking more than the recommended amount of alcohol can raise a woman's risk for many types of cancer. (2) For example, a recent study of 150,000 women published in Britain's *Journal of Cancer* found that when a woman drinks more than two drinks a day, every extra drink she

1. **enthused:** interested

* From Bonita L. Marks, "Sweat Inspiration," *Allure*, October 2001, 162.

4

consumes daily on a regular basis increases her breast cancer risk by 7 percent. (3) Drinking too much alcohol may also exacerbate[1] depression. (4) Alcohol can also transform prescription or over-the-counter drugs into toxic chemicals. (5) High doses of acetaminophen (Tylenol)—2,000 milligrams a day—mixed with alcohol can cause liver damage, while a regular aspirin regimen mixed with alcohol can trigger stomach bleeding. (6) Alcohol can lead women to gain weight, too. (7) Not only is alcohol highly caloric—a 12-ounce beer packs 144 calories; a seven-ounce daiquiri has about 200—but it can also lead to overeating. (8) Alcohol stimulates the appetite by increasing the production of saliva and gastric acids, and it can also lower inhibitions and a woman's diet resolve.*

Sentences 1–2 subject: ______________________________

Sentence 3 subject: ______________________________

Sentences 4–5 subject: ______________________________

Sentences 6–8 subject: ______________________________

Type(s) of supporting details: ______________________________

General topic of paragraph: ______________________________

Generalization: ______________________________

Implied main idea: ______________________________

Exercise 4.8

Read each paragraph and complete the sentence that follows to correctly state the paragraph's main idea.

1. On September 23, 1952, Richard Nixon, who was Dwight Eisenhower's running mate, went on television to deny accepting gifts from rich donors. The public responded favorably; Eisenhower and Nixon were elected president and vice president. On July 25, 1969, Senator Edward Kennedy gave a 14-minute televised address to deny any "immoral conduct" after driving his car off a bridge and losing his passenger, Mary Jo Kopechne, to drowning. Massachusetts voters reelected him in 1970. On March 4, 1987, President Reagan broadcast a speech from the same office and fully accepted responsibility for secretly giving Iran weapons in

1. **exacerbate:** worsen

* Adapted from Kristyn Kusek, "Toast to Your Health," *Real Simple*, August 2003, 110. © 2003.

4

exchange for the release of hostages. Reagan's job approval rating jumped from 42 percent to 51 percent, and he completed two full terms as president. On January 26, 1992, Bill and Hillary Clinton appeared on the *60 Minutes* television show to deny [his having had] an extramarital affair with nightclub singer Gennifer Flowers. Clinton went on to be elected president and served two terms.*

Politicians in trouble ______________________________

____

2. New York City is renowned[1] for its high-end, celebrity-chef food culture. It also offers a host of budget-priced options for good food and drinks. Many of the best meal deals are found in the ethnic enclaves[2] that dot the city. In addition to good values on down-home classics, New York serves up thrifty[3] East Indian curries, Moroccan couscous, Greek kebabs, West Indian callaloos, Senegalese *thiebu djen* (fish stews), Mexican chimichangas, and many more culinary[4] treats from around the globe.†

   New York City ______________________________

3. New Orleans lies below sea level, in a bowl bordered by levees[5] that fend off Lake Pontchartrain to the north and the Mississippi River to the south and west. The low-lying Mississippi Delta, which buffers the city from the gulf, is also rapidly disappearing. A year from now another twenty-five to thirty square miles of delta marsh—an area the size of Manhattan—will have vanished. An acre disappears every twenty-four minutes. Each loss gives a storm surge a clearer path to wash over the delta and pour into the bowl, trapping one million people inside and another million in surrounding communities. Extensive evacuation would be impossible because the surging water would cut off the few escape routes. Scientists at Louisiana State University, who have modeled hundreds of possible storm tracks on advanced computers, predict that more than 100,000 people could die.‡

   New Orleans ______________________________

1. **renowned:** famous
2. **enclaves:** areas
3. **thrifty:** economical; wisely managing money
4. **culinary:** related to food
5. **levees:** embankments that prevent rivers from overflowing

* Adapted from Richard Benedetto, "Using TV to Get Out of a Jam," *USA Today*, August 27, 2001, 64.

† From Jonell Nash, "A Cheap Bite of the Apple," *Essence*, October 2001, 156.

‡ Adapted from Mark Fischetti, "Drowning New Orleans," *Scientific American*, October 2001, 78.

4. In one experiment, researcher Ilene Bernstein gave a group of cancer patients Mapletoff ice cream an hour before they received nausea-provoking chemotherapy. A second group ate the same kind of ice cream on a day they did not receive chemotherapy. A third group got no ice cream. Five months later, the patients were asked to taste several ice cream flavors. Those who had never tasted Mapletoff and those who had not eaten it in association with chemotherapy chose it as their favorite. Those who had eaten Mapletoff before receiving chemotherapy found it very distasteful.*

   A dislike of a certain taste ______________________________

5. Peter Karafotas, 26, really likes the idea of a chocolate and strawberry wedding cake at his June 19 nuptials[1] in Washington, D.C., but a new temptation has him doubting his commitment. A chocolate-raspberry combo, he declares, also seems appealing. After several one-on-one visits with florists, Chris Coffman, 24, of Menlo Park, California, has settled on white bouquets and a modern, clean look for the centerpieces at his wedding reception, also this June. "We're doing heavy, square, clear-glass vases, some with glass beads, some with candles, and some with floating flowers," he says. But when it comes to wedding involvement, Jason Fox Jackson, 27, takes the groom's cake. The Texan spent four hours sewing beads on his bride's wedding gown before they said "I do" in December. "She was doing it by hand," he says. "I wanted to help."†

   Many grooms ______________________________

CHAPTER 4 REVIEW

Fill in the blanks in the following statements.

1. An __________ main idea is one that is suggested but not stated.
2. An implied main idea paragraph contains specific supporting details but no __________.

1. **nuptials:** wedding ceremony

* Adapted from Bernstein et al., *Psychology,* 6th ed. Boston: Houghton Mifflin, 2003, 193. Copyright © 2003 by Houghton Mifflin Company. Reprinted with permission.

† Adapted from Vicky Hallett, "Grooms for Improvement," *U.S. News and World Report,* March 22, 2004, www.usnews.com.

3. To determine the implied main idea of a paragraph, you can follow four steps:
   a. Find the ____________ of each sentence.
   b. Determine the ____________ of supporting details in the paragraph.
   c. Determine a general ____________ based on the specific details.
   d. Draw a ____________ from the supporting details and state an implied main idea in your own words.
4. An implied main idea, like one that's stated in a topic sentence, includes both the ____________ and what is being said about it.

Reading Selection

Practicing the Active Reading Strategy:

Before and While You Read

You can use active reading strategies before, as, and after you read a selection. The following are some suggestions for active reading strategies that you can perform before you read and while you read.

1. Skim the selection for any unfamiliar words. Circle or highlight any words you do not know.
2. As you read, underline, highlight, or circle important words or phrases.
3. Write down any questions about the selection if you are confused by the information presented.
4. Jot notes in the margin to help you understand the material.

One Man's Kids

by Daniel Meier

1 I teach first graders. I lived in a world of skinned knees, double-knotted shoelaces, riddles that I've heard a dozen times, stale birthday cakes, hurt feelings, wandering stories, and one lost shoe ("and if you don't find it my mother'll kill me"). My work is dominated by six-year-olds.

2 It's 10:45, the middle of snack, and I'm helping Emily open her milk carton. She has already tried the other end without success,

and now there's so much paint and ink on the carton from her fingers that I'm not sure she should drink it at all. But I open it. Then I turn to help Scott clean up some milk he has just spilled onto Rebecca's whale crossword puzzle.

3 While I wipe my milk- and paint-covered hands, Jenny wants to know if I've seen that funny book about penguins that I read in class. As I hunt for it in a messy pile of books, Jason wants to know if there is a new seating arrangement for lunch tables. I find the book, turn to answer Jason, then face Maya, who is fast approaching with a new knock-knock joke. After what seems like the tenth "Who's there?" I laugh and Maya is pleased.

4 Then Andrew wants to know how to spell "flukes" for his crossword. As I get to "u," I give a hand signal for Sarah to take away the snack. But just as Sarah is almost out the door, two children complain that "we haven't even had ours yet." I stop the snack midflight, complying with their request for graham crackers. I then return to Andrew, noticing that he has put "flu" for 9 Down, rather than 9 Across. It's now 10:50.

5 My work is not traditional male work. It's not a singular pursuit. There is not a large pile of paper to get through or one deal to transact. I don't have one area of expertise of knowledge. I don't have the singular power over language of a lawyer, the physical force of a construction worker, the command over fellow workers of a surgeon, the wheeling and dealing transactions of a businessman. My energy is not spent in pursuing, climbing, achieving, conquering, or cornering some goal or object.

6 My energy is spent in encouraging, supporting, consoling, and praising my children. In teaching, the inner rewards come from without. On any given day, quite apart from teaching reading and spelling, I bandage a cut, dry a tear, erase a frown, tape a torn doll, and locate a long-lost boot. The day is really won through matters of the heart. As my students groan, laugh, shudder, cry, exult[1], and wonder, I do, too. I have to be soft around the edges.

7 A few years ago, when I was interviewing for an elementary-school teaching position, every principal told me with confidence that, as a male, I had an advantage over female applicants because of the lack of male teachers. But in the next breath, they asked with a hint of suspicion why I chose to work with young children. I told them that I wanted to observe and contribute to the intellectual growth of a maturing mind. What I really felt like saying, but didn't, was that I loved helping a child learn to write her name for the first time, finding someone a new friend, or sharing in the hilarity of reading about Winnie the Pooh getting so stuck in a hole that only his head and rear show.

8 I gave that answer to those principals, who were mostly male, because I thought they wanted a "male" response. This meant talking about intellectual matters. If I had taken a different course and talked about my interest in helping children in their emotional development, it would have been seen as closer to a "female" answer. I even altered my language, not once mentioning the word "love" to describe what I do indeed love about teaching. My answer worked; every principal nodded approvingly.

9 Some of the principals also asked what I saw myself doing later in my career. They wanted to know if I eventually wanted

1. **exult:** rejoice

to go into educational administration. Becoming a dean of students or a principal has never been one of my goals, but they seemed to expect me, as a male, to want to climb higher on the career stepladder. So I mentioned that, at some point, I would be interested in working with teachers as a curriculum coordinator. Again, they nodded approvingly.

10 If those principals had been female instead of male, I wonder whether their questions, and my answers, would have been different. My guess is that they would have been.

11 At other times, when I'm at a party or a dinner and tell someone that I teach young children, I've found that men and women respond differently. Most men ask about the subjects I teach and the courses I took in my training. Then, unless they bring up an issue such as merit pay, the conversation stops. Most women, on the other hand, begin the conversation on a more immediate and personal level. They say things like "those kids must love having a male teacher" or "that age is just wonderful; you must love it." Then, more often than not, they'll talk about their own kids or ask me specific questions about what I do. We're then off and talking shop.

12 My job has no bonuses or promotions. No complimentary box seats at the ballpark. No cab fare home. No drinking buddies after work. No briefcase. No suit. (Ties get stuck in paint jars.) No power lunches. (I eat peanut butter and jelly, chips, milk, and cookies with the kids.) No taking clients out for cocktails. The only place I take my kids is to the playground.

13 Although I could have pursued a career in law or business, as several of my friends did, I chose teaching instead. My job has benefits all its own. I'm able to bake cookies without getting them stuck together as they cool, buy cheap sewing materials, take out splinters, and search just the right trash cans for useful odds and ends. I'm sometimes called "Daddy" and even "Mommy" by my students, and if there's ever a lull in the conversation at the dinner party, I can always ask those assembled if they've heard the latest riddle about why the turkey crossed the road. (He thought he was the chicken.)*

VOCABULARY

Read the following questions about some of the vocabulary words that appear in the previous selection. Circle the letter of the correct answer.

1. In paragraph 4, the author writes about "*complying* with their request for graham crackers." What does *complying* mean in this context?
   a. going along with their request
   b. disagreeing with their opinion
   c. discussing their request with them
   d. not going along with their request

* From Daniel Meier, "One Man's Kids," *The New York Times Magazine*, November 1, 1987. Reprinted by permission of the author.

2. What does *singular* mean in paragraph 5?
   a. ordinary
   b. undistinguished
   c. being the only one
   d. melancholy

3. In paragraph 7, the author writes "What I really felt like saying, but didn't, was that I loved helping a child learn to write her name for the first time, finding someone a new friend, or sharing in the *hilarity* of reading about Winnie the Pooh getting so stuck in a hole that only his head and rear show." From rereading this sentence, can you determine the meaning of the word *hilarity?*
   a. fun or merriment
   b. endeavor
   c. chore
   d. mastery

4. What does *complimentary* mean in paragraph 12?
   a. high up
   b. large
   c. luxurious
   d. free

Implied Main Ideas, Topics, Topic Sentences, and Supporting Details

Respond to each of the following questions about "One Man's Kids" by circling the letter of the correct answer.

1. Reread paragraphs 2 and 3 and look at the choices that follow. What is the implied main idea of these paragraphs?
   a. The author hates cleaning up during snack.
   b. The author has to do many things at once as a first-grade teacher.
   c. Snack is a very important time in a first grader's day.
   d. The crossword puzzle is a common homework assignment.

2. Reread paragraph 12 and look at the choices that follow. What is the implied main idea of this paragraph?
   a. The author's job is poorly paid.
   b. The author was smart to go into a profession that he loves.
   c. The author's job doesn't have any of the benefits that traditional male jobs in corporate America have.
   d. The author doesn't like wearing a tie.

3. Read paragraph 8. What is its topic?
   a. children's emotional development
   b. "male" vs. "female" reasons for teaching
   c. male principals
   d. love

4. Reread paragraph 13. Which of the following is the topic sentence?
   a. sentence 1.
   b. sentence 2.
   c. sentence 3.
   d. sentence 4.

5. Reread paragraph 11. Which of the following sentences is a MAJOR supporting detail?
   a. "At other times, when I'm at a party or a dinner and tell someone that I teach young children, I've found that men and women respond differently."
   b. "Most men ask about the subjects I teach and the courses I took in my training."
   c. "They say things like 'those kids must love having a male teacher' or 'that age is just wonderful; you must love it.'"
   d. "Then, more often than not, they'll talk about their own kids or ask me specific questions about what I do."

Practicing the Active Reading Strategy:
After You Read

Now that you have read the selection, answer the following questions using the active reading strategies that are discussed on pages 30–33.

1. Identify and write down the point and purpose of this reading selection.
2. Besides the vocabulary words included in the exercise on pages 200–201, are there any other vocabulary words that are unfamiliar to you? If so, write a list of them. When you have finished writing your list, look up each word in a dictionary and write the definition that best describes the word as it is used in the selection.
3. Predict any possible test questions that may be used on a test about the content of this selection.
4. How could you use the information contained in this selection? Does the information contained in the selection reinforce or contradict your ideas and experiences? Explain.

Questions for Discussion and Writing

Answer the following questions based on your reading of the selection. Write your answers on the blanks provided.

1. Do you think the author chose the right line of work? Why or why not?

____

____

2. Write an essay in which you argue whether it is more important to love your work or to be very well paid. ______________________________

____

3. This selection was written almost fifteen years ago. Do you think the author is still a first-grade teacher? Why or why not? ______________

____

4. Keeping in mind that this article was first published in 1987, do you think attitudes about gender roles in society have changed? Specifically, do you think that attitudes towards "traditional" male and female roles and professions have changed? Would the author's choice of work be more accepted today? Why or why not? ______________________

____

Vocabulary: The Definition/Restatement Context Clue

When you encounter an unfamiliar word as you read, you may be able to figure out its meaning by using context clues. The context of a word is its relationship to the other words, phrases, and sentences that surround it. Sometimes, these nearby elements offer clues you can use to get a sense of what a particular word means.

One type of context clue is definition or restatement. In this type of clue, either the word's meaning is directly stated, or synonyms are used to restate it. The following sentence, which comes from one of the paragraphs in Chapter 3, uses restatement:

> One important factor is making sure the punishment closely follows the child's ***transgression***, so that the child makes the connection between her wrongdoing and the consequences.
>
> The word *wrongdoing* is another way to say *transgession.*

Vocabulary Exercise 1

The following sentences all come from paragraphs in this chapter. In each one, underline the definition or restatement context clue that helps you understand the meaning of the boldfaced, italicized word:

1. The neuron's ability to communicate efficiently also depends on two other features: the "excitable" surface membrane of some of its fibers, and the minute gap, called a ***synapse,*** between neurons.

2. Soy milk doesn't have ***lactose*** (milk sugar,) which many people of Asian, Native American, and African descent can't easily digest.
3. ***Classical,*** or traditional, yoga—in which physical postures are used—is the type of yoga with which people are most familiar.
4. Exercise reduces or controls ***hypertension*** (abnormally high blood pressure,) and improves cholesterol levels.
5. Think of a ***jingle,*** or catchy tune, and it probably comes from a soft-sell ad.
6. Dr. Sears, though, advocates the ***"attachment parenting"*** approach in which parents hold and cuddle their babies in the "family bed" until the children fall asleep.
7. The name *Arkansas* comes from the Sioux word ***quapaw,*** which means "downstream people."
8. Recycling would be essential in all aspects of the mission, but ***regenerating*** systems tend to weigh more as well.

4

Vocabulary Exercise 2

In the following passage, circle the six words or phrases that are defined with definition/restatement context clues.

To understand diabetes, it's important to know a bit about how our body works. Here's a little biology lesson:

As mammals, we burn glucose (a form of sugar) as our predominant fuel. We eat food, it's digested and broken down into simpler components in the intestines, then it's transported to the bloodstream. The glucose component floats around to provide the body's cells with fuel. Glucose is moved into the cells by a hormone called insulin, produced in the pancreas. If the pancreas doesn't produce enough insulin or if the body's cells become resistant to insulin, the cells are starved for energy because the glucose stays in the bloodstream. This rise in blood sugar, detectable by your doctor, is diabetes.

There are two basic types of diabetes. Type 1, or juvenile diabetes, occurs when the pancreas fails to produce insulin. It's an autoimmune disease in which the immune system destroys insulin-making cells. As a result, there's zero insulin, so the cells consume other fuel, with deadly results.

Far more common is Type 2 diabetes. The number of sufferers has tripled in the past 30 years. That alarming increase has paralleled another American phenomenon—obesity, which also has tripled in the past few decades. The vast majority of people with Type 2 diabetes are overweight. Being too heavy reduces the body's sensitivity to insulin, leading to a rise in blood sugar.*

READING STRATEGY: SQ3R

In Chapter 1, you learned how to use active reading techniques to increase your comprehension of the material you read. One specific type of active reading strategy is called the **SQ3R method.** This abbreviation stands for

S urvey
Q uestion
R ead
R ecite
R eview

This series of five steps gives you a clear, easy-to-remember system for reading actively. Step 1 is to **survey** the text. "To survey" means to look over the text to preview it. Surveying gives you an overall idea of a reading selection's major topics, organizations, parts, and features. When you complete this step, you'll be able to form a mental framework that will allow you to better understand how specific paragraphs, sections, or chapters fit in. At this stage, your purpose is not to read the whole text but to get an overview of what to expect.

If you're preparing to read a longer text, such as a book, read over the title and glance through the table of contents to understand the major topics covered and how they are organized. Flip to one of the chapters and make yourself aware of its important features. A textbook, like this one, for example, may include a list of goals at the beginning of the chapter and a review summary at the end. It will probably also include headings that divide and identify sections of information. It's likely to emphasize key words or concepts with a distinctive typeface such as bold print.

Continued

4

* Adapted from Tedd Mitchell, M.D., "Get Moving on Diabetes," *USA Weekend,* November 2–4, 2001, 4. Reprinted with permission from the author.

Prior to reading a shorter selection—such as one particular chapter, an article, or an essay—survey it by reading any introductory material, the headings throughout, and the first sentence of each paragraph or each section. Read any review summaries or questions at the end of the chapter to get an idea of the major concepts covered in the selection. Also, glance over any illustrations and their captions.

The second step is to **formulate questions.** Turn the title and the headings into questions; then, when you read, you can actively look for the answers to those questions. For example, if the heading is "The Stamp Act Crisis," you could turn it into "What was The Stamp Act Crisis?" or "What caused The Stamp Act Crisis?" If the heading is "IQ Scores in the Classroom," you would create the question "What are the effects of IQ scores in the classroom?"

The next three steps are the three Rs of the SQ3R process. Step 3 is **read.** In this step, you read entire sentences and paragraphs in a section. However, you read only one section at a time; for example, in a textbook, you'd read from one heading to the next and then stop. As you read, look for the answers to the questions you formed in step 2. Mark the text as you go. Highlight or underline those answers and other important information. You may want to write the answers or other details in the margins.

Step 4 is to **recite.** Reciting means saying something aloud. After you read a section of material, stop and speak the answers to the questions you created in step 2. If you can't answer a question, reread the information until you can. Move on to the next section only when you can say the answers for the section you just read.

The last step of the SQ3R method is **review.** Review means "look at again." After you've read the entire selection, go back through it and see if you can still answer all of the questions you formed in step 2. You don't have to reread unless you can't answer a particular question.

Practice the SQ3R active reading method with the following passage from a psychology textbook:

Cells of the Nervous System

One of the most striking findings in current research on the cells of the nervous system is how similar they are to other cells in the body, and how similar all cells are in all living organisms, from bacteria to plants to humans. For example, bacteria, plant cells, and brain cells all synthesize[1] similar proteins when they are subjected to reduced oxygen or elevated temperatures. The implica-

1. **synthesize:** make

tions[1] of this similarity are clear: We can learn much about humans by studying animals, and much about brain cells by studying cells in simple organisms. For example, studies of viruses by cancer researchers led to the discovery of proteins that may be involved in the formation of memories in the brain. Cells of the nervous system share three characteristics with every other kind of cell in the body. First, they have an *outer membrane* that, like a fine screen, lets some substances pass in and out while blocking others. Second, nervous system cells have a *cell body* that contains a *nucleus*. The nucleus carries the genetic information that determines how a cell will function. Third, nervous system cells contain *mitochondria*, which are structures that turn oxygen and glucose into energy. This process is especially vital to brain cells. Although the brain accounts for only 2 percent of the body's weight, it consumes more than 20 percent of the body's oxygen. All of this energy is required because brain cells transmit signals among themselves to an even greater extent than do cells in the rest of the body.

Two major types of cells—called *neurons* and *glial cells*—allow the nervous system to carry out its complex signaling tasks so efficiently. **Neurons** are cells that are specialized to rapidly respond to signals and quickly send signals of their own. Most of our discussion of brain cells will be about neurons, but glial cells are important as well. *Glial* means "glue," and scientists have long believed that glial cells did no more than hold neurons together. Recent research shows, however, that **glial cells** also help neurons communicate by directing their growth, keeping their chemical environment stable, secreting chemicals to help restore damage, and even sending signals between neurons. Without glial cells, neurons could not function.

Neurons have three special features that enable them to communicate signals efficiently. The first is their structure. Although neurons come in many shapes and sizes, they all have long, thin fibers that extend outward from the cell body. When these fibers get close to other neurons, communication between the cells can occur. The intertwining of all these fibers with fibers from other neurons allows each neuron to be in close proximity[2] to thousands or even hundreds of thousands of other neurons.

Continued

1. **implications:** consequences
2. **proximity:** nearness

4

The fibers extending from a neuron's cell body are called *axons* and *dendrites*. **Axons** are the fibers that carry signals away from the cell body, out to where communication occurs with other neurons. Each neuron generally has only one axon leaving the cell body, but that one axon may have many branches. Axons can be very short or several feet long, like the axon that sends signals from the spinal cord all the way down to the big toe. **Dendrites** are the fibers that receive signals from the axons of other neurons and carry those signals to the cell body. A neuron can have many dendrites. Dendrites, too, usually have many branches. Remember that *a*xons carry signals *away* from the cell body, whereas *d*endrites *detect* those signals.

The neuron's ability to communicate efficiently also depends on two other features: the "excitable" surface membrane of some of its fibers, and the minute[1] gap, called a **synapse**, between neurons.*

Reading Visuals: Flow Charts

A **flow chart** is a visual aid composed of boxes, circles, or other shapes along with lines or arrows. The purpose of a flow chart is to represent the sequence of steps or stages in a process.

The parts of a flow chart are:

- **Title.** The title identifies the process or procedure summarized in the chart.
- **Boxes or other shapes.** Each box contains one step in the process. They are arranged either top to bottom or left to right.
- **Lines or arrows.** These show the sequence of steps.
- **Source line.** The source line, if applicable, identifies who collected or compiled the information in the chart.

These parts are labeled in the flow chart on page 209:

1. **minute:** tiny

* Adapted from Bernstein et al., *Psychology,* 4th ed. Boston: Houghton Mifflin, 1997, 177–178.

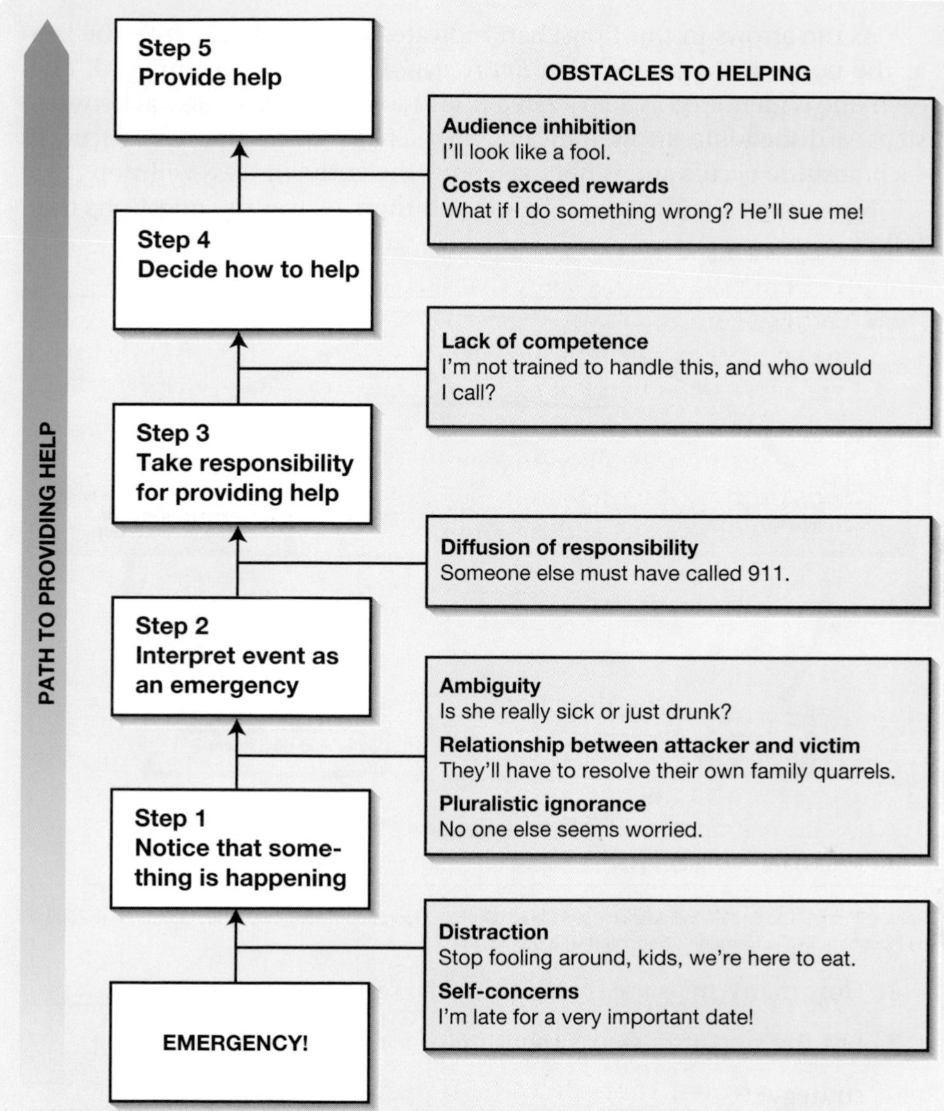
PATH TO PROVIDING HELP
Step 5
Provide help
OBSTACLES TO HELPING
Audience inhibition
I'll look like a fool.
Costs exceed rewards
What if I do something wrong? He'll sue me!
Step 4
Decide how to help
Lack of competence
I'm not trained to handle this, and who would I call?
Step 3
Take responsibility for providing help
Diffusion of responsibility
Someone else must have called 911.
Step 2
Interpret event as an emergency
Ambiguity
Is she really sick or just drunk?
Relationship between attacker and victim
They'll have to resolve their own family quarrels.
Pluralistic ignorance
No one else seems worried.
Step 1
Notice that something is happening
Distraction
Stop fooling around, kids, we're here to eat.
Self-concerns
I'm late for a very important date!
EMERGENCY!

The Five Steps to Helping in an Emergency
On the basis of their analysis of the decision-making process in emergency interventions, Latané and Darley (1970) outlined five steps that lead to providing assistance. But there are obstacles that can interfere; and if a step is missed, the victim won't be helped.

Excerpted from S. Brehm et al., *Social Psychology,* 5th ed. Boston: Houghton Mifflin, 2002, 361. Copyright © 2002 by Houghton Mifflin Company. Reprinted with permission.

To interpret a flow chart, first read the chart's title so you'll know what process is being summarized. Read each step in order, following the lines and arrows to understand their sequence.

Continued

4

As the arrows in this flow chart indicate, the steps begin with the box at the bottom, the one labeled *Emergency!* The steps move upward, and each one is identified as Step 1, Step 2, and so on. At each interval between steps, a dotted-line arrow indicates a specific obstacle that can occur. If each obstacle occurs and is not overcome, the entire process will stop.

Now, study the flow chart below and then answer the questions that follow.

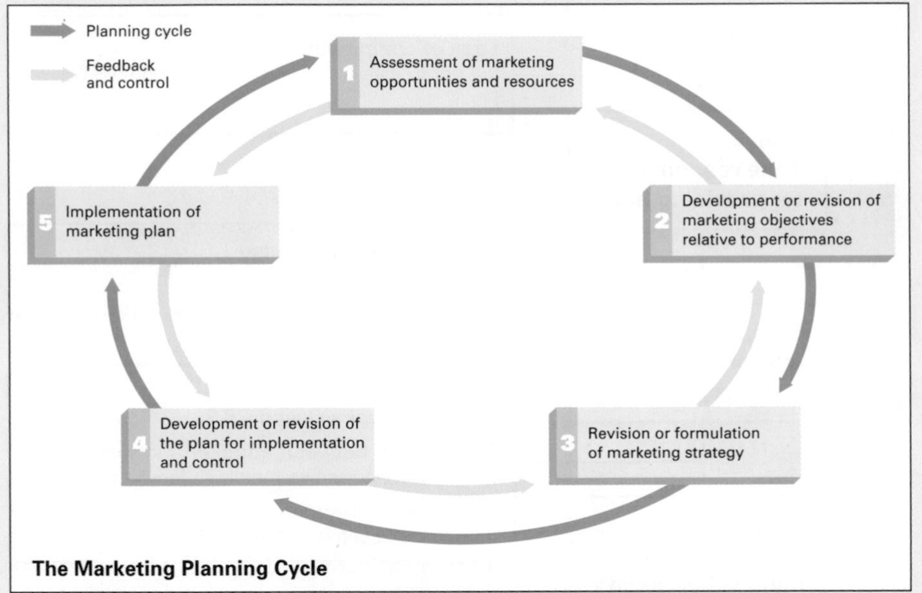

The Marketing Planning Cycle

Source: From Pride and Ferrell, *Marketing,* 11th ed. Boston: Houghton Mifflin, 2000, 40. Copyright © 2000 by Houghton Mifflin Company. Reprinted with permission.

1. How many steps are there in the Marketing Planning Cycle? ______
2. List the step after step 3 (revision or formulation of marketing strategy). ____
____
3. At what step do you actually implement a marketing plan? ______
4. According to this chart, can you implement a marketing plan immediately after you revise marketing objectives? ____________
5. When the whole planning cycle is reversed, what is it called?
____

CHAPTER 4 TESTS

Name ______________________________ Date ______________

TEST 1

After each group of sentences, circle the letter of the general sentence that includes all of the specific details given.

1. Galileo's[1] telescopes permitted the first enhanced views of heavenly bodies in human history.

   Galileo made dozens of telescopes in his lifetime and gave many away to interested colleagues and would-be patrons.[2]

   The telescopes may seem very simple instruments to us, but the twenty-fold magnification provided by the smaller instrument enabled Galileo to make celestial[3] observations that would help revolutionize humans' understanding of their physical world.*

   a. Galileo had many patrons.
   b. Galileo invented the first telescope, which was popular and quite sophisticated.
   c. Galileo's telescope led to the discovery of many new planets.
   d. The telescope is a simple but amazing instrument.

2. In 2003, at the invitation of the principal, police in Goose Creek, South Carolina, stormed a high school with a zero-tolerance policy, forced students to the floor at gunpoint, and handcuffed many in a futile[4] search for drugs.

   In October of that same year, a Lee County, Florida, boy was kicked out of a zero-tolerance school for a doodle that showed one stick figure shooting another.

1. **Galileo:** 17th c. astronomer and physicist
2. **patrons:** supporters
3. **celestial:** relating to the sky or heavens
4. **futile:** useless

* Adapted from Noble et al., *Western Civilization,* Vol. 1, 3rd ed. Boston: Houghton Mifflin, 2002, 573.

For additional tests, see the Test Bank.

And in September, a Montgomery County, Texas, teen was suspended and arrested for violating his school's drug policy by loaning his inhaler[1] to a classmate who was having a severe asthmatic[2] attack.*

a. The police are too harsh on teenagers.
b. Zero-tolerance policies sometimes punish students unfairly for trivial offenses.
c. Students shouldn't bring inhalers to school.
d. Some school officials have wisely adopted zero-tolerance policies.

3. One student who described a debilitating[3] medical condition in his college application essay was given 500 points.

If a student reports having been raised by a single parent, that student is given 250 points.

If your "personal circumstances" include having been a class president, you will receive 300 points.†

a. Colleges are assigning point values to "personal circumstances" that are described or listed on college applications.
b. The point system is unfair.
c. Colleges are giving more weight to students' extracurricular activities.
d. Students should slightly exaggerate their achievements on their college application essays.

4. One key to Starbucks's success is its well-conceived and implemented strategy for growth.

Another key to success is Starbucks's astute[4] promotional campaigns and commitment to quality.

Starbucks's owner, Howard Schultz, refuses to franchise[5] his stores, fearing a loss of control and a potential deterioration of quality.‡

a. Starbucks doesn't grow as fast as other chains.
b. Starbucks should not limit itself to selling only coffee.
c. A number of factors contribute to Starbucks's success.
d. Howard Schultz is a control freak.

1. **inhaler:** device that produces vapors to ease breathing
2. **asthmatic:** related to asthma, a respiratory disease
3. **debilitating:** causing a significant reduction in strength or energy
4. **astute:** showing shrewdness (keen awareness and intelligence)
5. **franchise:** grant the right for a person or group to sell a company's goods or services

* Adapted from "Zero Tolerance Takes Student Discipline to Harsh Extremes," no author credited, *USA Today*, January 2, 2004, 11a.

† Adapted from Mary Beth Marklein, "California Rewrites College Admissions," *USA Today*, January 28, 2002, 1D.

‡ Adapted from Griffin, *Management*, 7th ed. Boston: Houghton Mifflin, 2002, 258.

5. One thing you can do to lose weight is drink water, a diet beverage, or low-fat milk in place of the beverages you usually drink.

   Arienna Dunne takes tap and Irish dancing each week as part of her weight-loss program.

   If you are trying to lose weight, don't use food as a reward or withhold it as punishment.*

   a. Irish dancing is a great way to exercise.
   b. Fast food is terrible for you if you are on a diet.
   c. Certain changes in your eating and exercise habits will help you lose weight.
   d. Tap dancing alone will not help you lose weight.

6. Fat increases the risk of heart disease and high blood pressure in children.

   Once rare in children, Type 2 diabetes has skyrocketed in youngsters, largely because of weight.

   Fat also can raise a child's liver enzymes and cause nonalcoholic cirrhosis,[1] while teens can get gall bladder disease or even a brain condition, caused by increased pressure, called pseudotumor cerebri.†

   a. Being overweight can put a child's health at risk.
   b. Obesity in children is an epidemic in our country.
   c. Diet and exercise are the keys to a healthy lifestyle, even for children.
   d. Type 2 diabetes is on the rise in our country.

7. To deal with loss of revenue[2] and sinking employee morale,[3] chief executive officer John Chambers of network equipment maker Cisco Systems cut his annual pay to $1 and waived[4] rights to 2 million stock options valued at $44 million.

   Coca-Cola's Douglas Daft asked directors to defer any stock award and requested no raise on his $1.5 million salary.

   Citigroup's Sanford Weill told directors not to give him a bonus.‡

   a. CEOs make a lot of money.
   b. Many CEOs will lose money because of their companies' performances.
   c. Many CEOs are responding to hard times in their industries by taking pay cuts.
   d. CEOs get stock options instead of salaries sometimes.

1. **cirrhosis:** liver disease
2. **revenue:** income
3. **morale:** spirits or attitude
4. **waived:** gave up voluntarily

* Adapted from Susan Ferraro, "Pound by Pound," *The Daily News,* January 28, 2002, 36.

† Adapted from Susan Ferraro, "Pound by Pound," *The Daily News,* January 28, 2002, 36.

‡ Adapted and excerpted from Gary Strauss and Barbara Hansen, "Bubble Hasn't Burst on CEO Salaries Despite the Times," *USA Today,* March 31, 2003, www.usatoday.com.

8. Younger workers are at risk for losing their jobs because employers want skills and proven performance, not inexperience.

   High school and college-age students were disproportionately[1] represented in the high-tech industry, hit hard by the downturn in the economy; many of those workers are currently unemployed.

   Climbing unemployment has increased competition for jobs, causing older workers with more experience to take more entry-level jobs typically held by younger hires.*

   a. The high-tech industry is losing ground in the economy.
   b. Many dot-com companies have gone bankrupt.
   c. Unemployment is on the rise among young workers.
   d. Older workers resent younger workers.

9. Thomas Johansson, winner of the 2002 Australian Open in tennis, was said to be the sixteenth best player in the tournament.

   In twenty-four previous tournaments, he never had advanced beyond the quarterfinals.

   He came into the Australian Open with only six titles to his record since turning pro in 1994.†

   a. Thomas Johansson was the surprise winner of the 2002 Australian Open.
   b. People are not too enthusiastic about the way Johansson plays tennis.
   c. The heat at the Australian Open was very intense.
   d. Johansson doesn't play tennis very well.

10. Group therapy, which refers to the treatment of several clients under the guidance of a therapist, offers features not found in individual treatment.

    Family therapy involves treatment of two or more individuals from the same family.

    In couples therapy, improving communication between partners is one of the most important targets of treatment.‡

    a. Don't go to couples therapy unless you are in a relationship.
    b. Family therapy is very helpful to most families.
    c. There are different types of therapy situations available, depending on your needs.
    d. Group therapy is a lot of fun because you get to meet new people.

1. **disproportionately:** lacking in balance or proportion

---

* Adapted from Stephanie Armour, "Young Job Seekers Get Squeezed Out," *USA Today*, January 28, 2002, 1B.

† Adapted from Phil Brown, "Johansson Jumps from Bit Player to Big Time," *USA Today*, January 28, 2002, 12C.

‡ From Bernstein and Nash, *Essentials of Psychology*, 2nd ed. Boston: Houghton Mifflin, 2002, 464–465.

TEST 2

Read each of the following paragraphs and answer the questions that follow by circling the letter of the correct response.

A. (1) How accurate are the FBI's crime statistics? (2) First, these statistics reflect only those crimes reported to local police departments, and it is estimated that only two out of every five crimes are officially known to the police. (3) Second, because some types of crime are more likely to be reported than others are, the statistics may not account for large numbers of crimes. (4) Murders and auto thefts are almost always reported, whereas larceny[1] and rape victims, whether out of embarrassment or fear, or other reasons, may remain silent. (5) Third, the FBI's crime data include only eight types of criminal behavior, which means that most white-collar[2] crimes and drug crimes are excluded, despite the fact that their number is growing.*

1. The subject of sentence 2 is
   a. crimes.
   b. the FBI.
   c. the FBI's crime statistics.
   d. local police departments.

2. The subject of sentence 3 is
   a. types of crime.
   b. the FBI's crime statistics.
   c. criminals.
   d. crime reports.

3. The subject of sentence 5 is
   a. the FBI's crime data.
   b. types of criminal behavior.
   c. white-collar crimes.
   d. drug crimes.

4. The types of details that organize this paragraph are
   a. descriptive details or features.
   b. points of comparison.
   c. events.
   d. steps.

1. larceny: theft

2. white-collar: relating to workers whose work does not involve manual labor

* Adapted from Bowman and Kearney, *State and Local Government*, 5th ed. Boston: Houghton Mifflin, 2002, 450.

5. The general topic of this paragraph is
   a. crime.
   b. the FBI.
   c. the FBI's crime statistics.
   d. crime victims.

6. What kind of generalization could be made about the details stated in the paragraph?
   a. All of the statistics are very accurate.
   b. All of the statistics are based on partial or incomplete information.
   c. All of the statistics are increasing in number.
   d. All of the statistics have been carefully researched and compiled.

7. What is the implied main idea of this paragraph?
   a. Crime is on the rise.
   b. The FBI maintains accurate records of crimes committed in America.
   c. The FBI's crime statistics provide an incomplete picture of criminal activity.
   d. Criminal activity is one of this country's biggest problems.

B. (1) The Hispanic and Asian population rose about 70 percent during the 1990s in the twenty fastest-growing cities, many of them like Phoenix and Las Vegas in the Sun Belt, an analysis by the Brookings Institute shows. (2) An influx[1] of people from a variety of different cultures and backgrounds swelled the population in Rust Belt capitals such as Chicago. (3) Simultaneously, immigrants moved to suburbs, as in the cases of the Chinese influx into California's San Gabriel Valley, Indians in central New Jersey, Indochinese in Northern Virginia, and others around the country.*

8. The subject of sentence 1 is
   a. the Asian population.
   b. the Brookings Institute.
   c. the Hispanic and Asian population.
   d. Phoenix and Las Vegas.

9. The subject of sentence 2 is
   a. Rust Belt capitals.
   b. Chicago.

1. **influx:** flowing in

* Adapted from Samuel G. Freedman, "Recognize New Arrivals' Value," *USA Today,* May 16, 2001, 15A.

c. people from different backgrounds and cultures.
d. population.

10. The subject of sentence 3 is
    a. Chinese immigrants.
    b. Indochinese immigrants.
    c. immigrants.
    d. suburbs.

11. The types of details that organize this paragraph are
    a. examples.
    b. events.
    c. points of comparison.
    d. reasons.

12. The general topic of this paragraph is
    a. fast-growing cities.
    b. Indochinese immigrants.
    c. immigrants.
    d. Rust Belt capitals.

13. What kind of generalization could be made about the details stated in the paragraph?
    a. The cities and suburbs were all in the West.
    b. The cities and suburbs all grew in population.
    c. The cities and suburbs were all located in warm, sunny climates.
    d. The cities were all much nicer than the suburbs.

14. What is the implied main idea of this paragraph?
    a. Immigrants are settling in cities.
    b. Immigrants are settling in suburbs.
    c. The immigrant population rose in American cities and suburbs during the 1990s.
    d. Many Americans welcomed immigrants to their communities.

4

C. (1) Research has shown that when teachers are asked to nominate their best students or those with the most potential, they are more likely to nominate boys than girls. (2) They are especially likely to name boys as most skilled in mathematics. (3) Even when the differences between boys and girls is minimal, teachers who are asked to think of students who excel in language or social skill are more likely to name girls. (4) Boys receive more disapproval from teachers than girls do during preschool and elementary school, even when boys and girls engage in similar amounts of disruptive behavior. (5) Teachers pay more attention to a girl when she sits quietly in the front of the classroom, whereas the amount of attention paid to a boy is high regardless of where he sits. (6) Within elementary school classrooms, teachers tend to call on boys more often than girls and give them more explicit[1] feedback regard-

1. **explicit:** specific

ing their answers. (7) When girls answer, they are more likely to receive a simple acceptance from the teacher ("okay"), whereas boys tend to receive more praise, constructive criticism, or encouragement to discover the correct answer. (8) Thus, boys receive more explicit academic instruction and tend to dominate classroom interactions.*

15. The subject of sentence 5 is

 a. teachers.
 b. girls.
 c. classroom behavior.
 d. students.

16. The subject of sentence 6 is

 a. elementary school classrooms.
 b. teachers.
 c. boys.
 d. feedback.

17. Most of the details in this paragraph are

 a. descriptive details or features.
 b. points of comparison.
 c. effects.
 d. types.

18. The general topic of this paragraph is

 a. education.
 b. the differences between boys and girls.
 c. teachers' responses to boys and girls.
 d. male students.

19. What kind of generalization could be made about the details stated in the paragraph?

 a. The reactions are all different and based on gender.
 b. The reactions are all fair and reasonable.
 c. The reactions are all harmful for students.
 d. The reactions are all good for students.

20. What is the implied main idea of this paragraph?

 a. Teachers don't receive enough training in classroom management.
 b. Teachers treat children differently according to their sex.
 c. Education in America is unequal and unfair.
 d. Male students perform better than female students do in America's classrooms.

* Adapted from Bukatko and Daehler, *Child Development,* 5th ed. Boston: Houghton Mifflin, 2004, 487. Copyright © 2004 by Houghton Mifflin Company. Reprinted with permission.

CHAPTER 5
Transitions

GOALS FOR CHAPTER 5

- **Define the term *transition.***
- **Recognize common transitions used to indicate a series of items.**
- **Recognize common transitions used to indicate time order.**
- **Recognize common transitions used to indicate cause/effect.**
- **Recognize common transitions used to indicate comparison/contrast.**
- **Recognize common transitions used to indicate definition and examples.**
- **Recognize transitions in paragraphs organized according to more than one pattern.**
- **Practice the steps involved in summarizing a reading selection.**
- **Read and understand information in a pie chart.**

5

In Chapters 3 and 4, you learned how to recognize supporting details within paragraphs. To help you understand how those details are related to one another, paragraphs include transitions that help you follow the author's train of thought. To discover what you already know about transitions, take the following pre-test.

TEST YOURSELF

Circle the transition words in the following paragraphs.

1. Through the first four decades of the century, the *Journal,* the *Post,* and many of the other mass-circulation magazines thrived. During the 1920s, more specialized magazines made their successful debut. One type revolved around the idea of distilling information for busy people.

For example, *Reader's Digest,* a compendium[1] of "must read" articles, and *Time,* a weekly news summary, came out in 1922 and 1923, respectively. Both had their predecessors in magazine history, and both had their imitators. The second type of magazine reflected an elite, knowing cynicism[2] and humor that seemed to be the mark of the so-called Jazz Age, the 1920s. The *New Yorker,* for instance, was the most successful of these.*

2. Problems in life such as money troubles, illness, final exams, or unhappy relationships often create upsetting thoughts and worry. Consequently, upsetting thoughts create anxiety. These thoughts become particularly difficult to dismiss when you are under stress or feel incapable of dealing effectively with the problems you are worried about. So, as the thoughts become more persistent, anxiety increases. An action such as cleaning may temporarily relieve the anxiety, but that action does nothing to eliminate the obsessive thoughts. Therefore, they become compulsive, endlessly repeated rituals that keep the person trapped in a vicious circle of anxiety. Thus, social-learning theorists see obsessive-compulsive disorder as a learned pattern sparked by distressing thoughts.†

3. You, too, can bring back a lost art of communication by learning to whistle with your fingers. First, wash your hands. Then, move your pinkies in a V shape toward your mouth. Next, place them underneath your tongue, about an inch to an inch and a half past the tip, and lift your tongue slightly. Close your lips over your first knuckles and tighten them against

1. **compendium:** collection of various items

2. **cynicism:** attitude characterized by distrust of others' motives, virtue, or integrity

* From Turow, *Media Today*. Boston: Houghton Mifflin, 1999, 97.

† Adapted from Bernstein and Nash, *Essentials of Psychology,* 2nd ed. Boston: Houghton Mifflin, 2002, 423.

your fingers and teeth. Finally, press slightly against your tongue, pursing the lips as needed, and blow.*

4. If you want to train your dog Henry to sit and to "shake hands," you need to shape Henry's behavior. Shaping is accomplished by reinforcing *successive approximations,* or responses that come successively closer to the desired response. For example, you might first give Henry a treat whenever he sits down. Then, you might reinforce him only when he sits and partially lifts a paw. Next, you might reinforce more complete paw lifting. Eventually, you would require that Henry perform the entire sit-lift-shake sequence before giving the treat. Shaping is an extremely powerful, widely used tool. Animal trainers have used it to teach chimpanzees to roller-skate, dolphins to jump through hoops, and pigeons to play Ping-Pong.†

5. The excitement that the networks generated around TV led more and more people to buy TV sets. By 1960, more than 90 percent of homes had one. Instead of listening to network radio, people tended to watch network television. With network audiences declining, nervous station owners began to drop their affiliations[1] to look for other, nonnetwork ways to make money. Whereas 97 percent of all radio stations were affiliated with a network in 1947, only 50 percent were network affiliates in 1955. Now, looking back, it seems clear that radio was undergoing a revolution.‡

Transitions are words and phrases whose function is to show the relationships between thoughts and ideas. The word *transition* comes from the Latin word *trans,* which means "across." Transitions bridge the gaps across sentences and paragraphs and reveal how they are related.

1. **affiliations:** associations, connections

---

* Adapted from Bryan Mealer, "The Lost Art of Whistling with Your Fingers," *Esquire,* February 2002, 95.

† Adapted from Bernstein et al., *Psychology,* 5th ed. Boston: Houghton Mifflin, 2000, 191.

‡ From Turow, *Media Today.* Boston: Houghton Mifflin, 1999, 179.

5

Transitions make sentences clearer, so they help readers understand the ideas in a passage more easily. Without them, the readers have to figure out relationships on their own. For example, read these two sentences: **We've called ourselves African Americans, Japanese Americans, Mexican Americans, and Irish Americans. We're all just plain Americans.**

When you read these two sentences, which are not connected with a transition, you have to pause to figure out how they're related. Now look at how the addition of a transition more clearly reveals the contrast between the two thoughts. **We've called ourselves African Americans, Japanese Americans, Mexican Americans, and Irish Americans. *However,* we're all just plain Americans.**

Characteristics of Transitions

You should be aware of three characteristics of transitions:

1. Some of them are synonyms. In other words, they mean the same thing. For instance, the transitions *also, in addition,* and *too* all have the same meaning. Therefore, they are usually interchangeable with one another.

2. Some transitions can be used in more than one pattern of organization. For example, you may see the word *first* in both series and process paragraphs.

   First, you must choose a topic for your speech. (process)

   The ***first*** reason to assign your child chores is to develop his or her sense of responsibility. (series)

3. Different transitions can create subtle but significant changes in the meaning of sentences. For example, reread an earlier example that includes a contrast transition: **We've called ourselves African Americans, Japanese Americans, Mexican Americans, and Irish Americans. *However,* we're all just plain Americans.**

The transition *however* suggests a contradiction or reversal of the idea in the first sentence. Notice, though, how a different transition changes the relationship between the two sentences: **We've called ourselves African Americans, Japanese Americans, Mexican Americans, and Irish Americans. *Now,* we're all just plain Americans.**

Substituting the transition ***now,*** which is a time order word, suggests a change over time rather than a contradiction. Changing that one transition subtly alters the meaning of those two sentences.

As you read, then, you'll need to pay attention to transitions so you can accurately follow the train of thought within a reading selection. The remainder of this chapter explains and illustrates the different types of transition words that accompany various patterns of organization. (For more information about patterns of organization, see Chapter 6.)

Transition Words that Indicate a Series

Certain transition words show readers that the sentence will add another item to a series. A series may consist of examples, reasons, or some other kind of point. Here are some common series transitions:

Series Transitions

also	furthermore	finally
in addition	first, second, third	lastly
too	first of all	most importantly
another	and	moreover
one	for one thing	next

The following pairs of sentences illustrate the use of series transitions:

> If you know how to respond productively under pressure, stress can actually increase your energy. ***Also,*** good stress can boost your confidence and help you achieve your goals.
>
> Frequent memory lapses are one early warning sign of Alzheimer's disease. ***Another*** sign is getting lost or disoriented about the time or the place.
>
> When asked to name the key ingredients of a successful intimate relationship, people most often mention affection. ***In addition,*** they believe emotional expressiveness is very important.

Now, read a paragraph that includes series transition words (boldface, italicized). Notice how each transition indicates the addition of another item in the series:

> Three different temperature scales are commonly used in measuring heat intensity. ***One of these*** is the Fahrenheit temperature scale, which was devised by Gabriel Daniel Fahrenheit, a German scientist, in 1724. On this scale the freezing point of pure water is at 32 degrees (32°F), and the boiling point of water is at 212 degrees (212°F). There are thus 180 Fahrenheit degrees between the freezing point and the boiling point of water. The ***second,*** the Celsius temperature scale, was devised in 1742 by Anders Celsius, a Swedish astronomer. His objective was to develop an easier-to-use temperature scale; he did so by assigning a nice, round 100 Celsius degrees between the freezing and boiling

points of pure water. On the Celsius scale, the freezing point of water is at zero degrees (0°C), and the boiling point of water is at 100 degrees (100°C). (The Celsius scale is also sometimes referred to as the centigrade scale.) ***Third,*** the Kelvin temperature scale is an *absolute* temperature scale. That is, its zero point (0 K) is an absolute zero, the lowest possible temperature theoretically attainable. The divisions of the Kelvin scale are the same size as Celsius degrees, but they are called *kelvins* (abbreviated K) rather than degrees.*

This paragraph presents a series of three different kinds of temperature scales. The series transitions *one, second,* and *third* indicate each new kind.

Exercise 5.1

Fill in the blanks in the following sentences and paragraphs with appropriate series transitions. Choose words or phrases from the box on page 223. Try to vary your choices.

1. The first thing you should do when you are flying in a commercial airplane is to check to see where the exits are. ___________, make sure you know how to access your oxygen mask should the airplane cabin have a loss in pressure.
2. By age three or so, children begin to use auxiliary verbs[1] and to ask questions using *what, where, who,* and *why.* ___________, they begin to put together clauses to form complex sentences.†
3. There are a couple of other things we'll need for our trip. ___________, a canteen for fresh water would be helpful. ___________, sunscreen always comes in handy in case it gets hot and sunny. ___________, it is crucial that you remember to bring enough food for three days.
4. In 1993, Compaq Computer decided to change the way it organized its sales function. ___________, it wanted to cut the size of the group by one-third.

1. **auxiliary verbs:** verbs such as *have, can,* or *will,* which accompany the main verb

* Adapted from Sherman and Sherman, *Basic Concepts of Chemistry,* 6th ed. Boston: Houghton Mifflin, 1996, 40–41. Copyright © 1996 by Houghton Mifflin Company. Reprinted with permission.

† Adapted from Bernstein and Nash, *Essentials of Psychology,* 2nd ed. Boston: Houghton Mifflin, 2002, 234. Copyright © 2002 by Houghton Mifflin Company. Reprinted with permission.

__________, it wanted to reduce its overhead expenses. __________, the company wanted to enrich the jobs of the sales reps to make them more motivating and engaging. The key, managers realized, was to allow the sales representatives to work from home offices, eliminating both their commute time and the need to maintain a company office for them.*

5. To conduct an effective search on the Web, you need to be aware of a few factors. __________, search engines often provide a superficial[1] view of what might be available and often return an incomplete listing of their findings. Each of these engines uses different criteria for a search and will return information based on those criteria. __________, you can search for relevant information via links that you encounter. Links are a central component of the Web. __________, the Uniform Resource Locator[2] provides another way to investigate your topic. If you obtain the URL of a particular website that is likely to have information you can use, travel there directly by using the Open Location command and entering the URL.†

Transition Words that Indicate Time Order

Some transition words signal that the sentence is providing another event, step, or stage within a chronological order of details. Here is a list of common time-order transitions:

Time-Order Transitions

first, second, third	once	last
before	today	meanwhile
now	previously	finally
then	often	over time
after	as	in the end
while	when	during, in, on,
next	until	*or* by (*followed*
soon	later	*by a date*)
in the beginning	eventually	

1. **superficial:** shallow; related to the surface only
2. **Uniform Resource Locator (URL):** website address

* Adapted from Griffin, *Management,* 6th ed. Boston: Houghton Mifflin, 1999.
† Adapted from Andrews et al., *Public Speaking.* Boston: Houghton Mifflin, 1999, 151–152.

The following pairs of sentences illustrate the use of time-order transitions:

> ***In 1941,*** the Japanese attacked America's Pearl Harbor. ***In 1942,*** 120,000 Japanese-Americans were rounded up and imprisoned in internment[1] camps.
>
> Baseball's Mark McGwire held the record for home runs in a season. ***Then,*** the San Francisco Giants' Barry Bonds broke that record, hitting three more home runs in one season than McGwire.
>
> Eating breakfast foods that are high in sugar and carbohydrates, such as doughnuts, causes blood sugar to rise quickly. ***By mid-morning,*** blood sugar drops rapidly, making you feel lethargic[2] and irritable.

Now, read a paragraph that uses time-order transition words (boldfaced, italicized). Notice how each transition indicates another event in the timeline:

> Following certain guidelines will ensure that your interview will be efficient and productive. ***Before*** the interview, research the topic and plan your questions. Dress nicely to show that you take the interview seriously, and to show respect for the person you are interviewing. ***On the day of the interview,*** arrive on time. ***When*** you meet your expert, engage in a little small talk before you get to your prepared questions. ***After*** the initial tension is reduced, begin by asking your first question. ***Then,*** let the expert do most of the talking ***while*** you listen and take notes. ***At the end of the interview,*** summarize what you heard so the expert can verify the accuracy of your understanding. ***Soon after the interview,*** send the expert a thank-you note as a professional courtesy.*

This paragraph offers advice about each step of the interviewing process. Each new detail is introduced with a time-order transition to help the reader easily follow the order of the steps.

1. **internment:** confinement
2. **lethargic:** state of sluggishness and low energy

* Adapted from Michael Osborn and Suzanne Osborn, *Public Speaking,* 4th ed. Boston: Houghton Mifflin, 1997, 164. Copyright © 1997 by Houghton Mifflin Company. Reprinted with permission.

Exercise 5.2

Fill in the blanks in the following sentences and paragraphs with appropriate time-order transitions. Choose words or phrases from the box on page 225. Try to vary your choices.

1. Sixty-six percent of teachers now use computers in the classroom as part of their lesson plans. ___________, that number will rise to almost 100 percent.
2. Right now, Deena and her family live in a small apartment in Hoboken, New Jersey. ___________, they would like to move to a bigger place or perhaps even a house.
3. Fred put the steak on the grill to cook. ___________, Doris made a salad to serve with it.
4. Washing your own car is a satisfying endeavor.[1] Here's how you do it right. ___________, park in the shade so your car won't dry too quickly and spot. ___________, soak the exterior to loosen dirt so it won't scratch the finish when you wash. Keep the car wet during the entire process. ___________, use a soapy sponge to clean painted areas and a soft brush to clean tires and wheels. Open doors, hood, fuel door, and trunk to clean the jambs. Spray wheel wells to remove road grime and salt. ___________, dry with bath towels that have been washed without fabric softener, which can cause streaks. Let the car sit with doors, trunk, and hood open so remaining moisture can evaporate. ___________, apply a tire dressing to make that rubber shine. Every spring and fall, finish painted surfaces with paste wax.*
5. ___________, many scientists believed that the human lifespan (the maximum age to which the perfectly maintained, disease-free body could remain alive before it simply wore out and broke down) was infinitely extendible. The average lifespan early in the evolution of *Homo sapiens*[2] is thought to have been just twenty years. ___________ the beginning of the twentieth century, that figure had more than doubled—to a still-brief forty-seven. ___________, life expectancy (the number

5

1. **endeavor:** activity; effort toward a goal

2. **Homo sapiens:** the modern species of human beings

* Adapted from Barry Rice, "The Lost Art of Washing Your Own Car," *Esquire,* February 2002, 93.

of years you can expect to live before being claimed by illness or accident) has been exploding, with people in the developed world now able to live deep into their seventies and beyond. ___________, though, scientists understand that lifespan has remained fixed at a hard ceiling of about 125 years.*

Transition Words that Indicate Cause/Effect

Certain transition words indicate that an occurrence about to be presented in a sentence is either a reason for or a result of an occurrence presented in a previous sentence. These are the transitions that reveal cause or effect relationships between thoughts. The most common cause/effect transition words are listed below:

Cause/Effect Transitions

so	because of	due to
therefore	in response	hence
as a result	consequently	for this reason
thus	as a consequence	

The following pairs of sentences illustrate the use of cause/effect transitions:

The existing financial safety net for farmers proved inadequate. ***So,*** Congress approved a new bill that provides support for grain, cotton, and soybean producers.

Carrying a grudge around saps your energy and happiness. ***For this reason,*** you should learn to forgive the mistakes or thoughtlessness of other people.

Cigarettes cost more, and American culture has shifted away from smoking. ***As a result,*** there has been a dramatic drop in the number of teenagers who pick up the habit.

Next, read a paragraph that uses cause/effect transition words (boldfaced, italicized). Notice how each transition indicates another effect:

* Adapted from Jeffrey Kluger, "Can We Learn to Beat the Reaper?" *Time,* www.time.com/time/covers/1101020121/aging.html.

From the 1880s onward, popular newspapers increasingly nurtured people's fascination with the sensational.[1] Joseph Pulitzer, a Hungarian immigrant who bought the *New York World* in 1883, pioneered this trend by filling his newspaper with stories of disasters, crimes, and scandals. ***As a result,*** the *World*'s daily circulation increased from 20,000 to 100,000, and by the late 1890s, it had reached one million. ***Consequently,*** other publishers, such as William Randolph Hearst, who started an empire of mass-circulation newspapers, adopted Pulitzer's techniques. ***Hence,*** sensationalist journalism became a nationwide phenomenon.*

This paragraph is arranged according to the chain-reaction type of cause/effect. Each transition indicates that the detail is the result of a previous occurrence.

Exercise 5.3

Fill in the blanks in the following sentences and paragraphs with appropriate cause/effect transitions. Choose words or phrases from the box on page 228. Try to vary your choices.

5

1. ___________ added security measures at airports around the country, it is taking longer to get to your departure gates. ___________, you should leave extra time to get through all of the checkpoints.
2. Danny missed the notice from his professor that there was a test on Friday; ___________, he did very poorly.
3. Second hand smoke has been proven to be as dangerous as smoke that is directly inhaled from cigarettes, ___________ do your best to stay away from smokers.
4. ___________ of the unusual amount of rain on the East Coast this spring, the pollen count was very high.
5. "Net," abbreviated from "Internet," refers to the internetworking of computers around the world. Advances in software and hardware and a

1. **sensational:** arousing strong curiosity through exaggerated or shocking details

* Adapted from Norton et al., *A People and a Nation,* 5th ed., Vol. 2. Boston: Houghton Mifflin, 1998, 560.

common interface[1] allow people from around the globe to communicate and to exchange information almost instantaneously. __________, the Internet has grown exponentially.[2] New sites appear every minute, adding to the millions already there. Organizations, companies, corporations, agencies, schools, colleges, universities, libraries, repositories,[3] interest groups, and politicians have scrambled to establish a presence. __________, on the Internet you can encounter information and opinions on any topic imaginable, and not only in text form, but also in images, sound, and video.*

6. When the United States entered World War I in 1917, a team of psychologists was asked to develop group-administered tests that could identify the mental ability of army recruits and guide their assignment to appropriate jobs. Soldiers who could speak and read English were tested on mental tasks that required verbal skills, such as defining words, whereas the rest were asked to visualize objects and perform other nonverbal tasks. Unfortunately, the verbal tests contained items that were unfamiliar to many recruits. Further, tests were often given under stressful conditions in crowded rooms where instructions were not always audible[4] or, for non-English speakers, understandable. __________, almost half of the soldiers tested appeared to have a mental age of thirteen or lower. __________, testers were led to draw seriously incorrect conclusions about their lack of intelligence—especially in cases of those who did not speak English. __________, later tests developed by David Wechsler, were designed to correct some of the weaknesses of earlier ones.†

5

Transition Words that Indicate Comparison/Contrast

Paragraphs include comparison transitions to help readers see similarities between two or more things. They include contrast transitions to point out differences.

1. **interface:** point of interaction
2. **exponentially:** multiplying in large quantities
3. **repositories:** places where things are put for safekeeping
4. **audible:** able to be heard

* From Andrews et al., *Public Speaking*. Boston: Houghton Mifflin, 1999, 150–151.

† Adapted from Bernstein and Nash, *Essentials of Psychology,* 2nd ed. Boston: Houghton Mifflin, 2002, 238.

First, let's examine the comparison transitions, which appear in the list below:

Comparison Transitions

also	similarly	in the same way
too	in like manner	along the same line
likewise	just like, just as	in both cases

The following pairs of sentences illustrate the use of comparison transitions:

> Religious Sunni Muslims participate in prayer services in which they bow their heads toward the holy city of Mecca and recite verses from their holy book, the Quran. ***Likewise,*** Shiite Muslims worship in the same ways.

> Tobacco is a highly addictive substance that accounts for more deaths than do all other drugs, car accidents, suicides, homicides, and fires combined. ***Similarly,*** alcohol is a potentially addictive drug that can lead to major health problems.

> To nineteenth-century Americans, the West represented opportunity. The machine, ***too,*** fired American optimism; between 1860 and 1930, the United States Patent Office registered 1.5 million new inventions.

The following paragraph uses comparison transition words (boldfaced, italicized). Notice how each transition indicates another point of comparison:

Scientists are simulating a Martian lifestyle on Devon Island, a polar desert in the Canadian Arctic, because conditions there are like those on the planet Mars. The terrain of Devon Island is strikingly similar to the landscape of Mars. ***Like*** Mars, Devon Island is characterized by canyons and crevasses[1] created by, some scientists theorize, the movement of ancient glaciers. Both seem rocky and lifeless. ***As*** on Devon Island, researchers speculate, the seemingly dead rocks on Mars may contain microbial[2] life or fossils. The climate is similar, ***too.*** Mars is extremely cold. ***Likewise,*** Devon Island is cold, requiring scientists to wear protective suits with helmets. On Mars, scientists would conduct experiments. ***In the same way,*** researchers on Devon Island collect soil samples, study rocks, use sensors to search for water, and test a solar-powered robot that might actually be used someday on our neighboring planet.*

1. **crevasses:** deep cracks or chasms
2. **microbial:** relating to tiny life forms

* Adapted from John B. Carnett, "Mars Boot Camp," *Popular Science,* October 2001, 52–58.

Exercise 5.4

Fill in the blanks in the following sentences and paragraphs with appropriate comparison transitions. Choose words or phrases from the box on page 231. Try to vary your choices.

1. A table of contents in a book helps you find information contained in the pages of that book. __________, directories on the Internet offer extensive lists of Web pages, all grouped by topic.

2. Workers in many different types of professions have formed unions to ensure recognition of their profession's importance and adequate pay. Teachers are one group of professionals that formed a union. __________, nurses have a nurse's union to look out for them.

3. Meat is so packed with nutrients, it gave early humans a break from constant feeding, allowing them to eat at less regular intervals.[1] __________, lions and tigers didn't have to eat around the clock just to keep going.*

4. Islam and Christianity are similar in many ways. Islam is a monotheistic[2] religion that recognizes God (Allah) as the Creator. Christianity, __________, is monotheistic. Islam holds that God is omnipotent and omniscient.[3] __________, Christians believe in an all-powerful God. Followers of Islam believe that God has a unique relationship with humans and makes agreements or Covenants with them. __________, Christians believe that humans can have meaningful relationships with God. Both religions believe that humans have an eternal soul or spirit, which continues its existence after physical death. Those who practice Islam believe that God will judge each human after the end of the world and evaluate his or her actions in compliance with a moral code. Christians __________ believe that God will hold humans accountable for their deeds on Earth.†

5. In his studies of how infants form attachments to their caregivers, Harry Harlow isolated some newborn monkeys from all social contact. After a

1. **intervals:** amounts of time between two events or states
2. **monotheistic:** worshipping one god
3. **omnipotent and omniscient:** all-powerful and all-knowing

---

* Adapted from Michael D. Lemonick, "How We Grew So Big," *Time,* June 7, 2004.

† Adapted from "Islam and Christianity: Similarities and Differences," muslim-canada.org/islam_christianity.html.

5

year of this isolation, the monkeys showed dramatic disturbances. When visited by normally active, playful monkeys, they withdrew to a corner, huddling or rocking for hours. When some of the females had babies (through artificial insemination), they tended to ignore or even physically abuse them.

___________, humans who spend their first few years without a consistent caregiver exhibit many of the same problems. ___________ Harlow's deprived monkeys, abandoned children discovered at Romanian and Russian orphanages were withdrawn and engaged in constant rocking. Even after being adopted, the children were depressed, stared blankly, and demanded attention. ___________ the deprived monkeys lashed out at their own babies, some of the children could not control their own tempers and interacted poorly with their adopted mothers. Neurologists suggest that the dramatic problems observed in both isolated monkeys and humans are the result of developmental brain dysfunction and damage brought on by a lack of touch and body movement in infancy.*

Now, let's look at the contrast transitions:

Contrast Transitions

however	nevertheless	unfortunately
but	on the one hand/ on the other hand	in contrast
yet		conversely
although	unlike	even though
instead	rather	still
in opposition	on the contrary	nonetheless
in spite of	actually	whereas
just the opposite	despite	in reality
though	while	as opposed to

The following pairs of sentences illustrate the use of contrast transitions:

More than 8,000 fifth graders failed state reading and math tests. ***Yet,*** 75 percent of these children were promoted by principals to the sixth grade.

* Adapted from Bernstein et al., *Psychology*, 5th ed. Boston: Houghton Mifflin, 2000, 426.

Las Vegas, America's most colorful city, is best known for its casinos and showgirls. ***However,*** no less than five fine-art museums are determined to bring class and culture to the neon strip.

The common view is that the East has been so heavily logged that there are no old trees left. ***On the contrary,*** several forests in New York, Pennsylvania, New Hampshire, and Massachusetts contain trees as old as four or five hundred years.

Next, read a paragraph that includes contrast transition words (boldfaced, italicized). Notice how each transition indicates another point of contrast.

If you want whiter teeth, should you try one of the do-it-yourself whitening kits, or should you book an appointment with your dentist? The home kits and dentist treatments differ in terms of time, cost, and results. At-home bleaching, such as Crest's Whitestrips, contains tape or trays that you wear on your teeth from thirty minutes to three hours at a time over several weeks. ***In contrast,*** the dentist's treatment often includes lasers that speed the process, which takes only two or three sessions in the chair. The cost of the various treatments differs widely. Crest Whitestrips cost only about $44 for a 2-week supply, ***but*** dentist treatments can cost up to one thousand. The results, too, will differ. Crest guarantees "noticeably whiter" teeth. Dentists, ***however,*** are more specific; they say they can lighten the teeth eight to ten shades.*

5

Exercise 5.5

Fill in the blanks in the following sentences and paragraphs with the appropriate contrast transition. Choose words or phrases from the box on page 233. Try to vary your choices.

1. Many people feared the Second World War would be a repetition of the First. ____________, it was much bigger in every way.†
2. Jeff Moran and some friends from Troop 1320 dropped onto the lawn near Trading Post 13 one sweltering Tuesday morning during the Fifteenth Boy Scouts Jamboree at Fort A. P. Hill near Fredericksburg, Virginia.

* Adapted from Patty Rhule, "White Might," *USA Weekend,* October 5–7, 2001, 12.

† From Bulliet et al., *The Earth and Its Peoples,* Brief Edition. Boston: Houghton Mifflin, 2000, 539. Copyright © 2000 by Houghton Mifflin Company. Reprinted with permission.

__________ the heat wave, over the next ten days they would help 32,000 other Scouts burn through 76,000 hamburgers, 479,000 eggs, and 10 tons of beef stew.*

3. __________ we often think of a speech as "being over" when the speaker has delivered his or her conclusion, many times the conversation with the audience is just beginning.†

4. Hispanics living in the United States differ in more than places of origin and settlement. Cubans are much more likely to be political refugees,[1] __________ those from other countries tend to be economic refugees looking for a better life. Because primarily educated, professional Cubans fled their native country, they have largely gained a higher socioeconomic[2] status in the United States as well. For instance, almost 20 percent of Cuban Americans are college educated, roughly the same percentage as for Americans as a whole. __________, only 6 percent of Mexican Americans and 9 percent of Puerto Ricans have graduated from college. The numbers suggest that if Hispanics acted together, they would wield considerable clout.[3] __________, their diversity has led to fragmentation[4] and powerlessness.‡

5. Females and males physically differ in a number of ways, including the makeup of their chromosomes,[5] their genitalia,[6] and levels of certain hormones. Females are physically more mature at birth, __________ males show a special physical vulnerability during infancy. Compared with females, males are more likely to be miscarried, die in infancy, or develop hereditary diseases. Later in infancy and childhood, females walk, talk, and reach other developmental milestones earlier than males. Males, ______________, are more physically active and more likely to engage in vigorous rough-and-tumble play. By later childhood and adolescence,

5

1. **refugees:** people who flee in search of protection
2. **socioeconomic:** related to social or economic class
3. **clout:** influence
4. **fragmentation:** breaking into small, isolated groups or parts
5. **chromosomes:** in cells, the material that carries hereditary information
6. **genitalia:** sex organs

* Adapted from David France, "Scouts Divided," *Newsweek,* August 6, 2001, 45.

† From Andrews et al., *Public Speaking.* Boston: Houghton Mifflin, 1999, 287.

‡ Adapted from Barbour and Wright, *Keeping the Republic.* Boston: Houghton Mifflin, 2001, 135.

females reach puberty[1] earlier and males develop greater height, weight, and muscle mass than females.*

Transition Words that Indicate Definition

One final set of transition words are those that signal examples. Because the definition pattern or organization often includes one or more examples, this type of transition will often appear in definition paragraphs. However, transitions that indicate examples can appear in other types of paragraphs, too. Any time authors want to illustrate an idea or make it clearer, they often identify the beginning of an example with one of the following transitions:

Definition (Example) Transitions

for example	as an illustration	in one case
for instance	in one instance	more precisely
to illustrate	such as	specifically

The following pairs of sentences illustrate the use of example transitions:

Special operations troops are the United States military's elite forces. The army's Delta Force, ***for example,*** is a clandestine[2] unit that specializes in hostage rescue and high-risk missions.

A learning disability is defined as a significant discrepancy[3] between measured intelligence and academic performance. Thomas Edison, ***for instance,*** did not have a low IQ, yet he experienced problems with reading, writing, and math in school.

A joint venture is a partnership formed to achieve a specific goal or to operate for a specific period of time. ***In one case,*** the Archer Daniels Midland Company (ADM), one of the world's leading food processors, entered into a joint venture with Gruma SA, Mexico's largest corn and flour tortilla company.

1. **puberty:** stage at which an individual becomes capable of sexual reproduction
2. **clandestine:** secret or hidden
3. **discrepancy:** difference

* Adapted from Bukatko and Daehler, *Child Development,* 5th ed. Boston: Houghton Mifflin, 2004, 468. Copyright © 2004 by Houghton Mifflin Company. Reprinted with permission.

Now, read a paragraph that includes example transition words (boldfaced, italicized). Notice how the transitions introduce the two examples:

> A United States Pentagon publication defines asymmetric[1] warfare as "unanticipated or nontraditional approaches" that "exploit an adversary's vulnerabilities." More simply put: It is dirty fighting that gives the weak the best chance to defeat the strong. It often involves unexpected sneak attacks, which may occur in urban areas where civilians are present. ***For example,*** a 1983 guerilla[2] attack in Lebanon killed 241 American service members. ***In another instance,*** Somali militiamen downed two U.S. helicopters and killed eighteen American troops in 1993.*

Exercise 5.6

Fill in the blanks in the following sentences and paragraphs with appropriate example transitions. Choose words or phrases from the box on page 236. Try to vary your choices.

1. The speaker who wants to help the audience understand concepts that are complicated, abstract, or unfamiliar will give a speech of explanation. A professor's lecture, ___________, is a speech aimed at explaining abstract or difficult concepts to students.†
2. "Trade paperbacks" is a term that refers to standard-size books that have flexible covers. They are designed to sell primarily in so-called mass-market outlets ___________ newsstands, drug stores, discount stores, and supermarkets.‡
3. Specific gravity is the ratio of a substance's weight to the weight of an equal volume of pure water. ___________, a mineral that weighs four times as much as an equal volume of water has a specific gravity of 4. The precise specific gravity of an unknown mineral is generally determined in a laboratory, although relative specific gravity can also be helpful in the

5

1. **asymmetric:** unbalanced, unequal, uneven

2. **guerilla:** related to a member of an irregular military unit

* Adapted from Mark Mazzetti and Richard J. Newman, "The Far Horizon," *U.S. News and World Report,* October 8, 2001, 14–15.

† Adapted from Andrews et al., *Public Speaking.* Boston: Houghton Mifflin, 1999, 300.

‡ Adapted from Turow, *Media Today.* Boston: Houghton Mifflin, 2000, 105.

field in distinguishing between two apparently similar minerals. Minerals with a markedly higher specific gravity will feel much heavier relative to their size than minerals with a lower specific gravity will. ___________, gold, with a specific gravity of 19.3, feels much heavier than "fool's gold" (the mineral pyrite), which has a specific gravity of only 5.*

4. *Entrapment,* which is also known as *escalation of commitment,* occurs when commitment to a failing course of action is increased to justify investments already made. In numerous instances, groups, businesses, and governments have incurred huge costs because they kept throwing more money, time, and other resources into a project that should have been terminated long before. ___________ is British Columbia's escalation of its commitment to host a world's fair in 1986 despite rapidly growing budget deficits. ___________ is the U.S. government's escalation of the war in Vietnam in the mid-1960s despite mounting evidence that its strategy would not succeed. ___________ is the recent, massive construction project in Boston known as the "Big Dig," designed to turn a congested stretch of highway into a high-speed tunnel. These 7.5 miles of road were costing about $5 million a day—but with so much money already spent, no one could conceive of terminating the project.†

5. Senators opposed to a bill can engage in a *filibuster,* which is an effort to tie up the floor of the Senate in debate to stop the members from voting on a bill. ___________ a filibuster is considered "hardball politics." ___________, a filibuster occurred when southern senators temporarily derailed Minnesota senator Hubert Humphrey's efforts to pass the Civil Rights Act of 1964.‡

Transitions in Combinations of Patterns

Supporting details in paragraphs can be organized according to more than one pattern. For example, a paragraph may include *both* time-order details and effect details. In such paragraphs, it will be particularly important for you to notice transition words and phrases, for they will provide clues about the

* From Chernicoff and Fox, *Essentials of Geology,* 2nd ed. Boston: Houghton Mifflin, 2000, 29.

† Adapted from Brehm et al., *Social Psychology,* 5th ed. Boston: Houghton Mifflin, 2002, 282–283. Copyright © 2002 by Houghton Mifflin Company. Reprinted with permission.

‡ Adapted from Barbour and Wright, *Keeping the Republic.* Boston: Houghton Mifflin, 2001, 177–179.

various relationships among different kinds of details. For an example of a paragraph that includes more than one pattern and, therefore, different kinds of transitions, read the following:

> *Ecotourism* is relatively low-impact group travel or tour packages to destinations in nature. In other words, ecotourists travel to natural areas without disturbing the environment or contributing to the destruction of resources. ***For example,*** they might go to the South Pacific to see forests and endangered birds, or canoe down the Amazon in South America. Engaging in this type of travel has several benefits. It respects the diversity and fragility[1] of the environment of the Earth, so you won't cause more damage to natural resources or animal habitats. It ***also*** allows you to help support indigenous[2] cultures with your travel dollars. It offers you opportunities to broaden your horizons, ***too,*** because you travel off the beaten path into excitingly different places. ***Finally,*** it will help you rediscover your passion for life, for your experience is bound to help you discover something personal and meaningful.*

This paragraph begins with a *definition* of ecotourism that includes examples. Then, it offers a *series* of reasons for becoming an ecotourist. Therefore, it includes both example and series transitions.

5

Exercise 5.7

Read each of the following paragraphs and circle the transition words or phrases. Then, in the list below the paragraph, place a checkmark next to the two or three patterns used to organize the details.

1. In presidential campaigns, both candidates usually try to use statistics to defend their own views of how the economy is faring. Governor Bill Clinton created controversy when he claimed success in creating jobs in his own state of Arkansas. The governor, using statistics derived from the last two years, pointed to the dramatic increases in jobs. In contrast, the Bush campaign, using statistics covering a ten-year period, claimed that Arkansas had fared worse than the rest of the nation. Both sides were

1. **fragility:** easily damaged or destroyed
2. **indigenous:** living or growing in a certain area; native to

* Adapted from www.ecotourism.org website.

technically "right." But both sides were using a different set of figures to prove their point. Consequently, the media had to consistently point out that the two campaigns were projecting how much programs would cost, whether or not they would lead to tax increases, how many people would be employed, and the like, based on statistics that each side had carefully selected to reinforce its own position.*

_____ series
_____ time order
_____ cause/effect
_____ comparison/contrast
_____ definition

2. Three styles of leadership have been identified: authoritarian, laissez-faire, and democratic. The first type, the authoritarian leader, holds all authority and responsibility, with communication usually moving from top to bottom. This leader assigns workers to specific tasks and expects orderly, precise results. The leaders at United Parcel Service, for instance, employ authoritarian leadership. At the other extreme is the laissez-faire[1] leader, who gives authority to employees. With the laissez-faire style, subordinates are allowed to work as they choose with a minimum of interference. For example, leaders at Apple Computer are known to employ a laissez-faire style. The third type, the democratic leader, holds final responsibility but also delegates authority to others, who participate in determining work assignments. An example of this leadership style is the manager who employs a communication style that is active both upward and downward. Managers for both Wal-Mart and Saturn have used democratic leadership.†

5

1. **laissez-faire:** French for "let do," or "leave alone"

* From Andrews et al., *Public Speaking*. Boston: Houghton Mifflin, 1999, 199.

† Adapted from Pride et al., *Business*, 6th ed. Boston: Houghton Mifflin, 1999, 153.

_____ series
_____ time order
_____ cause/effect
_____ comparison/contrast
_____ definition

3. Knowing that radio stations use various pieces of data to make decisions on airplay, record executives have developed many ways to artificially boost the perceived popularity of a song. One technique used in the 1990s was to specially price singles from new artists in the hope that the low cost, say, under a dollar, would spur impulse sales. A similar technique is a "buy two singles, get one free" gimmick,[1] which aims to boost the sale of singles by lesser-known artists. The hope is that the artificial increase in their sales would land them on hit lists. Radio programmers would choose the songs for airplay, and this choice would, in turn, spur actual sales of the artists' albums. Other techniques at record promotion are even less ethical. There are reports that record company representatives have organized campaigns to flood stations with requests for a particular song. Another activity aimed at placing songs on radio stations is payola—a practice where a promotion executive bribes a station program director to include certain music on the playlist.*

_____ series
_____ time order
_____ cause/effect
_____ comparison/contrast
_____ definition

4. A debate that began in the late 1970s suggested that the content of curriculum taught in U.S. classrooms should reflect the diverse character of the nation's population, or be *multicultural*. It should, for instance, dispense knowledge about this country's diverse cultural groups. This multicultural

1. **gimmick:** device used to trick or cheat someone

* Adapted from Turow, *Media Today*. Boston: Houghton Mifflin, 1999, 221–222. Copyright © 1999 by Houghton Mifflin Company. Reprinted with permission.

approach was recommended for several reasons. First, advocates argued that the curriculum should better represent the actual contributions made by various cultural groups to this country's society. Second, a multicultural curriculum would educate children of majority status as to the many accomplishments and contributions to U.S. society by individuals of minority status. Third, multicultural education was perceived as a school reform movement that could improve the content and process of education within schools.*

_____ series
_____ time order
_____ cause/effect
_____ comparison/contrast
_____ definition

5. Halloween is a plastic holiday. Unlike Christmas, Easter, and their cousins from other cultures, Halloween lacks religious foundations. Unlike Thanksgiving and the Fourth of July, it has no patriotic underpinnings.[1] It even lacks the single-minded sentimentality of the synthetic Mother's Day. Instead, Halloween has been mauled[2] and molded to fit the needs of each generation. In the 1600s, Puritans[3] intent on survival in a new world and salvation in the next ignored it. In the next two centuries, a hard-pressed immigrant population let off steam in its honor. In the 1800s and early 1900s, a Victorian society tamed it. In the twentieth century, World Wars I and II and even Vietnam undermined it. And a newly powerful postwar nation gave it a social conscience.†

1. **underpinnings:** support or foundation
2. **mauled:** injured by beating or rough handling
3. **Puritans:** group of 16th and 17th century English Protestants who advocated strict religious observance and morality

* Adapted from Garcia, *Student Cultural Diversity: Understanding and Meeting the Challenge,* 3rd ed. Boston: Houghton Mifflin, 2002.

† Adapted from Ellen Feldman, "Halloween," *American Heritage,* October 2001, 69. Reprinted by permission of *American Heritage.*

_____ series

_____ time order

_____ cause/effect

_____ comparison/contrast

_____ definition

Exercise 5.8

The following groups of sentences have been scrambled. Number them in the order they should appear (1, 2, 3, etc.) so that they make sense. Use the transitions to help you figure out the right order. Then, in the list below each group, write a checkmark next to the pattern or patterns used to organize the details.

1. _____ From 1942 to 1943, fighting street by street, the Soviets managed to defend their city in what was arguably the pivotal[1] military engagement of World War II.

   _____ Although the Germans reached Stalingrad by late 1942, they could not achieve a knockout.

   _____ By the end of January 1943, the Soviets had captured what remained of the German force, about 100,000 men.

   _____ The victory came at an immense price: A million Soviet soldiers and civilians died at Stalingrad, but by February 1944, Soviet troops had pushed the Germans back to the Polish border.*

   Pattern(s) of organization:

   _____ series

   _____ time order

   _____ cause/effect

   _____ comparison/contrast

   _____ definition

2. _____ Finally, if you need to evacuate the aircraft, leave your bags on the plane.

   _____ You can increase your chances of surviving an airplane crash.

   _____ Also, you should listen to the flight attendants' preflight safety briefing.

   _____ For one thing, when you fly, wear clothing of natural fabrics and don't wear high heels.

1. **pivotal:** important, crucial

* Adapted from Noble et al., *Western Civilization,* 2nd ed. Boston: Houghton Mifflin, 1999, 666. Copyright © 1999 by Houghton Mifflin Company. Reprinted with permission.

5

____ In addition, examine the emergency hatches and figure out how they operate.*

Pattern(s) of organization:

____ series ____ comparison/contrast

____ time order ____ definition

____ cause/effect

3. ____ This reduced activity in the locus coeruleus, in turn, tends to cause cognitive changes and a release of inhibitions.

____ In particular, alcohol depresses activity in a specific region of the brain called the *locus coeruleus.*

____ Alcohol affects specific brain regions.

____ As a result, some drinkers talk loudly, act silly, or tell others what they think of them.†

Pattern(s) of organization:

____ series ____ comparison/contrast

____ time order ____ definition

____ cause/effect

5

4. ____ In literature, several twentieth-century novelists used the stream-of-consciousness technique, a type of narration in which the author presents a character's thoughts, feelings, and reactions with no comment or explanation.

____ Another example is William Faulkner's *The Sound and the Fury* (1922), in which much of the drama is seen through the eyes of a person with a learning disability.

____ One example is Virginia Woolf's *Jacob's Room* (1922), a novel made up of a series of internal monologues,[1] in which ideas and emotions from different periods of time bubble up randomly.

1. **monologues:** speeches made by one person

---

* Adapted from Sally B. Donnelly, "How to Survive a Crash," *Time,* November 13, 2000, 91.

† Adapted from Bernstein and Nash, *Essentials of Psychology,* 2nd ed. Boston: Houghton Mifflin, 2002, 135.

_____ James Joyce's *Ulysses* (1922), which abandoned conventional grammar and blended foreign words, puns, bits of knowledge, and scraps of memory together in bewildering confusion, is a third—and perhaps the most famous—example.*

Pattern(s) of organization:

_____ series _____ comparison/contrast

_____ time order _____ definition

_____ cause/effect

5. _____ However, tiredness, fever, headache, and major aches and pains probably indicate the flu.

_____ A cold and the flu are alike in some ways, but their symptoms and length differ.

_____ These flu symptoms can continue for several weeks and lead to more serious problems, like the lung disease pneumonia.

_____ A stuffy nose, sore throat, and sneezing are usually signs of a cold.

Pattern(s) of organization:

_____ series _____ comparison/contrast

_____ time order _____ definition

_____ cause/effect

CHAPTER 5 REVIEW

Fill in the blanks in the following statements.

1. ____________ are words and phrases whose function is to show the relationships between thoughts and ideas.
2. Some transitions are ____________; in other words, they mean the same thing.

* Adapted from McKay et al., *A History of Western Civilization,* 7th ed. Boston: Houghton Mifflin, 2003, 929–930. Copyright © 2003 by Houghton Mifflin Company. Reprinted with permission.

3. Some transitions can be used in more than one __________ of organization.
4. Different transitions can create subtle but significant changes in the __________ of sentences.
5. __________ transitions indicate the addition of another reason, example, type, or other point.
6. __________ transitions signal another event, step, or stage within a chronological order of details.
7. __________ transitions indicate either a reason for or a result of an occurrence presented in a previous sentence.
8. __________ transitions point out similarities, and __________ transitions point out differences.
9. __________ transitions illustrate ideas in definition paragraphs as well as other types of paragraphs.
10. __________ organized according to more than one pattern will often include different kinds of transitions.

Reading Selection

Practicing the Active Reading Strategy:

Before and While You Read

You can use active reading strategies before, as, and after you read a selection. The following are some suggestions for active reading strategies that you can perform before you read and while you read.

1. Skim the selection for any unfamiliar words. Circle or highlight any words you do not know.
2. As you read, underline, highlight, or circle important words or phrases.
3. Write down any questions about the selection if you are confused by the information presented.
4. Jot notes in the margin to help you understand the material.

Classical Conditioning: Learning Signals and Associations

1 At the opening bars of the national anthem, a young ballplayer's heart may start pounding; those sounds signal that the game is about to begin. A flashing light on a control panel may make an airplane pilot's adrenaline flow, because it means that something may be wrong. These people were not born with such reactions; they learned them from observed relations or associations between events in the world. The experimental study of this kind of learning was begun, almost by accident, by Ivan Petrovich Pavlov.

Pavlov's Discovery

2 Pavlov is one of the best-known figures in psychology, but he was not a psychologist. A Russian physiologist, Pavlov won a Nobel Prize in 1904 for his research on the digestive processes of dogs. In the course of this work, Pavlov noticed a strange phenomenon: His dogs sometimes salivated—the first stage of the digestive process—when no food was present. For example, the dogs began to salivate when they saw the assistant who normally brought their food, even if the assistant was empty-handed.

3 Pavlov devised a simple experiment to determine why salivation occurred in the absence of an obvious physical cause. First he performed a simple operation to divert a dog's saliva into a container, so that the amount secreted could be measured precisely. He then placed the dog in an apparatus similar to the one shown in Figure 5.1. The experiment had three phases.

4 In the first phase of the experiment, Pavlov and his associates confirmed that when meat powder was placed on the dog's tongue, the dog salivated, but it did not salivate in response to a neutral stimulus—a musical tone, for example. Thus, the researchers established the existence of the two basic components for Pavlov's experiment: a natural reflex (the dog's salivation when meat powder was placed on its tongue) and a neutral stimulus (the sound of the tone). A *reflex* is the swift, automatic response to a stimulus,

Figure 5.1
Apparatus for Measuring Conditioned Responses

In this more elaborate version of Pavlov's original apparatus, the amount of saliva flowing from a dog's cheek is measured, then recorded on a slowly revolving drum of paper.

such as shivering in the cold or jumping when you are jabbed with a needle. A *neutral stimulus* is one that initially does not elicit the reflex being studied, although it may elicit other responses. For example, when the tone is first sounded, the dog pricks up its ears, turns toward the sound, and sniffs around; but it does not salivate.

5 It was the second and third phases of the experiment that showed how one type of learning can occur. In the second phase, the tone sounded and then a few seconds later meat powder was placed in the dog's mouth. The dog salivated. This *pairing*—the tone followed immediately by meat powder—was repeated several times. The tone predicted the subsequent presentation of the meat powder, but the question remained: Would the animal learn this association? Yes. In the third phase of the experiment the tone was sounded and, even though no meat powder was presented, the dog again salivated. In other words, the tone by itself now elicited salivation.

6 Pavlov's experiment was the first laboratory demonstration of a basic form of *associative* learning. Today, it is called *classical conditioning*—a procedure in which a neutral stimulus is repeatedly paired with a stimulus that already triggers a reflexive response until the previously neutral stimulus alone evokes a similar response. Figure 5.2 shows the basic elements of classical conditioning. The stimulus that elicits a response without conditioning, like the meat powder in Pavlov's experiment, is called the **unconditioned stimulus (UCS).** The automatic, unlearned reaction to this stimulus is called the **unconditioned response (UCR).** The new stimulus being paired with the unconditioned stimulus is called the **conditioned stimulus (CS),** and the response it comes to elicit is the **conditioned response (CR).***

Figure 5.2
Classical Conditioning

Before classical conditioning has occurred, meat powder on a dog's tongue produces salivation, but the sound of a tone—a neutral stimulus—does not. During the process of conditioning, the tone is repeatedly paired with the meat powder. After classical conditioning has taken place, the sound of the tone alone acts as a conditioned stimulus, producing salivation.

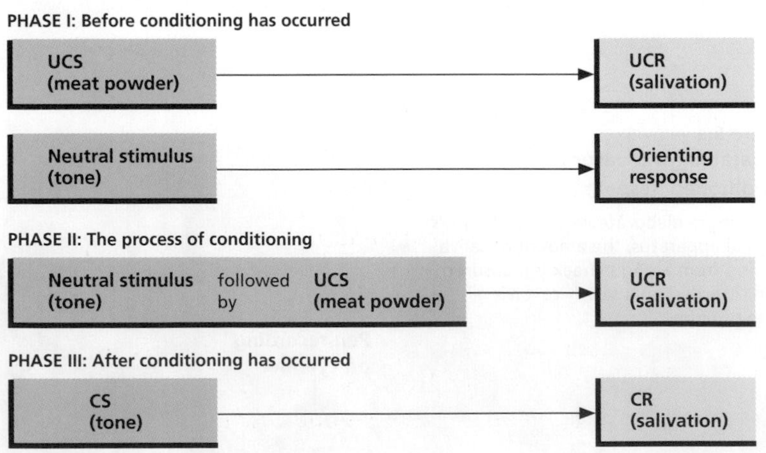

* From Bernstein et al., *Psychology*, 5th ed. Boston: Houghton Mifflin, 2000, 177–178. Copyright © 2000 by Houghton Mifflin Company. Reprinted with permission.

Vocabulary

Read the following questions about some of the vocabulary words that appear in the previous selection. Circle the letter of the correct answer.

1. In paragraph 1, what does the word *adrenaline* mean? "A flashing light on a control panel may make an airplane pilot's *adrenaline* flow, because it means that something may be wrong."
   a. anger
   b. a hormone in the body that is secreted due to stress
   c. blood
   d. saliva

2. In paragraph 2, Pavlov is referred to as having been a physiologist. What does a physiologist study?
   a. the human body and its parts
   b. animals
   c. plants
   d. insects

3. What is a stimulus? (paragraph 4)
   a. a reaction
   b. a response
   c. something that causes a response
   d. behavior

4. What does it mean to *elicit* something? "In other words, the tone by itself now *elicited* salivation." (paragraph 5)
   a. to draw
   b. to arrive
   c. to bring or draw something out
   d. to hide

Topic, Main Idea, Transitions, and Reading Visuals

Respond to the following questions by circling the letter of the correct answer.

1. What is the topic of paragraph 2?
   a. the Nobel Prize
   b. Pavlov's research
   c. experiments
   d. dogs

2. What is the main idea of paragraph 4?
   a. The first phase of Pavlov's experiment established the existence of a natural reflex and a neutral stimulus.
   b. A reflex is an automatic response to a stimulus.
   c. Music does not affect animals in any way.
   d. Dogs can be taught to enjoy good music.

3. Which of the following paragraphs begins with a transition word or phrase?
   a. paragraph 2
   b. paragraph 4
   c. paragraph 5
   d. paragraph 6

4. The two transitions in paragraph 5 are the
   a. series type
   b. time order type
   c. comparison/contrast type
   d. definition type

5. Which type of transition does NOT appear in paragraph 4?
   a. series
   b. time order
   c. cause/effect
   d. definition/example

6. According to Figure 5.2, in Phase III, a dog will
   a. salivate after being given meat powder.
   b. salivate after hearing a tone.
   c. salivate after hearing a tone while being given meat powder.
   d. stop salivating when given meat powder.

Practicing the Active Reading Strategy:

After You Read

Now that you have read the selection, answer the following questions, using the active reading strategies that are discussed on pages 30–33.

1. Identify and write down the point and purpose of this reading selection.
2. Besides the vocabulary words included in the exercise on page 249, are there any other vocabulary words that are unfamiliar to you? If so, write a list of them. When you have finished writing your list, look up each word in a dictionary and write the definition that best describes the word as it is used in the selection.
3. Predict any possible test questions that may be used on a test about the content of this selection.
4. How could you use the information contained in this selection? Does the information contained in the selection reinforce or contradict your ideas and experiences? Explain.

Questions for Discussion and Writing

Answer the following questions based on your reading of the selection. Write your answers on the blanks provided.

1. Did you find this selection interesting? Why or why not? Do the visuals that accompany the selection make the selection more or less interesting? Why? ______________________________

____

5

2. Think about your own life. Give one or two examples where you have been conditioned to respond in a certain way. ____________________

____

3. Summarize the three phases of classical conditioning. Use Pavlov's experiment as a guide. ____________________

____

Vocabulary: The Explanation Context Clue

In Chapter 4, you learned about the definition/restatement context clue. A second type of context clue is **explanation.** In this type of clue, the words, phrases, or sentences near an unfamiliar word will explain enough about that word to allow you to figure out its meaning. For example, read this next sentence, which comes from one of the paragraphs in this chapter:

> In 1941, the Japanese attacked America's Pearl Harbor. In 1942, 120,000 Japanese-Americans were rounded up and imprisoned in ***internment*** camps.

What does *internment* mean? There are a few explanation clues in this sentence. First of all, it's an adjective that describes a type of camp. Secondly, it's where people are imprisoned. Therefore, you can conclude that it must refer to a place where large numbers of people are confined or locked up.

5

Vocabulary Exercise 1

The following examples all come from paragraphs in this chapter and Chapter 4. In each one, use the explanation context clue to help you determine the meaning of the boldfaced, italicized word, and write a definition for this word on the blank provided.

1. A learning disability is defined as a significant ***discrepancy*** between measured intelligence and academic performance. Thomas Edison, for instance, did not have a low IQ, yet he experienced problems with reading, writing, and math in school. ____________________
2. For example, *Reader's Digest,* a ***compendium*** of "must-read" articles, and *Time,* a weekly news summary, came out in 1922 and 1923, respectively.

   ____
3. Finally, press slightly against your tongue, ***pursing*** the lips as needed, and blow. ____________________

4. Eating breakfast foods that are high in sugar and carbohydrates, such as doughnuts, causes blood sugar to rise quickly. By mid-morning, blood sugar drops rapidly, making you feel ***lethargic*** and irritable. ____________

5. *Ecotourism* is relatively low-impact group travel or tour packages to destinations in nature. In other words, ecotourists travel to natural areas without disturbing the environment or contributing to the destruction of resources. For example, they might go to the South Pacific to see forests and endangered birds, or canoe down the Amazon in South America. Engaging in this type of travel has several benefits. It respects the diversity and fragility of the environment of the Earth, so you won't cause more damage to natural resources or animal habitats. It also allows you to help support ***indigenous*** cultures with your travel dollars. It offers you opportunities to broaden your horizons, too, because you travel off the beaten path into excitingly different places. ____________

____

6. In today's busy world, do you have an understudy if something unexpected comes up? First, organize a handful of friends, neighbors, or relatives and ***deputize*** one another; you look out for them, and they look out for you. ____________

____

7. New York City is renowned for its high-end, celebrity-chef food culture. It also offers a host of budget-priced options for good food and drinks. Many of the best meal deals are found in the ethnic ***enclaves*** that dot the city. ____________

8. New Orleans lies below sea level, in a bowl bordered by ***levees*** that fend off Lake Pontchartrain to the north and the Mississippi River to the south and west. ____________

Vocabulary Exercise 2

Read the following passage, and then use explanation context clues to write a definition of each boldfaced, italicized word on the blanks provided:

If you tuned into Court TV recently, or even if you just glanced at the paper, it was hard to miss the Massachusetts case in which Thomas Junta, a 44-year-old truck driver, was convicted of involuntary manslaughter in the death of his son's hockey coach, Michael Costin. Even in the already dismal ***annals*** of American sports excess, this was a gruesome incident: while several children—including their sons—watched, Junta, who outweighed Costin by more than 100 pounds, pounded the other man senseless on the ice-rink floor. Yet those of us who spend much time in rinks have had to acknowledge that the Junta case shouldn't have come as a huge surprise. It was entirely ***foreseeable*** that when one enraged sports parent finally succeeded in killing another, it would be a hockey dad who was responsible.

In my experience, both as a coach and a spectator, hockey parents are worse than even Little League parents, who seem meek by comparison. Hockey parents are louder, more ***volatile,*** more apt to shout abuse at the players, the officials, and one another. At almost any game, there are the leatherlungs, too frenzied to sit, who stand and bang on the glass. It is not just the fathers, either. When my son was a peewee hockey player, two opposing moms got into a fight at our local rink, and the police had to be summoned to break them up.

What is it with hockey? To begin with, it is a fast, physical game that encourages players and spectators alike to burn at a much higher emotional temperature than does baseball or even football, both of which have built-in cooling-off periods. And hockey is, of course, the only game in which—on the professional level, anyway—fistfights routinely break out and in which it is customary for every team to carry on its ***roster*** an "enforcer," whose main job is to intimidate the opposition. The game has underlying it a longstanding cult of toughness. What casual fans—and apparently many parents—don't understand, though, is that a lot of hockey fighting is ***ritualistic.*** There is more pushing and posturing than there is actual punching, and the whole show—the pointing, the snarling, the chest-bumping—may actually serve as a kind of safety valve.

Junta's defense contended that the trouble all began because he was trying to stop the rough stuff. The practice Costin was supervising was supposed to be noncontact, but at the end of the session, some of the older boys began slashing and elbowing the younger ones, including Junta's son. Junta complained and was told, "That's hockey." The two men thereupon engaged in their own version of what happens when Darius Kasparaitis, say, squares off against Tie Domi,[1] and with no one to intervene except some scared kids, the role playing quickly turned deadly. . . .

1. Darius Kasparaitis and Tie Domi are two hockey players known for a very aggressive playing style that sometimes results in fighting.

5

. . . Hockey has become a kind of recipe for parental overinvolvement—an extreme example of what is happening to youth sports in general. In no other team sport, for example—except maybe swimming—do parents so religiously attend not just games but practices (and at a swimming practice there is a lot less for them to get excited about). Because youth hockey in this country still retains a certain ***novelty,*** moreover—and because so many parents are themselves new to the game—there is less of a reality check on parental ambition. Just a little success can fuel inflated dreams of college scholarships (which are in fact harder to come by in hockey than in almost any other sport) and even pro careers; it's not merely a player some parents are looking after—it's an investment.

And hockey may have become a vehicle for something else. Not even at a youth football game do you hear grown-ups cheer so loudly for hits and slams and ***bray*** so avidly for more. Why, at a time of nonstop parental effort to reduce risks for our kids, would we encourage them to play such a rough and aggressive game? Could it be that we are asking our offspring to discharge the frustrations and aggressions that we no longer have any outlet for? There is a better solution: adult hockey, which is also growing at an ***unprecedented*** rate and offers to the novice and the veteran alike the old-time satisfaction of bruising and getting bruised—and even scoring once in a while. If Thomas Junta and Michael Costin had both been playing hockey, instead of just watching the kids, Costin might still be alive.*

1. annals: ____________________
2. foreseeable: ____________________
3. volatile: ____________________
4. roster: ____________________
5. ritualistic: ____________________
6. novelty: ____________________
7. bray: ____________________
8. unprecedented: ____________________

* Adapted from Charles McGrath, "Ice Sturm," *New York Times Magazine,* January 20, 2002. Copyright © 2002 by the New York Times Company. Reprinted by permission.

READING STRATEGY: Summarizing

When you **summarize** a reading selection, you briefly restate, in your own words, its most important ideas. A summary usually focuses on the most general points, which include the overall main idea and some of the major supporting details. As a result, summaries are much shorter than the original material. A paragraph can usually be summarized in a sentence or two, an article can be summarized in a paragraph, and a typical textbook chapter can be summarized in a page or two.

Summarizing is an important reading skill that you will use for three specific academic purposes: studying, completing assignments and tests, and incorporating source material into research projects.

Studying. Writing summaries is an effective way to gain a better understanding of what you read. If you need to remember the information in a textbook chapter, for instance, you will know it more thoroughly after you have summarized its main ideas. Also, the act of writing down these ideas will help reinforce them in your memory.

Completing assignments and tests. Summaries are one of the most common types of college writing assignments. Professors in a variety of disciplines often ask students to summarize readings such as journal articles. Also, "summarize" is a common direction in tests that require written responses.

Incorporating source material into research projects. You will use summaries of other sources to support your ideas in research projects such as term papers.

To write a summary, follow these three steps:

1. Using active reading techniques, read and reread the original material until you understand it.
2. Identify the main idea and major supporting points. In particular, underline all of the topic sentences. You might also want to create an outline or map that diagrams the general and specific relationships among sentences (in a paragraph) or paragraphs (in an article or chapter).
3. Using your own words, write sentences that state the author's main idea along with the most important major details. Your paraphrase should be accurate; it should not add anything that did not appear in the original or omit anything important from the original. It should also be objective. In other words, don't offer your own reactions or opinions; just restate the author's points without

Continued

5

commenting on them. If you use a phrase from the original, enclose it in quotation marks to indicate that it is the author's words, not yours.

Follow the three steps described above to write a one- or two-paragraph summary of the following textbook passage:

Causes of the French Revolution

The example of the American Revolution was particularly important for France. The most populous country in Europe and among the most prosperous, France in the last half of the eighteenth century was a troubled society. The death of Louis XIV in 1715 had brought to the throne a five-year-old boy, Louis XV (1710–1774). Largely unconcerned with government, Louis was particularly interested in women, eating, and lock making. His son, Louis XVI (1754–1793), although well meaning, was weak and popularly seen as dominated by his wife, Marie Antoinette.

Neither of these monarchs, consequently, played a guiding role in the political life of the nation. A succession of ministers of varying ability governed the country, and policy lacked the consistency that an active monarch could have given it. Indicative[1] of the shift in political focus was the increasing marginalization[2] of Versailles[3] as the center of French culture and the return of Paris to that position.

In retrospect, historians after the French Revolution came to speak of France in the eighteenth century as the *ancien regime* (the old order). All phases of French life were dominated by an outmoded[4] social structure that endured primarily because it was legally defined and protected. All French citizens except the royal family were divided into three classes: the clergy, the nobility, and the third estate, by far the largest of the three, comprising the peasants, the artisans of the towns, and the middle class or *bourgeois*. Of France's twenty-four million people, only about 2 percent belonged to the clergy and nobility. Yet in a society in which land remained the greatest form of wealth, the other 98 percent owned only 60 percent of the landed property. This social group was the greatest force in causing the revolution.

1. **indicative:** pointing out; serving as a sign
2. **marginalization:** being confined to the outer or lower parts of society
3. **Versailles:** a city in north central France, known for its magnificent palace
4. **outmoded:** no longer in fashion

5

But there was a greater source of discontent among the third estate. The clergy and nobility paid almost no taxes. Moreover, while giving little or nothing to support it, the nobility enjoyed all the highest offices in the government; they also constituted the officer corps of the army. As for the clergy, this class had the right to levy[1] a tax, for its maintenance, on all agricultural goods produced by the third estate.

What made the situation volatile[2] was that for most of the eighteenth century the economy was expanding. Bankers, merchants, and other members of the middle class had accumulated great wealth, and many of the peasants were prosperous. Traditionally, there had been various avenues by which successful members of the third estate could work their way into the nobility, but in the course of the eighteenth century, these avenues had gradually been shut off by an aristocracy resolved not to dilute[3] its membership further. The upper bourgeois, therefore, felt excluded from the social and financial privileges to which their success entitled them.

Economic prosperity also entailed rising prices and higher living costs. The nobility and clergy, barred by law from entering commerce or industry to reap the profits of the boom, increasingly came to insist on their economic rights over the third estate. Indeed, this was the heyday[4] of lawyers employed by the upper classes to dredge up old, long-neglected rights over the peasantry. Moreover, although the bourgeoisie and the upper peasantry were profiting throughout most of the eighteenth century, the lower classes, at least in the last half of the century, saw their wages rise more slowly than prices and their standard of living fall.

The most immediate cause of the revolution, which began in the summer of 1789, was the government's financial crisis. Because some of the wealthiest elements in the country were exempt from taxation, the state could not balance its budget. An important element in the French public debt was the expense incurred by helping the Americans in their revolt against England. For years the enlightened advisers of the French king had endeavored[5] to abolish the tax privileges of the clergy and

Continued

5

1. **levy:** collect
2. **volatile:** violent, explosive
3. **dilute:** to make thinner or weaker
4. **heyday:** period of greatest popularity, success, or power
5. **endeavored:** worked

the nobility, but these two orders had solidly resisted the effort. The king could proclaim the necessary laws, but the courts, completely controlled by the nobility, would never enforce them. Finally, in 1788, the royal government simply abolished the old court system and created a new one.

The result was an aristocratic revolt: the army officers and the king's officials at Paris and in the provinces refused to serve, and the whole state was brought to a halt. Unable to persevere in the attempt at reform, the king (Louis XVI) acceded to the nobility's demands that, for the first time since 1614, a National Assembly be called to settle the nation's problems. The nobility clearly intended to gain more control over the king's government through an assembly that, by tradition, gave them and the clergy (dominated by the aristocracy) two votes, against one for the third estate.*

5

Reading Visuals: Pie Charts

In previous chapters, you've examined organizational charts and flow charts. A third kind of chart is called a **pie chart.** This visual aid is a circle that is divided into wedges or slices, like the pieces of a pie. The purpose of a pie chart is to show the composition of something; it indicates the amounts of each part that make up the whole. Each part is identified with a percentage or other quantity that indicates its size in relation to all of the other parts. One common use of pie charts is to represent financial information such as budgets or expenditures.

Pie charts contain the following parts:

- **Title.** The title identifies the whole entity that is being divided into parts.
- **Lines.** The lines radiate from the center of the circle, dividing the pie into pieces that represent the amount of each part. These pieces are different sizes because they are designed to be proportional to the whole.
- **Labels for names of parts.** Each piece is labeled to identify one part and its quantity in relation to the whole.

* Adapted from Frese Witt et al., *The Humanities*, 5th ed., Vol. 2. Boston: Houghton Mifflin, 1997, 290–291. Copyright © 1997 by Houghton Mifflin Company. Reprinted with permission.

- **Source line.** The source line identifies who collected or compiled the information.

These parts are labeled in the following pie chart.

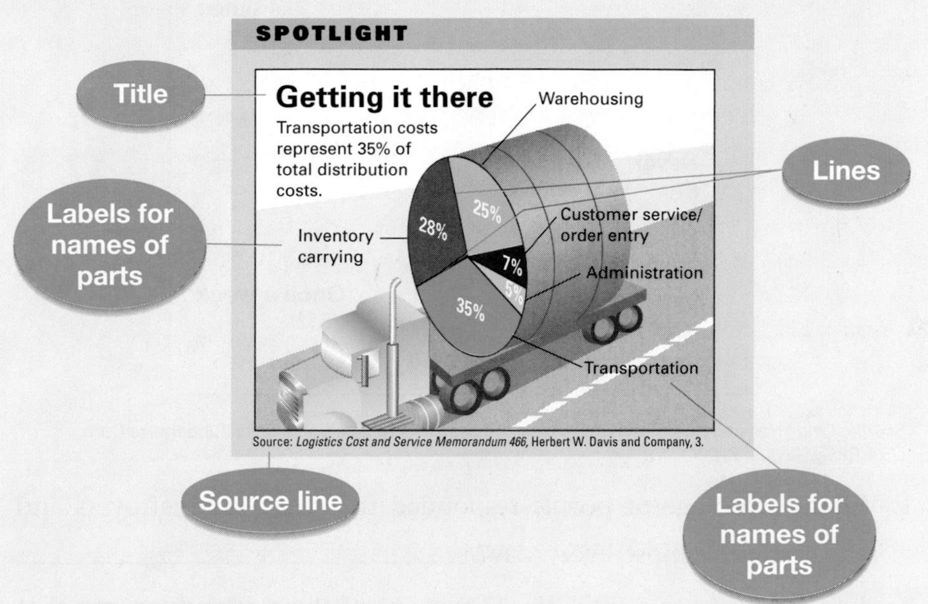

Source: "Getting It There," pie chart from *Logistics Cost and Service Memorandum 466*, Herbert W. Davis and Company, 3. Used by permission of Herbert W. Davis and Company.

To read a pie chart, first look at its title so you'll know the whole entity that is being divided. Then, read each label and amount. Try to summarize in your own words the relationships you see and notice the biggest part, the smallest part, and parts that are about equal.

The pie chart "Getting It There" shows the amounts of five different kinds of distribution costs involved in getting products to consumers. The largest piece of the pie is transportation costs, which account for 35 percent of all costs. Inventory carrying is the next biggest cost, and administration is the smallest. The percentages all add up to 100 percent to represent the whole. The pie chart is cleverly drawn as a load carried on a truck to increase visual interest.

Now, study the pie charts "Pop it into the microwave" and "Where the Gifts Go" and then answer the questions that follow.

Continued

5

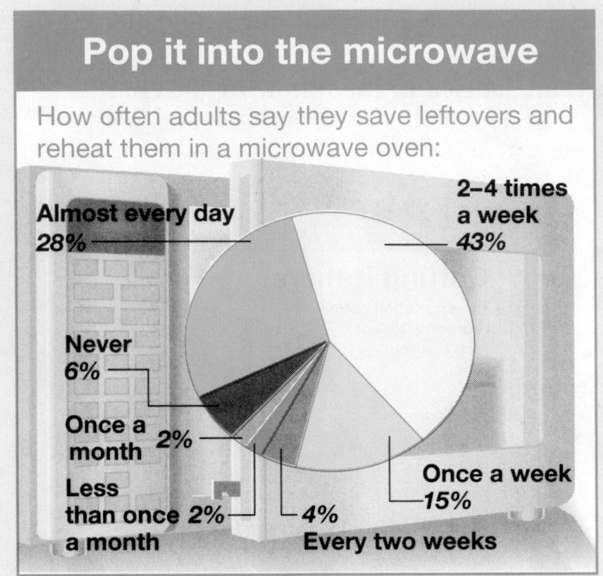

Source: Cindy Hall and Keith Simmons, Opinion Research Corp. International for Tupperware Corp. *USA Today,* August 2, 2001, ID.

5

1. What percentage of people responded that they save leftovers and reheat them almost every day? ____________
2. How many times a week do 43 percent of the respondents say that they save leftovers and reheat them? ____________
3. What percentage of people save and reheat once a month? ________
4. What percentage of people never save and reheat? ____________

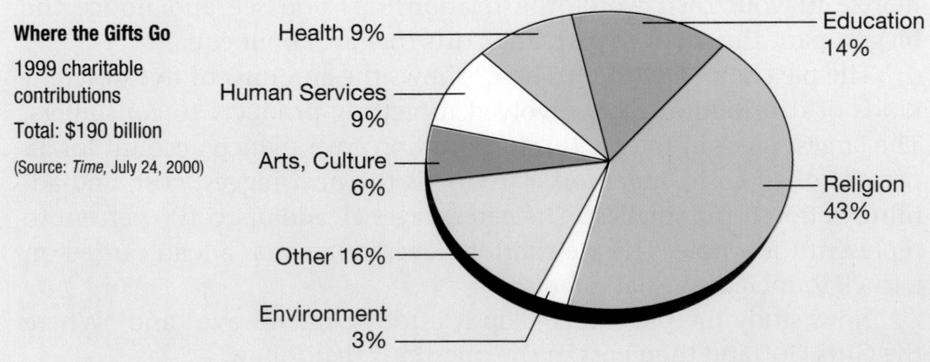

Source: Brehm et al., *Social Psychology*, 5th ed. Boston: Houghton Mifflin, 2002, 383. Copyright © 2002 by Houghton Mifflin Company. Reprinted with permission.

5. What were the total 1999 charitable contributions, according to the pie chart? ______

6. What percentage of charitable contributions went toward religious organizations? ______

7. Which group received the least amount of charitable contributions?

______

8. Which group received 6% of the charitable contributions represented on the pie chart? ______

5

CHAPTER 5 TESTS

Name ____ Date ____________________

TEST 1

Circle the letter of the best transition or set of transitions for the blanks in each of the sentences and paragraphs below.

1. Work during adolescence serves three important functions. __________, it facilitates the transition from school to work. __________, it provides structure for involvement in family- and school-related activities. __________, it provides an arena outside of home and school for gaining social experience and the material rewards needed to have an independent life with peers. How work influences adolescent mental health and adjustment depends on the type and level of workplace stress, the relevance of job-related skills to future careers, and the compatibility[1] between the demands and experiences of work and school.*

   a. First, Second, Finally
   b. Consequently, Thus, As a result
   c. First, Next, Meanwhile
   d. On the other hand, Conversely, In contrast

2. Why did Motorola, a successful company in the early and mid-1990s, experience a downward spiral that seemed almost irreversible? __________, Motorola fell behind in digital telephone technology and lost crucial market leadership to Finland's Nokia Group. The semiconductor market also shifted, leaving the firm's semiconductor business poorly positioned for new technologies and areas of new growth potential. __________, because the firm did about 24 percent of its business in Asia, the currency crisis that wracked[2] that continent also hit Motorola hard. __________, a $6 billion iridium communications satellite that the company invented,

1. **compatibility:** state of harmony or agreeable combination
2. **wracked:** destroyed

* From Seifert et al., *Lifespan Development,* 2nd ed. Boston: Houghton Mifflin, 2000, 373. Copyright © 2000 by Houghton Mifflin Company. Reprinted with permission.

For additional tests, see the Test Bank.

financed, and helped build missed its launch date, failed to attract customers, and eventually had to file for bankruptcy protection.*

a. First of all, Furthermore, Second
b. For one thing, Moreover, In addition
c. Hence, As a consequence, So
d. First, For example, For instance

3. Many of the country's biggest advertisers, including Coca-Cola, General Motors, and Procter & Gamble, are finding ways other than television commercials to put their goods and their messages in front of consumers.

_____________, Revlon is running minimovies in theaters, American Express airs short films on its web site, and General Motors' Hummer H2 gets almost as much face time as the TV crime specialists on *CSI Miami*.†

a. However
b. Therefore
c. For instance
d. Finally

4. Sometimes speakers aim to teach an audience how something works or how to do something. On a popular show, Emeril Legasse shows his television audience how to prepare gourmet meals. ___________, viewers can learn how to build a bookcase on *The New Yankee Workshop*.‡

a. Similarly
b. Next
c. On the contrary
d. As an illustration

5. Twenty years ago the personal computer was the province of a very small group of experts and hobbyists. ___________, one stands in virtually every office and in millions of U.S. households. ___________ 1985, when people said a "portable personal computer," they meant a suitcase-size box that weighed more than ten pounds and was difficult to lug onto a train or plane. ___________, slim "notebook" computers that weigh a couple of pounds are almost standard equipment for businesspeople who work regularly in train stations and airports. ___________, many students even use them to take notes in classes and libraries.§

a. Now, In, Today, Now
b. First, Second, Third, Lastly
c. So, Thus, Hence, As a consequence
d. For example, For instance, To illustrate, Specifically

* Adapted from Griffin, *Management,* 7th ed. Boston: Houghton Mifflin, 2002, 4.
† Adapted from Betsy Streisand, "Tuning Out TV," *U.S. News and World Report,* May 24, 2004, 46.
‡ Adapted from Andrews et al., *Public Speaking*. Boston: Houghton Mifflin, 1999, 299.
§ Adapted from Turow, *Media Today*. Boston: Houghton Mifflin, 1999, 293.

6. __________ great white sharks grow and reproduce slowly, their recent decline puts them at risk of extinction unless they are protected throughout their range. We need to find out more about their migration and movements, and how they utilize the South African coast, in order to evaluate whether the protection they receive in these waters is working. In 1991, South Africa became the first country to legally protect white sharks in its 200-mile Economic Exclusive Zone. __________, Namibia, Australia, the United States, and Malta have followed suit with similar legislation.*

   a. Similarly, On the contrary
   b. Next, For example
   c. Because, As a result
   d. As a result, Even though

7. There are routine ways in which safety is guaranteed in any organized society. __________ we have a police force to protect us from crime, we have a fire department to protect us from disaster.†

   a. For this reason
   b. Just as
   c. Conversely
   d. Soon

8. Schools run on things: pencils, books, paper, heat, hot lunches, sanitary toilets, lights, and construction paper, to name a few things. They need a facilitator to get these things. __________, principals keep teachers supplied so that they, in turn, can carry out the aims of the school.‡

   a. Specifically
   b. Eventually
   c. Unfortunately
   d. In contrast

9. Daily newspaper circulation has hovered around 60 million for the past quarter century, __________ the fact the nation's adult population has grown by more than a third. National and suburban dailies, __________, increased in number and circulation during the past few decades. __________ most of the three-thousand-plus suburban papers are weekly, a couple of hundred do appear at least five days a week.§

   a. in spite of, in contrast, Although
   b. likewise, too, In like manner

5

* Adapted from Ramon Bonfil, "Spying on Great White Sharks," *Wildlife Conversation,* March/April 2004, 7.

† Adapted from Andrews et al., *Public Speaking*. Boston: Houghton Mifflin, 1999, 329.

‡ Adapted from Ryan and Cooper, *Those Who Can, Teach,* 9th ed. Boston: Houghton Mifflin, 2000, 36.

§ Adapted from Turow, *Media Today*. Boston: Houghton Mifflin, 1999, 125.

c. now, then, Next
d. to illustrate, for example, For instance

10. Job rotation involves systematically moving employees from one job to another. A worker in a warehouse might unload trucks on Monday, carry incoming inventory[1] to storage on Tuesday, verify invoices on Wednesday, pull outgoing inventory from storage on Thursday, and load trucks on Friday. __________, the jobs do not change, but instead, workers move from job to job.*

a. For this reason
b. Over time
c. Thus
d. Nevertheless

11. Agriculture and settled village life emerged in Egypt around 5000 B.C. __________ 4000 B.C. villages had grown into towns, each controlling a strip of territory. About a thousand years __________, around 3100 B.C., the Nile Valley had become one unified kingdom of Egypt, with a capital city perhaps at Memphis. __________, around 3000 B.C., Menes, king of Upper Egypt, is said to have conquered Lower Egypt and united the two into a single realm.†

a. Hence, as a result, So
b. By, later, Then
c. One, another, Moreover
d. More precisely, in one case, For instance

12. Southerners opposed John Quincy Adams'[2] policies on tariffs[3] and finances __________ they feared the increase in federal power that his policies implied and __________ they disliked tariffs in general.‡

a. because, because
b. for one thing, furthermore
c. then, after
d. just as, despite

13. Adolescents who have atypical[4] physical characteristics because of inherited or acquired abnormalities sometimes face more serious psychological

1. **inventory:** the goods or materials a company or business has on hand
2. **John Quincy Adams:** sixth president of the United States
3. **tariffs:** taxes imposed by a government on imported or exported goods
4. **atypical:** not usual

* From Griffin, *Management,* 7th ed. Boston: Houghton Mifflin, 2002, 328.

† Adapted from Noble et al., *Western Civilization,* 3rd ed. Boston: Houghton Mifflin, 2002, 23.

‡ Adapted from Berkin et al., *Making America,* 2nd ed. Boston: Houghton Mifflin, 2001, 193.

problems regarding their bodies. ___________, children who are badly scarred or whose movements are spasmodic[1] must learn to cope with these added burdens.*

a. Conversely
b. Lastly
c. For example
d. Furthermore

14. ___________ Democrat Bill Clinton was in favor of "big government," George W. Bush, a Republican, favored smaller government and less intervention in the lives of ordinary citizens by government.

a. Before
b. Just as
c. Whereas
d. Also

15. Studies of how brain injuries affect memory provide evidence about the brain regions involved in various kinds of memory. ___________, damage to the hippocampus, which is part of the limbic system,[2] often results in anterograde amnesia, a loss of memory for an event occurring after the injury.†

a. Next
b. On the contrary
c. Secondly
d. For instance

16. For jurors, the believability of a witness often depends as much (or even more) on *how* the witness presents evidence as on the content or relevance of that evidence. Many jurors are impressed, ___________, by witnesses who give lots of details about what they saw or heard.‡

a. even though
b. similarly
c. meanwhile
d. for example

17. *Gerrymandering* is the process of drawing district lines to benefit one group or another, and it can result in some extremely strange shapes by the time the state politicians are through. ___________ of gerrymandering is partisan[3] gerrymandering, with the party controlling the redistricting process drawing lines to maximize the number of seats it wins. A

1. **spasmodic:** convulsive or jerky
2. **limbic system:** a group of interconnected deep brain structures
3. **partisan:** supporting one particular party, cause, or idea

* From Seifert and Hoffnung, *Child and Adolescent Development,* 5th ed. Boston: Houghton Mifflin, 2000, 446.

† From Bernstein et al., *Psychology,* 5th ed. Boston: Houghton Mifflin, 2000, 241.

‡ From Bernstein et al., *Psychology,* 6th ed. Boston: Houghton Mifflin, 2003, 246. Copyright © 2003 by Houghton Mifflin Company. Reprinted with permission.

5

Democratic legislature, __________, might draw a district so that it splits a conservative town or community, reducing its ability to elect a Republican representative.*

a. One example, for instance
b. One consequence, as a result
c. In spite, instead
d. In the beginning, in the end

18. __________ 1999, what seemed like a political miracle occurred: the federal government did not have a deficit.[1] That year it stopped spending more money than it collected in taxes. This was the first time since the early 1960s that there was no deficit. Of course, __________ all those years when the federal government did have an annual deficit, it had to borrow money to pay its bills. __________ 1999, the total amount of the national debt was more than 5 trillion dollars.†

a. Despite, in contrast to, Whereas
b. In one case, to illustrate, Specifically
c. Like, similar to, Along the same line
d. In, during, By

5

19. There are many TV shows whose primary subject is politics. __________, CNN and C-SPAN, sometimes called "America's Town Hall," offer news around the clock. __________ include weekend shows like *Meet the Press, Washington Week in Review,* and *Face the Nation,* which highlight the week's coverage of politics.‡

a. For example, Other examples
b. In contrast, Just the opposite
c. Therefore, For this reason
d. Today, Next

20. There are several reasons for joining a group. At a fundamental level, people may have an innate[2] need to belong to groups, stemming from evolutionary pressures that increased people's chances of survival and reproduction when in groups rather than in isolation. This need may __________ be driven by the desire to feel protected against threat and

1. **deficit:** shortfall of money; inadequate funds

2. **innate:** in-born

---

* From Barbour and Wright, *Keeping the Republic*. Boston: Houghton Mifflin, 2001, 161.

† Adapted from Wilson and DiIulio, *American Government,* 8th ed. Boston: Houghton Mifflin, 2001, 459.

‡ Adapted from Barbour and Wright, *Keeping the Republic*. Boston: Houghton Mifflin, 2001, 378.

uncertainty in everyday life. __________, people join specific groups in order to accomplish things that they cannot accomplish as individuals. Neither symphonies nor football games can be played by one person alone, and many types of work require team effort. __________, people join groups because of the social status and identity that they offer.*

a. therefore, Thus, Hence
b. also, Further, In addition
c. in addition, For one, Third
d. on the contrary, Just as, Likewise

TEST 2

Read each of the following paragraphs and respond to the questions that follow by circling the letter of the correct answer.

(1) Even though voters may not know a lot about the issues, that does not mean that issues play no role in elections or that voters respond irrationally to them. (2) For example, V. O. Key, Jr., looked at those voters who switched from one party to another between elections and found that most of them switched in a direction consistent with their own interests. (3) As Key put it, the voters are not fools.

(4) Moreover, voters may know a lot more than we suppose about issues that really matter to them. (5) They may have hazy, even erroneous,[1] views about monetary policy, Central America, and the trade deficit, but they are likely to have a very good idea about whether unemployment is up or down, prices at the supermarket are stable or rising, or crime is a problem in their neighborhoods. (6) And on some issues—such as abortion, school prayer, and race relations—they are likely to have some strong principles that they want to see politicians obey.

(7) Contrary to what we learn in our civics classes, representative government does not require voters to be well informed on the issues. (8) If it were our duty as citizens to have accurate facts and sensible ideas about how best to negotiate with foreign adversaries,[2] stabilize the value of the dollar, revitalize failing industries, and keep farmers prosperous, we might as well forget about citizenship and head for the beach. (9) It would be a full-time job, and

1. **erroneous:** wrong, incorrect 2. **adversaries:** opponents or enemies

* Adapted from Brehm, et al., *Social Psychology,* 5th ed. Boston: Houghton Mifflin, 2002, 267–268. Copyright © 2002 by Houghton Mifflin Company. Reprinted with permission.

then some, to be a citizen. (10) Politics would take on far more importance in our lives than most of us would want, given our need to earn a living and our belief in the virtues of limited government.*

1. Which of the following sentences starts with a definition/example transition?
   a. sentence 1
   b. sentence 2
   c. sentence 3
   d. sentence 4

2. Which of the following pairs of sentences start with series transitions?
   a. sentences 1 and 3
   b. sentences 4 and 6
   c. sentences 7 and 8
   d. sentences 7 and 9

3. Which sentence begins with a contrast transition?
   a. sentence 2
   b. sentence 4
   c. sentence 6
   d. sentence 7

4. Which of the following is NOT a type of transition found in paragraph 1?
   a. contrast
   b. definition
   c. time order
   d. series

5. Using your knowledge of transitions, identify the pattern that organizes the details in paragraph 2.
   a. definition
   b. time order
   c. series
   d. cause/effect

(1) For some time now, college textbook publishers have been struggling with a significant problem. (2) The subject matter that comprises a particular field, such as management, chemistry, or history, continues to increase in size, scope, and complexity. (3) Thus, authors feel compelled to add more and more information to new editions of their textbooks. (4) Publishers have also sought to increase the visual sophistication of their texts by adding more color and photographs. (5) At the same time, some instructors find it increasingly difficult to cover the material in longer textbooks. (6) Moreover, longer and more attractive textbooks cost more money to produce, resulting in higher selling prices to students.

(7) Publishers have considered a variety of options to confront this situation. (8) One option is to work with authors to produce shorter and more economical books. (9) Another option is to cut back on the complimentary supplements that publishers provide to instructors as a way of lowering the

* From Wilson and DiIulio, *American Government,* 8th ed. Boston: Houghton Mifflin, 2001, 201.

overall cost of producing a book. (10) Still another option is to eliminate traditional publishing altogether and provide educational resources via CD-ROM, the Internet, or other new media.

(11) Confounding[1] this situation, of course, is cost. (12) Profit margins in the industry are such that managers feel the need to be cautious and conservative. (13) As a result, they cannot do everything and must not risk alienating[2] their users by taking too radical a step. (14) Remember, too, that publishers must consider the concerns of three different sets of customers: the instructors who make adoption decisions, the bookstores that buy educational materials for resale, and students who buy the books for classroom use and then often resell them back to the bookstore.*

6. Which of the following sentences begins with a cause/effect transition?

a. sentence 6 c. sentence 10
b. sentence 8 d. sentence 13

7. Using your knowledge of transitions, identify the pattern that organizes the details in paragraph 2.

a. time order c. cause/effect
b. series d. definition/example

5

8. Which of the following sentences from paragraph 1 begins with a time-order transition?

a. sentence 2 c. sentence 5
b. sentence 3 d. sentence 6

(1) Managers in international businesses must attend to various organizing issues. (2) For example, General Electric has operations scattered around the globe. (3) The firm has made the decision to give local managers a great deal of responsibility for how they run their business. (4) In contrast, many Japanese firms give managers of their foreign operations relatively little responsibility. (5) As a result, those managers must frequently travel back to Japan to present problems or get decisions approved. (6) Managers in an international business must address the basic issues of organization structure and design, managing change, and dealing with human resources.†

1. **confounding:** worsening 2. **alienating:** turning away

* Adapted from Griffin, *Management,* 7th ed. Boston: Houghton Mifflin, 2002, 30.
† Adapted from Griffin, *Management,* 7th ed. Boston: Houghton Mifflin, 2002, 155.

9. Which of the following sentences does NOT begin with a transition?
   a. sentence 1
   b. sentence 2
   c. sentence 4
   d. sentence 5
10. Which of the following patterns is NOT represented in this paragraph through the use of a transition?
   a. definition/example
   b. contrast
   c. cause and effect
   d. time order

5

CHAPTER 6

Patterns of Organization

GOALS FOR CHAPTER 6

- Define the term *pattern* as it relates to paragraphs.
- Name the five broad patterns for organizing supporting details in paragraphs.
- Recognize words in topic sentences that indicate certain patterns.
- Recognize supporting details within a series pattern.
- Recognize supporting details within a time-order pattern.
- Recognize supporting details within a cause/effect pattern.
- Recognize supporting details within a comparison/contrast pattern.
- Recognize supporting details within a definition pattern.
- Take notes on a reading selection.
- Read and understand information in a line graph.

6

Now that you've practiced examining supporting details and transitions, you're ready to look at some common patterns for arranging those details. A **pattern** is a consistent form or method for arranging things. To find out what you already know about patterns of organization in paragraphs, take the pre-test below.

TEST YOURSELF

Look at the following paragraphs and decide which pattern of organization arranges the details. Write a checkmark next to the correct pattern in the list below each paragraph.

1. Most professional grill jockeys prefer charcoal to gas and with good reason. Charcoal generally burns hotter than gas, so you get a more truly grilled taste. Charcoal grills are more versatile than gas grills: it's easier to toss wood chips or herbs on the coals, and you get a better smoke flavor.

Not to mention the fact that they give you something to do during the barbecue (in other words, they require constant attention), which will make you feel like a real pit master, not a cook whose stove happens to be outdoors. Charcoal grills cost a lot less than gas grills, and you can use them to burn both charcoal and wood. Visit a barbecue festival, like Memphis in May or the Kansas City Royal, and you won't find a gas grill around for miles.*

_____ series
_____ time order
_____ cause/effect
_____ comparison/contrast
_____ definition

2. Any memory of a specific event that happened while you were present is defined as an *episodic memory*. It is a memory of an episode, or event, in your life. For example, what you had for dinner yesterday, what you did last summer, or where you were last Friday night are episodic memories.†

_____ series
_____ time order
_____ cause/effect
_____ comparison/contract
_____ definition

3. There are several unconventional ways to get yourself out of bed, as suggested by readers of Oprah Winfrey's magazine, *O*. One thing you can do if you are having trouble getting out of bed is to get a dog. As long as it has to go out, you have to get up. Another thing you can do is place a huge bird feeder outside the bedroom window so the neighborhood robins serve as your alarm clock. You can also do yoga. It is the most relaxing way to bring your energy level up. One reader suggested having children and remarked that it is less relaxing than yoga but equally effective!‡

_____ series
_____ time order
_____ cause/effect
_____ comparison/contrast
_____ definition

4. There are several healthy effects of eating a low-fat diet, particularly for patients with a history of heart disease or high cholesterol. You can lower your blood fats and maintain a healthy heart. Many patients have also

* Adapted from Steven Raichlen, "Cooking Outside: What Are Your Options?" *Consumers' Research*, August 2001, 29.

† Adapted from Bernstein and Nash, *Essentials of Psychology*, 2nd ed. Boston: Houghton Mifflin, 2002, 181. Copyright © 2002 by Houghton Mifflin Company. Reprinted with permission.

‡ Adapted from Melissa Gotthardt, "Rise and Shine," *O* Magazine, September 2001, 86.

6

reported lower cholesterol and a higher energy level than before. Studies have also shown that people who eat low fat or a diet rich in vegetables and grains feel better, live longer, and have more stamina[1] than those patients who do not change their diets or adapt a healthy lifestyle.

______ series ______ comparison/contrast

______ time order ______ definition

______ cause/effect

5. Before beginning an exercise program, there are several steps you should take. First, consult a doctor. Many people jump into an exercise program without getting confirmation from their physician that what they are about to undertake is safe and will be effective. Then, do research to decide what type of activity you want to engage in. For instance, if you are a homebody, joining a gym or a running group may not be the best thing for you to do, but doing indoor yoga or aerobic exercise may be the right thing for you to do. Next, start slow. People who start exercising at their peak level of heart rate immediately lose stamina[1] quickly and their motivation to exercise. And lastly, look for someone to exercise with. Studies have shown that those who begin an exercise program with a partner stay with the program longer and have greater success in the long run.

______ series ______ comparison/contrast

______ time order ______ definition

______ cause/effect

6

To help readers find and comprehend supporting details more easily, paragraphs are usually organized according to at least one particular pattern. A **pattern** is a consistent, predictable form or method for putting something together. So, if you learn the most common patterns found within paragraphs, you'll be able to:

1. Recognize supporting details more quickly and accurately.
2. Better understand the relationships among supporting details.

Both of these skills are essential to good reading comprehension.

This chapter presents five broad patterns of organization: series, time order, cause/effect, comparison/contrast, and definition. Each pattern type is

1. **stamina:** physical strength

illustrated by itself first, but it's important to realize that paragraphs often combine two or more of these patterns. The end of this chapter presents some examples of paragraphs that are organized according to two or more patterns.

Topic Sentences

As you read the example paragraphs and learn to recognize each pattern, note how the **topic sentence** often indicates the paragraph's pattern of organization. Alert readers know how to watch for clues within topic sentences, clues that indicate how the information is arranged. When you can see these clues, you'll be able to predict the paragraph's framework and see more easily how the details fit into it as you read.

Series

Many paragraphs organize supporting details as a series of items. A **series** is a number of things that come one after the other in succession. Series within paragraphs are often in the form of reasons, examples, types, or some other kind of point. Series of items all equally support the paragraph's topic sentence. The following paragraph, for example, presents a series of three reasons in support of the topic sentence:

> I oppose the construction of the new golf course because golf courses damage our natural environment. For one thing, to create a golf course, many acres of land have to be cleared of their natural vegetation and habitat, graded,[1] and planted with non-native grass, trees, and shrubs. Native plants and animals are destroyed or driven out of their homes. Often, local streams have to be diverted, negatively impacting freshwater aquatic life and sometimes destroying wetlands. Second, golf courses cause damaging chemical pollution. All of that pretty green grass requires fertilizers, pesticides, herbicides, and fungicides. These chemicals run off into and contaminate our streams, rivers, lakes, and the ocean. A golf course's acres of grass also need a lot of water, which can strain the local community's water supplies. Finally, a golf course increases air pollution, for the constant lawn-mowing releases harmful gases into the atmosphere. For all of these reasons, a golf course is a bad idea.*

1. **graded:** leveled or smoothed

* Adapted from Surfrider Foundation, "Golf Courses: Friend or Foe?" www.surfrider.org/a-z/golf.htm.

A series paragraph might also present a series of examples. This specific pattern is referred to as **illustration**, for it illustrates the main idea with specific examples. The following paragraph, for instance, includes a series of examples:

> Several conditions are known to cause the body to ease its own pain. For example, endorphins[1] are released by immune cells that arrive at sites of inflammation. And during the late stages of pregnancy, an endorphin system is activated that will reduce the mother's labor pains. An endorphin system is also activated when people believe they are receiving a painkiller even when they are not. This may be one reason for the placebo effect.[2] Remarkably, the resulting pain inhibition[3] is experienced in the part of the body where it was expected to occur, but not elsewhere. Physical or psychological stress, too, can activate natural analgesic[4] systems. Stress-induced release of endorphins may account for cases in which injured soldiers and athletes continue to perform in the heat of battle or competition with no apparent pain.*

This paragraph offers a series of four equal examples to explain the topic sentence:

Example #1:	sites of inflammation
Example #2:	labor pains
Example #3:	people who believe they are receiving painkillers
Example #4:	injured soldiers or athletes

6

Another specific kind of series pattern is **classification**, which sorts things into a series of groups, types, or categories. The following paragraph is an example of a classification:

> Often, unpopular teenagers are placed in one of two groups: *rejected adolescents* and *neglected adolescents*. Rejected adolescents are rarely named as friends by their peers, and they are actively disliked. Many show high levels of aggression, others are extremely withdrawn, and still others are aggressive and withdrawn. They show poor attitudes

1. **endorphins:** hormones that reduce the sensation of pain
2. **placebo effect:** beneficial effects that arise from a patient's expectations about treatment rather than the treatment itself
3. **inhibition:** blockage or suppression
4. **analgesic:** related to pain reduction

* Adapted from Bernstein et al., *Psychology,* 6th ed. Boston: Houghton Mifflin, 2003, 135. Copyright © 2003 by Houghton Mifflin Company. Reprinted with permission.

toward school (including low attendance and achievement) and discipline problems. Neglected teenagers are rarely named by their peers as best friends, but they are not actively disliked. Members of this group show little problem behavior but are not physically attractive, do not seem to have similar interests as other teens, and are not involved in activities socially valued by other adolescents.*

This paragraph classifies all unpopular teenagers into two groups, rejected and neglected. Minor supporting details then provide descriptive information about each group.

Yet another type of series pattern is **division**, which divides a subject into a series of main parts and describes each part. For example, read the following paragraph:

A landfill has six basic parts. The first is the bottom liner system. The bottom liner prevents the trash from coming in contact with the outside soil, particularly the groundwater. It is usually some type of durable, puncture-resistant synthetic plastic 30-100 millimeters thick. The second part of a landfill is the cells, the area where trash is stored. Within each cell is one day's worth of compacted garbage. The third part is the storm water drainage system, which collects rainwater that falls on the landfill. The landfill must be kept as dry as possible to prevent substances from leaking out of it, so plastic drainage pipes and storm liners collect water from areas of the landfill and channel it to drainage ditches surrounding the landfill's base. The fourth part, the leachate collection system, collects water that does manage to get into the cells. It collects the water that contains *leachates*, or contaminated substances. The methane collection system, the fifth part, collects the methane gas that is formed during the breakdown of the trash inside the landfill. This gas is then vented, burned, or even used as a fuel source. The sixth and last part of the landfill is the covering or cap. This covering seals the compacted trash from the air and prevents vermin[1] (birds, rats, mice, flying insects, etc.) from getting into the trash.†

This paragraph divides landfills into six main parts and describes each one.

6

1. **vermin:** small, destructive animals or insects

---

* Adapted from Kaplan, *Adolescence*. Boston: Houghton Mifflin, 2004, 194. Copyright © 2004 by Houghton Mifflin Company. Reprinted with permission.

† Adapted from Craig C. Freudenrich, "How Landfills Work," HowStuffWorks.com, http://people.howstuffworks.com/landfill6.htm.

In Chapter 3, you learned how to map major and minor supporting details. In a map of a series paragraph, each new reason, example, type, or part is a major detail. For example, read the following series paragraph:

> To ensure the respectful display of the American flag, an emblem of our nation's pride and ideals, certain fundamental rules have been developed. First, the flag is always hung with the blue union at the top at the observer's left. Second, when displayed with other flags, the flag of the United States should be in the center and at the highest point. Third, the flag should never touch anything beneath it, including the ground or the floor. Fourth, the flag should never be used as wearing apparel, bedding, or drapery. Fifth, the flag should never be written upon, nor should it be used as a receptacle[1] for holding, carrying, or delivering anything.*

The details in this paragraph are organized into a series of rules. The main idea is, "There are rules that Americans follow to display the national flag," and the paragraph states five rules that support that idea.

Rule #1: Hang with the blue union at top.

Rule #2: Display in middle of and higher than other flags.

Rule #3: Don't let it touch anything beneath it.

Rule #4: Don't use it as clothing, bedding, or drapery.

Rule #5: Don't write on it or carry anything in it.

If you were to map this paragraph, it would look like this:

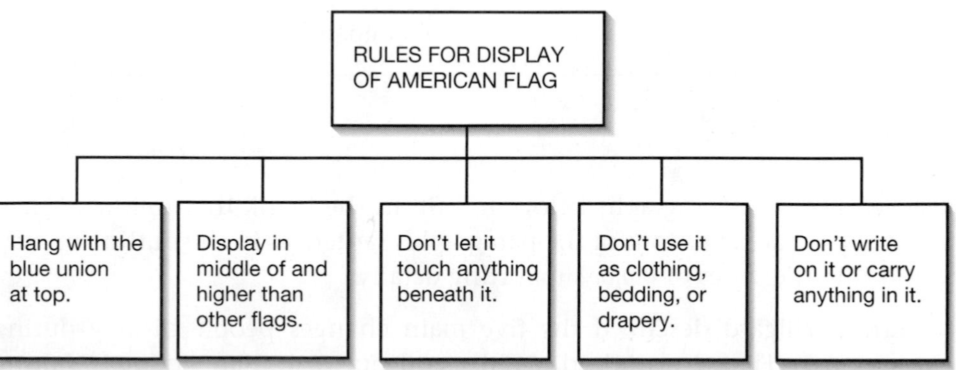

1. **receptacle:** container

* Adapted from *Our Flag* pamphlet. Roseland, NJ: Annin & Co., 1997.

6

Series of supporting details all equally develop the topic sentence, so they can often be presented in any order. Authors, however, may choose to arrange them according to their order of importance so they can emphasize one of the points by either presenting it first or saving it for last.

A paragraph's topic sentence will often indicate that the details will appear as a series of items. For example:

There are ***four types*** of dangerous drivers.

The Google Internet search engine is superior to all other search engines for ***three reasons.***

If you want to screen what your children see on the Internet, you can use ***one of several*** parental screening services such as Net Nanny, Cybersitter, or Cyber Patrol.

As you read, look for the following topic sentence words that indicate a series to follow.

Words and Phrases that Indicate a Series Pattern

Quantity word	***plus***	***a Series word***	
several		examples	kinds
many		reasons	characteristics
two, three, four, etc.		points	methods
a number of		classes	advantages
numerous		types	ways
		categories	forms
		groups	tips
		goals	

6

Exercise 6.1

Read each of the paragraphs below and fill in the blank that follows. Then, insert abbreviated versions of the paragraph's sentences in the outline or map to indicate the series of *major* supporting details.

1. Ernest Hilgard described the five main changes people display during hypnosis. First, hypnotized people tend not to initiate actions, waiting instead for the hypnotist's instructions. Second, subjects tend to ignore all but the hypnotist's voice and whatever it points out. Third, hypnosis enhances the ability to fantasize, so subjects more vividly imagine a scene or relive a memory. Fourth, hypnotized people display increased role

taking; they more easily act like a person of a different age or a member of the opposite sex, for example. Fifth, hypnotic subjects tend not to question if statements are true and more willingly accept apparent distortions of reality. Thus, a hypnotized person might shiver in a warm room if a hypnotist says it is snowing.*

Word(s) in the topic sentence that indicate a series: ________________

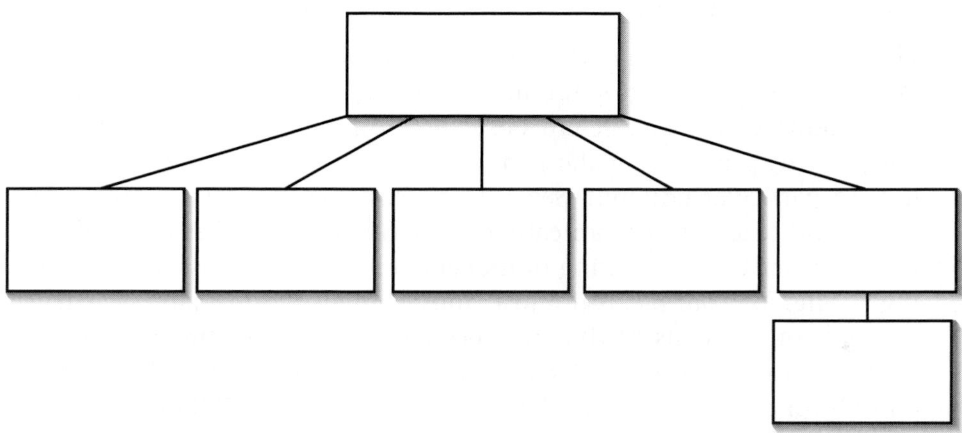

2. There are several things teachers can do to turn students' parents into allies. One way is to prepare a short statement to be carried home for the year. Stress that you and they are in a partnership to help their child and have a productive year. Further, let them know how to get in touch with you and that you are looking forward to meeting them. A second suggestion is that once you have established disciplinary and homework policies, a copy should be sent home for parental sign-off. Third, on the first day, get the home and office telephone numbers of each student's parent or parents. Fourth, it is a good idea to call all parents early in the fall. Finally, if problems with a particular student arise or persist throughout the year, insist on a parent visit.†

   Word(s) in the topic sentence that indicate a series: ________________

   I. ____

      A. ____

6

* Adapted from Bernstein et al., *Psychology*, 4th ed. Boston: Houghton Mifflin, 1997, 177–178.

† Adapted from Ryan and Cooper, *Those Who Can, Teach*, 9th ed. Boston: Houghton Mifflin, 2000, 60–61.

1. ______________________________
2. ______________________________

B. ______________________________

C. ______________________________

D. ______________________________

E. ______________________________

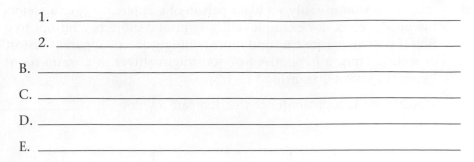

3. Three factors seem to underlie successful early childhood programs, whatever their format and curriculum. First, the staff of successful programs regard themselves as competent observers of children's educational needs and as being capable of making important decisions in tailoring a curriculum to particular children. Second, the vast majority of successful programs and teachers view an early childhood curriculum as an integrated whole rather than consisting of independent subject areas of skills. Singing a song, for example, is not just "music"; it also fosters language development, motor skills (if the children dance along), arithmetic (through counting and rhythm), and social studies (if the words are about people and life in the community). Third, successful early childhood programs involve parents, either directly as volunteers in the classroom or indirectly as advisers on governing boards, in certain school activities, or in additional services that support families.*

Word(s) in the topic sentence that indicate a series: ______________________________

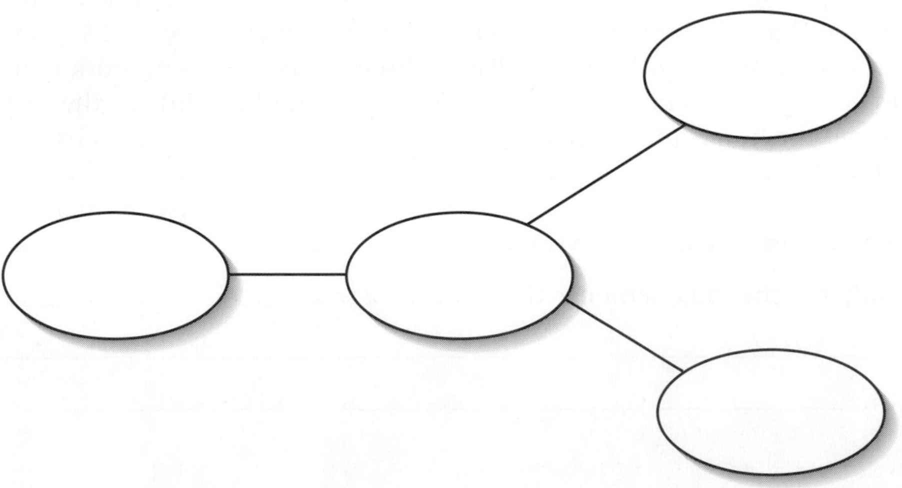

* Adapted from Seifert and Hoffnung, *Child and Adolescent Development,* 5th ed. Boston: Houghton Mifflin, 2000, 288.

4. Temple University psychologist Frank Farley, a longtime researcher on heroic behavior, says that there are three main types of heroes. The first type, "911[1] heroes," are those who protect people for a living, such as firefighters, police officers, paramedics, and security guards. The second type is the one-time "situational" hero that springs into action when an occasion calls for it. For example, a person who attacks an airplane hijacker or wrestles a gun from a would-be mugger is a situational hero. The last type of hero is the "sustained altruist,"[2] a person who often engages in heroic acts over a longer time; this type of hero is more interested in helping people than in making money or doing anything else.*

   Word(s) in the topic sentence that indicate a series: ______________________

   ____

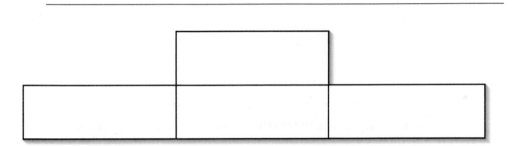

5. I've learned several ways to improve my stamina[3] so I can keep myself going. To begin with, you have to nourish your body and soul. The first thing I do when I get out of bed is meditate for five to ten minutes; that's the grounding work I must do for myself and what makes everything else possible. Second, I'm careful with my diet, and if I'm not, I can feel it. Third, when I get home at night, I don't automatically turn on the television. And fourth, every day I do some sort of exercise. I run four miles every other day—in the winter I do it inside; this morning I ran outside.†

   Word(s) in the topic sentence that indicate a series: ______________________

   ____

1. **911:** a reference to the 911 emergency phone number
2. **altruist:** someone who helps others
3. **stamina:** physical strength

* Adapted from Marilyn Elias, "Three Kinds of Heroes Emerge," *USA Today*, November 21, 2001, 1D.

† Adapted from Oprah Winfrey, "Secrets of the Staministas," *O* Magazine, September 2001, 196.

6

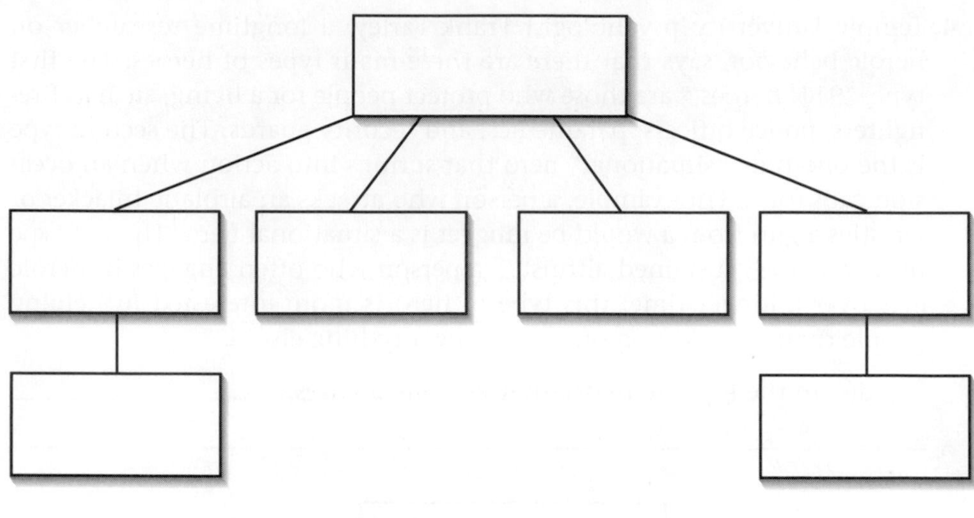

Time Order

The next common pattern for organizing details is time order. In **time-order** paragraphs, the details are arranged according to their chronological relationships. In other words, time-order paragraphs present details in the order they happened or should happen. Like the series pattern, the time-order pattern includes items that follow each other in succession to support a main idea. However, these series are events, stages, or steps presented in the order they occurred or should occur. Unlike series paragraphs, these details cannot be rearranged because they would no longer make sense.

6

Two types of time-order paragraphs are narrative and process. A **narrative** paragraph tells a story or recounts a sequence of events. Here is an example of a narrative paragraph that arranges details according to the time-order pattern:

> The American flag, also known as Old Glory, was born in 1777 and evolved into its present form by 1960. On June 14, 1777, Congress adopted the first official Stars and Stripes, which included 13 stars and 13 stripes to symbolize each of the original 13 American Colonies. In 1795, the flag was given 15 stars and 15 stripes to honor the admission of Vermont and Kentucky to the Union. On July 4, 1818, Congress restored the original 13 stripes and ordered the addition of a new star for each new state. By 1861, the flag had 34 stars. During the Civil War (1861–1865), the flag was not changed to reflect the secession[1] of the Southern states. From 1867 to 1959, fifteen more stars were added.

1. **secession:** withdrawal

The final fiftieth star was added on July 4, 1960, following Hawaii's admission into the Union, and the flag assumed its present form.*

In this paragraph, the supporting details are all events presented in the order they occurred:

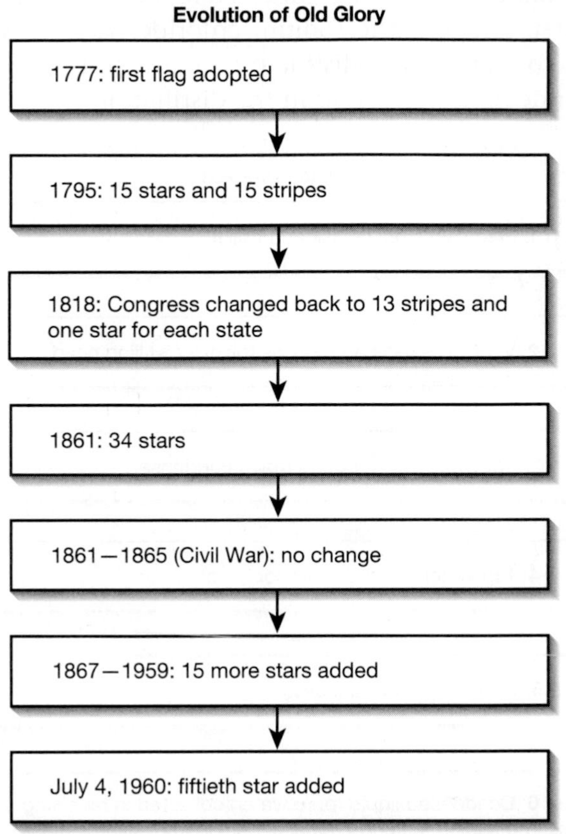

Evolution of Old Glory
1777: first flag adopted
1795: 15 stars and 15 stripes
1818: Congress changed back to 13 stripes and one star for each state
1861: 34 stars
1861—1865 (Civil War): no change
1867—1959: 15 more stars added
July 4, 1960: fiftieth star added

The second type of time-order paragraph is **process.** A process paragraph explains how something is done or could be done. Its details are organized in the steps or stages, in the order they occur. Here is an example:

Suppose you have a solution of sodium chloride and water. You want to separate the sodium chloride from the water and at the same time collect the purified water. You place the sodium chloride–water solution in the distillation[1] flask and heat it to boiling. As the solution boils, water in the form of vapor fills the flask and travels toward

1. **distillation:** related to the purification of a liquid through evaporation and condensation

* Adapted from "History of Old Glory," *News Herald*, Morganton, NC, September 23, 2001, 1C, 8C.

6

the distilling head. From there, the hot water vapor travels down the double-jacketed, water-cooled condenser. As the vapor travels down within the inner walls of the condenser, it is cooled by tap water running between the outer walls of the condenser. The water vapor condenses. The condensed liquid is collected in a receiving flask. Because only the water, and not the sodium chloride, vaporizes and passes through the condenser, the distillate contains only pure water. The sodium chloride remains behind in the distillation flask.*

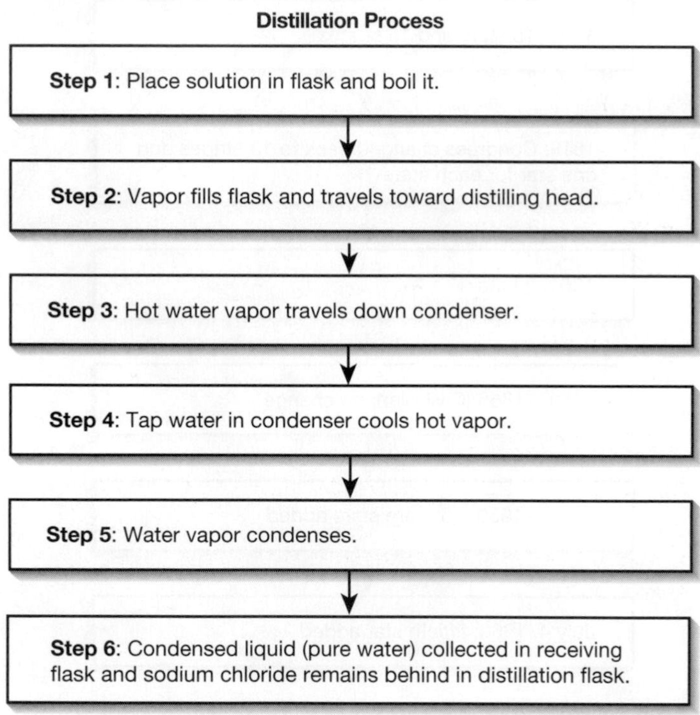

Distillation Process
Step 1: Place solution in flask and boil it.
Step 2: Vapor fills flask and travels toward distilling head.
Step 3: Hot water vapor travels down condenser.
Step 4: Tap water in condenser cools hot vapor.
Step 5: Water vapor condenses.
Step 6: Condensed liquid (pure water) collected in receiving flask and sodium chloride remains behind in distillation flask.

Topic sentences in time-order paragraphs will often indicate that a chronology will follow:

A young adult can follow ***three easy steps*** to establish a good credit record.

Construction of the United States Capitol Building began in 1793 and continued ***over the next hundred years.***

The history of antibiotics is marked by several key ***events.***

As you read, look for topic sentence words that indicate a time-order pattern.

* Adapted from Sherman and Sherman, *Basic Concepts of Chemistry*, 6th ed. Boston: Houghton Mifflin, 1996, 340.

Words and Phrases that Indicate a Time-Order Pattern		
Quantity word	***plus***	***Time-Order word***
several		events
two, three, four, etc.		steps
a number of		stages
over time		developments
in just one year		procedure
		process

Exercise 6.2

Read each of the paragraphs below and fill in the blank that follows. Then, write abbreviated versions of the paragraph's sentences in the outline or map to indicate the *major* time-order details.

1. There are several events that take place during jury selection. First, everyone who has been summoned to appear at jury duty must arrive by nine o'clock in the morning and assemble in the jury room. A few minutes later, the court clerk usually shows a movie outlining what is going to happen throughout the day as the jury is chosen for a particular trial. At around ten o'clock, twenty people are chosen from the jurors in attendance and are taken to a courtroom where a judge describes how the process is going to work. About thirty minutes later, ten people are called to sit in the jury box to be questioned by the lawyers in the case.

   Words in topic sentence that indicate time order: ____________________

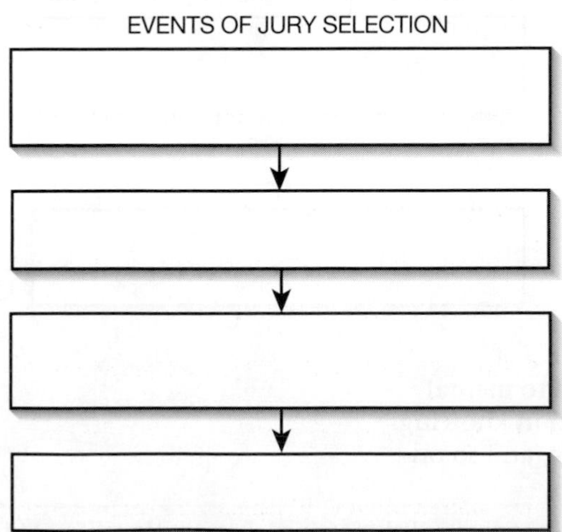

6

2. Research on memory suggests a certain procedure for taking and using notes effectively. First, realize that in note taking, more is not necessarily better. Taking detailed notes of everything requires that you pay close attention to unimportant as well as important content, leaving little time for thinking about the material. Next, once you have a set of lecture notes, review them as soon as possible so that you can fill in missing details. When the time comes for serious study, use your notes as if they were a chapter in a textbook. Finally, write a detailed outline and think about how various points are related. Once you have organized the material, the details will make more sense and will be much easier to remember.*

   Word(s) in topic sentence that indicate time order: ____________

   I. ____________

      A. ____________

      B. ____________

      C. ____________

3. The "preoperational period," a term used by Jean Piaget, a Swiss psychologist highly respected for his theory of cognitive[1] development, is divided into two stages: the *preconceptual stage* from age two to four and the *intuitive stage* from age four to six or seven. During the preconceptual stage, children begin to engage in symbolic thought by representing ideas and events with words and sentences, drawings, and dramatic play. As they begin to use symbols to stand for spoken words, they realize that writing represents meaning, a concept that is basic to reading comprehension. At the *intuitive stage,* children are rapidly developing these concepts. Most

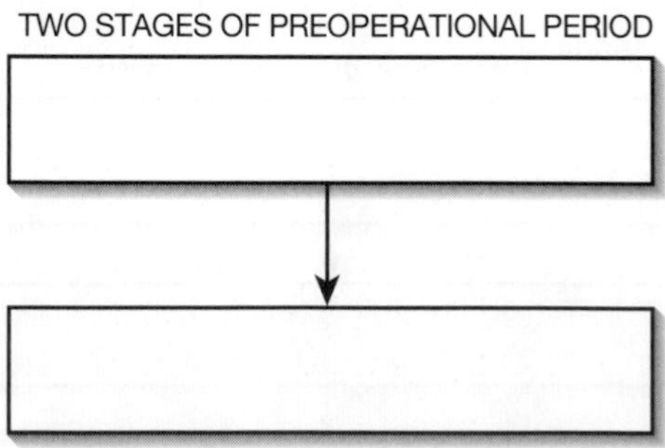

1. **cognitive:** related to mental processes involved in knowing, reasoning, judging, and so on

* Adapted from Bernstein et al., *Psychology*, 5th ed. Boston: Houghton Mifflin, 2000, 245.

children at this stage are unable to state the rules governing syntax,[1] but they do demonstrate grammatical awareness in their speech; that is, they are able to use words in a logical order as they form sentences.*

Word(s) in topic sentence that indicate time order: ____________________

4. George Polya, who is known as the "father of problem solving," created a four-step model for problem solving that will help you organize your thoughts and give you a general framework for solving any type of problem, whether it be a real-life situation or a textbook problem. Step one is to understand the problem. This consists of asking yourself a variety of questions to diagnose the situation. Step two is to devise a plan. In this step you come up with a plan to solve the problem by connecting what you know with what is unknown to you. The third step is to carry out the plan or actually solve the problem. Finally, look back at your work and be sure that it is correct.†

   Word(s) in topic sentence that indicate time order: ____________________

   I. ____

      A. ____

      B. ____

      C. ____

      D. ____

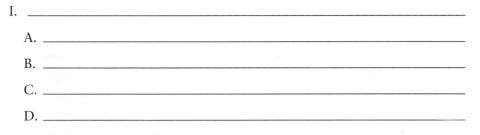

5. During childbirth, labor proceeds in three traditional stages. The first of the three stages begins with brief, mild contractions perhaps ten to fifteen minutes apart. These contractions become increasingly frequent and serve to alter the shape of the cervix,[2] preparing it for the fetus's descent and entry into the narrow birth canal. Near the end of the first stage, which on average lasts about eleven hours for firstborns and about seven hours for later-borns, dilation[3] of the cervix proceeds rapidly to allow passage through the birth canal. The second stage consists of the continued descent and the birth of the baby. This stage usually requires a little less than an hour for firstborns and about twenty minutes for later-borns. It also normally includes several reorientations of both the head and shoulders

1. **syntax:** rules and patterns for forming sentences
2. **cervix:** opening to the womb
3. **dilation:** widening

* Adapted from Burns et al., *Teaching Reading in Today's Elementary Schools*, 7th ed. Boston: Houghton Mifflin, 1999, 35. Copyright © 1999 by Houghton Mifflin Company. Used with permission.

† Adapted from Sherman and Sherman, *Essential Concepts of Chemistry*. Boston: Houghton Mifflin, 1999, 16–17.

to permit delivery through the tight-fitting passageway. In the third stage, which lasts about fifteen minutes, the placenta[1] is expelled.*

Words in topic sentence that indicate time order. ______________

____

I. ______________

A. ______________

B. ______________

C. ______________

II. ______________

A. ______________

B. ______________

III. ______________

Cause/Effect

When details are arranged in the cause/effect pattern, the paragraph intends to show how the details relate to or affect each other. Like a narrative paragraph, a cause/effect paragraph presents a series of occurrences. However, unlike a narrative, the cause/effect pattern reveals how one occurrence led to another. It might also demonstrate how a series of causes produced one particular effect, or result. The following diagrams will help you visualize some common types of cause/effect patterns:

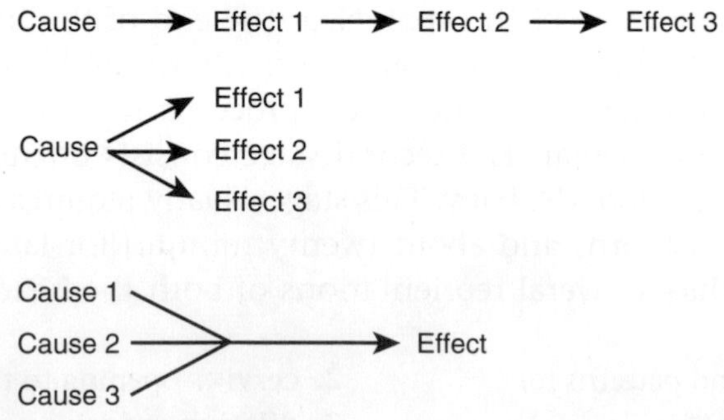

1. **placenta:** organ that encloses the fetus during pregnancy

* Adapted from Bukatko and Daehler, *Child Development,* 5th ed. Boston: Houghton Mifflin, 2004, 135. Copyright © 2004 by Houghton Mifflin Company. Reprinted with permission.

6

The first diagram shows a chain reaction of causes and effect, while the second one indicates a separate series of effects that are not related. The third diagram shows a pattern in which several unrelated causes together produce one particular effect.

For an example of the cause/effect pattern, read the following paragraph:

> Obesity is particularly difficult for adolescents who already are struggling to develop a comfortable and realistic view of their changing bodies. It can significantly impair teenagers' sense of themselves as physically attractive people and their overall identity development. In some cases, obesity can severely limit social opportunities due to both exclusion by peers and self-isolation. Because overweight adolescents do not conform to the social ideal of thinness, they also suffer from discrimination that limits their access to education, employment, housing, and health care.*

In this paragraph, one cause produces three main effects.

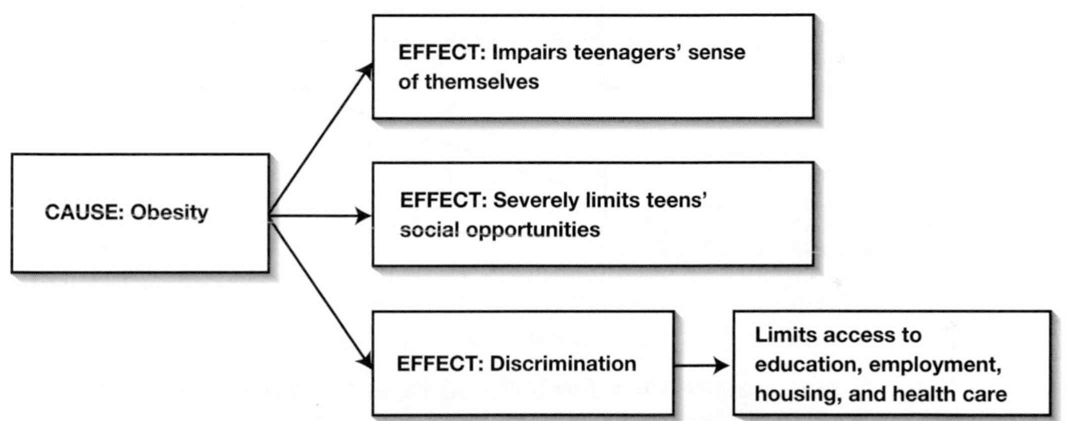

Here's a second example that is arranged according to a different cause/effect pattern.

> How could the stunning 1941 attack on Pearl Harbor[1] have happened? After all, American cryptanalysts[2] had broken the Japanese diplomatic code. Although the intercepted[3] Japanese messages told policymakers that war lay ahead, the intercepts never revealed naval

1. **Pearl Harbor:** American military base in Hawaii
2. **cryptanalysts:** people who decipher secret codes
3. **intercepted:** cut off or interrupted

* Adapted from Seifert et al., *Lifespan Development*, 2nd ed. Boston: Houghton Mifflin, 2000, 352. Copyright © 2000 by Houghton Mifflin Company. Reprinted with permission.

6

or military plans and never specifically mentioned Pearl Harbor. The base at Pearl Harbor was not ready—not on red alert—because a message sent from Washington warning of the imminence[1] of war had been too casually transmitted by a slow method and had arrived too late. Base commanders were too relaxed, believing Hawaii too far from Japan to be a target for all-out attack. Like Roosevelt's[2] advisers, they expected an assault at British Malaya, Thailand, or the Philippines. The Pearl Harbor calamity[3] stemmed from mistakes and insufficient information, not from conspiracy.*

In this paragraph, several causes produce one effect.

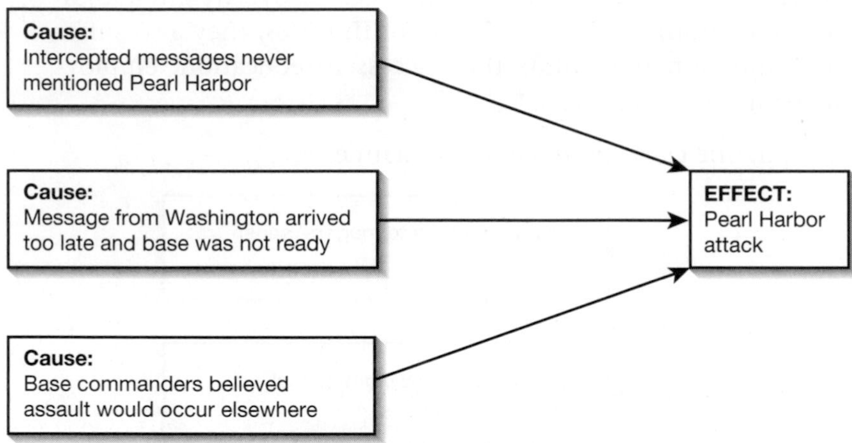

Topic sentences in cause/effect paragraphs will often indicate that an explanation of related occurrences will follow.

Fewer fans are attending football and baseball games ***because*** they are turned off by the commercialism[4] of these sports.

Ethical behavior in business ***results in*** a variety of benefits for an organization.

Parents who cater to their kids' every whim and demand too little of them in return will negatively ***affect*** their children's character development.

1. **imminence:** state of being able to happen
2. **Roosevelt:** Franklin D. Roosevelt, thirty-second president of the United States
3. **calamity:** disaster
4. **commercialism:** attitude that emphasizes profits

* Adapted from Norton et al., *A People and a Nation*, 5th ed. Vol. II. Boston: Houghton Mifflin, 1998, 774.

As you read, look for the following topic sentence words that signal a cause/effect pattern.

Words and Phrases that Indicate a Cause/Effect Pattern	
consequences	was caused by
effects	causes
results	chain reaction
outcomes	leads to
affect	factors
because	

Exercise 6.3

Read each paragraph below and fill in the blank that follows. Then, write abbreviated versions of the paragraph's sentences in the map to indicate the cause/effect relationships between the *major* supporting details.

1. Smoking is responsible for more preventable illnesses and deaths than any other single health-compromising behavior. Smoking is associated with cancer of the lung, larynx, oral cavity, and esophagus; it is also a major risk factor for other cancers throughout the body. Smoking is also related to cardiovascular illness and mortality. Smoking increases the risk

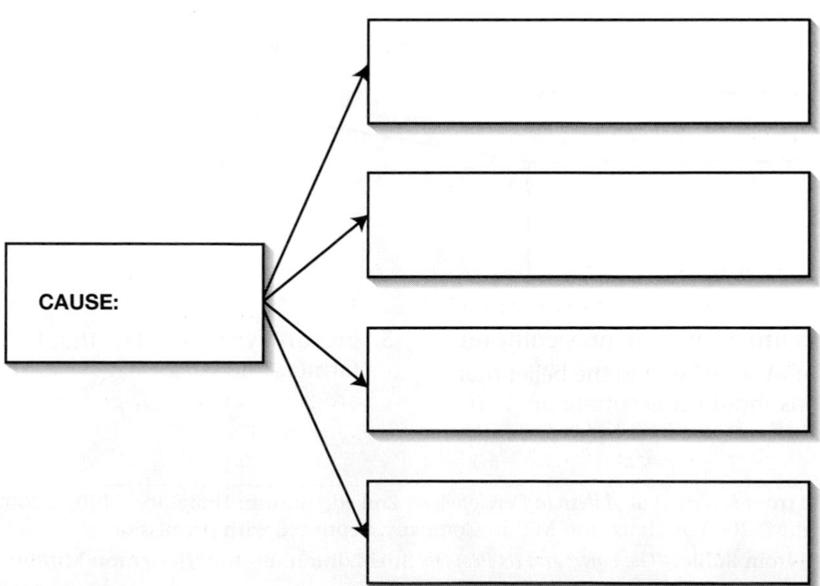

of emphysema, chronic bronchitis, peptic ulcers, cirrhosis of the liver, and respiratory disorders and aggravates the symptoms of allergies, diabetes, and hypertension. In women, smoking increases the risk of osteoporosis and lowers the age of menopause.*

Word(s) in topic sentence that indicate cause/effect order: ______________

2. Three causes sparked momentous[1] revolutions and nationalist[2] movements in Asia and Latin America between the years 1914 and 1945. One cause was the increasing poverty among the peasants and a widening of the gap between their incomes and those of the rich. The second cause was the appearance of a new generation of city people, many of them educated in Western ideas of equality and national independence, who were inspired by the rise of Japan and the Russian Revolution. The third cause of revolution was a growing alliance between this new urban generation and the dissatisfied peasantry.[3] Together they created the politics of mass participation by calling for social justice, national unity, and independence.†

Word(s) in topic sentence that indicate cause/effect order: ______________

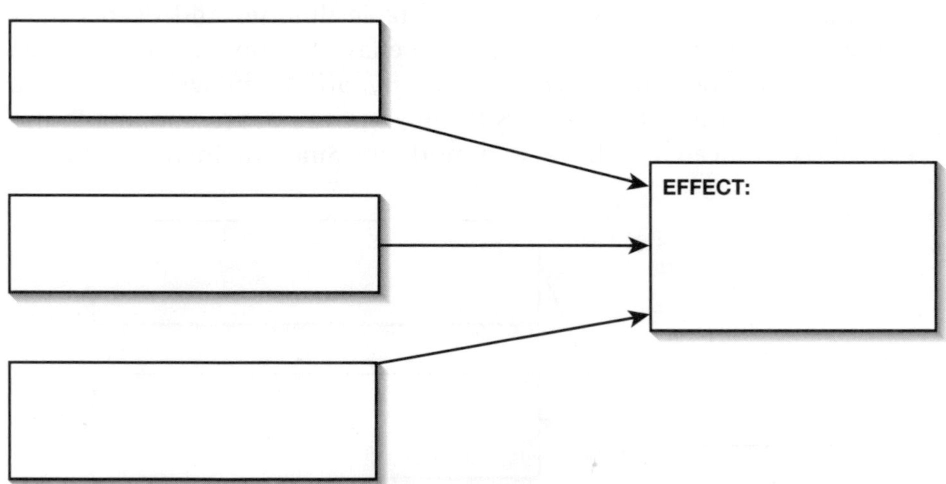

6

1. **momentous:** important, significant
2. **nationalist:** related to the belief that nations should concentrate on their own interests and act independently
3. **peasantry:** social class that includes farmers and laborers

* Adapted from Seifert et al., *Lifespan Development*, 2nd ed., Boston: Houghton Mifflin, 2000, 428. Copyright © 2000 by Houghton Mifflin Company. Reprinted with permission.

† Adapted from Bulliet, *The Earth and Its Peoples*, Brief Edition. Boston: Houghton Mifflin, 2000, 549.

3. Experts have identified several factors that lead to a child biting another person, whether it be a parent, caregiver, sibling, or another child. Biting often occurs when children are playing together in close quarters, in a family or preschool setting and may occur because of conflicts over favorite toys or snacks. It also happens more frequently during unstructured time, such as free playground periods, or when children are tired. Changing dynamics at home or in a childcare setting (brought on by such events as moving to a new room in a childcare center, having a new child come into a room, or the arrival of a new sibling) can cause stress, leading a toddler or preschooler to bite out of frustration or anger.*

Word(s) in topic sentence that indicate cause/effect order: ____________

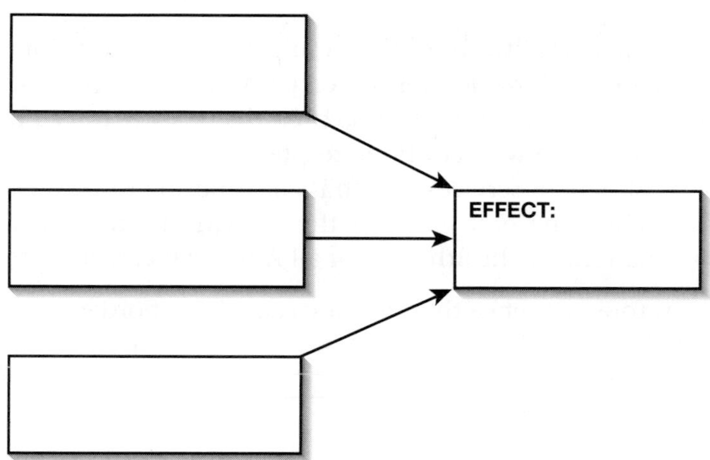

6

4. Research indicates that sending toddlers to day care has several positive effects. Toddlers in day care spend about 25 percent of their time interacting positively with other toddlers. They are more likely to express positive feelings and play competently with peers than with adults or when by themselves. Repeated contact with a peer in a familiar setting with a familiar caregiver and minimal adult interference appears to facilitate the development of peer friendship. Peer relationships during toddlerhood in turn may promote the development of positive friendships later in childhood. A recent longitudinal[1] study of the quality of children's relationships between infancy and nine years of age found that children's formation of

1. **longitudinal:** long-term

* Adapted from Laurie A. Cavanaugh, "Nipping Biting in the Bud," *Westchester Family*, October 2001, 32.

close friendships as toddlers predicted their positive ratings of their friendship quality as nine-year-olds.*

Word(s) in topic sentence that indicate cause/effect order: ____________

____

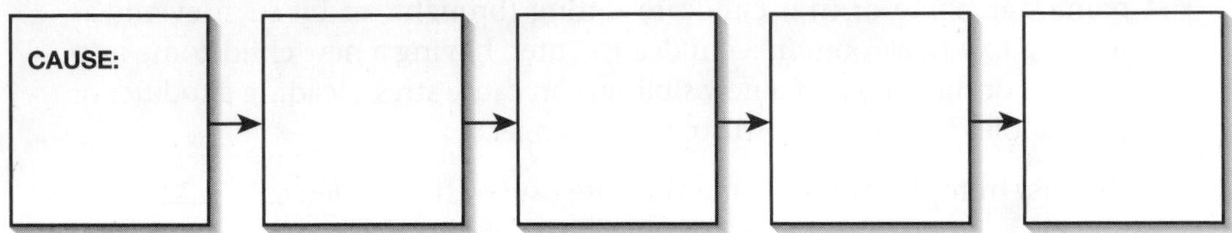

5. Medical malpractice litigation[1] that results in large awards for patients results in higher malpractice insurance premiums for doctors. For many physicians, these rates are soaring so high that they're forced to quit their profession. Of those who continue to practice, many are being forced to raise the cost of their services, which is contributing to skyrocketing medical costs. Thus, the end result of the growing number of malpractice claims is unaffordable health care for all American citizens.

Word(s) in topic sentence that indicate cause/effect order: ____________

6

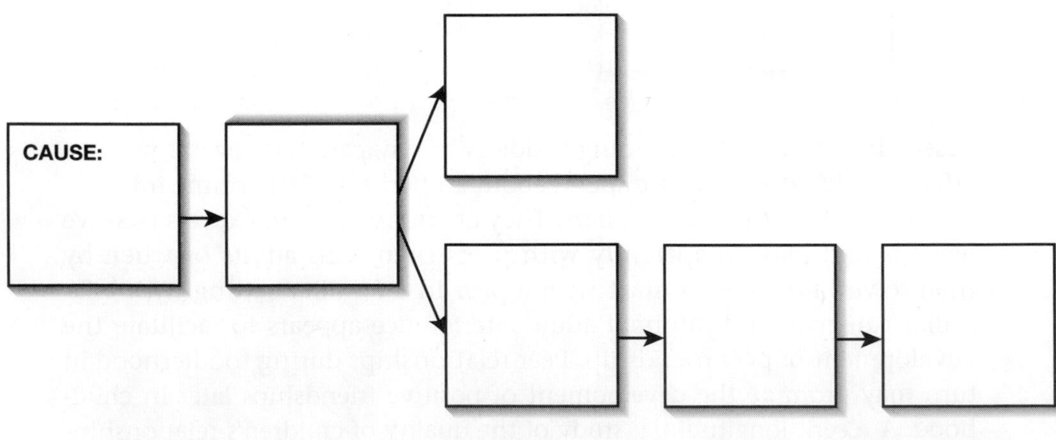

1. **litigation:** legal proceedings

* From Seifert et al., *Lifespan Development*, 2nd ed. Boston: Houghton Mifflin, 2000, 158. Copyright © 2000 by Houghton Mifflin Company. Reprinted with permission.

Comparison/Contrast

A third common pattern is comparison/contrast. **Comparison** means explaining the *similarities* between two or more things. **Contrast** means examining the *differences* between things. A paragraph can compare or contrast or do both.

In comparison/contrast paragraphs, the supporting details are in the form of points of comparison. In other words, the paragraph concentrates on certain aspects or features of the subjects and explores their likenesses and/or differences in those areas. For example, a comparison of two different male singing groups might focus on the similarities in their style, the subjects of their songs, and the audiences they attract. Paragraphs arrange the details in one of two ways. One option is to focus on each subject in turn. The following paragraph, which deals only with similarities, provides an example of this pattern:

> England's Stonehenge and the colossal statues on Rapa Nui, or Easter Island, share quite a few similarities. The monoliths that compose the circular Stonehenge are huge. Some of them weigh as much as 45 tons and measure seven feet tall. The transport of stones this size was a marvel of preindustrial age engineering. Modern scientists speculate that the stones were moved by laying each one on a sledge[1] and then pulling it with ropes over log rollers. Their purpose is still a mystery, but many believe that Stonehenge was some kind of temple used for sacred rituals. One theory claims that ancient Druids[2] conducted religious ceremonies, including human sacrifices, at the site. Similarly, the carved stones of Rapa Nui are gigantic. On average, each stands over 13 feet high and weighs about 14 tons. Like the stones of Stonehenge, they may have been moved from the quarries[3] where they originated with sledges, ropes, and logs. They may have had a sacred purpose as well; the people of Rapa Nui might have viewed them as ceremonial conduits[4] for communication with the gods.

This paragraph groups the points of comparison by subject, discussing first Stonehenge and then the statues of Rapa Nui. It would be outlined like this:

I. Similarities between Stonehenge and Rapa Nui

A. Stonehenge
1. Size
2. Transport
3. Purpose

6

1. **sledge:** low vehicle drawn by work animals, used to transport loads
2. **Druids:** an ancient order of priests
3. **quarries:** pits from which stones are cut or dug
4. **conduits:** pipes or channels

B. Statues of Rapa Nui
   1. Size
   2. Transport
   3. Purpose

A comparison/contrast paragraph can also be arranged so that it focuses on the points of comparison, alternating back and forth between the two subjects.

> Debit cards and credit cards may look alike, but there are important differences. A debit card, or check card, electronically subtracts the amount of your purchase from your bank account the moment the purchase is made. In contrast, when you use your credit card, the credit card company extends short-term financing, and you do not make a payment until you receive your next statement. Using a debit card means you do not pay an interest or finance charge for your purchase. If you use a credit card and do not pay off the balance when you receive your statement, you end up paying interest that results in higher costs for the items you buy. Finally, banks usually do not charge debit card users an annual fee. Many credit cards do.*

This paragraph contrasts three aspects of debit cards and credit cards: when you pay for the purchase, whether or not interest applies, and whether an annual fee applies. It would be outlined as follows:

I. Differences between debit cards and credit cards
   A. When you pay
      1. Debit cards
      2. Credit cards
   B. Interest
      1. Debit cards
      2. Credit Cards
   C. Annual fee
      1. Debit cards
      2. Credit cards

Topic sentences in comparison/contrast paragraphs often indicate that an explanation of similarities and/or differences is to follow:

> There are some fundamental ***differences*** between Greek and Roman mythology.

* Adapted from Pride et al., *Business*, 6th ed. Boston: Houghton Mifflin, 1999, 492–493.

6

In comparison to American women, many women in Middle Eastern countries have fewer rights, freedoms, and opportunities.

Research on identical twins has shown that they tend to demonstrate remarkable ***similarities*** in traits.

As you read, look for the following topic sentence words that indicate a comparison/contrast pattern.

Words that Indicate a Comparison/Contrast Pattern

similarities	differences
alike	different
likenesses	

Exercise 6.4

Read the following comparison/contrast paragraphs and answer the questions that follow. Circle the letter of the correct answer or write your answer on the blank provided.

Although my husband and I have many common interests, we couldn't be more different. Both of us love to go to the movies, but I love action/adventure movies, and he enjoys romantic comedies. We even eat differently at the movies—I love popcorn, while he enjoys chocolate. We also share a love of the outdoors, but while I love to go camping, hiking, and rafting, he enjoys just sitting in our backyard, reading the paper. We also enjoy eating good food, but while I love to cook, he hates it! However, he enjoys cleaning up after I cook a gourmet meal, so I can do the thing we both love to do—relax.

1. This paragraph (circle the letter of one answer)
   a. compares.
   b. contrasts.
   c. compares and contrasts.
2. What two subjects are being compared and/or contrasted? __________ and __________
3. How are the two subjects compared? List four similarities on the blanks provided.
   1. ______________________________
   2. ______________________________

6

3. ______________________________

4. ______________________________

4. How are they contrasted?

1. ______________________________

2. ______________________________

3. ______________________________

4. ______________________________

The single biggest factor determining differences between the House of Representatives and the Senate is size. With 100 members, the Senate is less formal; the 435-person House needs more rules and hierarchy in order to function efficiently. The Constitution also provides for differences in terms: two years for the House, six for the Senate (on a staggered basis—all senators do not come up for reelection at the same time). In the modern context, this means that House members never stop campaigning. Senators, in contrast, can suspend their preoccupation with the next campaign for the first four or five years of their terms and thus, at least in theory, have more time to spend on the affairs of the nation. The minimum age of the candidates is different as well: members of the House must be at least twenty-five years old, senators thirty. This again reflects the founders' expectation that the Senate would be older, wiser, and better able to deal with national lawmaking.*

5. This paragraph (circle the letter of one answer)
   a. compares.
   b. contrasts.
   c. compares and contrasts.

6. What two subjects are being compared and/or contrasted? ______________ and ______________

7. On what three differences between the two subjects does the paragraph focus?

   1. ____________
   2. ____________
   3. ____________

The comparisons between pro basketball player Stephon Marbury and high school player Sebastian Telfair (they are first cousins, once removed) are

* From Barbour and Wright, *Keeping the Republic*. Boston: Houghton Mifflin, 2001, 156.

inevitable. They grew up in the same housing project and played for the same school; both won city championships (Marbury got one, while Telfair is going for his third straight this spring); both have brothers who also played high-level basketball; and both are the subjects of books. Telfair says Marbury was a "role model, even if he didn't know it," and Sebastian was excited when his cousin was traded to the Knicks—he let out a whoop when he got the news on his cellphone during class.*

8. This paragraph (circle the letter of one answer)
   a. compares.
   b. contrasts.
   c. compares and contrasts.

9. What two subjects are being compared and/or contrasted?

   ______________________ and ______________________

10. On what five similarities between the two subjects does the paragraph focus?

    1. ______________________
    2. ______________________
    3. ______________________
    4. ______________________
    5. ______________________

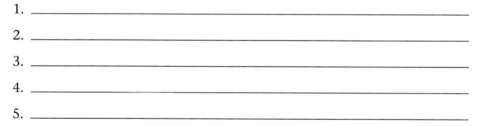

Dating norms in other cultures differ, sometimes drastically, from norms among most Americans. A survey of college students from a U.S. Midwestern state university and a Chinese university in Shanghai showed dating behaviors and attitudes that varied greatly. American college students held more liberal attitudes toward who initiates a date, dated younger, dated more frequently, and were more likely to develop a sexual relationship. Chinese students dated later, dated less frequently, and were less likely to develop a sexual relationship. American students in this sample had their first date during their 14th year, whereas the average age for Chinese students' first date was 18 years. Social pressure to date is greater in the United States, and the ability to have dates indicates popularity. In China, however, dating in junior high or even high school is considered somewhat unusual, and opportunities for

* From Chris Ballard, "Ready for the Big Time," *Sports Illustrated*, March 8, 2004, 42.

dating are more limited. American society encourages dating, whereas Chinese society frowns on it.*

11. This paragraph (circle the letter of one answer)
    a. compares.
    b. contrasts.
    c. compares and contrasts.

12. What two subjects are being compared and/or contrasted?

    ______________________ and ______________________

13. On what six differences between the two subjects does the paragraph focus?

    1. ______________________
    2. ______________________
    3. ______________________
    4. ______________________
    5. ______________________
    6. ______________________

Group therapy offers features not found in individual therapy treatment. First, group therapy allows the therapist to observe clients interacting with one another, whereas individual therapy relies on the patient and the therapist only. Second, clients often feel less alone as they listen to others and realize that many people struggle with difficulties at least as severe as their own. In contrast, individual therapy patients benefit from one-on-one contact with their therapists, who get to know their patients well during treatment. Third, group members can boost one another's self-confidence and self-acceptance as they come to trust and value one another. In a therapist-patient relationship, the patient must develop trust only with his or her therapist in order for the therapy to work in that setting. Fourth, clients learn from one another, which is something that obviously cannot happen in a one-on-one situation. They share ideas for solving problems and give one another honest feedback about their attitudes and behavior. Fifth, perhaps through mutual modeling, the group experience makes clients more willing to share their feelings and more sensitive to other people's needs, motives, and messages. In a one-on-one therapy situation, the patient shares his or her feelings with the therapist alone. Finally, group therapy allows clients to try out new skills in a

* From Kaplan, *Adolescence*. Boston: Houghton Mifflin, 2004, 204. Copyright © 2004 by Houghton Mifflin Company. Reprinted with permission.

supportive environment, whereas one-on-one patients can take what they've learned out into the world and try it out there.*

14. This paragraph (circle the letter of one answer)
    a. compares.
    b. contrasts.
    c. compares and contrasts.

15. What two subjects are being compared and/or contrasted? ______________

    ______________________________ and ______________________________

16. On what six similarities or differences between the two subjects does the paragraph focus?
    1. ______________________________
    2. ______________________________
    3. ______________________________
    4. ______________________________
    5. ______________________________
    6. ______________________________

Definition

6

One last pattern you should learn to recognize is the definition pattern. **Definition** usually states the meaning of a particular word, term, or concept, and then goes on to illustrate it with one or more examples. Textbooks often use this pattern to explain a term being introduced for the first time. The following paragraph is organized according to the definition pattern.

> Permanent whirlpools are not just ancient myths; these churning areas of ocean actually exist. A whirlpool is a marine phenomenon created by a combination of tide, current, wind, and seabed features. When fast-moving water flows over rocks, shelves, ridges, and peaks of the ocean floor, the water eddies[1] and swirls, creating extremely dangerous whirling waves that can grind up all ships that pass

1. **eddies:** moves in a circular motion, against the main current

* Adapted from Bernstein and Nash, *Essentials of Psychology,* 2nd ed. Boston: Houghton Mifflin, 2002, 464.

through incautiously, turning them into matchwood. There are just five whirlpools in the world that are wild enough and big enough and famous enough to earn the name. This most notorious of them all is the Maelstrom in Norway, which added a word for "violent or turbulent situation" to the English language. It is a huge area of furious water that appeared on maps as early as 1555 and still threatens sailors today.*

The example or examples within a definition paragraph may be arranged according to one of the other patterns. For example, the definition might be followed by a *series* of examples or other details. Or, one example might be told using the *time-order* format. This next paragraph is a good example:

For some people, anxiety takes the form of **panic disorder.** People suffering from panic disorder experience recurrent terrifying *panic attacks* that often come without warning or obvious cause and are marked by intense heart palpitations,[1] pressure or pain in the chest, dizziness or unsteadiness, sweating, and a feeling of faintness; often, victims believe they are having a heart attack. They may worry constantly about suffering future panic episodes and thus curtail activities to avoid possible embarrassment. For example, Geri, a thirty-two-year-old nurse, had her first panic attack while driving on a freeway. Afterward, she would not drive on freeways. Her next attack occurred while with a patient and a doctor in a small examining room. A sense of impending[2] doom flooded over her and she burst out of the office and into the parking lot, where she felt immediate relief. From then on, fear of another attack made it impossible for her to tolerate any close quarters, including crowded shopping malls. She eventually quit her job because of terror of the examining rooms.†

Topic sentences will often indicate that a definition will follow:

A triathalon ***is*** a long-distance race that usually includes phases of running, swimming, and bicycling.

Evolution can be ***defined*** as a process of changes that occur over several generations in a particular population.

1. **palpitations:** rapid, irregular beating 2. **impending:** upcoming, nearby

* Adapted from Simon Winchester, "In the Eye of the Whirlpool," *Smithsonian,* August 2001, 84–94.

† Adapted from Bernstein, *Psychology,* 4th ed. Boston: Houghton Mifflin, 1997, 503.

One *meaning* of Zen is the process of identifying and reducing attachments to the beliefs, attitudes, and ideas that cause human suffering.

As you read, look for the following topic sentence words that may indicate a definition pattern.

Words that Indicate a Definition Pattern

means	definition
meaning	is/are
define	

Exercise 6.5

Read each of the following definition paragraphs and answer the questions that follow. Write your answers on the blanks provided.

(1) A social movement is a widely shared demand for change in some aspect of the social or political order. (2) In the nineteenth century, for example, there were various movements that sought to reduce immigration to this country or to keep Catholics or Masons[1] out of public office. (3) Broad-based religious revivals, such as the nineteenth century's Second Great Awakening, have also been social movements. (4) There have been several feminist social movements, too, in this country's history, in the 1830s, the 1890s, the 1920s, and the 1960s. (5) The civil rights movement of the 1960s was a demand for change, as was the environmentalist movement of the 1970s.*

1. What term is defined in this paragraph? ______________________

2. Which sentence states the definition? ______________________

3. How many examples are given as illustrations? ______________________

4. Which pattern organizes the examples? ______________________

(1) The word *crater* (Greek *krater*) means bowl-shaped, and lunar craters are small- and large-diameter depressions believed to be caused by the impact

1. **Masons:** Freemasons, a fraternal and charitable organization with secret rites and signs

* Adapted from Wilson and DiIulio, *American Government: The Essentials*, 9th ed. Boston: Houghton Mifflin, 2004, 231–232. Copyright © 2004 by Houghton Mifflin Company. Reprinted with permission.

6

and explosion of small and large meteorites. (2) The craters are rather shallow (their depths are small in comparison with their diameters), and their floors are located below the lunar surface. (3) The moon's South Pole-Aiken impact basin is the largest known in the solar system, with a diameter of 2500 km (1550 miles) and a depth that averages about 12 km (7.4 miles). (4) The youngest impact basin on the moon is Orientale, which is about 1000 km across and was formed 3.8 billion years ago.*

5. What word is/are defined in this paragraph? ______________________

6. Which sentence(s) states the definition? ______________________

7. How many examples are given as illustrations? ______________________

8. Which pattern organizes the examples? ______________________

(1) Many public schools in the United States are adopting a "uniform only" policy regarding how their students dress. (2) What is a uniform? (3) A uniform is a standard outfit worn by both girls and boys at their school. (4) Taking their cue from parochial[1] schools around the country, some school administrators are requiring students, who formerly wore whatever they wanted to school, to wear a uniform that is determined by the school and sold only at specific locations. (5) It is the equivalent of a dress code with the "dress" being mandated by the school administration. (6) An example of this would be blue pants, white shirt, and a tie for boys, and for girls, a jumper, white blouse, and knee socks. (7) Some schools have even determined that students should wear a specific type of shoe, but many still allow students and their parents to pick the shoes to go with the uniform.

9. What word is defined in this paragraph? ______________________

10. Which sentence states the definition? ______________________

11. How many examples are given as illustrations? ______________________

12. Which pattern organizes the examples? ______________________

(1) In a simple sense, e-business, or electronic business, can be defined as the organized effort of individuals to produce and sell, for a profit, the products and services that satisfy society's needs through the facilities available on the Internet. (2) American Online, or AOL, is an example of

1. **parochial:** relating to a church parish

* Adapted from Shipman et al., *An Introduction to Physical Science*, 9th ed. Boston: Houghton Mifflin, 2000, 445.

an e-business that invented itself on the Internet. (3) Another example is Amazon.com, which gives customers anywhere in the world access to the same virtual[1] store of books, videos, and CDs. (4) And at e-Bay's global auction site, customers can, for a small fee, buy and sell almost anything.*

13. What term is defined in this paragraph? ____________________

14. Which sentence states the definition? ____________________

15. How many examples are given as illustrations? ____________________

16. Which pattern organizes the examples? ____________________

(1) Most young people would like to have more influence, status, and popularity. (2) These goals are often achieved through identification with an authority figure or a role model. (3) A role model is a person you most admire or are likely to emulate.[2] (4) Preschoolers are most likely to identify their parents as their role models. (5) At this early stage, parents are seen as almost perfect, as real heroes. (6) During early elementary school, children begin to realize that their parents have flaws, and they search for other heroes—perhaps a popular athlete, a rock star, or an actor. (7) During later stages of development, new role models are adopted.†

17. What term is defined in this paragraph? ____________________

18. Which sentence states the definition? ____________________

19. How many examples are given as illustrations? ____________________

20. Which pattern organizes the examples? ____________________

6

Combination of Patterns

Often, paragraphs include more than one pattern of organization. The major supporting details may be arranged according to one pattern, and minor details are arranged according to another. For example, read the following paragraph:

In 1994, the Women's Bureau of the Department of Labor conducted a landmark survey of how working women in America feel

1. **virtual:** existing in computers   2. **emulate:** imitate

* Adapted from Pride, Hughes, and Kapoor, *Business*, 7th ed. Boston: Houghton Mifflin, 2002, 104–105. Copyright © 2002 by Houghton Mifflin Company. Reprinted with permission.

† Adapted from Reece and Brandt, *Effective Human Relations in Organizations*, 7th ed. Boston: Houghton Mifflin, 1999, 151.

about their jobs. More than a quarter of a million women told of their concerns and experiences. After the results of the survey were studied, the workplace was identified as the greatest single source of stress. The causes of such stress can range from the anxieties produced by corporate downsizing to factors that result in physical disorders such as carpal tunnel syndrome.[1] Stress also can result from simply a feeling on the part of the individual worker that he or she is not appreciated on the job or is being overwhelmed by family obligations.*

This paragraph is mostly a cause/effect paragraph that explains two major causes of stress in the workplace. However, it begins with some time order details regarding a 1994 survey about how workers in America feel about their jobs.

Here is one more example:

Time-starved Americans now spend as much time eating out as they do eating at home. How often do you pick up a quick lunch at a Burger King or Taco Bell? In the 1950s and 1960s, this trend was just beginning. Consumers wanted more restaurants and fast-food outlets. As a result, McDonald's, Wendy's, Big Boy, White Castle, Pizza Hut, Godfather's Pizza, and other fast-food outlets flourished. The trend toward eating away from home reached a fevered pitch in the late 1970s, when the average number of meals per person eaten out (excluding brown-bag lunches and other meals prepared at home but eaten elsewhere) exceeded one per day. In the 1980s, people wanted the fast food but didn't want to go get it. By emphasizing delivery, Domino's Pizza and a few other fast-food outlets became very successful. In the 1990s, the "takeout taxi" business—where restaurant food is delivered to homes—grew 10 percent per year.†

Most of the details in this paragraph are arranged in the time-order (narrative) pattern. The paragraph points out the development of the fast-food trend over five decades. The results of consumer desires are also included, so this paragraph combines the time-order and cause/effect patterns.

6

1. **carpal tunnel syndrome:** pain, numbness, and weakness in the thumb and fingers

* Adapted from Andrews et al., *Public Speaking*. Boston: Houghton Mifflin, 1999, 124.

† Adapted from Boyes and Melvin, *Fundamentals of Economics*. Boston: Houghton Mifflin, 1999, 45. Copyright © 1999 by Houghton Mifflin Company. Reprinted with permission.

Exercise 6.6

In the list following each paragraph, write a checkmark beside each pattern used to organize the supporting details.

1. In denial, impulses and associated ideas reach awareness, but their implications[1] are rejected or denied. For example, an unwillingness to check on medical symptoms could indicate the presence of denial, as does "gallows[2] humor," the tendency of soldiers to engage in banter and jest as they near an engagement with the enemy. While denial may be functional for soldiers marching off to combat, it can be damaging for the individual. To deny the possible diagnostic implications of a persistent swelling that may be symptomatic of cancer is to risk the possible consequences of failing to take advantage of early treatment. Denial can also result in profound psychological consequences as, for example, when one refuses to acknowledge negative traits in a potential spouse.*

   _____ series
   _____ time order
   _____ cause/effect
   _____ comparison/contrast
   _____ definition

2. Soaring eagles have the incredible ability to see a mouse move in the grass from a mile away. Similarly, cats have the amazing ability to see even in very dim light, thanks to special "reflectors" at the back of their eyes. Through natural selection, over time, each species has developed a visual system uniquely adapted to its way of life. The human visual system has also adapted to many things well: it combines great sensitivity and great sharpness, enabling people to see objects near and far, during the day and night. Our night vision is not as acute[3] as that of some animals, but our color vision is excellent. This is not a bad tradeoff, since being able to appreciate a sunset's splendor seems worth an occasional stumble in the dark.†

   _____ series
   _____ time order
   _____ cause/effect
   _____ comparison/contrast
   _____ definition

1. **implications:** significance
2. **gallows:** related to the place where executions by hanging occur
3. **acute:** sharp

* From Feshbach et al., *Personality*, 4th ed. Boston: Houghton Mifflin, 1996, 84. Copyright © 1996 by Houghton Mifflin Company. Reprinted with permission.

† Adapted from Bernstein et al., *Psychology*, 5th ed. Boston: Houghton Mifflin, 2000, 107.

6

3. Finland and the United States approach education differently. Children in Finland start at age 7, two years later than children in the United States start. Educational spending in Finland is only $5,000 a year per student, there are no gifted programs, as there are in America, and there are often 30 Finnish children in one classroom. In America, class sizes tend to be smaller. Therefore, one would expect America's schools to be better. On the contrary, an international survey showed that Finland is number one in the world in literacy and in the top five in both math and science. Many experts attribute Finland's high academic ranking to the higher quality and social standing of its teachers. Educators must have at least a master's degree, and teaching is a highly respected profession. Universities in Finland have to turn down the majority of applicants for teaching programs. In contrast, American schools often have trouble finding enough teachers for a profession that is not highly regarded.*

_____ series _____ comparison/contrast

_____ time order _____ definition

_____ cause/effect

4. There are five major problems with bureaucracies:[1] red tape, conflict, duplication, imperialism, and waste. Red tape refers to the complex rules and procedures that must be followed to get something done. Conflict exists because some agencies seem to be working at cross-purposes with other agencies. (For example, the Agricultural Research Service tells farmers how to grow crops more efficiently, while the Agricultural Stabilization and Conservation Service pays farmers to grow fewer crops or to produce less.) Duplication (usually called "wasteful duplication") occurs when two government agencies seem to be doing the same thing, as when the Customs Service and the Drug Enforcement Administration both attempt to intercept illegal drugs being smuggled into the country. Imperialism refers to the tendency of agencies to grow without regard to the benefits that their programs confer or the costs they entail. Waste means spending more than is necessary to buy some product or service.†

1. **bureaucracies:** governments administered by different departments

6

* From Lizette Alvarez, "Educators Flocking to Finland, Land of Literate Children," *New York Times*, April 9, 2004, www.nytimes.com.

† From Wilson and DiIulio, *American Government: The Essentials*, 9th ed. Boston: Houghton Mifflin, 2004, 395. Copyright © 2004 by Houghton Mifflin Company. Reprinted with permission.

_____ series _____ comparison/contrast

_____ time order _____ definition

_____ cause/effect

5. An overwhelming amount of evidence shows that social support has therapeutic[1] effects on both our psychological and physical health. David Spiegel, of Stanford University's School of Medicine, came to appreciate the value of social connections many years ago when he organized support groups for women with advanced breast cancer. Spiegel had fully expected the women to benefit, emotionally, from the experience. But he found something else he did not expect: These women lived an average of eighteen months longer than did similar others who did not attend the groups. In another study, Lisa Berkman and Leonard Syme surveyed seven thousand residents of Alameda County, California; conducted a nine-year follow-up of mortality rates; and found that the more social contacts people had, the longer they lived. This was true of men and women, young and old, rich and poor, and people from all racial and ethnic backgrounds. James House and others studied 2,754 adults interviewed during visits to their doctors. He found that the most socially active men were two to three times less likely to die within nine to twelve years than others of similar age who were more isolated.*

_____ series _____ comparison/contrast

_____ time order _____ definition

_____ cause/effect

6

CHAPTER 6 REVIEW

Fill in the blanks in the following statements.

1. A __________ is a consistent, predictable form or method for putting something together.
2. Patterns help readers find ________________ and understand their relationships.

1. **therapeutic:** having healing powers

* Adapted from Brehm et al., *Social Psychology*, 5th ed. Boston: Houghton Mifflin, 2002, 528. Copyright © 2002 by Houghton Mifflin Company. Reprinted with permission.

3. Five broad patterns for organizing details include __________, __________, __________, __________, and __________.
4. __________ often include clues to a paragraph's pattern of arrangement.
5. A __________ is a number of things that follow each other in succession. Series in paragraphs may be examples, reasons, types, or other points.
6. __________ paragraphs, which include narratives and processes, arrange details chronologically.
7. __________ paragraphs explain how supporting details are related to each other.
8. __________ paragraphs examine two or more subjects' similarities, differences, or both.
9. The __________ pattern includes a term's meaning plus one or more examples as illustration.
10. Paragraphs often use a combination of __________ to organize supporting details.

Reading Selection

Practicing the Active Reading Strategy:

Before and While You Read

You can use active reading strategies before, as, and after you read a selection. The following are some suggestions for active reading strategies that you can perform before you read and while you read.

1. Skim the selection for any unfamiliar words. Circle or highlight any words you do not know.
2. As you read, underline, highlight, or circle important words or phrases.
3. Write down any questions about the selection if you are confused by the information presented.
4. Jot notes in the margin to help you understand the material.

Women React to Pain Differently Than Men

by Rita Rubin

1 Recent studies now show that pain is not gender neutral. From the intensity of their pain to the way they deal with it, men and women are different, suggests a growing body of evidence. One result, many scientists say, is that women's pain is not taken as seriously as men's. "Pain is not simply a physical experience," says Diane Hoffmann, director of the Law & Health Care Program at the University of Maryland School of Law. "Men and women have been shown to give different meaning to their pain."

2 Two common scenarios illustrate some of the differences between the sexes: A man awakens with chest pain and writes it off as indigestion. His wife urges him to go to the emergency room, where he is diagnosed as having a heart attack. In contrast, a woman awakens with chest pain and thinks she might be having a heart attack. She goes immediately to the emergency room, where all tests of her heart function are normal. Doctors throw up their hands and send her on her way.

3 Possible explanations for these differences are complex, ranging from the physiological to the cultural. It's not clear whether women actually feel pain more intensely, as some—but not all—laboratory experiments have found, or whether they simply tend to describe their pain more expansively. "It's complicated, because you have to separate out reporting style," says Arthur Barsky, director of psychiatric research at Brigham and Women's Hospital in Boston. "What's a twinge for you may be an agonizing, crushing pain for me. It's hard to separate the vocabulary from the actual sensual experience."

4 Anita Tarzian, a health law researcher at the University of Maryland and a hospice[1] nurse, notes that women do have thinner skin and a higher density of nerve fibers than men. And estrogen, the so-called female hormone, influences women's pain response in many ways, Tarzian says. Fluctuations in hormone levels might contribute to variations in the severity of women's pain symptoms across the menstrual cycle, during pregnancy and immediately after delivery, and during and after menopause.

5 Menstrual cramps and childbirth themselves might help explain differences in how women and men perceive pain, scientists say. "We have a regular experience of pain that can be somewhat severe," says Anita Unruh, an occupational therapist and social worker at Dalhousie University in Halifax, Nova Scotia. "You have to learn to be attuned to when pain is actually abnormal."

6 When women feel pain, their brains don't respond the same as men's do, says psychologist Karen Berkley of Florida State University. Because women are brought up to be more nurturing than men, Berkley says, they're more likely to regard pain as a call to action. In other words, she says, women tend to think, "OK, it hurts. Now, let's go do something about it." Men, on the other hand, are taught from boyhood that crying and other expressions of distress are

1. **hospice:** related to a program that provides care for terminally ill people

for sissies, Barsky says. And, partly because women tend to seek medical help more often than men, their pain complaints are often less likely to be taken seriously, says Tarzian, who with Hoffmann wrote a paper titled "The Girl Who Cried Pain: A Bias Against Women in the Treatment of Pain" in an issue of *The Journal of Law, Medicine & Ethics*.

7 Some doctors might discount a woman's pain because they think it's all in her head. Even if doctors do acknowledge the validity of a woman's pain, they may think she has a higher pain tolerance because she's built to give birth, Tarzian and Hoffmann write. Either way, they say the outcome is the same: less aggressive treatment of women's pain.

8 Further complicating matters are the reasons for women's pain, or the apparent lack thereof. Women are far more likely than men to suffer from painful conditions with no obvious cause, such as migraines or fibromyalgia, characterized by tender, aching muscles. "The whole issue of just treating symptoms isn't dealt with much in medical education," Barsky says. "The real objective is to make a diagnosis and treat the under-lying problem." Doctors are at a loss when confronted by patients whose pain has no obvious cause, he says. As a result, says James Campbell, director of the pain treatment center at Johns Hopkins Hospital in Baltimore, "people who have illnesses that are not well understood end up getting rotten care."

9 That shouldn't dissuade women from seeking medical advice when they feel pain, Unruh says. "You have to trust your own knowledge about who you are and what your body is like," she says. Women need to tell their doctor when they are seeking information rather than treatment and ask themselves, "Do I have a pain to worry about or not?" Unruh says. "A good doctor will say when he or she doesn't know."*

Vocabulary

Read the following questions about some of the vocabulary words that appear in the previous selection. Circle the letter of the correct answer.

1. In paragraph 1, what do you think *gender neutral* means?
   a. the same for men and women
   b. different for men and women
   c. more intense for men
   d. less intense for women
2. What is *indigestion*? (paragraph 2) "A man awakens with . . . *indigestion*."
   a. cramps
   b. inability to digest
   c. leg pain
   d. headache
3. "Possible explanations for these differences are complex, ranging from the *physiological* to the cultural." (paragraph 3) What does *physiological* mean?
   a. related to the brain
   b. related to the functions of the body
   c. the study of illnesses
   d. the study of plants

* Adapted from Rita Rubin, "Women React to Pain Differently Than Men," *USA Today*, October 9, 2001, 10D.

4. What are *fluctuations*? (paragraph 4) "*Fluctuations* in hormone levels might contribute to variations in the severity of women's pain symptoms. . . ."

   a. ideas
   b. moments
   c. changes
   d. definitions

5. "Because women are brought up to be more *nurturing* than men. . . ." (paragraph 6) What does it mean to be *nurturing*?

   a. helping to grow or develop
   b. helping to decide
   c. providing shelter
   d. providing food

6. What does it mean to *dissuade*? (paragraph 9) "That shouldn't *dissuade* women from seeking medical advice when they feel pain. . . ."

   a. encourage
   b. protect
   c. discourage
   d. enhance

Main Ideas, Supporting Details, Patterns of Organization, and Transitions

Respond to the following questions by circling the letter of the correct answer.

1. What pattern organizes the details in paragraph 4?

   a. time order
   b. series
   c. cause/effect
   d. comparison/contrast

2. In paragraph 4, what word or phrase is defined?

   a. estrogen
   b. nerve fibers
   c. hospice
   d. hormone

3. In paragraph 6, what pattern organizes the details?

   a. time order
   b. series
   c. cause/effect
   d. comparison/contrast

4. What is the implied main idea of paragraph 2?

   a. Men often get indigestion.
   b. Men have more heart attacks than women.
   c. Men and women react differently to pain, which confuses doctors.
   d. Women don't have heart attacks.

5. Which of the following is a comparison/contrast transition that appears in the reading selection?

   a. on the other hand
   b. and
   c. as a result
   d. because

6

Practicing the Active Reading Strategy:

After You Read

Now that you have read the selection, answer the following questions, using the active reading strategies that are discussed on pages 30–33.

1. Identify and write down the point and purpose of this reading selection.
2. Besides the vocabulary words included in the exercise on pages 314–315, are there any other vocabulary words that are unfamiliar to you? If so, write a list of them. When you have finished writing your list, look up each word in a dictionary and write the definition that best describes the word as it is used in the selection.
3. Predict any possible test questions that may be used on a test about the content of this selection.
4. How could you use the information contained in this selection? Does the information contained in the selection reinforce or contradict your ideas and experiences? Explain.

Questions for Discussion and Writing

Answer the following questions based on your reading of the selection. Write your answers on the blanks provided.

1. State one interesting fact that you learned from this selection. Why was this fact interesting to you? ______________________________

____

2. Do you think that the information in this selection stereotypes men and women? Why or why not? Does the author provide enough evidence to support her assertion that "pain is not gender neutral"? Why or why not?

____

____

3. What do you think Diane Hoffmann means in paragraph 1 when she says, "Men and women have been shown to give different meaning to their pain?" Do you agree? If so, provide an example from your own life where this was true. ______________________________

____

4. Research men's and women's different attitudes toward health, and/or medical treatment. How do these attitudes influence each gender's be-

haviors? Compare and/or contrast their different approaches to health and well-being. ____________________

____

Vocabulary: The Example Context Clue

You've learned that a *context clue* is a word, phrase, or sentence that helps you understand the meaning of an unfamiliar word you encounter as you read. In Chapter 4, you practiced recognizing the definition/restatement context clue. In Chapter 5, you learned about the explanation context clue. The **example** is a third type of context clue that can give you a sense of a particular word's definition. In this type, an example somewhere near a word provides an illustration that allows you to draw a conclusion about the word's meaning. For example, read the following sentence, which comes from one of the paragraphs in this chapter:

> Singing a song, for example, is not just "music"; it also fosters language development, ***motor skills*** (if the children dance along), arithmetic (through counting and rhythm), and social studies (if the words are about people and life in the community).

What does the term *motor skills* mean in this sentence? You get a clue in the form of the phrase *if the children dance along*. If dancing is an example of using motor skills, then they must have something to do with moving the body. Therefore, you can conclude that *motor skills* means "the performance of movements."

6

Vocabulary Exercise 1

The following sentences all come from paragraphs in this chapter and previous chapters. In each one, underline the example context clue that helps you understand the meaning of the boldfaced, italicized word. Then, on the blank provided, write a definition for the boldfaced, italicized word.

1. They may worry constantly about suffering future panic episodes and thus ***curtail*** activities to avoid possible embarrassment. For example, Geri, a thirty-two-year-old nurse, had her first panic attack while driving on a freeway. Afterward, she would not drive on freeways. ____________
2. It also happens more frequently during ***unstructured*** time, such as free playground periods, or when children are tired. ____________
3. From the 1880s onward, popular newspapers increasingly nurtured people's fascination with the ***sensational.*** Joseph Pulitzer, a Hungarian immigrant who bought the *New York World* in 1883, pioneered this trend

by filling his newspaper with stories of disasters, crimes, and scandals. ______________________________

4. [Tennis players] Tilden and Johnston played five acts of incredible ***melodrama,*** with a thrill in every scene, with horrible errors leading suddenly to glorious achievements, with skill and courage and good and evil fortune. ______________________________

5. Countless monuments, from the pyramids of Egypt to ordinary tombstones, have suffered drastic deterioration from freezing water, hot sunshine, and other ***climatic*** forces. ______________________________

6. The types of fat in these oils can improve the levels of cholesterol and other ***lipids*** in your blood and combat the narrowing of arteries that often occurs with age. ______________________________

7. In addition to good values on down-home classics, New York serves up thrifty East Indian curries, Moroccan couscous, Greek kebabs, West Indian callaloos, Senegalese thiebu djen (fish stews), Mexican chimichangas, and many more ***culinary*** treats from around the globe. ______________________________

8. This covering seals the compacted trash from the air and prevents ***vermin*** (birds, cats, mice, flying insects, etc.) from getting into the trash. ______________________________

6

Vocabulary Exercise 2

In each of the following passages, underline the example context clues that help define the boldfaced, italicized words.

A. Any candle factory worth its wicks will produce 1,000 to 2,000 varieties. Candles are highbrow ***horticulture,*** with creations of Bulgarian Roses and Mexican Orange Blossom. Candles are ***cuisine,*** in flavors of Oatmeal Cookie, Candy Corn, and Toasted Marshmallow. Appealing to Generation X, there are Jumpin' Java candles with whipped wax "served" in Irish coffee mugs. There are hometown candles with ***regional*** flavors: That's not a leafy clump of weeds burning on your coffee table! It's a kudzu candle from Mississippi. And no fewer than ten varieties are considered ***aphrodisiacs.*** Ylang Ylang, for example, is said to inspire romance.*

B. The scientific study of memory has influenced the design of the electrical and mechanical devices that play an increasingly important role in our lives. Designers of the computers, VCRs, cameras, and even stoves are faced with a choice: Either place the operating instructions on the ***contraptions*** themselves, or assume that the user remembers how to operate them. Understanding the limits of both working memory and long-term memory has helped designers distinguish between information that is likely to be stored in (and easily retrieved from) the user's memory, and information that should be presented in the form of labels, instructions, or other ***cues*** that reduce memory demands. Placing unfamiliar or hard-to-recall information in plain view makes it easier to use the device as intended, and with less chance of errors.

Psychologists have influenced advertisers and designers to create many other "user-friendly" systems. For example, in creating toll-free numbers, they take advantage of ***chunking,*** which provides an efficient way to maintain information in working memory. Which do you think would be easier to remember: "1-800-447-4357" or "1-800-GET-HELP"? Similarly, automobile designers ensure that the turn signals on your car emit an audible cue when turned on, a feature that reduces your memory load while driving.†

READING STRATEGY: Taking Notes

Learning how to take notes effectively is a vital skill for college students. You will often be tested on the information in reading selections such as textbook chapters, so you will need to make sure you're using all of the tools at your disposal to understand and retain this information.

Continued

* Adapted from Dennis McCafferty, "Stop and Smell the Candles," *USA Weekend,* July 27–29, 2001, 12.

† Adapted from Bernstein et al., *Psychology,* 5th ed. Boston: Houghton Mifflin, 2000, 245.

One of those tools is an active reading technique known as note taking. **Taking notes** means recording in writing the major information and ideas in a text. You might choose to take these notes in the margins of the book itself, or in a notebook, or on separate sheets of paper.

Regardless of where you write them, notes offer two important benefits. First of all, writing down information and ideas helps you to remember them better. For many people, taking the extra time to handwrite the main points helps implant those points in their memory more securely. As a result, retention and test performance tend to improve. Secondly, good notes are often easier to study because they provide the student with a condensed version of the main points.

Good notes always begin with highlighting or underlining main ideas or key terms as you read, just as you learned to do in Chapter 1. When you write notes, they might take one or more of the following forms:

- **A list of the main ideas in all of the paragraphs.** Put them in your own words and condense them whenever possible. Don't try to include all of the details, just the most important points.
- **A summary of the chapter or article** (for an overview of this strategy, see Chapter 5).
- **An outline.** In previous chapters of this book, you've practiced filling out outlines that reveal the relationships between the details. You can use a Roman numeral outline, but the notes are usually for your eyes only, so you could also adopt or create a more informal system. No matter what kind of outline you use, though, make sure it clearly demonstrates the general and specific relationships between the ideas.

6

No matter what form they take, effective notes always possess three important characteristics. They should be:

1. *Neat.* Skip lines between points and write legibly.
2. *Clearly organized.* Group related points together so they're easier to remember.
3. *Factual and objective.* Like summaries, notes should be free of your own opinions.

Actively read the following section from a management textbook. Then, take notes by creating a list of the paragraphs' main ideas, by writing a summary, or by outlining the selection.

Exploding Myths about Small Businesses

Mistaken notions can become accepted facts if they are repeated often enough. Such is the case with failure rates and job creation for small businesses. Fortunately, recent research sets the record straight.

The 80-Percent-Failure-Rate Myth. An often-repeated statistic says that four out of five small businesses will fail within five years. This 80 percent casualty[1] rate is a frightening prospect for anyone thinking about starting a business. But a recent study by Bruce A. Kirchhoff of the New Jersey Institute of Technology found the failure rate for small businesses to be *only 18 percent during their first eight years.* Why the huge disparity?[2] It turns out that studies by the U.S. government and others defined business failure much too broadly. Any closing of a business, whether because someone died, sold the business, or retired, was recorded as a business failure. In fact, only 18 percent of the 814,000 small businesses tracked by Kirchhoff for eight years went out of business with unpaid bills. This should be a comfort to would-be entrepreneurs.[3]

The Low-Wage-Jobs Myth. When it came to creating jobs during the 1980s and 1990s, America's big businesses were put to shame by their small and midsize counterparts. Eighty percent of the new job growth was generated by the smaller companies; massive layoffs were the norm at big companies. Critics, meanwhile, claimed that most of the new jobs in the small-business sector went to low-paid clerks and hamburger flippers. Such was not the case, according to a Cambridge, Massachusetts, study by researcher David Birch.

After analyzing new jobs created in the United States between 1987 and 1992, Birch found that businesses with fewer than 100 employees had indeed created most new jobs. Surprisingly, however, only 4 percent of those small firms produced 70 percent of that job growth. Birch calls these rapidly growing small companies "gazelles,"[4] as opposed to the "mice"

Continued

1. **casualty:** related to harm, loss, or injury
2. **disparity:** inequality, unlikeness
3. **entrepreneurs:** people who start and operate new businesses
4. **gazelles:** small, swift mammals with horns

6

businesses that tend to remain very small. For the period studied, the gazelles added more high-paying jobs than big companies eliminated. Gazelles are not mom-and-pop operations.[1] They tend to be computer software, telecommunications, and specialized engineering or manufacturing firms. So, while small businesses do in fact pay on average less than big companies do, they are not low-wage havens.

Again, as in the case of failure rates, the truth about the prospects of starting or working for a small company is different—and brighter—than the traditional fallacy[2] suggests.

Career Opportunities in Small Business

Among the five small-business career options listed in Table 6.1, only franchises require definition. The other four are self-defining. A franchise is a license to sell another company's products and/or to use another company's name in business. Familiar

Table 6.1 Career Opportunities in Small Business

Small-Business Career Options	Capital Requirements	Likelihood of Steady Paycheck	Degree of Personal Control	Ultimate Financial Return
1. **Become an independent contractor/consultant**	Low to moderate	None to low	Very high	Negative to high
2. **Take a job with a small business**	None	Moderate to high	Low to moderate	Low to moderate
3. **Join or buy a small business owned by your family**	Low to high	Low to high	Low to high	Moderate to high
4. **Purchase a franchise**	Moderate to high	None to moderate	Moderate to high	Negative to high
5. **Start your own small business**	Moderate to high	None to moderate	High to very high	Negative to very high

1. **mom-and-pop operations:** small businesses run by families
2. **fallacy:** false or incorrect idea

6

franchise operations include McDonald's, the National Basketball Association, and Holiday Inn. Notice how each of the career options in Table 6.1 has positive and negative aspects. There is no one best option. Success in the small-business sector depends on the right combination of money, talent, hard work, luck, and opportunity. Fortunately, career opportunities in small business are virtually unlimited.

Entrepreneurship

According to experts on the subject, "**entrepreneurship** is the process by which individuals—either on their own or inside organizations—pursue opportunities without regard to the resources they currently control." In effect, entrepreneurs look beyond current resource constraints when they envision new possibilities. Entrepreneurs are preoccupied with "how to," rather than "why not." Conversations about entrepreneurship these days invariably turn to tales of Internet billionaires. Actual statistics offer a more sobering outlook: "A 1999 study by ActivMedia found 47 percent of revenue-generating Web sites produce less than $10,000." But who is to say *your* $10,000 Web site won't become your ticket to the billionaires' club? Entrepreneurs, as we discuss next, are risk takers—and all they want is a chance.

We refer to entrepreneurs in large companies as *intrapreneurs*. Although intrapreneurs are needed to pump new blood into large organizations, our focus here is on entrepreneurs who envision, start, and operate whole new businesses. Entrepreneurship is thriving today from Argentina to Poland to Malaysia to China, thanks to the global swing toward market-based economies.

A Trait Profile for Entrepreneurs. Exactly how do entrepreneurs differ from general managers or administrators? According to the trait profiles in Table 6.2, entrepreneurs tend to be high achievers who focus more on future possibilities, external factors, and technical details. Also, compared with general administrators, entrepreneurs are more comfortable with ambiguity[1] and risk taking. It is important to note that entrepreneurs

Continued

6

1. **ambiguity:** doubtfulness or uncertainty

Table 6.2 Contrasting Trait Profiles for Entrepreneurs and Administrators

Entrepreneurs tend to	Administrators tend to
Focus on envisioned futures	Focus on the established present
Emphasize external/market dimensions	Emphasize internal/cost dimensions
Display a medium-to-high tolerance for ambiguity	Display a low-to-medium tolerance for ambiguity
Exhibit moderate-to-high risk-taking behavior	Exhibit low-to-moderate risk-taking behavior
Obtain motivation from a need to achieve	Obtain motivation from a need to lead others (i.e., social power)
Possess technical knowledge and experience in the innovative area	Possess managerial knowledge and experience

Source: Philip D. Olson, "Choices for Innovation-Minded Corporations," *The Journal of Business Strategy,* 11 January–February 1990: Exhibit 1, 44. Reprinted by permission of Emerald Group Publishing Limited, Bradford, U.K.

are not necessarily better or worse than other managers—they are just different.

Entrepreneurship Has Its Limits. Many successful entrepreneurs have tripped over a common stumbling block. Their organizations outgrow the entrepreneur's ability to manage them. Entrepreneurs generally feel stifled[1] by cumbersome[2] and slow-paced bureaucracies.[3] A prime example is Victor Kiam, who became famous with his television advertisements proclaiming that he liked his Remington electric razor so much that he bought the company. In 1991, Kiam admitted, "The company got too big for my entrepreneurial style. . . . A lot of things were falling through the cracks." Remington's costs got out of control, and the company lost 25 percent of its U.S. market share for men's electric shavers. Kiam eventually turned the day-to-day management of his company over to David J. Ferrari, a corporate turnaround specialist. Kiam's case is not unique. Entrepreneurs who launch successful and growing companies face a tough dilemma: either grow with the company or have the courage to step aside and turn the reins over to professional

1. **stifled:** smothered or suffocated; held back
2. **cumbersome:** difficult or troublesome
3. **bureaucracies:** governments administered by different departments

managers who possess the administrative traits needed, such as those listed in Table 6.2.*

Reading Visuals: Line Graphs

A **graph** is a visual aid composed of lines or bars that correspond to numbers or facts arranged along a vertical axis, or side, and a horizontal axis. The purpose of a graph is to show changes or differences in amounts, quantities, or characteristics. Two types of graphs are the line graph and the bar graph. Each one presents information differently. The bar graph is covered in Chapter 7 of this text.

A **line graph** is composed of points plotted within a vertical axis and a horizontal axis and then connected with lines. Line graphs typically reveal changes or trends in numerical data over time. They demonstrate how two factors interact with each other. The vertical axis is labeled with increments of time, such as years or minutes. The vertical axis is labeled with quantities. For each point in time, a dot on the graph indicates the corresponding quantity. Then, these dots are all connected to show upward and downward movement.

Line graphs contain the following parts:

- **Title.** The title points out the type of numbers being examined. It corresponds to the label of the vertical axis.
- **Vertical axis.** This line, which runs up and down, is divided into regular increments of numbers that correspond to the type of data being tracked. This axis is labeled to identify what that type of data is.
- **Horizontal axis.** This line, which runs from left to right, is divided into segments of time. It, too, is labeled to identify the kind of time factor being used.
- **Points.** Numerical data is plotted at the points where numbers and time factors intersect on the grid. These points may be labeled with specific amounts.
- **Lines.** Points are connected with lines to show trends.
- **Source line.** The source line identifies who collected or compiled the information in the graph.

Continued

* Adapted from Kreitner, *Management,* 8th ed. Boston: Houghton Mifflin, 2001, 30–32. Copyright © 2001 by Houghton Mifflin Company. Reprinted with permission.

6

These parts are labeled on the following line graph.

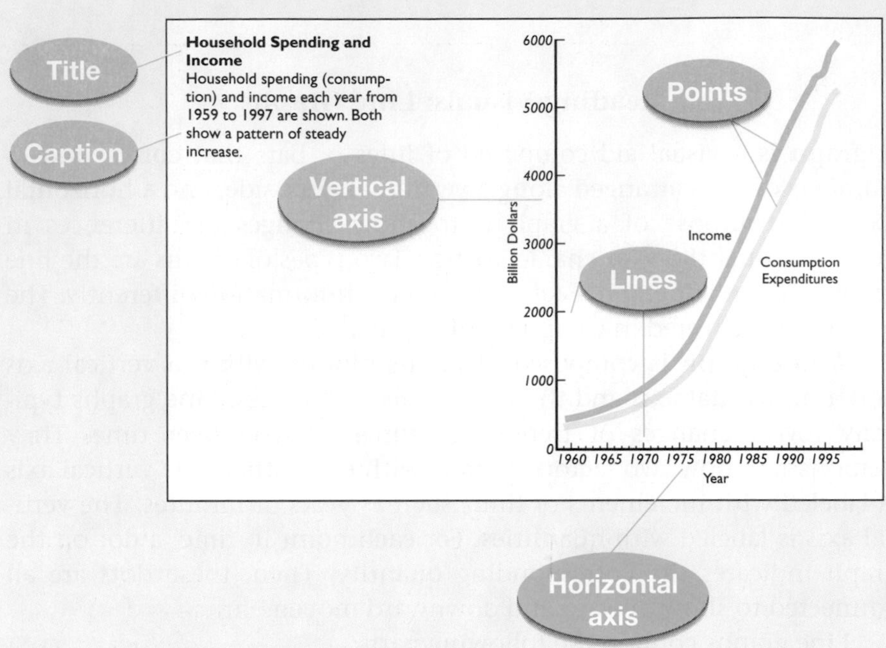

Source: Boyes and Melvin, "Household Spending and Income," *Fundamentals of Economics.* Boston: Houghton Mifflin, 1999, 147.

6

To read a line graph, begin with the title. Read it carefully to understand the numerical value on which the graph focuses. Then, read the labels on the vertical and horizontal axes to understand what two factors are interacting. Finally, examine the line that connects the points and try to state in your own words the trends being revealed by the numbers. Do the numbers increase, decrease, or both? When? How much overall change has occurred during the time span indicated on the horizontal axis?

As the title indicates, the line graph above illustrates how household spending compares with household income. The vertical axis is divided into billion dollar increments. The horizontal axis is divided into years. The points plotted on this grid are connected by two different colored lines, which are labeled. These two lines clearly reveal that between 1959 and 1997, income steadily increased and expenditures kept pace. The caption beneath the figure's title points out that conclusion, too.

Number of African Americans, Hispanics, and Women of All Races Serving in Congress, 1901–2001

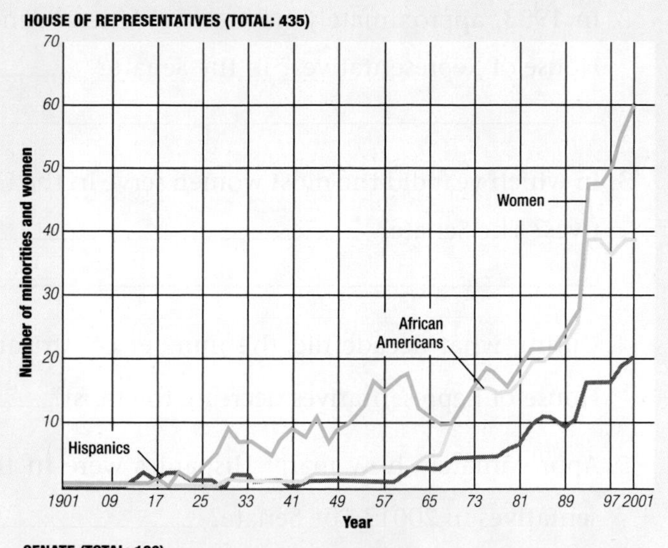

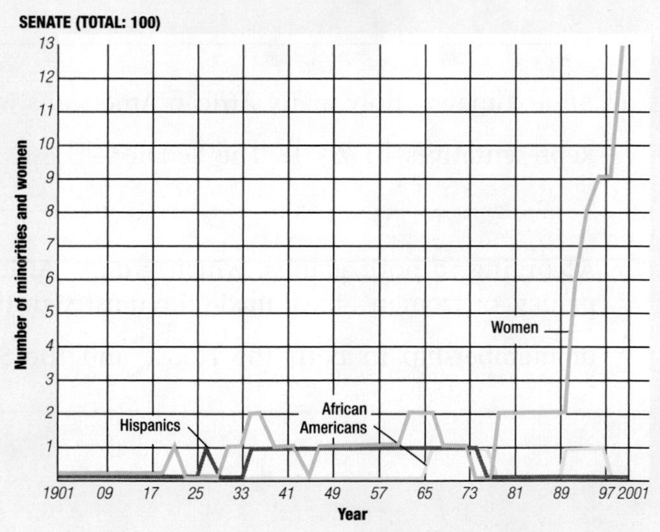

Source: Barbour and Wright, *Keeping the Republic.* Boston: Houghton Mifflin, 2001, 163.

Now, study the two line graphs above and then answer the questions that follow.

1. What is the subject of the first line graph? The second graph?

____

____

____

Continued

6

2. In 1933, approximately how many African Americans were in the House of Representatives? In the Senate? ____________________

____

3. In which year did the most women serve in the House of Representatives? The Senate? ____________________

____

4. During what decade did the number of African Americans in the House of Representatives decrease the most? ____________________

5. Approximately how many Hispanics were in the House of Representatives in 2001? The Senate? ____________________

____

6. Approximately how many African Americans were in the House of Representatives in 2001? The Senate? ____________________

____

7. According to both graphs, which group—African Americans, Hispanics, or women—have made the most significant gains in terms of membership in both the House and the Senate? ____________________

____

CHAPTER 6 TESTS

Name ______________________________ Date ______________

TEST 1

Read each of the following topic sentences. Circle the letter of the clue word that indicates a specific pattern.Then circle the letter of the correct pattern from the list.

The difference between a depressant and a stimulant is that depressants slow down central nervous system activity and stimulants speed it up.*

1. What clue word(s) indicate(s) a pattern?

   a. difference c. between
   b. slow down d. speed it up

2. What pattern is indicated by this topic sentence?

   a. cause/effect c. definition
   b. comparison/contrast d. time order

One side effect of drugs may be the potential for abuse.†

3. What clue word indicates a pattern?

   a. side c. may
   b. effect d. potential

4. What pattern is indicated by this topic sentence?

   a. cause/effect c. time order
   b. definition d. series

The ease of recalling words near the end of a list is called the *recency effect.*

5. What clue word(s) indicate(s) a pattern?

   a. ease c. near
   b. recalling d. is called

6. What pattern is indicated by this topic sentence?

   a. cause/effect c. comparison/contrast
   b. definition d. time order

* Bernstein and Nash, *Essentials of Psychology,* 2nd ed. Boston: Houghton Mifflin, 2002.
† Bernstein and Nash, *Essentials of Psychology,* 2nd ed. Boston: Houghton Mifflin, 2002.

For additional tests, see the Test Bank.

6

Coercive power is defined as power that is based on threatened or actual punishment.*

7. What clue word(s) indicate(s) a pattern?
   a. Coercive power
   b. is defined as
   c. based on
   d. threatened or actual punishment

8. What pattern is indicated by this topic sentence?
   a. cause/effect
   b. comparison/contrast
   c. time order
   d. definition

For many decades the Supreme Court allowed Congress to pass almost any law authorized by the Constitution.

9. What clue word(s) indicate(s) a pattern?
   a. For many decades
   b. allowed
   c. almost any law
   d. authorized

10. What pattern is indicated by this topic sentence?
    a. time order
    b. series
    c. definition
    d. cause/effect

One consequence of sticking to the 65-miles-per-hour speed limit is a reduction in gas consumption.

11. What clue word(s) indicate(s) a pattern?
    a. gas
    b. can be
    c. one consequence
    d. speed

12. What pattern is indicated by this topic sentence?
    a. definition
    b. cause/effect
    c. comparison/contrast
    d. time order

There are several striking facts about American welfare policy.†

13. What clue word(s) indicate(s) a pattern?
    a. There are
    b. several striking facts
    c. American
    d. welfare policy

14. What pattern is indicated by this topic sentence?
    a. definition
    b. cause/effect
    c. time order
    d. series

* From Kreitner, *Management*, 8th ed. Boston: Houghton Mifflin, 2001, 462.

† From Wilson and DiIulio, *American Government*, 8th ed. Boston: Houghton Mifflin, 2001, 411, 481.

6

England offers perhaps the clearest contrast with the United States.

15. What clue word indicates a pattern?
    a. offers
    b. perhaps
    c. contrast
    d. with

16. What pattern is indicated by this topic sentence?
    a. definition
    b. cause/effect
    c. time order
    d. comparison/contrast

In just one year, enrollment in the Arabic language class at my college increased dramatically.

17. What clue word(s) indicate(s) a pattern?
    a. in just one year
    b. enrollment
    c. class
    d. increased

18. What pattern is indicated by this topic sentence?
    a. definition
    b. time order
    c. series
    d. cause/effect

Phobias[1] have several characteristics.

19. What clue word(s) indicate(s) a pattern?
    a. have
    b. several characteristics
    c. can be named
    d. defined

20. What pattern is indicated by this topic sentence?
    a. series
    b. time order
    c. cause/effect
    d. comparison/contrast

TEST 2

Read each of the following paragraphs and respond to the questions that follow by circling the letter of the correct answer.

Three factors in particular can affect a president's popularity: the cycle effect, the economy, and unifying[2] or divisive[3] current events. The cycle effect, the first important factor, refers to the tendency for presidents to begin their terms of office with relatively high popularity ratings, which decline as they move through their four-year terms. The second important factor that consistently influences presidential approval is the state of the economy. At least

1. **phobias:** intense fears
2. **unifying:** bringing together
3. **divisive:** creating disagreement

since Franklin D. Roosevelt,[1] the government has taken an active role in regulating the national economy, and every president promises economic prosperity. In practice, presidential power over the economy is quite limited, but we nevertheless hold our presidents accountable for economic performance. Third, newsworthy events can influence presidential approval. In general, unifying events help, and divisive events hurt.*

1. What words in the topic sentence indicate a specific pattern?

   a. three factors; affect
   b. in particular
   c. president's popularity
   d. the economy

2. Which pattern arranges the details in this paragraph?

   a. series
   b. definition
   c. cause/effect
   d. time order

Meiosis involves the following steps. First, the twenty-three chromosomes[2] of the egg (or sperm) cell duplicate themselves. Then they break up into smaller pieces and randomly exchange segments of genetic material with one another. Next, the new chromosome pairs divide to form two separate cells. Finally, the two new cells divide again. Each of the four new cells contains a unique set of genetic material in its twenty-three chromosomes, one-half the usual number of chromosomes carried by all other cells.†

3. What word(s) in the topic sentence indicate(s) a specific pattern?

   a. Meiosis
   b. involves
   c. the
   d. following steps

4. Which pattern arranges the details in this paragraph?

   a. time order
   b. definition
   c. cause/effect
   d. comparison/contrast

By all odds the most powerful indicator of judicial power can be found in the kinds of remedies that the courts will impose. A **remedy** is defined as a judicial order setting forth what must be done to correct a situation that a judge believes to be wrong. In ordinary cases, such as when one person sues another, the remedy is straightforward; the loser must pay the winner for some injury that he or she has caused, the loser must agree to abide by the terms of

1. **Franklin D. Roosevelt:** the thirty-second president of the United States
2. **chromosomes:** in cells, proteins that transmit hereditary information

* Adapted from Barbour and Wright, *Keeping the Republic*. Boston: Houghton Mifflin, 2001, 203–204.

† From Seifert et al., *Lifespan Development*, 2nd ed. Boston: Houghton Mifflin, 2000, 64. Copyright © 2000 by Houghton Mifflin Company. Reprinted with permission.

a contract he or she has broken, or the loser must promise not to do some unpleasant thing, like dumping garbage on a neighbor's lawn.*

5. What word(s) in the topic sentence indicate(s) a specific pattern?
   a. order
   b. setting forth
   c. to correct
   d. is defined as

6. Which pattern arranges the details in this paragraph?
   a. cause/effect
   b. time order
   c. series
   d. definition

The Appalachian mountain range and the Ouachitas mountain system are similar in a few ways. The Appalachian mountain range extends from Newfoundland to Alabama and then continues a short distance below the Gulf Coastal Plain, where it is covered by younger sediments.[1] Another mountain system, the Ouachitas, similar in age and structure to the Appalachians, extends across Arkansas, Oklahoma, and Texas down into northern Mexico. The two mountain systems are also alike in that they are divided along their lengths and widths into a number of provinces[2] that differ in rock type, structure, and age.†

7. What word(s) in the topic sentence indicate(s) a specific pattern?
   a. Appalachian; Ouachitas
   b. mountain range
   c. similar
   d. are

8. Which pattern arranges the details in this paragraph?
   a. definition
   b. cause/effect
   c. time order
   d. comparison/contrast

6

When anger surfaces, we usually have several options. If another driver pulls out in front of your car and almost causes an accident, you will likely feel fear followed by anger. One option is to suppress the angry feelings. Another option is to give way to irrational thinking and act out your angry feelings. You may be tempted to pull alongside the other driver and make a threatening gesture or shout obscenities. A final option would have you do nothing and just live with the feelings of anger that have surfaced during this incident.‡

1. **sediments:** materials produced by the weathering of rock
2. **provinces:** areas of land

* From Wilson and DiIulio, *American Government*, 8th ed. Boston: Houghton Mifflin, 2001, 423.

† Adapted from Dolgoff, *Essentials of Physical Geology*. Boston: Houghton Mifflin, 1998, 372. Copyright © 1998 by Houghton Mifflin Company. Reprinted with permission.

‡ Adapted from Reece and Brandt, *Effective Human Relations in Organizations*, 7th ed. Boston: Houghton Mifflin, 1999, 234–235.

9. What word(s) in the topic sentence indicate a specific pattern?
   a. When
   b. anger surfaces
   c. have
   d. several options

10. Which pattern arranges the details in this paragraph?
    a. definition
    b. cause/effect
    c. comparison/contrast
    d. series

Boys and girls tend to view moral problems differently. As they grow up, boys learn to think more often in terms of general ethical principles that they can apply to specific moral situations. They might learn that deceiving is always bad in principle and evaluate a specific instance of deception of a friend against this generalization. Girls, on the other hand, tend to develop an ethic of care, a view that integrates principles with the contexts in which judgments must be made. A girl therefore may think deception is usually bad but also believe deception is ethical in certain circumstances, such as when a friend needs reassurance about the quality of a term paper that is actually mediocre[1] but took a lot of time and effort.*

11. What word(s) in the topic sentence indicate(s) a specific pattern?
    a. boys and girls
    b. view
    c. problems
    d. differently

12. Which pattern arranges the details in this paragraph?
    a. comparison/contrast
    b. definition
    c. series
    d. time order

6

Although the delegates[2] supported the broad principles of the Virginia Plan,[3] they were in sharp disagreement over many specific issues. The greatest controversy centered on representation in the legislative branch. The Great Compromise resolved this controversy at the convention.[4] Another compromise settled the issue of how representatives were to be chosen. State legislatures would select senators, and a state's eligible voters would elect members

1. **mediocre:** ordinary; moderate in quality
2. **delegates:** representatives; people who attend a conference or convention
3. **Virginia Plan:** 14 proposals to create a more powerful central government and give states proportional representation in the legislature
4. **convention:** Constitutional Convention of 1787

* Adapted from Seifert et al., *Lifespan Development*, 2nd ed. Boston: Houghton Mifflin, 2000, 362. Copyright © 2000 by Houghton Mifflin Company. Reprinted with permission.

of the House of Representatives. The final stumbling block over representation was the question of who was to be counted in determining a state's population. The Three-Fifths Compromise[1] settled this issue.*

13. What word(s) in the topic sentence indicate(s) a specific pattern?
    a. broad principles
    b. were
    c. sharp disagreement
    d. many specific issues

14. Which pattern arranges the details in this paragraph?
    a. time order
    b. series
    c. cause/effect
    d. definition

During the late 19th century, several developments in mass transportation allowed people to move faster and farther. By the 1870s, horse-drawn vehicles were disappearing from city streets, replaced by motor-driven conveyances.[2] Cable cars (carriages that moved by clamping onto a moving underground wire) came first. By the 1880s, cable-car lines operated in Chicago, San Francisco, and many other cities. Then in the 1890s, electric-powered streetcars began replacing horse cars and cable cars. Designed in Montgomery, Alabama, and Richmond, Virginia, electric trolleys spread to nearly every large American city. Between 1890 and 1902, the total extent of electrified track grew from 1,300 to 22,000 miles. In a few cities, companies raised track onto trestles,[3] enabling vehicles to travel without interference above jammed downtown streets.†

15. What word(s) in the topic sentence indicate(s) a specific pattern?
    a. several developments
    b. mass transportation
    c. allowed
    d. faster and farther

16. Which pattern arranges the details in this paragraph?
    a. time order
    b. definition
    c. cause/effect
    d. comparison/contrast

The present system of traffic control is inconvenient and dangerous, and there are serious consequences resulting from this less-than-perfect system. Three children have been seriously injured in the last year on First Street

1. **Three-Fifths Compromise:** decision to include three-fifths of slaves during a headcount of a state's population
2. **conveyances:** vehicles for transportation
3. **trestles:** horizontal beams or bars held up by two pairs of supporting legs

* Adapted from Berkin et al., *Making America*, brief 2nd ed. Boston: Houghton Mifflin, 2001, 137.
† Adapted from Norton et al., *A People and a Nation*, 6th ed. Boston: Houghton Mifflin, 2001, 520. Copyright © 2001 by Houghton Mifflin Company. Reprinted with permission.

while attempting to cross an unguarded crossing. At the crossing on the by-pass, several accidents have resulted when oncoming traffic has failed to stop for the red light. Traffic jams causing long delays and increasing psychological stress on drivers occur every weekday during the rush hours. Directions showing lanes in which to turn, painted on the street, are completely worn away by the end of the winter.*

17. What word(s) in the topic sentence indicate(s) a specific pattern?
    a. inconvenient and dangerous
    b. consequences; resulting
    c. present system
    d. less-than-perfect system

18. Which pattern arranges the details in this paragraph?
    a. comparison/contrast
    b. cause/effect
    c. time order
    d. series

A television network is an organization that distributes programs, typically by satellite and microwave relay, to all its linked stations so that the programs can be broadcast at the same time. ABC, CBS, Fox, and NBC are the broadcast networks that regularly reach the largest number of people. They are advertiser supported, as are two smaller television networks, the Warner Brothers (WB) Network and United Paramount Network (UPN). The Public Broadcasting Service (PBS) is the network for noncommercial stations.†

19. What word in the topic sentence indicates a specific pattern?
    a. is
    b. organization
    c. typically
    d. broadcast

20. Which pattern arranges the details in this paragraph?
    a. definition
    b. cause/effect
    c. time order
    d. comparison/contrast

6

* Adapted from Andrews et al., *Public Speaking*. Boston: Houghton Mifflin, 1999, 172.

† Adapted from Turow, *Media Today*. Boston: Houghton Mifflin, 1999, 270. Copyright © 1999 by Houghton Mifflin Company. Reprinted with permission.

CHAPTER 7
Inferences

GOALS FOR CHAPTER 7

- **Define the term *inference.***
- **Explain how inferences are made.**
- **State three reasons for asking readers to make inferences.**
- **Use guidelines to make accurate inferences from reading selections.**
- **Write an entry in a reading journal.**
- **Read and understand information in a bar graph.**

Reading selections don't always state everything you should know about a subject. Instead, you're expected to figure out information that's not actually in the text by drawing inferences, or conclusions. To see how well you already do this, take the test below.

TEST YOURSELF

Read the following sentences and answer the questions that follow. Circle the letter of the correct answer.

When I returned home from the store, I took off my wet clothes and dried my hair.

1. What you can infer about the weather?
   a. It was dry and sunny.
   b. It was raining.
   c. It was warm.
   d. It was cold.

Dolores spent the day raking leaves.

2. What can you infer about the season?
   a. It was autumn or fall.
   b. It was spring.
   c. It was summer.
   d. It was winter.

Frances is on a fixed income, so she uses coupons when she shops at the grocery store.

7

3. What can you infer about coupons?
   a. They are the same as money.
   b. They can only be used at the grocery store.
   c. They can save you money at the grocery store.
   d. They are good to use only with certain items.

Earphones on, eyes on the computer screen, the ninth grader types the word he hears: I-M-I-G-E-S. Wrong, the computer tells him. He tries again: I-M-U-G-E-S. Still wrong. He starts the next word. T-E-C-N-O-L in a flash of frustration, he leaves the spelling program and clicks into a reading drill, where he correctly answers questions about the Blue Man group, and then, calmer, he returns to the spelling program.*

4. What can you infer about the ninth grader from this passage?
   a. He is not a good speller.
   b. He is not computer literate.
   c. He is very computer literate.
   d. He is working on a computer in his home.

While wearing either a sweater or swimsuit in front of a mirror, male and female students took a challenging standardized math test. All students' scores on this test were adjusted based on their scores from standardized college entrance math examinations. The men's scores were unaffected by what clothes they were wearing. The women's scores were affected. Women did significantly worse on the test if they were wearing a swimsuit than if they were wearing a sweater.†

5. What can you infer about women from this passage?
   a. They do poorly on math tests.
   b. They feel uncomfortable around men.
   c. They feel uncomfortable in bathing suits.
   d. They like to wear sweaters all year round.

7

Inferences

Writers do not write down everything they want you to understand about a topic, but they expect you to figure out this information anyway. How? They

* From Tamar Lewin, "In Cities, a Battle to Improve Teenage Literacy, *New York Times*, April 14, 2004, www.nytimes.com.

† Adapted from Brehm et al., *Social Psychology*, 5th ed. Boston: Houghton Mifflin, 2002, 172. Copyright © 2002 by Houghton Mifflin Company. Reprinted with permission.

know you make inferences while you read. An **inference** is a conclusion you draw that's based upon the stated information, the implied information, and your own knowledge of the subject. You made one type of inference when you learned how to determine implied main ideas in Chapter 4. When you consider a group of related supporting details and draw a conclusion about the point they suggest, you're inferring that main idea. But you make many more kinds of smaller inferences, too, as you read. For example, read the following passage.

> A woman's voice in the dark, a voice that meant death. That is what they talk about, the children who survived, even as the decades pass and their hair grays. Not just about the two famous killers with a flashlight and a gun wresting a boy from his bed, but about those who helped them. Simeon Wright, who was lying next to his cousin Emmett Till[1] that fateful Mississippi night, remembers the intruders well enough. But he also recalls a third man out on the porch. And he repeats his deceased father Mose's recollection that "they took Emmett out to the truck to ask 'Is this the one?' And a female voice said, 'He's the one.'" Mose Wright used to repeat this often.*

After you read this short passage, did you conclude that many years ago, in the middle of the night, Emmett Till was abducted and killed by two men in revenge for something he said or did to a woman? If you did, you made several inferences to reach that conclusion. First of all, the paragraph never says exactly when this crime took place, but decades have passed and the children who survived now have gray hair, so you concluded that it happened quite a long time ago. Next, the passage never says that Emmett Till was abducted. But you figured that out based on the information that the men, one with a gun, "wrest" the boy from his bed. How do you know that Emmett was murdered? You based that conclusion on the information that the other children "survived." Also, the two men who took Emmett from his bed are called "killers," and the woman's voice "meant death." How do you know the murder was an act of revenge? The men have a woman outside identify him to make sure they have the right person.

7

1. In 1955, the murder of fourteen-year-old Emmett Till fueled support for the civil rights movement, especially black Americans' boycott of the segregated buses in Montgomery, Alabama, later that same year. Although Roy Bryant and J. W. Milam stood trial for Till's murder and were acquitted, Milam later confessed to the crime.

* Adapted from David Van Biema, "Revisiting a Martyrdom," *Time,* May 24, 2004, 57.

Therefore, even though the passage does not tell you exactly what happened, you still understand because of your ability to make inferences. "To infer" means "to read between the lines." You see more than what is actually there because you bring your own knowledge, experiences, and observations to your reading, allowing you to fill in the gaps. For instance, you've seen cars broken down on the side of the highway. Therefore, when you see a parked car on the shoulder of the interstate and people standing next to it, you conclude that the vehicle has malfunctioned and the people are stranded, so they're waiting for a ride and a tow truck. You apply these same experiences and observations as you read.

Here is another example that illustrates how you use your previous knowledge to make inferences.

> A man showed up at a Citizen's Bank in Connecticut on a Monday at 3:08 P.M., wearing a mask and carrying a note. From the window, bank workers—who had just closed shop eight minutes before—watched as the man pulled futilely[1] on the locked door before fleeing in a truck. A police sergeant witnessed the suspect throwing the mask and a note out the truck window, and Michael Maslar, 45, later surrendered without incident. Maslar was arrested and was being held on $500,000 bail.*

This passage expects you to conclude that the man who was arrested intended to rob the bank. It asks you to recall your memory of news stories, observations, or personal experiences that have taught you that a man who tries to enter a bank with a mask and a note and then "flees" when he can't get in is planning to commit a crime. Did you also infer that the would-be robber wasn't very bright? If you did, you based that conclusion on the information that the bank closed before the man showed up. Although a 3:00 o'clock closing time seems early for a bank, the passage does not mention that it was unusual, leaving the reader to believe that the man should have researched his intended target before trying to carry out his scheme.

7

As you read the next passage, think about what knowledge you must possess in order to make the right conclusions.

> Rich Boland, who directs stress management operations for Pittsburgh, passed out hundreds of teddy bears to FBI agents and state

1. **futilely:** uselessly

* Adapted from "Would-be Banker Tripped Up By Bank's Closing," www.usatoday.com/news/nweird/nweird.htm, October 16, 2001.

troopers combing through a plane crash site. "Initially," Boland says, "I thought it might be a bit of an issue—here are these big, burly[1] state police officers and I'm going to give them a teddy bear." But when the agents heard the cuddly critters were available, "people were coming up and asking, 'Hey, you got any more of those bears?'"*

First of all, the passage asks you to interpret why Mr. Boland would be passing out teddy bears at a plane crash site. You rely on your knowledge and experiences that teddy bears are comforting to children, so Mr. Boland thought they might help adults involved in a stressful situation. Then, the passage asks you to infer why "big, burly police officers" might not want a teddy bear. Like Boland, most readers would assume that "tough" grown-ups are too old for teddy bears. Therefore, they would reject them as a means of comfort. Finally, what can you infer from the information that FBI agents were seeking the bears? You would infer that the second inference is incorrect: teddy bears are comforting to adults, too.

Exercise 7.1

Look at the following comic strips and photographs and write a checkmark next to each accurate inference.

Snuffy Smith reprinted with special permission of King Features Syndicate.

1. _____ Jughaid and his mother are preparing to celebrate Easter.

   _____ Jughaid has not been collecting all the eggs.

   _____ The woman wants to cook chicken for dinner.

   _____ This woman and her son are wealthy poultry farmers.

1. **burly:** heavy, strong, and muscular

* Adapted from Olivia Barker, "Reliable Teddy Bears Are Huggable Healing For Grief," *USA Today,* October 12, 2001, 1D.

7

TANK McNAMARA

by Jeff Millar & Bill Hinds

2. _____ Tiger Woods feels sorry for the Rapanui people who live on Easter Island.

_____ Tourists plan to boycott Easter Island because they are frightened of the Rapanui people.

_____ The people of Easter Island do not understand how to make money.

_____ The people of Rapanui gave Tiger Woods one of their colossal statues to pay him for playing in their tournament.

© Tim Boyle/Newsmakers/Getty Images

3. _____ This couple won a lottery.
   _____ This couple lives in Chicago.
   _____ The man and woman are both retired.
   _____ The man in the photo is giving his money to charity.

© Jonathan Barth/BarthPhoto.com

4. _____ The people at the desks are from Canada.
   _____ The women are students comparing notes.
   _____ The students have just taken a test.
   _____ The women are angry at each other.

© Gamma

5. _____ This cliff is in Arizona.

_____ This man in the photo is a stunt man.

_____ The man bought the chairs at Wal-Mart.

_____ The man in the photo is crazy.

Exercise 7.2

Read the following paragraphs and respond to the questions that follow by circling the letter of the correct answer.

Seldom has an unsurprising finding elicited the near delirium[1] of the NASA scientists who announced last week that, on close inspection, a patch of Mars was once sopping[2] wet. James Garvin, the agency's lead scientist for lunar and Mars exploration, bubbled with glee as he described the water-deposited minerals that the six-wheeled Mars rover Opportunity found after it rambled over a gray plain to a ledge of exposed rock. Exulted[3] Garvin, "Unbelievable!".*

1. **delirium:** excitement
2. **sopping:** soaked, drenched
3. **exulted:** rejoiced

* From Charles Pitt, "Ancient Water Buoys Hopes of Past Life," *U.S. News and World Report,* March 15, 2004, 71.

7

1. What can you infer about the Mars rover?
   a. He is an astronaut.
   b. It is a machine.
   c. It is a type of boat.
   d. It was destroyed when it fell off a cliff into water.

I have memories of Dad coming home from work and wrestling with me on the floor. I remember my mom holding my hand and walking me to the library, and eating Ritz crackers while I sat amazed as she answered the questions on *Jeopardy!*[1] correctly. I remember Easy-Bake Ovens and learning math by counting pinto beans. There were Tootsie Roll pops and even a pet chick (one of those colored ones they used to sell at Easter) that I named Chicken Noodle. I have memories of fishing with my dad and vacations in Florida every year on my birthday.*

2. What does the author want you to infer about her childhood from this passage?
   a. She had a happy childhood.
   b. She didn't like her parents.
   c. She wished she had been raised by her biological parents.
   d. She was depressed as a child.

One of the defining moments of my life came in the fourth grade—the year I was Ms. Duncan's student. I really came into myself in her class. For the first time, I wasn't afraid to be smart. She encouraged me to read as much as I could, and she often stayed after school to work with me. For many years after that, I had one goal for myself: I would one day become a fourth-grade teacher who would win the Teacher of the Year Award.

Ron Clark is living my dream. I met him last fall in Los Angeles. He'd not only traveled from East Harlem to Los Angeles to receive his award but he'd raised more than $25,000 to bring his entire class with him. As I watched the video about Ron's life and his decision to relocate from North Carolina to one of the toughest areas of Harlem, I was moved to tears. What I saw in Ron that day left me humbled and inspired—I could literally feel his deep sense of love for and connection with his students.†

1. ***Jeopardy!:*** a television game show

* From Tina Wesson, "On Being . . . Adopted," *Rosie,* November 2001, 71.
† Adapted from Oprah Winfrey, "Mr. Clark's Opus," *O* Magazine, November 2001, 110.

3. What can you infer about Ron Clark from this passage?
   a. He had a profound effect on the writer of this passage.
   b. He was one of Ms. Duncan's students.
   c. He never thought he'd win.
   d. He had never been to Los Angeles before.

Telltale holes, each about the size of a dime, recently started appearing in the soft spring earth beneath big trees on the University of Maryland campus in College Park. Entomologist[1] Mike Raupp can hardly contain his excitement. In a few weeks, the massive community known as Brood X will suddenly emerge from the ground after lurking underfoot for 17 years. Billions of them will fly clumsily around 15 eastern states in a brief mating frenzy, shrieking in a daytime din[2] that can rival a jet engine.*

4. What can you infer about Brood X?
   a. They are fish.
   b. They are insects.
   c. They are rats.
   d. They are tropical birds.

Howard Schultz, CEO of Starbucks Coffee Company, grew up in a lower-middle-class family in federally subsidized[3] housing in Brooklyn. His father was a blue-collar worker who held a variety of jobs. Schultz says, "He was not valued as a worker; the system he was part of beat him down, and he became a bitter person who lost his self-esteem." Schultz is now working hard to make sure every employee feels valued and respected. At Starbucks the employee, not the customer, comes first. This policy is based on the belief that enthusiastic, happy employees will keep customers coming back. Starbucks offers workers an employee ownership plan, excellent training programs, full medical and dental benefits (available even to part-time employees), and career advancement opportunities.†

5. What does the author want you to infer about Howard Schultz's memories of his father?
   a. They don't mean anything.
   b. They are responsible for shaping his philosophy toward his workers at Starbucks.
   c. They created his determination to become a very wealthy man.
   d. They contributed toward his success at Starbucks.

1. **entomologist:** scientist who studies insects
2. **din:** loud noise
3. **subsidized:** supported with financial assistance

---

* Adapted from Nell Boyce, "Summer of the Cicada," *U.S. News and World Report,* April 19, 2004, 70.

† Adapted from Reece and Brandt, *Effective Human Relations in Organizations,* 7th ed. Boston: Houghton Mifflin, 1999, 4.

Writers rely on readers' ability to make inferences for three reasons. First of all, passages that spelled out every detail would be boring and tedious to read. Second, they would be unnecessarily long. And finally, they would deprive readers of the pleasure they experience in figuring out some things for themselves.

Guidelines for Making Accurate Inferences

How can you make sure you're drawing the right conclusions from information in a text? Follow these guidelines.

- **Focus only on the details and information provided, and don't "read in" anything that's not there.**

It's surprisingly easy to take just a little bit of information and jump to unfounded conclusions. For example, think back to the earlier example about the murder of Emmett Till. What do you suppose Emmett Till did to the woman who identified him? The men killed him for his misdeed, so you might conclude that Till assaulted her in some way. However, the passage does not reveal exactly what Till did. (In fact, he is reported to have whistled at the wife of one of the men who killed him.) Now, without looking back at the passage, answer this question: Did a third person escape being charged with Emmett Till's murder? Did you answer yes? Why? You probably inferred that because Till's cousin Simeon Wright recalls a third man out on the porch, there were three killers rather than just two. Actually, though, we don't get enough information to be able to answer that question, so we should not leap to possibly inaccurate conclusions.

Next, read another passage.

> One of two escaped inmates holed up in a North Texas house freed his two captives early today, then shot the second fugitive to end the standoff. While jail escapee John Leroy Weston slept inside the house, his partner, Joe Bob Smith, helped free the two hostages, whose hands had been tied. The hostages then escaped through a bathroom window, law enforcement officers said. Harold Thompson and his wife, Dede, fled to shelter behind hay bales near the house. Before Smith could escape, officers said, Weston awoke and the two suspects began talking. Law officers, who had been negotiating with Smith, then heard gunfire at 3:50 A.M. Smith surrendered and Weston was sent to a hospital for treatment of a wound to the abdomen. A large cache[1] of weapons was found inside the farmhouse. Smith, who was unhurt, surrendered after the shooting

1. **cache:** hiding place

7

> and was taken to Wilson County Jail, where arraignment[1] was scheduled for later this morning. The freed hostages were uninjured.*

Would it be accurate to infer from this passage that the house is in a rural area? Yes, that's correct. Why? Because the hostages take shelter behind hay bales near the house and because the house is referred to as a farmhouse. Could you infer that one inmate shot the other one with a gun? Most readers would. However, the passage refers only to "weapons" and a "wound in the abdomen." Though it's unlikely, the weapons could have been crossbows. Why did one of the fugitives free the hostages and shoot his fellow escapee? We're told only that he had been negotiating with law officers. We can infer that they talked him into ending the standoff.

- **Don't ignore any details.**

The details provide the important clues. For instance, in the earlier example, was Emmett Till kidnapped during the day? The passage says that the woman's voice was "in the dark," the killers had a flashlight, and the children were in bed. If you conclude that the crime occurred during the day, you have ignored these details.

Here's another paragraph in which you must notice the details to make the right inferences:

> Like other dutiful mothers, Lisa Jillani took her newborn daughter, Samantha, to the doctor for required immunizations. As months passed, she began to notice "a gradual fading away" in her daughter. After the fourth of five sets of shots, Samantha "acted like she was in her own little world," Jillani said. ". . . She acted like she was drunk sometimes."
>
> Samantha, now 9, was 3 when she was diagnosed with sensory integration dysfunction, a milder-than-autism[2] disorder. Doctors couldn't identify a cause. After some research, Lisa and her husband, A. J., agreed that their second daughter, Madison, now 5, would get no vaccinations.
>
> The Jillanis' pediatrician refused to see them any more. And when Madison was born, the couple felt hospital nurses and doctors tried to intimidate them into accepting shots. "It was just a very hostile experience that I didn't think other people should have to go through," Lisa

7

1. **arraignment:** calling an accused person into a court of law to answer the charge made against him or her
2. **autism:** abnormal withdrawal and concentration upon oneself

* Adapted from Angela K. Brown, Associated Press, "Escapee Frees Hostages, Shoots Other Fugitive," *News Herald,* Morganton, NC, October 15, 2001, 7A. Reprinted with permission of The Associated Press.

said. A few months later, she started PAVE (People Advocating Vaccine Education), a group that advises parents not to vaccinate their children.*

Now, try to recall the details as you consider whether or not the following inferences are correct:

Lisa and A. J. Jillani believe that vaccinations caused their daughter Samantha to develop sensory integration dysfunction.

Samantha's doctors agreed with the Jillanis' conclusion.

Many doctors and nurses join the PAVE organization.

Think about how the details affect the inferences you make. The first statement is correct because the Jillanis did some research after their first daughter became ill and because they subsequently refused to allow their second daughter to be vaccinated. The second statement, however, is incorrect. The passage says Samantha's doctors could not identify the cause of her illness. The third statement is incorrect, too. The Jillanis' pediatrician would no longer treat their children, and hospital doctors and nurses pressured them to vaccinate their second child. Therefore, it would be correct to infer that most doctors and nurses advocate immunizations and incorrect to infer that they would want to join a group that advises against immunizations.

- **Make sure nothing contradicts your conclusion.**

Try not to overlook one or more details that may conflict with any preliminary conclusion you make about a passage. For example, read the following:

The mighty Tyrannosaurus rex deserved its reputation for viciousness, but in some ways, T. rex was a T. wreck, research suggests. The fearsome thunder-lizards lived wretched lives, says Wyoming paleontologist Robert Bakker. "They were beat up, limping, had oozing sores, were dripping pus and disease ridden, and had to worry about their children starving and other T. rexes coming in and kicking them out." Bakker, of the Wyoming Dinosaur Society, bases his characterization on research conducted by Elizabeth Rega, a physical anthropologist[1] at Western University in Pomona, California, and University of Iowa paleontologist[2] Chris Brochu. The pair have

1. **anthropologist:** scientist who studies the origins and development of human beings
2. **paleontologist:** scientist who studies prehistoric life forms

* Adapted from Karen Garloch, "Debate Simmers Over Vaccinations," *Charlotte Observer,* Charlotte, NC, October 15, 2001, 1E, 4E. Reprinted with permission from the *Charlotte Observer.* Copyright owned by the *Charlotte Observer.*

examined three T. rexes, including Sue, one of the most complete specimens in the world. Sue's lower leg bone had an infection that healed but probably leaked pus at times. "I don't know if this would have debilitated[1] the animal, but it probably would have been really smelly in life," says Rega, who presented her findings at the recent meeting of the Society of Vertebrate Paleontology at Montana State University–Bozeman. Sue also had several broken ribs, and several bones in her spine and tail had stiffened and begun to fuse.*

In this passage, you can infer that the Tyrannosaurus rex dinosaur was often injured. Can you also infer that the three T. rex specimens the paleontologists studied ultimately died of old age? Probably not. Not only is there no information to support that conclusion, most of the details actually contradict it. An animal suffering from multiple wounds, infections, and broken bones probably did not live long enough to be considered "old."

- **Don't let stereotypes and/or prejudices color your interpretation.**

When you think back to that story about Lisa Jillani and her People Advocating Vaccine Education group, did you infer that she and her husband were wrong to deny their second child immunizations? The only information in the passage that supports this conclusion is the doctors' and nurses' reactions to the parents' refusal to allow their baby to be vaccinated. If you agree with the doctors and nurses, you probably will be prejudiced against the Jillanis and their decision, and you will likely judge their decision to be irresponsible. You should be aware that some of your inferences will be colored by your own personal beliefs and attitudes, and that these can lead us to form generalizations that may be incorrect.

For example, read the following passage.

Scientists claimed bittersweet[2] victory in the experiment that used technology they hope can be used to shore up the numbers of endangered

1. **debilitated:** made weak or feeble

2. **bittersweet:** bitter and sweet at the same time

* Adapted from Michelle Healy, "T. Rex Played Hard, Lived Hard," *USA Today,* October 16, 2001, 7D.

animals. The Asian gaur, a bull calf named Noah, was born Monday at Trans-Ova Genetics in Sioux Center, Iowa, and died Wednesday. It was a project that united the technology of cloning with that of an interspecies birth.

Noah was the first animal to gestate[1] in the womb of another species and survive through the late stages of fetal development. Five other cows that became pregnant with cloned gaur fetuses spontaneously aborted the fetuses. To create Noah, scientists used the single cell of a dead gaur implanted into a cow's egg. They first removed the DNA from the cow's egg, ensuring that the interspecies pregnancy produce a gaur, not a gaur-cow mix.

Gaur, native to India and Burma, are brownish-black animals with white legs, a pronounced shoulder hump, and horns that curve inward. The largest of wild cattle, an adult male gaur can reach a shoulder height of six feet and weigh up to a ton with horns two feet long.

"The data collected clearly indicates that cross-species cloning worked, and as a scientist, I'm pleased," said Philip Damiani, a researcher with Advanced Cell Technology. "Despite this setback, the birth of Noah is grounds for hope," said Robert Lana, vice president of Medical and Scientific Development at ACT. "We still have a long way to go, but as this new technology evolves, it has the potential to save dozens of endangered species."

Bessie, an ordinary black and white Angus cow, gave birth under the watchful gaze of geneticists. The experiment cost Advanced Cell Technology around $200,000, Damiani said.*

Would you say that Noah died and the other cows aborted their fetuses because nature disagrees with human attempts at cloning? If you answered "yes," you're letting your opinions about cloning color your interpretation of the information. Actually, the scientists believed that they were successful in their experiment, and they express optimism about their future attempts. Yet, many people who oppose cloning for moral or religious reasons might conclude that the animals' deaths are proof that scientists should not be tampering with such technology.

1. **gestate:** develop in the womb

* Adapted from "Rare Ox Clone Dies After Birth," as it appears at http://my.abcnews.go.com, October 19, 2001. Reprinted with permission of The Associated Press.

Exercise 7.3

Read the following passages and circle the letter of the correct answer for each of the questions that follow.

In July 1861, Georgia matron[1] Gertrude Clanton Thomas wrote, "Events transcending in importance anything that has ever happened within the recollection of any living person in our country, have occurred since I have written in my journal. War has been declared." Fort Sumter in South Carolina had surrendered; Lincoln had called for 75,000 troops; four more southern states—Virginia, North Carolina, Arkansas, and Tennessee—had left the Union; the newly formed Confederate government had moved from Montgomery, Alabama, to Richmond, Virginia; and thousands of troops had passed through Augusta, Georgia, on their way to the front. "So much has taken place," Gertrude Thomas declared, "I appear to be endeavoring to recall incidents which have occurred many years instead of months ago."*

1. What can you infer about the war that Gertrude is referring to?
   a. It was the Civil War.
   b. It was World War I.
   c. It was the Revolutionary War.
   d. It was the War of 1812.
2. What can you infer from this passage about how Gertrude feels about the events?
   a. She was angry about what had happened.
   b. She was overwhelmed by all that had happened.
   c. She was frightened.
   d. She was happy and excited.
3. What can you infer about Gertrude?
   a. She probably supported the Confederate government.
   b. She probably supported keeping the Union intact.
   c. She probably opposed the war.
   d. If women had been able to vote, she would have voted for Lincoln.

Deena Karabell had lived in her New York City apartment for 15 years, so when she fell ill in 1983, she never suspected that her apartment itself could

1. **matron:** a married woman or widow

---

* Adapted from Boyer et al., *The Enduring Vision,* 5th ed., Boston: Houghton Mifflin, 2004, 437. Copyright © 2004 by Houghton Mifflin Company. Reprinted with permission.

be to blame. Over the next 15 years she grew progressively weaker. Finally, in the spring of 1998, she lost 30 pounds and went into anaphylactic shock[1] three times. She literally lay dying in her bedroom when a hired nurse noticed a strong odor of mold in the closet. Suddenly, things clicked. Karabell's family moved her out immediately. Today—at a safe distance from the mold—she is almost back to normal. "People are amazed at my recovery," she says."*

4. What can you infer about the cause of Deena's illness from this passage?
   a. Her closet was making her sick.
   b. The mold in the closet was making her sick.
   c. The starch in the nurse's uniform was making her sick.
   d. Deena's apartment was infested with bugs.

5. What can you infer about mold from this paragraph?
   a. It can be deadly.
   b. It thrives in apartments.
   c. It grows predominantly in New York City apartments.
   d. Only nurses can detect the existence of mold.

When Helena Rubinstein was growing up in Krakow, Poland, in the 1880s, her mother issued her the following piece of advice: "Women influence the world through love. Outer charm and inner beauty will give you the power to control your own life and hold the love of the man you will marry." The extent to which Rubinstein, who died in 1965 at the age of 94, employed love as a management tool while she was revolutionizing the way Americans thought of their faces is open to question. But she certainly exhibited other personal characteristics, such as a raging competitiveness, and a sharp tongue that could have put Sandra Bernhardt[2] to shame. In 1951, for example, Rubinstein was told by a journalist from the *Los Angeles Times* that her arch rival, Elizabeth Arden,[3] had suffered an accident—one of Arden's horses had bitten the cosmetics queen's finger off. Rubinstein replied, "I'm so sorry. Is the horse all right?"†

6. What can you infer about Helena Rubinstein from this paragraph?
   a. She continued living in Poland all of her life.
   b. She owned her own cosmetics company.
   c. She was in business with Elizabeth Arden.
   d. She did not like horses.

1. **anaphylactic shock:** sudden, severe, and sometimes fatal allergic reaction
2. **Sandra Bernhardt:** a comedienne
3. **Elizabeth Arden:** cosmetics company executive

* From Anne Underwood, "A Hidden Health Hazard," *Newsweek,* December 4, 2000, 74.

† From Rebecca Mead, "The Makeup Madame," *Allure,* October 2001, 232.

7

7. What can you infer about Rubinstein's feelings for Elizabeth Arden?
    a. She enjoyed Arden's company immensely.
    b. She liked Arden and often went horseback riding with her.
    c. She did not like Arden.
    d. She liked both Arden and her horse.

My conversation with the insurance agent went as I'd expected. She assumed, correctly, that the house my husband and I were buying (and were to move into with our two children) was protected by deadbolt locks and smoke detectors. She was satisfied the wood stove had been properly installed. She wasn't concerned about the lack of hydrants on our country road; a pond a quarter mile away would provide plenty of water in case of a fire. Only one fact troubled her. "You've got the size of the house listed as 1,200 square feet," she said. "That's just the first floor, right?" No, I said. That's the whole house, first and second floors. She paused. "That can't be," she insisted.*

8. What can you infer about the insurance agent?
    a. She thinks the house is too small for the author and her family.
    b. She loves small houses.
    c. She thinks families with children should buy houses with two stories.
    d. She likes being an insurance agent.

9. What can you infer about the author of this selection?
    a. She doesn't like climbing stairs.
    b. She doesn't like her insurance agent.
    c. She wishes the house were bigger.
    d. She thinks the house is big enough for her family.

10. What can you infer about the house in the selection?
    a. It is the size of a barn.
    b. It is smaller than the average American home.
    c. It is smaller than the house the author used to live in.
    d. It is much bigger than the average American home.

7

Exercise 7.4

Read the following passages and then write a checkmark beside all of the accurate inferences in the list.

* Adapted from Barbara Stith, "When Half as Big Is More Than Enough," *Newsweek,* April 30, 2001, 22.

1. Any dog can sleep all day. The profoundness of my dog's laziness comes not from his immobility[1] but from his almost predatory[2] pursuit of ease. Example: He long ago learned that he can avoid the inconvenience of walking down the hall for a drink of water before bedtime by standing beside my own bedside cup of water and making a discontented, growly noise that sounds and functions exactly like a fussy old man clearing his throat. I am supposed to hold the cup under his nose for him so he can lap up all the water, then get out of bed to refill it. When I return, he will be sitting on my pillow, having taken my warm place on the bed. This happens every night. It used to be cute.*

   _____ 1. The dog sleeps in the bed with the narrator.

   _____ 2. The narrator loves his dog.

   _____ 3. The narrator works as a dog trainer.

   _____ 4. The dog is very old.

   _____ 5. The dog is disabled.

2. If there are 1,000 square feet in the two-bedroom flat, then a good 80 percent of that space is devoted to Jim Breidenbach's passion. Yes, there are those commemorative[3] programs that vendors hawk at most sporting events. But much of Breidenbach's collection consists of one-of-a-kind items, like a poster from the 1971 Muhammad Ali/Joe Frazier fight at Madison Square Garden. He has part of a seat from the old Madison Square Garden in one bedroom. He also has the ticket stub from the last hockey game played at the old Garden at 50th Street and Eighth Avenue—right next to a ticket stub from the first hockey game played at the new one. And somebody could just about outfit a whole hockey team in sticks, jerseys, and pucks in Breidenbach's apartment.†

   _____ 1. Jim Breidenbach is a fanatical sports fan.

   _____ 2. Jim Breidenbach lives in Brooklyn, New York.

   _____ 3. Jim Breidenbach is not married.

7

1. **immobility:** lack of movement
2. **predatory:** victimizing others for one's own gain
3. **commemorative:** serving as a reminder or memorial to something

* Adapted from David Dudley, "The Laziest Dog in the World," *Modern Maturity,* January/February 2002, 54.

† Adapted from Clem Richardson, "Stuck on Pucks," *New York Daily News,* March 22, 2004, 15.

_____ 4. Jim Breidenbach has an impressive collection of sports memorabilia.

_____ 5. Jim Breidenbach enjoys hockey.

3. Located in the heart of Tokyo's government district, the Kasumigaseki subway station is one of the city's busiest stations. But what strikes a Westerner accustomed to American subways is the almost surreal[1] orderliness of the place. People line up at appointed places. Trains arrive at precisely scheduled times a few minutes apart. Uniformed attendants are posted throughout the gleaming, well-lit station—a dependable oasis of rational order in the hectic urban whirlwind that is modern Tokyo.*

_____ 1. Tokyo does not have many subways.

_____ 2. People like to decorate Tokyo subway stations with graffiti (spray-painted artwork).

_____ 3. Americans do not line up at appointed places in subway stations.

_____ 4. Tokyo's subways are the world's most modern and technologically advanced.

_____ 5. Trains at American subway stations are often late.

4. Every surface in my bathroom is covered with bottles of face moisturizer, body lotion, volumizer, night cream, and eye serum.[2] On the shelves in my shower, I have nine shampoos, five conditioners, and ten bath gels. When I leave every morning, I cart six mascaras and twelve lip glosses in my makeup bag, just for the day, just for the office. I find myself wandering into beauty boutiques and drugstores every day scanning whether I'd truly tried each beauty potion available in the store.†

_____ 1. The author shops a lot.

_____ 2. The author is allergic to many cosmetics.

_____ 3. The author cares about her appearance.

_____ 4. The author enjoys using body lotion, shampoo, bath gels, and other beauty products.

_____ 5. The author is in her twenties.

1. **surreal:** having on odd, dreamlike quality

2. **serum:** fluid

* Adapted from Malcolm Jones, "Notes from the Underground," *Newsweek,* April 30, 2001, 78.

† Adapted from Linda Wells, "The High Road, and the Low," *Allure,* October 2001, 70.

7

5. Even now, at 63, when my mother speaks of home, she does not mean the house that she and my father rented before I was born. She does not mean the house they bought soon after I turned five, or even the one after that, a bigger house, perched on the edge of a ravine. What she means by home—what she has always meant—is my grandmother's 100-acre farm in Dacada, Wisconsin: the white clapboard house at the end of a country road, yes, but also the barn and the milk house across the courtyard, the smokehouse and the chicken coop out back. What she means is the gently sloping hill that rolls from the root-cellar door down to the apple orchard, the grape arbor reaching long and low to either side, humming with bees. She means the twin cherry trees my grandfather planted before his death, and the view from the vegetable garden: flat fields stretching in all directions; weathered fence posts crowned with meadowlarks; the clean, dark line where the land meets the sky.*

_____ 1. The author's mother is confused and may have Alzheimer's disease.[1]

_____ 2. The author's mother is dead.

_____ 3. The author's mother has very fond memories of her childhood home.

_____ 4. The author did not like her grandparents' home.

_____ 5. Dacada, Wisconsin, is a rural town.

Making Inferences in Literature

When you read literary selections, such as novels, short stories, poetry, plays, and essays, you'll often be required to make inferences. Creative writers tend to describe situations, people, objects, and ideas with specific details, and then they let the reader draw conclusions based on those details. Therefore, improving your ability to make inferences will help you understand and

1. **Alzheimer's disease:** a disease marked by progressive loss of mental capacity

* From A. Manette Ansay, "One Hundred Acres," *Real Simple,* October 2001, 149. Reprinted by permission.

7

appreciate literature more. For example, read this passage from the classic novel *Wuthering Heights* by Emily Brontë:

> One fine summer morning—it was the beginning of harvest, I remember—Mr. Earnshaw, the old master, told Joseph what was to be done during the day, he turned to Hindley, and Cathy, and me—for I sat eating my porridge[1] with them—and he said, speaking to his son, "Now, my bonny man, I'm going to Liverpool to-day, what shall I bring you? You may choose what you like: only let it be little, for I shall walk there and back: sixty miles each way, that is a long spell!"
>
> Hindley named a fiddle, and then he asked Miss Cathy; she was hardly six years old, but she could ride any horse in the stable, and she chose a whip.
>
> He did not forget me, though he was rather severe sometimes. He promised to bring me a pocketful of apples and pears, and then he kissed his children good-bye, and set off.*

The reader can draw several important conclusions from this brief passage. First, we learn about the kind of person Mr. Earnshaw is. He's about to undertake a long journey, but he's thinking about bringing back presents for his children. He obviously loves them and wants to make them happy by giving them gifts. What can you infer about the speaker of this passage? Is the person telling the story male or female? There's nothing in the passage that indicates the speaker's gender. Is the narrator one of Mr. Earnshaw's children? No, the narrator must be a servant or employee. Cathy and Hindley will get expensive gifts—a fiddle and a whip—but the narrator will receive only apples and pears. The narrator also tells us that Mr. Earnshaw "did not forget me," suggesting that he brings gifts for others besides his children. This, too, is a further indication of his kindness.

7

Next, take a look at a passage from Mark Twain's nonfiction memoir entitled *Life on the Mississippi:*

> My father was a justice of the peace, and I supposed he possessed the power of life and death over all men and could hang anybody that offended him. This was distinction enough for me as a general thing; but the desire to be a steamboatman kept intruding, nevertheless. I first wanted to be a cabin-boy, so that I could come out with a white apron on and shake a tablecloth over the side, where all my comrades

1. **porridge:** soft food made by boiling oatmeal or another meal in water or milk

* Adapted from Emily Brontë, *Wuthering Heights*. New York: Bantam, 1947.

could see me; later I thought I would rather be the deckhand who stood on the end of the stage-plank with the coil of rope in his hand, because he was particularly conspicuous.[1] But these were only day-dreams,—they were too heavenly to be contemplated as real possibilities. By and by one of our boys went away. He was not heard of for a long time. At last he turned up as apprentice engineer or 'striker' on a steamboat. This thing shook the bottom out of my Sunday-school teachings. That boy has been notoriously worldly, and I just the reverse; yet he was exalted[2] to this eminence,[3] and I left in obscurity and misery. There was nothing generous about this fellow in his greatness. He would always manage to have a rusty bolt to scrub while his boat tarried[4] at our town, and he would sit on the inside guard and scrub it, where we could all see him and envy him and loathe him. And whenever his boat was laid up he would come home and swell around the town in his blackest and greasiest clothes, so that nobody could help remembering that he was a steamboatman; and he used all sorts of steamboat technicalities in his talk, as if he were so used to them that he forgot common people could not understand them. He would speak of the "labboard" side of a horse in an easy, natural way that would make one wish he was dead. And he was always talking about "St. Looy" like an old citizen; he would refer casually to occasions when he "was coming down Fourth Street," or when he was "passing by the Planter's House," or when there was a fire and he took a turn on the brakes of "the old Big Missouri;" and then he would go on and lie about how many towns the size of ours were burned down there that day. Two or three of the boys had long been persons of consideration among us because they had been to St. Louis once and had a vague general knowledge of its wonders, but the day of their glory was over now. They lapsed into a humble silence, and learned to disappear when the ruthless "cub"-engineer approached. This fellow had money, too, and hair oil. Also an ignorant silver watch and a showy brass watch chain. He wore a leather belt and used no suspenders. If ever a youth was cordially[5] admired and hated by his comrades, this one was. No girl could withstand his charms. He "cut out" every boy in the village. When his boat blew up at last, it diffused[6] a tranquil contentment among us such as we had not known for months. But when he came home the

1. **conspicuous:** obvious, easy to notice
2. **exalted:** elevated
3. **eminence:** high rank or standing
4. **tarried:** remained, stayed, lingered
5. **cordially:** warmly; strongly felt
6. **diffused:** spread

next week, alive, renowned,[1] and appeared in church all battered up and bandaged, a shining hero, stared at and wondered over by everybody, it seemed to us that the partiality[2] of Providence[3] for an undeserving reptile had reached a point where it was open to criticism.*

What can you infer from this passage about how the author and his fellow townspeople feel about steamboatmen? Many clues in the passage tell readers that they greatly admire the men who work on the boats. Do the author and his friends really hate the boy who goes off to work on a steamboat? No, they are jealous of him. The author tells us that he dreams of being a steamboatman, so he and his friends envy the boy for his job, his money, his attractiveness to girls, and his heroism when he survives an explosion. Is the boy humble about his job? No, he likes to advertise the fact that he is a steamboatman and uses his position to increase his status in the community.

Poetry is yet another type of literature that requires the reader to make inferences. As a matter of fact, poetry is such a condensed form of expression that it relies heavily on the reader's ability to draw the right conclusions. For example, read the following poem by Theodore Roethke:

My Papa's Waltz†

The whiskey on your breath
Could make a small boy dizzy;
But I hung on like death:
Such waltzing was not easy.

We romped until the pans
Slid from the kitchen shelf;
My mother's countenance[4]
Could not unfrown itself.

The hand that held my wrist
Was battered on one knuckle;
At every step you missed
My right ear scraped a buckle.

1. **renowned:** famous
2. **partiality:** prejudice or favor
3. **Providence:** God
4. **countenance:** facial expression

---

* *Source:* Mark Twain, *Life on the Mississippi.*

† *Source:* "My Papa's Waltz," copyright 1942 by Hearst Magazines, Inc., from *The Collected Poems of Theodore Roethke* by Theodore Roethke. Used by permission of Doubleday, a division of Random House, Inc.

7

You beat time on my head
With a palm caked hard by dirt,
Then waltzed me off to bed
Still clinging to your shirt.

The poet expects you to make a number of inferences based on the details he includes. What kind of person is the father? He's got whiskey on his breath and battered and dirty hands. These details suggest that he's a hard-working, rough sort of person. He may even be drunk. What can you conclude about father and son's "dance"? Their movements cause pans to fall from shelves, the child scrapes the father's buckle, and his father "beats time" on his head. The mother disapproves probably because their game is making noise and a mess. All of these details suggest that the game is rough, too. Does the child enjoy this game? He says he "hung on like death" as they "romped," and he clings to his father's shirt. He also calls their game a "waltz," which is a graceful, elegant dance. His actions and his description of their game seem to indicate that he likes it. Also, he's a boy, and experience tells us that boys tend to enjoy rough-and-tumble games. The reader must examine these details carefully, though, to make the right interpretation.

Exercise 7.5

Read the following selection by Mitch Albom from his book, *Tuesdays with Morrie*. Although the selection is only four short paragraphs, you can infer a lot about Morrie, the narrator, and the nature of their relationship. Respond to the questions that follow by circling the letter of the correct answer.

The First Tuesday: We Talk About the World

1 Connie opened the door and let me in. Morrie was in his wheelchair by the kitchen table, wearing a loose cotton shirt and even looser black sweatpants. They were loose because his legs had atrophied[1] beyond normal clothing size—you could get two hands around his thighs and have your fingers touch. Had he been able to stand, he'd have been no more than five feet tall, and he'd probably have fit into a sixth grader's jeans.

2 "I got you something," I announced, holding up a brown paper bag. I had stopped on my way from the airport at a nearby supermarket and purchased some turkey, potato salad, macaroni salad, and bagels. I knew there

1. **atrophied:** wasted away

was plenty of food at the house, but I wanted to contribute something. I was so powerless to help Morrie otherwise. And I remembered his fondness for eating.

3 We sat at the kitchen table, surrounded by wicker chairs. This time, without the need to make up sixteen years of information, we slid quickly into the familiar waters of our old college dialogue, Morrie asking questions, listening to my replies, stopping like a chef to sprinkle in something I'd forgotten or hadn't realized. He asked about the newspaper strike, and true to form, he couldn't understand why both sides didn't simply communicate with each other and solve their problems. I told him not everyone was as smart as he was.

4 Occasionally, he had to stop to use the bathroom, a process that took some time. Connie would wheel him to the toilet, then lift him from the chair and support him while he went. Each time he came back, he looked tired.*

1. Which can you infer about Morrie from the selection?
   a. He is a young man.
   b. He is seriously ill.
   c. He has lived his life in a wheelchair.
   d. He is married to Connie.
2. What can you infer about Morrie and the narrator's relationship?
   a. They have just met.
   b. They met two years earlier.
   c. They have known each other a fairly long time.
   d. They often argue.
3. What can you infer about the location of the meeting between Morrie and the narrator?
   a. They are visiting in Morrie's hospital room.
   b. They are at a college campus.
   c. They are in Detroit.
   d. They are in Morrie's home.
4. From the information provided, what do you think the narrator does for a living?
   a. He is a college professor.
   b. He works for a newspaper.
   c. He takes care of Morrie.
   d. He is a wheelchair salesman.

7

* From *Tuesdays with Morrie*, by Mitch Albom, copyright © 1997 by Mitch Albom. Used by permission of Doubleday, a division of Random House, Inc.

CHAPTER 7 REVIEW

Fill in the blanks in the following statements.

1. An ___________ is a conclusion you draw that's based upon the stated information.
2. ___________ use their knowledge, experiences, and observations to help them make inferences.
3. Writers ask readers to make inferences to keep their writing ___________, ___________, and fun for the reader.
4. To make accurate inferences, readers should avoid ___________ information that's not in a text. Conversely, they should not ignore any details provided.
5. To make accurate inferences, readers should make sure nothing ___________ a conclusion, and they should avoid letting stereotypes or ___________ affect their conclusions.

Reading Selection

Practicing the Active Reading Strategy:

Before and While You Read

You can use active reading strategies before, as, and after you read a selection. The following are some suggestions for active reading strategies that you can perform before you read and while you read.

1. Skim the selection for any unfamiliar words. Circle or highlight any words you do not know.
2. As you read, underline, highlight, or circle important words or phrases.
3. Write down any questions about the selection if you are confused by the information presented.
4. Jot notes in the margin to help you understand the material.

The Diary of a Young Girl

by Anne Frank

Wednesday, July 8, 1942

Dearest Kitty,

1 It seems like years since Sunday morning. So much has happened it's as if the whole world had suddenly turned upside down. But as you can see, Kitty, I'm still alive, and that's the main thing, Father says. I'm alive all right, but don't ask where or how. You probably don't understand a word I'm saying today, so I'll begin by telling you what happened Sunday afternoon.

2 At three o'clock (Hello had left but was supposed to come back later), the doorbell rang. I didn't hear it, since I was out on the balcony, lazily reading in the sun. A little while later, Margot appeared in the kitchen doorway looking very agitated. "Father has received a call-up notice from the SS,"[1] she whispered. "Mother has gone to see Mr. van Daan." (Mr. van Daan is Father's business partner and a good friend.)

3 I was stunned. A call-up: everyone knows what that means. Visions of concentration camps[2] and lonely cells raced through my head. How could we let Father go to such a fate? "Of course he's not going," declared Margot as we waited for Mother in the living room. "Mother's gone to Mr. van Daan to ask whether we can move to our hiding place tomorrow. The van Daans are going with us. There will be seven of us altogether." Silence. We couldn't speak. The thought of Father off visiting someone in the Jewish Hospital and completely unaware of what was happening, the long wait for Mother, the heat, the suspense—all this reduced us to silence.

4 Suddenly the doorbell rang again. "That's Hello," I said.

5 "Don't open the door!" exclaimed Margot to stop me. But it wasn't necessary, since we heard Mother and Mr. van Daan downstairs talking to Hello, and then the two of them came inside and shut the door behind them. Every time the bell rang, either Margot or I had to tiptoe downstairs to see if it was Father, and we didn't let anyone else in. Margot and I were sent from the room, as Mr. van Daan wanted to talk to Mother alone.

6 When she and I were sitting in our bedroom, Margot told me that the call-up was not for Father, but for her. At this second shock, I began to cry. Margot is sixteen—apparently they want to send girls her age away on their own. But thank goodness she won't be going; Mother had said so herself, which must be what Father had meant

1. **the SS:** a unit of Germany's Nazi Party, which served as German dictator Adolph Hitler's personal guard and special security force; a call-up notice from the SS was a command to report for removal to a concentration camp

2. **concentration camps:** camps where prisoners of war, enemies, and political prisoners are locked up, typically under harsh conditions

when he talked to me about our going into hiding. Hiding . . . where we would hide? In the city? In the country? In a house? In a shack? When, where, how . . . ? These were questions I wasn't allowed to ask, but they still kept running through my mind.

7 Margot and I started packing our most important belongings in a schoolbag. The first thing I stuck in was this diary, and then curlers, handkerchiefs, schoolbooks, a comb and some old letters. Preoccupied by the thought of going into hiding, I stuck the craziest things in the bag, but I'm not sorry. Memories mean more to me than dresses.

8 Father finally came home around five o'clock, and we called Mr. Kleiman to ask if he could come by that evening. Mr. van Daan left and went to get Miep. Miep arrived and promised to return later that night, taking with her a bag full of shoes, dresses, jackets, underwear, and stockings. After that it was quiet in our apartment; none of us felt like eating. It was still hot, and everything was very strange.

9 We had rented our big upstairs room to a Mr. Goldschmidt, a divorced man in his thirties, who apparently had nothing to do that evening, since despite all our polite hints he hung around until ten o'clock.

10 Miep and Jan Gies came at eleven. Miep, who's worked for Father's company since 1933, has become a close friend, and so has her husband Jan. Once again, shoes, stockings, books, and underwear disappeared into Miep's bag and Jan's deep pockets. At eleven-thirty they too disappeared.

11 I was exhausted, and even though I knew it'd be my last night in my own bed, I fell asleep right away and didn't wake up until Mother called me at five-thirty the next morning. Fortunately, it wasn't as hot as Sunday; a warm rain fell throughout the day. The four of us were wrapped in so many layers of clothes it looked as if we were going off to spend the night in a refrigerator, and all that just so we could take more clothes with us . . . I was wearing two undershirts, three pairs of underpants, a dress, and over that a skirt, a jacket, a raincoat, two pairs of stockings, heavy shoes, a cap, a scarf and lots more. I was suffocating even before we left the house, but no one bothered to ask me how I felt.

12 Margot stuffed her schoolbag with schoolbooks, went to get her bicycle and, with Miep leading the way, rode off into the great unknown. At any rate, that's how I thought of it, since I still didn't know where our hiding place was.

13 At seven-thirty we too closed the door behind us; Moortje, my cat, was the only living creature I said goodbye to. According to a note we left for Mr. Goldschmidt, she was to be taken to the neighbors, who would give her a good home.

14 The stripped beds, the breakfast things on the table, the pound of meat for the cat in the kitchen—all of these created the impression that we'd left in a hurry. But we weren't interested in impressions. We just wanted to get out of there, to get away and reach our destination in safety. Nothing else mattered.

15 More tomorrow.

*Yours, Anne**

* From Anne Frank, *The Diary of a Young Girl*. Copyright © 1991, the Anne Frank-Fonds, Basel, Switzerland. Used by permission of Anne Frank-Fonds.

Vocabulary

Read the following questions about some of the vocabulary words that appear in the previous selection. Circle the letter of the correct answer.

1. What does it mean to be *agitated*? "A little while later Margot appeared in the kitchen doorway looking very *agitated*." (paragraph 2)

   a. happy
   b. joyful
   c. depressed
   d. disturbed

2. "Margot and I started packing our most important *belongings* in a schoolbag." (paragraph 7) What does *belongings* mean?

   a. possessions
   b. underwear
   c. legal documents
   d. boots

3. "I was *suffocating* even before we left the house, but no one bothered to ask me how I felt." (paragraph 11) What does it mean to be *suffocating* in this context?

   a. overly chilly
   b. overly hot
   c. happy
   d. depressed

Main Ideas, Inferences, Patterns of Organization, and Transitions

Respond to the following questions by circling the letter of the correct answer.

1. Can you infer who "Kitty" is?

   a. Kitty is Anne's best friend.
   b. Kitty is the name that Anne gave her diary.
   c. Kitty is another cat in the Frank household.
   d. Kitty is the nickname that Anne has given Margot.

2. What can you infer about the relationship between Anne and Margot?

   a. They are sisters.
   b. They are best friends.
   c. They are cousins.
   d. They are not blood relatives.

3. Based on the information presented in the selection, the date of the diary entry (July 8, 1942), the fact that Anne lives in Europe, and the fact that Margot was called up by the SS, what can you infer about the Franks?

   a. They are Catholic.
   b. They are Africans.
   c. They are Jewish.
   d. They are Dutch.

4. Based on your reading of this selection, what can you infer about Miep and Jan Gies?
   a. They are committed to helping the Franks.
   b. They are going to take care of the cat when the Franks leave the house.
   c. They will provide Margot with a good home.
   d. They will eventually turn the Franks in to the SS.
5. What can you infer about the mood in the Frank house from this diary entry?
   a. The Franks are happy-go-lucky.
   b. The Franks are extremely tense.
   c. The Franks are depressed.
   d. The Franks are joyful.
6. What pattern of organization arranges the details in paragraph 8?
   a. series
   b. time order
   c. comparison/contrast
   d. definition
7. What type of transition helps the reader follow the pattern in paragraph 2?
   a. series
   b. time order
   c. comparison/contrast
   d. cause/effect
8. Which sentence states the main idea of paragraph 7?
   a. "Margot and I started packing our most important belongings in a schoolbag."
   b. "The first thing I stuck in was this diary, and then curlers, handkerchiefs, schoolbooks, a comb, and some old letters."
   c. "Preoccupied by the thought of going into hiding, I stuck the craziest things in the bag, but I'm not sorry."
   d. "Memories mean more to me than dresses."

Practicing the Active Reading Strategy:

After You Read

Now that you have read the selection, answer the following questions, using the active reading strategies that are discussed on pages 30–33.

1. Identify and write down the point and purpose of this reading selection.
2. Besides the vocabulary words included in the exercise on page 366, are there any other vocabulary words that are unfamiliar to you? If so, write a list of them. When you have finished writing your list, look up

each word in a dictionary and write the definition that best describes the word as it is used in the selection.

3. Predict any possible test questions that may be used on a test about the content of this selection.
4. How could you use the information contained in this selection? Does the information contained in the selection reinforce or contradict your ideas and experiences? Explain.

Questions for Discussion and Writing

Answer the following questions based on your reading of the selection. Write your answers on the blanks provided.

1. What hints are you given about Anne as a person from this passage, if any? Based on her diary entry, think about what kind of person Anne was and create a description. Use examples from her diary entry. ________

____

2. If you were in a similar situation and had to leave your home suddenly, would memories mean more to you than dresses, as Anne states in paragraph 7? Describe how you would react in a similar situation. What would you bring on such a journey and why? __________________

____

3. Conduct research about Anne Frank, and write a summary of what happened to her and her family. ____

____

Vocabulary: The Contrast Context Clue

In Chapters 4, 5, and 6, you learned about the three different types of context clue: definition/restatement, example, and explanation. One last type of context clue is **contrast.** In this type of clue, nearby words, phrases, or sentences may give the *opposite* meaning of the unfamiliar word, allowing you to conclude what it means by noticing this contrast. For example, read this next sentence, which comes from one of the paragraphs in this chapter.

> That boy had been notoriously worldly, and I just the reverse; yet he was exalted to this ***eminence,*** and I left in obscurity and misery.

If you're wondering what *eminence* means, you can look to the remainder of the sentence, which includes a contrast clue. The word is contrasted with "obscurity and misery"; therefore, it must mean "famous, with high rank or standing."

Vocabulary Exercise 1

The following examples all come from paragraphs in Chapters 5, 6, and 7. In each one, use the explanation context clue to help you determine the meaning of the boldfaced, italicized word, and write a definition for this word on the blank provided.

1. Second, the vast majority of successful programs and teachers view an early childhood curriculum as an ***integrated*** whole rather than consisting of independent subject areas of skills. ______________________
2. Carrying a ***grudge*** around saps your energy and happiness. For this reason, you should learn to forgive the mistakes or thoughtlessness of other people. ______________________
3. The numbers suggest that if Hispanics acted together, they would wield considerable ***clout,*** but their diversity has led to fragmentation and powerlessness. ______________________
4. Thus, the otherwise ***staid*** *New York Times* resorted to wild hyperbole to summarize a 1920 tennis match between Bill Tilden, the national champion, and challenger William Johnston. ______________________
5. Again, as in the case of failure rates, the truth about the prospects of starting or working for a small company is different—and brighter—than the traditional ***fallacy*** suggests. ______________________

Vocabulary Exercise 2

In the following passage, underline the contrast context clues that help define the boldfaced, italicized words.

12 Things You Must Know to Survive and Thrive in America

Those of us with forebears[1] branded by history hold in our hearts an awful truth: to be born black and male in America is to be put into shackles[2] and then challenged to escape. But that is not our only truth, or even the one most relevant. For in this age of new possibilities, we are learning that the shackles forged in slavery are far from ***indissoluble,*** that they will yield, even break, provided that we attack them shrewdly.

Today's America is not our grandfathers' or even our fathers' America. We are no longer forced to hide our ambition while masking our bitterness with a grin. We don't face, as did our forefathers, a society committed to relentlessly humiliating us, to forcing us to play the role of inferiors in every civilized sphere. This doesn't mean that we are on the verge of reaching that lofty state of exalted[3] consciousness that sweeps all inequities away. What it does mean is that we have a certain social and cultural leeway: that, in a way our forefathers could only dream about, we are free to define our place in the world. That freedom is nowhere near absolute. But today's obstacles are not nearly as daunting[4] as those faced by our ancestors. It's the difference between stepping into the ring with both hands ***lashed*** behind your back and stepping in with one hand swinging free. Still, if the one hand is all you have, you must use it twice as well as your opponent uses his. And because you have so much less room for error, you must fight strategically, understanding when to retreat and when to ***advance*** and how to deflect the blows that inevitably will come your way. You must understand, in short, how to compete in this new arena, where the rules are neither what they seem nor quite what they used to be. So what I have set out below is a list of things that may help us in our competition.

Complain all you like about the raw deal you have gotten in life, but don't expect those complaints to get you anywhere. America likes winners, not whiners. And one of the encouraging developments of this new, more enlightened age is that Americans even, at times, embrace winners who are black.

Don't let the glitter blind you. Almost invariably when I have spoken to people who have made their living selling drugs, they talk a lot like "Frank," who said, "I didn't want to be the only dude on the streets with busted-up shoes, old clothes." They talk of the money, the women, the cars, the gold chains—the glamour, the glitter of the dealer's life. Only later do most acknowledge that the money, for most dealers, is not all that good, and that

1. **forebears:** ancestors
2. **shackles:** devices used to restrain someone
3. **exalted:** elevated
4. **daunting:** discouraging

even when it is, it generally doesn't last very long—partly because the lifestyle so often leads to either prison or an early grave. Maybe you don't care about that. Nonetheless, I urge you to realize that you have a better chance (providing you prepare for it) of getting a big job at a major corporation than of making big money for a long time on the streets—and the benefits and security are a hell of a lot better.

Recognize that being true to yourself is not the same as being true to a stupid stereotype.[1] A few years ago when I visited Xavier University, a historically black college in New Orleans, I was moved by a student who proudly proclaimed the university to be a school full of nerds. At a time when many black men and boys are trying their best to act like mack-daddies and badass muthas, Xavier (which sends more blacks to medical schools than any other university) is saying that it has another image in mind: blackness really has nothing to do with projecting a manufactured, crude street persona. Xavier celebrates accomplishment instead of ***denigrating*** it, and it makes no apologies for doing so. We desperately need to promote archetypes[2] other than rappers, thugs, and ballplayers of what it is possible and desirable for us to be—if for no other reason than that so few of us can find success on such limited terrain.[3]

Expect to do better than the world expects of you; expect to live in a bigger world than the one you see. One of the most unfortunate realities of growing up as a black male in America is that we are constantly told to lower our sights; we are constantly nudged, unless we are very lucky and privileged, in the direction of ***mediocrity.*** Our dreams, we are told in effect, cannot be as large as other folks' dreams; our universe, we are led to believe, will be smaller than that of our nonblack peers. When Arthur Ashe wrote that his "potential is more than can be expressed within the bounds of my race or ethnic identity," he was speaking for all of us. For those of us who are accustomed to hearing, "You will never amount to much," dreams may be all that give us the strength to go on. And as we dream big dreams, we must also prepare ourselves to pursue them, instead of contenting ourselves with fantasies of a wonderful existence that will be forever beyond our reach.

Don't expect support for your dreams from those who have not accomplished very much in their lives. The natural reaction of many people (especially those who believe they share your background) is to feel threatened or intimidated or simply to be dismissive if you are trying to do things they have not done themselves. Don't share your dreams with failures; people who have not done much in their own lives will be incapable of seeing the potential in yours.

1. **stereotype:** an oversimplified generalization about a group
2. **archetypes:** original models or ideal examples
3. **terrain:** ground

7

That is certainly not true in all cases, but it is true much too often. You owe it to yourself to tune out the voices around you telling you to lower your sights.

If someone is bringing out your most self-destructive tendencies, acknowledge that that person is not a friend. No one should toss away friendship. People who will care for you, who will support and watch out for you, are a precious part of a full and blessed life. But people who claim to be friends are not always friends in fact—as Mike Gibson, an ex-prisoner who is now a Morehouse student, ultimately learned. His time behind bars taught Gibson to "surround myself with people who want to see me do good." On the streets he learned that when things got tough, the very buddies who had encouraged him to break the law were nowhere to be found: "When I was in the cell, I was there by myself. . . . I always found myself alone." It's easy to be seduced by those who offer idiotic opinions disguised as guidance.

Don't be too proud to ask for help, particularly from those who are wiser and older. Mathematician Philip Uri Triesman has had astounding success teaching advanced mathematics to black students who previously had not done very well. Unlike Chinese-American students who typically studied ***en masse,*** blacks, he had discovered, tended to study alone. For blacks, the solitary study ritual seemed to be a matter of pride, reflecting their need to prove that they could get by without help. By getting them, in effect, to emulate[1] some of what the Chinese-Americans were doing, Triesman spurred the black students to unprecedented levels of accomplishment. Whether in schools, in the streets, or in corporate suites, too many of us are trying to cope alone when we would be much better off if we reached out for help.*

READING STRATEGY: Keeping a Reading Journal

In Chapter 1 of this book, you learned that active readers are those who interact with the text by thinking about what they read and by consciously trying to connect the text's information to their own experiences and beliefs. One useful strategy for understanding and absorbing new information you read is to keep a reading journal, a notebook in which you record your thoughts about the things you read. These thoughts could include a brief summary of the selection, a list of new

7

1. **emulate:** imitate

* Adapted from Ellis Cose, "12 Things You Must Know to Survive and Thrive in America." Reprinted by permission of Don Congdon Associates, Inc. Originally published by *Newsweek* and published in *The Envy of the World* (Pocket Books, 2002). Copyright © 2002 by Ellis Cose.

ideas or new information you learned, or your reactions to or opinions about the text.

Keeping a reading journal offers two important benefits. First of all, the act of writing helps your thoughts become clearer. You may have some vague ideas or reactions after finishing a text. When you write them down, however, you'll find that trying to find the right words to express what you think will actually result in a better understanding of those thoughts. Therefore, the act of writing your response becomes a tool for learning about what that response is. A second benefit comes from creating a written record of your ideas. An entry for each article, chapter, or essay you read for a class, for example, can provide you with a handy reference for study. Later, when you're preparing for a test or completing an assignment, you can simply reread your entries to refresh your memory about the content of each text.

To keep a reading journal, obtain a notebook with blank pages inside. Immediately after you read a text, first write down its title, the author's name, and the date you read it or finished reading it. Then, let your purpose for reading the text determine the type of response you compose. If you'll be expected to discuss the content of the selection in class or write about its topic for an assignment, you may want to record several or all of the following.

- A brief summary of the text.
- Your reaction (your feelings or your own opinions about the subject).
- Your judgment of the selection's merit or accuracy.
- A comparison of this work to other works you've read.
- Your experiences or observations that either support or refute the text's ideas and conclusions.
- Your questions about the text.

If you're reading for your own pleasure or to expand your general knowledge about a particular topic, you might want to focus on just one or two of the items in the list above. No matter what your purpose, though, plan to put forth the little bit of extra effort it takes to better understand what you've read.

Read the following article and then write a reading journal entry that includes at least three of the items in the bulleted list above.

Continued

7

Howard Gardner's Multiple Intelligences Theory

Book learning is only one kind of intelligence. Researchers have found other categories of intelligence that are changing our definition of what it means to be smart.

Those who study intelligence are divided between two camps. Some believe intelligence is a single ability measured by IQ tests, and others think intelligence is multifaceted. Howard Gardner, a professor at Harvard University's Graduate School of Education, belongs to the second camp. Author of *Frames of Mind* (1983) and *Multiple Intelligences: The Theory in Practice* (1993), Gardner argues that we have seven intelligences. In 1996, Gardner added an eighth intelligence to his theory: *naturalistic*. Everyone possesses these intelligences to some degree, but some people may show greater strength in one or more areas. Gardner also believes that we can encourage the development of our intelligences and that we can learn to use them to our advantage.

Linguistic. This intelligence is characterized by skill with words and a sensitivity to their meanings, sounds, and functions. If your linguistic intelligence is high, you probably learn best by reading.

Logical-Mathematical. This intelligence is characterized by skill with numbers, scientific ability, and formal reasoning. If your logical-mathematical intelligence is high, you probably learn best by taking a problem-solving approach to learning. Outlining or making charts and graphs may be good study techniques for you.

Bodily-Kinesthetic. This intelligence enables people to use their bodies skillfully and in goal-oriented ways such as playing a sport or dancing. If your bodily intelligence is high, you may be able to learn more effectively by combining studying with some physical activity.

Musical. This intelligence is characterized by the ability to find meaning in music and other rhythmical sounds and to reproduce them either vocally or with an instrument. If your musical intelligence is high, you may want to choose a career in music or engage in leisure activities that allow you to pursue your musical interests. Although studying to music is a distraction for some, you may find that it aids your concentration.

Spatial. This intelligence is characterized by the ability to perceive the world accurately and to mentally reorganize or reinterpret those perceptions. For example, an artist perceives accurately what a bowl of fruit looks like—the colors and sizes of the fruit and how the fruit is arranged. However, the artist's painting of the bowl of fruit is a new interpretation—the artist's mental image of the bowl of fruit—and this image may distort the sizes or change the colors of the fruit. If your spatial intelligence is high, you may learn best by finding ways to visualize or restructure the material that you want to learn.

Interpersonal. This intelligence is characterized by the ability to read people's moods and intentions and to understand their motives. Empathy is another characteristic of interpersonal intelligence. *Empathy* is the ability to identify with another person's feelings. People who have a high degree of interpersonal intelligence may be said to have "good people skills." If your interpersonal intelligence is high, you may learn best by collaborating with others on projects or by participating in a study group.

Intrapersonal. This intelligence is characterized by self-knowledge: the ability to read your own emotions, to understand what motivates you, and to use that understanding to shape your behavior. If your intrapersonal intelligence is high, you should be able to make use of all of your other intelligences to find the best study methods that will work for you.

Naturalistic. This intelligence is the ability to perceive the world from an environmental perspective: feeling, sensing, and relating to your environment through its natural features and rhythms. For example, people living in remote cultures become skilled at coping with nature, navigating without maps, and surviving in a hostile climate. For others, this intelligence may reveal itself in curiosity about nature, love of the outdoors, or special ability in the natural sciences.

Gardner's theory of multiple intelligences (MI) is widely accepted among educators. However, opinions about the theory's usefulness differ. Some psychologists and educators praise Gardner for raising public awareness about the many facets of intellectual ability. But others are concerned because the theory has never been formally tested, and because Gardner's naturalistic

Continued

intelligence, unlike his original seven, does not seem to be an independent category. Instead, it may be a special application of one or more other intelligences. In any case, it is well to remember that most employers place great value on verbal and math skills, believing that they are stronger predictors of success at work. The practical value of Gardner's theory may be that it encourages students to discover and use all of their talents and intellectual capacities to create success in college and in life.

To pursue this topic further, do an online search using these keywords: *learning styles, multiple intelligences, Howard Gardner.**

Reading Visuals: Bar Graphs

In Chapter 6, you learned about line graphs. A second kind of graph is a **bar graph.** Bar graphs indicate quantities of something with bars, or rectangles. These bars can run upward from the horizontal axis, or sideways from the vertical axis of the graph. Each bar is labeled to show what is being measured. While the line graph includes a time factor, the bar graph may not; it focuses on varying quantities of some factor or factors, although it may include several sets of bars that correspond to different time periods.

A bar graph includes the following parts:

- **Title.** The title reveals the entity that's being measured. Depending on how the graph is arranged, this subject may correspond to either the vertical or the horizontal axis.
- **Vertical axis.** This line, which runs up and down, is labeled with either a kind of quantity or the entities being measured.
- **Horizontal axis.** This line, which runs from left to right, is labeled to identify either a kind of quantity or the entities being measured.
- **Bars.** Each bar rises to the line on the grid that matches the quantity it represents. Each bar may be labeled with a specific number.
- **Key.** If entities are broken down into subgroups, the graph may include bars of different colors to represent each group. In that case, a key, or explanation of what each color signifies may accompany the graph.
- **Source line.** The source line identifies who collected or compiled the information in the bar graph.

* From Kanar, *The Confident Student,* 5th ed. Boston: Houghton Mifflin, 2004, 36–37. Copyright © 2004 by Houghton Mifflin Company. Reprinted with permission.

These parts are labeled on the bar graph below.

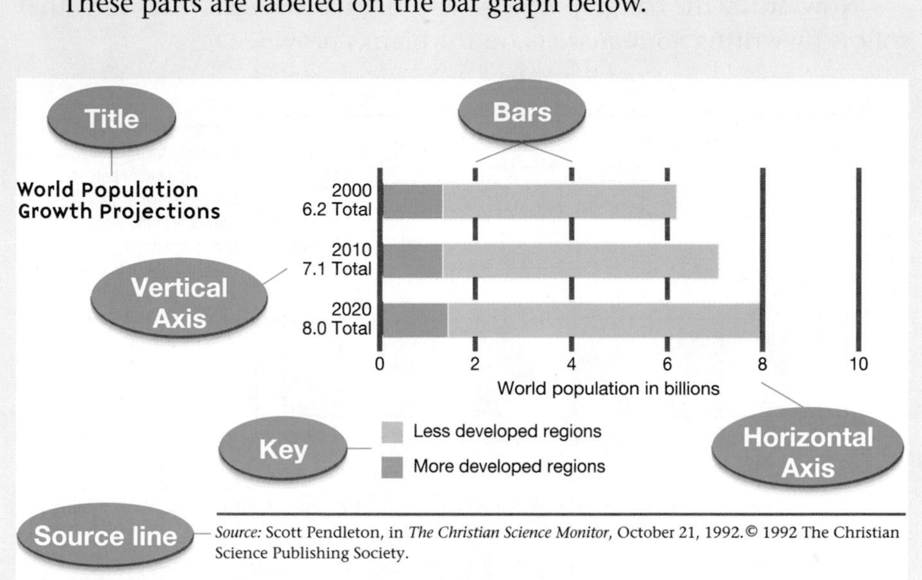

To interpret the information in a bar graph, read the title first to find out what is being measured. Next, read the labels of the vertical and horizontal axes to understand how the graph is arranged and what type of quantity is being used. Finally, examine each bar, and try to state, in your own words, the relationship among them. Which entity is largest? Smallest? Are there large discrepancies between two or more of the entities?

The bar graph above shows the current world population, as well as projections for the next twenty years. Among the notable relationships indicated by the bars are the following.

- By 2020, the overall world population is expected to increase by 1.8 billion people.
- More developed regions (indicated by the darker portions of the bars) will show very little increase in population.
- Less developed regions (indicated by the lighter portions of the bars) of the world will be responsible for the increase in population.

Notice how the graph includes a key that identifies what each color signifies.

Continued

Now, study the bar graph below and then answer the questions that follow by writing your answers on the blanks provided.

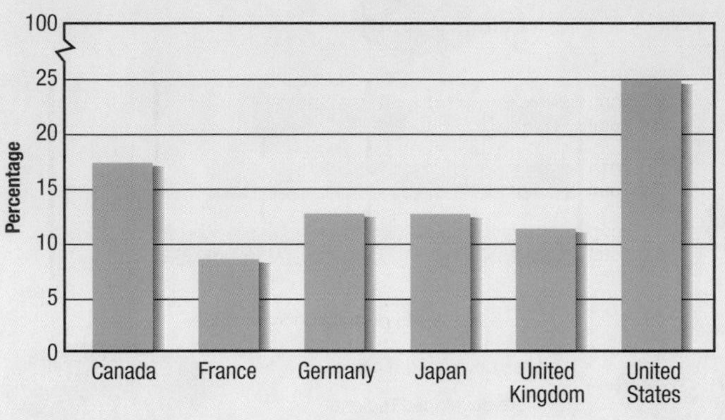

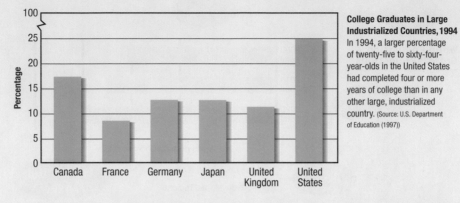

College Graduates in Large Industrialized Countries, 1994
In 1994, a larger percentage of twenty-five to sixty-four-year-olds in the United States had completed four or more years of college than in any other large, industrialized country. (Source: U.S. Department of Education (1997))

Source: Seifert et al., *Lifespan Development*, 2nd ed. Boston: Houghton Mifflin, 2000, 453. Copyright © 2000 by Houghton Mifflin Company. Reprinted with permission.

1. What is the subject of this bar graph? ______________________

____

2. What percentage, approximately, of Japanese students in the twenty-five to sixty-four-year-old range completed four or more years of college? ______________________

3. Which country had the least number of graduates, according to this graph? ______________________

4. Which country had the most number of graduates? __________

____

5. What is the source of this information? ______________________

____

7

Name ____ Date ____________________

TEST 1

Read the following sentences and answer the questions that follow. Circle the letter of the correct answer.

Every night, I read a book to my son before he goes to bed.

1. What can you infer about the son?
   a. He cannot read because he is young.
   b. He doesn't like to read.
   c. He has a lot of homework.
   d. He's afraid of the dark.

Carlos spent the morning mowing his lawn in the hot sun.

2. What can you infer about what season it is?
   a. spring
   b. fall
   c. summer
   d. winter

Only one person, Cal Ripken, has played more consecutive baseball games than Lou Gehrig, the original "Iron Man" and the person who previously held the record.

3. What can we infer about how many games Lou Gehrig played?
   a. He didn't play that many games.
   b. He retired early.
   c. He played only in certain games.
   d. He played in many consecutive baseball games and had a long-standing record.

Bill and Melinda Gates have donated more than $24 billion dollars to help fund medical care in Third World countries.

4. What is one thing we can infer about Bill and Melinda Gates?
   a. They are extremely wealthy.
   b. They don't know what to do with their money.
   c. They should not have gotten involved in this problem.
   d. They have too much time on their hands.

For additional tests, see the Test Bank.

Elmore Leonard is a writer, which is like saying Michael Jordan is a basketball player.*

5. What can we infer about Elmore Leonard?
   a. He is a writer.
   b. He plays basketball with Michael Jordan.
   c. He is an exceptional writer, just as Michael Jordan is an exceptional basketball player.
   d. He is going to retire only to come back and play basketball for the Washington Wizards.

Tiger Woods blamed the United States Golf Association for the difficult course conditions at a recent U.S. Open. Woods criticized the USGA for the dry and slick greens, saying, "I think they lost control of the golf course." He blamed the media for creating distractions during the tournament. He blamed everyone but himself for his play in a U.S. Open.†

6. What can you infer about Tiger Woods's performance at the U.S. Open?
   a. He led in all rounds of golf.
   b. He did very poorly.
   c. He blames the media the most for his bad play.
   d. He did extremely well.

7. What can you infer about Tiger Woods's state of mind after playing at the Open?
   a. He was upset and making excuses for his bad play.
   b. He was enthusiastic about playing at the Open again.
   c. He was looking forward to retiring from golf permanently.
   d. He was interested in finding another sport to play.

Michelle was interested in finding out the value of a diamond pin her grandmother had given her, so she logged on to appraiseit.com to see if she could get an online appraisal. After she filled out information, one of the site's appraisers valued the pin at $200.00. She also submitted her information to appraisalday.com and was told that the pin would be worth about $3,000. A visit to the Sotheby's online appraisal service gave her an estimate at around $7,000. Michelle was more confused than when she didn't know what the pin was worth at all and decided to take the advice of a jeweler who recommended she visit a professional appraiser in person.‡

* From Pete Hamill, "Elmore Leonard Spares a Moment," *Daily News*, February 6, 2002, 36.

† Adapted from Rich Cimini, "Woods Pours Whine as Drought Goes On," *Daily News*, June 21, 2004, 59.

‡ Information adapted from Michelle Slatalla, "Antiques Web Show," *Rosie*, February 2002, 44–45.

8. What can you infer about online appraisal sites?
   a. They are very reliable.
   b. The estimates they give will vary widely, so it is better to show the piece in question to an appraiser.
   c. Sotheby's is an auction house in New York and shouldn't be trusted.
   d. Online appraisal sites are illegal.

Salt Lake City was host to the 2002 Winter Olympics. The city prepared for seven years for the Games. Some people complained about the overall expense of hosting the games; others said the money should have been spent on housing the homeless. Some fretted[1] about security issues or the possible degradation of the Utah mountains. Still others feared that all the people coming into Salt Lake City would result in a loss of lifestyle for Salt Lake natives.*

9. What can you infer about the reaction to the Olympic Games being in Salt Lake City?
   a. Everyone was thrilled that Salt Lake had been chosen to host the Games.
   b. Most everyone feels that housing the homeless is a major priority.
   c. Not everyone was thrilled about the fact that Salt Lake was host to the Olympic Games.
   d. The people of Salt Lake City felt that the mountains in Salt Lake City were beyond repair.

Soon after Stan Leon, a gifted student-athlete who plans on attending a university that specializes in aeronautical science, was born in East Los Angeles in 1984, his mother, Olga, was abandoned by his biological father. Olga also had symptoms of mental illness that has afflicted her all of her life. Her sister Angelica took baby Stan to Guadalajara, Mexico, to live with his grandparents and returned to Los Angeles to care for her own daughters. Olga was in and out of their lives during that time. Two baby sisters appeared and were sent to live with the grandparents as well. Stan recalls holding his sisters on the train back to California when he was five. He lived with a number of his aunts and cousins in a small house in Glendale. But when he was eight, raising Olga's three children became too much for the struggling family, and Stan and his sisters were taken into foster care.†

7

1. **fretted:** worried

---

* Adapted from Deedee Corradini, "Olympic Investment Grows Beyond Host City's Hopes," *USA Today,* February 6, 2002, 13A.

† Adapted from Susan Littwin, "Self-Made Stan," *Rosie*, February 2002, 54–55.

10. What can we infer about Stan Leon from this paragraph?
    a. Stan has triumphed over adversity by staying in school and planning to attend college.
    b. Stan plays football and baseball.
    c. Stan's foster parents didn't love him like Olga did.
    d. Stan enjoyed living in foster care.

11. What can we infer about Olga from this paragraph?
    a. She suffered from manic depression.
    b. She was not equipped to raise her three children because of her circumstances.
    c. She was very young when she had Stan.
    d. She tried to find a good job.

Ever since last summer, Dillon has started looking and acting different than before. He has grown nearly two inches in the last six months, a fact that his mother comments on with pride, but also with a note of dismay when his clothing no longer fits. Sometimes Dillon would prefer that no one notice the changes. He was well coordinated and athletic in school sports just a year or two ago, but now he feels clumsy, trips over himself, and bumps into things. He can't even count on his voice. Sometimes it sounds normal, and other times it sounds as deep as his father's; worst of all, it sometimes bounces out of control, cracking and breaking at embarrassing moments.*

12. What can we infer about Dillon from this passage?
    a. He is going through puberty.
    b. He has an incurable disease.
    c. He is alone in his experiences, for none of his friends are going through what he's experiencing.
    d. He will never be a professional athlete.

7

The New England Patriots football team was dismissed as mediocre, called lucky when they moved through the NFL playoffs, and seen as sacrificial lambs in the Super Bowl. To the estimated 1.2 million fans who packed the streets of Boston and City Hall Plaza on a cold February day in 2002, however, the Patriots were simply super. The players took the opportunity to revel with their fans, and defensive back Lawyer Milloy asked the crowd, "City of Boston, it's been a long time coming, huh?"†

* Adapted from Seifert et al., *Lifespan Development*, 2nd ed. Boston: Houghton Mifflin, 2000, 337. Copyright © 2000 by Houghton Mifflin Company. Reprinted with permission.

† Adapted from "Pats Party in Boston," no author credited, *Sports Wire, Daily News,* February 6, 2002, 74.

13. What can we infer about the New England Patriots from this paragraph?
    a. They didn't win the Super Bowl, but the fans had a party for them anyway.
    b. They won the Super Bowl, overcoming their underdog status.
    c. The fans didn't expect them to win anything.
    d. The fans did not pay attention to Lawyer Milloy's speech.

I have two Ivy League[1] master's degrees—and two left thumbs. In my case, I am not a "white collar" or "blue collar" worker but "green collar"—laying down lush, hydroseeded lawns. When the truck driver from Quebec arrived with an 18-wheeler full of mulch and I began conversing in near-flawless Parisian French about his long journey and breakfast of croissants,[2] my boss's eyes lit up. But when it came time to tell him to "attach the metal chain to the forklift and remove the pallets,"[3] all I could muster was a stare. Evidently I'd been absent from French class the day trucking was covered. I was reduced to grunting and clutching at his sleeve to convey the message.*

14. What can we infer about the author of this paragraph?
    a. He went to Harvard.
    b. He went to Yale and Harvard.
    c. His academic degrees did not equip him to do the work he is currently doing.
    d. He is very strong.

What goes on in the single parent's mind when he or she contemplates dating? There will be questions like "Will my child like this person?" "How will he/she treat my kids?" and "How much work will marriage add to my already complicated life?" Unless a date is truly exceptional, parents will think long and hard about whether or not kids will be better off with another adult in the household.†

15. What can we infer about single parents and dating?
    a. Single parents don't like to date.
    b. Single parents want to date other single parents.
    c. Single parents think about what effect dating will have on their children.
    d. Single parents need support groups.

1. **Ivy League:** an association of eight prestigious universities and colleges in the northeastern U.S.
2. **croissants:** crescent-shaped rolls
3. **pallets:** platforms for moving cargo or freight

---

* Adapted from Bob Muldoon, "White-Collar Man in a Blue-Collar World," *Newsweek*, February 4, 2002, 13.

† Adapted from Diane Chambers, "To Remarry or Not to Remarry . . . ," *Westchester Parent*, February 2002, 74.

7

TEST 2

A. Read each of the passages and circle the letter of the correct answer for each of the questions that follow.

For as far back as I can remember, my grandfather always seemed larger than life. My earliest memory of him was of the summer I visited Puerto Rico before he and Abuela returned to New York to live closer to all of us. For the last few years, they were living in San Turce where they ran a small bodega[1] just minutes from their home. I was only four at the time and remember feeling so small amidst all the canned and boxed goods. Despite this, I looked forward to bringing Abuela his café con leche at or around noon. Abuela would prepare it with a calculated efficiency that I marveled at. I looked on in awe, fully convinced that I could never master such a complicated task and my heart ached to be able to do something so grand—especially for him.

Abuela would measure each spoonful of coffee and stir it into boiling water in an awaiting pot. As she blended the two elements together, the air would be transformed and filled with a fragrance so intense it seemed to possess the powers of a magical potion. I could readily imagine its effectiveness in any tale: one sip and surely you would be cast under its spell, willing to do anything for just one more taste. What followed confirmed my thoughts. This brew was first poured into a cloth funnel to separate the coffee grounds. Abuela would then blend the dark liquid into the simmering milk, which was always heated to perfection. Goldilocks[2] would have emphatically approved. For it was "Not too hot, not too cold, but just right!" The final step was adding the secret ingredient. Abuela would use a large soup spoon to add sugar to the completed café con leche. Scoop after scoop—unos, dos, nueve, cinco—(1, 2, 9, 5) confounding my youthful counting abilities, was added until she deemed it perfect and then she would add more spoonful for good measure. Abuelo's café had to be as sweet as he.*

1. What can you infer about how the author feels about her grandfather from this passage?
   a. She is afraid of him.
   b. She has a deep love for him.
   c. She doesn't know him very well.
   d. She thinks that he is old and foolish.

1. **bodega:** a small Hispanic grocery store

2. **Goldilocks:** character from the fairy tale "Goldilocks and the Three Bears"

* Excerpted from Lillian Diaz-Imbelli, "El Viejo." Reprinted by permission of the author. Ms. Lillian Diaz-Imbelli, Director of Admission at Loyola School in New York City wants to encourage all who read this story to keep their own family narratives alive.

2. From the coffee ritual, what can you infer about Abuelo and Abuela's relationship?
   a. Abuela loves her husband very much.
   b. Abuela is losing patience with her husband.
   c. Abuelo thinks that his wife takes too much time to prepare his coffee.
   d. Abuela wishes her husband would take less sugar in his coffee.

3. What can you infer about the author's family from this selection?
   a. They are Italian.
   b. They are from Latin America.
   c. They are Puerto Rican.
   d. They all live in the United States.

My cousin, Georgie, as I still called him, although he would have turned 60 soon, suffered from minimal brain damage at birth. He stuttered, never graduated from high school, and worked at a grocery store named Jubilee. He loved it there, driving through the early morning darkness to open the place, to make sure the shopping carts were all in order, to greet the first customers of the day who stopped by for the morning paper and a doughnut.

After Georgie died, as people came through the funeral home, they told stories of a man I never knew. There was the story about a woman who broke her hip doing the "Jubilee Shuffle" with him. There were people who said he knew which shopping cart they wanted, although for the life of me I don't know how he could tell one from another. And there was the woman at the post office who said he'd often bring her cookies, although she'd always protest. He was the first person many saw in the morning, and to them, that was a great comfort.*

4. What can we infer about Georgie from the selection?
   a. He was well loved by the people who shopped at the grocery store.
   b. Nobody really knew him.
   c. He had no responsibility at the store.
   d. Georgie stuttered when he was nervous.

5. What can we infer about the author's relationship with his cousin?
   a. The author didn't go to school with his cousin.
   b. The author and Georgie were second cousins.
   c. The author and Georgie were first cousins.
   d. The author learned more about Georgie at his funeral than he knew from firsthand experience.

7

* Adapted from Craig Wilson, "Cousin Georgie's Cart Was Filled with Joyful Stories," *USA Today*, January 30, 2002, 1D.

Last Halloween my five-year-old son entered a pumpkin-decorating contest at his school. He was so proud of his entry—a wild combination of carvings, painting, and feathers he had constructed all by himself with his own kindergartner's sense of art. He lugged it proudly to the school cafeteria, and we placed it among the other entries, a very creative bunch of witch pumpkins, snowman pumpkins, scary pumpkins, even a bubble-gum blowing, freckle-faced pumpkin wearing a baseball cap. "Wow," I thought to myself. "The judges are going to have a tough time choosing a winner."

I guess the judges must have thought the same thing because they didn't choose one. When we returned to the school cafeteria for the annual fall dinner that evening, we saw that all the pumpkins had been awarded the same black and gold ribbon. My son, eagerly searching to see if he'd won, kept asking me, "Which pumpkin won? Where's the winner?"

What could I say? "Well, it looks like everyone won. Look: you got a ribbon, honey!"

Kids are smart. That didn't satisfy him. "Yeah, but who *won*?" he asked. You could almost hear him asking himself, "What's the point of having a contest if you're not going to pick a winner?"*

6. What can you infer about the author's son's reaction to the fact that there were no winners of the pumpkin contest?
   a. He had no reaction.
   b. He was really happy that no one won.
   c. He was disappointed that a winner had not been chosen.
   d. He was going to start crying.

7. What can you infer about what the author thinks of the collection of pumpkins at the contest?
   a. She thought that there were a lot of good ones and that competition was going to be stiff.
   b. She didn't think about them at all.
   c. She thought her son's was the best one.
   d. She thought that all of them were better than her son's.

8. What can you infer about how the author felt about the fact that there were no winners?
   a. She didn't think it was a good idea to not pick a winner or winners and thought it would be hard to explain to her son why there were no winners.
   b. She thought the judges did the right thing.

* Adapted from Suzanne Sievert, "It's Not Just How We Play That Matters," *Newsweek*, March 19, 2001, 12. © 2001 Newsweek, Inc. All rights reserved. Reprinted by permission.

7

c. She thought that none of the pumpkins deserved to win.
d. She didn't give it much thought at all.

The new driveway cuts through the trees that border my property. From my doorstep, I can hear my old friends falling; a little more light comes in my windows every day. Across the road, the SOLD sign goes up among the trees at the top of the hill. I hear that eight houses will be built on what is now untouched woods.

I've lived on my 1½-acre wooded lot in Landenberg, Pennsylvania, for one year, in a house that was built in 1954. The surrounding area has already changed. I'm 31 years old and I hear myself saying, "Back in my day, that development was nothing but trees." Just like my dad talks about how he used to ride horses along a road that's now called Kirkwood Highway in Delaware, where you can get a taco, a lube job, a massage, and a new pair of shoes all at one intersection. Every intersection.*

9. When the author refers to his "old friends" in the first sentence, about whom can you infer he is talking?
   a. driveways
   b. trees
   c. college friends
   d. childhood friends

10. What can you infer about how the author feels about the new real estate developments in his area?
    a. He is delighted; his property values will go up tremendously.
    b. He doesn't think about it much.
    c. He is sad that trees are being cut down to make way for houses, roads, and stores.
    d. He is going to move.

B. Read the following passages and then write a checkmark beside the inferences in the list that are accurately based upon the information given.

11. It was a beautiful day at the beach—blue sky, gentle breeze, calm sea. I knew these things because a man sitting five feet from me was shouting them into his cellular telephone, like a play-by-play announcer. "IT'S A BEAUTIFUL DAY," he shouted. "THE SKY IS BLUE, AND THERE'S A BREEZE, AND THE WATER IS CALM. . . ."

    Behind me, a woman, her cell phone pressed to her ear, was pacing back and forth. "She DIDN'T," she was saying. "No, she DIDN'T. She DID? Really? Are you SERIOUS? She did NOT. She DID? No, she DIDN'T. She DID. NO, she . . ."

7

* From Sean Clancy, "The Problem in Our Own Backyards," *Newsweek*, January 21, 2002, 10.

And so on. This woman had two children, who were frolicking in the surf. I found myself watching them, because the woman was surely not. A giant squid could have surfaced and snatched the children, and this woman would not have noticed. Or, if she had noticed, she'd have said, "Listen, I have to go, because a giant squid just. . . . No! She didn't! She DID! No! She . . ."*

_____ The author hates people.

_____ The author has a problem with people who use their cell phones in public places.

_____ The author thinks the woman was not a very good mother because she wasn't watching her children.

_____ The author loves squid.

_____ The author doesn't have a lot of patience in general.

12. Hiawatha was in the depths of despair. For years, his people, a group of five Native American nations known as the Iroquois, had engaged in a seemingly endless cycle of violence and revenge. Iroqouis families, villages, and nations fought one another, and neighboring Indians attacked relentlessly. When Hiawatha tried to restore peace within his own Onondaga nation, an evil sorcerer caused the deaths of his seven beloved daughters. Grief-stricken, Hiawatha wandered alone into the forest. After several days, he experienced a series of visions. First he saw a flock of wild ducks fly up from the lake, taking the water with them. Hiawatha walked onto the dry lakebed, gathering the beautiful purple-and-white shells that lay there. He saw the shells, called wampum, as symbolic "words" of condolence[1] that, when properly strung into belts and ceremoniously presented, would soothe anyone's grief, no matter how deep. Then he met a holy man named Deganawidah (the Peacemaker), who presented him with several wampum belts and spoke the appropriate words—one to dry his weeping eyes, another to open his ears to words of peace and reason, and a third to clear his throat so that he himself could once again speak peacefully and reasonably. Deganawidah and Hiawatha took the

7

1. **condolence:** sympathy with a person who has experienced pain, grief, or misfortune

* Adapted from Dave Barry, "Ban Cell Phones—Unless You're Attacked by Giant Squid," *Miami Herald*, August 19, 2001. Copyright, 2001, Tribune Media Sevices, Inc. All Rights Reserved. Reprinted with permission.

wampum to the five Iroquois nations. To each they introduced the ritual of condolence as a new message of peace.*

_____ Hiawatha was a very spiritual man.

_____ Hiawatha was a great warrior and battle commander.

_____ The other nations were open to Hiawatha's gesture of peace.

_____ Hiawatha never recovered from the death of his daughters.

_____ Hiawatha was very forgiving.

13. Gina Pell, of San Francisco, sent an e-mail to her sister asking her to set up a dinner with her sister's boyfriend. What Pell didn't say in the e-mail—because she was in a hurry—was that she wanted to introduce him to some friends who might help his career. "Somehow my request opened the floodgates for her pent-up resentment about how I treat her like a secretary and how it was inappropriate for me to hang out with her boyfriend," Pell says. "Rather than try to clarify the situation, I responded with a scathing, critical e-mail in typical haughty[1] older-sister fashion." The heated exchange got more and more intense, and finally boiled over. They didn't speak for a year. Today, they make a point of calling each other when potentially sensitive questions arise in e-mail.†

_____ Gina and her sister think that communicating by phone is more appropriate and effective in certain situations.

_____ Gina Pell did not communicate effectively on e-mail with her sister.

_____ Gina and her sister don't really like each other.

_____ Gina regrets that she responded with a "scathing, critical e-mail" message to her sister.

_____ Gina's sister and her boyfriend broke up right after the e-mail exchange.

14. It was dark. Not even a moon to light the way. Patricia Yaska and April Kameroff perched nervously in a boat slowly snaking down Alaska's Kuskowim River. Fog shrouded the mountains that ordinarily served as

1. **haughty**: proud and condescending

* Excerpted from Boyer et al., *The Enduring Vision*, 5th ed., Boston: Houghton Mifflin, 2004, 1. Copyright © 2004 by Houghton Mifflin Company. Reprinted with permission.

† Adapted from Janet Kornblum, "E-Mail's Limits Create Confusion, Hurt Feelings," *USA Today*, February 5, 2002, 6D.

landmarks. The beams from their handheld searchlights were useful. Two boys lay seriously injured after a head-on collision by all-terrain vehicles on a gravel trail about 30 miles away from Aniak. The river was the only way to reach them. Roads were nonexistent and the skies too murky to fly.*

_____ The two women are rescue workers.

_____ The women mentioned were wearing light jackets in the cold weather.

_____ The two boys had been speeding.

_____ The trek to rescue the kids was very dangerous.

_____ The river was very cold.

15. With perfect composure, the 18-year-old El Juli draws the bull past him in one, two, three, four, five quick passes. He wraps the cape around his torso like a sari,[1] pulling the animal in a tight spin, and soon leads the bull into the dance of his life. At one point they charge each other so fast—the ultimate game of chicken—that it seems they will collide in a ball of hair and bone and death. But El Juli dodges at the last instant. Outraged, the bull chases off after El Juli and nearly pins him against the wall, bellowing in frustration when he leaps over the five-foot barricade.†

_____ El Juli is Spanish for "young man."

_____ El Juli is a bullfighter.

_____ Bullfighting is dangerous work.

_____ The bull is old and feeble.

_____ El Juli is good at what he does.

7

1. **sari:** lightweight cloth outerwear garment worn mostly by women in India and Pakistan

* Adapted from Robert C. Yeager, "Everyday Heroes: Kicking Ash," *Reader's Digest*, February 2002, 29.

† Adapted from Elizabeth Gilbert, "Glory in the Afternoon," *Reader's Digest*, February 2002, 92.

CHAPTER 8

Purpose and Tone

GOALS FOR CHAPTER 8

- Define the term *critical reading*.
- List the three purposes for writing.
- Define the term *bias*.
- Explain why readers should learn to detect bias in texts.
- Identify examples of positive and negative bias.
- Define the terms *connotative meaning* and *denotative meaning*.
- Recognize connotative meanings of words.
- Define the term *tone*.
- Recognize different types of tone in reading selections.
- Explain and apply the steps of the REAP strategy.
- Read and understand information in a diagram.

The author's **purpose** is the reason he or she wrote the text. The **tone** of the text reflects the author's attitude about his or her topic. This chapter will focus on both purpose and tone. Complete the test below to see how much you already know.

TEST YOURSELF

Circle the letter of the correct answer for each question that follows the passages below.

Though charter schools are freed from some policies and regulations that govern traditional public schools, they must still adhere to state testing rules and are judged by testing results. In addition, though the charters get state money through per-pupil expenditures, they get no help paying for facilities and other capital expenses. Most charters can't afford to own a building or to

8

provide cafeterias, gyms, or libraries. Charter schools say that these issues hamper their ability to provide the innovation they feel could enhance student performance.*

1. What is the primary purpose of the above passage?
   a. to inform
   b. to entertain
   c. to persuade

Charter schools, indeed all public schools, must do more than make parents feel good. Fostering high academic standards and improving student achievement must be the primary goals. Those schools failing to do so cannot be tolerated. State officials, and we the public, must make sure they are not.†

2. What is the primary purpose of the above passage?
   a. to inform
   b. to entertain
   c. to persuade

Like to go to the beach, do you? Swim? Surf? Fish? Snorkel? Scuba dive? Wait! What can you be thinking? Don't you read the papers? Watch TV? Don't you know sharks are massing along our coastlines, biting bathers, eating people? Should you risk an attack by these JAWS wanna-bes?‡

3. What is the tone of the paragraph above?
   a. nostalgic
   b. angry
   c. alarmed
   d. sorrowful

Researchers find that many affluent[1] schools let kids solve real-world math problems and read stories that spark their interest. Low-income students, meanwhile, are apt to be seated in rows, kept busy with meaningless worksheets and endless practice tests that focus on vowel sounds or arithmetic rules to be memorized and recited without understanding. Reforms that aim for higher scores on standardized tests just intensify the worst form of instruction for the have-nots[2].§

4. Does this passage reveal positive bias, negative bias, or is it neutral?
   a. positive bias
   b. negative bias
   c. neutral

8

1. **affluent:** wealthy

2. **have-nots:** those with little material wealth

---

* Adapted from "Charter Schools," *Charlotte Observer*, November 14, 2001, 18A.

† Adapted from "Charter Schools," *Charlotte Observer*, November 14, 2001, 18A.

‡ From Downs Matthews, "Taking the Bite Out," *Wildlife Conservation*, December 2001, 38.

§ Adapted from Alfie Kohn, "More Testing Is No Answer," *USA Today*, July 31, 2001, 14A.

In the past, curtailing information in wartime has had disastrous results. Recall the secret bombing of Cambodia in 1969, when President Nixon kept even Congress in the dark. The North Vietnamese, the ones who could put Americans at risk, were well aware of the attacks. Americans were left out of the equation, eventually adding to anger over the war.

Today, the Bush administration is packaging its attempts to restrict information as a way to protect the war effort—when in fact they could do the opposite. The moves violated the very spirit of freedom that America is fighting for. They risk obliterating[1] the checks on government decisions that come when lawmakers and the general public know what the administration is doing.*

5. What is the author's tone in the paragraph above?

   a. amused
   b. critical
   c. neutral
   d. admiring

Now that you have mastered the basics of reading presented in the previous chapters of this text, you are ready to begin to probe a text more deeply to understand *what* it says and *how* it says it through critical reading.

Critical reading does not mean reading to criticize or find fault with a text. Instead, **critical reading** involves noticing certain techniques the writer is using to try to convince you of the validity and worth of his or her ideas or information. Once you learn to recognize these techniques, you are better able to evaluate a reading selection and decide what it means to you.

The ultimate goal of critical reading is critical thinking, an important skill in all areas of life, not just your academic courses. Critical thinkers don't just believe everything they hear or read. Instead, they approach new ideas and information with a healthy skepticism. They have learned how to analyze texts and ideas to not only understand them better, but also to decide whether they should accept those ideas, reject them or think about them further.

This chapter and Chapter 9 will help you develop your own critical reading skills by showing you how to examine important features of a text as you evaluate it. In particular, you'll get some practice with asking four key questions to further guide your analysis:

What is the author's purpose?

Does the author reveal bias or a certain tone?

1. **obliterating:** destroying

* "Moves to Block Information from Public Go Too Far," *USA Today,* October 16, 2001, 14A.

What is the main point and the evidence offered to support the author's claim?

Does the text attempt to distract you from the real issue or to oversimplify it?

This chapter will address the first two questions, and Chapter 9 will cover the other two questions. When you actively search for the answers to these questions, you're examining the features of a text that will indicate its validity.

Purpose

To begin to read more critically, the first question you should ask yourself as you read any text is: *What is the author's purpose?* Every book, article, or any other document you read has a purpose behind it. The writer recorded his or her thoughts for one or more of three main purposes:

1. **Entertain:** to entertain or amuse you
2. **Inform:** to give you more information about a topic
3. **Persuade:** to convince you to change an attitude, belief, or behavior

Everything you read has been written for at least one of these purposes. It's important to realize, too, that a particular reading selection can have more than one purpose. For example, a persuasive essay can also be informative. An entertaining novel might also teach you something new. Good reading comprehension includes the ability to recognize these different purposes so you'll know what the author wants you to do with the information.

Purpose: To Entertain

Some works are written to either entertain or amuse you. Much creative writing, such as novels, stories, poems, and plays, is created solely for the reader's enjoyment. For example, read the following newspaper column:

8

> The glue might stick a burly construction worker's hardhat to a steel beam, but it was having a difficult time securing the dangling quarter section of a plastic snake.
>
> My thumb and forefinger bonded instantly, but I could never form a tight seal on the snake's backside.
>
> Snake, of course, begins with the letter "s," which was why I was patching up the damaged toy critter at 7:15 A.M., with a tube of super-strength glue. It was show-and-tell day in kindergarten and students were encouraged to bring an item that began with the letter of the

week. Though we had had days to come up with a Slinky or a slingshot or a spatula, we waited until the last possible minute to paw through the closets and toy boxes, adding to the frenzy of our early morning routine.

"You put her clothes on her," I told my wife as we hauled 50 pounds of semicomatose child to the couch, "and I'll find something for show-and-tell."

In a perfect world, a father and daughter would join together in a mutual quest for knowledge, searching hand in hand for items that would fulfill the educational objectives of show-and-tell and, perhaps, just perhaps, grow a little closer along the way. But in my world, a man in his underwear tried desperately to glue a broken snake while yelling at his daughter to wake up and put on her shoes.

The snake, which was nearly severed in a tug-of-war mishap months earlier, would not survive a day at school intact without being glued, but the glue was not cooperating. I had to do some quick thinking, or my daughter would have nothing to show and tell, which I feared would haunt her throughout her academic career. I knew somewhere in her permanent record would be the notation, "Child has above-average intelligence and adequate social skills, but her unwillingness to participate in show-and-tell denotes a pattern of behavior that will likely culminate in a stint in training school or marriage at 16 to a heavily tattooed 37-year-old parolee who runs the Scrambler for the Scuzz Brothers Traveling Carnival."

I discarded the snake and searched for other "s" items, but I was panicked by the approaching school bell and disoriented from the glue fumes. There were hundreds of toys, scattered around the house, but none seemed to start with "s."

In the kitchen I found salt, but I knew this was not the time to take any white, powdery substance to school. I preferred not to see my child turn up on the FBI's top 20 terrorist list.

"Yes, hello, Mr. Hollifield? This is John Ashcroft[1] calling. Sorry to bother you, but we have taken your daughter into custody, confiscated a quantity of an unknown white powder, and are now searching for a reputed accomplice, described as a broken snake."

The Stillson wrench was too heavy, and the saw was too sharp. I looked for Spam in the cupboard, but we were all out.

1. **John Ashcroft:** served as U.S. Attorney General when several people died as a result of anthrax, a white powder that was transmitted through the mail

8

> A stump? It was too late to dig one up.
>
> Spleen? I'm really not sure where one is located.
>
> Statue of Liberty commemorative beer mug? I can't part with that.
>
> I made one more dive into the auxiliary toy box and came up with a Scooby-Doo hand puppet and a small Superman figure. I held them both up and asked my daughter to choose.
>
> "I don't want to go to school," was her overwhelming favorite.
>
> Eventually, after much more hysteria, my wife, daughter, Scooby, and Superman were on their way. With an hour or so to kill before work, I turned my attention back to the snake. Glue didn't fix him, but duct tape sure did. Tape . . . that's a "t" word. I'll keep that in mind.*

The sole purpose of this story is to entertain you and make you laugh. How do you know? It's a personal story, for one thing. And, it includes humor such as exaggeration and amusing descriptions. It makes no attempt to teach you anything or convince you of something.

Purpose: To Inform

Much writing is intended to increase your knowledge or understanding about a subject. A work with an informative purpose is designed to teach you something. Textbooks, most of the newspaper, and reference works such as encyclopedias are created with an informative purpose in mind. For example, read this passage from an American government textbook.

> Today, many Americans have come to the view that the Antifederalists[1] were right about the need for some type of term limits in Congress. When around 95 percent of House incumbents[2] are reelected, people worry that popular control of Congress has weakened, while state and local officials complain that there is no room for them to move up the political ladder. A 1992 survey showed that about 80 percent of Americans felt there should be a limit on the number of terms to which a senator or member of the House can be elected.
>
> The contemporary term-limit movement began in the fall of 1990, when term-limit measures passed in three statewide initiatives (California, Colorado, and Oklahoma). By 1994 twenty-two states had voted, in most places by large majorities, to impose limits on the

8

1. **Antifederalists:** those who opposed the ratification (approval) of the U.S. Constitution
2. **incumbents:** people who currently hold public offices

* Adapted from Scott Hollifield, "Spam, Spatula, or Scooby For Show & Tell," *News Herald,* October 19, 2001, 4A. Used by permission of the author.

number of years their representatives could serve in Congress, but the Supreme Court has ruled that such state-imposed limits on members of Congress are unconstitutional.

Proposals that would place a lifetime limit on legislative service would result in an amateur legislature. Let us assume, as many supporters of these measures do, that amateurs in Congress would act out of personal conviction rather than from the desire to be reelected. Reelection-minded professional politicians must be concerned about what their constituents think and want; principled amateur legislators need not be. Would a congress composed of such legislators be good or bad, better or worse? The answer, of course, depends largely on whether you favor representative or direct democracy.*

The topic of this passage is term limits, a debatable issue. Yet, the writers attempt to present neutral and factual information about the subject. They are not attempting to persuade you to think one way or another, so the purpose here is simply informative.

Purpose: To Persuade

Works with a persuasive purpose attempt to convince you to change a belief, an attitude, or a behavior. These readings are said to be arguments, for they argue a point in hopes of getting the reader to agree. An editorial in a newspaper, for example, may argue that you should support a particular cause. A self-help book may urge you to think and act differently to improve a personal problem. An essay in a magazine might attempt to convince you to interpret a current event in a certain way. For example, look at the following excerpt from a "My Turn" essay that originally appeared in *Newsweek*.

> It occurred to me that for any society to be great, it has to do two things. It must reward hardworking, talented people like Derek Jeter[1], then strongly encourage those people to share their rewards thoroughly and intelligently with their fellow citizens. I know that money won't solve all problems (give a kid a loving environment over a few extra bucks any day). But why should there be 34 students in each of my classes instead of 25, and why should the ceiling in the gym at my school be too low for us to even shoot a basket?

1. **Derek Jeter:** shortstop for the New York Yankees baseball team

* Adapted from Wilson and DiIulio, *American Government,* 8th ed. Boston: Houghton Mifflin, 2001, 320–322.

8

> I'm sure that Mr. Jeter has lots of demands on his money, and my guess is that he gives a fair amount of it pretty generously. But I wonder if he realizes that if he wanted to, he could build a new public school. After all, he'll never be able to spend all of that money in a lifetime. He could change the lives of the thousands of Bronx kids who root for him and are a big part of the reason that he can make so much money doing what he loves in the first place.*

In this excerpt, the author hopes to persuade the reader to agree with the opinion that wealthy sports stars like Derek Jeter should use some of the money they earn to help people. Specifically, the writer is arguing that Jeter should build a school for some of his young fans. This opinion is debatable, of course, so the writer offers some reasons (for instance, Jeter should help the kids who made him rich in the first place) in support of his point of view.

Determining the Purpose

When you read a passage, how can you determine the author's purpose? The passage itself will usually provide a number of clues that will help you decide on the author's intentions.

The Main Point An entertaining passage may not have a main point at all, or the main point may focus on something that the writer learned from some experience. The main point of an informative passage will usually state a fact or describe some state of affairs without offering any judgment about it. The main point of a persuasive passage, however, will be an opinion. Its persuasive purpose is often indicated with words like *should, must,* and *have to,* for the author wants to convince the reader to change a belief or a behavior.

The Supporting Details In entertaining passages, supporting details are often stories or descriptions, both of which might be humorous. In an informative passage, the details take the form of facts that can be verified, and they do not offer the writer's opinions about those details. A persuasive passage, too, can include facts; however, watch also for more opinions that are used to justify the main point.

8

The Sources of the Information In an entertaining passage, there are usually no sources provided. An informative passage will often cite sources, and those sources will usually be informative in nature themselves. Persuasive passages may cite sources as well, but those sources may very well be ones that favor the author's point of view.

* From Michael Lupinacci, "Jeter: Put Your Money Where Your Fans Are," *Newsweek*, May 21, 2001, 14. © 2001 Newsweek, Inc. All rights reserved. Reprinted by permission.

The Author Pay attention to any information you get about the writer's background, qualifications, experience, and interests, for these characteristics will help you evaluate what he or she intended by writing the passage. Sometimes, authors will directly state their purpose by announcing it or by summarizing their credentials. They may offer you some details about their background that led them to write about the topic. However, even if a text reveals little or nothing about the writer, you will still be able to gain a sense of who the writer is and what he or she hopes to achieve. The words authors choose, and even the way they put their sentences together, can reveal a great deal about their feelings, their attitudes, and their goals. Specifically, you can learn to recognize bias and to determine the tone of a text, which are discussed in the next section.

You should get in the habit of examining all these aspects of a reading selection so that you can begin to think more critically about the ideas and information it includes.

Exercise 8.1

Circle the letter of the primary purpose of each of the following passages.

The Plague had eliminated as much as a third of the European population over a five-year period. Smallpox was never that devastating in Europe, becoming endemic[1] and occasionally outbreaking. Widespread resistance reduced the losses to local impacts of about 10 percent. However, introduction of smallpox to America quite rapidly depleted the population. For example, the Spanish attempted to settle Hispanola[2] for sugar cane plantation in 1509. By 1518 every single one of the 2.5 million aboriginals[3] had perished, and the labor population had to be restored with African slaves.*

1. In this passage, the author's primary purpose is to
   a. entertain.
   b. inform.
   c. persuade.

1. **endemic:** widespread in a particular region or among a certain group of people
2. **Hispanola:** island of the West Indies east of Cuba
3. **aboriginals:** people who have existed in a region from the beginning

* Adapted from "Smallpox: History," October 22, 2001, http://seercom.com/bluto/smallpox/history.html.

8

I know there are questions about sports in society: Are they overemphasized? Do brawling parents at kids' games foretell a cycle of "sports rage"? Is the XFL[1] a precursor of sports horrors to come?

But for most of us, sports offer more than questions. For families, they offer a physical place to be together away from work or school. For kids, they offer—often at critical times in their lives—a way to connect with each other and work toward common goals. For me, sports became a collection of personal moments, a mental album of boys growing to men.

Sports gave my sons, my wife, and me a center, a source of endless conversation. I have no doubt my sons are better people for having competed in sports. My family is closer. John and James, my sons, are best friends. I don't think either of them misses sports or practice, and I'm not sure they yet appreciate everything sports gave them. But I do know that those who say that America is obsessed with sports, or that schools that stress sports too much are missing an important point. Sports can be a bond that brings and holds families together. And I'm sad the last game is over.*

2. In this passage, the author's primary purpose is to

   a. entertain.
   b. inform.
   c. persuade.

I love Halloween because it reminds me of a simpler, more innocent time—a time when I dressed up as a goblin and ran around the neighborhood shouting, "Trick or treat!"

But that was last year. This year I think I'll have a more subdued costume. Maybe I'll dress up as a large piece of lumber and carry around a cardboard box labeled "Interest Rates," and every few steps, I'll drop it. Get it? It's the Federal Reserve "Board." Dropping interest rates! Ha-ha! I bet *that* will get a big reaction from the neighborhood kids. Probably in the form of eggs.

That's the problem with kids today: They don't know what Halloween is all about. It has been commercialized to the point where our young people think it's just fun and games. They know nothing about the somber origin of this holiday, which dates back to 1621, when the Pilgrims,[2] having survived a difficult first winter in America, decided to express their thanks by dressing up in comical outfits with knickers and hats shaped like traffic cones (ordinarily, the Pilgrims wore bowling attire) and then went around playing pranks with

8

1. **The XFL:** was a football league started by the McMahon family, who are famous for their involvement in professional wrestling. The XFL does not exist as an organization anymore.
2. **Pilgrims:** English settlers who founded Plymouth Colony in 1620

* Adapted from John Baer, "Wins and Losses Are Not What I Remember," *Newsweek,* April 16, 2001, 13. © 2001 Newsweek, Inc. All rights reserved. Reprinted by permission.

what—tragically—turned out to be their last remaining roll of toilet paper. And thus, as you can imagine, their second winter was no picnic, either.

That is what Halloween is about, but try explaining it to these spoiled kids today, with their inexhaustible supplies of Charmin[1].*

3. In this passage, the author's primary purpose is to

   a. entertain.
   b. inform.
   c. persuade.

Was Elvis' song "That's All Right" the birth cry of rock 'n' roll? Or is that all wrong?

On July 5, 1954, Elvis Presley stepped into Sun Studio in Memphis to record "That's All Right," his first single. The event has been declared the birth date of rock 'n' roll by a host of commercial celebrators, from BMG, which controls his catalog, and Elvis Presley Enterprises to the Hard Rock Cafe and the Memphis Convention & Visitors' Bureau.

But rock's genesis has long been debated by critics, historians and pioneers themselves. (Little Richard and Chuck Berry might have a beef with Elvis.) "Obviously, it's a pretty nuanced[2] thing to stick a needle in the timeline and say it's the moment rock 'n' roll was birthed," says Alan Light, editor of music magazine *Tracks*. "There's never a definitive answer, partly because there's no simple, universal definition of rock to begin with."

"It's impossible to pin the birth of rock on one day or even one year," says Pete Howard, publisher of *Ice* magazine. "One could make a strong argument for the late '40s as well as the early '50s. It was a long, gradual process. July 5, 1954, is probably the best single date to settle on, even though it's like trying to pick the date live music began," he says. "We do it just for fun, because people love lists and anniversaries. If Elvis were alive, he'd probably argue for Wynonie Harris' 'Good Rockin' Tonight' or Jackie Brenston's 'Rocket 88.'"†

4. In this passage, the author's primary purpose is to

   a. entertain.
   b. inform.
   c. persuade.

You may not be serving your country in an official status, but you can help those who are. Let the families of military personnel know you recognize their efforts and appreciate what they do. By helping a military family, you are supporting and giving peace of mind to a military member who is risking so much for us.

1. **Charmin:** a brand of toilet paper 2. **nuanced:** subtle

* Adapted from Dave Barry, "Hairum-Scarum," *Boston Globe Magazine,* October 28, 2001, 6. Copyright, 2001, Tribune Media Services, Inc. All Rights Reserved. Reprinted with permission.

† Adapted from Edna Gundersen, "Elvis' First Single Crowns Rock's 50th Anniversary," *USA Today,* July 2, 2004, 4E.

If you know a family suffering through deployment,[1] consider adopting them. Invite them over for meals, offer to help baby-sit, help fix that leaky faucet. If they are able to correspond with the deployed member, provide a few long-distance phone calls or stationery. Or if you have computer skills, help set up a family Web site or e-mail account. Use your photography skills so the deployed spouse can have an updated picture of the family. If you're a business owner, post job openings at the Family Support Center on base, hold Military Appreciation Days, and provide military discounts.*

5. In this passage, the author's primary purpose is to

   a. entertain.
   b. inform.
   c. persuade.

Exercise 8.2

Circle the letter that corresponds to the primary purpose of each of the following passages.

Frankly, it seems pretty easy to come up with a new exercise. You just take something people are already doing—like eating—and add "ercise." Or say it's cardio-friendly. So how's about:

R.C. Colaerobics: Soda shopping? Don't just grab a Coke. Stretch waaaaay down to reach the Royal Crown! Your abs will be glad—and so will your wallet!

Karaoke[2] Swim: Tired of singing on that stupid bike? Start singing as you swim across the pool! Pounds peel away as you struggle to clear your lungs and stay afloat. You go, gurgle!

Lego Lifts: Step 1: Invite a child to play with Legos on your rug. Step 2: Have child leave after "cleaning up." Step 3: Remove your socks and run around. Yeow! Ouch. There's another one he missed! You're hopping your way to health!†

1. In this passage, the author's primary purpose is to

   a. entertain.
   b. inform.
   c. persuade.

1. **deployment:** bringing troops into action, ready for combat
2. **karaoke:** performance in which someone sings the words to a song

* Adapted from Patty Erickson, "Honor Military Families," *Charlotte Observer*, November 11, 2001, 3D. Copyright, 2001, Knight Ridder/Tribune Media Services. Reprinted with permission.

† From Lenore Skenacy, "I'm Rock Hard Thanks to Lie-ercize," *Daily News*, June 13, 2004, 47.

In his book *The Revolt of the Elites*, the late Christopher Lasch wrote that only in the course of argument do "we come to understand what we know and what we still need to learn. . . . We come to know our own minds only by explaining ourselves to others." If we wish to be engaged in serious argument, Lasch explained, we must enter into another person's mental universe and put our own ideas at risk.

Exactly. When a friend launches an argument and your rebuttal sounds tinny[1] to your own ears, it shouldn't be that hard to figure out that something's wrong—usually, that you don't really agree with the words coming out of your own mouth. Arguing can rescue us from our own half-formed opinions.*

2. In this passage, the author's primary purpose is to
   a. entertain.
   b. inform.
   c. persuade.

Somewhere along the line, *The Times* got out of the news business and into the nation building business. Its primary intent is no longer to provide objective information and fair-minded analysis to its readers, but to convince them to support a brave new world in the U.S. The power of *The Times* is being used to promote the formation of a new America, a bright, shining progressive city on a hill of steep government entitlements.[2]

Why should you care what an individual newspaper does? Even with a circulation of more than a million, most Americans don't read *The Times*. But consider this: Every morning, the powerful barons and anchor people who run the network TV news operations read *The Times* first thing. They often take editorial direction from the paper, sometimes duplicating story selection and even point of view. All-news radio does the same thing, and *The Times'* wire goes out to thousands of newspapers across the country and around the world. This is one extremely powerful outfit.†

3. In this passage, the author's primary purpose is to
   a. entertain.
   b. inform.
   c. persuade.

Truck-only toll (TOT) lanes, which are the brainchild of Robert Poole, an engineer who oversees transportation studies at the Reason Foundation, are

8

1. **tinny:** weak, thin, flimsy

2. **government entitlements:** guaranteed benefits to particular groups

* From John Leo, "Instead of Arguments, We Get Shouts and Insults," *Daily News*, June 15, 2004.

† From Bill O'Reilly, "The Worst of Times," *Daily News*, June 21, 2004. By permission of Bill O'Reilly and Creators Syndicate, Inc.

extra lanes that would be added to our nation's highways to separate cars from trucks in an attempt to expand capacity, improve traffic and move freight more efficiently. This year, Poole identified 10 stretches of interstate highways in 16 states, including I-80 through Illinois and Iowa, as ideal for testing TOT lanes. But trucking industry leaders are wary. They worry about the financial burden of truckers being forced to pay more tolls, especially on roads they already use for free. "Separating cars and trucks, for the trucking industry, would be an improvement," says Darrin Roth of the American Trucking Associations. "The issue becomes how do you pay for it."

But TOT lanes are gaining favor in Congress. That's mainly because the Federal Highway Administration has predicted a 31 percent increase in truck freight by 2015. Last year, 77 million trucks hauled 13.2 billion tons of freight. Combined with the growth of other traffic, the nation's highways are rapidly approaching capacity. TOT lanes would allow highways to be widened without using tax dollars. Construction would be paid for with toll money.*

4. In this passage, the author's primary purpose is to
   a. entertain.
   b. inform.
   c. persuade.

Does the lie-detector, or polygraph, test really work? Many people think it is foolproof, but scientific opinion is still split. Some researchers report accuracy rates of about 90 percent. Others say that such claims are exaggerated and misleading. One well-documented problem is that truthful persons too often fail the test. For example, a study of polygraph records obtained from police files revealed that although 98 percent of suspects later known to be guilty were correctly identified as such, 45 percent of those who were eventually found innocent were judged deceptive. A second problem is that the test can be faked. Studies show that you can beat the polygraph by tensing your muscles, squeezing your toes, or using other countermeasures while answering the control questions, which ask yes-no questions that are not relevant to the crime. By artificially inflating the responses to the "innocent" questions, one can mask the stress that is aroused by lying on the crime-relevant questions.†

5. In this passage, the author's primary purpose is to
   a. entertain.
   b. inform.
   c. persuade.

---

* Adapted from Debbie Howlett, "Truckers Leery of Toll-Lanes Idea," *USA Today*, June 28, 2004, 3A.

† Adapted from Brehm et al., *Social Psychology,* 5th ed. Boston: Houghton Mifflin, 2002, 446. Copyright © 2002 by Houghton Mifflin Company. Reprinted with permission.

8

Bias and Tone

One of the main reasons to determine an author's purpose is so that you can detect any bias the author might have about his or her subject. **Bias** is an inclination toward a particular opinion or viewpoint. The term describes our tendency to feel strongly that something is right or wrong, positive or negative. Even authors who try to present information neutrally, without revealing any of their own feelings about the topic, will often allow their own prejudices to creep into their writing. Conversely, authors can also make their bias perfectly clear. They often do so in hopes that they will influence the reader to agree. Therefore, the second question you should ask yourself as you read any text is: *Does the author reveal bias or a certain tone?*

Recognizing Bias

Authors communicate their bias by using words that urge the reader to feel a certain way about a topic. Many of these words are emotional, and they provoke strong reactions in readers, encouraging them to feel either positive or negative. For example, the word *recruiter* is a respectful term, but the word *headhunter* is negative and derogatory. In the following pairs of sentences, the first sentence includes words that are relatively neutral. Notice how the substitution of a few more emotional words injects bias into the statement.

Neutral: Pharmaceutical company representatives influence doctors to write prescriptions for their products by giving them gifts and buying them meals.

Emotional: Pharmaceutical company salesmen seduce doctors into hawking their products by showering them with gifts and wining and dining them.

Neutral: Prisoners serving life sentences should lose all of their freedoms, including their right to procreate[1] with their spouses.

Emotional: Convicted criminals do not deserve any freedoms, including the right to make babies while they're locked up.

Neutral: Drive-in movie theaters are not obsolete; on the contrary, those still in operation are improving their technology to increase their number of customers.

1. **procreate:** conceive and produce children

Emotional: Some drive-in movie theaters are still thriving; their cutting-edge, crystal-clear pictures and stereo sound are attracting a new generation of customers who will create a new golden age like the 1950s.

In the second sentence of each pair, you can see that the choice of words makes the author's opinion more emotionally forceful.

Exercise 8.3

In each of the following statements, underline the words or phrases that reveal the author's bias. Then, on the blank, write POSITIVE if the words encourage you to feel positive about the subject and NEGATIVE if they urge you to feel negative.

1. This summer, TV is giving us too much of a bad thing. With Fox and NBC in the forefront, the networks have offered viewers an unusually full schedule of flat sitcoms, dull dramas and cheap, mean-spirited, copycat reality shows. Viewer response has been a resounding "no thanks."* ____________

2. That the world has changed in meaningful ways since 1954 is beyond question. Oprah Winfrey and her activities were driving forces in many of those changes. Her enormously influential talk show, her philanthropic work with children in Africa and elsewhere, her popular book club and magazine, her empowering spiritual message, her contribution (by action and example) to improving race relations—all speak to the human family, touching hearts and leaving each one uplifted .† ____________

3. When we think of felines, we think of selfish, indulgent, petulant independence. It's a personality that makes us slightly uneasy: While we believe we have a certain level of control—after all, we do feed and house this beast—we also know that the cat is quite capable of acting against immediate best interests by biting the finger of the hand that feeds it. You can't relax around a cat, which is why cats may be this era's pet. We can't relax anymore, period. Cats mock our pretensions to power, show no gratitude, hide when we want to display them to company. They are tiny terrorists, reminders of our vulnerability.‡ ____________

* Adapted from Robert Bianco, "Networks Are Sweating Out Their Own Long, Hot Summer," *USA Today*, June 30, 2004, 3D.

† Sidney Poitier, "Heroes and Icons: Oprah Winfrey," *Time*, April 26, 2004, 123.

‡ Adapted from Robert Lipsyte, "Uncertain Times Turn Us into Cat People," *USA Today*, June 30, 2004, 13A.

8

4. Joe Torre is proud of the way his New York Yankee baseball team has hugged New York, proud to believe his Yankees are as much a family as famed football coach Vince Lombardi's Green Bay Packers were.*

____

5. Unfortunately, NBC's *Lost* is reason to make you hate reality TV all over again. *Lost* features six players, strangers split into three teams competing for $200,000. They're dropped in the middle of an unknown, remote location and must find their way back to New York. The fun of this is supposed to be in watching Americans struggle with foreign cultures and landscapes and the occasional airborne illness. In fact, *Lost* ends up feeling like a bad National Geographic special. The trek around the world unfolds so slowly that the show's disembodied narrator often resorts to giving us useless geographical and historical information about the country in play. And *Lost* jumps around among the teams so often and in such discombobulated ways, we end up feeling as disoriented as riders disembarking from the Tilt-a-Whirl at the fair.† _______________

Connotative and Denotative Meanings

When you are evaluating a text and trying to decide whether the author reveals a certain bias, you will want to notice any connotative meanings attached to the words that the author chose. While the **denotative meaning** of a word refers to its literal, dictionary definition, the **connotative meaning** of the word refers to all of the associations and emotions that people tend to attach to that word. The denotative meaning of the word *father*, for example, is "the male parent of a child." However, the word also carries connotative meanings for many people. For some people, usually those who had positive experiences with their own fathers, the word carries a positive connotation. For others, who had negative experiences, the word may carry a negative connotation.

Connotations of words are attached by people; therefore, they vary from individual to individual. However, many words have absorbed general positive or negative associations. As the chart on page 408 shows, connotations are relative. The word *fearless*, for example, may be neutral to some people and have positive connotations for others, but it seems more neutral, or even positive, when compared to a word like *reckless*.

8

* Adapted from Ian O'Connor, "Torre Keeps N.Y. All in the Family, " *USA Today,* October 25, 2001.
† Adapted from Marc Peyser, "Reality on Foot," *Newsweek,* September 10, 2001, 61.

Positive	Neutral	Negative
diminutive	short	stunted
cuisine	food	grub
eccentric	different	odd
part company	leave	abandon
cottage	cabin	shack
brave	fearless	reckless

Exercise 8.4

For each pair of words, write a checkmark in the blank beside the one that has the more **positive** connotation.

1. ______ scent ______ odor
2. ______ disabled ______ crippled
3. ______ cop ______ police officer
4. ______ assertive ______ aggressive
5. ______ housewife ______ stay-at-home mom
6. ______ abortion ______ reproductive freedom
7. ______ blind ______ visually impaired
8. ______ sweat ______ perspire
9. ______ downsized ______ fired
10. ______ vomit ______ spit up
11. ______ passed away ______ died
12. ______ fat ______ voluptuous
13. ______ old ______ mature
14. ______ fib ______ lie
15. ______ cheap ______ inexpensive
16. ______ stroll ______ straggle
17. ______ flawed ______ irregular

18. ______ disagreement ______ argument

19. ______ lie around ______ relax

20. ______ poor ______ disadvantaged

Determining Tone

In addition to communicating either an overall positive or negative view about a subject, an author can also reveal a more specific attitude, or **tone.** For example, the author may be angry, critical, or sarcastic about his subject. These attitudes express more particular types of negative bias. Or, an author might be excited, sympathetic, amused, or awed. These are some examples of positive bias. Of course, authors can present their ideas and information with a neutral, objective tone, too. The following series of passages illustrates how changing a few words here and there results in a very different tone.

This passage illustrates a **neutral tone:**

Nearly 13 years after a suitcase checked onto Pan Am Flight 103 exploded over Lockerbie, Scotland, killing 189 Americans, checked luggage still isn't examined effectively for explosives. Airlines continue not to follow the few government directives that exist to ensure that some checked baggage is screened. Just this month, government inspectors discovered laxity[1] at major airports, including high-tech, $1-million scanners that weren't being used. In spite of dramatic efforts to increase airport security, the vast majority of baggage transported in cargo holds still goes unscreened.*

This passage illustrates a **critical tone:**

Nearly 13 years after a suitcase checked onto Pan Am Flight 103 exploded over Lockerbie, Scotland, ***senselessly*** killing 189 Americans, airlines are still ***turning a blind eye*** to ***potentially dangerous*** checked luggage. Airlines continually ***flout*** even the ***flimsy*** government directives that exist to ensure that at least some checked baggage is screened. Just this month, government inspectors ***exposed unforgivable laziness*** at major airports, where employees ***couldn't be bothered to even turn on*** high-tech $1-million scanners that were ***sitting there collecting dust.*** In spite of dramatic efforts to increase airport security, the airlines ***obviously believe that ignorance is bliss.*** They

1. **laxity:** lack of rigor, strictness, or firmness

* Adapted from "Checked Bags Unscreened, Despite Terrorist Threat," *USA* Today, October 22, 2001, 14A.

8

just keep ***tossing*** the unscreened luggage into cargo holds and ***pretending that bombs don't exist.***

This passage illustrates a **sympathetic tone:**

Nearly 13 years after a suitcase checked onto Pan Am Flight 103 exploded over Lockerbie, Scotland, killing 189 Americans, ***overwhelmed*** airlines are still ***having a hard time*** conducting effective examinations for explosives. Overworked airline staffs ***struggle*** to comply with government directives that exist to ensure that some checked baggage is screened. Just this month, government inspectors found that ***undertrained and underpaid*** airline employees were not using high-tech, $1-million scanners. In spite of dramatic efforts to increase airport security, airlines just don't have the time or manpower to screen ***the huge mountain of luggage passengers insist on bringing with them.***

The first paragraph is relatively neutral. It includes mostly factual information that is free of emotional words, with the exception of *laxity* in the third sentence. Therefore, the reader is not encouraged toward any particular feeling or attitude. The second version, however, is clearly critical. Words and phrases like *turning a blind eye, flouts,* and *unforgivable laziness* leave no doubt in the reader's mind about the author's attitude, and they encourage the reader to blame the airlines for the problem. Notice, though, how the tone changes to one of sympathy in the third version. In that paragraph, the boldfaced, italicized words and phrases suggest that we should feel sorry for the *overwhelmed* airlines, which are not to blame for the problem. The third version also suggests that passengers cause the problem by bringing too much luggage.

Exercise 8.5

Read each of the paragraphs below and then use the boldfaced, italicized words to help you circle the letter of the correct tone in the list that follows.

1. Seabiscuit was one of the most ***remarkable*** thoroughbred racehorses in history. From 1936 to 1940, Americans thronged to racetracks to watch the small, ungainly[1] racehorse become a ***champion.*** He had an awkward gait but ran with ***dominating speed;*** he was mild-mannered yet ***fiercely competitive;*** and he was stubborn until he became compliant.*

   a. critical
   b. admiring
   c. neutral

1. **ungainly:** clumsy, lacking grace

* From "Mammals and Events: Seabiscuit (1933–1947)," PBS.org,http://www.pbs.org/wgbh/amex/seabiscuit/mammalsevents/m_seabiscuit.html.

8

2. The time has come for this ***archaic***[1] process we call the primary season—a ***long, drawn-out,*** state-by-state process—to be abolished and replaced by a true national primary. The 2004 election should be the last for this old system. In our current process, by the time the first three or four states have voted and the news media have declared the trends and expected results, the party moguls have the stage set for their guy or gal. This ***disenfranchises***[2] voters. Every registered American citizen deserves the opportunity to enter the voting booth and express a choice totally uninfluenced by exit polls and media ***rhetoric.***[3] There should be one day of national primary voting across the country. I suggest the first Tuesday nearest the Fourth of July. What a significant date to exercise our freedom and patriotic duty. This method should eliminate the ***problem*** of "He or she who has the most money, wins."*

   a. neutral
   b. critical
   c. admiring

3. Plucked by Ronald Reagan[4] in 1981 from a state appeals court in Arizona to be the first female on the Supreme Court, Sandra Day O'Connor established a reputation for seeking ***sensible*** outcomes on a case-by-case basis rather than developing a sweeping legal philosophy. Her ***elegant,*** personal 2003 autobiography was titled *The Majesty of the Law.* But her own ***majestic qualities are refreshingly devoid of regal pretense.***[5] They are marked instead by the ***humility and tolerance and restraint*** that are the true foundations of the constitutional principles that she endeavors both to balance and to obey.†

   a. admiring
   b. angry
   c. neutral

4. President Kennedy filled his cabinet (his so-called Ministry of Talent) with ***able*** and ***experienced*** leaders from both political parties, all of them ***men of commitment.*** Forsaking private-sector compensation, private life's leisures, and, to a considerable extent, privacy itself, they were ***genuinely dedicated*** to fulfilling this nation's destiny as a "beacon . . . to

8

1. **archaic:** outdated
2. **disenfranchises:** deprives citizens of their rights
3. **rhetoric:** persuasive language
4. **Ronald Reagan:** fortieth president of the United States
5. **pretense:** false appearance

* Adapted from James Talley, "Adopt One-Day, National Primary," *USA Today,* January 2, 2004, 11A.

† Adapted from Walter Isaacson, "Scientists and Thinkers: Sandra Day O'Connor," *Time,* April 26, 2004, 104.

the rest of the world," as the Founding Fathers had dreamed. Americans of widely differing backgrounds shared that ***spirit of dedication*** to the public interest.*

a. insulting.
b. neutral.
c. admiring.

5. Here's a real financial ***scandal***—one presided over by your very own federal government. Wage and salary earners are paying an ***utterly disproportionate*** share of national taxes. They are carrying corporations and foreign companies that are getting away with daylight ***robbery.*** In the boom years from 1996 through 2000, when profits went through the roof, over 60 percent of American companies, doing nearly $2.5 trillion in gross income, paid no income taxes. None. Some 71 percent of foreign companies, doing three quarters of a trillion dollars, also paid no federal income taxes. This is ***outrageous, intolerable, and unfair.***†

a. neutral
b. angry
c. admiring

Below is a list of more words that are often used to describe tone.

admiring praising, favoring, or supportive
amused humorous or playful
angry feeling displeased or hostile
arrogant boastful; feeling of being superior to others
ashamed feeling embarrassed or guilty
bewildered confused
bitter very angry
caring concerned and interested
conceited vain; having a high opinion of oneself
concerned troubled and anxious
critical expressing disapproval or strong disagreement
defensive protective; prepared to withstand attack
disgusted feeling sickened or irritated
distressed anxious and upset; disturbed
doubting disbelieving; distrusting, skeptical
enthusiastic excited and supportive
excited emotionally aroused and active
frightened apprehensive, fearful

* Adapted from Ted Sorensen, "Patriotic Pride," *Town and Country,* July 2001, 74.

† From Mortimer B. Zuckerman, "An Intolerable Free Ride," *U.S. News and World Report,* May 17, 2004, 80.

humorous	funny or witty
impassioned	full of passion or emotion
indignant	angered by something unjust, mean, or unworthy
insulted	offended and angry
insulting	being rude or offensive
ironic	saying the opposite of what you mean
irreverent	disrespectful
joyful	cheerful, glad, pleased
lighthearted	not serious; carefree
mocking	making fun of something; ridiculing
nostalgic	longing for the past
optimistic	expecting the best; hopeful about the future
outraged	extremely angry
passionate	expressing very strong feelings
pessimistic	expecting the worst to happen
playful	full of fun and high spirits
pleading	begging; arguing earnestly for something
praising	approving, admiring; pointing out the virtues of something
remorseful	bitterly regretful for past misdeeds
respectful	showing high regard; treating someone or something as having worth
reverent	expressing a feeling of deep awe or respect
sad	feeling down, depressed, or hurt
sarcastic	mean and hurtful
scolding	openly criticizing or reprimanding
scornful	treating as though unworthy
sentimental	very emotional
serious	with deep concern about important matters
solemn	serious and deeply earnest
suspicious	believing someone guilty of wrongdoing
sympathetic	understanding the feelings of others
threatening	expressing an intention to inflict pain or damage
worried	concerned or frightened about what will happen

8

Exercise 8.6

Read each paragraph and circle the letter of the correct tone.

1. Widely described as the crown jewel of NASA's science program, the Hubble Space Telescope ranks among the world's most important astronomical observatories. In addition to providing years of beautiful photos

of the cosmos, it has yielded remarkable discoveries of black holes, explosive ancient galaxies, star births and star deaths, among many others. In 1998, Hubble observations of distant exploding stars astounded astronomers by revealing that our universe is expanding at an accelerating rate, a discovery that overturned decades of thought about the nature of the universe. If the telescope is allowed to expire in 2007, more will be lost than the new instruments and gyroscopes[1] worth about $200 million that will go unused with the cancellation of the shuttle servicing mission. Steven Beckwith, head of the Space Telescope Science Institute in Baltimore, says these scientific advancements, among others, will be missed:

- Better measures of those distant exploding stars to uncover the "dark energy" behind the universe's runaway expansion.
- Closer looks at those explosive ancient galaxies, or quasars, to determine how the first star clusters formed after the big bang.
- No planned telescope will, like Hubble, look at visible light from stars, leaving a hole in NASA's Great Observatory program.*

a. bewildered
b. praising
c. doubting
d. excited

2. It's not easy being a mother these days. Most work outside the home in addition to their parenting duties. Because of the high divorce rate, many are rearing their children alone or with only part-time help from fathers. In 2001, an ABC news columnist did some research that suggested if you paid mothers for all the things they do, they would draw down about $500,000 a year.

Moms face a daunting task, whether they have other jobs or not. First, they must make their way through a labyrinth[2] of advice based on vast amounts of research, much of it conflicting. Whatever they do, they're bound to find some study that says they did the wrong thing, didn't do the right thing, or otherwise somehow permanently damaged their offspring.

8

1. **gyroscopes:** devices that consist of a spinning disk or wheel that can maintain its orientation regardless of movement to its base
2. **labyrinth:** maze

* Adapted from "Achievements Would Be Lost in Space," no author credited, *USA Today,* February 10, 2004, 7D.

Then there's the whole problem of keeping their children healthy amidst an incessant barrage of messages seducing them to eat more sugar- and carbohydrate- and fat-loaded snack foods. And of teaching them values in a society that worships materialism. And of helping them find a path through a world filled with diverse beliefs, an explosion of knowledge and information, and moral ambiguity.

But most mothers run the gauntlet[1] of conflicting messages, struggle to figure it all out, sacrifice as mothers always have and nurture their children to the best of their ability. And most children thrive despite the forces that complicate theirs' and their mothers' lives.*

a. ashamed
b. indignant
c. threatening
d. sympathetic

3. I was brought up in Europe. I came to the United States at age 25 in 1963, and for the past 41 years, I have been disturbed by the eating habits of Americans. Americans have come to demand that an endless quantity of foods be available at all times. I have seen them pile food on their plates at buffet-style restaurants. However, seldom have I seen them eat all of the items they put on their plates. Some restaurants, in a smart move, have had to resort to posting signs such as, "You may take as much as you want, but please eat all that you take."

In my country, it is only after a person eats everything on his or her plate that he or she goes back to the buffet to get more food. Piling everything on a plate and giving little thought to what you're eating—or little thought to whether or not the food realistically can be consumed—is pure gluttony[2] and uncivilized. Usually, our eyes are bigger than our stomachs. It's time for Americans to learn to take smaller portions and eat what they put on their plates. It all starts in the home, being educated by parents who should set good examples.

America needs to wake up and learn good food manners.†

a. humorous
b. optimistic
c. disgusted
d. respectful

1. **run the gauntlet:** a reference to getting through a form of punishment in which a person is forced to run through two lines of people who try to strike him or her

2. **gluttony:** excess in eating and drinking

* Excerpted from "No Job Can Ever Be More Challenging or More Important Than That of a Mom," *Asheville Citizen-Times*, May 9, 2004, A12. Copyright 2004, Asheville, NC Citizen-Times. Reprinted with permission.

† From Ingrid Lander, Longmont, CO, "Americans Lack Good Eating Habits at Buffet Table," *USA Today*, March 17, 2004, 12A.

4. Random checkpoints such as those employed by the Click it or Ticket program have not only become commonplace—they're becoming accepted as normal. This is a disturbing development to civil libertarians.[1] Dragnets[2] used to be reserved for the FBI's Ten Most Wanted. Now they're used to enforce compliance with "lifestyle laws" on the one hand—and more subtly, to give the police an easy means of being able lawfully (the term is used loosely) to pull people over, just to check them out and to look for other "violations." So much less trouble than having to come up with probable cause, or get a warrant based on fact-supported suspicions.

   Americans are less and less troubled by the idea of being subjected to these random searches and "once-overs" by police, even when they have done absolutely nothing wrong. But although the Supreme Court may have "constitutionalized" random searches and similar heavy-handed tactics such as are increasingly favored by the authorities, that doesn't make them constitutional. It's hard to imagine a more un-American concept than a random roadblock—or giving police sanction to (for all practical purposes) arrest people for personal choices that are no business of the state's.*

   a. frightened
   b. indignant
   c. sad
   d. worried

5. President Ronald Reagan was a hero to me. I became a citizen of the United States when he was president, and he is the first president I voted for as an American citizen. He inspired me and made me even prouder to be a new American. President Reagan symbolized to me what America represented—hope, opportunity, freedom. He made us remember that the United States stood for something great and noble. Once again, it was all right to stand tall and believe in this country, and in ourselves. He made each of us, no matter our station in life, feel part of something larger and grander. He saw America as an "empire of ideals," and he advanced those ideals to the world.

   Why are people everywhere so deeply and personally affected by Ronald Reagan's legacy? Because his leadership profoundly influenced not only America, but also the world. He embodied the very things that

8

1. civil libertarians: people actively concerned with protecting the rights guaranteed to individuals by law

2. dragnets: systems of coordinated procedures used to catch criminals

* Excerpted from Eric Peters, "The Federal Government Wants You to Buckle Up," *Consumers Research*, July 2003, 43. Reprinted by permission of the publisher.

all people desire, the same things that draw immigrants like myself to the United States: an unfailing optimism, a devotion to freedom and a belief in the goodness of humankind. He is a role model for any of us who have been granted the public trust as an elected leader. He led a life of public service with common sense and uncommon purpose. And he taught me something very special about this country: That here, the greatest power is not derived from privilege; it is derived from the people. President Reagan's unshakable faith in the people reminds us that despite the challenges we face, by the power of our collective resolve, we are a mighty force for goodness and progress.*

a. concerned
b. reverent
c. pessimistic
d. playful

CHAPTER 8 REVIEW

Fill in the blanks in the following statements.

1. ____________ means noticing certain techniques the writer is using to convince you of the validity and worth of his or her ideas or information.
2. You can use four critical reading __________ to guide your interpretation of a text. These questions focus on the author's ________, the presence of ________ or a certain ________, the main point and the ________, and __________ that may be present.
3. Writers record their thoughts for one or more of three main purposes: to ________, to ___________, or to ___________.
4. A work created solely for the reader's enjoyment or amusement has an ___________ purpose.
5. A work with an ___________ purpose is designed to teach you something.
6. Works with a ___________ purpose attempt to convince you to change a belief, an attitude, or a behavior.
7. ________ is an inclination toward a particular opinion or viewpoint.

* From Arnold Schwarzenegger, "Ronald Reagan: My Hero, and an Eternal Light for the World," *USA Today*, June 9, 2004, 11A.

8

8. The __________ meaning refers to a word's literal dictionary definition. The __________ meaning of a word refers to the emotions or associations that people attach to it.
9. __________ is the author's specific attitude about his or her subject.

Reading Selection

Practicing the Active Reading Strategy:

Before and While You Read

You can use active reading strategies before, as, and after you read a selection. The following are some suggestions for active reading strategies that you can perform before you read and while you read.

1. Skim the selection for any unfamiliar words. Circle or highlight any words you do not know.
2. As you read, underline, highlight, or circle important words or phrases.
3. Write down any questions about the selection if you are confused by the information presented.
4. Jot notes in the margin to help you understand the material.

You've Got Mail, But How About Romance?

by Susan Lendroth

1 When is the last time you found a letter in your mailbox? Not the false intimacy of a sweepstakes offer or a chatty update from your local congressman, but an actual letter written just to you. If you're like most of us, it's been a long, long while.

2 Most of the time life is too hectic to notice the lack of letters. After all, it's not as if my mailbox is ever empty. Quite the opposite—the slot bulges with coupon packs and "limited-time offers," a glossy medley of junk. Interspersed through that weekly take are bills and an occasional newsletter from my health-care provider. Letters are as rare as hens' teeth.

3 I sometimes wonder if we are witnessing the end of an era. Will handwritten correspondence all but disappear in favor of e-mail and the ubiquitous telephone? If so, we will lose more than the occasional note in the postbox; we will lose the romance of mail.

4 Years ago I checked my mailbox eagerly each day. What was inside? Tissue-thin letters from overseas, parcels tied with string, envelopes stuffed with snapshots? Anything was possible in that split second before the mailbox door creaked open.

5 My mother gave me a book that my grandfather received on his bar mitzvah in 1905, *The Secret Service of the Post Office Department.* Two golden mailbags are embossed on the front cover, crossed like swords on a heraldic shield. I like to think of them as mailbags rampant,[1] their padlocks swinging proudly on metal clasps to deter the "depredators upon the mails" who people the book's twenty-three chapters.

6 I fell in love with the idea of mail at an early age, even creating my own by gluing used postage stamps on old envelopes. At 12 I discovered pen pals, starting a parade of exotic mail from Poland, Australia and Japan. Once an envelope contained folded origami cranes, another time fragile pieces of amber found on the shore of the Baltic Sea. When I left home for college and a teaching job overseas, letters linked me to my family and friends, giving us the chance to share the minutia of our daily lives.

7 But the world changed. Phone rates dropped; e-mail debuted. No one seems to have time to write letters by hand anymore. Even Christmas cards are filled with colorful newsletters created on the family computer rather than scribbled personal notes. And I am as guilty as everyone else, flashing messages around the globe at the touch of a keyboard, receiving almost instantaneous replies. E-mail is popcorn correspondence—light, quick, fun, sometimes a little salty. Press the delete key, and the words vanish as if they had never been.

8 I miss the tangible world of letters, slitting open the envelopes, unfolding the pages. I miss their individuality, the personality that rides the curve of the ink.

9 At an exhibition about George Washington, I lingered over the glass cases where his correspondence lay displayed, tracing the peaks and valleys of his handwriting. He crossed out mistakes with precise rows of little loops. Where he paused to dip his pen, the words were momentarily darkened from the infusion of fresh ink. Pen stroke by pen stroke he wrote orders to his troops, letters to friends, and ideas to shape a nation. Who will ever feel that connection with a modern president whose secretary types his notes on a laptop?

10 Of course, the transition away from the personal began long before e-mail. My grandfather lamented my lack of penmanship. He wrote with the flourishes of the Edwardian era, I with the unruly scrawl of a kid used to lined notepaper.

11 Greeting-card companies created cards for everyone and every occasion. Now we need never be troubled by having to write anything more taxing than our names.

12 Finally, the post office banned the use of twine around domestic packages, ensuring that everything is wrapped with smooth, dull uniformity. A few years back I received a parcel from Malaysia. Bright stamps festooned the rustling paper, which was secured with brown cords and red sealing wax. I carefully snipped the package open at one

1. **rampant:** rearing on the hind legs, like the animals on heraldic shields

end to preserve it—a memento of a fast-vanishing age.

13 Recently I made an effort to turn back the tide by writing letters to five friends, pages and pages on pale blue parchment. Within days they all answered—by e-mail.

14 My mailbox continued to groan under the weight of innumerable catalogs and credit-card offers. Once in a while a stray postcard worms its way into the heap. A flicker of the old romance flares, allowing me to imagine briefly that there exists somewhere a letter-writing world with wax-sealed parcels and crossed mailbags rampant. I hope someone there sends me a letter.*

Vocabulary

Read the following questions about some of the vocabulary words that appear in the previous selection. Circle the letter of the correct answer.

1. In paragraph 2, the author refers to her mail as a "glossy *medley* of junk." What does *medley* mean in this context?
   a. mixture
   b. hybrid
   c. confusion
   d. depression
2. When something is *ubiquitous*, what does that mean? (paragraph 3)
   a. scarce
   b. rare
   c. all over
   d. dirty
3. In paragraph 5, the author writes, "Two golden mailbags are embossed on the front cover, crossed like swords on a *heraldic* shield." What does *heraldic* mean?
   a. relating to birds
   b. relating to fish
   c. relating to cranes
   d. relating to designs on armor
4. What is a synonym for "*depredator*"? (paragraph 5)
   a. looter
   b. dog lover
   c. outdoorsman
   d. bird watcher
5. What is *origami*? (paragraph 6)
   a. a raw fish dish
   b. the Japanese art of paper folding
   c. a type of Chinese baking
   d. shipbuilding in the Philippines

*From Susan Lendroth, "You've Got Mail, But How About Romance?" *Newsweek*, June 4, 2001, 14. © 2001 Newsweek, Inc. All rights reserved. Reprinted by permission.

6. When the author writes in paragraph 8 that she misses the "tangible world of letters," what does she mean?
   a. She misses receiving paper letters, which can be held in the hand and felt.
   b. She misses her laptop and all of the fonts she can create with a touch of a button.
   c. She doesn't really miss anything; it is just an expression.
   d. She misses traveling abroad and seeing how words are written in other languages.
7. In paragraph 12, the author writes that "Bright stamps *festooned* the rustling paper. . . ." What does *festooned* mean?
   a. destroyed
   b. marred
   c. erased
   d. decorated

Purpose, Tone, Bias, Patterns of Organization, Topic Sentences, and Implied Main Ideas

Respond to the following questions by circling the letter of the correct answer.

1. What is the primary purpose of the reading selection?
   a. to inform
   b. to persuade
   c. to entertain
2. The overall tone of this essay is
   a. angry.
   b. nostalgic.
   c. amused.
   d. worried.
3. Reread paragraph 8. When the author writes about letters in this paragraph, she reveals
   a. positive bias.
   b. negative bias.
   c. no bias (she's neutral).
4. Reread paragraph 9. When the author writes about George Washington and his letters, she reveals
   a. positive bias.
   b. negative bias.
   c. no bias (she's neutral).
5. The pattern that organizes the details in paragraph 6 is
   a. series.
   b. time order.
   c. cause/effect.
   d. comparison/contrast.

6. Which of the following is the topic sentence of paragraph 7?
   a. "But the world changed."
   b. "Phone rates dropped; e-mail debuted."
   c. "No one seems to have time to write letters by hand anymore."
   d. "Even Christmas cards are filled with colorful newsletters created on the family computer rather than scribbled personal notes."

7. What is the implied main idea of paragraph 9?
   a. George Washington was not a very good writer.
   b. Paper letters help us feel a connection with the writer.
   c. Letters were critical to the founding of America.
   d. George Washington was a better president than any other since.

Practicing the Active Reading Strategy:

After You Read

Now that you have read the selection, answer the following questions using the active reading strategies that are discussed on pages 30–33.

1. Identify and write down the point and purpose of this reading selection.
2. Besides the vocabulary words included in the exercise on pages 420–421, are there any other vocabulary words that are unfamiliar to you? If so, write a list of them. When you have finished writing your list, look up each word in a dictionary and write the definition that best describes the word as it is used in the selection.
3. Predict any possible test questions that may be used on a test about the content of this selection.
4. How could you use the information contained in this selection? Does the information contained in the selection reinforce or contradict your ideas and experiences? Explain.

Questions for Discussion and Writing

Answer the following questions based on your reading of the selection. Write your answers on the blanks provided.

1. The author feels very passionately about the art of letter writing. Has technology changed the way you do something in your life, causing you to miss out on something else? If so, what is it? For example, do you

enjoy watching home movies that were made before video? If so, why? Or, do you enjoy watching old movies that can only be seen in black and white? Think of an example from your own life and write about it. ____

____

2. Do you feel strongly about the art of letter writing or do you prefer to talk on the phone or e-mail your friends and family? Why do you prefer one over the other? Is it the immediacy of e-mail or phoning that makes it either desirable or undesirable as a communication medium? Discuss your feelings. ____

____

3. How have advances in communication technology improved business and personal relationships? Have these advances had any negative impacts? If so, what are they? ____

____

Vocabulary: Formal vs. Informal Language

When you read, you should be able to distinguish between formal and informal language. **Formal language** is usually serious, businesslike, and often sophisticated. This is the type of language that is most prevalent in scholarly, academic, and professional writing. Most textbooks, college assignments, and business reports, for example, are written using formal language. **Informal language** is closer to that of conversation. It's more casual, often including colloquial (everyday) words, slang terms, idioms (expressions like "She's trying to butter me up"), and even humor.

The level of formality in a reading selection helps the reader know how the author feels about his or her subject. A passage or document written in a formal style communicates the author's belief that the subject is important and significant. A more informal style can suggest that the author is more lighthearted about the topic.

When a text is written in a more formal style, the reader may have to make more of an effort to understand it. One way to increase your comprehension is to use active reading, the technique you learned about in Chapter 1 of this text. When you read actively, you look up the definitions of unfamiliar words, underline or highlight main ideas, and jot down notes and questions. All of these tactics will help you better understand the formal language of an academic or professional text. You can also use the SQ3R technique you practiced in Chapter 4. Surveying a text, turning its headings into questions, and then reading it, reciting the answers to the questions, and reviewing the information will most likely increase your understanding of a text with a formal style. Or, you might prefer to apply the REAP reading strategy presented at the end of this chapter. Experiment with using different strategies to find the ones that help you comprehend the more advanced vocabulary and more complex sentences of a formally written text.

To understand the difference between formal and informal language, first take a look at a formal statement from one of the passages in this chapter:

> Researchers find that many ***affluent*** schools let kids solve real-world math problems and read stories that spark their interest. ***Low-income*** students, ***meanwhile,*** are apt to be seated in rows, kept busy with meaningless worksheets and endless practice tests that focus on vowel sounds or ***arithmetic*** rules to be ***memorized and recited without understanding.***

The sentences in this passage are complex, and the boldfaced, italicized words and phrases are serious and formal. Notice, though, how rewriting the statement and substituting some different words makes the statement more colloquial and casual:

> Researchers find that ***rich kids*** get ***cool*** assignments like real-world math problems and interesting stories. But ***poor kids*** are given ***lame busywork*** assignments they ***don't*** really ***get.***

Vocabulary Exercise 1

Use the boldfaced, italicized words in each of the following sentences, which come from Chapters 7 and 8, to decide whether the language is formal or informal. On the blank alongside each sentence, write FORMAL if the language is formal and INFORMAL if the language is informal.

8

1. Reelection-minded professional ***politicians*** must be ***concerned*** about what their ***constituents*** think and want; ***principled*** amateur legislators ***need not be.*** ________
2. Give a ***kid*** a loving environment over a few extra ***bucks*** any day. ________
3. And thus, as you can imagine, their second winter ***was no picnic,*** either. ________

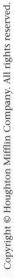

4. The ***profoundness*** of my dog's laziness comes not from his ***immobility*** but from his almost ***predatory pursuit of ease.*** ________

5. Soda shopping? Don't just ***grab*** a Coke. Stretch ***waaaaay*** down to reach the Royal Crown! Your ***abs*** will be glad—and so will your wallet! ________

6. Her elegant, personal 2003 autobiography was titled *The Majesty of the Law.* But her own majestic qualities are ***refreshingly devoid of regal pretense.*** They are marked instead by the humility and tolerance and restraint that are the ***true foundations of the constitutional principles*** that she ***endeavors*** both to balance and to obey. ________

7. When his boat blew up at last, it ***diffused a tranquil contentment*** among us such as we had not known for months. But when he came home the new week, alive, ***renowned,*** and appeared in church all battered up and bandaged, a shining hero, stared at and wondered over by everybody, it seemed to us that the ***partiality of Providence*** for an undeserving reptile had reached a point where it was ***open to criticism.*** ________

Vocabulary Exercise 2

On the blank at the end of each passage, write FORMAL if the language is formal and INFORMAL if the language is informal.

1. We may talk the lean talk. But we are walking—make that waddling—the fat walk. The days of "reduced-fat" snacking aren't dead, but they're in intensive care. Perhaps no one knows that better than Andrea Ratliff. She can't stomach low-fat anything. She recently bought some Yoplait no-fat yogurt—and chucked it before finishing the container. She bought some fat-substitute Wow potato chips—and never finished the bag. She's even got a half gallon of Edy's Vanilla fat-free ice cream stashed in her freezer—with just one spoonful eaten out of it. It's been there for a month. "All you're doing is paying a lot of money for stuff that tastes lousy," says Ratliff. "The more fat they take out of something, the worse it tastes, and the more it costs."* ________

2. Consumers report that they are confused by the media's constant barrage of often-conflicting nutritional advice that leads many to eschew

* Adapted from Bruce Horovitz, "Low-fat Industry Loses Out as Consumers Favor Flavor," *USA Today*, October 15, 2001, 2B.

nutritional advice altogether. In a time of unprecedented obesity and diet-related disease in the United States, the U.S. Department of Agriculture's food pyramid was designed as a clear, concise guide to healthy eating. It has become an international icon of nutrition and should be supported in its present form.

Harvard professor Walter Willett's revision of the USDA pyramid, with its base level of "daily exercise and weight control" is at best vaguely worded and confusing and at worse a very dangerous eating plan. That healthy foods such as white rice, white bread, potatoes, and pasta are in the "use sparingly" category is the first clue that Willett's advice is not grounded in sound science.* ________

3. The thermometer read thirty-six degrees when I walked out the back door at first light to inspect my tomato patch. They're coming along nicely, and if the weather holds, we should be eating summer tomato sandwiches by, oh, mid-December anyway. Shoot, we've had young 'uns faster than this year's 'mater crop has come in.

   We've had several frost warnings, but overall it's been warm, which is why I think we might be lucky enough to have 'mater sandwiches for Christmas dinner.

   The leaves are coming off the trees at a rapid clip now, and even the weakening fall sunlight is doing the Big Boys and the Better Boys a world of good. Right now it's a race against the calendar, and my neighbor is betting Jack Frost will get the tomatoes before I do.

   Me? All I want for Christmas is a good ol' 'mater sammich—the thicker the better. Maybe two, now that I think about it.† ________

READING STRATEGY: REAP

- **REAP (Read-Encode-Annotate-Ponder)** is a strategy that guides you to respond to a text to improve your reading and thinking skills. This method provides you with a system of four steps. When you follow these steps, you'll be training yourself to look deeper into the texts you read so you can more fully understand and evaluate them. As a result, your comprehension and critical thinking skills will improve.

8

* Adapted from Robert N. Pyle, "Letters," USA Today, August 6, 2001, 12A.

† Adapted from Jack Betts, "Trials of a Shade-tree Farmer," *Charlotte Observer*, November 14, 2001, 18A. Reprinted with permission from the *Charlotte Observer*. Copyright owned by the *Charlotte Observer*.

- **Step 1: READ.** The first step involves carefully reading the text to understand the author's ideas and information.
- **Step 2: ENCODE.** Next, you translate the text's message into your own words. This step asks you to paraphrase the ideas or information to put them in language you understand.
- **Step 3: ANNOTATE.** To annotate means to write notes or comments about a text. You can record these in the margins of the text, or in a notebook, or on separate sheets of paper. These notes can take the form of objective summaries or more subjective reactions to the ideas and information. For example, you could jot down your own feelings, opinions, or judgments.
- **Step 4: PONDER.** Finally, you continue reflecting on what you have read and the notes you have written. In this stage, you also read or discuss other people's responses to the same text in order to more fully explore its content. This sharing can take place formally in classroom settings, or informally, outside of the classroom.

Here is a sample passage annotated according to the REAP method.

Does Watching Violence on Television Make People More Violent?

If observational learning is important, then surely television—and televised violence—must teach children a great deal. For one thing, it is estimated that the average child in the United States spends more time watching television than attending school. Much of what children see is violent; prime-time programs in the United States present an average of 5 violent acts per hour; some Saturday morning cartoons include more than 20 per hour. As a result, the average child will have witnessed at least 8,000 murders and more than 100,000 other acts of televised violence *before graduating from elementary school.*

Children must be affected by all the violence they see on TV.

Psychologists have speculated that watching so much violence might be emotionally arousing, making viewers more likely to react violently to

Research suggests that watching TV violence increases violent reactions to frustration, aggressive behavior, and aggressive thoughts and feelings.

Continued

8

frustration. Televised violence might also provide models that viewers imitate, particularly if the violence is carried out by attractive, powerful models—the "good guys," for example. And recent research suggests that exposure to media violence can trigger or amplify viewers' aggressive thoughts and feelings, thus increasing the likelihood that they will *act* aggressively.

Many have argued that, through one or more of these mechanisms, watching violence on television causes violent behavior in viewers. Indeed, in 1993 a National Academy of Science report concluded that "overall, the vast majority of studies, whatever their methodology, showed that exposure to television violence resulted in increased aggressive behavior, both contemporaneously[1] and over time." An American Psychological Association commission on Violence and Youth reached the same conclusion.

National scientific and psychological organizations believe that watching violent TV increases aggressive behavior.

Three types of evidence back up the claim that watching violent television programs increases violent behavior. Some evidence comes from anecdotes and case studies. Children have poked one another in the eye after watching the Three Stooges[2] appear to do so on television. And adults have claimed that watching TV shows prompted them to commit murders or other violent acts matching those seen on the shows.

Anecdotes and case studies show a link between violent TV and violent behavior.

Second, many longitudinal[3] studies have found a correlation[4] between watching violent television programs and later acts of aggression and violence. One such study tracked people from the time they were six or seven (in 1977) until they reached their early twenties (in 1992).

Long-term studies show a link between violent TV and violent behavior.

8

1. **contemporaneously:** happening at the same time
2. **Three Stooges:** three slapstick film comedians of the mid-20th century
3. **longitudinal:** long-term
4. **correlation:** relationship

Those who watched more violent television as children were significantly more aggressive as adults and more likely to engage in criminal activity. They were also more likely to use physical punishment on their own children, who themselves tended to be much more aggressive than average. These latter results were also found in the United States, Israel, Australia, Poland, the Netherlands, and even Finland, where the number of violent TV shows is very small.

Finally, the results of numerous laboratory experiments also support the view that TV violence increases aggression among viewers. In one study, groups of boys watched violent or nonviolent programs in a controlled setting and then played floor hockey. Boys who had watched the violent shows were more likely than those who had watched nonviolent programs to behave aggressively on the hockey floor. This effect was greatest for those boys who had the most aggressive tendencies to begin with. More extensive experiments in which children are exposed for long periods to carefully controlled types of television programs also suggest that exposure to large amounts of violent activity on television results in aggressive behavior.*

Lab experiments show the same link.

There is a lot of evidence that suggests that TV violence increases real-life violence, but other factors may be at work, too. I know many people who watch violent programs but don't lash out aggressively.

Now, practice the REAP method yourself by reading and annotating the following passage. Then, discuss your reactions with a partner or a group of your classmates.

Earth Day Has Seen Great Gains, But Earth Can Do Better

When the first Earth Day was observed in 1970, raw sewage was being dumped into rivers and lakes, smog forced California

Continued

8

* Adapted from Bernstein et al., *Psychology,* 5th ed. Boston: Houghton Mifflin, 2000, 203–204.

schoolchildren indoors at recess, and the Cuyahoga River in Cleveland was so fouled with oil and industrial waste that it had caught fire. The growing environmental disaster spurred Congress and presidents of both parties to act. Among the landmark laws passed from 1970 to 1980 were the Clean Air Act, Clean Water Act and the Superfund toxic waste cleanup law.

As the nation observes Earth Day this year, a great deal has changed for the better. Children born in the USA today have cleaner air to breathe and water to swim in than most of their parents did. Air pollution emissions have been slashed 25%. The amount of clean waterways has jumped from 10% in 1972 to about 60% today. Drinking water is safer. And more than half of the nation's worst toxic waste dumps have been cleaned up.

But serious problems remain. Air pollution causes 70,000 premature deaths a year in America, according to the World Health Organization. About 40% of U.S. rivers and lakes remain too polluted for fishing or swimming. "Laws like the Clean Air Act and the Clean Water Act helped tremendously," says Sen. Jim Jeffords, I-Vt, senior member of the Environment and Public Works Committee. "But we've still got a long way to go, and the polluters would like us to go backward, not forward."

Since 1970, emissions of the six major pollutants that cause smog, soot, acid rain and breathing problems have been cut by 25% even as Americans consumed more energy (up 42%) and drove more miles (up 149%). Still, in 2001, more than 133 million Americans lived in areas where air quality was unhealthful at times because of high levels of at least one pollutant, according to the Environmental Protection Agency. Air pollution aggravates asthma and irritates lungs.

When Congress passed the Clean Water Act in 1972, only 10% of waterways were considered clean. Today, about 60% of waterways are safe for fishing and swimming. But the law has fallen short of its goal to make all waterways "swimmable and fishable" by 1983. Part of the problem is that the law is not always enforced. More than 60% of industrial and municipal plants violated their Clean Water Act permit limits in the first six months of 2002, according to a new report based on EPA data by the U.S. Public Interest Research Group.

It is safe to drink the water almost everywhere in America. In 2002, 94% of people served by community water systems got drinking water that met all health-based standards, vs. 79% in 1993. But the recent discovery of lead in the drinking water of Washington, D.C., homes has spurred legislation by Jeffords to overhaul the federal Safe Drinking Water Act to provide better notification of high lead levels. Lead can delay physical and mental development in children.

The discovery 26 years ago of toxic pollution from a former chemical plant seeping into the Love Canal neighborhood in Niagara Falls, N.Y., spurred creation of the Superfund program to clean up the nation's worst toxic waste sites. Since then, about 850 have been cleaned up. But the pace has slowed as a federal trust fund created to clean up the sites has run out of money. A tax on oil and chemical companies that paid for the trust fund expired in 1995, and Congress has not renewed it. Toxic waste cleanup now must compete for limited federal dollars. Meanwhile, the site that started it all, Love Canal, finally was declared clean in March 2004.*

Reading Visuals: Diagrams

A **diagram** is a visual aid that includes a pictorial illustration, usually in the form of a drawing created by hand or by computer. The purpose of diagrams is to clarify and condense written information through images so they are very common in instruction manuals and textbooks. They often illustrate processes or sequences of information.

A diagram typically contains these parts.

- **Title.** The title identifies the subject of the drawing.
- **A picture or series of pictures.** Diagrams communicate information through images.
- **Labels.** Parts or areas of the images will often be labeled to identify what they are.

Continued

8

* Adapted from Erin Kelly, "Earth Day Has Seen Great Gains, But Earth Can Do Better," *USA Today,* April 19, 2004, 8D.

- **Key.** A diagram that contains special symbols, colors, or shading will usually include a key to explain what these features represent.

These parts are labeled on the diagram below.

HOW IT WORKS

Title

The Polygraph Test

A polygraph machine records physiological signs and how they change in response to questioning. An examiner then interprets these changes to determine whether the subject is being less than truthful. The polygraph test was invented by medical student John Larson in 1921 and has been used in law enforcement since 1924.—NICOLE FOULKE

A. Two pneumonic tubes wrapped around the subject's chest and abdomen measure the rate and degree of respiration.

B. A blood pressure cuff, or sphygmomanometer, is wrapped around the subject's bicep to measure cardio-vascular activity.

C. Two electrodes attached to the ring and index finger of one hand measure skin conductance response [that is, perspiration].

D. An analog-to-digital converter turns mechanical data into digital data that is then displayed on a computer screen.

E. The examiner asks various questions to determine the subject's physiological norm. Measuring change from the norm in the polygraph reading, the examiner determines if and when a subject is being deceptive.

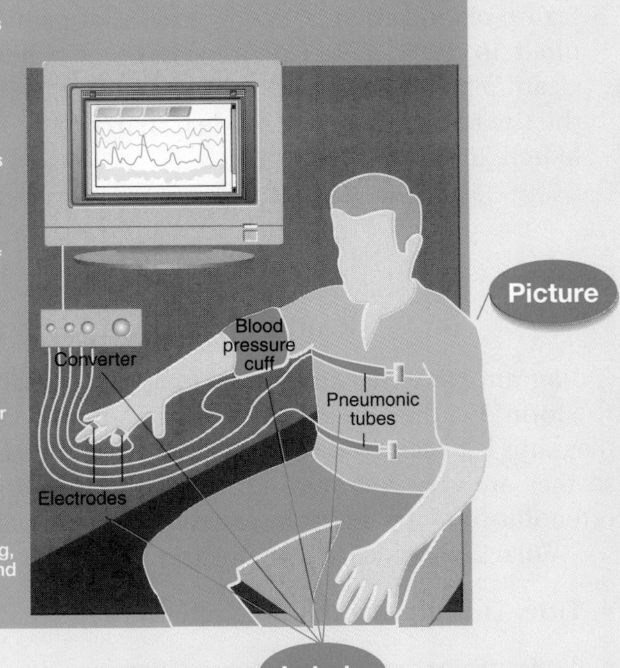

Source: Nicole Foulke, "The Polygraph Test," *Popular Science*, October 2001, 85. Used by permission of *Popular Science*.

Reading a diagram begins with understanding the subject and main point identified in the title. Then, you can examine the labeled parts of the diagram to understand how they illustrate that point. Also, make sure you review the key to help you draw accurate conclusions.

The diagram on page 432 illustrates the components of a polygraph machine. This line drawing not only labels each part, it also indicates where each part is placed on the person being tested. The column at the left briefly summarizes the five steps the examiner completes to administer the test.

Now, study the diagram below and then answer the questions that follow.

The Impact of Leading Questions on Eyewitness Memory

After seeing a filmed traffic accident, people were asked, "About how fast were the cars going when they (smashed, hit, or contacted) each other?" As shown here, the witnesses' responses were influenced by the verb used in the question; "smashed" was associated with the highest average speed estimates. A week later, people who heard the "smashed" question remembered the accident as being more violent than did people in the other two groups.

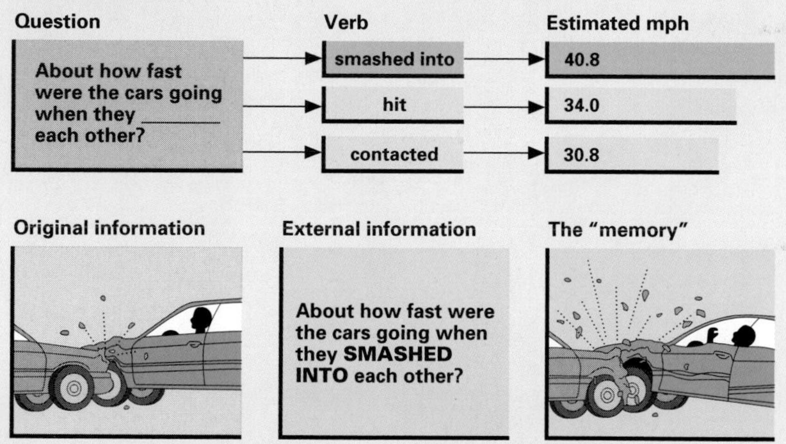

Source: Bernstein et al., *Psychology*, 5th ed., 2000, Boston: Houghton Mifflin, 239.

1. What is the topic of this diagram? ______________________

2. What verb or vocabulary word was associated with the highest estimated miles per hour? What verb was associated with the lowest?

____

3. What is "external information" in this diagram? ______________

Continued

4. Are the illustrations for the original information and the "memory" the same? If not, how do they differ? ____________________

____

5. What are the three different miles per hour associated with "smashed into," "hit," and "contacted"? ____________________

____

CHAPTER 8 TESTS

Name ______________________________ Date ______________

TEST 1

Circle the letter that corresponds to the primary purpose of each of the following passages.

1. When the Internet burst on the popular scene in the early 1990s, its advocates argued that it heralded a so-called virtual community that offered rich new forms of human contact. But two years ago, a Stanford University political scientist, Norman H. Nie, touched off a bitter dispute by reporting that data from a big survey indicated that the Internet was an isolating medium—that the more time people spent using the Internet, the less time they were likely to spend in face-to-face human contact.

   Despite his critics, who argued that Internet interaction is its own form of human contact, Mr. Nie is standing by his thesis. In a chapter to appear in the coming book *The Internet in Everyday Life,* edited by Barry Wellman and Caroline Haythornthwaite, Mr. Nie and two of his colleagues, D. Sunshine Hillygus and Lutz Ebring, report the findings of a new survey of how 6,000 Americans spend their time each day. The study concludes that Internet use at home has a strong negative impact on time spent with friends and family, while Internet use at work decreases the time spent with colleagues. . . .

   Mr. Nie, who was co-inventor of a research tool widely used by social scientists, the Statistical Package for the Social Sciences, was a political scientist at the University of Chicago and a senior study director at the National Opinion Research Center before coming to Stanford in 1998 to establish the Stanford Institute for the Quantitative Study of Society. He is openly skeptical of the argument made by the Internet's defenders that the medium increases the number of social contacts of its users. "The question is not the number of friends you have, it's the time you spend with them," he said.*

   a. to inform   c. to entertain
   b. to persuade

* From John Markoff, "Compressed Data: How Lonely Is the Life That Is Lived Online?" *New York Times,* January 21, 2002. http://www.nytimes.com. Copyright © 2002 by the New York Times Co. Reprinted by permission.

For additional tests, see the Test Bank.

8

2. Scientists plumbing the bubbling, black depths of a geothermal hot spring in Idaho have discovered a unique community of microbes[1] that thrive without sunlight or oxygen. Scientists say the organisms are very similar to life as it might exist on Mars and other planets.

   The one-celled organisms, Archaea, grow by consuming the hydrogen produced by hot water reacting with bedrock 600 feet below the Beaverhead Mountains. They produce tiny amounts of methane as a byproduct of their weird metabolism. Although types of Archaea have been found before, this community is unlike anything else on Earth, because of the concentration.

   Most life on Earth flourishes not only in the presence of water, but relies also on oxygen, sunlight, and organic carbon. Conditions on the rest of the planets—and perhaps beyond the solar system—are far more hostile.*

   a. to inform c. to entertain
   b. to persuade

3. Walt Disney has taken over my daughter's brain. She's not even two, but she's already obsessed with the Disney cartoon versions of *Snow White, Cinderella* and *Sleeping Beauty,* all of which have the same plot: The heroine is beautiful, but sad. Or in a coma. But wait! Here comes a handsome prince! He kisses her! She's happy! Everybody's happy! Even the woodland creatures are dancing!

   I have big problems with this. For one thing, if you see a squirrel dancing, you are looking at the final stages of rabies. For another thing, I don't want my daughter growing up believing that Handsome Prince Equals Lifetime Happiness, which is the basic Disney message. The alleged exception is *Beauty and the Beast,* wherein the beautiful heroine falls in love with a creature who makes the Wolf Man look like Hugh Grant. The enlightened message of this story, we are led to believe, is: Appearance doesn't matter! Inner beauty is what counts! But this message goes down the toilet at the end when the spell on the beast is finally broken and he is revealed to be—you guessed it—Gary Condit[2].†

   a. to inform c. to entertain
   b. to persuade

8

4. A new, book-length study to be published this month says that the negative impact of divorce on both children and parents has been exaggerated

1. **microbes:** tiny life forms
2. **Gary Condit:** is the U.S. congressman from California who claimed to know nothing about the disappearance of Chandra Levy, a former federal intern with whom he had an affair

* From "Found: Life on Earth That Could Exist on Mars," *New York Times,* January 17, 2002, www.nytimes.com.

† From Dave Barry, "Daughter, 2, Will Be Allowed to Date in 2048," *Miami Herald,* January 27, 2002. Copyright, 2002, Tribune Media Services, Inc. All Rights Reserved. Reprinted with permission.

and that only about one-fifth of youngsters experience any long-term damage after their parents break up. One of the most comprehensive studies to date, the research will bring balm to the souls of parents who have chosen to end their marriages. It probably also will incense those who see divorce as undermining American society. After studying almost 1,400 families and more than 2,500 children—some of them for three decades—trailblazing researcher E. Mavis Hetherington finds that 75 percent to 80 percent of children from divorced homes are "coping reasonably well and functioning in the normal range." Eventually they are able to adapt to their new lives.*

a. to inform
b. to persuade
c. to entertain

5. Local resident Carl Sutton was recognized by Fayetteville, Arkansas, officials Monday for his "unique and patriotic" ability to name all 50 United States. "I am proud to call Carl Sutton one of Fayetteville's own," said Mayor Gordon Semple, who awarded Sutton a special citation[1] at the city's American Legion Hall. "Very few people possess the skill to name all 50 states of the Union-without consulting reference materials. Yet, relying only on his intellect and his powers of retention, Carl has achieved the near-impossible. He is a true American hero."

Sutton's state-recitation aptitude[2] has drawn national attention, resulting in guest spots on TV talk shows, lecture dates in elementary and secondary schools, and goodwill visits to hospitals, nursing homes, and military bases. However, the 46-year-old delivery driver for Tyson Foods remains modest and somewhat bewildered by the acclaim.[3] "I only graduated from high school and never attended college, so when people say I'm a hero or a genius, I have a hard time believing them," Sutton told reporters. "I didn't have the advantages others have, so I'm just grateful to God for endowing me with this gift. I do not take it for granted, because I know how much it means to so many people."

Sutton then concluded his remarks with his customary, keenly anticipated recitation of the 50 states in alphabetical order. Those who have heard Sutton's celebrated recitation inevitably express wonderment. "I have a hard time just remembering which states border my own," said Joseph Russo, an insurance-claims adjuster from Harwich, MA. "Heck, I can't remember how to spell my own state. But this Sutton guy, he's amazing." But for all the adulation, Sutton refuses to rest on his laurels.

1. **citation:** an official commendation (praise or award)
2. **aptitude:** talent
3. **acclaim:** praise, approval

* From Karen S. Peterson, "Kids, Parents Can Make Best of Divorce," *USA Today,* January 14, 2002, 1A.

Not content to dazzle others with his perfect state recall, he has taught himself the names of the territories currently under U.S. jurisdiction.*

a. to inform c. to entertain
b. to persuade

6. What do smart, articulate, no-nonsense women do as they break through the glass ceiling of their profession? If television talk-show host Greta Van Susteren is any indication, they change their faces. Literally. Van Susteren is the latest high-profile example of a low-profile cultural truth: How women look is more important than how they think.

Van Susteren, a hot media property who commands a strong following, jumped from CNN to Fox last month. The move gave her time, and perhaps Fox gave her a nudge, to have plastic surgery. Her show, *On the Record,* debuted on February 4, 2002. The lead-in had important words flashing across the screen and around the show's title: "determined," "experienced," "courageous." Presumably these were meant to describe Van Susteren. Then she appeared. Her eyes were tilted up at the corners and seemed bigger. Her famously crooked mouth had mostly lost its crook. Where her hair had often been an afterthought at CNN, it had the perfect sheen and placement of custom coiffure[1] at Fox. She sat at a table, which fully revealed her short skirt and legs. Van Susteren had been physically transformed to approximate the idealized woman that Fox viewers expect. She looked anything but courageous.

Van Susteren is a reminder of the minimalization of American women by American culture. Look at TV shows and commercials. Check out magazine ads and stories. Listen to water-cooler jokes and the gossip about female leaders' hairstyles. Women are reduced to the sum of our visible parts. We don't need Afghan-style *burqas*[2] to disappear as women. We disappear in reverse—by revamping and revealing our bodies to meet externally imposed visions of female beauty. What you see is not what women have got, but it's first in importance.†

a. to inform c. to entertain
b. to persuade

8

1. **coiffure:** hairstyle

2. ***burqas:*** head-to-toe coverings worn by women in some Islamic countries

* Adapted from "Hero Citizen Can Name All 50 States," *The Onion*, Vol. 37, No. 13 (April 12, 2001). Reprinted with permission of THE ONION. Copyright 2001 by ONION, INC. www.theonion.com.

† From Robin Gerber, "Why Turn Brilliant Lawyer into Barbie with Brains?" *USA Today,* February 11, 2002, 17A. Reprinted by permission of Robin Gerber. Author of *Leadership The Eleanor Roosevelt Way* (Penguin/Putnam, 2002), Senior Scholar, Academy of Leadership, University of Maryland.

7. I strongly disagree with Fareed Zakaria's characterization of the leadership at today's college and university campuses. Far from being "fund-raising bureaucrats" on "privileged perches," hundreds of college presidents contribute each day to the national policy debate, direct path-breaking research, educate our next generation of leaders, and help generate billions of dollars for state economies. Don't mistake a miscommunication at Harvard [between university president Lawrence Summers and Cornel West of its Afro-American Studies department] for the decline of the American academic presidency.*

   a. to inform
   b. to persuade
   c. to entertain

8. Some signs you've hired a bad lawyer: (1) Begins every sentence with, "As Ally McBeal[1] once said . . ."; (2) Whenever he says, "Your Honor," he makes those little quotation marks in the air; (3) Keeps citing the legal case of Godzilla vs. Mothra;[2] (4) Giggles every time he hears the word *briefs*; (5) Just before trial, he whispers, "the judge is the one with the little hammer, right?"†

   a. to inform
   b. to persuade
   c. to entertain

9. Scientists are discovering that viral infections may damage your arteries. A provocative[3] preliminary study at the University of Texas Medical School in Houston revealed that heart patients who'd had a flu shot were 67 percent less likely to experience a second heart attack than those who hadn't. Another study suggests that older people who had a cold-sore virus were twice as likely to have a heart attack or die from heart disease as people who didn't. An Italian study found evidence that chronic infections, such as sinusitis, bronchitis, and even urinary-tract infections might raise the risk of hardened arteries.‡

   a. to inform
   b. to persuade
   c. to entertain

1. **Ally McBeal:** fictional lawyer on a television show
2. **Godzilla, Mothra:** fictional monsters in Japanese films
3. **provocative:** interesting

* From David Ward, "At the Top of the Ivory Tower," *Newsweek,* January 28, 2002, 14.

† Adapted from "Laughter, the Best Medicine," and "Late Show with David Letterman (CBS)," *Reader's Digest,* February 2002, 132.

‡ From Sue Ellin Browder, "The Heart Quiz That Could Save Your Life," *Reader's Digest,* February 2002, 144.

8

10. I am a 47-year-old Long Islander who has lived in Switzerland for more than 14 years and has come to terms with the fact that one does not have to indulge. I enjoy food tremendously, and I finally decided to lose weight, but without giving up the good things in life. It will be two years in June that I have slowly lost weight and kept it off. I have now lost 40 pounds. I eat what I like, but only in half portions. I maintain a well-balanced diet and feel very healthy. Fad diets don't do the trick. Why even write about these senseless diets when they actually are unhealthy? One should be writing about the stories of people who have maintained a well-balanced healthy diet and have kept the weight off for one or two years.*

    a. to inform
    b. to persuade
    c. to entertain

TEST 2

A. After reading each passage, circle the letter of the answer that includes the word(s) that reveal(s) the author's bias. Then circle the letter of the type of bias in the passage.

If the prospect of being reduced to tears by a puppet show makes you shudder with embarrassment, it's probably a good thing you weren't at Manhattan's City Center last week. There, a group of first-rate performers, with help from four cuddly creatures designed in the Jim Henson Company's New York Muppet Workshop, opened Thursday in a new production of *Carnival,* which, sadly, was scheduled to run only through Sunday.

The 1961 musical focuses on a lonely, naive young woman who finds work in a carnival, and the more jaded but equally forlorn puppeteer who falls for her. A once-great dancer whose prowess[1] was shattered by a war injury, he can only connect with her through his puppets—and even they face competition from a slick magician called Marco the Magnificent. It's an unabashedly[2] sentimental tale, even by old-fashioned musical standards, and we know from the moment our hero and heroine meet what their fate will be. Still, this lush, whimsical, gorgeously spirited revival was as irresistible as the parade of balloons and bon-bons on display in one of several delectable[3] production numbers.

1. **prowess:** skill or ability
2. **unabashedly:** without embarrassment
3. **delectable:** pleasing, delightful

* From Judith A. Kramer-Herrer, "Enjoy Healthy Food," *USA Today*, February 7, 2002, 14A.

8

In fact, the entire show looked good enough to eat, with sumptuous[1] costumes and fanciful sets—fashioned with consultants Martin Pakledinaz and John Lee Beatty—engulfed in lighting designer Peter Kaczorowski's vivid hues. Director/choreographer Kathleen Marshall also contributed spectacle and sass, peppering the concert with athletic dance routines and winking references to the scripts clutched on stage.*

1. Words that reveal the author's bias about the production include
   a. shudder, embarrassment
   b. gorgeously spirited, delectable, sumptuous
   c. sadly, lonely, naive
   d. jaded, forlorn

2. The author's bias is
   a. positive. b. negative.

That chirpy songbird Britney Spears has popped up with more mindless drivel.[2] The diva[3]-in-training stars in *Crossroads,* which is less a movie than a mind-numbingly dull road trip that offers plenty of opportunity for girlish high jinks, radio duets, and adorable mugging. A role model (sigh) for young girls and a sex symbol for young boys, Spears is ever mindful of looking her cutest. OK, we're covered there, but acting is another thing. Sure, she tries to emote (she cries, pouts, bursts into fits of giggles), but it's all one note. Not since *That Thing You Do!* have we been subjected so repeatedly to a movie tune. Not only must we hear her warble[4] "I'm not a girl, not yet a woman" several times, we must also endure her intoning the lyrics as "poetry." Such foolishness proves Britney's still a girl, not yet an actress.†

3. Words that reveal the author's bias include
   a. chirpy songbird, popped.
   b. cutest, adorable.
   c. mindless drivel, mind-numbingly dull, foolishness.
   d. warble, lyrics.

1. **sumptuous:** of a size or splendor suggesting great expense
2. **drivel:** stupid talk
3. **diva:** a singer who is talented, but temperamental and conceited
4. **warble:** sing with embellishments like trills (fluttering sounds)

* Adapted from Elysa Gardner, "Puppets of *Carnival* Pull at the Heartstrings," *USA Today,* February 11, 2001, 13B.

† Adapted from Claudia Puig, "Spears' One-Note Acting Sends *Crossroads* Astray," *USA Today,* February 15, 2002, 13B.

8

4. The author's bias is
   a. positive. b. negative.

If ever the urge to step on a bug were justifiable, the Asian longhorned beetle is the bug that justifies it. We are so used to the thought of scourges[1] that come in microbial[2] sizes, like foot-and-mouth disease, that it is almost shocking to grasp the size of this particular scourge. An adult Asian longhorned beetle can be up to an inch and a half long, and is black-bodied with white spots and long mottled[3] black antennae. The beetles entered New York in 1996 in solid-wood packing material from China, where they are uncontrolled, and they immediately began devastating trees in Greenpoint. Since then they have turned up in Bayside and Amityville, and in sections of Chicago. Now the beetles have been found in two maples in Central Park.*

5. Words that reveal the author's bias include
   a. urge, microbial, adult.
   b. beetle, China, Chicago.
   c. black-bodied, white spots, mottled black antennae.
   d. scourges, devastating.

6. The author's bias is
   a. positive. b. negative.

It is the land that God forgot, and its long silence may be broken by the hands of men. The Arctic National Wildlife Refuge is an opus[4] crowned from hope because our forefathers decided that it would shine if left alone. They were insightful, for it still shines. But the refuge now faces possible toxicity[5] brought by greed. It is difficult to fathom such disgrace. The indigenous[6] people and animal inhabitants of the refuge deserve emancipation.[7] The magnificent tundra has been left alone for the simple, understandable reason of continuing the preservation of natural splendors and, ultimately, of keeping this valuable tradition.†

1. **scourges:** sources of widespread destruction
2. **microbial:** characteristic of tiny life forms
3. **mottled:** spotted or marked with different colors
4. **opus:** creative work
5. **toxicity:** poisoning
6. **indigenous:** originating or living in a particular environment
7. **emancipation:** freedom

---

* Adapted from "Beware the Asian Longhorned Beetle," no author credited, *New York Times,* February 16, 2002, www.nytimes.com.

† Adapted from Joel Koslosky, "Letters," *Miami Herald,* February 13, 2002, www.miami.com.

7. Words that reveal the author's bias include
   a. shines, magnificent, natural splendors.
   b. forefathers, ultimately.
   c. tundra, indigenous, animal inhabitants.
   d. silence, men, alone.

8. When describing the Arctic Refuge, the author's bias is
   a. positive. b. negative.

Figure skating dominates the Winter Olympics precisely because it's a circus. As a sport, it's never going to be anything but nonsense. As train-wreck entertainment, it's riveting. This is a sport whose popularity skyrocketed after Harding[1] conspired with her then-husband and a buffoonish[2] thug named Shane Stant to whack rival Nancy Kerrigan's knee and take her out of the Olympic trials in 1994. It's a sport where the stunning caprice[3] of the judges and the amazing goofiness of the performers are assets, not detriments[4].*

9. Words that reveal the author's bias include
   a. riveting, popularity, stunning.
   b. nonsense, train-wreck, caprice, goofiness.
   c. sport, performers, Winter Olympics.
   d. figure skating, judges, trials.

10. The author's bias is
   a. positive. b. negative.

B. Read each passage and circle the letter of the correct tone.

I came to the Olympic Winter Games to watch the men's 90-meter ski jump, which gets its name from the fact that a sane person would have to drink a 90-meter-high glass of gin before he would even consider attempting this sport. Of course, ski jumping was not invented by sane people. It was invented by Norwegians. These are people who eat a dish called "lutefisk," which can be either an entree or an industrial solvent.[5] So they think nothing of flinging themselves off cliffs.

8

1. **Tonya Harding:** a figure skater
2. **buffoonish:** clown-like
3. **caprice:** tendency to change one's mind unpredictably
4. **detriments:** things that cause harm or damage
5. **solvent:** substance capable of dissolving another substance

* Adapted from King Kaufman, "Fixing Figure Skating Would Kill It," Salon.com, February 16, 2002, www.salon.com.

If you've ever watched ski jumping on television, you've probably asked yourself: How do they DO that? How is it POSSIBLE? The answer to that question is two words—two words that define the spirit and essence of this amazing sport. Those words are: computer graphics. The "jumpers" are actually suspended by cables about a foot off the ground in a studio in Los Angeles. Also "Bob Costas"[1] is an elaborate puppet operated by four people.

No, I'm kidding. I personally watched the ski jumpers here hurtle down an incredibly steep ramp, launch themselves off the end, soar through space long enough to qualify for beverage-cart service, then somehow land on their skis and slide, triumphantly, to the underwear-changing station. After each jump, two enthusiastic dudes would get on the public-address system and analyze it for the crowd. Most events at these Olympics have enthusiastic announcer dudes who are really, really into the sport, and thus are able to explain it in terms that only they understand. At ski jumping, they were always saying helpful things like: "Wow! He got a real huge float off his V!"

The 90-meter ski jump was won by—and in my opinion, this is a growing scandal here—three foreign persons. At a press conference afterward, one of them, Sven Hannawald of Germany, was asked if he could explain ski jumping to people who've never done it. Through an interpreter, he answered: "If everybody tried, they would probably need very good insurance."*

11. The tone of this passage is
    a. critical.
    b. amused.
    c. neutral.
    d. outraged.

A steel autopsy table in a red-tiled room is the last resting place for nearly every manatee that dies in Florida. And it is rarely unoccupied these days. Biologists at the Florida Marine Mammal Pathobiology Laboratory here say 53 of the state's several thousand manatees died in January [of 2002], 18 of them from collisions with powerboats. That is the highest figure in a single month since officials began keeping records in 1974. In 2001, 325 manatees died, 81 of them killed by boats. The deaths from boating have continued despite the creation of a network of refuges and slow-speed boating zones, and a result is one of the country's most intense debates over an endangered species.

8

1. **Bob Costas:** television commentator for the Olympic Games

* Adapted from Dave Barry, "Competitive Ski Jumping Is a Weighty Issue," *Miami Herald*, February 13, 2002. Copyright, 2002, Tribune Media Services, Inc. All Rights Reserved. Reprinted by permission.

Boaters and marina builders say deaths are mounting simply because manatees are more numerous. Many biologists say the likely cause is growing fleets of fast boats. Florida registered 860,000 powerboats in 2001, nearly twice as many as in 1976. But the debate is about more than the manatee, the slow-moving weed-munching underwater mammal that has long been a popular symbol of Florida's subtropical ecology. Manatees have become caught up in the wider battle over balancing the needs of wildlife and the rights of legions of boaters and shorefront property owners.*

12. The tone of this passage is

a. critical.
b. amused.
c. neutral.
d. sarcastic.

Gee, let's tell all the children in the land to read teen magazines so they can become materialistic clones! Let's tell them that Britney Spears is "cool!" and that the Backstreet Boys[1] are "totally dreamy!" And while we're at it, let's make the kids feel really bad about themselves if they don't look like they're made of plastic. Hell, with magazines like this, it's no wonder there are 12-YEAR-OLDS that want breast implants. Hey kids! Just ask Mommy and Daddy to buy you an entire new body! If they really love you, they will.†

13. The tone of this passage is

a. amused.
b. sympathetic.
c. neutral.
d. sarcastic.

In the 29-year-history of the Endangered Species Act, the government has sometimes looked thoughtless in placing the well-being of animals above the needs of people. But rarely, if ever, have those who administer the act looked as inept[2] as the National Academy of Sciences made them look last week. The academy registered its opinion in one of the most controversial endangered-species decisions of recent years: the cutoff of irrigation water last summer to more than 1,000 farms in southern Oregon and Northern California in order to save endangered suckerfish and local salmon. Farms turned to dust, livelihoods were threatened, and violence was barely avoided. Now the academy's preliminary report says the decision was rooted in inadequate science. Low

1. **Britney Spears and the Backstreet Boys:** performers who were popular with adolescents

2. **inept:** foolish, incompetent

* Adapted from Andrew C. Revkin, "How Endangered a Species?" *New York Times,* February 12, 2002, Copyright © 2002 by the New York Times Co. Reprinted with permission.

† Adapted from http://www.i-mockery.com/minimocks/destroy2/default.asp.

water levels caused by a combination of drought and irrigation from Upper Klamath Lake never threatened the suckerfish. And the salmon may actually have been hurt by the government's efforts.

This is hardly the first time enforcement of the Endangered Species Act has seemed to turn into an absurd battle of man vs. beast. Fights involving bugs, fish, birds, and even rare plants have roiled[1] the nation for decades, delaying construction of hospitals, highways, and homes. But the Klamath case isn't about political differences as much as it is about competence and patience under pressure.*

14. The tone of this passage is
    a. neutral.
    b. amused.
    c. critical.
    d. sympathetic.

Scientists in Texas have cloned a cat, opening the door to what some experts say will be the first large-scale commercial use of cloning—to reproduce beloved pets. The effort was supported by a company, Genetic Savings and Clone, of College Station, Texas, and Sausalito, California, which wants to offer cloning to dog and cat owners. It is investing $3.7 million in the project. . . .

The cloned cat, called cc, for carbon copy, is a genetically identical copy of a two-year-old female cat, Rainbow, that was not anyone's pet. But Rainbow and cc do not look alike, illustrating that identical twin cats may not have identical coats. . . .

For now, Mr. Hawthorne said, the company was storing tissue from cats and dogs, for a fee, so that owners could try to have their pets cloned in the future. He added that the company would consider trying to clone the cats of carefully selected customers. "They will have to understand that we are in a research mode for at least the next year," he said. "They will have to be patient and realize that they would be expected to bear some of the research costs." Mr. Hawthorne said he could not estimate what cat cloning would cost. Cloning experts say that if their experience is any guide, Genetic Savings and Clone will not lack for interested pet owners.†

15. The tone of this passage is
    a. critical.
    b. sympathetic.
    c. admiring.
    d. neutral.

8

1. **roiled:** stirred up

* Adapted from "Rushed Decision Endangers Species and People, Too," no author credited, *USA Today,* February 11, 2002, 15A.

† Adapted from Gina Kolata, "What Is Warm and Fuzzy Forever? With Cloning, Kitty," *New York Times,* February 15, 2002, www.nytimes.com. Copyright © 2002 by the New York Times Co. Reprinted by permission.

My two-year-old daughter Sophie plays Snow White 814,000 times per day, using little figurines to act out the parts. Snow White is played by Snow White. The seven dwarfs are played by six dwarfs (Sleepy is currently missing). The wicked witch is played by a Fisher-Price Little People construction worker, who wears a hard hat, as if to say: "I may be evil incarnate,[1] but, dang it, I am not exempt from OSHA[2] regulations!" The poison apple is played by a plastic apple from Sophie's play kitchen. It's roughly ten times the size of Snow White's head; even if she didn't eat it, this thing could SCARE her into a coma. The handsome prince is usually played by a handsome prince, although recently he was misplaced, so Snow White was awakened from her coma by a romantic kiss from: a sheep. It's from the Fisher-Price farm set, and as sheep go, it's reasonably handsome.

Over and over, in Sophie's little hands, these figurines act out the story: Snow White is put to sleep by the giant mutant apple; she is awakened by the handsome prince/sheep; everybody dances around happily, including the hard-hat witch.

But I am not happy. I am eager for Sophie to reach a more-mature age—say, three—so that I can explain to her, as a concerned father, that men, especially handsome men, are vermin scum. I will inform her that she will not be allowed to date until she is a minimum of 47 years old, and even then her dates will have to be unattractive. I will keep horses in the garage, and if a man wishing to date my daughter fails to spook them, I will politely ask him to leave, from behind the machine gun that I will keep mounted on a tripod in the foyer, next to a sign that says: "Kiss THIS, Prince Charming."

I'm just kidding, of course. I may be a protective dad, but I'm also a realistic and reasonable person. She can date at 46.*

16. The tone of this passage is

a. critical.
b. amused.
c. neutral.
d. admiring.

Country boy. Braggart. Jester. Rebel. Daredevil. Heroic champion athlete. Muhammad Ali symbolizes so much of our unconscious American identity and so much of what it is about us that has universal appeal. In Ali, who almost always had a white trainer, we see the frontiersman in buckskin learning from the Indians how to best handle the dangers of the woods. In his chanting of doggerel[3] before fights and speaking of himself as "so pretty" and

1. **incarnate:** with human form
2. **OSHA:** Occupational Safety and Health Administration
3. **doggerel:** bad poetry

---

* Adapted from Dave Barry, "Daughter, 2, Will Be Allowed to Date in 2048," *Miami Herald,* January 27, 2002. Copyright, 2002, Tribune Media Services, Inc. All Rights Reserved. Reprinted with permission

8

"the greatest," he was heir to the charismatic insolence[1] and humor that have always defined our national bad boys. Considered laughable when challenging Sonny Liston for the heavyweight championship in 1964, Ali turned out to be as surprising as the troops who wore rags on their feet and followed George Washington to take down the British Empire and turn the world upside down. In his trash talking to his opponents, the press, and anyone else who would listen, he connected things as seemingly opposite as Dave Crockett's braggadocio[2] and the aggressive posturing of the black streets and locker rooms where he grew up. His startling wit was as exhilarating as those flying pies in American slapstick movies[3].*

17. The tone of this passage is
    a. admiring.
    b. neutral.
    c. critical.
    d. sarcastic.

Dean Kamen, the inventor of the Segway Human Transporter, an electric scooter, positively gushes at the idea of rendering walking obsolete. "When you stand on this machine, it kind of walks for you," he told *The Today Show.* He is not alone in his enthusiasm. The networks, news magazines, and major newspapers have all joined in the hype, as have some big names of the high-tech world. Bigger than the PC, said Apple's Steve Jobs. Bigger than the Internet, said Kleiner-Perkins' John Doerr. Though not, presumably, bigger than our sedentary[4] butts will be. Americans will soon have the opportunity to purchase their very own two-wheel human transport system for the low, low price of $3,000. The federal government is already on board for several hundred at $4,000 a wheel. Soon, obscenely fat postal workers and park rangers across the nation will be scooting around perspiration free.†

18. The tone of this passage is
    a. amused.
    b. sarcastic.
    c. admiring.
    d. critical.

8

1. **insolence:** insulting, rude, or disrespectful behavior
2. **braggadocio:** empty bragging
3. **slapstick movies:** comedies with chases, collisions, and practical jokes
4. **sedentary:** not moving

* Adapted from Stanley Crouch, "An American Original," *Time,* December 24, 2001, 75.

† Adapted from Christopher Orlet, "Segway's Assault on Walking," Salon.com, December 7, 2001, www.salon.com.

CHAPTER 9

Critical Reading

GOALS FOR CHAPTER 9

- **Identify the two basic elements of an argument.**
- **Define the terms *point* and *support*.**
- **List the characteristics of a sound main idea.**
- **List the two essential qualities of sound evidence.**
- **Match a point with relevant support.**
- **Explain the difference between a fact and an opinion.**
- **Label statements either facts or opinions.**
- **Distinguish informed opinions from uninformed opinions.**
- **Define the term *logical fallacies*.**
- **Define the following terms: *circular reasoning, red herring, hasty generalizations, faulty cause and effect, non sequitur, false comparison, false alternative, argument to the person, bandwagon appeal, testimonial*.**
- **Identify different types of logical fallacies in passages.**
- **Explain the three purposes of skimming and describe the steps involved in skimming a text.**
- **Read and understand information in a map.**

Chapter 9 continues to explore critical reading by focusing on **arguments**, texts with a persuasive purpose. To discover how well you already recognize the features of both effective and ineffective arguments, complete the test below.

TEST YOURSELF

Read the following passages. Circle the letter of the correct answer for each question.

9

Since 1990, stock car racing has caused 260 deaths. Among them have been 29 spectators, five of whom were children. Another 200 drivers and bystanders have suffered traumatic injuries. Racing, of course, is inherently dangerous, but the racing industry can implement changes to pursue remedies for this shocking carnage.[1] Driver equipment should be improved. Spectator movement should be better controlled and fans better protected by fencing. Basic emergency care provisions should be required. Drivers should be subjected to reliable screening and licensing. Safety data should be pooled and analyzed. More research is needed into safety.*

1. In the paragraph above, which of the following sentences states a fact?
   a. "Another 200 drivers and bystanders have suffered traumatic injuries."
   b. "Driver equipment should be improved."
   c. "Spectator movement should be better controlled and fans better protected by fencing."
   d. "More research is needed into safety."

2. In the paragraph above, which of the following sentences states an opinion?
   a. "Since 1990, stock car racing has caused 260 deaths."
   b. "Among them have been 29 spectators, five of whom were children."
   c. "Another 200 drivers and bystanders have suffered traumatic injuries."
   d. "Racing, of course, is inherently dangerous, but the racing industry can implement changes to pursue remedies for this shocking carnage."

As a New Jersey resident, I'm opposed to the ban on cellphone use while driving, a law that goes into effect today. There's debate about whether using a cellphone is any more distracting than changing a CD, eating a sandwich or quelling[2] the kids in the back seat or whether the problem is having one hand on the wheel, dialing a number or just the talking itself. Indeed, what about the simple act of talking to a passenger? Many drivers tend to turn to look at their passengers during conversation. Isn't this as bad or even worse than using a cellphone? From now on, no more talking in the vehicle! I can also say from experience that untangling my cellphone from the wires of a hands-free earplug is more disruptive than simply picking up the handset could ever be. And if the problem instead is "having one hand on the wheel," as postulated[3] by some critics, then that seems the next thing to legislate: Drivers, keep two

1. **carnage:** slaughter
2. **quelling:** quieting
3. **postulated:** argued

* Adapted from "Racing Kills," *Charlotte Observer*, November 11, 2001, 2D.

hands on the steering wheel at all times! 10 o'clock and 2 o'clock positions! Furthermore, car manufacturers, don't put CD players in cars anymore! What will legislators do next to ensure our safety? Well, at least there's enough to keep them busy as they increasingly seek to control our lives.*

3. Which sentence in the above paragraph states the author's point?
   a. "As a New Jersey resident, I'm opposed to the ban on cellphone use while driving, a law that goes into effect today."
   b. "There's debate about whether using a cellphone is any more distracting than changing a CD, eating a sandwich or quelling the kids in the back seat or whether the problem is having one hand on the wheel, dialing a number or just the talking itself."
   c. "And if the problem instead is 'having one hand on the wheel,' as postulated by some critics, then that seems the next thing to legislate: Drivers, keep two hands on the steering wheel at all times!"
   d. "Furthermore, car manufacturers, don't put CD players in cars anymore!"

We must put a stop to raunchy cheerleading dance routines. Moves like hip thrusts and shaking bottoms are just not appropriate for young girls representing a school.

4. What logical fallacy is contained in the passage above?
   a. red herring
   b. argument to the person
   c. circular reasoning
   d. hasty generalization

School districts must train and employ more English as a Second Language (ESL) teachers immediately. Either we get more ESL teachers, or we teach all schoolchildren the Spanish language.

5. What logical fallacy is contained in the passage above?
   a. circular reasoning
   b. argument to the person
   c. false alternative
   d. bandwagon appeal

In Chapter 8, you learned how to begin to read critically by asking two questions:

What is the author's purpose?

Does the author reveal bias or a certain tone?

* Adapted from Jim Caruso, "Legislators Overreach with Cellphone Ban," *USA Today*, July 1, 2004, 14A.

In this chapter, you will continue to expand your critical reading skills by gaining practice in asking two more questions:

> What is the main point and the evidence offered to support the claim?
>
> Does the text attempt to distract you from the real issue or to oversimplify it?

In particular, you will focus on recognizing and evaluating arguments, which are texts with a persuasive purpose.

The Two Components of Argument: Point and Support

If you think about it, you encounter quite a few arguments as you move through your day. Advertisers try to persuade you to buy a certain product or service. Your children try to convince you to take them somewhere. Your supervisor or coworkers encourage you to complete a task a certain way. A friend or loved one tries to persuade you to go to a particular restaurant or watch a particular TV program. These attempts to influence your thoughts or behaviors are called *arguments*.

In Chapters 2 and 3 of this book, you learned how to recognize the main idea and supporting details in a paragraph. Reading selections that have a persuasive purpose—in other words, arguments—contain these two elements, too. However, we usually refer to them as the *point* and the *support*. All arguments contain these elements.

The **point** of the argument is the belief or attitude an author wants you to accept. It always raises the question "Why?" For example, look at the following statement. ***You should get your hair cut at the Fantastic Hair Beauty Salon.*** If a friend of yours said this to you, you would naturally wonder what reasons are behind this opinion. Why would you agree with this statement and act upon it? Your friend might offer these details:

> *Reason #1:* The prices are reasonable.
>
> *Reason #2:* The stylists have many years of experience, so they are good at cutting and styling.
>
> *Reason #3:* The stylists listen carefully to each customer so they can give you the style you want.

These details are the support that proves the point. Support, therefore, is defined as the specific reasons, facts, examples, or other details the author offers to convince the reader to accept the point.

Exercise 9.1

On the blanks next to the statements in each group, write a **P** if a statement is the point and **S** if the statement offers support for the point.

1. _____ Laughter is good for your health.

   _____ Laughter lowers stress hormones.

   _____ Laughter helps digestion and sleep.

2. _____ Many common household items, such as nail clippers and tweezers, are being banned from carry-on luggage.

   _____ Airline security has become very tight in the last few months.

   _____ Federal marshals are on guard at every major airport in the United States.

3. _____ The staff manages blood drives in times of need.

   _____ The organization solicits donations for causes around the world.

   _____ The American Red Cross does many good things for citizens both domestically and abroad.

4. _____ Having a good day planner is essential to doing well in college.

   _____ A day planner can help you keep your assignments organized.

   _____ You can plan your study time, your work schedule, and your leisure activities so you know when to do each.

5. _____ With just a point and click, you can find the item you want and add it to your electronic "shopping bag."

   _____ Many catalog shoppers are finding that it's fun and easy to shop online from their favorite catalogs.

   _____ Some sites even have "virtual models" on which you can try on the clothing items you would like to buy.

It is important to recognize the author's main point or position and the evidence that supports it. Scrutinizing these two aspects of the text will help you determine the text's validity. Therefore, a critical reader always asks the question: *What is the main point and the evidence offered to support it?*

First of all, consider the author's point. In Chapters 2 and 3, you learned to recognize stated and unstated main ideas. A critical reader not only identifies the author's main idea but also examines it further to decide whether it is valid or not. In particular, you should evaluate these characteristics of a main idea.

- **Is it significant?** Does the main idea seem important? Does it impact a lot of people? Not every point has to have huge or far-reaching implications, of course, but some ideas are obviously more worthy of attention than others.
- **Is it reasonable?** Does the idea seem logical, or does it seem weird or far-fetched? Even if an idea seems outlandish, you should not necessarily reject it. Some innovative thoughts probably seemed ridiculous at first, so you should reserve judgment until you've given the author an opportunity to explain. However, an idea that seems particularly dubious should put you on the alert, causing you to pay even more careful attention to the evidence offered as proof.
- **Is it appropriately qualified, or limited?** Beware of ideas that are expressed in absolute terms, as though they apply to everyone in every situation, with no exceptions. Authors are free to make generalizations, of course, but if they insist that the idea is universal, it may not be as valid as when they limit it with words like *most, many, several, a lot, quite a few,* and so forth.
- **Does it allow for other possibilities?** There are many different interpretations of the world around us, so reasonable authors often admit to that by using words such as *possibly, may be, could be, seems, appears, apparently,* and *seemingly*, that suggest that their idea offers *one* viewpoint, not the *only* viewpoint.

After you evaluate the main point of a reading selection, you're ready to examine the evidence offered in support of that idea. Evidence comes in many forms, including facts, statistics, examples, expert testimony, observation, experience, and opinions. A critical reader weighs all of the evidence presented to decide whether it provides a firm basis of support for accepting an idea. Weighing the evidence involves looking first at whether the evidence is *adequate*. Does the author provide enough support, or is he or she trying to convince you on the basis of just one or two observations or examples? Some opinions or ideas are more informed than others, so you should add up the total amount of evidence and decide if it truly offers enough support. In addition, you should evaluate the kinds of evidence offered. Is it all derived from the author's personal experience, or is it based, at least in part, on verifiable facts and research? Be aware, too, that some paragraphs don't offer any real evidence at all; they merely repeat the main idea or offer irrelevant information that doesn't support the point.

Matching the Point with Relevant Support

To be effective, the support offered for a point must be relevant. In other words, a specific example, fact, or reason must directly relate to the point. If it doesn't, then the author has not truly supported his or her opinion. For example, what if your friend who recommends the Fantastic Hair Beauty Salon told you to go there because the owner is a member of the Chamber of Commerce? Would that be a good reason why you should get your hair cut there? Probably not. That information is not relevant to the point.

Exercise 9.2

Each point is followed by six support statements. Circle the letter beside each statement that provides RELEVANT support for the point.

1. Benjamin Franklin made many important scientific discoveries and advancements.
   a. He made eight voyages across the Atlantic Ocean to Europe during his lifetime.
   b. He invented the lightning rod, which protects buildings and ships from lightning damage.
   c. He invented the Franklin stove, an iron furnace stove that allowed people to warm their homes less dangerously.
   d. Ben created bifocals to help people see both near and far.
   e. Ben had poor vision and needed glasses to read.
   f. People remember Ben for his contributions to the creation of America's democratic government.

2. We should continue to send humans into outer space.
   a. The discoveries astronauts make while in outer space benefit future generations of human beings.
   b. The volume and variety of the samples the Apollo astronauts collected on the moon helped science better understand not only the moon but also all of the planets, including Earth.
   c. Without regular maintenance and periodic upgrades from astronauts, the magnificent Hubble telescope in orbit around Earth would have become just a piece of space junk by now.

d. Robots that take photographs and analyze soil samples are useful for planetary exploration.
e. Presidents Nixon and Carter dismantled the whole Apollo-program infrastructure[1] to save money in the 1970s.
f. Many wealthy people would be willing to pay large sums of money for a trip into outer space.*

3. There is a lot of scholarship money available for college just waiting to be found; all you have to do is know where to look for it and apply for it.
   a. You can check out several thick scholarship reference books that are in your local library.
   b. Scholarships can help you pay for your college tuition.
   c. Many students apply for scholarships every year.
   d. One great place to look for obscure scholarships that many people don't know about is on the Internet.
   e. Talk with your school's counseling department; they are a good source for scholarship information.
   f. My friend went to college on a full scholarship.

4. Fathers should consider leaving work to become the primary care providers for their preschool children.
   a. According to the U.S. Census Bureau, about 207,000 men are stay-at-home dads.
   b. Fathers who stay at home rather than work find that their relationships with their children improve.
   c. Women report that when their husbands take on the care of the children, both husband and wife feel a closer bond, which improves the marriage.
   d. When mothers work outside the home while fathers care for the children, mothers tend to feel jealous of their husbands' time with the kids.
   e. Even stay-at-home dads rarely do their share of household chores, leaving the majority of housework to their wives.
   f. In families with stay-at-home dads, problems with finding child care are usually nonexistent.†

1. **infrastructure:** foundation or base of an organization or system

9

* Adapted from Alcestis Oberg, "Humans in Space Serve Science, Future Citizens," *USA Today,* April 1, 2004, 11A.

† Adapted from Andy Hoffman, "Don't Call Him Mr. Mom," *Working Mother,* August 9, 1999, www.workingmother.com.

5. World War II captivates our memories while World War I leaves only a vague impression, but for Western Europe, the century's first war was bloodier than the second.
   a. The British Empire lost 908,000 men in World War I and 329,000 in World War II.
   b. France lost 1,385,000 in World War I and 210,671 in World War II.
   c. World War I included trench warfare, in which soldiers from one side's trenches climbed into no man's land[1] to attack the other side's trenches, only to be slaughtered by the deadliest weapon of the war, the machine gun.
   d. British Prime Minister Winston Churchill was outraged by the carnage[2] of World War I.
   e. World War I produced gripping poetry by such British writers as Wilfred Owen, W. B. Yeats, and Sigfried Sassoon.
   f. Sigfried Sassoon won high honors for valor as an infantry officer but eventually turned against the war and threw his medals in a river.*

Exercise 9.3

For each group of supporting statements, circle the letter of the point that they support.

1. **Supporting statements:**

   City parks help to raise property values.
   City parks improve air quality and health.
   Parks contribute to a city's image and bring tourism to the area.

   Choose one of the following points:
   a. The park system is understaffed.
   b. Private funds are essential to maintaining city parks.
   c. Parks are an important asset in a city.
   d. Some cities have better parks than other cities.

1. **no man's land:** the land between two armies on a battlefield

2. **carnage:** slaughter

* Adapted from Ed Williams, "On Veterans Day, Thoughts on War and Peace," *Charlotte Observer,* November 11, 2001, 3D.

2. Supporting statements:

Anorexia[1] has many long-term effects, including cardiac irregularities, kidney failure, and sudden death.

It is very difficult to recover from anorexia, a serious eating disorder, and many people who suffer from it die.

People, and in particular teenage girls, who suffer from anorexia usually weigh below 100 pounds.

Choose one of the following points:

a. Anorexia affects teenage girls only.
b. Anorexia causes long-term health effects that can be serious to life-threatening.
c. Doctors don't know why people suffer from anorexia.
d. Strides towards a cure for sufferers of anorexia are being made.

3. Supporting statements:

In 1961, John F. Kennedy[2] introduced the Omnibus Housing Plan, which was designed to clear slum housing and bring urban renewal to the inner cities of the United States.

The Area Redevelopment Act of 1961, another Kennedy program, helped revive depressed areas such as the Appalachian countryside and the textile towns of New England.

Many of Kennedy's other programs were designed to help the poor.

Choose one of the following points:

a. John F. Kennedy was committed to helping the poor and underprivileged in the United States during his presidency.
b. John F. Kennedy was a very busy person who worked at least fourteen hours per day.
c. Lyndon Johnson, who succeeded Kennedy in office, inherited some of the finest programs a president ever created.
d. Kennedy's programs achieved too little, too late.

4. Supporting statements:

Many athletes who hold world records still train intensely, even after they have achieved great feats.[3]

1. **anorexia:** eating disorder characterized by fear of obesity, aversion to food, and severe weight loss
2. **John F. Kennedy:** thirty-fifth president of the U.S.
3. **feats:** noteworthy deeds or accomplishments

Many people who have built multimillion dollar businesses still work fourteen-hour days.

Some artists who have created many great works still work many days and nights in an attempt to create another great work of art for all to enjoy.

Choose one of the following points:

a. Some people are capable of achieving great things.
b. Most people are underachievers.
c. People with a high need for achievement seek to master tasks even after significant accomplishments.
d. Athletes achieve more than nonathletes.*

5. Supporting statements:

Jim has Barry Bonds's rookie baseball card, which is very valuable since Bonds broke the home run record in 2001.

Jim's Mickey Mantle card is probably worth $2,000.

Jim keeps his entire baseball card collection in a safety deposit box at the bank.

Choose one of the following points:

a. Jim enjoys collecting Barry Bonds baseball cards.
b. Jim has a very valuable baseball card collection.
c. At $22 a month, Jim's safety deposit box is a significant expense.
d. Jim will never part with his collection.

Distinguishing Fact from Opinion

As you begin to recognize points and support, you will need to distinguish between facts and opinions. **Facts** are information that is presented in a way that is verifiable. They are based upon direct experience and observation, so they often include specific data such as numbers, dates, times, or other statistics. They also include information like names of people, places, or events. Therefore, facts can be proven. The following statements are all examples of facts:

Figure skater Michelle Kwan earned thirty-one perfect scores, more than any other female in the sport.

* Adapted from Bernstein and Nash, *Essentials of Psychology,* 2nd ed. Boston: Houghton Mifflin, 2002, 274.

So many products are priced $10.99, $15.99, and $199.99 because research has shown that people think prices that end in nine are a bargain.

Women in troubled marriages are three times more likely than women with stressful jobs to be hospitalized for heart problems.

You should be aware as you read that a statement presented as a fact can be incorrect. Writers are not always right, and, sometimes, they include inaccurate information by accident or even on purpose. If that's the case, how does a reader know what to believe? That question will be answered more fully in a later section of this chapter.

Opinions are statements that express beliefs, feelings, judgments, attitudes, and preferences. They cannot be verified because they are based on an individual's perceptions of the world. Thus, they are subject to change as a person modifies his or her views. They can also be argued or disputed. Here are some examples of each kind of opinion.

BELIEF: If you want to live an ethical life, you must follow the Ten Commandments.[1]

FEELING: We should be ashamed of our failure to get homeless people the help they need.

JUDGMENT: People who don't keep their lawns neatly trimmed are lazy and inconsiderate toward their neighbors.

ATTITUDE: A mother with a preschooler should not work outside the home full time.

PREFERENCE: Singers should not try to improve upon "The Star-Spangled Banner"[2] because the melody is fine the way it was written.

When you are trying to decide whether a statement is a fact or an opinion, you can look for some clue words that often appear in statements of opinion. One kind of clue is words that indicate the relative nature of something, words like *bigger, most important, strangest,* and *silliest.* These words relate and compare the subject to something else. For example, notice the boldfaced, italicized words in the following opinions:

The ***best*** time of the year to control wasps is in June after the queen has established her colony and while the colony is still small.

1. **Ten Commandments:** the ten laws God gave to Moses
2. **"The Star Spangled Banner":** America's national anthem

Oprah Winfrey[1] is the ***most*** powerful woman in America.

For many reasons, multimedia encyclopedias are much ***better*** than traditional printed encyclopedias.

Another kind of clue is words that either qualify or limit statements or turn them into absolutes. Qualifying words and phrases include *some, several, many, quite a few, a lot, most, a majority, large numbers, usually, often, sometimes, frequently, seldom,* and *rarely.* Absolute words and phrases include *all, every, never, each, always, none*, and *no*. For example, notice the boldfaced, italicized words in the following opinions:

Everyone should get a flu vaccine every October before flu season hits in November.

Many kids who are taking Ritalin[2] for attention deficit/hyperactivity disorder should not be using the drug.

The majority of handgun owners in America are Republicans who are out of touch with the violence problem.

One last type of clue is words or phrases that admit there are other possibilities. These terms include *may be, could be, seems, appears, probably, possibly, apparently,* and *seemingly.* This type of clue is boldface italic in the following examples:

Children of very involved mothers ***may*** not have adequate opportunities to be independent and make mistakes because their mothers are always there to smooth the way.

Inflammation in the blood stream ***might*** be a reliable predictor of a heart attack.

Patrick has been very cranky lately; ***possibly,*** he's not getting enough sleep or he's overworked.

Just as they know that some "facts" may be inaccurate, critical readers are also aware that some opinions are more valid than others. Everyone has opinions, but they may not always be sound. First of all, some opinions can be unreasonable. For example, many opinions that include the absolute words mentioned earlier can be too all inclusive to be valid. An author who claims, for example, that *everyone* feels a certain way or that *all* things of a certain

1. **Oprah Winfrey:** popular television talk-show host
2. **Ritalin:** drug that helps calm people with attention deficit/hyperactivity disorder

type share some characteristic is probably not allowing for reasonable exceptions. Second, some opinions are based on shaky or inadequate evidence. Some people believe, for example, that the Holocaust never happened, and they manage to ignore all of the proof that it *did* happen. A later section in this chapter will further discuss how to evaluate the evidence to determine whether an opinion is informed or uninformed.

So, why do you need to recognize the difference between a fact and opinion? The distinction matters because you are going to see both used to explain and support ideas in reading selections. If you need to evaluate whether a text is valid, you'll have to sort out what is definitely true from what the writer *believes* to be true. Understanding the difference allows you, the reader, to make more sound interpretations and, thus, more reliable judgments about the worth of information and ideas.

Exercise 9.4

Read the following statements carefully and then label each of them **F** if it is a fact and **O** if it is an opinion.

_____ 1. I think Toyotas are the most reliable cars on the road today.

_____ 2. *Newsweek* is a very informative magazine.

_____ 3. *Rugrats* is my son's favorite show.

_____ 4. The weatherman on the news said that last Saturday was the hottest day of the year.

_____ 5. The Great Wall of China is a magnificent structure.

Exercise 9.5

Read the passages and then label each of the sentences in the list **F** if it offers a fact and **O** if it offers an opinion.

A. (1) American servicemen and women get the best that American TV has to offer. (2) From California's March Air Reserve Base, the American Armed Forces Radio and Television Service (AFRTS) gives the roughly 80,000 off-duty service people, their families, and civilian employees stationed around the globe a little bit of home with its 24-hour programming on four channels. (3) "Our mission," says programming chief Larry Marotta, "is to take the 150 channels we have in the States and provide a 'best of' for the servicemen."

(4) The service has its pick of selections from ABC, CBS, Fox, NBC, UPN, and WB, plus nearly 150 cable channels, which offer shows free or for a minimal charge. (5) NBC's *ER* and Fox's *Boston Public* run on Wednesdays; NBC's *Will & Grace* and ABC's *NYPD Blue* air on Thursdays. (6) Saturday features such highly rated shows as NBC's *Law & Order*, CBS's *Everybody Loves Raymond*, and UPN's *Star Trek: Voyager*. (7) There are no commercials except for armed forces promos and public service announcements. (8) And there's a prime-time no-rerun policy.*

_____ Sentence 1 _____ Sentence 5

_____ Sentence 2 _____ Sentence 6

_____ Sentence 3 _____ Sentence 7

_____ Sentence 4 _____ Sentence 8

B. (1) To me, presenting an engagement ring is the height of romantic gestures, and I don't believe women should play much of a role in its purchase. (2) Other than announcing a preference on metal or a stone's cut, they shouldn't dictate its precise design. (3) And they certainly should not mandate its expected value. (4) An engagement ring represents a guy's commitment to the woman in his life, not his commitment to make her ring finger stand apart amid her friends and family. (5) The value of the ring is in its sentiment, represented by the effort a man puts into its selection, not the dollars he puts into its acquisition.†

_____ Sentence 1

_____ Sentence 2

_____ Sentence 3

_____ Sentence 4

_____ Sentence 5

C. (1) *E Pluribus Unum* means "out of many, one." (2) No other country on earth is as multiracial and multicultural as the United States of America. (3) This diversity is a popular topic and common buzzword in newspaper and magazine articles focusing on the future of American organizations.

* Adapted from Kevin V. Johnson, "Over There, U.S. Troops Get Selective TV Service," *USA Today*, January 29, 2002, 1D.

† From Jeff D. Opdyke, "Bridging the Engagement-Ring Divide," *The Sun News*, May 30, 2004, 11D.

(4) The strength of many other nations lies in their homogeneity.[1] (5) Japan is mostly made up of persons of Japanese descent, and their economy and business transactions reflect this heritage. (6) The People's Republic of China is populated mostly with persons of Chinese ancestry, whose values and culture are a major part of their global economic strength. (7) But America has always been the "melting pot" of all the world's cultures. (8) This diversity now represents the country's biggest crisis as well as its greatest opportunity.*

____ Sentence 1

____ Sentence 2

____ Sentence 3

____ Sentence 4

____ Sentence 5

____ Sentence 6

____ Sentence 7

____ Sentence 8

D. (1) Rod Stewart was a respectable rock 'n' roll star for five years, and a slave to styles and celebrity for the next 25. (2) At his concert Friday night, however, he chose his set so wisely, and performed with such easy affability[2] and such a remarkable absence of attitude, he tweaked the proportion to his favor. (3) The show was front loaded with early favorites such as "The First Cut Is the Deepest" and "Reason to Believe," which were evidence enough of Stewart's youthful accomplishments. (4) Those rough-and-tumble fusions of rock, folk, and country established him as an artist with an appealing original vision, and a husky rasp of a singing voice to match. (5) Happily, Stewart's is the sort of voice that ages well. (6) He still can't sing a tune, but at 57 Stewart's as soulful an interpreter as ever—a quality that's been subsumed[3] in the last couple of decades by his jet-set lifestyle, which became more interesting than his music.†

____ Sentence 1

____ Sentence 2

____ Sentence 3

____ Sentence 4

____ Sentence 5

____ Sentence 6

E. (1) Your child may be at risk of being swept up in one of the fastest growing health epidemics to hit kids in recent years. (2) That's the bad news.

1. **homogeneity:** state of being similar
2. **affability:** pleasantness
3. **subsumed:** classified under a general category or principle

* Adapted from Reece and Brandt, *Effective Human Relations in Organizations,* 7th ed. Boston: Houghton Mifflin, 1999, 388–389.

† Adapted from Joan Anderman, "Soulful Stewart Has Aged Well," *Boston Sunday Globe,* October 28, 2001, A25. Copyright 2001 by Globe Newspaper Co. (MA). Reproduced with permission of Globe Newspaper Co. (MA) in the format Textbook via Copyright Clearance Center.

(3) The good news is that protecting your kid may be as simple as turning off the tube, hoofing it around the block, or stocking the fridge with fruits and veggies instead of cakes and cookies. (4) One out of every four children in this country is dangerously overweight. (5) And with increasing obesity rates, there has been an explosion in Type 2 diabetes, a disease once so rarely seen in children it was called "adult-onset diabetes." (6) Ten years ago, it accounted for just 4 percent of diabetes cases in children. (7) But today, that figure has jumped to as high as 45 percent in some parts of the country. (8) Of the children diagnosed with Type 2 diabetes, 85 percent are obese. (9) "It's a very serious problem" says Janet H. Silverstein, M.D., the American Academy of Pediatrics' representative on the U.S. Health Care Financing Administration's Diabetes Quality Improvement Project Leadership Council. (10) "It is really an epidemic."*

_____ Sentence 1

_____ Sentence 2

_____ Sentence 3

_____ Sentence 4

_____ Sentence 5

_____ Sentence 6

_____ Sentence 7

_____ Sentence 8

_____ Sentence 9

_____ Sentence 10

Informed vs. Uninformed Opinion

Some opinions are more informed than others; that is, they are supported by a sound body of factual or verifiable information. Uninformed opinions are those that are based on an insufficient amount of evidence, questionable facts, or on simply more opinions instead of solid proof. For example, read the following paragraph.

> The population of orca whales off the coast of Washington is in decline, down more than 20 percent in six years. Scientists say that people are to blame. Adoring whale watchers are disrupting the whales' feeding and mating behaviors and polluting their air and water. Because of people's interference, seven whales died during the summer of 2001. The easiest way to find those still alive is to search for the flotilla[1] of slow-moving boats that constantly surrounds them.

1. **flotilla:** small fleet

* Adapted from Debra Gordon, "The Type 2 Diabetes Epidemic," *Westchester Family*, October 2001, 26. Used by permission of the author.

9

Researchers estimate that whale watching is now worth tens of millions of dollars, and they're concerned that noise from the boats is contributing to the problem.*

This paragraph offers the opinion that people who like to watch whales are contributing to their deaths. In support of this point, the author mentions that the reasons include disruption of the whales' behaviors, noise, and pollution caused by the whale watchers' boats. However, no real evidence—no facts or data—is ever offered to support these speculations. Therefore, this opinion is relatively uninformed. Without any concrete evidence, it's difficult to accept the point of this argument.

Exercise 9.6

Read the paragraphs that follow and decide whether each offers an informed opinion or uninformed opinion. Place a checkmark on the blank beside the correct answer.

1. I am all for allowing candidates to spend their own fortunes when running for office. These self-made millionaires and billionaires have worked hard, made a great deal of money, and see a new challenge in running for public office and making a difference. In the case of California's Michael Huffington, his millions—he spent $28 million in a losing 1994 Senate race—did not get him elected. In the case of Jon Corzine, a Democrat from New Jersey, I say good for him.

   I say let them spend it. They worked hard for it. They earned it. They made it. And now they should have the right to spend as much of it as they choose.†

   _____ Informed _____ Uniformed

2. All together, Americans are tremendously generous, but many folks of modest means probably give even more than they should (bless their hearts) while many of the most fortunate give remarkably little. On average, Americans at almost all income levels give about 3 percent of their income to charity—a lot for those struggling to get by, not much at all for the well off. One very decent millionaire I know felt too stressed to grant an important $10,000 request because, he said, he had just spent $80,000 on wall coverings.

* Adapted from Carol Kaesuk Yoon, "Struggle to Survive for an 'Urban Whale,'" *New York Times*, October 16, 2001, www.nytimes.com.

† From Richard Unger, "Let Candidates Use Their Own Money," "Letters," *USA Today*, November 9, 2001, 16A.

Contrast that with the late Oseola McCarty, a Mississippi laundress of very modest wants (she never owned a car and walked a mile for groceries) who, at 87, astonished the world by giving $150,000—her life savings—to establish a college scholarship.*

_____ Informed _____Uninformed

3. Public schools are better than private schools. In my opinion, public schools are more diverse in their student population. You never see a diverse student population in a private school class, yet public school classes often have students from all over the globe.

   Public schools also offer more programs, and have better teachers. People think private school teachers are better educated than public school teachers, but they're not. Public school teachers are very knowledgeable and caring.

   Public school buildings are more modern because many were built in the 1970s, like the ones in my town. The buildings in my town are clean, fairly new, and updated often. Private school buildings are often from the early 1900s and look it. For this reason, and the others mentioned above, I think public schools are better.

   _____ Informed _____ Uninformed

4. I must take issue with the conclusion that military schools outscore civilian schools. The data presented simply do not justify the conclusion that military students are attaining higher test scores. The scores reported for the Nation's Report Card exam were only in the area of eighth-grade writing, a trivial and statistically insignificant component of the entire scope of skills for all grades. The only scores that are statistically significant are SAT scores. Military students scored worse on the SAT[1] in math and equal in verbal compared with students overall. One could make the case that SAT scores are the best measure of an overall education, since they measure students after they've completed all grades. If military students in the eighth grade score better than average on a writing test, they must then lose ground later in their education to end up average at the end of high school.†

   _____ Informed _____ Uninformed

1. **SAT:** Scholastic Aptitude Test, a college entrance exam

---

* Adapted from Andrew Tobias, "Smart Ways To Be Generous," *Parade Magazine*, November 4, 2001, 20.

† Adapted from Burt Ward, "Letters," *USA Today*, October 15, 2001, 16A.

5. I agree that businesses need to be willing to suffer short-term losses in order to provide stability for their employees and, in the big picture, for the economy as a whole. The president of my company made in excess of $12 million last year in total compensation. Last week, he made an announcement regarding layoffs and terminations totaling more than 12,000 workers. He himself has indicated no plans to cut his own pay, and I am unaware of any other top executives at our organization who plan to take a reduction in their pay. If the business leaders of our country want the state of the economy to improve, then they have to be willing to sacrifice a little, too. If they invest in their employees, then employees won't continue to fear the loss of their positions, and we'll begin to spend again.*

____ Informed ____ Uninformed

In addition to evaluating whether the evidence is adequate, you should consider whether the evidence seems *accurate*. Where does the author get the information? If you are provided with any details about the sources of the evidence, you should examine those details to decide how trustworthy the information is. Even facts can be misrepresented or misinterpreted, so it's important to know who collected them and what methods they used.

Exercise 9.7

Read each of the following passages. Then, respond to the questions that follow by circling the letter of the correct answer or by writing your answer on the blank provided.

America cannot solve its energy problems by finding more oil in our own lands. Proponents[1] of Arctic drilling say that the Arctic National Wildlife Refuge alone could provide us with enough oil to significantly reduce Americans' dependence on foreign oil. They claim the Arctic could yield 1.5 million barrels a day at peak production in, say, 2020. That is a significant amount of oil. However, it also assumes the discovery of 15 billion barrels under the refuge's coastal plain, which the United States Geological Survey regards as an extremely remote possibility. Official estimates of "economically recoverable" oil are in fact much lower than 15 billion barrels. Yet even if the most optimistic estimates prove to be right, the Arctic reserves—or any other

9

1. **proponents:** supporters

* Adapted from Velvet Key, "Letters," *USA Today*, October 1, 2001, 14A.

major domestic discoveries, for that matter—would not guarantee anything approaching energy independence. The reason is simple: according to the U.S. Department of Energy, this country accounts for about 25 percent of global oil consumption but only has about 3 percent of proven global oil reserves. Even if we can generate 1.5 million barrels a day, we still need 2.5 million to meet demand.*

1. The main point of this passage can be paraphrased
   a. Americans are far too dependent on sources of foreign oil.
   b. Americans consume too much energy.
   c. Drilling in the Arctic National Wildlife Refuge will damage the environment of that area.
   d. Drilling in the Arctic National Wildlife Refuge is not the solution to America's energy problems.

2. Is the evidence mostly facts or mostly opinions?
   a. mostly facts   b. mostly opinions

3. Would you say that this opinion is informed or uninformed?
   a. informed   b. uninformed

4. Would you say this evidence is accurate or inaccurate? Why or why not?

___

American women should not have their faces injected with Botox, the poison that smoothes wrinkles. Women who do this are risking their health in the quest for an unattainable ideal of beauty manufactured by the multibillion dollar cosmetics, fashion, and diet industries. Women should know better than to believe the myth that only the wrinkle-free are attractive, and they should have enough self-esteem to resist this message from corporations. When women use Botox, their faces may be smooth, but they also look like paralyzed robots with only one facial expression. And they teach their daughters that it's acceptable to disfigure themselves in an attempt to achieve physical perfection.

5. The main point of this passage can be paraphrased
   a. People who use Botox to rid their faces of wrinkles are damaging their health.
   b. For many reasons, women should not use Botox.
   c. The cosmetics, fashion, and diet industries care only about money.
   d. Modern women have very little self-esteem.

* Adapted from "Enlightenment on Energy," *New York Times*, October 22, 2001, http://www.nytimes.com. Copyright © 2001 by the New York Times Co. Reprinted with permission.

6. Is the evidence presented mostly facts or opinions?
   a. mostly facts   b. mostly opinions
7. Would you say that this opinion is informed or uninformed?
   a. informed   b. uninformed
8. Would you say this evidence is adequate and accurate? Why or why not?

   ____

   ____

Children don't need all of their time scheduled. I am a stay-at-home mom with a six-year-old and a four-year-old. I don't schedule play dates. My girls don't go to dance, gymnastics, piano or trampoline lessons, music lessons, or soccer camp. They don't want to, and that's fine with me. When they are ready they will join a sport or ask me to take lessons in something that interests them. For now, our time off is just that—our time off. We stay outside and do absolutely nothing structured: we go for walks, ride bikes, go to the beach, a park, or a picnic. Or they stay inside drawing, painting, playing school, playing games, singing, dancing, reading books, playing dress up. When a child is left with time and no pressure, her imagination blossoms. She becomes creative, introspective, and curious. My four-year-old daughter is reading level-two books because she has the time to just sit and look at the books and sound out the words. Sometimes, her older sister helps her—because she also has the time. The opportunity for children to have time to just do nothing at all is one of the greatest gifts that can ever be given to a child. And they will surely remember, years from now, those lazy, hot summer afternoons, sitting in the blazing sun, eating a Popsicle, getting all sticky, and running away from the bees.*

9. The main point of this passage can be paraphrased
   a. Young children should not be forced to learn until they are ready.
   b. Children will learn to like to read on their own if parents and teachers will stop pushing them.
   c. Parents should not fill up their children's free time with lessons, sports, and other structured activities.
   d. Imaginative, creative children are happy children.
10. Is the evidence mostly facts, mostly opinions, or a combination of both?
   a. mostly facts.
   b. mostly opinions.
   c. combination of facts and opinions.

9

* Excerpt from Bianca Scelfo, "Letters," *Newsweek,* May 27, 2002, 24. Used by permission of the author.

11. Is the main point adequately supported? Why or why not. ___________

____

____

I Love Lucy isn't just a great example of a situation comedy; it pretty much invented the situation comedy form. Fifty years later, the show is still absolutely hilarious. Who can forget, for example, the episode in which Lucy and Ethel get jobs in a candy factory and can't package the candy on the conveyer belt fast enough? That episode still makes us all howl with laughter. There wasn't anything that Lucille Ball wouldn't do to entertain us. She was the most talented comedienne who's ever lived, and her total commitment to the show made it great. As a result, it had a profound influence on television, and there will never be another show to equal it.

12. The main point of this passage can be paraphrased
    a. *I Love Lucy* was the first and one of the best television situation comedies.
    b. The candy factory episode of *I Love Lucy* was the best episode.
    c. Lucille Ball was the funniest comedienne on television.
    d. No show has ever been as entertaining as *I Love Lucy*.

13. Is the evidence mostly facts or mostly opinions?
    a. mostly facts
    b. mostly opinions

14. Would you say that this evidence is adequate and accurate? Why or why not?

____

____

Logical Fallacies

When you are evaluating the main point or evidence in a text, you should be aware that authors can try to divert you away from what's really the issue. They can also oversimplify so that you're more inclined to accept a particular viewpoint. Sometimes, authors use these tactics intentionally to manipulate readers. But sometimes, authors—especially inexperienced ones—can also use such tactics without realizing they're doing so. They may unknowingly allow faulty evidence or careless thinking to creep into their writing. Regardless of the writer's intention, however, the reader should learn to recognize the most

9

common **logical fallacies**, the errors in reasoning that weaken the quality of the evidence presented. Get in the habit of asking the fourth critical reading question: *Does the text attempt to distract you from the issue or oversimplify the point or the evidence?* By learning to recognize these distractions, you'll never be misled by an author's tricks or mistakes in thinking. Some fallacies you should watch out for are illustrated in the rest of this chapter.

Fallacies Related to a Lack of Sound Evidence

Some errors in reasoning arise due to a lack of good evidence in defense of an idea. Three specific fallacies of this kind are *circular reasoning,* the *red herring,* and the *hasty generalization.*

Circular reasoning is simply repeating the main idea in different words without adding any reasons or evidence that actually supports that idea. In other words, the sentence or paragraph merely circles back to where it began without adding any new development. The following statements, for example, include circular reasoning:

We should prevent teenagers from driving. They're just not old enough to handle driving.

We must not permit scientists to engage in stem-cell[1] research on newly formed embryos. These embryos may not look like babies, but we should not destroy them for scientific experiments.

To end school shootings, we have to remove children's access to guns. If a kid can't get his hands on a gun, then he can't blow away his classmates, right?

The second sentence in each example does not offer any proof for the point. Instead, it merely states the point again in different words.

The **red herring** is an idea or information that distracts you from the real issue or point. The term comes from a smelly fish that was used to confuse tracking dogs following a scent trail. Similarly, a red herring in a text leads the reader down an irrelevant path. Authors can inadvertently or intentionally toss these into passages when they run out of valid evidence, or when they want to disguise the fact that their evidence is flimsy. The following statements all include red herrings.

Taxpayers should not have to pay the pensions of ex-presidents. We live in a country where the rich just keep getting richer and the poor keep getting poorer.

9

1. **stem-cell:** related to unspecialized cells that give rise to specific, specialized cells, such as blood cells

Children who commit murder should be tried as adults. Too many parents are not disciplining their children, so it's no surprise that these kinds of crimes are happening.

Sport utility vehicles should be taken off the American car market. Americans think they're superior to all other nations, and Europeans are tired of their arrogant boasting.

These examples state a point and then, rather than offering some proof or evidence, they quickly change the subject to something related but irrelevant.

One last fallacy related to a lack of good evidence is the **hasty generalization.** This happens when the author bases a conclusion on very little evidence. The generalization is hasty because it's made without enough proof to support it. The following examples all demonstrate hasty generalizations:

A firefighter in our community was killed last week in a burning building. That just goes to show that our fire department is not concerned enough about the safety of its employees.

One study showed that pet owners experience lower stress levels. People who work in high-stress occupations, therefore, should all go get themselves a cat or a dog.

Winters in New England are still freezing, so the theory of global warming is obviously inaccurate.

In all three of these examples, one instance or incident is the sole basis for the writer's conclusion. Therefore, all of these generalizations are hasty because they do not arise from enough evidence.

Exercise 9.8

Read each of the following statements and then circle the letter of the type of fallacy it includes.

1. One woman in the news said her cancer went into remission[1] after she began practicing yoga, so yoga must cure cancer.

   a. circular reasoning c. hasty generalization
   b. red herring

1. **remission:** subsiding of disease symptoms

2. Marcy isn't mature enough to see that movie. She's just too childish to go.
   a. circular reasoning
   b. red herring
   c. hasty generalization

3. People who are unemployed shouldn't get unemployment checks. The lines are too long at all government offices anyway.
   a. circular reasoning
   b. red herring
   c. hasty generalization

4. A tree fell in our backyard last night. All of the trees in our yard must have weak roots.
   a. circular reasoning
   b. red herring
   c. hasty generalization

5. Our town's officials are all corrupt. They are more concerned with lining their own pockets than with bringing improvements to our community.
   a. circular reasoning
   b. red herring
   c. hasty generalization

Fallacies That Involve Faulty Relationships

Another group of fallacies describes those errors in reasoning that depend on flawed relationships between ideas or events. Sometimes, authors try to link two events together when, in actuality, they might not be related. This is called **faulty cause and effect**, and it incorrectly suggests that one thing caused another while it ignores other factors that might be involved. Here are some examples of faulty cause and effect:

> Orlando's tourist attractions cost too much. That's why tourism is down this year.
>
> Shark attacks are at a record high, so there must be an overpopulation of sharks in coastal waters.
>
> If we don't ban all sport utility vehicles, we'll never see reasonable gasoline prices again.

All three of these examples ignore the fact that other factors may account for the effect given.

A second fallacy of this type is called the ***non sequitur,*** which is Latin for "it does not follow." In a *non sequitur*, a conclusion does not logically follow from the evidence presented. The following statements all include *non sequiturs*:

9

The Big Green Corporation was recently fined for dumping toxic waste, which is just like dumping your household trash into your neighbor's yard. Their top executives are probably guilty of sexual harassment, too.

The cigarette boat is a favorite among boating enthusiasts in Miami. Many tourists must rent the boat while visiting South Florida.

Two people were killed when their small-engine plane struck a tree. The pilot must have been drunk.

A third fallacy that presents a flawed relationship is the false comparison. **False comparisons** attempt to draw an analogy, or comparison between two situations that are not truly parallel. Though they may, on the surface, include some similarities, closer scrutiny reveals some significant differences that make a comparison invalid. Look, for example, at the following faulty comparisons:

Posting the Ten Commandments[1] in classrooms would be just like returning racial segregation to our nation's schools.

If you're going to take away America's guns, you might as well take away their cars, too. After all, a vehicle can be a lethal weapon as well.

Letting a professional but disabled golfer ride in a golf cart during tournaments is just like letting a kid in a wheelchair join a soccer team.

Because of some very significant differences, the comparisons in these examples are invalid. In the first example, tacking a document to a wall is, of course, nothing like separating children of different races into different schools. The second comparison is faulty because the main purpose of a car is not to harm, while a gun's is. In the third example, a disabled golfer's performance is not affected by riding in a golf cart, while a child in a wheelchair cannot play the sport of soccer at all.

A choice between **false alternatives** is also known as an either-or fallacy. This is a technique authors use to try to reduce an issue to just two choices and then ask you to select between those alternatives. It is a fallacy that ignores additional alternatives, as well as the complexity or "gray areas" of a subject. The statements below all include false alternatives.

Either we stop letting elementary school kids use calculators in math class, or we accept the fact that kids in other countries will always be better at math than our children.

NASA[2] must start letting millionaires pay for rides on space shuttles. If it doesn't, Americans will withdraw their support of the space program.

1. **Ten Commandments:** the ten laws God gave to Moses
2. **NASA:** National Aeronautics and Space Administration

You can either believe in the myth of evolution,[1] or you can accept the truth of creationism.[2]

The first example reduces a complex problem to two choices: either we let kids use calculators and accept their low achievement in math, or we ban calculators and watch our kids outperform kids all over the world. Obviously, these two choices greatly oversimplify the issue. The second example also provides only two possibilities: either we let millionaires ride space shuttles, or we watch the space program end. These are clearly not the only two options available. The third example insists on two absolute choices that ignore other alternatives.

Exercise 9.9

Read each of the following passages and then circle the letter of the specific fallacy it includes.

1. Babe Ruth was a loveable figure in baseball in the 1920s. He often made the headlines because of his charitable actions, such as visiting sick children in hospitals. He did have a reputation as a boozer and womanizer, but I believe it was always overstated. If he were a constant carouser,[3] he couldn't have put up all those winning figures in pitching and batting.*

   a. faulty cause/effect c. false comparison
   b. *non sequitur* d. false alternative

2. Kids are like cars. Just like you shouldn't buy a car you can't control, you shouldn't have kids if you can't control them.†

   a. faulty cause/effect c. false comparison
   b. *non sequitur* d. false alternative

3. You can support stem-cell[4] research, or you can get used to living in a world where there are no cures for any diseases.

   a. faulty cause/effect c. false comparison
   b. *non sequitur* d. false alternative

1. **evolution:** the gradual process of change and development due to natural selection (survival of the fittest)
2. **creationism:** position that the Bible's account of the world's creation is literally true
3. **carouser:** one who drinks and goes to parties
4. **stem-cell:** related to unspecialized cells that give rise to specific, specialized cells, such as blood cells

* Adapted from Harry Wilson, "Babe Ruth, the King of Swat," *News Herald*, Morganton, NC, July 30, 2001, 4A.

† Adapted from Alice Stein, "Letters," *Time,* August 27, 2001, 9.

4. John uses food stamps to buy groceries. He's probably too lazy to work.
   a. faulty cause/effect c. false comparison
   b. *non sequitur* d. false alternative

5. Either tuition for college is reduced or people will give up on their dream of completing a college education.
   a. faulty cause/effect c. false comparison
   b. *non sequitur* d. false alternative

A Fallacy That Takes the Form of a Personal Attack

One particular type of fallacy attacks the person who holds the opposing viewpoint. It diverts the reader's attention from the real evidence by focusing on deficiencies in the opponent's character. Known as an **argument to the person**, or the Latin *ad hominem,* this fallacy resorts to discrediting an individual rather than dealing with the argument itself. Here are examples of arguments to the person:

College football coaches should not be making million-dollar salaries. Most of them are just has-beens with gigantic egos anyway.

The people who criticize MTV as being childish or immature should look in the mirror. They're all just a bunch of middle-aged ex-hippies who smoked too much pot in the 1960s and 1970s.

Dr. Paul Wilson, a physical education professor, wants to ban dodge ball from schools. He's obviously just a wimp who got his feelings hurt a few too many times during his childhood P. E. classes.

All three of these examples do not offer a sound reason in support of the point. Instead, they include personal attacks on the character or background of those who believe the opposing viewpoint.

Fallacies That Appeal to What Other People Believe

One final pair of fallacies involves appeals based on what others think or believe. They attempt to convince the reader that, because a certain person or group accepts an idea, the reader should accept it, too. This type of fallacy includes *bandwagon appeals* and *testimonials.*

Bandwagon appeals are suggestions that the reader should accept an idea simply because everyone else accepts it as true. They encourage the reader to jump on the "bandwagon" and go along with the crowd. This fallacy misleads in two ways. First of all, its claim that "everyone" feels the same way is probably inaccurate. Also, it assumes that "everyone" is right. The following statements include bandwagon appeals:

Millions of Americans have bought the new Wonder Widget. That's why you should buy one, too.

Many people watched the Madonna concert on HBO. You should watch it, too; you'll really like it.

Everyone who lives in New York City roots for the New York Yankees baseball team. If you move here, you should root for them, too.

Another appeal to others' beliefs is known as the **testimonial.** This fallacy suggests that because a certain individual, usually a celebrity such as a sports hero or movie star, believes an idea to be true, the reader should believe it, too. Obviously, advertisers use this technique often. Companies are willing to pay famous people huge sums of money to endorse their products because people tend to view a product favorably if they like or admire the person who is offering the testimonial. Yet, the celebrity's opinion really has little to do with the product's quality or worth, so a testimonial is a type of misleading fallacy. These statements all include testimonials:

Michael Jordan[1] wears Nike shoes, so you should, too.

Respected and admired former President Jimmy Carter does not agree with anything President George W. Bush is doing. Therefore, President Bush must not be doing his job very well.

If Oprah Winfrey[2] says we should sing the national anthem at every sporting event, then that's exactly what we should do.

All three of these examples argue that the point must be true because a celebrity says it is.

Exercise 9.10

Read each of the following examples and then circle the letter that corresponds to the specific fallacy it includes.

1. Berkin bags, the trendy new purses from Hermes, are all the rage in New York City this year. Everyone has to have one, even though the cheapest

1. **Michael Jordan:** a former professional basketball player
2. **Oprah Winfrey:** popular television talk-show host

one costs $4,500. You won't be cool without one if you're a woman living in the Big Apple[1]. They are particularly great if you have a lot of stuff to carry around, which most women in New York City do. You'll have plenty of room for all of your makeup, Palm Pilot, brush, and even a small dog, if you have one!

a. argument to the person c. testimonial
b. bandwagon appeal

2. Actress Nicole Kidman says that text.com has the best prices on textbooks and encourages students to buy all of their texts from the website. I bought all of this semester's texts from the site because they must have the best prices. I didn't even check out any of the other textbook sites.

   a. argument to the person c. testimonial
   b. bandwagon appeal

3. Most people who host talk shows today make too much money. They are just people who want to spend an hour talking about themselves anyway. They don't really care about the people they are supposed to be interviewing; they just go on and on about themselves, and I think the shows are boring. Also, these talk show hosts all have checkered[2] pasts that include failed marriages, drug abuse, and eating disorders, so their advice just isn't worth all that money they earn.

   a. argument to the person c. testimonial
   b. bandwagon appeal

4. Anyone with any sense at all should vote "yes" on the school funding issue. Everyone we know is going to vote for it. It only makes sense to do so. You should vote "yes" on the issue so that the funding passes.

   a. argument to the person c. testimonial
   b. bandwagon appeal

5. Television talk show host Maury Povich thinks that his wife, Connie Chung, is the best interviewer in news today. Therefore, she must be a great interviewer.

   a. argument to the person c. testimonial
   b. bandwagon appeal

1. **the Big Apple:** New York City

2. **checkered:** marked by great changes or shifts in fortune

Deciding for Yourself

Once you are able to evaluate the main point and the evidence, separate fact from opinion, and recognize logical fallacies, you should be able to better evaluate whether a text is valid or worthy. Then, you can determine what you should do about the new ideas or information. Should you accept them as true? Should you change your own opinions in response? Should you reject the text outright? Or should you resolve to gather more information before you respond? Critical readers know how to scrutinize a text so they can decide for themselves.

CHAPTER 9 REVIEW

Fill in the blanks in the following statements.

1. Attempts to influence your thoughts or behaviors are called ________.
2. All arguments contain two elements: the ________ and the ________.
3. The ________ of an argument is the belief or attitude an author wants you to accept.
4. ________ is defined as the specific reasons, facts, examples, or other details the author offers to convince the reader to accept the point.
5. A sound main point is usually ________, reasonable, ________ ________, and mindful of other possibilities.
6. Sound evidence is both ________ and ________.
7. To be effective, the support for a point must be ________; in other words, it must directly relate to the point.
8. ________ are information that is verifiably true.
9. ________ are statements that express beliefs, feelings, judgments, attitudes, and preferences.
10. Statements of opinion often contain ________ words that indicate the relative nature of something.

9

11. ____________ opinions are supported by a sound body of factual or verifiable information, while ____________ opinions are those that are based on an insufficient amount of evidence, questionable facts, or simply more opinions instead of solid proof.
12. ________________ are errors in reasoning.
13. Fallacies related to a lack of sound evidence include ________________, the red herring, and the ________________.
14. Fallacies that involve faulty relationships include faulty cause and effect, the ____________, false comparisons, and ________________.
15. The ____________________ is a form of fallacy that includes a personal attack.
16. Two fallacies that appeal to others' beliefs are the ______________ and the ____________.

Reading Selection

Practicing the Active Reading Strategy:

Before and While You Read

You can use active reading strategies before, as, and after you read a selection. The following are some suggestions for active reading strategies that you can perform before you read and while you read.

1. Skim the selection for any unfamiliar words. Circle or highlight any words you do not know.
2. As you read, underline, highlight, or circle important words or phrases.
3. Write down any questions about the selection if you are confused by the information presented.
4. Jot notes in the margin to help you understand the material.

Pill-Popping Replaces Healthy Habits

by Steven Findlay

1 If you watch enough TV these days, you might get the impression that there's a prescription drug for just about anything that ails you. And that's about right. In recent years, more and better drugs have come along to treat the chronic diseases and conditions afflicting us: arthritis, diabetes, asthma, coronary-artery narrowing, heartburn, allergies, depression and erectile dysfunction.

2 U.S. pharmacies dispensed more than 3 billion prescriptions in 2003, up from about 2 billion a decade ago. We love our medicines. And why not? They are so easy, and they usually work. We take more and more of them, even as we complain bitterly about their prices and rail against the pharmaceutical industry.

3 But another perspective goes down less easily: Although many Americans don't get the medicines they need, as a nation, we are fast becoming overly reliant on a slew[1] of drugs that essentially substitute for a healthy lifestyle. Most of us don't routinely eat wholesome foods in moderate quantity, stay active or manage our body weight. One in five of us still smoke. When the inevitable consequences follow, we count on pills to counter the ills that our human weaknesses engender and our culture fosters (think ubiquitous fast, fatty foods and physical education's demise in schools).

4 This has every bit as much impact on the steeply rising national tab for prescription drugs as their prices do. Unless Americans, individually and collectively, begin to take more responsibility for their own health, that tab may rise to a point where more serious limits will be imposed on our access to drugs.

5 The predicted costs of medicines compelled Congress to limit the drug benefit it added to Medicare to stay within a self-imposed 10-year budget of $400 billion. Now the Bush administration has raised that projection to $534 billion, even as the AARP[2] and others begin to push to expand the new benefit.

6 The drug industry correctly notes that many medicines can save money by preventing hospitalizations or nursing-home care and reducing disability. But it's just as true that the industry's success builds on our failure. Growth in costs could be reduced sharply if more people took basic steps to maintain their health and so needed fewer drugs or other medical care.

7 Consider the cholesterol-lowering drugs known as statins. They are among the most widely prescribed medicines: Sales topped $13 billion in 2002, up from $1.8 billion a decade earlier. Lipitor alone earned Pfizer more than $6 billion last year in the U.S., the most of any drug. Some 15 million Americans take a statin daily.

8 Statins are highly effective, lowering the risk of heart attack and stroke by an average 20 percent to 30 percent among people at risk. But their use has soared largely because more and more people are identified as "at risk" due to obesity, clogged arteries, diabetes and high blood pressure,

1. **slew:** large amount

2. **AARP:** American Association of Retired Persons

which, in turn, are linked to overeating, poor diet and lack of sufficient physical activity.

9 In 2001, for example, a National Institutes of Health panel changed the at-risk standard for "bad" (LDL) cholesterol and said many more people with other heart-disease-risk factors also should lower their cholesterol. This pushed the number of Americans who need to lower their cholesterol from 13 million to 36 million. The panel urged people to eat better and exercise more—but tellingly, its leaders noted that drugs might be an easier solution. "We used to say to try lowering (cholesterol) with diet first, but now we say that if your LDL is above 130 and you have coronary disease, you should be on drug therapy," Scott Grundy, a physician and the panel's chairman, told *The Wall Street Journal*. For people with LDL levels between 100 and 130, he added, "We think the evidence justifies the majority going on drugs."

10 Recent studies add to the momentum. One showed the benefits of lowering LDL to 70 or 80. Two studies last year revealed that children and teens with high LDL levels show early signs of heart disease. These studies, trumpeted in the media, largely were seen as further evidence that even more Americans, maybe up to 50 million, could benefit from statins.

11 Less noticed was a study out last July that found that a diet rich in fiber and soy protein lowered LDL levels about as much as a statin. OK, OK: Soy protein may be too much to ask. But a large body of research shows that a healthy, balanced diet and regular exercise can keep high cholesterol at bay for most of us—and yields multiple other benefits to boot, including a lower risk of some cancers.

12 The cholesterol story is not unique. This same dynamic plays out for other ills and the drugs that treat them: high blood pressure, type 2 diabetes, certain kinds of pain, sleep disturbances, heartburn, even mild depression. Yes, millions of Americans with such conditions need medicines. But millions of us are self-afflicted with such ills because we can't or won't get our lifestyle acts together.

13 We devour fad diets, such as Atkins and South Beach. But obesity rates have climbed steadily for 20 years. Two-thirds of us now are overweight. What we really want—admit it—is a trusty, safe anti-fat pill. Indeed, that's the Holy Grail[1] of the pharmaceutical industry.

14 The looming question is whether we can afford in the long run to allow the drug industry to bail us out of our bad habits. Drugs will get better, but not cheaper. It's our choice: Let drug costs spiral upward and drug firms capitalize on our weaknesses. Or take charge of our own health and reduce the overall need for pills.*

1. **Holy Grail:** The Holy Grail is generally considered to be the cup from which Christ drank at the Last Supper and the one used by Joseph of Arimathea to catch Christ's blood as he hung on the cross. (From The Holy Grail website, http://www.lib. rochester.edu/camelot/grlmenu.htm, The Camelot Project at the University of Rochester.) In the time of King Arthur and according to that legend, pursuit of the Grail was the highest spiritual pursuit. It is used here to represent something magical and unattainable.

* Adapted from Steven Findlay, "Pill-Popping Replaces Healthy Habits," *USA Today,* February 5, 2004, 15A.

Vocabulary

Read the following questions about some of the vocabulary words that appear in the previous selection. Circle the letter of each correct answer.

1. In paragraph 1, the author uses the word *chronic* to describe diseases. In this context, what does *chronic* mean?
   a. final
   b. happening over and over again
   c. minor
   d. disturbing

2. "We take more and more of them, even as we complain bitterly about their prices and *rail* against the pharmaceutical industry." (paragraph 2) In this context, what does *rail against* mean?
   a. criticize
   b. disagree with
   c. agree with
   d. throw around

3. "When the inevitable consequences follow, we count on pills to counter the ills that our human weaknesses *engender* and our culture fosters." (paragraph 3) What does *engender* mean?
   a. disgust c. adjust
   b. obey d. produce

4. "[T]hink *ubiquitous* fast, fatty foods and physical education's demise in schools." (paragraph 3) What does *ubiquitous* mean?
   a. disappearing c. ever-present
   b. never-ending d. inexpensive

5. What does it mean to keep something or someone *at bay?* (paragraph 11)
   a. to keep close c. to keep at arm's length
   b. to keep safe d. to keep in a box

Critical Reading

Are the following sentences from the reading selection facts or opinions? On the blank after each statement, write FACT if it's a fact and OPINION if it's an opinion.

1. "In recent years, more and better drugs have come along to treat the chronic diseases and conditions afflicting us: arthritis, diabetes, asthma,

9

coronary-artery narrowing, heartburn, allergies, depression and erectile dysfunction." ______________

2. "We love our medicines." ______________

3. "One in five of us still smoke." ______________

4. "When the inevitable consequences follow, we count on pills to counter the ills that our human weaknesses engender and our culture fosters (think ubiquitous fast, fatty foods and physical education's demise in schools)."______________

5. "What we really want—admit it—is a trusty, safe anti-fat pill."__________

Circle the letter of the correct answer.

6. What is Steve Findlay's tone in this selection?
   a. amused
   b. critical
   c. sad
   d. delighted

7. How can the main point of the selection be paraphrased?
   a. Americans tend to replace a healthy lifestyle with medicines.
   b. Drug companies make too much money and Americans suffer.
   c. Drug companies make false promises about their drugs.
   d. Americans spend a lot of money on fad diets.

8. Is the evidence presented mostly facts or mostly opinions?
   a. mostly facts
   b. mostly opinions

9. Would you say that the evidence is adequate and accurate? Why or why not? ____

____

____

10. One could argue that the statement, "Unless Americans, individually and collectively, begin to take more responsibility for their own health, that tab may rise to a point where more serious limits will be imposed on our access to drugs" is an example of
   a. an argument to the person.
   b. faulty/cause effect.
   c. false alternative.
   d. a testimonial.

Practicing the Active Reading Strategy:

After You Read

Now that you have read the selection, answer the following questions using the active reading strategies that are discussed on pages 30–33.

1. Identify and write down the point and purpose of this reading selection.
2. Besides the vocabulary words included in the exercise on page 484, are there any other vocabulary words that are unfamiliar to you? If so, write a list of them. When you have finished writing your list, look up each word in a dictionary and write the definition that best describes the word as it is used in the selection.
3. Predict any possible test questions that may be used on a test about the content of this selection.
4. How could you use the information contained in this selection? Does the information contained in the selection reinforce or contradict your ideas and experiences? Explain.

Questions for Discussion and Writing

Answer the following questions based on your reading of the selection. Write your answer on the blanks provided.

1. Do you agree or disagree with the following statement from the selection? "Although many Americans don't get the medicines they need, as a nation, we are fast becoming overly reliant on a slew of drugs that essentially substitute for a healthy lifestyle." Why? Write a paper in which you explore your opinion on this statement. ______________________

   ____

2. "But a large body of research shows that a healthy, balanced diet and regular exercise can keep high cholesterol at bay for most of us—and *yields multiple other benefits to boot,* including a lower risk of some cancers." Conduct some additional research to find out what some of the other multiple benefits of a balanced diet and regular exercise might be and summarize your findings in a short essay. ______________________

   ____

3. The author of this selection mentions both the Atkins diet and the South Beach diet. Go online and research both diets. Write a paper in which you

summarize the basic rules of each diet, their purported health benefits (beyond weight loss), and their success rates. ______________________________

____

Vocabulary: Figures of Speech

Figures of speech are creative comparisons between things that have something in common. An author uses figures of speech because they are clever, interesting, vivid, and imagistic. In other words, they tend to create pictures, or images, in the reader's mind. An author also includes figures of speech because they help readers understand something new and unfamiliar by comparing it to something already known or understood. Four types of figures of speech are *analogies, similes, metaphors,* and *personification.*

An **analogy** is an extended comparison between two things or ideas. This chapter included, in the section about logical fallacies, some examples of false analogies, which are comparisons that are flawed. However, when used correctly, analogies can aid readers in grasping new concepts. For example, look at the following analogy:

> I like to think of my friends as two parts of an egg-and-ham sandwich: Some friends are like egg-laying chickens, and some are like ham-producing hogs. The chickens can come by and lay an egg and keep on moving without any big sacrifice. But for you to enjoy the ham, that hog has to make the ultimate sacrifice. When you go through an ordeal like being fired from your job, your friends are on trial with you. You learn pretty quickly which ones are chickens and which ones are hogs who will actually put themselves on the line for you. All I can say is, thank God for those hogs.*

In this passage, the author compares some friends to chickens and other friends to hogs. This analogy helps the reader better understand how friends differ based on how much they help during a crisis.

A **simile** is much like an analogy, but briefer. Rather than being developed over several sentences, a simile is usually just a phrase inserted into a sentence. It compares one thing or idea to another by using the words *like* or *as*. For example, look at this example:

> And *Lost* jumps around among the teams so often and in such discombobulated ways, we end up feeling ***as disoriented as riders disembarking from the Tilt-a-Whirl at the fair.***

* Adapted from Tavis Smiley, "How a Pink Slip Can Fire You Up," *USA Weekend,* August 31–September 2, 2001, 10.

This simile compares the show's viewers to people who have just ridden a spinning ride at a fair.

A **metaphor** makes a more direct comparison by stating that something actually *is* something else rather than just *like* it. For example, read this next sentence:

> Cats are tiny terrorists, reminders of our vulnerability.

Cats are not actually terrorists, but this metaphor says they are to create an interesting and informative comparison.

One last type of figure of speech is **personification,** which compares nonhuman objects or animals to humans by giving them human abilities or characteristics. When we say the wind is ***whistling*** through the trees or the fire engine's siren ***screams*** in the night, we're giving the wind and the siren human abilities. Here's another example:

> Over the last several months, hundreds of Magellanic penguins have been washing ashore near Rio de Janeiro, 2,000 miles north of their usual haunts. The wayward birds may be signs of a massive climate shift in the South Atlantic: warming may have altered ocean circulation so as to ***nudge*** the cold-water currents (which the penguins follow for chow) thousands of miles off course.*

In this example, global warming has been given the human ability to nudge, or gently push, something.

Vocabulary Exercise 1

The following sentences all come from Chapters 7, 8, and 9. In each one, underline the figure of speech. Then, on the blank provided, write the two things or ideas that are being compared.

1. In spite of dramatic efforts to increase airport security, airlines just don't have the time or manpower to screen the huge mountain of luggage passengers insist on bringing with them. ______________________

____

2. Uniformed attendants are posted throughout the gleaming, well-lit station —a dependable oasis of rational order in the hectic urban whirlwind that is modern Tokyo. ______________________

* From Sharon Begley, "The Mercury's Rising," *Newsweek,* December 4, 2000, 52.

3. Uniformed attendants are posted throughout the gleaming, well-lit station—a dependable oasis of rational order in the hectic urban whirlwind that is modern Tokyo. ______

4. Moms face a daunting task, whether they have jobs or not. First, they must make their way through a labyrinth of advice based on vast amounts of research, much of it conflicting. ______

______

5. But most mothers run the gauntlet of conflicting messages, struggle to figure it all out, sacrifice as mothers always have and nurture their children to the best of their ability. ______

6. His startling wit was as exhilarating as those flying pies in American slapstick movies. ______

7. The Arctic National Wildlife Refuge is an opus crowned from hope because our forefathers decided that it would shine if left alone.

______

Vocabulary Exercise 2

Underline the five figures of speech in the following passage and label each one according to its specific type.

I am standing in Quebec's most fashionable hotel bar, trying to look cool. It is, as they say, "the season," and the place is packed. Wearing their finest Gore-Tex and down and wool, patrons slurp vodka from heavy square tumblers. Candles gutter on sparkling cocktail tables, and an eerie light filters through a wall made of what looks like frosted glass. From hidden speakers Jim Morrison[1] croons, "Come on, baby, light my fire." But besides the tiny candles, there is no fire. Walls, windows, tables, chairs, even the bar itself—everything is frozen solid. And I'm trying hard to look cool to hide the fact that I am really, really cold.

Unlike the thousands of other visitors to Quebec City who snuggle into bed in cozy inns, I have booked a deer pelt here, at North America's first Ice Hotel. Its founder, 38-year-old Jacques Desbois, got the idea to build it when

1. **Jim Morrison:** 1960s rock star

he read about a similar hotel in northern Sweden. Rounding up backers wasn't easy (they were reluctant to invest in a structure that would stand for three months and be bulldozed every spring—go figure), but he had enough capital by November 2000 to begin construction. Six weeks and $325,000 later, he had an Ice Hotel.

All day, I have the sense of floating around in a fun house, watching tourists duck in and out of hidden doorways and disappear behind ice columns like playful penguins. But as the sun goes down, the day-trippers thin out, until there's only a clutch of red-nosed folks at the bar—the overnight guests. At nine o'clock we gather for our prebedtime meeting, held in a clubhouse close by the Ice Hotel. Besides offering a place for us to stow our luggage and eat breakfast, the clapboard structure provides a rare commodity around these parts—heat.

It's only 20 degrees inside the hotel, so tell me again: Why am I here? An answer comes with my first glimpse of the Ice Hotel underneath the stars. This, I think, is how it's supposed to be seen, glowing like a fairy-tale cottage on a dark night. Inside, candles have been lit on every icy nightstand, and sleeping bags have been spread across the deep pelts on our mattresses. In my bedroom, "the Geometric," the circles and squares etched into the snowy walls cast dark shadows in the flickering candlelight, and the triangular window is a frosty black.

I order a shot of vodka from the bar for courage, and then rush back to my bedroom. There, I do 20 jumping jacks for warmth, and in one frantic motion I pry off my shoes, peel off my coat, and dive into my bag, cinching a drawstring around my neck like a sausage casing. I squeeze my eyes shut and pray for sleep, but there is a problem. My face is cold. I try to pull my hat down over my eyes and nose, and rest my frozen cheek on my mittened hands. But a thin stream of air sneaks through the tiny gap created by my hands and chills me to my double-socked toes.

Now I'm sitting up, squirming, yanking on cords and zippers and snaps until I finally find—a hood! I pull it over my head and sink back into a cave of darkness. I wait. And wait. And wait. Minutes crawl by . . . then hours. I am ready to call it quits and repair to the crash room when all of a sudden, miracle of miracles, blue light is seeping through the window. It is dawn. A staffer tiptoes into my room and sets a cup of coffee beside my bed. As the smell of it wafts into my hood, I realize that I have made it through the night. I am an adventurer, I am alive, I am also—can it be?—warm. But they're crazy if they think I am ever leaving this bag.*

9

* Adapted from Shea Dean, "My Holiday On Ice," *Reader's Digest,* November 2001, 114–117. Used by permission of the author.

READING STRATEGY: Skimming

When you look at an Internet Web site for the first time, do you read every word on your computer screen? Of course not. Instead, your eyes probably flick around over the pictures and text, reading individual words or phrases as you try to form a general impression of the site and its content. You do the same thing when you're standing in a store, deciding whether to buy a magazine. You flip through the pages, glancing at the titles of the articles and at the pictures, as you try to determine if the magazine is worth your money. This is called *skimming,* and it's also a useful strategy for reading printed materials.

When you skim a text or a passage, you're not looking for specific details or information (that's called *scanning,* which is discussed in another chapter). Instead, you're trying to get some sense of the content and organization. In particular, you skim a reading selection to get an idea of the author's subject, main point, overall focus, or purpose.

Skimming should never be a substitute for reading. It will not give you a full understanding of a text or a passage. However, skimming is useful for three particular purposes: previewing, evaluating a source's worth or relevancy, and reviewing.

Previewing. Skimming a reading selection—for instance, a chapter in a textbook or a journal article—will provide you with a "big picture" of what you're about to read. As a result, when you do finally read the text, you'll have a framework for understanding the specific details.

Evaluating. Skimming is also useful for research. You don't have time to read every single article you find when you're looking for information about a research topic. Skimming gives you a way to determine if a particular book or article relates to your project and is worth reading in detail later.

Reviewing. Finally, you can skim a text after reading it as a way of reviewing the information. Therefore, skimming can be a valuable technique for studying and remembering information.

To skim a text or a passage, follow these steps:

1. Glance over the title and all of the headings.
2. Quickly read the first sentence of each paragraph. Authors often state their main ideas at the beginnings of paragraphs, so reading these first sentences can help you get a sense of the major points.

Continued

3. Quickly move your eyes in a zig-zag pattern over the words in the text. At the same time, ask yourself, *What's this about?* and *What's the point?* Try to answer those questions by noticing words or phrases that are highlighted with bold print, italics, or some other kind of distinctive typeface. As you practice skimming, you'll become better at noticing key words or concepts even when they're not highlighted. You'll find that after a while these words will begin to jump out at you as you run your eyes over the passage.

Follow the three steps described above to skim the following passage from a business textbook. Then, answer the questions after the passage.

What Is Money?

The members of some remote societies exchange goods and services through barter, without using money. A barter system is a system of exchange in which goods or services are traded directly for other goods or services. One family may raise vegetables and herbs, and another may weave cloth. To obtain food, the family of weavers trades cloth for vegetables, provided that the farming family is in need of cloth.

The trouble with the barter system is that the two parties in an exchange must need each other's products at the same time, and the two products must be roughly equal in value. So even very isolated societies soon develop some sort of money to eliminate the inconvenience of trading by barter.

The Functions of Money

Money aids in the exchange of goods and services for resources. But that is a rather general (and somewhat theoretical) way of stating money's function. Let's look instead at three *specific* functions money serves in any society.

Money as a Medium of Exchange A medium of exchange is anything accepted as payment for products, services, and resources. This definition looks very much like the definition of money. It is meant to, because the primary function of money is to serve as a medium of exchange. The key word here is *accepted*. As long as the owners of products, services, and resources accept

9

money in an exchange, it is performing this function. Of course, these owners accept it because they know it is acceptable to the owners of other products, services, and resources, which *they* may wish to purchase. For example, the family in our earlier example can sell their vegetables and use the money to purchase cloth from the weavers. This eliminates the problems associated with the barter system.

Money as a Measure of Value A measure of value is a single standard, or yardstick, used to assign values to, and compare the values of, products, services, and resources. Money serves as a measure of value because the prices of all products, services, and resources are stated in terms of money. It is thus the "common denominator" we use to compare products and decide which we will buy. Imagine the difficulty you would have in deciding whether you can afford new Nike running shoes if they were priced in terms of yards of cloth or pounds of vegetables—especially if your employer happened to pay you in toothbrushes.

Money as a Store of Value Money received by an individual or firm need not be used immediately. It may be held and spent later. Hence, money serves as a store of value, or a means of retaining and accumulating wealth. This function of money comes into play whenever we hold on to money—in a pocket, a cookie jar, a savings account, or whatever.

Value that is stored as money is affected by *inflation*. As prices go up in an inflationary period, money loses purchasing power. Suppose you can buy a Sony stereo system for $1,000. Your $1,000 has a value equal to the value of that stereo system. But suppose you wait and don't buy the stereo immediately. If the price goes up to $1,050 in the meantime because of inflation, you can no longer buy the stereo with your $1,000. Your money has *lost* purchasing power because it is now worth less than the stereo. To determine the effect of inflation on the purchasing power of a dollar, economists often refer to a consumer price index. The consumer price index measures prices of a fixed amount of goods bought by a typical consumer, including food, transportation, shelter, utilities, clothing, and medical care. The base amount for the consumer price index is 100 and

Continued

was established by averaging the cost of the items included in the consumer price index over the 1982 to 1984 time period.

Important Characteristics of Money

To be acceptable as a medium of exchange, money must be easy to use, trusted, and capable of performing the three functions just mentioned. To meet these requirements, money must possess the following five characteristics.

Divisibility The standard unit of money must be divisible into smaller units to accommodate small purchases as well as large ones. In the United States, our standard is the dollar, and it is divided into pennies, nickels, dimes, quarters and half-dollars. These coins allow us to make purchases of less than a dollar and of odd amounts greater than a dollar. Other nations have their own divisible currencies: the euro in France and Germany, and the yen in Japan, to mention a few.

Portability Money must be small enough and light enough to be carried easily. For this reason, paper currency is issued in larger *denominations*—multiples of the standard dollar unit. Five-, ten-, twenty-, fifty-, and hundred-dollar bills make our money convenient for almost any purchase.

Stability Money should retain its value over time. When it does not, people tend to lose faith in their money. On October 27, 1987, when stock markets around the world took a deep plunge, the New York Stock Exchange lost approximately 8 percent of its total dollar value in one day. Although there were many reasons for the decline, one important reason heard time and again was the instability of foreign currencies in Hong Kong, Japan, and other nations in the Pacific Rim. When money becomes extremely unstable, people may turn to other means of storing value, such as gold and jewels, works of art, and real estate. They may even use such items as a medium of exchange in a barter system. During upheavals in Eastern Europe in the 1980s and early 1990s, farmers traded farm products for cigarettes because the value of cigarettes was more stable than each nation's money.

Durability The objects that serve as money should be strong enough to last through reasonable usage. No one would appreciate

9

(or use) dollar bills that disintegrated as they were handled or coins that melted in the sun. To increase the life expectancy of paper currency, most nations use special paper with a high fiber content.

Difficulty of Counterfeiting If a nation's currency were easy to counterfeit—that is, to imitate or fake—its citizens would be uneasy about accepting it as payment. Thus, countries do their best to ensure that it is very hard to reproduce their currency. Typically, countries use special paper and watermarks and print intricate designs on the currency to discourage counterfeiting.*

1. What is the topic of this entire passage? ______________________
2. According to the major headings, what two aspects of this topic are discussed in this passage? ______________________

____
3. How many functions does money serve? ______________________
4. How many characteristics does effective money possess? __________

Reading Visuals: Maps

A **map** is a visual depiction of an area and its physical characteristics. Maps illustrate spatial relationships; for example, they show sizes and borders and distances from one place to another. They can also be used to make comparisons. For instance, a map of the United States may color in the states who apply the death penalty in red, and color those that don't, blue.

Here are the parts of a map.

- **Title.** The title identifies either the area itself, or the relationship between different areas.
- **A diagram of the area.** A map includes a proportionate drawing that represents the geographical features and spatial relationships.
- **Key.** Many maps incorporate symbols, so the key explains what these symbols mean.

Continued

9

* Adapted from Pride et al., *Business,* 6th ed. Boston: Houghton Mifflin, 1999, 478–481.

- **Labels.** Maps will usually label parts or features that help the reader understand the overall point stated in the title.
- **Source line.** The source line identifies who collected or compiled the information shown in the map.

The map below labels all of these parts.

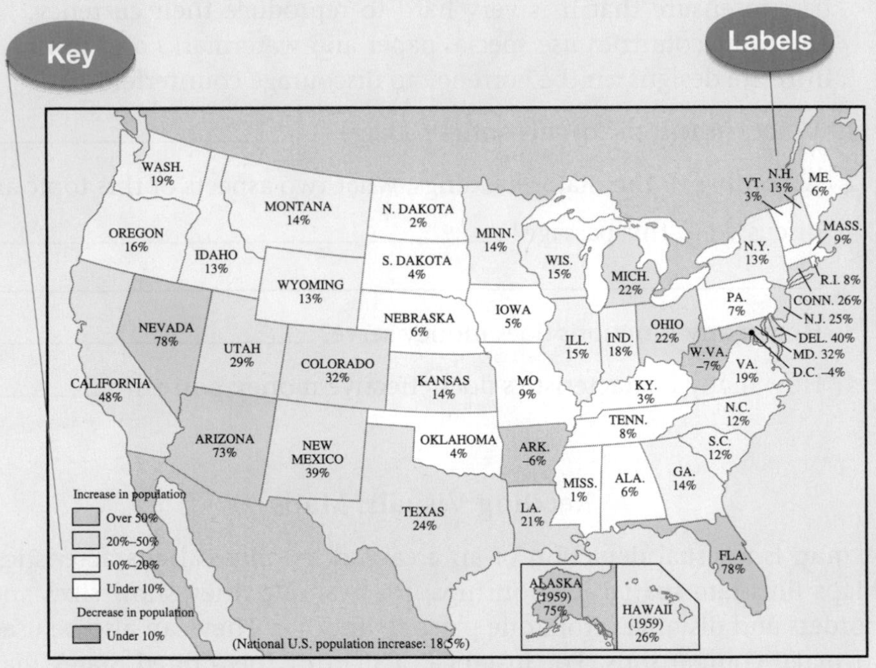

Rise of the Sunbelt, 1950–1960 *The years after the Second World War saw a continuation of the migration of Americans to the Sunbelt states of the Southwest and the West Coast.*

Source: Norton et al., *A People and a Nation,* 5th ed.,Vol. 2. Boston: Houghton Mifflin, 1998, 833.

To interpret a map, read the title first to understand the idea or information on which you should focus. Then, familiarize yourself with symbols in the key (including the scale that indicates distance) and read the labels that name different areas. If the map is illustrating some comparison, try to state in your own words a conclusion based on that comparison.

The map shown above shows population increases in each state of America from 1950 to 1960. As the title of the map indicates, the

9

percentages reveal an especially large increase in Sunbelt states of the Southwest and West Coast. The key in the bottom left-hand corner indicates that the states with the biggest increases—Nevada, Arizona, Florida, and Alaska—are colored in dark blue. Those states that experienced a 20 to 50 percent gain are colored in light blue, and so on. These colors help the reader quickly see the major relationships depicted by the visual.

Now, study the map below and then answer the questions that follow.

Electoral College

This distorted map, in which the states are sized according to their number of electoral votes, demonstrates the electoral power of the more populous states.

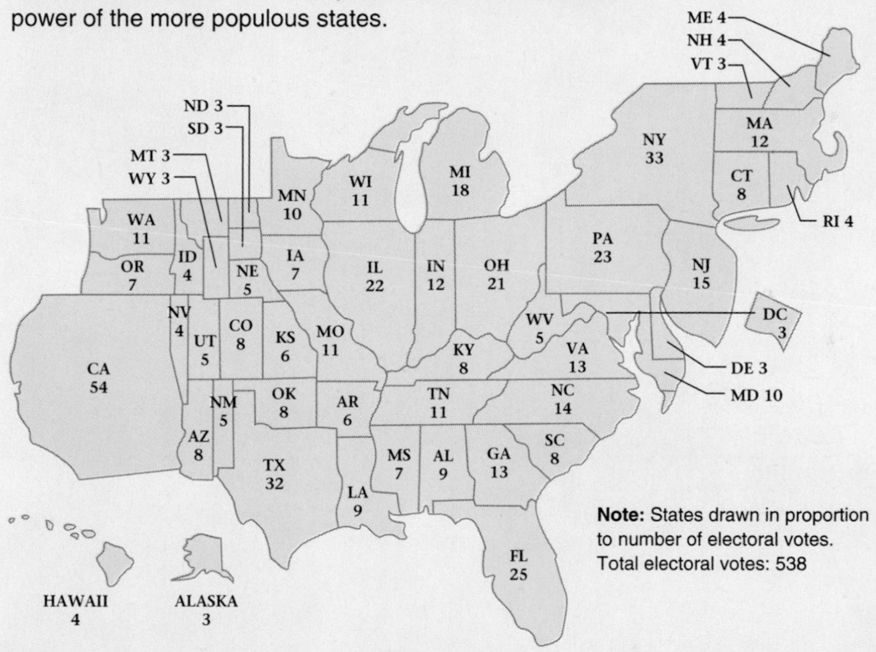

Source: Barbour and Wright, *Keeping the Republic*, Brief Ed. Boston: Houghton Mifflin, 2001, 357–358.

1. Name three states that have more than twenty electoral votes.

____

____

Continued

2. Name three states that have fewer than ten electoral votes. ________

____

3. Why do some states have more electoral votes than others? ________

____

4. What is the total number of electoral votes in the nation? ________

5. Which state has the largest number of electoral votes? ________

6. Why are the states distorted in this map? ________________

____

____

Name ______________________________ Date ______________

TEST 1

A. On the blanks next to the statements in each group, write a **P** if a statement is the point and **S** if the statement offers support for the point.

1. _____ Beginning with the natural-childbirth movements and breast-cancer activism of the 1970s, inspired by AIDS patients who refused to take no for an answer, Americans have increasingly demanded more information and more control.

   _____ People who once took orders from their physicians are now willing only to take advice.

   _____ They look for information on Web sites, in newspapers and magazines, and in conversations with friends, so that cocktail parties sometimes sound more like hospital waiting rooms than social events.

   _____ The greatest advance in health care in our lifetime has not been transplants or new pharmaceuticals; it has been the rise of the informed consumer.*

2. _____ Hispanics make up 12.5 percent of the U.S. population, but Hispanic actors had 4.9 percent of all roles studied.

   _____ Using many of the same categories found in the 2000 census, *USA Today* tallied and compared statistics about the age, race, and gender of the actors and characters in 2001 movies and found that they do not reflect real life.

   _____ Males and females are close to half and half in real life, but in the movies, men dominate 65 percent to 35 percent in all roles surveyed and 75 percent to 25 percent in starring roles.

   _____ In America, the median[1] age for females is slightly older than for males, 36.5 vs. 34, but the actors are older than the actresses in the movies studied, with median ages 38 vs. 30.†

1. **median:** average

---

* From Anna Quindlen, "In a Peaceful Frame of Mind," *Newsweek,* February 4, 2002, 64.

† From Susan Wloszczyna and Anthony DeBarros, "Reel Life vs. Real Life," *USA Today,* February 13, 2002, 1A.

For additional tests, see the Test Bank.

3. _____ Classmates.com attracts 15 million visitors a month.

_____ Classmates.com ranks No. 20 on Jupiter Media Metrix's list of top-traffic websites.

_____ Classmates.com is one of the most popular sites on the Web.

_____ In 2002, the number of visitors to Classmates.com tripled.*

4. _____ During the time of the ancient Roman Empire, criers were paid to scream out messages about products for sale.

_____ Archaeologists have found a three-thousand-year-old ad for a run-away slave that was written in Thebes on papyrus.[1]

_____ In medieval England, shopkeepers often posted a boy or man at the entrance to their shop to shout at the top of his lungs about the goods in the store.

_____ Advertising is as old as selling itself.†

5. _____ Skateboarding comes close to swimming in terms of working all muscle groups.

_____ Pushing off builds the calves and thighs while crouching strengthens the knees.

_____ As the body bobs up and down, muscles in the stomach and back are worked.

_____ The arms are used for balancing, like a tightrope walker uses a pole, so they get a workout, too.

_____ As the skater seeks equilibrium,[2] the shoulders flex and the neck muscles roll.‡

B. Each point below is supported by six statements. Circle the letters beside the three statements that provide RELEVANT support for the point.

6. Theodosius II enjoyed the longest imperial reign in Roman history and was responsible for marvelous developments in Roman society during that time.

1. **papyrus:** ancient material on which to write

2. **equilibrium:** balance

* Adapted from Jefferson Graham, "Web Site Chaperones Classmate Reunions," *USA Today,* February 12, 2002, 13B.

† Adapted from Turow, *Media Today.* Boston: Houghton Mifflin, 1999, 320.

‡ Adapted from "Boards Give a Full Body Workout," no author credited, *USA Today,* June 30, 2004, http://www.usatoday.com/usatonline/20040630/6329117s.htm.

9

a. Along with his wife and sister, he both added and beautified important buildings.
b. Theodosius created a comprehensive law code in 438 that brought together all Roman laws issued since Constantine and arranged them in systematic fashion.
c. Theodosius reigned from 408–450.
d. Theodosius was not particularly tall.
e. After Theodosius died in 450, the Eastern Empire endured seventy-seven years of rule by military men who lacked the culture, vision, or administrative capacity of their predecessors.[1]
f. Theodosius and his family made Rome a real intellectual center by promoting learning.*

7. Pet ownership in our county should be limited to a total of six dogs/cats, with the seventh pet requiring a special permit.
   a. All pet owners should be encouraged to spay/neuter[2] their pets to help reduce pet overpopulation.
   b. In the United States today, 39 percent of households own at least one dog, and 34 percent own at least one cat.
   c. Studies have shown that owning a pet is good for your health, for pets can help reduce stress.
   d. Limiting the number of pets a person can own would help to protect dogs and cats from neglect and abuse.
   e. If we keep pet ownership to a maximum of six animals, we will help to protect the health and safety of the public.
   f. Putting a cap on the number of pets one can own will reduce the complaints that neighbors of multi-pet owners make to authorities.

8. Like Oregon, our state should encourage insurance companies to offer rates based on how far a person drives, rather than a fixed rate for everyone.
   a. "Pay-as-you-drive" insurance would lower many drivers' insurance rates, for the less they drove, the less they would pay.
   b. Nationwide, insurance companies are charging motorists too much for too little coverage.
   c. Per-mile insurance rates would encourage motorists to drive less, reducing their chances of being an accident and decreasing congestion overall.

1. **predecessors:** ones who came before

2. **spay/neuter:** perform a surgical procedure on an animal to eliminate its ability to reproduce

* Adapted from Noble et al., *Western Civilization*, 3rd ed. Boston: Houghton Mifflin, 2002, 225.

d. Pay-as-you-drive insurance rates would ultimately reduce energy consumption and the exhaust gases that contribute to global warming.
e. People who have not received any tickets or been in any accidents usually get the best insurance rates.
f. Auto insurance regulations vary widely from state to state.*

TEST 2

Read each passage and respond to the questions that follow by circling the letter of the correct answer.

Although China continues to engage in human rights abuses, the United States goes out of its way to establish and continue trade relations with China. Is it because China has such a large population? The United States only sees dollar signs when it comes to China. That is why it makes it too hard to stand by and watch the isolationist[1] practices that the United States engages in when it comes to its relationship with its neighbor, Cuba. The United States continues its embargo, ban on travel, import, export, and immigration with this island-nation for no good reason. Not too many years ago, the United States fought a terrible and tragic war with Vietnam, and now holds hands with the same enemies it fought to oust.[2] Is Cuba any worse in its practices than China and Vietnam? I don't think so. It is time to move on, forget the past, and establish good relations with this culturally rich island of Cuba.

1. Which sentence states the main point of this paragraph?
   a. "Although China continues to engage in human rights abuses, the United States goes out of its way to establish and continue trade relations with China."
   b. "The United States only sees dollar signs when it comes to China."
   c. "It is time to move on, forget the past, and establish good relations with this culturally rich island of Cuba."
   d. "Not too many years ago, the United States fought a terrible and tragic war with Vietnam, and now holds hands with the same enemies it fought to oust."

2. Which of the following is NOT evidence given in support of the point?
   a. ". . . the United States goes out of its way to establish and continue trade relations with China."

1. **isolationist**: related to the policy of avoiding relations with other countries
2. **oust**: remove from power

* Adapted from Elisa Murray, "Driving a Hard Bargain," *Grist Magazine*, November 3, 2003, www.gristmagazine.com/soapbox/murray110303.asp.

b. "The United States continues its embargo, ban on travel, import, export, and immigration with this island-nation for no good reason."
c. "Not too many years ago, the United States fought a terrible and tragic war with Vietnam, and now holds hands with the same enemies it fought to oust."
d. "The United States only sees dollar signs when it comes to China."

3. The evidence is mostly

a. facts. b. opinions.

One reason to oppose and abolish the Olympic Games is because they were set up to foster peace and harmony, but they simply provide another arena for the continuation of violence between individuals in events and between states in the struggle for power and status. Many sports, such as boxing, archery, and the javelin, are modeled on skills for war. A number of sports involve violence themselves, including ostensibly[1] "noncontact" sports such as basketball. The intense competition and partisanship[2] linked to sports often cause spectators to become aggressive. Also, the awarding of the 1896 Games to Athens stimulated Greek nationalism,[3] leading to a war with Turkey in 1897.*

4. Which sentence states the point of this paragraph?

a. "One reason to oppose and abolish the Olympic Games is because they were set up to foster peace and harmony, but they simply provide another arena for the continuation of violence between individuals in events and between states in the struggle for power and status."
b. "Many sports, such as boxing, archery, and the javelin, are modeled on skills for war."
c. "A number of sports involve violence themselves, including ostensibly 'non-contact' sports such as basketball."
d. "Also, the awarding of the 1896 Games to Athens stimulated Greek nationalism, leading to a war with Turkey in 1897."

5. Which of the following is NOT evidence given in support of this point?

a. Many sports are modeled on skills for war.
b. The Olympic Games include noncontact sports like basketball.
c. A number of sports in the Olympic Games are violent.
d. The 1896 Olympic Games led to a war between Greece and Turkey.

1. **ostensibly:** supposedly; in appearance
2. **partisanship:** supporting one particular cause, idea, or party
3. **nationalism:** the belief that one's nation should act independently rather than in partnership with other nations

* Adapted from Brian Martin, "Ten Reasons to Oppose All Olympic Games," www.uow.edu.au/arts/sts/bmartin/pubs/96freedom.html.

9

6. The evidence is

   a. mostly facts. b. mostly opinions.

Drilling for oil is not as bad as naysayers claim. New technologies have dramatically reduced the infrastructure needed to extract oil from the ground. For instance, drilling for oil in the Arctic National Wildlife Refuge would affect only about 2,000 acres, a fraction of the more than 19 million refuge acres. Even with older technologies, though, wildlife preservation has occurred successfully side by side with petroleum extraction. In Louisiana alone, for example, there are over 1,600 oil and gas wells in areas that include fragile wetlands, home to migratory birds and other delicate animal species. Even offshore oil rigs bestride[1] America's richest marine-life zones and cause no damage to the environment.*

7. Which sentence states the point of this paragraph?

   a. "Drilling for oil is not as bad as naysayers claim."
   b. "New technologies have dramatically reduced the infrastructure needed to extract oil from the ground."
   c. "Even with older technologies, though, wildlife preservation has occurred successfully side by side with petroleum extraction."
   d. "Even offshore oil rigs bestride America's richest marine-life zones and cause no damage to the environment."

8. Which of the following is NOT evidence given in support of this point?

   a. New technologies have reduced the infrastructure needed to drill for oil.
   b. Petroleum extraction can coexist with wildlife preservation.
   c. Louisiana is home to many migratory birds and other animal species.
   d. Offshore oil rigs do not damage the environment.

9. The evidence is

   a. mostly facts. c. a blend of facts and opinions.
   b. mostly opinions.

My daughter goes to school in a wealthy school district. She started using computers at age 5 in kindergarten, and continues, at age 9, to visit the computer lab twice a week for instruction. Computers have become part of everyday life in many schools. However, it is a sad reality that while we offer money, clothing, and food to the poorest of children in many areas, we leave them behind when it comes to technology. In order to survive and thrive in today's competitive job market, all of our citizens are going to have to be proficient in computer use. But sadly, many poor children never see a com-

9

1. **bestride:** straddle; span

* Adapted from Mortimer B. Zuckerman, "Speaking Truth About Energy," *U.S. News and World Report,* February 18, 2002, 68.

puter during their academic careers and are doomed to take on menial[1] jobs that require no technological fluency.[2] It is our duty, as a citizenry, to make sure that every child, regardless of economic background, is introduced to and instructed in the use of computers. Today's managers and hirers want people who are able to work basic computer programs. This is a part of life on the job, every day. If we are able, as a country, to expose all of our children to computers, many have the opportunity to make a good living in a job market that places the utmost importance on technological knowledge.*

10. Which sentence states the point of this paragraph?
    a. "My daughter goes to school in a wealthy school district."
    b. "Computers have become part of everyday life in many schools."
    c. "However, it is a sad reality that while we offer money, clothing, and food to the poorest of children in many areas, we leave them behind when it comes to technology."
    d. "Today's managers and hirers want people who are able to work basic programs."

11. Which of the following is NOT given as evidence in support of this point?
    a. "My daughter goes to school in a wealthy school district."
    b. "Computers have become part of everyday life in many schools."
    c. "If we are able, as a country, to expose all of our children to computers, many have the opportunity to make a good living in a job market that places the utmost importance on technological knowledge."
    d. "Today's managers and hirers only want people who are able to work basic programs."

12. The evidence is
    a. facts. b. opinions. c. a blend of both.

There are practical benefits to spam, those unsolicited offers you receive in the form of e-mail messages. Spam offers great lessons in what works and what doesn't. When you spend time reviewing the pitches strangers are sending you every morning and afternoon, it becomes painfully evident why your own job applications and sales letters yield so few results. You never open an e-mail from someone you don't know? Better make more contacts. You never open an e-mail with a vague subject line? Better start making your own subject lines clearer and simpler. You never read an e-mail longer than five lines? Better learn to say clearly what you want to offer in four lines, obviously. This might strike

1. **menial:** appropriate for a servant
2. **fluency:** ability to express oneself with ease and grace

* Adapted from Robert J. Walker, "Computers Should Be Made Available to Children of Low-Income Families," *USA Today Magazine*, September 1997, 64.

some foes of spam as treasonous,[1] but have you ever stopped to consider that you might actually want some of what the spammers are pushing? In the few seconds it takes to click through and delete your daily mound of spam, there's a chance you might come across an agreeable offer. And is it just me, or are the spammers beginning to learn? I think spam is getting better. The sheer ease of sending gazillions of pitches that recipients complain about so bitterly is matched by the wondrous simplicity of the "delete" button. Spammers are becoming more sophisticated and less rude by the month, I believe. Ten years hence, when spammers have learned from the ruthless Darwinian[2] process of being clicked or filtered into oblivion, those who are left in business are going to be some of the most focused and sharp-minded salespeople the world has ever known. They'll know so much about selling things, we prospects will actually be glad to hear from them. Millions of us, not just unhinged[3] types like me. And what about beachcombing? If the Internet can be surfed, then should the surf not wash up daily detritus[4] on the cyber coast? Spam is the flotsam and jetsam[5] we find strewn on the beaches of our in boxes after the storms of the night.*

13. Which sentence states the point of this paragraph?
    a. "There are practical benefits to spam, those unsolicited offers you receive in the form of e-mail messages."
    b. "Spam offers great lessons in what works and what doesn't."
    c. "Spammers are becoming more sophisticated and less rude by the month, I believe."
    d. "Spam is the flotsam and jetsam we find strewn on the beaches of our in boxes after the storms of the night."

14. Which of the following is NOT given as evidence in support of this point?
    a. Spam can help you improve your own persuasive writing.
    b. You might find an agreeable offer in your spam.
    c. Spam is helping salespeople learn better how to sell things.
    d. The "delete" button is a marvelous invention.

15. The evidence is
    a. mostly facts.
    b. mostly opinions.
    c. a blend of facts and opinions.

1. **treasonous:** betraying, disloyal
2. **Darwinian:** related to Charles Darwin, whose theory of evolution explained that the strongest survive and prosper while the weak are eliminated
3. **unhinged:** unbalanced
4. **detritus:** debris, fragments
5. **flotsam and jetsam:** wreckage, floating debris, and cargo thrown overboard

9

* Adapted from Mark Griffith, "The Joy of Junk Mail," *Salon,* November 14, 2001, www.salon.com. Used by permission of Salon.com.

CHAPTER 10

Reading Longer Selections

GOALS FOR CHAPTER 10

- **Define the term *thesis statement*.**
- **Recognize the topic and thesis statement of longer reading selections.**
- **Define the term *headings* and explain the purpose of headings.**
- **Identify major and minor supporting details in longer reading selections.**
- **Determine implied main ideas in longer reading selections.**
- **Recognize patterns of organization in longer reading selections.**
- **Identify transitions in longer reading selections.**
- **Apply reading strategies to longer passages.**
- **Explain the difference between skimming and scanning, and scan a text for information.**

Now that you've practiced improving your comprehension of paragraphs and short passages, you're ready to move on to reading longer passages. To see how well you already comprehend longer selections, complete the following test.

TEST YOURSELF

As you continue in your academic career, you will be asked to read longer and more challenging selections, many of which will come from textbooks. Read the following selection from a college textbook. Take some time to complete this test and warm up for the longer, more challenging readings you will encounter in the rest of this chapter. If you come across any difficult or unfamiliar words, consult your dictionary.

Situational Communication Anxiety

1 Many of us experience communication anxiety in certain situations, such as admitting to a touchy roommate that we forgot to mail the letters he or she asked us to mail, telling a spouse about a shopping spree, alerting a boss to a major mistake we have made, and so forth. In fact, some of us tend to experience communication anxiety fairly consistently in certain recurring situations—asking someone for a date, being called on in class, being interviewed for a job, and so forth.

2 **Situational communication anxiety** (anxiety tied to the situation) occurs because of certain features of the situation, of course. For example, we are especially likely to experience communication anxiety in *novel* situations—situations we're not used to. If you have never before been called as a witness in a court case, for example, it would not be unusual for you to experience at least some anxiety when you are called.

3 Anxiety is also tied to situations that seem to involve *scrutiny* and *evaluation.* Most of us don't like the feeling of being put under a microscope by others, and most of us become anxious at the idea of being evaluated by others. Being called on to work a physics problem on the blackboard and then explain it to the class would induce at least some anxiety in most of us, for example.

4 Anxiety is also common in situations that allow for only *complete success or failure.* Perhaps this is why asking someone for a date is anxiety inducing for some people. It may also explain the anxiety sometimes experienced during those door-to-door sales you may have had to do to raise money for school organizations. There is a clear success/failure indicator in these and similar situations, and the outcome is uncertain.

5 Situations of excessive *formality* are often anxiety inducing as well, partly because we have a sense that we are supposed to play by rules of which we are not fully aware. This is one reason that job interviews are anxiety inducing, for example (not to mention the scrutiny and success/failure dimensions). There is a sense that the interview is supposed to proceed according to the interviewer's unstated rules rather than according to the familiar rules of ordinary conversation.

6 A sense of *incompetence* in a given situation will also induce anxiety in some individuals. For example, some people will experience communication anxiety if a conversation about movies turns to the topic of foreign films and they know nothing about foreign films, or a conversation about sports turns to cricket and they know nothing about cricket.

7 Thus, because of certain features of specific situations, most of us will experience at least a bit of communication anxiety from time to time. Whether this is a good thing or a bad thing depends upon how the anxiety affects the communication event. Suppose, for example, that Al has so much anxiety

about a job interview that he decides not to go; Beth has considerable anxiety, handles it badly, and blows the interview; Chris has just as much anxiety but handles it well and lands the job; Dale has almost no anxiety but respects the situation and lands the job; and Earl, with no anxiety whatsoever, is so oblivious to the demands of the situation that he blows the interview. Assuming that all were equally qualified, anxiety had costs for Al and Beth but not for Chris. And the absence of anxiety had costs for Earl but not for Dale.

8 In short, situational communication anxiety is common. It is not necessarily a bad thing, and in fact may be a good thing, as long as it does not severely disrupt our communication efforts. For those who consider their situational anxiety to be so frequent or so severe that they want to do something about it, the most direct solution is usually to identify the situational *feature* responsible for the anxiety, and then deal with the feature. For novel situations, gain experience so that the situation is no longer novel; for formal situations, become familiar with the new rules; for success/failure situations, come to accept and learn from an occasional failure; for incompetence situations, either develop competence or learn to deemphasize the ego; and for scrutiny and evaluation situations, learn how the sense of scrutiny and evaluation is often exaggerated.*

1. What is the topic of this selection?
   a. communication
   b. anxiety
   c. situational communication anxiety
   d. incompetence

2. Which of the following sentences states the thesis of this selection?
   a. "In fact, some of us tend to experience communication anxiety fairly consistently in certain recurring situations—asking someone for a date, being called on in class, being interviewed for a job, and so forth." (paragraph 1)
   b. "Anxiety is also tied to situations that seem to involve scrutiny and evaluation." (paragraph 3)
   c. "Being called on to work a physics problem on the blackboard and then explain it to the class would induce at least some anxiety in most of us, for example." (paragraph 3)
   d. "For those who consider their situational anxiety to be so frequent or so severe that they want to do something about it, the most direct solution is usually to identify the situational *feature* responsible for the anxiety, and then deal with the feature." (paragraph 8)

* Adapted from Suzanne Osborn and Michael T. Motley, *Improving Communication*. Boston: Houghton Mifflin, 1999, 101–102. Copyright ©1999 by Houghton Mifflin Company. Used with permission.

3. Which of the following is a *major* supporting detail from the selection?
   a. "In fact, some of us tend to experience communication anxiety fairly consistently in certain recurring situations—asking someone for a date, being called on in class, being interviewed for a job, and so forth." (paragraph 1)
   b. "A sense of *incompetence* in a given situation will also induce anxiety in some individuals." (paragraph 6)
   c. "For example, some people will experience communication anxiety if a conversation about movies turns to the topic of foreign films and they know nothing about foreign films, or a conversation about sports turns to cricket and they know nothing about cricket." (paragraph 6)
   d. "If you have never before been called as a witness in a court case, for example, it would not be unusual for you to experience at least some anxiety when you are called." (paragraph 2)
4. Which of the following is a *minor* supporting detail from the selection?
   a. "In fact, some of us tend to experience communication anxiety fairly consistently in certain recurring situations—asking someone for a date, being called on in class, being interviewed for a job, and so forth." (paragraph 1)
   b. "Situations of excessive *formality* are often anxiety inducing as well, partly because we have a sense that we are supposed to play by rules of which we are not fully aware." (paragraph 5)
   c. "Anxiety is also common in situations that allow for only *complete success or failure.*" (paragraph 4)
   d. "For example, some people will experience communication anxiety if a conversation about movies turns to the topic of foreign films and they know nothing about foreign films, or a conversation about sports turns to cricket and they know nothing about cricket." (paragraph 6)
5. What pattern organizes the details in paragraphs 2–6?
   a. comparison/contrast
   b. time order
   c. series
   d. cause/effect
6. What pattern is indicated by the transition that begins paragraph 7?
   a. comparison/contrast
   b. time order
   c. series
   d. cause/effect
7. What is the tone of this selection?
   a. annoyed
   b. serious
   c. amused
   d. sarcastic

So far, this book has focused mainly on helping you improve your reading comprehension by increasing your awareness and understanding of important features in *paragraphs*. But what about longer selections, those that are composed of multiple paragraphs? You may be wondering if you'll have to learn a whole new set of concepts in order to understand long selections such as chapters or articles. Fortunately, the answer is no. Many of the same principles apply to reading longer passages. This chapter, therefore, will focus on applying the information you've already learned in previous chapters to help you get more out of a reading composed of more than one paragraph.

Topic, Main Idea, and Thesis

In Chapter 2 of this book, you learned about topics, main ideas, and topic sentences. Like paragraphs, longer reading selections contain all three of these elements. A longer selection such as an essay or an article will be about a topic, and it will make a point about that topic just as a paragraph's topic sentence states the main idea.

However, in a longer reading selection, the main point is usually referred to as a *thesis*. The **thesis** is the one idea or opinion the author wants readers to know or to believe after they have read the piece. Just like the paragraph's topic sentence, the thesis includes the subject plus what is being said about that subject. You'll notice when you read the following thesis statements that they sound a lot like topic sentences.

> The restaurant was invented in Paris in the twenty-five-year period right before the French Revolution.
>
> Political analysts Cokie and Steve Roberts have defined the American spirit as a combination of six essential traits: diversity, tolerance, resilience, ingenuity, patriotism, and faith.
>
> Some of the greatest inventions in the world were made by the Chinese.

Rather than being developed in one paragraph, however, a thesis statement generally presents an idea that needs several paragraphs of explanation. It is often a point that is broader than one you would see in a topic sentence. That is why it takes longer to explain.

The thesis statement almost always appears near the beginning of the selection, most often in the opening paragraph. It is the main idea that will be developed throughout the rest of the piece. It may be useful here to recall what you learned about the terms *general* and *specific*. These concepts apply to longer readings, too. Just as paragraphs include a general topic and a specific point about that topic, longer selections also focus on one particular idea about a broader subject.

To find the thesis statement, determine first what the subject is. What does the opening paragraph seem to be about? Then look for a sentence that includes both this topic and a particular point about that topic.

A longer selection will still include topic sentences, too. Each paragraph will present a particular idea, just like those you studied in Chapter 2, and many of these paragraphs will state the point in a topic sentence that appears at the beginning, in the middle, or at the end of the paragraph. The major difference, however, is that these paragraphs do not stand alone; instead, they are smaller units within a larger whole.

For an illustration of how a longer selection includes a topic, a thesis statement, and topic sentences, read the following passage.

TOPIC
THESIS

> My research suggests three basic guidelines for greeting and departure touches in developing relationships. First, acquaintances and friends who are not yet close generally limit their touches in terms of the body regions involved. That is, they almost always restrict their initiation of contact to what I call "nonvulnerable body parts"—the arm, elbow, or shoulder. The other areas of the body, which I call "vulnerable body parts," are touched almost exclusively by persons who are close family members, romantic partners, and close friends—although many of the touches with these persons are also directed to nonvulnerable body zones. What is more, persons who are not close seldom touch both sides of the body in greetings or departures. A two-handed touch to both arms or both shoulders is a much more intimate touch than a contact to only one arm or shoulder. It might seem that the hand would be a safe place to touch, but actually, a casual touch on the hand of another often has intimate connotations[1] and may be seen as flirtatious.[2] The one exception, of course, if the formal handshake. This gesture is actually a very cautious symbol of trust. Some people have speculated that it originally represented an attempt to show that neither person had a weapon. (If this is accurate, it is not surprising that until very recently the handshake has been used predominantly among men.)

TOPIC SENTENCE

> The second guideline of ritualistic greeting and departure touches is that they should be brief. Generally, people who have initiated a touch take their hand away as soon as they have said, "Hi, how are you?" or "Nice talking to you; see you later." When a touch lasts for even a few seconds beyond the initial greeting or the final departure phases, it will often be misinterpreted, unless the people are close. This is true even for the handshake. Although some Latin Americans prolong handshaking

1. **connotations:** suggestions, associations
2. **flirtatious:** communicating romantic or sexual interest

for five or more seconds, persons from the United States are flustered by this gesture and wonder what the other person is trying to communicate. Similarly, a prolonged touch to the arm or shoulder during greetings or departures may suggest aggressiveness or excessive warmth, and a long touch to the hand is likely to have a sexual connotation, regardless of the sex of the persons involved. Hand holding is rather strictly limited to close relationships between the opposite sexes, or between children and their parents or caretakers.

A third guideline is that it is usually best to start with greeting touches in these brief, nonintrusive contacts. Ritual departure touches are more rare among acquaintances than among friends (except for the obligatory[1] handshake at the end of a business interaction) and suggest that the relationship has progressed to a level of somewhat greater involvement.* TOPIC SENTENCE

Applying the Active Reading Strategy

In Chapter 1 of this book, you learned about active reading, a strategy of marking a text so that you will understand and retain the information better. As you recall, active reading includes underlining, highlighting, circling or boxing key words or phrases in a text. It can also include making notes in the margins of the text. If you were to actively read the passage about touching, it might look like this.

My research suggests three basic guidelines for greeting and departure touches in developing relationships. First, acquaintances and friends who are not yet close generally limit their touches in terms of the body regions involved. That is, they almost always restrict their initiation of contact to what I call "nonvulnerable body parts"—the arm, elbow, or shoulder. The other areas of the body, which I call "vulnerable body parts," are touched almost exclusively by persons who are close family members, romantic partners, and close friends—although many of the touches with these persons are also directed to nonvulnerable body zones. What is more, persons who are not close seldom touch both sides of the body in greetings or departures. A two-handed touch to both arms or

3 guidelines for greeting/departure touching

1 Limited to certain body regions

not close → "non-vulnerable" parts

close → "vulnerable" parts

intimate touching:
– both sides of body
– two-handed touch
– touch on the hand

Continued

1. **obligatory:** required, expected

* From Martin S. Remland, *Nonverbal Communication in Everyday Life*. Boston: Houghton Mifflin, 2000, 252–253. Copyright © 2000 by Houghton Mifflin Company. Reprinted with permission.

both shoulders is a much more intimate touch than a contact to only one arm or shoulder. It might seem that the hand would be a safe place to touch, but actually, a casual touch on the hand of another often has intimate connotations and may be seen as flirtatious. The one exception, of course, is the formal handshake. This gesture is actually a very cautious symbol of trust. Some people have speculated that it originally represented an attempt to show that neither person had a weapon. (If this is accurate, it is not surprising that until very recently the handshake has been used predominantly among men.)

handshake: symbol of trust

2 Brief

The second guideline of ritualistic greeting and departure touches is that they should be brief. Generally, people who have initiated a touch take their hand away as soon as they have said, "Hi, how are you?" or "Nice talking to you; see you later." When a touch lasts for even a few seconds beyond the initial greeting or the final departure phases, it will often be misinterpreted, unless the people are close. This is true even for the handshake. Although some Latin Americans prolong handshaking for five or more seconds, persons from the United States are flustered by this gesture and wonder what the other person is trying to communicate. Similarly, a prolonged touch to the arm or shoulder during greetings or departures may suggest aggressiveness or excessive warmth, and a long touch to the hand is likely to have a sexual connotation, regardless of the sex of the persons involved. Hand holding is rather strictly limited to close relationships between the opposite sexes, or between children and their parents or caretakers.

Prolonged touch suggests
– aggressiveness
– excessive warmth
– sexual message

3 Greeting touches common; departure touches only between friends

A third guideline is that it is usually best to start with greeting touches in these brief, nonintrusive contacts. Ritual departure touches are more rare among acquaintances than among friends (except for the obligatory handshake at the end of a business interaction) and suggest that the relationship has progressed to a level of somewhat greater involvement.

In longer selections, sections of the text will often be labeled with headings. **Headings** are like mini-titles that identify the topic of one part of a longer work like a chapter or an article. They help the reader understand the focus of a particular section of text, and they also reveal how various sections are related to each other. Look at the following example.

Emotional Styles

A good starting point for achieving emotional control is to examine your emotional style. How do you deal with emotions? Your style started taking shape before birth and evolved over a period of many years. As an adult, you are likely to display one of four different emotional styles when confronted with strong emotions.

Suppressing Your Emotions
Many people have learned to suppress their feelings as much as possible. Some have developed intellectual strategies that enable them to avoid dealing directly with emotional reactions to a situation. In response to the loss of a loved one, a person may avoid the experience of grief and mourning by taking on new responsibilities at work. This is not, of course, a healthy way to deal with grief. Some people become upset but keep their anger bottled up inside. Controlling your anger does not mean ignoring injustices by others. The inability to express emotions has been linked to a number of mental and physical health problems. Research indicates that migraine headaches and back pain can sometimes be traced to suppressed emotions. Some heart attack patients are victims of their inhibited anger. They have blocked the feeling of anger and avoided the expression of this emotion toward the person or situation that provoked the feeling.

Capitulating[1] to Your Emotions
People who display this emotional style see themselves as the helpless victims of feelings over which they have no control. By responding to emotion in this manner, one can assign responsibility for the "problem" to external causes, such as other people or unavoidable events. For example, Paula, a busy office manager, is frustrated because her brother-in-law and his wife frequently show up unannounced on weekends and expect a big meal. Paula has a tight schedule during the week, and she looks forward to quiet weekends with her family. She has never expressed her anger to anyone because the uninvited guests are, after all, "family." People who capitulate to

1. **Capitulating:** surrendering

their emotions often experience feelings of helplessness and simply suffer in silence.

Overexpressing Your Emotions

In a work setting, everyone needs to be seen as a responsible and predictable person. Angry outbursts can damage credibility. One of the quickest ways to lose the respect and confidence of the people you work with is to display a lack of emotional control. Foul and vulgar language in conjunction with an angry outburst can seriously damage a person's image.

One acceptable way to release anger is to sit down with pen and paper and write a letter to the person who triggered your wrath. Don't worry about grammar, spelling, or punctuation—just put all your angry thoughts on paper. Write until you have nothing more to say. Then destroy the letter. Once you let go of your fury, you will be ready to deal constructively with whatever caused you to become upset.

Accommodating Your Emotions

An emotion can be thought of as a feeling that influences our thinking and behavior. Accommodation means you are willing to recognize, accept, and experience emotions and to attempt to react in ways appropriate to the situation. This style achieves an integration of one's feelings and the thinking process. People who display the accommodation style have adopted the "think before you act" point of view. Let's assume that as you are presenting a new project proposal at a staff meeting, someone interrupts you and strongly criticizes your ideas. The criticism seems to be directed more at you than at your proposal. Anger starts building inside you, but before responding to the assailant, you pause and engage in some rational thinking. During the few seconds of silence, you quickly make a mental review of the merits of your proposal and consider the other person's motives for making a personal attack. You decide the person's comments do not warrant a response at this point. Then you continue with your presentation, without a hint of frustration in your voice. If your proposal has merit, the other members of the group will probably speak on your behalf.

Do we always rely on just one of the four emotional styles? Of course not. Your response to news that a coworker was killed in an auto accident may be very different from your response to a demeaning comment made by your boss. You may have found appropriate ways to deal with your grief but have not yet learned to avoid lashing out at persons who trigger your anger. Dealing with our emotions is a very complex process. Selecting the most appropriate response can be very challenging.*

The passage above is just one section of a longer textbook chapter called "Achieving Emotional Balance in a Chaotic World." The topic of this one particular section is identified in the heading "Emotional Styles." Then, this section is subdivided into four smaller sections with subheadings that reveal the topic of each one.

Exercise 10.1

Read the selection below and then respond to the questions that follow by circling the letter of the correct answer.

Bigger Muscles, Bigger Problems

1 Anabolic steroids can cause a panoply[1] of side effects, both physical and psychological. Their adverse effects can appear soon after you begin to take them, or they may be delayed.

2 Although this toxicity[2] can affect any organ system, it's the androgenic[3] aspects that are the most apparent and important for long-term abusers of steroids. Oddly, men may become more like women and vice versa. Here's why it happens: When a man takes large amounts of testosterone or anabolic steroids for a prolonged period, some is converted into female hormone (estrogen). This is in addition to the small amounts of estrogen normally present (each of the sexes has some of the other's hormones). While you're taking steroid supplements, your testes—which normally make testosterone—become lazy and quit. After all, why should they bother to produce the hormone when you're doing the job for them with your pills and injections? So these now-dormant glands shrink and eventually lose their ability to make the male hormone. Sperm count is reduced, and you can become infertile. Then, when you quit providing the outside source and have to depend on your own pro-

1. **panoply:** wide variety
2. **toxicity:** poisonousness
3. **androgenic:** related to hormones that develop and maintain masculine characteristics

* Adapted from Reece and Brandt, *Effective Human Relations in Organizations*, 7th ed. Boston: Houghton Mifflin, 1999, 238–240.

duction of testosterone, your body isn't making it. So what you have on board is mostly estrogen. The male would-be bodybuilder or athlete may then develop enlarged breasts (gynecomastia), female distribution of fatty deposits, and soft muscles. Gynecomastia is permanent; other changes may not be.

3 In women, the net increase of testosterone from anabolic steroids can result in masculinization by suppressing estrogen production. This means excessive growth of body hair in the wrong places, loss of hair (alopecia) and menstrual abnormalities. Fortunately, many of these complications are reversible over time.

4 Adolescents who use steroids (many of them 10th- to 12th-graders) have problems of their own. These include premature closure of the growth centers in their bones, leaving them shorter than their peers. That's bad enough, but the major problems these kids have are behavioral. Some become bipolar[1] or depressed, aggressive and addicted to steroids in much the same way they can get hooked on amphetamines (speed). What's more, injecting steroids with shared needles also risks exposure to HIV-AIDS or hepatitis.

5 There is no proof that anabolic steroids really enhance agility, skill, cardiovascular capacity or overall athletic performance. But most athletes and their trainers think they do significantly increase muscle mass, strength and endurance. If that's true, how can you compare performances among athletes? How can you tell when a world record set by an "abstainer" has been broken by a "steroid junkie"? That's why the International Olympic Committee has banned the use of more than 40 anabolic steroids.

6 Even though some men and women do tolerate steroids, and some toxicity is reversible, overall the benefits are not worth the risk, in my opinion. There's enough illness in the world without looking for more trouble. These drugs can ruin you *and* the sport in which you are trying to excel.*

1. What is the topic of this entire selection?

   a. hormones
   b. sports medicine
   c. anabolic steroids
   d. testosterone

2. Which of the following sentences states the thesis of this selection?

   a. "Anabolic steroids can cause a panoply of side effects, both physical and psychological."
   b. "Their adverse effects can appear soon after you begin to take them, or they may be delayed."

1. **bipolar:** a disorder marked by episodes of mania and depression

* From Dr. Isadore Rosenfeld, "Bigger Muscles, Bigger Problems," *Parade*, April 4, 2004, 20–22. Reprinted with permission from *Parade* and Dr. Isadore Rosenfeld, copyright © 2004.

c. "Adolescents who use steroids have problems of their own."
d. "There is no proof that anabolic steroids really enhance agility, skill, cardiovascular capacity or overall athletic performance."

3. Which of the following statements functions as a topic sentence in this selection?
   a. "Their adverse effects can appear soon after you begin to take them, or they may be delayed." (paragraph 1)
   b. "Adolescents who use steroids (many of them 10th- to 12th-graders) have problems of their own." (paragraph 4)
   c. "But most athletes and their trainers think they do significantly increase muscle mass, strength and endurance." (paragraph 5)
   d. "There's enough illness in the world without looking for more trouble." (paragraph 6)

4. Look at paragraph 4 and apply the active reading strategy. Which of the phrases below would you underline or highlight? Circle all that apply.
   a. Adolescents who use steroids
   b. many of them 10th to 12th graders
   c. problems
   d. premature closure of the growth centers
   e. leaving them
   f. That's bad enough
   g. bipolar or depressed, aggressive and addicted
   h. amphetamines (speed)
   i. exposure to HIV-AIDS or hepatitis

Supporting Details

Longer reading selections also contain both major and minor supporting details, just as paragraphs do. The diagram below summarizes how the parts of a paragraph correspond to those of many longer selections. Each box represents a different paragraph.

In other words, a longer selection spreads the major supporting details over several paragraphs. Each of these major details is the topic of a separate paragraph, and each is developed with the examples, anecdotes, explanations, or other information that functions as minor details. Here is an example of a longer selection that labels the major and minor details.

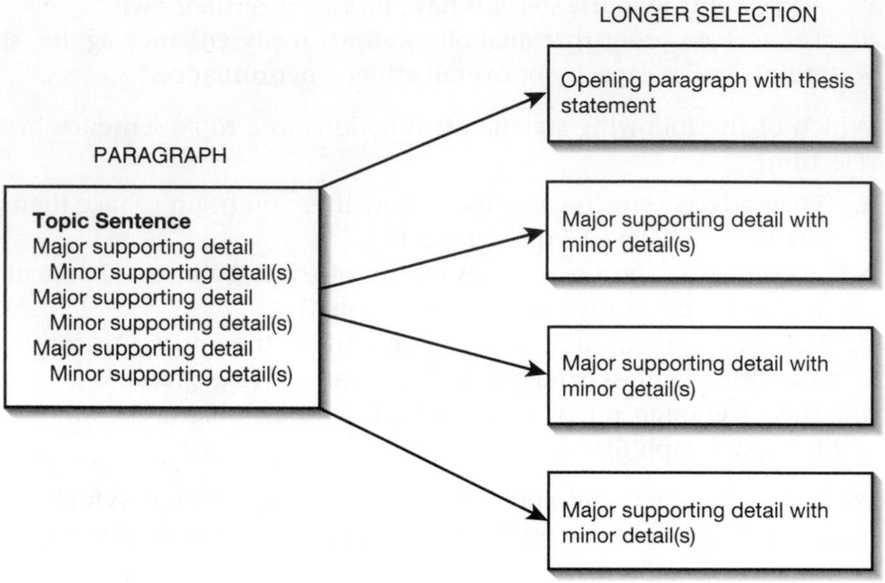

Patterns of Speaking

People often make judgments about others based on their speech patterns. If you slur your words, mispronounce familiar words, or speak with a dialect that sounds unfamiliar to your audience, you may be seen as uneducated or socially inept.[1] When you sound "odd" to your listeners, their attention will be distracted from what you are saying to the way you are saying it. In this section we cover articulation, enunciation, pronunciation, and dialect as they contribute to or detract from speaking effectiveness. *THESIS*

MAJOR DETAIL **Articulation.** Articulation refers to the way you produce individual speech sounds. Some people have trouble making certain sounds. For example, they may substitute a *d* for a *th*, saying "dem" instead of "them." Other sounds that are often misarticulated include *s*, *l*, and *r*. *Minor details* Severe articulation problems can interfere with effective communication, especially if the audience cannot understand the speaker or the variations suggest low social or educational status. Such problems are best treated by a speech pathologist, who retrains the individual to produce the sound in a more acceptable manner.

MAJOR DETAIL **Enunciation.** Enunciation refers to the way you pronounce words in context. In casual conversation it is not unusual for people to slur their words—for example, saying "gimme" for "give me." However, careless enunciation causes credibility problems for public speakers. Do you

1. **inept:** foolish, incompetent

say "Swatuh thought" for "That's what I thought"; "Harya?" for "How are you?", or "Howjado?" for "How do you do?" These lazy enunciation patterns are not acceptable in public speaking. Check your enunciation patterns on the tape recordings you have made to determine if you have such a problem. If you do, concentrate on careful enunciation as you practice your speech. Be careful, however, to avoid the opposite problem of inflated, pompous,[1] and pretentious[2] enunciation. Very few speakers can make this work without sounding phony. You should strive to be neither sloppy nor overly precise. Minor details

Pronunciation. Pronunciation involves saying words correctly. It includes both the use of the correct sounds and the proper accent on syllables. Because written English does not always indicate the correct pronunciation, we may not be sure how to pronounce words that we first encounter in print. For instance, does the word *chiropodist* begin with an *sh*, a *ch*, or a *k* sound? MAJOR DETAIL Minor details

In addition to problems pronouncing unfamiliar words, you may find that there are certain words you habitually mispronounce. For example, how do you pronounce the following words?

government *library*
February *picture*
ask *secretary*
nuclear *just*
athlete *get*

Unless you are careful, you may find yourself slipping into these common mispronunciations: Minor details

goverment *liberry*
Febuary *pitchur*
aks *sekaterry*
nuculer *jist*
athalete *git*

Mispronunciation of such common words can damage your ethos.[3] Most of us know what words we chronically mispronounce and are able to pronounce them correctly when we think about it. The time to think about it is when you are practicing and presenting your speech.

1. **pompous:** having a high opinion of oneself
2. **pretentious:** claiming a high position or status; showing off
3. **ethos:** character

MAJOR DETAIL

Dialect. A dialect is a speech pattern typical of a geographic region or ethnic region. Your dialect usually reflects where you were raised or lived for any length of time or your cultural and ethnic identity. In the United States there are three commonly recognized dialects: eastern, southern, and midwestern. Additionally, there are local variations within the broader dialects. For example, in South Carolina one finds the Gullah dialect from the islands off the coast, the Lowcountry or Charlestonian accent, the Piedmont variation, and the Appalachian twang. And then there's always "*Bah-stahn*" where you buy a "*lodge budded pup con*" at the movies!

Minor details

Minor details

There is no such thing in nature as a superior or inferior dialect. However, there can be occasions when a distinct dialect is a definite disadvantage or advantage. Listeners prefer speech patterns that are familiar to their ears. Audiences may also have stereotyped preconceptions about people who speak with certain dialect patterns. For example, those raised in the South often associate a northeastern dialect with brusqueness[1] and abrasiveness, and midwesterners may associate a southern dialect with slowness of action and mind. You may have to work to overcome these prejudices against your dialect.*

In this selection, four of the topic sentences announce major supporting details, the four different speech patterns mentioned in the thesis statement. Then each major detail is developed with one or more paragraphs of minor details.

Applying the Taking Notes Reading Strategy

In Chapter 6 of this book, you practiced taking notes, an important skill for success in college. As you learned earlier, notes can take the form of lists of main ideas or an outline. If you were to use the outline note taking strategy for the passage about speech patterns, the result might look like this:

I. Four Patterns of Speaking
   A. Articulation (pronunciation of speech sounds)
      1. Problems can interfere with communication
      2. Problems best treated by a speech pathologist

1. **brusqueness:** abruptness, bluntness

* Adapted from Osborn and Osborn, *Public Speaking*, 4th ed. Boston: Houghton Mifflin, 1997, 364–366.

B. Enunciation (way words are pronounced in context)
 1. Conversational slurring inappropriate for public speaking
 2. Check enunciation by tape recording your speech
 3. Avoid overly precise enunciation, too

C. Pronunciation (saying words correctly)
 1. Unfamiliar words
 2. Familiar words

D. Dialect (pattern typical of geographical region or ethnic group)
 1. Eastern, southern, midwestern
 2. Stereotypes and prejudices

Exercise 10.2

Read the selection below and respond to the questions that follow by circling the letter of the correct answer.

Group Development

1 Most theories and models of group development agree that groups pass through various stages as they develop. One model that many group researchers endorse is the five-stage version proposed by Bruce Tuckman in the 1960s. We'll examine this model in detail because it provides a solid general view of group development.

2 Tuckman believed that groups develop while passing through five stages over time. In the first stage, groups go through an orientation period that Tuckman referred to as *forming*; group members spend time getting to know each other. At this point their interactions are rather polite, tentative[1] and exploratory as members tactfully try to gain some understanding of one another. In some cases the interactions may even be guarded, especially among members who aren't initially comfortable revealing information about themselves. However, as members become more comfortable in the latter part of the forming stage, the interactions become less superficial. This is followed by a period of conflict called the *storming* stage, in which group members have moved beyond polite conversation and actually begin disagreeing with each other, questioning each other's ideas and beliefs, and openly revealing who they are. This second stage results in tension and stress within the group and can also lead to the formation of coalitions—small cohesive groups—within the larger group. The conflict that occurs at this time is actually necessary to the cohesion of the group. Groups that never experience conflict probably consist of members who are uninterested and uninvolved.

1. **tentative:** uncertain, hesitant

3 In the third stage, a structure-building stage that Tuckman referred to as *norming*, group members become more cohesive and establish unity among themselves. Trust increases, roles are defined, norms develop, and the group members become more "tightly knit" as they begin to understand what their roles; goals, and procedures are. In short, the group members become more organized and resolve many of their early conflicts about goals, roles, and authority. During the fourth stage, members are focused on productivity or *performing*. It typically takes a while before a group is productive; after the members have a better feel for each other, have formed some bonds, and have developed a sense of organizational structure, performance can follow. Of course, some groups never make it to this stage; having stagnated[1] at the norming stage, they fail to reach their potential in terms of productivity. Examples of unproductive groups can be found in numerous studies of combat groups, civic groups, and personal-growth groups. On the other hand, we have all experienced groups that were truly productive and reached the performing stage. It is exhilarating, indeed, to be part of a group that grows and matures into a productive arm of society, whether at work, church, home, or school.

4 The final stage involves the dissolution[2] of the group, or what Tuckman called *adjourning*. This stage can be planned for, as when a work group charged with a particular project dissolves because the project is finished or when a student group breaks up because the class is over and there is no other reason for the group to exist. Sometimes, however, groups dissolve due to lack of performance, lack of funding, or group members' dissatisfaction. The organization itself may decide that a particular group is no longer successful or useful and reassign its members to other projects and perhaps other groups. At other times, work groups are dissolved for financial reasons, as when group members are laid off or asked to take on more work that necessitates their being pulled out of the group. Indeed, the adjournment of work groups can be quite stressful, regardless of the reason for the dissolution. If a group has successfully completed an important project and then faces dissolution, its members may well experience stress as well as distress, unhappiness, and a void that needs to be filled. After all, people take great pride in their successful endeavors, and when the group they were so successful in is disbanded, they may have a difficult time adjusting. Of course, when a group is adjourned due to lack of performance or some other unexpected reason, this, too, can be quite stressful, leaving members feeling that they have failed or weren't given a fair opportunity. In such circumstances they may blame management or even turn on other group members.*

1. **stagnated:** stopped developing 2. **dissolution:** breaking up

* Adapted from Paul E. Levy, *Industrial/Organizational Psychology*. Boston: Houghton Mifflin, 2003, 355–357. Copyright © 2003 by Houghton Mifflin Company. Reprinted with permission.

1. Which of the following sentences states the thesis of the selection?
   a. "Most theories and models of group development agree that groups pass through various stages as they develop." (paragraph 1)
   b. "Tuckman believed that groups develop while passing through five stages over time." (paragraph 2)
   c. "In the third stage, a structure-building stage that Tuckman referred to as *norming*, group members become more cohesive and establish unity among themselves." (paragraph 3)
   d. "The final stage involves the dissolution of the group, or what Tuckman called *adjourning*." (paragraph 4)

2. Which of the following is a *major* supporting detail?
   a. "Most theories and models of group development agree that groups pass through various stages as they develop." (paragraph 1)
   b. "Tuckman believed that groups develop while passing through five stages over time." (paragraph 2)
   c. "In the third stage, a structure-building stage that Tuckman referred to as *norming*, group members become more cohesive and establish unity among themselves." (paragraph 3)
   d. "Trust increases, roles are defined, norms develop, and the group members become more "tightly knit" as they begin to understand what their roles, goals, and procedures are." (paragraph 3)

3. Which of the following is a *minor* supporting detail?
   a. "Most theories and models of group development agree that groups pass through various stages as they develop." (paragraph 1)
   b. "In the first stage, groups go through an orientation period that Tuckman referred to as *forming*: group member spend time getting to know each other." (paragraph 2)
   c. "The final stage involves the dissolution of the group, or what Tuckman called *adjourning*." (paragraph 4)
   d. "Indeed, the adjournment of work groups can be quite stressful, regardless of the reason for the dissolution." (paragraph 4)

4. Apply the note taking strategy to this passage and create a brief outline of Tuckman's model of group development.

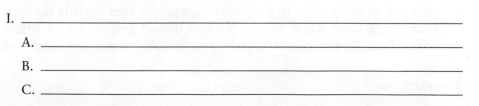

   I. ______________________________
      A. ______________________________
      B. ______________________________
      C. ______________________________

D. ______________________________

E. ______________________________

Implied Main Ideas

In Chapter 4 of this book, you learned to determine the main idea of a paragraph when it is not actually stated. Longer selections, too, will occasionally ask you to infer the author's overall point. You do this using the same procedure you used for paragraphs; however, you make adjustments for the multiple paragraphs. Instead of examining the topic of each sentence, for instance, you study the topic and point of each *topic sentence* and then add up those details to draw your conclusion. For example, read the following passage:

A Trip to India for the Pillsbury Doughboy

The Pillsbury Doughboy has landed in India to pitch a product that he had just about abandoned in America: plain old flour.

Pillsbury, the Diageo PLC unit behind the pudgy[1] character, has a raft of higher-margin products such as microwave pizzas in other parts of the world but discovered that in this tradition-bound market, it needs to push the basics.

Even so, selling packaged flour in India is almost revolutionary, because most Indian housewives still buy raw wheat in bulk, clean it by hand, store it in huge metal hampers, and every week carry some to a neighborhood mill, or *chakki*, where it is ground between two stones.

To help reach those housewives, the Doughboy himself has gotten a makeover. In TV spots, he presses his palms together and bows in the traditional Indian greeting. He speaks six regional languages.

Pillsbury is onto a potentially huge business. India consumes about 69 million tons of wheat a year, second only to China. (The United States consumes about 26 million tons.) Much of India's wheat ends up as *roti*, a flat bread prepared on a griddle that accompanies almost every meal. In a nation where people traditionally eat with their hands, roti is the spoon. But less than 1 percent of all whole wheat flour, or *atta*, is sold prepackaged. India's climatic extremes and

1. **pudgy:** chubby

deplorable[1] roads make it difficult to maintain freshness from mill to warehouse, let alone on store shelves.

Then there are the standards of the Indian housewife, who is determined to serve only the softest, freshest roti to her family. "Packaged flour sticks to your stomach and is bad for the intestines," says Poonam Jain, a New Delhi housewife.

Pillsbury knows that ultimately it won't make fistfuls of dough from packaged flour. Its aim is to establish its flour business and then introduce new products to carry its customers up to more lucrative products.

That payoff may take a decade or two. "As a food company, we have to be where the mouths are," says Robert Hancock, marketing director for Europe and Eurasia. "We'll get our rewards later."

Starting a flour operation meant turning back the clock for Pillsbury. Though it was born as a U.S. flour-milling company 130 years ago, the Diageo unit all but exited from that business in the early 1990s to focus on products such as frozen baked goods and ice cream. The food giant thought of introducing high-value products when it first explored India. But it quickly learned that most Indians don't have enough disposable income for such fare. Many lack refrigerators and ovens, too.

Pillsbury is betting that flour will generate sales volumes to compensate for the razor-thin profit margins. "We wanted a product with huge and widespread mainstream appeal," Mr. Hancock says.

Pitching packaged flour meant overcoming thousands of years of tradition. "I'd never met women so intimately involved with the food they prepare," recalls Bill Barrier, who led a Pillsbury team that spent 18 months trying to decode Indian wheat and consumers.

Marketing managers climbed into the attics where housewives store their wheat and accompanied them to their tiny neighborhood flour mills. "Anywhere else, flour is flour," says Samir Behl, vice president of marketing for Pillsbury International. "In India, the color, aroma, feel between the fingers, and mouth feel are all crucial."

Pillsbury had hoped to establish contracts with existing mills, but inspectors found hygiene and safety at some to be appalling. Pillsbury scouts visited forty plants, where they encountered mice, rotting wheat, and treacherous machinery. They often left coated in fine flour dust, whose presence is a severe fire hazard. In fact, when the electricity went out during a visit to one mill, Pillsbury executives were dumbfounded to see one worker light a match in the dark.

1. **deplorable:** terrible

Pillsbury eventually found two mills capable of the required standards. But even then, their rollout was delayed by several months because the company rejected 40 percent of the wheat delivered to the mills after the 1998 harvest.

Many focus groups and lab tests later, Pillsbury came up with its packaged wheat blend, Pillsbury Chakki Fresh Atta. Godrej-Pillsbury Ltd., its joint venture here, launched the flour in southern and western India last year. The blue package, which features the Doughboy hoisting a roti, has become the market leader in Bombay, India's largest city. . . .*

This selection never actually states a thesis. Instead, it asks the reader to infer that a company can successfully overcome a number of obstacles to introduce a product into a new market if it takes the time to learn that market and understand the potential new customers' needs and desires. You arrive at that conclusion by considering the details of this story. First, the passage describes the obstacles to selling flour in India, including India's traditions and standards. Then, it explains how Pillsbury tackled those problems. Finally, it mentions that Pillsbury flour now leads the market in Bombay. Therefore, you can conclude that the whole passage intends to point out the importance of understanding a new market to sell products there.

Applying the Reading Journal Strategy

In Chapter 7 of this book, you learned about a reading strategy that involves keeping a journal of your thoughts about and responses to a text. A reading journal can include summaries of a text, or your feelings and opinions about the subject. It might also consist of your questions, your judgment of a text, or a comparison of a work to other works you've read. Here is a journal entry for the passage about Pillsbury flour in India.

> *"A Trip to India for the Pillsbury Doughboy"*
> *Robert Kreitner, Management, 8th ed., p. 112.*
> *November 1, 20—*

This reading interested me for several reasons. First of all, I learned more about Indian culture. I had no idea that Indian women were using such old-fashioned methods to get ingredients for their bread. I also didn't know that roti is such an important staple of the Indian diet. Secondly, I found

* Adapted from Kreitner, *Management,* 8th ed. Boston: Houghton Mifflin, 2001, 112.

Pillsbury's strategy fascinating. To achieve a long-term goal—introducing their more expensive products into Indian society—they had to start with flour. The company's success story is a clear illustration of how critical it is to know the consumer. If a business does not truly understand what the prospective buyer wants or needs, it cannot hope to sell its product or service. I'll remember this powerful example when I graduate and start my own graphic design business. I'd like to know more, though, about Pillsbury's marketing strategies. This article doesn't really explain how they convinced Indian consumers to try the new flour product.

Exercise 10.3

Read the passage below and respond to each question that follows by circling the letter of the correct answer.

"And What Did You Do for Someone Today?"

1 When I was a child, we observed Father's Day by walking to the local Methodist church and listening to my father preach. We didn't have a car—my dad believed he could not "support Mr. Ford"[1] on a minister's salary and still see that all of his seven children went to college. While we understood it was a special day—my mother would have something exceptional like a roast or a turkey cooking in the oven—in many ways it was not all that different from any other day. As soon as my brothers and sisters and I got home, we'd all gather around the dining-room table, where we took turns answering our father's daily question: "And what did you do for someone today?"

2 While that voice and those words always stuck in my mind, they often got pushed aside by more immediate concerns: long hours in medical school, building a career in medical research, getting married, raising children and acquiring the material accouterments[2] every father wants for his family. All the hallmarks of a "successful" life, according to today's standards. When

1. **Mr. Ford:** Henry Ford, early 20th century manufacturer of automobiles
2. **accouterments:** outward forms of recognition; trappings

these goals were met and that busy time of life was over, retirement followed on Hilton Head Island, S.C.

3 My wife and I built our home in a gated community surrounded by yacht clubs and golf courses. But when I left the compound and its luxurious buffer zone for the other side of the island, I was traveling on unpaved roads lined with leaky bungalows.[1] The "lifestyle" of many of the native islanders stood in jarring contrast to my cozy existence. I was stunned by the disparity.[2]

4 By means of a lifelong habit of mine of giving rides to hitchhikers—remember, I grew up without a car—I got to talking to some of these local folks. And I discovered that the vast majority of the maids, gardeners, waitresses and construction workers who make this island work had little or no access to medical care. It seemed outrageous to me. I wondered why someone didn't do something about that. Then my father's words, which had at times receded to a whisper, rang in my head again: "What did you do for someone today?"

5 So I started working on a solution. The island was full of retired doctors. If I could persuade them to spend a few hours a week volunteering their services, we could provide free primary health care to those so desperately in need of it. Most of the doctors I approached liked the idea, so long as their life savings wouldn't be put at risk by malpractice suits. They also wanted to be relicensed without a long, bureaucratic[3] hassle. It took one year and plenty of persistence, but I was able to persuade the state legislature to create a special license for doctors volunteering in not-for-profit clinics, and got full malpractice coverage for everyone from South Carolina's Joint Underwriting Association for only $5,000 a year.

6 The town donated land, local residents contributed office and medical equipment and some of the potential patients volunteered their weekends stuccoing[4] the building that would become the clinic. We named it Volunteers in Medicine and we opened its doors in 1994, fully staffed by retired physicians, nurses, dentists and chiropractors as well as nearly 150 lay[5] volunteers. That year we had 5,000 patient visits; last year we had 16,000.

7 Somehow word of what we were doing got around. Soon we were fielding phone calls from retired physicians all over the country, asking for help in starting VIM clinics in their communities. We did the best we could—there are now 15 other clinics operating—but we couldn't keep up with the need.

1. **bungalows:** small houses or cottages
2. **disparity:** inequality
3. **bureaucratic:** related to a government that consists of many different departments
4. **stuccoing:** putting a durable finish on exterior walls
5. **lay:** nonprofessional

Yet last month I think my father's words found their way up north, to McNeil Consumer Healthcare, the maker of Tylenol. A major grant from McNeil will allow us to respond to these requests and help establish other free clinics in communities around the country.*

1. What is the implied main idea of this entire longer selection?
   a. The author's father taught him to help others, and doing so has improved his life.
   b. Retirement is boring, and people should stay busy.
   c. In America, the gap between the rich and the poor is very wide.
   d. The author had a poor relationship with his strict father.

2. Which of the following supporting details helps the reader figure out the implied main idea?
   a. "When I was a child, we observed Father's Day by walking to the local Methodist church and listening to my father preach." (paragraph 1)
   b. "The town donated land, local residents contributed office and medical equipment and some of the potential patients volunteered their weekends stuccoing the building that would become the clinic." (paragraph 6)
   c. "As soon as my brothers and sisters and I got home, we'd all gather around the dining-room table, where we took turns answering our father's daily question: 'And what did you do for someone today?'" (paragraph 1)
   d. "My wife and I built our home in a gated community surrounded by yacht clubs and golf courses." (paragraph 3)

3. Many of the supporting details are in the form of:
   a. examples.
   b. events and causes.
   c. reasons.
   d. points of comparison and contrast.

4. Which of the following components of a reading journal—a summary of the selection, your feelings about the selection, your opinion about the subject, your questions, your judgment of the selection, a comparison of this work to other works you've read, or a combination of a few of these things—lends itself to this reading selection? If you were to write a reading journal entry for this selection, what would it look like and why? Would you record your feelings about this text or merely summarize it?

* Adapted from Jack McConnell, M.D., "And What Did You Do for Someone Today?" *Newsweek*, June 18, 2001, 13. © 2001 Newsweek, Inc. All rights reserved. Reprinted by permission.

Write a brief journal entry to demonstrate your answers to these questions.

Patterns of Organization

Chapter 6 of this book explained five common patterns of organization (series, time order, cause/effect, comparison/contrast, and definition) used to arrange supporting details within paragraphs. Conveniently, longer selections are organized according to the very same patterns. Here is an example of a passage that's organized with a series of types:

In one study Sidney Verba and Norman Nie analyzed the ways in which people participate in politics and came up with six forms of participation that are characteristic of six different kinds of U.S. citizens. TYPE #1 About one-fifth (22 percent) of the population is completely inactive: they rarely vote, they do not get involved in organizations, and they probably do not even talk about politics very much. These inactives typically have little education and low incomes and are relatively young. At the opposite extreme are the complete **activists,** constituting about one-TYPE #2 ninth of the population (11 percent). These people are highly educated, have high incomes, and tend to be middle-aged rather than young or old. They tend to participate in all forms of politics.

Between these extremes are four categories of limited forms of par-TYPE #3 ticipation. The *voting specialists* are people who vote but do little else; they tend not to have much schooling or income and to be substantially TYPE #4 older than the average person. *Campaigners* not only vote but also like to get involved in campaign activities. They are better educated than the average voter, but what seems to distinguish them most is their interest in the conflicts, passions, and struggle of politics: their clear identification with a political party; and their willingness to take strong positions. TYPE #5 *Communalists* are much like campaigners in social background but have a very different temperament: they do not like the conflict and tension of partisan[1] campaigns. They tend to reserve their energy for community activities of a more nonpartisan nature—forming and joining organizations to deal with local problems and contacting local officials TYPE #6 about these problems. Finally, there are some *parochial participants* who do not vote and stay out of election campaigns and civic associations

1. **partisan:** favoring one particular party, cause, person, or idea

but are willing to contact local officials about specific, often personal, problems.*

This selection offers a series of ways people participate in politics. Most of the passage describes six different types of U.S. citizens depending on their degree of political involvement.

This next passage is organized with the time order pattern:

> The rotating and revolving motions of planet Earth were concepts not readily accepted at first. In early times most people were convinced that Earth was motionless and that the sun, moon, planets, and stars revolved around Earth, which was considered the center of the universe. This concept, or model, of the solar system is called the Earth-centered or **geocentric model.** Its greatest proponent[1] was Claudius Ptolemy, about A.D. 140.
>
> Nicolaus Copernicus (1473–1543), a Polish astronomer, developed the theory of the Sun-centered model, or **heliocentric model,** of the solar system. Although he did not prove that Earth revolves around the sun, he did provide mathematical proofs that could be used to predict future positions of the planets.
>
> After the death of Copernicus in 1543, the study of astronomy was continued and developed by several astronomers, three of whom made their appearance in the last half of the sixteenth century. Notable among these was the Danish astronomer Tycho Brahe (BRAH-UH) (1546–1601), who built an observatory on the island of Hven near Copenhagen and spent most of his life observing and studying the stars and planets. Brahe is considered the greatest practical astronomer since the Greeks. His measurements of the planets and stars, all made with the unaided eye (the telescope had not been invented), proved to be more accurate than any made previously. Brahe's data, published in 1603, were edited by his colleague Johannes Kepler (1571–1630), a German mathematician and astronomer who had joined Brahe during the last year of his life. After Brahe's death, his lifetime of observations were at Kepler's disposal and provided him with the data necessary for the formulation of three laws known today as Kepler's laws of planetary motion.
>
> Kepler was interested in the irregular motion of the planet Mars. He spent considerable time and energy before coming to the conclusion

1. **proponent:** supporter

* Adapted from Wilson and DiIulio, Jr., *American Government*, 8th ed. Boston: Houghton Mifflin, 2001, 138.

that the uniform circular orbit proposed by Copernicus was not a true representation of the observed facts. Perhaps because he was a mathematician, he saw a simple type of geometric figure that would fit the observed motions of Mars and the other known planets.*

Longer passages are more likely to use a combination of patterns to organize details. This next selection from a textbook, for example, combines different patterns to explain the effects of drugs.

The Varying Effects of Drugs

Unfortunately, chemical properties that give drugs their medically desirable main effects, such as pain relief, often create undesirable side effects as well.

Substance Abuse. One side effect may be the potential for abuse. **Substance abuse** is a pattern of use that causes serious social, legal, or interpersonal problems for the user. Of course, as a culture changes, the drugs that cause personal, social, and legal problems may also change.

Substance abuse can lead to psychological or physical dependence. People displaying **psychological dependence** on a drug will continue to use it despite its adverse affects. They need the drug for a sense of well-being, and become preoccupied with getting the drug if it is no longer available. However, they can still function without the drug. Psychological dependence can occur with or without *physical dependence*, also known as *addiction*. **Addiction** is a physiological state in which there is not only a strong craving for the drug, but in which using the drug becomes necessary to prevent an unpleasant **withdrawal syndrome.** Withdrawal symptoms vary depending on the drug, but they often include an intensification of craving for the drug and physical effects generally opposite to those of the drug itself.

Physical dependence can develop gradually, without a person's awareness. As the addiction progresses, the person may also develop drug **tolerance,** a condition in which increasingly larger drug doses are required to produce the same effect. Scientists now believe that the changes in the brain that underlie addiction may be similar to those that occur during learning. With the development of tolerance, many addicts need the drug just to prevent the negative effects of not taking it. However, most researchers believe that a craving for

* Adapted from Shipman et al., *An Introduction to Physical Science,* 9th ed. Boston: Houghton Mifflin, 2000, 381–382.

the positive effects of drugs is what keeps addicts coming back to drug use.

The potential for "normal" people to develop drug dependence should not be underestimated. (If you're a coffee drinker, think about how you'd feel without that morning "jolt.") All addictive drugs stimulate the brain's "pleasure centers," regions that are sensitive to the neurotransmitters dopamine and endorphin. Neuron activity in these areas of the brain produces intensely pleasurable feelings. It also helps generate the pleasant feelings of a good meal or a "runner's high." Thus, addictive drugs have the capacity for creating tremendously rewarding effects in most people.*

This passage not only defines several negative results of drug use, but it also explains the causes and effects of psychological and physical dependence on drugs.

Applying the SQ3R Reading Strategy

In Chapter 4 of this book, you were introduced to one specific type of active reading strategy called *SQ3R*. The SQ3R strategy involves completing a five-step process—(1) Survey; (2) Question; (3) Read; (4) Recite; (5) Review—to improve reading comprehension. For example, if you applied this strategy to the passage about drugs, you would first survey the material to get an idea of what it's about. The heading announces that this section, which comes from a longer textbook chapter, is about the effects of drugs, and the first sentence indicates that the section will focus on *negative* effects.

Step 2 of SQ3R involves turning headings into questions. This passage contains two headings. We could write:

What are the varying effects of drugs?

above the first one, and

What is substance abuse?

What are its causes and effects?

near the second heading.

Continued

* Adapted from Bernstein and Nash, *Essentials of Psychology,* 2nd ed. Boston: Houghton Mifflin, 2002, 133–134.

Third, we read to find answers to those questions. You could mark the text as follows:

What are the varying effects of drugs?
What is substance abuse?
What are its causes and effects?

The Varying Effects of Drugs

Unfortunately, chemical properties that give drugs their medically desirable main effects, such as pain relief, often create undesirable side effects as well.

Substance Abuse. One side effect may be the potential for abuse. **Substance abuse** is a pattern of use that causes serious social, legal, or interpersonal problems for the user. Of course, as a culture changes, the drugs that cause personal, social, and legal problems may also change.

Side effect

Side effect

Side effect

Side effect

Substance abuse can lead to psychological or physical dependence. People displaying **psychological dependence** on a drug will continue to use it despite its adverse affects. They need the drug for a sense of well-being, and become preoccupied with getting the drug if it is no longer available. However, they can still function without the drug. Psychological dependence can occur with or without *physical dependence,* also known as *addiction*. **Addiction** is a physiological state in which there is not only a strong craving for the drug, but in which using the drug becomes necessary to prevent an unpleasant **withdrawal syndrome.** Withdrawal symptoms vary depending on the drug, but they often include an intensification of craving for the drug and physical effects generally opposite to those of the drug itself.

Physical dependence can develop gradually, without a person's awareness. As the addiction progresses, the person may also develop drug **tolerance,** a condition in which increasingly larger drug doses are required to produce the same effect. Scientists now believe that the changes in the brain that underlie addiction may be similar to those that occur during learning. With the development of tolerance, many addicts need the drug just to prevent the negative effects of not taking it. However, most researchers believe that a craving for the positive effects of drugs is what keeps addicts coming back to drug use.

The potential for "normal" people to develop drug dependence should not be underestimated. (If you're a coffee drinker, think about how you'd feel without that morning "jolt.")

All addictive drugs stimulate the brain's "pleasure centers," regions that are sensitive to the neurotransmitters dopamine and endorphin. Neuron activity in these areas of the brain produces intensely pleasurable feelings. It also helps generate the pleasant feelings of a good meal or a "runner's high." Thus, addictive drugs have the capacity for creating tremendously rewarding effects in most people. *Causes*

Next, after you've read the entire passage, go back and say aloud the answers to each question until you feel confident that you know them. Finally, in the final review step, cover the text with your hand or a piece of paper and try to answer each question to review what you've learned.

Exercise 10.4

Read the passage below and respond to each question that follows by circling the letter of the correct answer.

Types of Memory

1 In which hand does the Statue of Liberty hold her torch? When was the last time you made a phone call? What part of speech is used to modify a noun? Your attempt to answer the first question is likely to elicit a visual image. To answer the second, you must remember a particular event in your life. The third question requires general knowledge that is unlikely to be tied to a specific event. Some psychologists suggest that answering each of these questions requires a different type of memory. How many types of memory are there? No one is sure, but most research suggests that there are at least three basic types, and each is named for the kind of information it handles: episodic, semantic, and procedural.

2 Any memory of a specific event that happened while you were present is an episodic memory. It is a memory of an episode in your life. What you had for dinner yesterday, what you did last summer, or where you were last Friday night are episodic memories. Semantic memory contains generalized knowledge of the world—such as that twelve items make a dozen—that does not involve memory of a specific event. So you would answer the question "Are wrenches pets or tools?" using your semantic memory, because you don't have to remember a specific episode in which you learned that wrenches are tools. As a general rule, people convey episodic memories by saying, "I remember when . . ." whereas they convey semantic memories by

saying, "I know that. . . ." Procedural memory involves knowledge of how to do things, such as riding a bike, reading a map, or playing tennis. A procedural memory often consists of a complicated sequence of movements that cannot be described adequately in words. For instance, a gymnast might find it impossible to describe the exact motions in a particular routine.

3 Many activities require all three types of memory. Consider the game of tennis. Knowing the official rules or the number of sets needed to win a match involves semantic memory. Remembering which side served last requires episodic memory. And knowing how to hit the ball involves procedural memory.

4 Recalling all three kinds of memories can be either intentional or unintentional. When you deliberately try to remember something, such as where you went on your last vacation, you are relying on explicit memory. In contrast, implicit memory involves the unintentional recollection and influence of prior experiences. For instance, while watching a movie about a long car trip, you might begin to feel slightly anxious because you subconsciously recall a time you had engine trouble on such a trip. Implicit memory operates automatically and without conscious effort. In fact, people are often unaware that their actions have been influenced by previous events. Because some influential events cannot be recalled even when people try to do so, implicit memory has been said to involve "retention without remembering."*

1. Which of the following sentences states the thesis of this selection?
   a. "No one is sure, but most research suggests that there are at least three basic types, and each is named for the kind of information it handles: episodic, semantic, and procedural." (paragraph 1)
   b. "Any memory of a specific event that happened while you were present is an episodic memory." (paragraph 2)
   c. "Many activities require all three types of memory." (paragraph 3)
   d. "Recalling all three kinds of memories can be either intentional or unintentional." (paragraph 4)

2. Which pattern organizes most of the *major* supporting details?
   a. time order
   b. comparison/contrast
   c. cause/effect
   d. series

3. If you were to apply the SQ3R strategy to paragraph 1 of the selection, which of the following questions would be most appropriate to ask?
   a. What are the different types of memory?
   b. What is the definition of an episodic memory?
   c. In which hand does the Statue of Liberty hold her torch?
   d. What are the three questions you should ask yourself about memory?

* From Bernstein and Nash, *Essentials of Psychology*, 2nd ed. Boston: Houghton Mifflin, 2002, 181.

4. What is the answer to the question you selected in question #3?
   a. intentional or unintentional
   b. episodic, semantic, and procedural
   c. implicit and explicit
   d. conscious and subconscious

Transitions

As you learned in Chapter 5 of this book, paragraphs include transitions, words that signal relationships between sentences. Longer reading selections employ transitions for the very same purpose, but they also show how whole *paragraphs* are related to one another. As you read the following example of a series passage, notice how the boldfaced, italicized transitions help you understand the relationships between the major details.

Money Demand

Why do you hold money? What does it do for you? What determines how much money you will hold? These questions are addressed in this section. Wanting to hold more money is not the same as wanting more income. You can decide to carry more cash or keep more dollars in your checking account even though your income has not changed. The quantity of dollars you want to hold is your demand for money. By summing the quantity of money demanded by each individual, we can find the money demand for the entire economy. Once we understand what determines money demand, we can put that demand together with the money supply and examine how money influences the interest rate and the equilibrium level of income.

First of all, people use money for transactions, to buy goods and services. The transactions demand for money is a demand to hold money in order to spend it on goods and services. Holding money in your pocket or checking account is a demand for money. Spending money is not demanding it; by spending it you are getting rid of it.

If your boss paid you the same instant that you wanted to buy something, the timing of your receipts and expenditures would match perfectly. You would not have to hold money for transactions. But because receipts typically occur much less often than expenditures, money is necessary to cover transactions between paychecks.

People ***also*** hold money to take care of emergencies. The precautionary demand for money exists because emergencies happen. People never know when an unexpected expense will crop up or when actual expenditures will exceed planned expenditures. So they hold money as a precaution.

Finally, there is a speculative[1] demand for money, a demand created by uncertainty about the value of other assets. This demand exists because money is the most liquid[2] store of value. If you want to buy a stock, but you believe the price is going to fall in the next few days, you hold the money until you are ready to buy the stock.

The speculative demand for money is not necessarily tied to a particular use of funds. People hold money because they expect the price of any asset to fall. Holding money is less risky than buying the asset today if the price of the asset seems likely to fall. For example, suppose you buy and sell fine art. The price of art fluctuates over time. You try to buy when prices are low and sell when prices are high. If you expect prices to fall in the short term, you hold money rather than art until the prices do fall. Then you use money to buy art for resale when the prices go up again.*

Applying the REAP Reading Strategy

In Chapter 8, you were introduced to REAP, a strategy for increasing reading comprehension. REAP is a four-step process that includes: (1) Read; (2) Encode; (3) Annotate; and (4) Ponder. If you applied this strategy to the passage about money demand, you would first carefully read the selection. Next, you would put the ideas into your own words (encode) and write them down (annotate). If you applied the Encode and Annotate steps to the passage about money demand, it might look like this:

1. **speculative:** related to reasoning that is based on inconclusive evidence
2. **liquid:** readily available as spendable cash

* Adapted from Boyes and Melvin, *Fundamentals of Economics*. Boston: Houghton Mifflin, 1999, 278–279.

Money Demand

Why do you hold money? What does it do for you? What determines how much money you will hold? These questions are addressed in this section. Wanting to hold more money is not the same as wanting more income. You can decide to carry more cash or keep more dollars in your checking account even though your income has not changed. The quantity of dollars you want to hold is your demand for money. By summing the quantity of money demanded by each individual, we can find the money demand for the entire economy. Once we understand what determines money demand, we can put that demand together with the money supply and examine how money influences the interest rate and the equilibrium level of income.

Wanting more income and wanting to hold more money are not the same thing. The amount of money you want to hold is your demand for money.

Money demand influences interest rates and income levels.

First of all, people use money for transactions, to buy goods and services. The transactions demand for money is a demand to hold money in order to spend it on goods and services. Holding money in your pocket or checking account is a demand for money. Spending money is not demanding it; by spending it you are getting rid of it.

One reason we hold money is for spending it on stuff.

If your boss paid you the same instant that you wanted to buy something, the timing of your receipts and expenditures would match perfectly. You would not have to hold money for transactions. But because receipts typically occur much less often than expenditures, money is necessary to cover transactions between paychecks.

You have to hold money to buy stuff because you aren't paid the second you want something.

People ***also*** hold money to take care of emergencies. The precautionary demand for money exists because emergencies happen. People never know when an unexpected expense will crop up or when actual expenditures will exceed planned expenditures. So they hold money as a precaution. ***Finally,*** there is a speculative demand for money, a demand created by uncertainty about the value of other assets. This demand exists because money is the most liquid store of value. If you want to buy a stock, but you believe the price is going to fall in the next few days, you hold the money until you are ready to buy the stock.

Another reason to hold money is to have cash in case of emergencies.

Third, you need money because it's the asset you can use most quickly and easily.

The speculative demand for money is not necessarily tied to a particular use of funds. People hold money because they

We hold money until we think the price is right for something we want.

Continued

expect the price of any asset to fall. Holding money is less risky than buying the asset today if the price of the asset seems likely to fall. For example, suppose you buy and sell fine art. The price of art fluctuates over time. You try to buy when prices are low and sell when prices are high. If you expect prices to fall in the short term, you hold money rather than art until the prices do fall. Then you use money to buy art for resale when the prices go up again.

The final step of REAP is Ponder. During this last stage of the process, you reflect upon what you've read and discuss it with others. For example, you could compare your annotations with those of your classmates, and you could discuss your reactions to the ideas. You could apply your own experiences to the information. Do you hold money for emergencies? You could also think critically about the text. For instance, you might decide that the author did not cover all of the reasons for holding money. Are there others?

Exercise 10.5

Read the passage below and respond to each question that follows by circling the letter of the correct answer.

Fighting That Ticket

1 If you sincerely believe you've been wrongly issued a traffic ticket, our legal system provides you the opportunity to fight it. You'll find, however, that getting the ticket was the easy part—getting out of it can be a bit more complicated for the average motorist. What follows amounts to using the very same, often absurdly complex, rules that were used to nail you to work things to your own advantage. Payback can be sweet!

2 First of all, ask for and get a "continuance"—a change of the court date listed on your summons to a later date. Most jurisdictions will grant a continuance as a matter of course; all you have to do is call or visit the court clerk's office and file a request. So why request a continuance? Simple. The cop who issued you the ticket is the state's witness against you. If he doesn't show up to give testimony, the charge against you will likely be dismissed by the judge, since there is no evidence against you.

3 Failing that, continue to request those continuances; sometimes you can string this process out for up to a year. Worst case, you've put off the day of reckoning and made life a little more aggravating for the "revenue collectors." Make them earn the money they intend to pry from your wallet!

4 The second thing you must do is exercise another one of your rights. File a motion (indeed, many motions) for what is called "discovery" at the clerk of courts's office to obtain records of things that will be used against you during your trial. These include the training records of the officer, the devices he used, their maintenance/calibration[1] records, etc. If any of these are not provided to you expeditiously[2] and prior to the court date, it is grounds for dismissal.

5 Many times, the records will, in fact, fail to be coughed up—or will reveal out-of-date calibrations (such as those for radar guns). The bureaucracy can be as inept[3] as you imagine it to be, so anything you can find that challenges the legal basis of the ticket you were issued is ammunition for your cause. If it's a speed-limit bust, demand access to the records revealing the process by which the posted speed limit for that stretch of road was established; if it does not accord with state law (and there are definite legal requirements and processes governing the setting of posted speed limits; they can't just put up a sign), you are on your way to being home free.

6 The basic idea here is to let them know you plan to fight tooth and nail—and will insist on every legal right and technicality available to you under the law. In some jurisdictions, you even have the right to request a jury trial to contest a traffic ticket. Don't hesitate to make such a demand. Many courts will quickly tire of this game after a very short while and dismiss the case.*

1. Which of the following sentences states the thesis of this passage?
   a. "If you sincerely believe you've been wrongly issued a traffic ticket, our legal system provides you the opportunity to fight it." (paragraph 1)
   b. "Payback can be sweet!" (paragraph 1)
   c. "First of all, ask for and get a 'continuance'—a change of the court date listed on your summons to a later date." (paragraph 2)
   d. "In some jurisdictions, you even have the right to request a jury trial to contest a traffic ticket." (paragraph 6)

2. What two patterns of organization are used to arrange the supporting details?
   a. series and time order
   b. time order and cause/effect
   c. comparison/contrast and cause/effect
   d. series and comparison/contrast

1. **calibration:** related to the checking or adjusting of an instrument of measurement
2. **expeditiously:** quickly and on time
3. **inept:** foolish, incompetent

* From Eric Peters, "Fighting That Ticket," *Consumers' Research*, July 2001, 33. Used by permission of the publisher.

3. Which of the following sentences begins with a time-order transition?
   a. "If you sincerely believe you've been wrongly issued a traffic ticket, our legal system provides you the opportunity to fight it." (paragraph 1)
   b. "First of all, ask for and get a 'continuance'—a change of the court date listed on your summons to a later date." (paragraph 2)
   c. "Many times, the records will, in fact, fail to be coughed up—or will reveal out-of-date calibrations (such as those for radar guns)." (paragraph 5)
   d. "Many courts will quickly tire of this game after a very short while and dismiss the case." (paragraph 6)
4. Using the REAP strategy, write a brief annotation for each of the following paragraphs: 2, 3, 4, and 5.

CHAPTER 10 REVIEW

Fill in the blanks in the following statements.

1. Like paragraphs, longer reading selections include a __________ and a __________.
2. The main idea of a longer passage is usually called a __________.
3. A thesis statement includes the __________ along with what is being said about that subject.
4. __________ are mini-titles that identify the topic of one section of a longer work like a chapter or an article.
5. Like paragraphs, longer reading selections include __________ and __________ supporting details.
6. Though not as common, a longer reading selection can offer an __________ main idea.
7. Longer reading selections, like paragraphs, organize supporting details according to common __________, and they include __________ to show how paragraphs are related to one another.

Vocabulary: Review

You've covered many important vocabulary concepts in Chapters 1–9 of this book. The following exercise, which draws sentences from the passages in Chapter 10, will give you practice reviewing several of these concepts.

A. On the blank following each paragraph, write the synonyms that the sentence or passage includes for the boldfaced, italicized word or phrase.

1. One acceptable way to release ***anger*** is to sit down with pen and paper and write a letter to the person who triggered your wrath. Don't worry about grammar, spelling, or punctuation—just put all your angry thoughts on paper. Write until you have nothing more to say. Then destroy the letter. Once you let go of your fury, you will be ready to deal constructively with whatever caused you to become upset.

   Two synonyms for the boldfaced, italicized word: ____________________

2. Research indicates that migraine headaches and back pain can sometimes be traced to ***suppressed*** emotions. Some heart attack patients are victims of their inhibited anger. They have blocked the feeling of anger and avoided the expression of this emotion toward the person or situation that provoked the feeling.

   Three synonyms for the boldfaced, italicized word: ____________________

3. . . . careless enunciation causes credibility problems for public speakers. Do you say "Swatuh thought" for "That's what I thought"; "Harya?" for "How are you?"; or "Howjado?" for "How do you do?" These ***lazy*** enunciation patterns are not acceptable in public speaking. Check your enunciation patterns on the tape recordings you have made to determine if you have such a problem. If you do, concentrate on careful enunciation as you practice your speech. Be careful, however, to avoid the opposite problem of inflated, pompous, and pretentious enunciation. Very few speakers can make this work without sounding phony. You should strive to be neither sloppy nor overly precise.

   Two synonyms for the boldfaced, italicized word: ____________________

B. Look up the boldfaced, italicized words in a dictionary and determine which definition best describes how each word is being used. Write that definition on the blank provided.

4. . . .we are especially likely to experience communication anxiety in ***novel*** situations—situations we're not used to. ____________________

5. In women, the ***net*** increase of testosterone from anabolic steroids can result in masculinization by suppressing estrogen production. __________

6. If you want to buy a ***stock***, but you believe the price is going to fall in the next few days, you hold the money until you are ready to buy the stock. ____________________

7. People never know when an unexpected expense will ***crop*** up or when actual expenditures will exceed planned expenditures. ______________

____

C. In each of the following sentences, underline the context clue that helps you understand the meaning of the boldfaced, italicized word, and write what kind of context clue (definition/restatement, example, explanation, or contrast) it is on the blank provided.

8. Paula has a tight schedule during the week, and she looks forward to quiet weekends with her family. She has never expressed her anger to anyone because the uninvited guests are, after all, "family." People who ***capitulate*** to their emotions often experience feelings of helplessness and simply suffer in silence. ______________

9. Let's assume that as you are presenting a new project proposal at a staff meeting, someone interrupts you and strongly criticizes your ideas. The criticism seems to be directed more at you than at your proposal. Anger starts building inside you, but before responding to the ***assailant***, you pause and engage in some rational thinking. ______________

10. It typically takes a while before a group is productive; after the members have a better feel for each other, have formed some bonds, and have developed a sense of organizational structure, performance can follow. Of course, some groups never make it to this stage; having ***stagnated*** at the norming stage, they fail to reach their potential in terms of productivity.

____

11. This second stage results in tension and stress within the group and can also lead to the formation of ***coalitions***—small cohesive groups—within the larger group. ______________

12. India's climatic extremes and ***deplorable*** roads make it difficult to maintain freshness from mill to warehouse, let alone on store shelves. ______________

13. Pillsbury had hoped to establish contracts with existing mills, but inspectors found hygiene and safety at some to be ***appalling***. Pillsbury scouts visited forty plants, where they encountered mice, rotting wheat, and treacherous machinery. ______________

D. In each of the following sentences, which come from passages in this chapter and previous chapters, underline the figure of speech (analogy, metaphor, simile, or personification).

14. Brainstorming is a technique for finding solutions, creating plans, and discovering new ideas. When you are stuck on a problem, brainstorming can break the logjam.
15. The bureaucracy can be as inept as you imagine it to be, so anything you can find that challenges the legal basis of the ticket you were issued is ammunition for your cause.
16. The truth is that when we think about North Dakota, which is not often, we picture it as having the same year-round climate as Uranus. In contrast, SOUTH Dakota is universally believed to be a tropical paradise with palm trees swaying on surf-kissed beaches.

READING STRATEGY: Scanning

The last time you went to a restaurant hungry for a particular dish, like fried chicken, did you read every word of the menu before placing your order? You probably didn't. Instead, you glanced over the lists and descriptions of the items available until you found the ones that included fried chicken, and you probably ignored most of the other sections of the menu. This is called **scanning,** and it is a useful strategy to use when you are searching for a particular piece of information. You also scan when you look for a certain topic in a book's table of contents or index, or when you read a visual aid like a table. You are scanning when you look at classified ads, telephone books, dictionaries, or a list of websites generated by an Internet search engine.

When you scan a text, you don't read the whole thing; rather, you run your eyes over the page, reading words or phrases here and there until you discover what you are looking for. Though this seems like skimming, the strategy explained in Chapter 9, it is different because when you scan, you know what you are looking for. When you skim, you don't; you are just trying to gain a general understanding of a text and/or its main features.

Continued

When might scanning be appropriate for longer texts such as chapters or articles? If you are looking for an answer to a particular question, or if you are searching for a specific fact, name, or other type of detail, scan the text to find what you need. Scanning is often useful, then, for completing assignments or for refreshing your memory about some piece of information you remember reading about. If you need to form a complete understanding of the ideas in a text, however, you'll have to read it more thoroughly.

The following list of websites was generated from a search for "cell phones" and "health."* Scan this list and then answer the questions that follow.

1. Write the numbers of two websites that you could consult if you were researching whether or not cell phones damage human health. ______________________________

____

2. Write the numbers of two websites you could access if you're researching the addition of E911 (the E stands for *enhanced* because an emergency dispatcher can pinpoint the caller's location) to cell phones. ______________________________

____

3. If you're interested in devices that protect you from cell phone radiation, which two websites should you consult? ______________

____

4. Out of the eight websites listed, which one has nothing to do with cell phones' or cell phone devices' potential to damage health or protect health? ______________________________

____

YAHOO!

Search Results cell phones health [Search] Advanced Search Help

Your search: **cell phones health** Categories | **Web Sites** | Web Pages | News | Research Documents

Sponsor Matches (What are Sponsor Matches?)

Web Site Matches (sites in Yahho! Directly that match your search) **1 - 8 of 8** | Web Page Matches

1. ZDNet: Adding E911 to **cell phones** a no-brainer - article discussing the benefits of E911.
   http://www.zdnet.com/eweek/stories/general/0,11011,2572781,00.html
   More sites about: Emergency Services > Enhanced 911

2. Cellular Phone Antennas and Human **Health** - addresses the issue of whether base station transmitter/antennas for cellular **phones**, PCS **phones**, and other types of portable transceivers are a risk to human **health**.
   http://www.mcw.edu/gcrc/cop/cell-phone-health-FAQ/toc.html
   More sites about: Cellular Telephones Issues > **Health**

3. SmartReminders - sends email messages to desktops, **cell phones**, or pagers for weather, **health**, sports, product recalls, dates, and more.
   http://www.smartreminders.com/
   More sites about: Calendars > Reminder Services

4. Cellphones and **Health** - offers a compilation of research papers, articles, and reports.
   http://www.electric-words.com/cell/rindex.html
   More sites about: Cellular Telephones Issues > **Health**

5. Wireless Developer Network - Locating Your Location Based Service Provider - article discussion of the various **cell** phone location technologies and E911.
   http://www.wirelessdevnet.com/channels/lbs/features/newsbite11.html
   More sites about: Emergency Services > Enhanced 911

6. A-1 Hearing Aid Center - provides hearing tests, custom hearing aids, tinitus maskers, and custom ear pieces for **cell phones**, noise, and swimming.
   http://www.a1hearingaidcenters.com/
   More sites about: California > San Diego > Audiology Clinics and Practices

7. MagMed - offers the RayMaster, to reduce the effects of **cell** phone, computer, and microwave electromagnetic radiation.
   http://www.magmed.net/
   More sites about: Shopping > Alternative **Health** > Products

8. WaveShield Rhode Island - distributors of **health** protection devices for **cell** phone radiation.
   http://www.waveshieldri.com/
   More sites about: Safety Products > Radiation Shielding

http://search.yahoo.com/bin/search?p=cell+phones+health

* Yahoo search on cell phones/health, October 2, 2001. http://search.yahoo.com/bin/search?p=cell+phones+health. Reproduced with permission of Yahoo!. © 2000 by Yahoo! Inc. Yahoo! and the Yahoo! logo are trademarks of Yahoo! Inc.

Name ______________________________ Date ________________

COMBINED SKILLS TEST 1

Read the selection below and respond to each question that follows by circling the letter of the correct answer.

Development and Memory

1 The ability to remember facts, figures, pictures, and objects improves as we get older and more expert at processing information. But take a minute right now and try to recall anything that happened to you when you were, say, one year old. Most people can accurately recall a few autobiographical memories from age five or six but remember virtually nothing from before the age of three.

2 Psychologists have not yet found a fully satisfactory explanation for this "infantile amnesia." Some have suggested that young children lack memory encoding and storage processes. Yet children of two or three can clearly recall experiences that happened weeks or even months earlier. Others suggest that infantile amnesia occurs because very young children lack a sense of self. Because they don't even recognize themselves in a mirror, they may not have a framework for organizing memories about what happens to them. However, this explanation would hold for only the first two years or so, because after that, children do recognize their own faces, and even their taped voices.

3 Another possibility is that early memories, though "present," are implicit rather than explicit. Implicit memories form automatically and can affect our emotions and behavior even when we do not consciously recall them. Note, however, that children's implicit memories of their early years, like their explicit memories, are quite limited. For example, Nora Newcombe and Nathan Fox showed photographs of young children to a group of ten-year-olds. Some of the photos were of preschool classmates whom the participants had not seen since they were five years old. They explicitly recalled 21 percent of their former classmates, and their skin conductance (a measure of emotion) indicated that they had implicit memories of an additional 5 percent. Yet these youngsters had no memory of 74 percent of their preschool pals. Adults, however, can correctly identify 90 percent of photographs of high school classmates they have not seen for thirty years.

4 Other explanations of infantile amnesia suggest that our early memories are lost because we do not yet have the language skills to talk about, and thus

solidify, those memories. Still others say that early memories are stored, but because the schemas[1] we used in early childhood to mentally represent them have changed, we no longer have the retrieval cues necessary to recall them. A related possibility is that early experiences tend to be fused into generalized event representations, such as "going to Grandma's" or "playing at the beach," so that it becomes difficult to remember any specific event. Research on hypotheses such as these is beginning to unravel the mystery of infantile amnesia.*

1. What is the topic of this selection?
   a. infants
   b. infantile amnesia
   c. memory
   d. psychologists

2. Which of the following sentences from the selection best expresses the main idea of the entire selection?
   a. "The ability to remember facts, figures, pictures, and objects improves as we get older and more expert at processing information." (paragraph 1)
   b. "Most people can accurately recall a few autobiographical memories from age five or six but remember virtually nothing from before the age of three." (paragraph 1)
   c. "Psychologists have not yet found a fully satisfactory explanation for this 'infantile amnesia.'" (paragraph 2)
   d. "Other explanations of infantile amnesia suggest that our early memories are lost because we do not yet have the language skills to talk about, and thus solidify, those memories." (paragraph 4)

3. In paragraph 4, what does *hypotheses* mean?
   a. theories
   b. recollections
   c. goals
   d. topics

4. Which of the following is NOT a major supporting detail in this selection?
   a. "Some have suggested that young children lack memory encoding and storage processes." (paragraph 2)
   b. "Another possibility is that early memories, though 'present,' are implicit rather than explicit." (paragraph 3)
   c. "For example, Nora Newcombe and Nathan Fox showed photographs of young children to a group of ten-year-olds." (paragraph 3)

1. **schemas:** patterns used to explain reality or experience

* From Bernstein and Nash, *Essentials of Psychology*, 2nd ed. Boston: Houghton Mifflin, 2002, 315–316.

d. "Other explanations of infantile amnesia suggested that our early memories are lost because we do not yet have the language skills to talk about, and thus solidify, those memories." (paragraph 4)

5. Which of the following sentences begins with a contrast transition?

a. "But take a minute right now and try to recall anything that happened to you when you were, say, one year old." (paragraph 1)
b. "Because they don't even recognize themselves in a mirror, they may not have a framework for organizing memories about what happens to them." (paragraph 2)
c. "For example, Nora Newcombe and Nathan Fox showed photographs of young children to a group of ten-year-olds." (paragraph 3)
d. "Other explanations of infantile amnesia suggest that our early memories are lost because we do not yet have the language skills to talk about, and thus solidify, those memories." (paragraph 4)

6. Which pattern of organization arranges the *major* supporting details in this selection?

a. cause/effect
b. comparison/contrast
c. series
d. time order

7. The author's tone in this selection is

a. serious.
b. amused.
c. sarcastic.
d. joyful.

8. What can you infer from the statement "Adults, however, can correctly identify 90 percent of photographs of high school classmates they have not seen for thirty years" ?

a. Everyone has fond memories of high school.
b. By the time we're in high school, our memories are fully formed.
c. Most adults tend to live in the past.
d. Looking through high school yearbooks is a popular pastime for many adults.

9. What is the implied main idea of paragraph 4?

a. Parents should be careful about what they say to their children because kids form lasting impressions when they're still very young.
b. Psychologists will probably never figure out why we have infantile amnesia.
c. The development of language is still a mysterious process.
d. There are several theories about why we have infantile amnesia.

10. Reread the selection using the SQ3R method: Survey the reading; formulate questions; read the selection; recite; and review.

COMBINED SKILLS TEST 2

Read the selection below and respond to each question that follows by circling the letter of the correct answer.

The Brain Game

1 When Lori and Rich Boulware of Kendall Park, N.J., hit the road recently, their navigational radars were tuned into different frequencies. Rich used a mental map, while Lori used landmarks to get around. As the couple tried to get around a tricky area of town, Rich said, "Turn left on Webster," while Lori said, "You have to turn before the ice cream cone." Dr. Helen Fisher, an expert in gender differences, says the Boulwares are not unusual in their navigational skills. "Women go from one object to another. . . . A man will say, go two miles down the road and then head east. That's very different from saying go down to the shoe store and take a left at the high stone wall."

2 But these differences begin long before people get their driver's licenses. The Boulwares are already observing major differences in the way their three children communicate, particularly their two eldest—Jordan, 11, and Jerika, 9. Lori Boulware says her daughter Jerika describes her day with a lot more drama than her son. "Everything is about relationships," she said. "I know who was whose best friend today and who fought with who and what boy likes who. Jordan has no interest in that kind of stuff at all. Jordan would be happy to just say, 'My day was fine.'" Do the Boulwares' family stories sound familiar? If so, you're not alone. Fact is, men and women are very different in the way they speak, behave, solve problems, and even remember where the car keys are.

Size Isn't Everything

3 The reasons behind these differences have fueled arguments for generations and continue to do so today. Is it our biology, or our culture? Many scientists say it's all in our heads, or, more precisely, in the way men's and women's brains are designed and the way they function. A century ago, the discovery that female brains were about 10 percent smaller than male brains was cited as proof that women could never be as smart as men—contributing to their status as second-class citizens. We now know that size isn't everything when it comes to brainpower. Our I.Q.s are the same. In fact, the highest recorded I.Q. belongs to a woman, a writer named Marilyn vos Savant.

4 There are other, perhaps more significant, differences that distinguish male and female brains. Male brains are wired to move information quickly within each side—or hemisphere—of the brain. This gives them better spatial abilities. They can see an object in space, and react quickly. In women's brains,

areas of the cerebral cortex—linked to language, judgment and memory—are more densely packed with nerve cells than men's brains. This allows them to process that information more effectively. Fisher explained that the corpus callosum, which she describes as a "big highway between the two sides of the brain," is larger in women toward the rear than it is in men. "Hence," she said, "the two sides of the brain are better interconnected" in women. This means that women can absorb and analyze all sorts of information from the environment simultaneously. This makes women more adept at multitasking, while men tend to do better tackling one thing at a time.

Hard-Wired in the Womb?

5 Scientists are developing new ways of looking inside the working brain—to see just how it's wired. Diagnostic tests such as Functional MRIs, which can measure blood flow, electrical activity and energy use, are being used to give researchers pictures of our brains in action. Drs. Ruben and Raquel Gur, a husband and wife neuroscience team at the University of Pennsylvania, put men and women inside an MRI and studied how their brains responded to various verbal and spatial tasks. In each case, the men's brains "lit up" in a few specific areas, while the women's brains showed activity in many areas—for both spatial and verbal tasks. Ruben Gur said the men's brain activity became completely focused, while women did exactly the opposite, activating other parts of their brain. Researchers have found that the male brain's ability to focus on one area works better for spatial tests, while the female brain's approach is better for verbal tests. Scientists are still trying to figure out why that's the case.

6 The differences, researchers say, begin in the womb. At first, all fetuses' brains are virtually the same. At about nine weeks, however, testosterone[1] surges through the male fetus, not only creating a boy's body but actually hard-wiring the brain to be male. Without testosterone to spur those changes, girls develop "female" brains.

7 Michael Lewis, director of the Institute for the Study of Child Development at the Robert Wood Johnson Medical School in New Jersey, has documented behavioral differences in children as young as one year of age. In one study, Lewis placed toddler boys and girls behind a barrier, blocking them from reaching their mothers. The male and female children had very different strategies for getting past the barrier. Lewis said, "The boy child wants to get back to mom and it's going to climb over that barrier. It's going to knock it down. It's gonna push on it. It's gonna try to go around the side." The girls' strategy? According to Lewis, they "get help from another person."

1. **testosterone:** a hormone responsible for male characteristics

Interestingly, the female children got out from behind the barrier faster than the boys. They showed distress, and their mothers came and picked them up.

An Old Brain in a Modern Culture

8 The degree to which individuals' behavior is determined by their physiological make-up remains a hotly debated question. Lewis points out that children grow up in a world that reinforces boy and girl differences—through cartoons, commercials, clothing—and their behavior as adults will be shaped by these social cues. Anne Fausto-Sterling, a biologist at Brown University, thinks these external influences are so substantial that we shouldn't study the brain in isolation. "I balk at the notion that our brains are hard-wired," Fausto-Sterling said. "Our brains develop, and they develop new connections. So, you never have development outside of culture and experience," she said. Fausto-Sterling, like Lewis, pointed out that children are bombarded with "heavily gendered messages." Fausto-Sterling said these messages "start earlier than we can imagine."

9 Some researchers say the perception that men excel in motor and spatial skills while women are stronger in the verbal department is not just an over-parodied[1] stereotype. Evolutionary scientists claim it all began with our ancient ancestors. Fisher said it all goes back to the hunter-gatherer days. Women needed verbal and emotional skills to cajole[2], educate and discipline their babies, while men needed spatial skills out on the hunt. "We've got an old brain in a very modern culture."

From the Classroom to Career Choices

10 Researchers are also trying to understand why boys and girls often show stark differences in academic performance. In grade school, girls usually outshine the boys in every subject, including math. In high school, however, it's a different subject altogether. Lewis noted that "early math really isn't math. It's really more language problems." Once puberty[3] hits, boys get a second surge of testosterone and their math and spatial abilities climb dramatically—but some researchers don't exactly know what the connection is. By the time high school kids take their SATs[4], boys outscore girls in the math section by 7 percent. Fisher said, "It's quite remarkable how much better boys become at all kinds of spatial skills, mechanical skills, engineering skills, when that surge of testosterone comes on them." Meanwhile, estrogen starts flooding the girls'

1. **parodied:** ridiculed, mocked, made fun of
2. **cajole:** urge with gentle and repeated pleading, teasing, or flattery
3. **puberty:** stage of adolescence during which an individual becomes capable of sexual reproduction
4. **SAT:** Scholastic Aptitude Test, a college entrance exam

bodies, and experts think that boosts helps them develop stronger verbal and memory skills. According to Fisher, a woman's verbal ability climbs rapidly during the middle of the monthly menstrual cycle, when estrogen levels peak.

11 Some researchers say these physiological differences may predispose men and women to gravitate toward certain careers. Fisher notes that despite the move toward equal employment opportunity in the U.S. job market, some 85 percent of the architects in America are still men, and 90 percent of the mechanics are still men. She said she's not at all surprised that men gravitate to those jobs that need and require mechanical spatial skills. Meanwhile, 94 percent of all speech therapists are women, and 99 percent of all pre-school and kindergarten teachers are female.

12 Fausto-Sterling cautions that an over-emphasis on innate brain differences may unfairly limit an individual's opportunities. "By saying something is innate we shut doors and say, 'Well, this is just the way it is.' We close down possibilities. For every woman I think of who's sort of stereotypically female, I can think of one who isn't, and the same for men." Michael Lewis agrees. "Even if there are dispositions we're born with, it doesn't mean environments can't alter them. The thing we know about brains now, that we didn't know ten years ago, is that the brain is not a static organ. It's changing throughout our lives," Lewis said.

Beauty and the Brain

13 Differences in the way male and female brains work don't just affect our career choices or academic aptitudes, they control the way we perceive beauty, and they may affect how our bodies deal with stress and disease. While romantics believe love comes from the heart, scientists know it starts with the brain. When the brain sees something it likes—a very distinct message is transmitted throughout the body. Researchers have learned that beauty taps into a part of the brain called the limbic system, which deals with craving and reward. Dr. Nancy Etcoff, a Harvard psychologist, has been studying how the brain responds to beauty. She observed that the so-called reward area in men's brains lit up when they were shown pictures of beautiful women. The same reward circuitry is triggered for many different pleasures, researchers say. Some people will respond similarly to a good meal, cocaine will trigger the same reaction in addicts. When men were shown photos of attractive men, however, there was no activity in the brain's reward center at all. Women responded differently to the photos. "They wanted to get a second look, not only at the beautiful men, but at the beautiful women," Etcofff said.

Depression and Women

14 Because the two halves of their brains are better connected, women may be more prone to emotional problems. Women make up some two-thirds of those who suffer from depression. Some researchers say the root of this may lie in the

balance of estrogen[1] and other chemicals in the female brain. Depression in females usually begins after age 13, when puberty and estrogen kick in. It is most prevalent during a woman's childbearing years, and drops off after menopause.

15 Autoimmune diseases also affect more women than men. Dr. Esther Sternberg of the National Institutes of Health said women sufferers of these diseases outnumber men by a two-to-one ratio. Again, researchers think that estrogen is behind it. The hormone plays a major role in the immune system. When released, it acts in delicate balance with other hormones in the brain, including those that fight stress. When estrogen and other hormones are in equilibrium, the immune system fights off disease. If the balance is off, however, the immune system can fall asleep at the switch, making you vulnerable to colds and flu, or it can become hyper-alert and begin attacking your own body. This can lead to autoimmune diseases.

16 But researchers are working on new medicines that may target the root of the problem. They're working to develop drugs that focus on the brain to control illnesses that devastate the body. Sternberg said, "We have a whole new category of drugs that we can begin to develop and test, and use to treat . . . a whole host of autoimmune diseases."*

1. What is the topic of this selection?
   a. brains
   b. gender differences in behavior
   c. academic performance of girls versus boys
   d. critical thinking

2. Based on the information presented in paragraph 14, what can you infer about the role female hormones play in depression in women?
   a. Female hormones have no effect on depression in women.
   b. Female hormones decrease the likelihood of depression in women.
   c. Female hormones increase the likelihood of depression in women.
   d. Female hormones are more likely to cause bipolar disorder than depression in women.

3. The selection contains mostly
   a. facts. b. opinions.

4. The author's opinion is
   a. informed. b. uninformed.

1. **estrogen:** a hormone responsible for female characteristics.

* "The Brain Game," ABCNews.com, July 31, 2002. Courtesy of ABCNEWS.com.

5. In paragraph 4, what two patterns organize the details?
   a. comparison/contrast and cause/effect
   b. time order and cause/effect
   c. definition and series
   d. comparison/contrast and series

6. What is the main idea of paragraph 11?
   a. Women usually aren't encouraged to enter male-dominated professions.
   b. There are more openings for jobs requiring mechanical spatial skills than for jobs requiring other kinds of skills.
   c. Men and women choose different kinds of careers, in part, because of their biological differences.
   d. The workplace is sexist and discriminates against women.

7. Which pattern organizes the details in paragraph 6?
   a. series
   b. comparison/contrast
   c. time order
   d. definition

8. Which of the following sentences best states the thesis of the entire selection?
   a. "The Boulwares are already observing major differences in the way their three children communicate, particularly their two eldest—Jordan, 11, and Jerika, 9." (paragraph 2)
   b. "The reasons behind these differences have fueled arguments for generations and continue to do so today." (paragraph 3)
   c. "Differences in the way male and female brains work don't just affect our career choices or academic aptitudes, they control the way we perceive beauty, and they may affect how our bodies deal with stress and disease." (paragraph 13)
   d. "Because the two halves of their brains are better connected, women may be more prone to emotional problems." (paragraph 14)

9. Which of the following paragraphs begins with a contrast transition?
   a. paragraph 1
   b. paragraph 2
   c. paragraph 3
   d. paragraph 14

10. Write a summary of the key points of this article.

COMBINED SKILLS TEST 3

Read the selection following and respond to each question that follows by circling the letter of the correct answer.

I Confess I Used Carbohydrates in My Wild Youth

1 I probably shouldn't admit this to you younger readers, but when my generation was your age, we did some pretty stupid things. I'm talking about taking CRAZY risks. We drank water right from the tap. We used aspirin bottles that you could actually open with your bare hands. We bought appliances that were not festooned with helpful safety warnings such as "DO NOT BATHE WITH THIS TOASTER."

2 But for sheer insanity, the wildest thing we did was—prepare to be shocked—we deliberately ingested carbohydrates.

3 I know, I know. It was wrong. But we were young and foolish, and there was a lot of peer pressure. You'd be at a party, and there would be a lava lamp blooping away, and a Jimi Hendrix record playing (a "record" was a primitive compact disc that operated by static electricity). And then, when the mood was right, somebody would say: "You wanna do some 'drates?" And the next thing you know, there'd be a bowl of pretzels going around, or crackers, or even potato chips, and we'd put these things into our mouths and just . . . EAT them.

4 I'm not proud of this. My only excuse was that we were ignorant. It's not like now, when everybody knows how bad carbohydrates are, and virtually every product is advertised as being "low-carb," including beer, denture adhesives, floor wax, tires, life insurance and Viagra. Back then, we had no idea. Nobody did! Our own MOTHERS gave us bread!

5 Today, of course, nobody eats bread. People are terrified of all carbohydrates, as evidenced by the recent mass robbery at a midtown Manhattan restaurant, where 87 patrons turned their wallets over to a man armed only with a strand of No. 8 spaghetti. ("Do what he says! He has pasta!") The city of Beverly Hills has been evacuated twice this month because of reports—false, thank heavens—that terrorists had put a bagel in the water supply.

6 But as I say, in the old days we didn't recognize the danger of carbohydrates. We believed that the reason you got fat was from eating "calories," which are tiny units of measurement that cause food to taste good. When we wanted to lose weight, we went on low-calorie diets in which we ate only inedible foods such as celery, which is actually a building material, and grapefruit, which is nutritious, but offers the same level of culinary satisfaction as chewing on an Odor Eater.

7 The problem with the low-calorie diet was that a normal human could stick to it for, at most, four hours, at which point he or she would have no biological choice but to sneak out to the garage and snork down an entire bag of Snickers, sometimes without removing the wrappers. So nobody lost weight, and everybody felt guilty all the time. Many people, in desperation, turned to disco.

8 But then along came the bold food pioneer who invented the Atkins Diet: Dr. Something Atkins. After decades of research on nutrition and weight gain—including the now-famous Hostess Ding Dong Diet Experiment, which resulted in a laboratory rat the size of a Plymouth Voyager—Dr. Atkins discovered an amazing thing: Calories don't matter! What matter are carbohydrates, which result when a carbo molecule and a hydrate molecule collide at high speeds and form tiny invisible doughnuts.

9 Dr. Atkins' discovery meant that—incredible though it seemed—as long as you avoided carbohydrates, you could, without guilt, eat high-fat, high-calorie foods such as cheese, bacon, lard, pork rinds and whale. You could eat an entire pig, as long as the pig had not recently been exposed to bread.

10 At first, like other groundbreaking pioneers such as Galileo[1] and Eminem[2], Dr. Atkins met with skepticism, even hostility. The low-calorie foods industry went after him big time. The Celery Growers Association hired a detective to—yes—stalk him. His car tires were repeatedly slashed by what police determined to be shards of Melba toast.

11 But Dr. Atkins persisted, because he had a dream—a dream that, some day, he would help the human race by selling it 427 million diet books. And he did, achieving vindication for his diet before his tragic demise in an incident that the autopsy report listed as "totally unrelated to the undigested 28-pound bacon cheeseburger found in his stomach."

12 But the Atkins Diet lives on, helping millions of Americans to lose weight. The irony is, you can't tell this by looking at actual Americans, who have, as a group, become so heavy that North America will soon be underwater as far inland as Denver. Which can only mean one thing: You people are still sneaking Snickers. You should be ashamed of yourselves! Got any more?*

1. Which of the following paragraphs begins with a time order transition?

   a. paragraph 1
   b. paragraph 2
   c. paragraph 5
   d. paragraph 11

2. What can you infer about the author's opinion of low-carbohydrate diets like the Atkins diet?

   a. He thinks that they are great.
   b. He thinks that they are silly and unrealistic in nature.
   c. He doesn't have an opinion.
   d. He thinks that they will cause cancer.

1. **Galileo:** seventeenth-century astronomer and physicist
2. **Eminem:** a popular rap singer

* Dave Barry, "I Confess I Used Carbohydrates in My Wild Youth," *Miami Herald,* March 28, 2004. Copyright, 2004, Tribune Media Services, Inc. All Rights Reserved. Reprinted with permission.

3. The author's tone is
   a. serious.
   b. amused.
   c. admiring.
   d. outraged.
4. Which of the following sentences states a fact?
   a. "I probably shouldn't admit this to you younger readers, but when my generation was your age, we did some pretty stupid things." (paragraph 1)
   b. "We drank water right from the tap." (paragraph 1)
   c. "People are terrified of all carbohydrates, as evidenced by the recent mass robbery at a midtown Manhattan restaurant, where 87 patrons turned their wallets over to a man armed only with a strand of No. 8 spaghetti." (paragraph 5)
   d. "Many people, in desperation, turned to disco." (paragraph 7)
5. Which of the following paragraphs begins with a contrast transition?
   a. paragraph 4
   b. paragraph 5
   c. paragraph 6
   d. paragraph 10
6. In paragraph 11, the word *vindication* means
   a. justification or support for.
   b. free publicity.
   c. enthusiasm.
   d. praise.
7. What pattern organizes the details in paragraph 3?
   a. definition
   b. comparison/contrast
   c. cause/effect
   d. time order
8. What is the purpose of this selection?
   a. to entertain
   b. to inform
   c. to persuade
9. What can you infer from paragraph 10 about celery and Melba toast?
   a. They are low-carb foods.
   b. They are low-fat foods.
   c. They are high-calorie foods.
   d. They are junk foods.
10. Write a reading journal entry based on this selection.

COMBINED SKILLS TEST 4

Read the selection following and respond to each question that follows by circling the letter of the correct answer.

Dual-Earner Couples

1 In a **dual-earner couple**, both members are employed and maintain a family life. According to the U.S. Bureau of Labor Statistics, 75 percent of all women between the ages of 25 and 54 were in the U.S. labor force in 1994. Seventy percent of those in this age category had children under the age of 18. In 1996, the percentage of married couples who both worked was more than 60 percent. And in 1997, according to the Census Bureau, only 17 percent of U.S. households matched the traditional model of a Dad who brought home the wages and a Mom who stayed home and took care of the kids. Currently, dual-earner couples make up over 45 percent of the labor force. According to a recent survey by Catalyst, a research group that focuses on working women, 85 percent of participants named increased income as the biggest advantage of a dual-earner situation. Fifty-six percent noted that a lack of time was the biggest challenge. As one IBM executive put it: "Dual-career couples are telling us that they're not cash-poor. They're telling us, 'We make enough money. But we don't have time to spend it because we're focused on our jobs and the demands of those jobs.'"

2 In a recent interview in *Forbes* magazine, Ralph Gomory, president of the Sloan Foundation and former director of the research labs at IBM, shared an interesting view on the idea that everyone is working harder and putting in more hours. "It's not that one individual is working longer so much as that two people are now doing three jobs. In the past, one person did the working job and the other one brought up the family, took care of the home, built a social network. . . . It was never recognized as a job. But it was." In other words, the dual-earner couple has added a third job to what used to be only two. Now, there are two jobs outside the home and one inside.

3 Needless to say, this situation takes more effort and is more difficult. When it comes to taking care of the home and the kids, men still do less than their fair share, even when their wives are working full time. In 1977, American men spent a little over one hour per day doing household tasks. Today, they spend a little more than two hours per day. Women, on the other hand, average about 3 hours per day on chores. The inequality is much worse in Japan. There, a government survey found that husbands in dual-earner families devote less than eight minutes per day to housework. Their income-earning wives, however, spend over three hours on domestic duties.

4 Little academic research has focused on dual-earner couples in the past. However, interest has been increasing. One recent study, for instance, looked at the effects of work and non-work influences on the career satisfaction of dual-earner couples in Hong Kong. This study found some interesting results. First, work-related factors are better than non-work-related factors at predicting career satisfaction. Both husbands and wives prefer supervisor support and the chance to make the most of their skills on the job. They also want to feel

as though they are an important part of the organization. Second, the only non-work-related factor that was important to both husbands and wives was satisfaction with child-care arrangements. Third, and this surprised the authors, the results for both husbands and wives were parallel. In other words, the same factors seemed to be important predictors of career satisfaction for both husbands and wives. Thus, there is considerable agreement about what these partners see as essential to making their dual-earner situation successful.

5 A second recent study also surveyed dual-earner couples, but its focus was on predictors of marital satisfaction rather than career satisfaction. Work-related stress can affect one's family life and vice versa, and this study looked at the effects of work on the families of dual-earner couples. Job insecurity, time pressures at work, poor supervisor-employee relations, and work-family conflict affected marital satisfaction. These difficulties were experienced indirectly, however. They caused, for example, job exhaustion and symptoms like headaches and heart palpitations. In other words, husbands and wives who perceived a lack of job security or who worked under time pressure tended to be tired at work and had more headaches. The same was true for those who didn't get along with their supervisors or experienced work-family conflict in general. When severe stress at work caused exhaustion and illness, people were more likely to report lower levels of marital satisfaction. The situation was exactly the same for men as for women. The authors of this study concluded that gender differences in work experiences, though still present, are fading.

6 A third recent study has taken a different approach by surveying over 170 career-oriented college women in the United States. The survey asked these women about their expectations and desires regarding future careers and family life. Participants were limited to those who said they saw themselves in a dual-career marriage. Based on their responses, the authors classified each student as one of two types. One type expects a *conventional dual-career marriage,* in which the female takes primary responsibility for the home and the children while adding a career to her responsibilities. The other type expects a *role-sharing dual-career marriage,* in which both spouses actively pursue careers and actively involve themselves in the household and parenting.

7 Interestingly, women who expected a role-sharing marriage were significantly more likely than the other group to be committed to a lifelong, consuming career. They were also higher in self-esteem. Perhaps the higher self-esteem of these women allowed them to consider a less conventional option. In addition, having a spouse who would involve himself in managing the household and parenting the children was important to those looking for a role-sharing marriage. Having an involved spouse was not as important to those looking for a more conventional dual-career relationship. The authors concluded that many college-educated women today are thinking about their futures differently than earlier generations did. No longer must women

choose between a career and a family. Today's college-educated women believe that both are possible. Fortunately, many are leading the way in demonstrating how to make this work.*

1. The topic of this selection is

   a. work.
   b. men and women.
   c. dual-earner couples.
   d. marital satisfaction.

2. Which of the following patterns organize the details in paragraph 1?

   a. definition and time order
   b. time order and series
   c. comparison/contrast and series
   d. definition and series

3. The purpose of this selection is

   a. to persuade.
   b. to inform.
   c. to entertain.

4. According to the author of the selection, how is the term *conventional dual-career marriage* defined?

   a. Both members of the marriage are employed and maintain a family life.
   b. The female maintains primary responsibility for the home and the children while simply adding a career to her responsibilities.
   c. Both spouses actively pursue careers and actively involve themselves in the household and parenting.
   d. Both spouses are exclusively involved in the household and parenting, to the exclusion of their careers.

5. Which of the following sentences from paragraph 4 is a *minor* supporting detail?

   a. "Little academic research has focused on dual-earner couples in the past."
   b. "One recent study, for instance, looked at the effects of work and non-work influences on the career satisfaction of dual-earner couples in Hong Kong."
   c. "First, work-related factors are better at predicting career satisfaction."
   d. "Both husbands and wives prefer supervisor support and the chance to make the most of their skills on the job."

6. The pattern that organizes the details in paragraphs 4–6 is

   a. time order.
   b. series.
   c. definition.
   d. cause/effect.

* Adapted from Paul E. Levy, *Industrial/Organizational Psychology.* Boston: Houghton Mifflin, 2003, 333–335. Copyright © 2003 by Houghton Mifflin Company. Reprinted with permission.

7. The pattern that organizes the major supporting details in paragraph 4 is
   a. time order.
   b. definition.
   c. cause/effect.
   d. comparison/contrast.

8. What pattern organizes the details in paragraph 3?
   a. time order
   b. comparison/contrast
   c. cause/effect
   d. series

9. Which of the following paragraphs begins with a series transition?
   a. Paragraph 2
   b. Paragraph 3
   c. Paragraph 6
   d. Paragraph 7

10. Reread the selection using the REAP strategy.

COMBINED SKILLS TEST 5

Read the selection below and respond to each question that follows by circling the letter of the correct answer.

I Know That Only Cowards Can Be Brave

1 "You're so brave," friends say when I show them my photographs from my recent trek to remote Zaskar and Ladakh, high on the Tibetan Plateau. Looking at the photographs, I can't believe it myself. Did I really hike 300 miles across glaciers, ice bridges, and 11 mountain passes as high as 18,000 feet? If I didn't have the photo, I wouldn't believe that I crossed a churning river on a flimsy rope-and-plank bridge so scary that even the sure-footed ponies had to be blindfolded. Yet I feel compelled to tell people that it is because I am *not* brave that I do these things. In fact, anxiety once ruled my life—and sometimes still does. I still close my eyes whenever I see a television commercial for a roller coaster. Yet, despite sounding like a female Woody Allen[1], I am one of the new group called "adventure travelers." In the last few years about 30 million American tourists have gotten their adrenaline highs—spelunking[2], dude ranching[3], river rafting, or scuba diving. Are we to assume that so many people are brave? My experience tells me otherwise.

2 One obvious reason people trek is to see astonishingly beautiful scenery and unusual wildlife. But a major reason we trek is to reinvent ourselves, to

1. **Woody Allen:** American actor, writer, and filmmaker
2. **spelunking:** exploring caves
3. **dude ranching:** participating in activities, such as horseback riding, on a ranch

shed some fear or another that has burdened us. I have met trekkers who are afraid of horses, precipices, swaying rope bridges, zippered tents, or catching a horrible disease. Sleeping-bag manufacturers, take note: my informal research shows that many travelers harbor a secret fear of mummy-style bags. Fortunately, I don't have this particular fear. I have enough others.

3 Years ago I moved to Arizona from Australia. As a single parent, with no relatives to rely on, I lived in torment that if something happened to me, my kids would be orphaned. My neurosis escalated to the point that I was uncomfortable leaving the house. I'd panic when driving, standing in line at the bank, or buying groceries. I envied friends who took trips to Tahiti and Rome. Was I destined to be just an armchair traveler reading *National Geographic*?

4 Partly to reclaim my independence, and partly to give my preteen children a better role model, I began timidly venturing out with friends. Eventually I was able to travel by myself, and took my first solitary airplane trip from Tucson, Arizona, to San Francisco. A friend made me a reassuring tape of encouragement ("Breathe slowly and deeply. Your heart is beating slower. You're totally relaxed.") to play on my headset. I discovered that my imagination was responsible for many of my anxieties.

5 After I moved to Hawaii, and with my children now teenagers, I ran in the Honolulu Marathon, to teach myself about setting and achieving a physical goal. Next, I took trips to the Neighbor Islands, where I rented a car and explored the islands by myself. Over the years I learned some important lessons: to trust myself, to ask for help, to avoid toxic people who ridicule anxiety.

6 To celebrate my fiftieth birthday in 1994, I took my first trip overseas without friends or family. I selected Bhutan because so little had been written about it, and I had no preconceived notions about it. With 11 others I trekked about 400 miles, into Laya, the remote heart of the Himalaya. The lessons I had learned paid off. I recited my mantra[1], "Slow and steady. Switch off the imagination." I was exhilarated by the vistas of eternal snows, and by the chance to meet nomadic[2] herdsmen and visit Buddhist monasteries. Yes, sometimes I was afraid. But I never once felt as though I could not manage.

7 Since then, I've traveled alone to Australia, India, and Nepal—all former impossible dreams. I haven't overcome my fears so much as learned to cope with them. I understand that my fear of heights is apparently innate; researchers think it's a phobia that's wired into our brains from our ancestral days in the treetops. Knowing my limitations—I doubt I'll ever try parachuting—has helped me to establish attainable goals. Not that it's easy. I once had to hold a fellow trekker's hand and be helped across nightmarish slopes that disappeared into bottomless gorges. We inched our way along a trail that had

1. **mantra:** a sacred verbal formula repeated in prayer or meditation
2. **nomadic:** traveling around; not settling in one place

been hand-carved hundreds of years ago out of a sheer vertical cliff face in India's Great Zaskar Range. My heart was beating so loudly that even the sound of boulders and ice chunks crashing into the river thousands of feet below couldn't drown it out. But I made it. Fear is two-way. I've been empowered by helping fellow adventurers with fears. One trekker lay curled in a fetal position, watching in terror as I removed a spider the size of a soup bowl from her tent.

8 As I browse through the glossy adventure-company brochures, I fantasize about the trips I intend to take. Maybe we'll meet on Kilimanjaro, Kailas, or Machu Picchu. You'll know me—I'm the one whose ritual on reaching a mountaintop is to high-five my fellow trekkers, and then remind the surrounding mountains at the top of my voice, "Only cowards can be truly brave."*

1. The topic of this selection is
   a. Tibet.
   b. facing fears.
   c. traveling.
   d. family life.

2. What is the main idea of this selection?
   a. Traveling is very educational.
   b. One can't be a good mother and a world traveler at the same time.
   c. People who travel all the time are restless souls who are running from their problems.
   d. Many adventure travelers, who are not necessarily brave, seek to shed some fear that plagues them.

3. Based on your reading of paragraph 3, what do you think the word *neurosis* means?
   a. emotional disturbance
   b. happiness
   c. joy in life
   d. depression

4. Which of the following sentences begins with a time-order transition?
   a. "Since then, I've traveled alone to Australia, India, and Nepal—all former impossible dreams." (paragraph 7)
   b. "Yet I feel compelled to tell people that it is because I am *not* brave that I do these things." (paragraph 1)
   c. "One obvious reason people trek is to see astonishingly beautiful scenery and unusual wildlife." (paragraph 2)
   d. "In fact, anxiety once ruled my life—and sometimes still does." (paragraph 1)

* From Sandra Kimberley Hall, "I Know That Only Cowards Can Be Brave," *Newsweek*, September 6, 1999, 14. © 1999 Newsweek, Inc. All Rights Reserved. Reprinted by permission.

5. Which of the following patterns organizes the *major* supporting details in paragraph 5?
   a. time order
   b. series
   c. cause/effect
   d. comparison/contrast

6. Which of the following sentences from the selection states the author's opinion?
   a. "Since then, I've traveled alone to Australia, India, and Nepal—all former impossible dreams." (paragraph 7)
   b. "Years ago I moved to Arizona from Australia." (paragraph 3)
   c. "Fear is two-way." (paragraph 7)
   d. "To celebrate my fiftieth birthday in 1994, I took my first trip overseas without friends or family." (paragraph 6)

7. What inference can you draw from the sentence "One trekker lay curled in a fetal position, watching in terror as I removed a spider the size of a soup bowl from her tent"?
   a. The author and the other trekker shared a tent.
   b. The other trekker was afraid of spiders.
   c. The other trekker was very cold.
   d. The author is not afraid of spiders.

8. Which of the following inferences can you make based on this whole selection?
   a. The author is married now.
   b. The author's friends don't like to travel as much as she does.
   c. The author is physically fit.
   d. The author is a travel writer for a magazine.

9. What is the implied main idea of paragraph 3?
   a. The author wanted to travel, but her fears held her back.
   b. Arizona is a better place to live than Australia.
   c. The author suffered from agoraphobia, the fear of open places.
   d. There's no place like home.

10. Write a reading journal entry based on this selection.

INDEX